Sutterer-Kipping

Platform Work Directive

Platform Work Directive

Article-by-Article Commentary

edited by

Amélie Sutterer-Kipping

2026

BECK • HART • NOMOS

Published by
Nomos Verlagsgesellschaft mbH & Co. KG, Waldseestraße 3-5, 76530 Baden-Baden, Germany,
email: service@nomos.de

Co-published by
Verlag C.H.Beck GmbH & Co. KG, Wilhelmstraße 9, 80801 München, Germany,
email: bestellung@beck.de

and

Hart Publishing, Kemp House, Chawley Park, Cumnor Hill, Oxford, OX2 9PH, United Kingdom,
online at: www.hartpub.co.uk

Published in North America by Hart Publishing,
An Imprint of Bloomsbury Publishing 1385 Broadway, New York, NY 10018, USA
email: mail@hartpub.co.uk

ISBN 978 3 7560 2423 0 (NOMOS Print)
ISBN 978 3 7489 7533 5 (NOMOS ePDF)
ISBN 978 3 406 84747 9 (C.H.BECK)
ISBN 978 1 0480 0496 0 (HART)

First Edition 2026

Foreword

Digitalisation is transforming the world of work, with digital labour platforms at the heart of this change. Millions of individuals across Europe already work through such digital platforms, often without legal clarity regarding their employment status or the data collected and processed by automated systems that organise their work. The Directive (EU) 2024/2831 of the European Parliament and of the Council of 23 October 2024 (Platform Work Directive) is the European Union's ambitious attempt to improve the working conditions in platform work.

This English-language 'Platform Work Directive – Article-by-Article Commentary' is the first commentary to systematically analyse and contextualise the Platform Work Directive within the broader EU social policy framework. It explores links to existing legal instruments, including the P2B Regulation, the GDPR and the AI Act, and highlights the challenges involved in transposing the Directive into the national legal frameworks of the Member States.

The commentary has been written by a team of experts from seven countries. At the time of writing, the Platform Work Directive had entered into force but not yet been transposed into the national legal frameworks of the Member States. The commentary is an invitation to start a discussion on how the Platform Work Directive should be interpreted and implemented. It can serve as a tool to assist with the transposition of the Platform Work Directive into national law and as a guide to interpreting the national implementing legislation, ensuring it aligns with the Platform Work Directive. The commentary also takes into account the expert groups' report, dated 12 January 2026. While this report is not binding and does not represent the official position of the European Commission, it provides guidance on interpreting the individual articles.

I would like to express my gratitude to my colleague, Athanasios Tragiannis, for his invaluable contribution and dedication to the project, and to the Hugo Sinzheimer Institute, and in particular to Ernesto Klengel, for their constant support and encouragement throughout this journey. I would also like to express my sincere gratitude to the authors for their expertise, professionalism, patience and cooperative spirit. Without their commitment, this project would not have been possible. I would like to conclude by extending my gratitude to the editorial team, especially to Matthias Knopik, for their excellent cooperation.

Munich, July 2026 Amélie Sutterer-Kipping

CONTENTS

Contents

CHAPTER V
REMEDIES AND ENFORCEMENT

PART III
COUNTRY REPORTS

Authors

Jeremias Adams-Prassl is Professor of Law and Associate Dean (Research) at the Faculty of Law, Oxford University, and a Fellow of Magdalen College. He read law at Oxford, Paris and Harvard Law and holds an honorary doctorate in law from Lund University. His research focuses on technology, innovation policy and the future of work in the European Union and beyond, supported by grants and prizes including an ERC Starting Grant and a Philip Leverhulme Prize.
Arts. 7–12

Edoardo Ales is Professor of Labour Law at the University of Naples Parthenope. He is a member of the Scientific Committee of the Marco Biagi Foundation, where he also serves as Coordinator of the Observatory on Participatory Management. He is Co-director of the journal *Diritti Lavori Mercati International.*
Country Report Italy

Christian Berger is a socio-economist and lawyer currently working as a political advisor for the Austrian Federal Minister for Women, Science and Research. He is a lecturer at the Vienna University of Economics and Business, the University of Applied Sciences FH Wien, and the Johannes Kepler University Linz. He is a member of the editorial board of the journal *Kurswechsel.*
Legal Policy Background (Chap. I)

Dr. Ilda Durri is a legal researcher in EU social policy at the European Social Observatory (OSE) in Brussels, where her expertise focuses on the future of work and the digitalisation of labour markets.
Legal Policy Background (Chap. I)

Michael Gogola is Head of the Legal Department of the GPA trade union in Austria. He focuses on issues relating to employment law and social policy, and publishes on these topics.
Country Report Austria

Ann-Christine 'Ankie' Hartzén is Associate Professor in the Department of Business Law at Lund University School of Economics and Management. She is specialised in labour law and her research focuses on the interaction between EU law and the Swedish model with a special interest in the situation of precarious workers. She has published on issues such as the European Social Dialogue, in-work poverty, fixed-term work and the minimum wage directive for which she also was invited as an expert to the Swedish Parliament Committee on the Labour Market.
Platform economy & collective bargaining (Chap. III)

Christina Hießl (Hiessl) is Professor of Labour Law at KU Leuven (Belgium), Invited Professor of Social Welfare at Yonsei University (Seoul), and editor of an extensive edited Article-by-Article Commentary on EU Labour Law. As part of a project commissioned by the European Commission (DG EMPL) to inform EU-level policy making, she keeps track of and analyses case law developments related to platform work and algorithmic management across Europe.
Arts. 3–5, Country Report Benelux

Authors

Johannes Höller is a fully qualified lawyer, PhD candidate at the Faculty of Law of the European University Viadrina Frankfurt (Oder), Germany and former doctoral student at the Hugo Sinzheimer Institute for Labour and Social Security Law. His research focuses on mobilization in platform work and the labor law assessment of the digital communication channels of Art 20 Platform Work Directive.
Art. 20

Eva Kocher is Professor of Civil Law and Labour Law and Head of the Center for Interdisciplinary Labour Law Studies (C*LLaS) at the Law Faculty of European University Viadrina Frankfurt (Oder), Germany. Her research focuses on European and German labour law, feminist legal studies and anti-discrimination law. She is the author of numerous books and articles, including the book 'Digital Work Platforms at the Interface of Labour Law' (2022); with Lorena Poblete, she co-edited the book 'Digital Intermediaries in Domestic and Care work' (forthcoming 2026).
Art. 20

Rüdiger Krause is Professor of Civil Law and Labour Law and Director of the Institute for Labour Law at the Georg-August-University Göttingen (Germany). He is the author of numerous books, articles and legal opinions, primarily on German and European Labour Law, including several contributions on platform work, data protection in the workplace, artificial intelligence and other aspects of the digitalisation of the world of work. He is also co-editor of the German Labour Law Journal 'Soziales Recht'.
Country Report Germany

Juliana Londoño Polo is a PhD Researcher and Lecturer in the Department of Private, Business and Labour Law at Tilburg University. Her work explores how labour law and industrial relations systems can be opened up to the self-employed, with a particular focus on the obstacles to meaningful collective rights that persist beyond competition law. Her broader research interests include the platform economy, worker representation structures, and comparative labour law.
Arts. 13–15, 19

Grégoire Loiseau is Professor of Private Law at the University of Paris 1 Panthéon-Sorbonne. Specialising in labour law and digital law, he serves as Director of the Master's Degree (Master 2) in Social Law Pratice and Co-Director of the Master's Degree (Master 2) in Artificial Intelligence and Governance. He is also Co-Editor-in-Chief of the labour law journal *Bulletin Joly Travail.*
Country Report France

Federica Palmirotta is a Postdoctoral Researcher in Labour Law. She earned her PhD in Labour Law from the Marco Biagi Department of Economics, University of Modena and Reggio Emilia – Marco Biagi Foundation, with a dissertation focused on algorithmic discrimination. She also serves as a Conciliator within the Certification Commission established at the Marco Biagi Foundation.
Country Report Italy

Ilaria Purificato is a Research Fellow in Labour Law at the University of Modena and Reggio Emilia – Marco Biagi Foundation, where she obtained her PhD with a dissertation on platform work. She is also a member of the Editorial Secretariat of the journal *Diritti Lavori Mercati International* and of the *Quaderni Fondazione Marco Biagi* editorial team. Her research interests include labour rights in the context of digital transformation and workers' participation.
Country Report Italy

Silvia Rainone is a Senior Researcher at the European Trade Union Institute (ETUI) and lecturer in labour law at the Université Libre de Bruxelles (ULB). Her research explores how labour law and industrial relations frameworks can respond to digitalisation, corporate fragmentation and new forms of work organisation.
Arts. 13–15, 19

Iacopo Senatori is Associate Professor of Labour Law at the University of Modena and Reggio Emilia. He serves on the Scientific Committee of the Marco Biagi Foundation, where he also coordinates the Observatory on Digital and Multilocal Work. He is also Coordinator of the Editorial Board of the *Quaderni Fondazione Marco Biagi.*
Country Report Italy

Michael 'Six' Silberman is a Postdoctoral Researcher in the iManage Project at the University of Oxford, contributing to research on the regulation of algorithmic management. He is also a consultant on digitalisation to the International Trade Union Confederation. Silberman has previously worked as a trade union official and software engineer.
Arts. 7–12

Amélie Sutterer-Kipping is Head of the Labour and Social Security Law Department at the Hugo Sinzheimer Institute of the Hans Böckler Foundation. She completed her doctoral thesis at Georg-August-University Göttingen and Université Paris 1 Panthéon-Sorbonne as part of a cotutelle programme. Her thesis, for which she was awarded the Franco-German Dissertation Prize 2024, deals with the labour and social law protection of low-income self-employed persons in Germany and France. Amélie Sutterer-Kipping teaches European Labour and Economic Law at the European Academy of Labour at the University of Frankfurt. Her research and lecturing focus on platform work, algorithmic management in the workplace, gender discrimination and equal pay.
Introduction, Interaction between P2B Reg. and Platform Work Directive (Chap. II), Arts. 7–12

Athanasios Tragiannis is a PhD Researcher at the University of Cologne and works at the Hugo Sinzheimer Institute for Labour and Social Security Law. His research focuses on the concept of the employee in German and EU labour law. He is a scholarship holder of the Hans Böckler Foundation.
Arts. 7–12, Country Report Greece

Noelia de Torres Bóveda is a Teaching and Research Assistant at the Faculty of Law of the Universidad Complutense de Madrid in Spain.
Country Report Spain

Authors

Johannes Warter is a Post-Doctoral University Assistant in the Department of Labour Law and Business Law at the University of Salzburg since 2018. In his research and teaching, he addresses the diverse aspects of Austrian and European labour law, social law, and data protection law. His particular research focus lies in the area of digitalisation at the intersection with labour law and social law.
Arts. 1–2, Country Report Austria

Abbreviations

AB	Amtsblatt (Official Journal)
ABR	Case-register code for German Federal Labour Court proceedings in labour-court matters
ACM	Association for Computing Machinery
ADMS	Algorithmic Decision-Making Systems
AI	Artificial Intelligence
AIS	Automatic Identification System
al.	alia (and others)
AMS	Automated Monitoring Systems
AP	Arbeitsrechtliche Praxis
ArbVG	Arbeitsverfassungsgesetz (Austrian Labour Constitution Act)
ARD	Arbeitsrechtlicher Dienst
Art(s).	Article(s)
ASoK	Arbeits- und SozialrechtsKartei
ASVG	Allgemeines Sozialversicherungsgesetz
AuR	Arbeit und Recht
AZR	Case-register code for German Federal Labour Court revision proceedings
BAG	Federal Labour Court (Germany)
BeckRS	Beck-Rechtsprechung
BMAS	Federal Ministry of Labour and Social Affairs (Germany)
BT	Bundestag (German Federal Parliament)
BV	Works Agreement
Cass.	Cour de cassation (French Supreme Court)
CCOO	Comisiones Obreras (Spanish trade union confederation)
cf.	compare
CFR	Charter of Fundamental Rights
CFREU	Charter of Fundamental Rights of the European Union
CGIL	Confederazione Generale Italiana del Lavoro
CJEU	Court of Justice of the European Union
CLLPJ	Comparative Labor Law & Policy Journal
CML	Common Market Law
CML Rev.	Common Market Law Review
CNN	Cable News Network
COD	Codecision procedure / ordinary legislative procedure
COLLEEM	Collaborative Economy and Employment
COM	European Commission document
com.	commentary / comment
Comm. com. électr.	Communication commerce électronique
DEE	Dikaio Epicheiriseon kai Etairion / Δίκαιο Επιχειρήσεων και Εταιριών
DEN	Deltio Ergatikis Nomothesias / Δελτίον Εργατικής Νομοθεσίας
DGB	German Trade Union Confederation
DLPs	Digital Labour Platforms
DMA	Digital Markets Act
DRdA	Das Recht der Arbeit

Abbreviations

DSA	Digital Services Act
DSL	Diritto della sicurezza sul lavoro
e.g.	for example
EC	European Community
ECHR	European Convention on Human Rights
ECJ	European Court of Justice
ECLI	European Case Law Identifier
Econ. Ind. Dem.	Economic and Industrial Democracy
ECtHR	European Court of Human Rights
EEC	European Economic Community
EELR	European Equality Law Review
EErgD	Epitheorisis Ergatikou Dikaiou / Επιθεώρηση Εργατικού Δικαίου
EfDD	Europe of Freedom and Direct Democracy
EllDni	Elliniki Dikaiosyni / Ελληνική Δικαιοσύνη
ELLJ	European Labour Law Journal
EP	European Parliament
EPolD	Epitheorisi Politikis Dikonomias / Επιθεώρηση Πολιτικής Δικονομίας
ESC	European Social Charter
et	and
etc.	and so on
ETUC	European Trade Union Confederation
ETUI	European Trade Union Institute
EU	European Union
EUR	Euro(s)
Eur. J. Ind. Rel.	European Journal of Industrial Relations
EuZA	Europäische Zeitschrift für Arbeitsrecht
EuZW	Europäische Zeitschrift für Wirtschaftsrecht
FNV	Federatie Nederlandse Vakbeweging
GDPR	General Data Protection Regulation
gGmbH	non-profit limited liability company (Germany)
GmbH	limited liability company (Germany)
GRUR	Gewerblicher Rechtsschutz und Urheberrecht
HAG	Heimarbeitsgesetz
HR	Human Resources
i.e.	that is
IG	Industriegewerkschaft
IDPL	International Data Privacy Law
IIC	International Review of Intellectual Property and Competition Law
IJoC	International Journal of Communication
ILLeJ	Italian Labour Law e-Journal
ILO	International Labour Organization
ILR	International Labour Review
J.	Journal
Ind. Law J.	Industrial Law Journal
Int. J. Comp. Labour Law Ind. Relat.	International Journal of Comparative Labour Law and Industrial Relations

Int. J. Sel. Asses.	International Journal of Selection and Assessment
J. Work Health Saf. Regul.	Journal of Work Health and Safety Regulation
JCP	JurisClasseur périodique / La Semaine juridique
JCP S	La Semaine Juridique – Social
JZ	JuristenZeitung
KJ	Kritische Justiz
KZfSS	Kölner Zeitschrift für Soziologie und Sozialpsychologie
LAG	Regional Labour Court (Germany)
LD	Lavoro e Diritto
LDE	Lavoro Diritti Europa
LLI	Labour & Law Issues
LRDT&PS	Labos. Revista de Derecho del Trabajo y Protección Social
LS	Lex Social
MGL	Massimario di giurisprudenza del lavoro
MLR	Modern Law Review
New Pol. Econ.	New Political Economy
New Technol Work Employ	New Technology, Work and Employment
NJOZ	Neue Juristische Online-Zeitschrift
mn.	marginal number (Randnummer)
NL	Netherlands
NZA	Neue Zeitschrift für Arbeitsrecht
NZA-Beil.	Neue Zeitschrift für Arbeitsrecht – Beilage
NZA-RR	Neue Zeitschrift für Arbeitsrecht – Rechtsprechungs-Report
OECD	Organisation for Economic Co-operation and Development
OGH	Oberster Gerichtshof (Austria)
OJ	Official Journal (EU)
OJLS	Oxford Journal of Legal Studies
OSH	Occupational Safety and Health
p.	page
P2B	Platform-to-Business
PDF	Portable Document Format
RdA	Recht der Arbeit
RDS	Revista de Derecho Social
RDS&E	Revista de Derecho Social y Empresa
RDSS	Rivista del Diritto della Sicurezza Sociale
RDT	Revue de droit du travail
REDT	Revista Española de Derecho del Trabajo
REJL&SS	Revista de Estudios Jurídico Laborales y de Seguridad Social
RIDL	Rivista italiana di diritto del lavoro
RSF J. Social Sciences	RSF: The Russell Sage Foundation Journal of the Social Sciences
RT&SS CEF	Revista de Trabajo y Seguridad Social. CEF
seq.	and the following
seqq.	and the following (plural)
SER	Socio-Economic Review

Abbreviations

SMEs	Small and Medium-sized Enterprises
SOU	Statens offentliga utredningar (Swedish Government Official Reports)
SR	Soziales Recht
SWD	Commission Staff Working Document
TaBV	Case-register code for complaint proceedings in German labour-court decision proceedings
T&D	Trabajo y Derecho
TFEU	Treaty on the Functioning of the European Union
TL	Temas Laborales
TPWC	Directive on transparent and predictable working conditions in the European Union
TRA	Tijdschrift Recht en Arbeid
UGT	Unión General de Trabajadores
UK	United Kingdom
Work Organ. Labour Glob.	Work Organisation, Labour & Globalisation
WSI	Wirtschafts- und Sozialwissenschaftliches Institut
WSI-Mitt.	WSI-Mitteilungen
ZAS	Zeitschrift für Arbeits- und Sozialrecht
ZdiW	Zeitschrift für das Recht der digitalen Wirtschaft
ZESAR	Zeitschrift für europäisches Sozial- und Arbeitsrecht
ZFA	Zeitschrift für Arbeitsrecht
ZRP	Zeitschrift für Rechtspolitik
ZUM	Zeitschrift für Urheber- und Medienrecht
ZVglRWiss	Zeitschrift für Vergleichende Rechtswissenschaft

Introduction

I. General features

1 The Platform Work Directive prioritises the protection of persons performing platform work. A first objective is to ensure that persons performing platform work are correctly classified as employees or self-employed persons, thereby combatting the practice of bogus self-employment. Secondly, the Platform Work Directive has established a regulatory framework specifically tailored to the digital organisation of work at the European level for the first time. This framework is designed to address the specific risks associated with the organisation of work through algorithms in the context of platform work for which general labour and data protection law has not yet provided adequate protective measures.

II. Structure of the Platform Work Directive

2 The Platform Work Directive is an EU Directive pursuant to Art. 288(3) TFEU. Following a series of unsuccessful votes and extensive amendments to the Commission's draft, a consensus was finally reached in March 2024 between the European Parliament and the Council on the regulation of working conditions in platform work, resulting in the adoption of the Platform Work Directive. The Platform Work Directive was published in the Official Journal on 11 November 2024 and entered into force on 1 December 2024.

3 Unlike a Regulation, which is directly and uniformly applicable in all Member States, a Directive must first be incorporated in Member States' national legal framework. For the Platform Work Directive, transposition into national law is required by 2 December 2026 (Art. 29). The Platform Work Directive has been prepared as a **minimum harmonisation act**. The national transposition measure must achieve the objectives and the minimum requirements set by the Directive. However, the Platform Work Directive does not prevent Member States from granting more favourable conditions, including via collective agreements (Art. 26).

4 The Platform Work Directive is divided into six chapters.

5 **Chapter I** sets out **general provisions**, especially on the regulatory objectives, the personal, territorial and material scope of the provisions (Arts. 1, 2). Art. 2 contains **definitions** of the central terms of the Platform Work Directive. Art. 3 addresses the protection of persons performing platform work who work through intermediaries. It ensures that they receive the same level of protection within subcontracting chains as those with a direct contractual relationship with a digital labour platform. **Chapter II** contains provisions for the **determination of the correct employment status** of persons performing platform work. **Chapter III** sets out a regulatory framework for the use of **algorithmic management** (Arts. 7–12). Art. 13 concerns collective rights (**information and consultation rights of workers' representatives**). Art. 15 allows the **representatives of persons performing platform work to exercise rights afforded to workers' representatives.**

6 The Platform Work Directive also applies to self-employed persons and their representatives, insofar as the protection of personal data of such self-employed persons is

concerned. Accordingly, the provisions to improve the protection of personal data in context of algorithmic management set out in Arts. 7–11 as well as Art. 17 and Chapter V apply to them.

7 **Chapter IV** lays down **transparency obligations**. Arts. 16 and 17 require that digital labour platforms declare work performed by platform workers to the competent national authorities and to provide information about the activities of the platform. **Chapter V** regulates **remedies and enforcement** of the obligations of the Platform Work Directive. It essentially requires digital labour platforms to provide communication channels for persons performing platform work (Art. 20). Final provisions are found in **Chapter VI** (promotion of collective bargaining in platform work, non-regression and more favourable provisions, entry into force).

III. Contents of the Commentary

8 The opening chapter of the commentary situates the Platform Work Directive within its legal and policy context (**Part I**). It begins by examining legal and legislative initiatives and developments taken by Member States to address issues of platform work, before moving on to instruments and measures at the EU level. It concludes with a detailed overview of the legislative process of the Platform Work Directive.

9 Chapter II of Part I addresses the interaction between the P2B Regulation and the Platform Work Directive. The P2B Regulation served as a model for the Platform Work Directive in many respects. The P2B Regulation sets out information and transparency obligations for digital platforms, thereby ensuring a fair, transparent and predictable online business environment for businesses that sell goods or services to consumers through these platforms. The Platform Work Directive itself only refers to the P2B Regulation on one occasion, in Art. 11(5), where it gives precedence to the P2B Regulation in cases where decisions made or supported by an automated decision-making system are subject to human review. This raises the question of how the Platform Work Directive interacts with the other provisions of the P2B Regulations. What protective provisions are in place for self-employed persons offering their goods or services via platforms? Chapter II of Part I provides a detailed exploration of these questions.

10 Part I (Chapter III) of this commentary concludes with an examination of the Nordic model, which is well known for its extensive collective bargaining coverage. It explores the role of collective agreements in regulating platform work, with a particular focus on the experiences made in Sweden.

11 **Part II** of this commentary focuses on the **interpretation** of the key articles of the Platform Work Directive. The Platform Work Directive is subject to **autonomous interpretation** to ensure the Directive's full practical effectiveness and the uniform application of the terms across all Member States. No conclusions can be drawn from national law. Therefore, the articles are interpreted in the context of EU law and in light of the case law of the European Court of Justice. Each interpretation starts with a list of the legislative texts and the relevant recitals for their interpretation. The intention of the legislators is read from the recitals in the sense of a **historical interpretation**. The recitals represent results of the negotiations and are essential for interpreting the operative provisions of the Platform Work Directive. The regulatory purpose is set out in Art. 1(1) and provides the basis for a **teleological interpretation** of the Directive. All provisions in the Platform Work Directive are understood as provisions that were created to improve the working conditions of platform workers and the protection of personal data of all persons performing platform work. Essential elements to achieve these aims include

the introduction of measures to facilitate the determination of the correct employment status of persons performing platform work, as well as measures to promote transparency, fairness, human oversight, safety and accountability in the algorithmic management of platform work. Transparency with regard to platform work is a key element of the Platform Work Directive, including in cross-border situations. Consequently, the prohibitions must be implemented in such a way that there are meaningful improvements for platform workers and persons performing platform work.

From a **systematic point of view** the Platform Work Directive is only one of many 12
pieces of legislation currently in force that apply to digital platforms. In addition to the Platform Work Directive there are the GDPR, the P2B Regulation and the AI Act. The **interaction between** these legal acts and the Platform Work Directive is also explored either as a separate contribution in Part I, Chapter 2 or in Part II of the commentary (Art. 1 mn. 12 et seqq.) and in the preliminary remarks to Arts. 7–12 (mn. 39 et seqq. and mn. 55 et seqq.).

The Platform Work Directive establishes a regulatory framework for algorithmic 13
management for the first time. To aid understanding of these key provisions of the Platform Work Directive, Arts. 7–12 are preceded by preliminary remarks explaining the concept of algorithmic management, its role in platform work and the Directive's approach to addressing algorithmic management. The preliminary remarks conclude with an explanation of how the Directive interacts with related legal acts, such as the GDPR and the AI Act.

To provide a comprehensive interpretation of Arts. 13 to 15, it is essential to explore 14
the collective dimension of the Platform Work Directive in its entirety. Arts. 13 to 15 should not be interpreted word by word in the conventional sense. Instead, the commentary on these articles provides a more comprehensive overview of the role of workers' representatives and representatives of self-employed persons, and their collective labour rights under the Platform Work Directive.

Part III analyses the impact of the Platform Work Directive on the national systems 15
of selected Member States. The country reports provide a detailed overview of the current legal situation in each country and the challenges and opportunities that Member States are facing when transposing the Platform Work Directive into their national legal frameworks. There are significant differences between Member States. While some Member States, such as Spain or France, have already enacted legislation with different approaches even before the Platform Work Directive entered into force, others, such as Germany, have remained inactive. As *Franz Gamillscheg*[1] wrote over 50 years ago, the experiences of other countries can provide valuable insights and serve as a model for one's own legal system. However, they can also serve as a warning against the mistakes that other countries have already made in their regulation of platform work.

[1] Gamillscheg, 'Arbeitsrecht und Rechtsvergleichung' in Kraus/Bracht (eds), Recht im Dienste der Menschenwürde, Festschrift für Herbert Kraus, Würzburg 1964, p. 95.

PART I
CONTEXT OF THE DIRECTIVE

Chapter I
Legal policy background

Literature: Aloisi/Rainone/Countouris, 'An unfinished task? Matching the Platform Work Directive with the EU and international "social acquis"', ILO Working Paper 101, 12/2023; Bjerre/Ilsøe/Larsen, 'Report on the Comparative Analysis of Case Studies of Social Actors' Innovative Strategies', Origami project, Milano 2025; Bourgery-Gonse, 'EU-Parlament: Einigung zur Plattformarbeit trotz Schlammschlacht. Euractiv (2023); Berger/Gogola, 'Plattformarbeit: mehr als nur ein Gig. Rechtliche Fragen und gewerkschaftliche Herausforderungen' in Raschauer/Tomaschek (eds), Nachhaltige Arbeitswelten. Überlegungen zu einer zukunftsfähigen Gestaltung von Arbeit, Münster 2024, p. 97; Daugareilh/Degryse/Pochet, 'The Platform Economy and Social Law: Key Issues in Comparative Perspective', ETUI Research Paper – Working Paper 2019.10, Brussels 2019; Degner/Kocher, 'Arbeitskämpfe in der "Gig-Economy"? Die Protestbewegungen der Foodora- und Deliveroo- Riders und Rechtsfragen ihrer kollektiven Selbstorganisation', Kritische Justiz 2018, 247; Deinert/Maksimek/Sutterer-Kipping, 'Die Rechtspolitik des Sozial- und Arbeitsrechts', HSI-Schriftenreihe Band 30, Frankfurt am Main 2020; De Stefano/Durri/Stylogiannis/Wouters, 'Platform work and the employment relationship', ILO Working Paper 27, Geneva 2021; De Stefano, 'The EU Commission's proposal for a Directive on Platform Work: an overview', ILLeJ 2022, 1; Durri/Stylogiannis/Wouters, 'The Platform Work Directive: a milestone or a nothingburger' in Sabato/Ghailani/Spasova S. (eds), Social policy in the European Union: state of play 2024, Social Europe amidst the security and competitiveness paradigms, ETUI and OSE Brussels 2025, p. 81; Durri, 'Connecting the dots between the Platform Work Directive and some existing EU social acquis: A missed opportunity for the Platform Work Directive', OSE Paper Series, Research Paper No. 69, European Social Observatory, Brussels 2025; Durri, 'Casual work arrangements and platform-based work: The casual work agenda as a way to enhance the labour protection of platform workers', Bulletin of Comparative Labour Relations, Alphen aan Rijn 2023; Hauben/Lenaerts/Wayert, 'The platform economy and precarious work', Study requested by the EMPL Committee, Luxembourg 2020; Gramano, 'Guidelines on Collective Agreements for Solo Self-Employed' in Hiessl (ed), EU Labour Law A Commentary, Alphen aan Rijn 2025, p. 1195; Gramano, 'Art. 101 AEUV' in Hiessl (ed), EU Labour Law A Commentary, Alphen aan Rijn 2025, p. 77; Gruber-Risak/Warter/Berger, 'Grundlagenpapier: Plattformarbeit – was tun?', Wien 2020; Gruber-Risak/Berger, 'Plattformarbeit in der EU' (AK Policy Paper), Wien 2021; Gruber-Risak/Warter, Die EU-Richtlinie zur Verbesserung der Arbeitsbedingungen in der Plattformarbeit, Das Recht der Arbeit (RdA) 2024, 267; Hiessl, Case Law on the Classification of Platform Workers: Cross-European Comparative Analysis and Tentative Conclusions, Comparative Labour Law & Policy Journal 2024, 1; Hiessl, Statusfragen in der Plattformarbeit: Europäische Arbeitnehmer- und Arbeitgeberkonzepte auf dem Prüfstand, Soziales Recht 2024, 128; Kilhoffer/De Groen/Lenaerts/Smits/Hauben/Waeyaert/Giacumacatos/Lhernould/Robin-Olivier, 'Study to gather evidence on the working conditions of platform workers (VT/1018/032)', Publications Office of the European Union, Luxembourg 2019; Kocher, Digitale Plattformarbeit – die Verantwortung von Marktorganisatoren, Zeitschrift für Europäisches Privatrecht, ZEuP 2021, 606; OECD: 'What Have Platforms Done to Protect Workers During the Coronavirus (Covid-19) Crisis?', Paris 2020a; OECD: 'Employment Outlook 2020: Worker Security and the Covid-19 Crisis', Paris 2020b; Piasna/Zwysen/Drahokoupil, 'The platform economy in Europe. Results from the second ETUI Internet and Platform Work Survey', ETUI Working Paper 2022.05, Brussels 2022; Prassl, Humans as a Service: The Promise and Perils of Work in the Gig Economy, Oxford University Press 2018; Pulignano/Marà/Franke/Muszynski, 'Informal employment on domestic care platforms: A study on the individualisation of risk and unpaid labour in mature market contexts', Transfer: European Review of Labour and Research 2023, 323; Risak, 'Fair working conditions for platform workers. Possible regulatory approaches at the EU level', Friedrich Ebert Stiftung, Berlin 2018; Schusta/Berger, 'Ein wichtiger Paradigmenwechsel: Ausnahme von kollektiven Verträgen vom EU-Kartellrecht zur Schaffung von Marktgegenmacht', A&W-Blog, Wien 2023; Seifert, 'Kollektivverträge für wirtschaftlich abhängige Selbständige und unionsrechtliches Kartellverbot', HSI-Schriftenreihe Band 42, Frankfurt am Main 2022; Spasova/Marenco, 'The politics behind EU legislation on platform work: institutional synergies and a novel constellation of players' in Vanhercke/Sabato/Spasova (eds), Social policy in the European Union: state of play 2022, Policymaking in a permacrisis (2023), p. 69; Sutterer-Kipping, 'Platform Work Directive' in Hiessl (ed), EU Labour Law A Commentary, Alphen aan Rijn 2025, p. 702; UNCTAD, 'Business e-commerce sales and the role of online platforms', UNCTAD Technical notes on ICT for development, No. 1, Geneva 2024.

A. The long way home: The regulation of platform work in European labour law

I. Background and context

1 Activities such as shopping, food preparation and delivery, cleaning, repairs, transport services, text and translation services, tutoring, graphic design, fitness services, dating services, childcare services, care for the sick and elderly, medical examinations and therapies, and car or flat sharing are all handled, paid for and provided digitally or on site as services via online platforms. The growth rates of the platform economy, and the booming subscription and sales trends on platforms demonstrate the great importance of these new forms of communication, lifestyle and work. Services offered by international work and service platforms, such as *Delivery Hero*, *Just Eat Takeaway*, *Uber*, *Bolt*, *Care.com*, have become even more important as a result of the coronavirus pandemic.[1] The protracted global lockdowns and the consequent increase in unemployment have boosted demand for platform services, leading to a corresponding rise in the number of persons performing platform work. The variety of platforms' business models is nearly unlimited, and it varies by both country and operator.[2] **Digital labour platforms** differ from platforms serving individual users, for example social media, and from those that facilitate the trade of goods or services, including e-commerce and business-to-business platforms.[3] Digital labour platforms use **automated monitoring and decision-making systems** to **organise work** performed by individuals, based on the **request of the service recipient.**[4] Platform work makes life easier for many people by

[1] OECD 2020a, What Have Platforms Done to Protect Workers During the Coronavirus (Covid-19); OECD 2020b, Employment Outlook 2020: Worker Security and the Covid-19 Crisis.
[2] Prassl, p. 12.
[3] ILO 2021, p. 31.
[4] Recital 19 Platform Work Directive.

providing quick, simple and low-cost access to services. They also offer many people alternative ways to earn some income.[5]

Due to the rapid global expansion of e-commerce and the platform-based service industry, even before the COVID-19 pandemic, the platform economy has gained considerable economic importance, especially in urban areas.[6] 2

The business model is based on short-term, platform-based assignments, in which people often earn their living through a large number of small-scale contractual relationships. Platform work functions as a digital model of work organisation and service provision independent of stationary production or labour, goods and service markets. A special feature of this type of work organisation is that predominantly (supposedly) self-employed individuals provide individual services for changing contractual partners on demand and within the framework of a decentralised, demand-driven (just-in-time) and algorithm-based system. By building their business model on the commitment of unorganised individuals, the platform economy exploits the **grey areas** between the **legal status** and the **reality** of dependent wage labour and (often economically dependent) self-employment. Given that classification as an employee remains a gateway to labour and social protection at Member State and EU level, a growing group of economically dependent **platform workers** are falling outside the scope and protection of labour law and social security law.[7] This means that, although the reality of the work relationship between parties shows that these individuals are employees, the formal classification as self-employed deprives them of entitlements such as the minimum wage (where it exists), collective bargaining, working time and health protection, the right to paid leave or improved access to protection against work accidents, unemployment and sickness benefits, as well as contributory old-age pensions.[8] 3

The amount of work carried out via platforms is still increasing. According to the European Commission, around 28 million people had jobs through online platforms in 2021. However, it is estimated that around 5.5 million of these persons were incorrectly classified as self-employed. As of 2025, around 43 million persons are working through online platforms.[9] However, many of them face precarious working conditions, involuntary self-employment and very low wages are not uncommon in this sector.[10] Several studies by the European Commission show that more than half of the people working via platforms earn less than the statutory minimum hourly wage that applies in the country in which they work.[11] **Platform work** is likely to **expand in the future**,[12] both in terms of the **number of workers** involved and its reach into **new sectors**.[13] 4

In this chapter, the terms 'platform worker' and 'worker' is used in a broad sense to refer to all persons who perform work via a platform and does not strictly align with the legal definition set out in Art. 2 of the Platform Work Directive. The distinction between 'platform workers' and 'persons performing platform work' is made only in Section B (The Platform Work Directive – high and low lights) and C (Guidelines on collective 5

---

[5] ILO 2021, p. 243 seqq.

[6] UNCTAD 2024, Business e-commerce sales and the role of online platforms.

[7] See in particular Prassl, p. 73 et seqq.

[8] De Groen et al., p. 64 et seq.; Kilhoffer et al., p. 247.

[9] European Commission 2021a, European Commission, Improving Working Conditions in Platform Work. Fact Sheet by the European Commission, <https://ec.europa.eu/social/BlobServlet?docId=24991&langId=en> (last accessed: 11.12.2025).

[10] See in general Eurofound 2018.

[11] Piasna/Zwysen/Drahokoupil, p. 42 seq.

[12] ILO 2019, p. 44.

[13] Prassl, 'The Platform Work Directive' (YouTube, 2022) <https://www.youtube.com/watch?v=Q9tHaDDSPiw&t=50s> (last accessed: 10.12.2025).

agreements regarding the working conditions of self-employed persons), where specific provisions of the Platform Work Directive are discussed.

1. Challenges related to working conditions

a) *Employment Status*

6 Platform work **blurs the boundaries between employment and self-employment** and the responsibilities between platforms, workers and clients.[14] Bogus self-employment deprives platform workers who are in fact employees from accessing basic labour and social rights.

7 Furthermore, platform work is characterised by **complex employment relationships** that involve **multiple parties**. Platforms typically argue that they play the role of intermediaries, matching supply and demand for specific services, and often explicitly refute the role of employer in their terms and conditions. However, persons performing platform work through intermediaries face the same risks of misclassification and algorithmic management, as those who directly work with the platform.[15]

b) *No protection against the termination of their relationship*

8 Platforms can end relationships with platform workers by **deactivating their accounts**, often **without giving workers prior notice** or providing any **explanation** for the decision. The vast majority of platform workers lack any opportunity to request clarification, engage in dialogue with a human contact person, or contest the decisions issued.[16]

c) *Social protection*

9 Platform workers usually have **limited access to social protection**. The situation arises because platform workers are often deemed self-employed, engaged on (very) short-term contracts, or involved in tasks that are not recognised as economic activities.[17] Their classification as self-employed deprives them of both **legal and effective access** to social protection. For platform workers, achieving effective access to social protection and benefits can be challenging because eligibility conditions, such as long qualifying periods, are hard to meet.[18]

d) *Earnings*

10 Most platform workers do not earn sufficient income through their platform work activities to make a living. They are **paid by task** rather than by hour; work is broken into small tasks, and they may lack bargaining power. Platform workers sometimes must pay a fee to the platform and cover work-related costs, such as gas, insurance and other costs, including providing their own materials and equipment.[19] **Low remuneration** finally contributes to **income uncertainty**. In addition to low remuneration, platform

---

[14] Recital 6 Platform Work Directive.

[15] Recital 24 Platform Work Directive.

[16] Recital 8 Platform Work Directive.

[17] Kilhoffer et al., p. 71.

[18] Council of the European Union, 'Proposal for a directive of the European Parliament and of the Council on improving working conditions in platform work – General approach', 7.6.2023, 10107/23, 10 seqq. <https://data.consilium.europa.eu/doc/document/ST-10107-2023-INIT/en/pdf> (last accessed: 15.12.2025).

[19] Kilhoffer p. 74.

workers also face issues related to **non-payment**, even though the client retains the work.[20]

e) Working time

In practice, the flexibility to choose whether, when and how long to work is often far more restricted than it appears, as platform workers may be required to log in during certain working hours, particularly during peak hours when labour demand is highest. Algorithm-driven schedules can lead to **unpredictable and anti-social working hours**, which can be excessively short or long and may often include **unpaid stand-by periods**.[21] These unpaid intervals may involve waiting for tasks, commuting between client locations, or engaging in emotional labour.[22] 11

2. Algorithmic management

The business model in the platform economy is characterised by the absence of traditional hierarchical structures and the apparent autonomy of platform workers. Algorithms exert control comparable to the managerial prerogatives of employers. **Control is not always direct** and can be exercised indirectly through the evaluation of work performance using **feedback, rating, and reputation** systems. The results of these evaluations, including the acceptance or rejection of work by platform workers, are then used to assign future jobs, thereby influencing shift/working hours and the type of jobs offered to platform workers.[23] At the same time, platforms also need a reliable and constantly available workforce. This requires a certain degree of predictability in work performance. Rating, sanction, and incentive systems play an important role in ensuring this. 12

Algorithmic management can lead to a **magnified surveillance** over workers, '**increase power imbalances** and **opacity about decision-making**'.[24] Platform workers typically lack information about which personal data algorithms use, how these algorithms make decisions and how their behaviour influences automated decision making.[25]

3. Conclusion

To **sum up**, platform work often blurs the line between employment and self-employment, leaving many platform workers misclassified as independent contractors and without basic labour or social rights. Platforms can terminate platform workers' access by deactivating accounts without notice, explanation, or the possibility to appeal. Because they are usually treated as self-employed or hired for very short tasks, platform workers have limited access to social protection and often cannot meet eligibility requirements for benefits. 13

Earnings are typically low and unstable: platform workers are paid per task, have little bargaining power, must cover their own expenses, and may even face non-payment. 14

[20] Commission Staff Working Document, Analytical document, Accompanying the document, Consultation document, Second phase consultation of social partners under Article 154 TFEU on a possible action addressing the challenges related to working conditions in platform work, 15.6.2021, C(2021) 4230 final, 69 link: <Protecting people working through platforms: Commission launches second-stage consultation of social partners – Employment, Social Affairs & Inclusion – European Commission> (last accessed: 15.12.2025).

[21] Durri, p. 154.

[22] Durri, p. 184; Pulignano et al, Transfer: European Review of Labour and Research 2023, 323 (326).

[23] Sutterer-Kipping in Hiessl, p. 702 (708); Kocher, p. 618.

[24] Recital 4 Platform Work Directive.

[25] Recital 8 Platform Work Directive.

The promise of flexible working time remains a mirage in many cases, as algorithms dictate when platform workers should be online, and much time spent waiting or on standby goes unpaid. Algorithmic management further shapes access to work through ratings and opaque automated decisions, increasing surveillance, power imbalances, and dependency.

II. Legal and legislative initiatives and developments

1. National courts dealing with employment status of platform workers

15 This line of critique outlined above was accompanied by legal activism and advocacy and led to numerous **Supreme Courts'** disputes in various EU Member States, with first *Uber* drivers and subsequently riders driving the development of case law against bogus self-employment.[26] The two main sectors of platform work most affected by legal disputes are **passenger transport** and **food delivery**, with the central issue revolving around the **employment status** of platform workers. A comparison of the judicial outcomes shows that, in most cases, national courts found that an employment relationship with the platform was present. However, the heterogeneity of platforms and the frequent changes to their terms and conditions make it difficult to identify consistent patterns in national case law.[27]

16 In **France**, for example, the *Cour de Cassation*[28] classified *Uber* drivers as employees in 2020, following the *Take Eat Easy* decision in 2018.[29] In that case, drivers' acceptance and cancellation rates were monitored, and their accounts were temporarily suspended after three refusals. Similar decisions have been made by delivery platforms in **Italy** and **Spain**.[30] In **Germany**, the Federal Labour Court[31] in 2021 focused on the platform's organisational structure. Although crowd workers were not contractually required to accept offers, the platform was designed so that only by accepting a certain number of orders could registered and trained users improve their status and receive more lucrative orders. The Federal Labour Court considered this incentive system to be a means of steering crowd workers' behaviour towards their employment needs without the necessity of specific instructions. According to the Federal Labour Court, this resulted in indirect control from the platform (→ Germany mn. 16).

2. National legislation on working conditions and social protection of platform workers

17 In addition to national case law on employment status in platform work, attempts were made to regulate platform work at the national level even before the Platform Work Directive.

18 In **France**, the 2016 *Loi El Khomri* introduced a framework in which social security obligations stemmed from a platform's social responsibility rather than its legal responsibility as an employer. It inserted specific provisions into the French Labour Code for

---

[26] See for an overview of the decisions Hiessl Comparative Labour Law & Policy Journal 2024, 1 (5 et seqq.).

[27] Hiessl SR 2024, 128 (130).

[28] Cour de Cassation 4.3.2020 arrêt n° 374 (19–13.316) – ECLI:FR:CCAS:2020:SO00374 (ruling on Uber).

[29] Cour de Cassation 28.11.2018 arrêt n° 17–20.079 (ruling on Take eat easy).

[30] Corte di Cassazione 24.1.2020 n. 1663/2020 (ruling on Foodora); Tribunal Supremo, 23.9.2020 – 4746/2019 (ruling on Glovo).

[31] BAG 1.12.2020 – 9 AZR 102/20, NZA 2021, 552 (ruling Roamler).

self-employed workers using one or more digital platforms to provide personal services (Art. L. 7241–1 and Art. L. 7342–1).[32] These workers are covered by core collective labour rights and are entitled to insurance for work accidents and professional diseases, training and continued education. The *Loi 2019–1428 du 24 décembre d'orientation des mobilités* also obliged ride-hailing and delivery service platforms to provide self-employed workers with relevant information.

In **Italy**, a 2019 Legislative Decree[33] broadened the personal scope of Art. 2 of the existing legal framework,[34] extending full employment and labour protections to 'workers whose personal performance is organised by the client, including through digital platforms,' unless a collective agreement provides otherwise.[35] In addition, a new chapter[36] was introduced to regulate self-employed delivery couriers operating in urban areas with bicycles or motor vehicles, for cases in which they do not fall within the scope of Art. 2. (→ Italy mn. 1).

In **Spain**, there has even been a law since July 2021, the so-called *Ley Riders*[37], which follows the Spanish Supreme Court decision for the Case of Glovo.[38] It establishes a rebuttable presumption in favour of an employment relationship focusing exclusively on delivery platforms. (→ Spain mn. 4) Furthermore, the law introduces algorithmic transparency provisions, by making it mandatory for platform companies to display to all platform workers the decision-making process of algorithms, which affects their working conditions, access to, and termination of their relationship with the platform.

3. Collective bargaining

In **Denmark**, a company agreement was concluded in 2018 between the cleaning platform ***Hilfr*** and the *United Federation of Danish Workers* (3F) (the Nordic approach. Chap. III mn. 4). The agreement enabled platform workers to choose employee status and gain the related benefits, while still keeping the possibility to work as freelancers. It had a tangible impact on platform workers' conditions, as an increasing proportion of tasks were carried out by employees – known as '*super Hilfrs*' – who received minimum wages, pension contributions, holiday pay, and sick leave.[39] This agreement was renegotiated in 2024 and it contains rules also on **algorithmic management**. 19

In **Austria**, a sectoral agreement was concluded in 2019 covering all **bicycle couriers**.[40] It sets out rules on **working hours** and **wage**, overtime and night work pay, equipment provision, procedures for resolving disputes, and **social protections** such as paid leave and sick days. This agreement was renegotiated in 2021, 2022, 2023 and 2024.[41] 20

---

[32] LOI n°2016–1088 du 8 août 2016 relative au travail, à la modernisation du dialogue social et à la sécurisation des parcours professionnels.

[33] Legislative Decree of 3 September 2019, n.101 disposizioni urgenti per la tutela del lavoro e per la risoluzione di crisi aziendali.

[34] Legislative Decree of 15 June 2015, n. 81 disciplina organica dei contratti di lavoro e revisione della normativa in tema di mansioni, a norma dell'articolo 1, comma 7, della legge 10 dicembre 2014, n. 183.

[35] De Stefano et al., p.21.

[36] Capo V-bis, Articolo 47-bis, comma 1, Legislative Decree n. 81 of 15 June 2015.

[37] Royal Decree-Law 9/2021.

[38] Tribunal Supremo 23.9.2020 – 4746/2019 (ruling on Glovo).

[39] Bjerre/Ilsøe/Larsen, p. 9.

[40] Collective Agreement for bicycle couriers, valid from 1.1.2023 (WKO, 2023) <https://www.wko.at/kollektivvertrag/kollektivvertrag-fahrradboten-2023> (last accessed: 10.12.2025).

[41] The union VIDA has terminated the collective bargaining agreement for bicycle couriers, effective September 30, 2025. However, as of 2026, uniform minimum standards regarding working conditions, pay, and rights will also apply to new employment relationships for independent contractors (the largest group of platform workers in Austria) through the conclusion or application of collective bargaining

21 In **Spain**, a company agreement was initially signed in 2021 between ***Just Eat* Spain** and the trade unions *Comisiones Obreras* (*CCOO*), *Unión General de Trabajadores* (*UGT*), and the *Federation of Independent Workers of Commerce* (*FETICO*).[42] It covers **salary** revisions, career development pathways for delivery staff and the extension of **working hours** within employment contracts. The company commits to informing employee representatives about the use of **algorithms** or **AI systems** that affect working conditions.

4. Instruments and Actions at EU Level

22 At the same time, the European Union has also been turning its attention to platform work.

23 The EU institutions first turned their attention to the legal issues raised by online platforms in **2015–2016**, beginning with the **Communication on the Digital Single Market Strategy**,[43] followed by the **Communication on the European Agenda for the Collaborative Economy.**[44]

24 The European agenda for the collaborative economy seeks to clarify the concepts of collaborative platforms and platform work. At that time, however, the European Commission still referred the question of the employment status of service providers exclusively to the competence of the Member States.[45]

25 The proclamation of the **European Pillar of Social Rights** (EPSR) in Gothenburg on 17 **November 2017**, which comprises 20 principles in three main areas – equal opportunities and access to the labour market, fair working conditions, and social protection and social inclusion – was a significant catalyst for the Directive. The endorsement of the EPSR offered a key framework for regulating working conditions as the labour market confronted emerging challenges. As a result of its proclamation, it has served as the **basis for several new guidelines, recommendations and other instruments.** For example, one of the pillars' roll-out initiatives was the adoption by the European Parliament and the Council in June 2019 of a **Directive on Transparent and Predictable Working Conditions.**[46] This Directive extends important safeguards against working time unpredictability also to platform workers, who are already employees.

26 In **June 2019**, a **Platform-to-Business** (P2B) **Regulation** aimed at promoting **fairness and transparency for business users of online intermediation services** directly addresses the platform economy. However, it does not cover employees, but **only self-employed** persons, who act in a **professional capacity** rather than as private individuals. Numerous platforms are likewise excluded from the Regulation's scope, such as *Uber* and *Deliveroo*, which do not merely offer online intermediation services (→ Chapter

---

agreements (BMASGPK, 2025) <https://www.sozialministerium.gv.at/Themen/Arbeit/Arbeitsrecht/Freie-Dienstverh%C3%A4ltnisse.html> (last accessed: 24.3.2026).

[42] Just Eat Company Agreement (CCOO, 2021), <https://www.ccoo-servicios.es/archivos/Acuerdo%20Sindicatos%20JUST%20EAT(1).pdf> (last accessed: 10.12.2025).

[43] European Commission, 'Communication from the Commission to the European Parliament, the Council, the European Economic and Social Committee and the Committee of the Regions, A Digital Single Market Strategy for Europe', 6.5.2015, COM(2015) 192 final.

[44] European Commission, 'Communication from the Commission to the European Parliament, the Council, the European Economic and Social Committee and the Committee of the Regions, A European agenda for the collaborative economy', 2.6.2016, COM(2016) 356 final.

[45] European Commission 'Communication from the Commission to the European Parliament, the Council, the European Economic and Social Committee and the Committee of the Regions, A European agenda for the collaborative economy', 2.6.2016, COM(2016) 356 final, 12 et seqq., 15.

[46] Directive (EU) 2019/1152 of the European Parliament and of the Council of 20 June 2019 on transparent and predictable working conditions in the European Union, OJ L 186/105, 11.07.2019.

P2B mn. 27).[47] The fundamental problem of precarious working conditions in the platform economy thus remained unresolved in EU law.

27 Improving working conditions in platform work became a prominent priority on the **EU agenda** with the publication in **July 2019** of the **von der Leyen I political guidelines**[48] for the 2019–2024 European Commission. Commission President *Ursula von der Leyen* pointed out that 'digital transformation brings fast change that affects our labour markets' and promised to 'look at ways of improving the labour conditions of platform workers, notably by focusing on skills and education'.[49] This intention was reiterated in *von der Leyen's* letter of intent annexed to the State of the Union address of **September 2020**, in which improving the labour conditions of people working in the platform economy was highlighted as one of the key new initiatives for 2021.[50] The **Mission Letter to *Nicolas Schmit***, the former European Commissioner for Jobs and Social Rights, also contains a similar passage, though it focuses more on working conditions: 'Dignified, transparent and predictable working conditions are essential to our economic model. I want you to closely monitor and enforce existing EU law in this area and to look at ways to improve the labour conditions of platform workers'.[51]

28 In **November 2019**, the Council adopted a **Recommendation on Access to Social Protection for Workers and the Self-employed.**[52] Although not legally binding, it sets out a common direction across the EU to make **social protection systems more inclusive**, particularly in response to new and non-standard forms of work, including platform work.

29 **In October 2020**, the European Commission work programme 2021 announced a **legislative initiative** for the end of 2021 on improving the **working conditions in platform work**, following a two-stage consultation of the social partners.

30 Concerns expressed by EU institutions, Member States, social partners, and civil society regarding platforms' impact on employment and the heightened risks for the platform workers concerned prompted the European Commission to launch a consultation process. On 24 **February 2021**, the European Commission launched **the first stage of consultations** with the social partners, which was open until 7 April 2021. The purpose of this first-stage social partner consultation was to gather the perspectives of European social partners on **whether EU action is needed** and, if so, on the **appropriate direction such action should take** to improve working conditions in platform work.[53]

---

[47] Hauben/Lenaerts/Wayert, p. 53.

[48] Von der Leyen, Political guidelines 2019–2024, A Union that strives for more- My agenda for Europe, <commission.europa.eu/document/download/063d44e9-04ed-4033-acf9-639ecb187e87_en?filename=political-guidelines-next-commission_en.pdf> (last accessed: 05.10.2025).

[49] Von der Leyen, Political guidelines 2019–2024, A Union that strives for more – My agenda for Europe, p. 10 <commission.europa.eu/document/download/063d44e9-04ed-4033-acf9-639ecb187e87_en?filename=political-guidelines-next-commission_en.pdf> (last accessed: 5.10.2025).

[50] Von der Leyen, Mission Letter to Nicolas Schmit, Commissioner-designated for Jobs, 2019 p. 5 <https://commissioners.ec.europa.eu/system/files/2022-11/mission-letter-nicolas-schmit_en.pdf> (last accessed: 11.12.2025).

[51] Von der Leyen, Mission Letter to Nicolas Schmit, Commissioner-designated for Jobs, 2019 p. 5 <https://commissioners.ec.europa.eu/document/download/acd12257-a614-47f1-ae25-40354d402460_en?filename=mission-letter-nicolas-schmit_en.pdf > (last accessed: 11.12.2025).

[52] Council Recommendation of 8 November 2019 on access to social protection for workers and the self-employed, OJEU 2019/C 387/01, https://eur-lex.europa.eu/legal-content/EN/TXT/?uri=uriserv:OJ.C_.2019.387.01.0001.01.ENG&toc=OJ:C:2019:387:TOC (last accessed: 24.03.2026).

[53] European Commission, 'Protecting people working through platforms: Commission launches a first-stage consultation of the social partners' (Press Release, 2021) <https://ec.europa.eu/commission/presscorner/detail/en/ip_21_686> (last accessed: 10.12.2025).

The Commission received 14 replies from social partners across the EU.[54] The consultations reflected a divergence between employer organisations and trade unions. While trade unions sought stronger measures on employment status, algorithmic transparency and access to rights,[55] employers stressed autonomy of national systems and warned against undermining legitimate self-employment.[56] Based on the replies received, the Commission concluded that further EU-level action is required to safeguard fundamental labour standards and rights for platform workers.[57]

31 The **second-stage consultation** with social partners was launched by the European Commission on 15 June and remained open until 15 **September 2021**. The purpose of the consultation was to gather social partners' views on a **potential legislative or non-legislative instrument** and its **possible content**.[58] Many employers were sceptical about a binding Directive covering all forms of platform work, arguing for non-legislative or more flexible instruments.[59] Trade unions tended to favour stronger binding instruments to ensure minimum standards across the EU.[60] While trade unions argued for the employment status to be at the core of any action, employers emphasised that platform work is very diverse and often the person genuinely is self-employed, so a 'one-size-fits-all' rule or a strong presumption of employment might undermine flexibility. In the consultation document, social partners were asked whether they were willing to enter into negotiations with a view to reaching an agreement under Art. 155 TFEU.[61] Nevertheless, **no agreement** could be reached: 'Their positions differed dramatically on the desired legal nature as well as on the content of such an initiative.'[62]

[54] European Parliamentary Research Service, 'Improving the working conditions of platform workers, Pre-legislative synthesis of national, regional and local positions on the European Commission's initiative' (European Parliament, 2021) <https://www.europarl.europa.eu/RegData/etudes/BRIE/2021/698839/EPRS_BRI%282021%29698839_EN.pdf?utm_source> (last accessed: 10.12.2025).

[55] ETUC, 'ETUC reply to the First phase consultation of social partners under Article 154 TFEU on possible action addressing the challenges related to working conditions in platform work' (ETUC, 2021) <https://www.etuc.org/sites/default/files/document/file/2021-04/ETUC%20reply%20to%20the%20First%20phase%20consultation%20of%20social%20partners%20%20platform%20work.pdf?utm_source> (last accessed: 10.12.2025).

[56] Business Europe, 'First phase social partner consultation on possible action addressing the challenges related to working conditions in platform work' (Business Europe, 2021) <https://www.businesseurope.eu/wp-content/uploads/2025/02/2021-04-06_platform_work_-_final_response_1st-phase_consultation_-82f-1.pdf?utm_source> (last accessed: 10.12.2025).

[57] European Commission – Press release, 'Protecting people working through platforms: Commission launches second-stage consultation of social partners' (European Commission, 2021) <https://ec.europa.eu/commission/presscorner/api/files/document/print/en/ip_21_2944/IP_21_2944_EN.pdf> (last accessed: 10.12.2025).

[58] European Commission – Press release, 'Protecting people working through platforms: Commission launches second-stage consultation of social partners' (European Commission, 2021) <https://ec.europa.eu/commission/presscorner/api/files/document/print/en/ip_21_2944/IP_21_2944_EN.pdf> (last accessed: 10.12.2025).

[59] World Employment Confederation, '2nd stage consultation of social partners under Article 154 TFEU on possible action addressing challenges related to working conditions in platform work' (World Employment Confederation, 2021) <https://weceurope.org/uploads/2021/09/WEC-Europe-position-2nd-stage-Consultaton-platform-work-15-Sept-2021.pdf?utm_source> (last accessed: 10.12.2025).

[60] ETUC, 'ETUC reply to the Second phase consultation of social partners under Article 154 TFEU on possible action addressing the challenges related to working conditions in platform work' (ETUC, 2021) <https://www.etuc.org/en/document/etuc-reply-second-phase-consultation-social-partners-under-article-154-tfeu-possible?utm_source> (last accessed: 10.12.2025).

[61] Consultation Document, 'Second-phase consultation of social partners under Article 154 TFEU on possible action addressing the challenges related to working conditions in platform work', 15.6.2021, (SWD(2021) 143 final) <https://ec.europa.eu/social/main.jsp?catId=89&furtherNews=yes&langId=en&newsId=10025> (last accessed: 15.12.2025).

[62] Spasova/Marenco, p. 78.

The **European Parliament** adopted a **resolution** on 16 September 2021 in which MEPs called on the European Commission to submit a proposal for a Directive on platform workers that would promote fair and transparent working conditions.[63] 32

After extensive consultations, which did not result in an agreement, the European Commission highlighted the importance of taking EU action in this area[64] and finally presented a **draft Directive on Improving working conditions in platform work** on 9 **December 2021**.[65] Many of the platform-specific challenges were addressed in the European Commission's impact assessment.[66] According to the Commission's proposal, a person performing platform work would be presumed an employee if at least **two of five control-related criteria** were satisfied. These included: remuneration set by the platform; requirements on appearance or conduct; electronic monitoring; limited discretion over working hours or task refusal; and constraints on working for other clients. This approach has been criticised by many scholars, who argue that the Commission has failed to recognise that, in many Member States, the presence of just one of the criteria set out in Art. 4 is sufficient to establish the existence of an employment relationship. Another criticism was that the Commission's concept of presumption was too closely aligned with the traditional subordination criterion instead of addressing the specific characteristics of platform work.[67] The proposal establishes a right to **transparency** concerning the use and functioning of **automated monitoring and decision-making systems**, together with **human oversight** of their effects on working conditions, in order to safeguard platform workers' fundamental rights and occupational health and safety. It also creates mechanisms through which platform workers can raise concerns and request the **review of automated decisions**. These rights apply to both employees and genuinely self-employed workers. Furthermore, the proposal aims to increase **transparency and traceability** in platform work to help authorities enforce current labour and social protection rules. It specifies that digital labour platforms that act as employers must report platform work to the authorities of the Member State where it occurs. 33

The Directive would also improve authorities' insight into active platforms by providing access to **key data**, such as the number of platform workers, their employment status and their usual terms and conditions. 34

On **19 May 2022**, the rapporteur *Elisabetta Gualmini* (S&D) presented her draft report, which contained 186 amendments aimed at greater binding force and more extensive rights for platform workers and their representatives.[68] The **European Parliament's Committee on Employment and Social Affairs** (EMPL) adopted the **report** prepared by *Gualmini* on 12 **December 2022**, by 41 votes to 12, amending the proposal in several ways.[69] The European Parliament's version of the employment presumption 35

---

63 Legislative Observatory European Parliament, European Parliament resolution of 16 September 2021 on fair working conditions, rights and social protection for platform workers – new forms of employment linked to digital development (2019/2186(INI)) <Document summary | Legislative Observatory | European Parliament> (last accessed: 14.12.2025).

64 Recital 15 Platform Work Directive.

65 European Commission, 'Proposal for a Directive of the European Parliament and of the Council on improving working conditions in platform work', 9.12.2021, COM(2021) 762 final.

66 European Commission, 'Proposal for a Directive of the European Parliament and of the Council, On improving working conditions in platform work accompanying impact assessment', 9.12.2021, SWD(2021) 396 final.

67 De Stefano ILLeJ 2022, 1 (4); Aloisi/Rainone/Countouris, p. 14 et seq.

68 European Parliament, 'Report on the proposal for a directive of the European Parliament and of the Council on improving working conditions in platform work', 21.12.2022, A9–0301/2022. Available at: <https://www.europarl.europa.eu/doceo/document/A-9-2022-0301_EN.html>.

69 European Parliament, Report on the proposal for a directive of the European Parliament and of the Council on improving working conditions in platform work, 21.12.2022, A9–0301/2022.

was considered as 'the most interventionist and worker-friendly one', as there were **no criteria** for triggering it.[70] Instead, the party seeking to rebut the presumption would have been required to prove that two cumulative conditions were met: first, that the platform exercised neither control nor direction; and second, that the platform worker was normally engaged in an independently established trade, profession, or business of the same nature as the work performed. Furthermore, the report enhances **data-protection measures** and mandates **human oversight** over all decisions affecting working conditions. It also promotes the right to **collective bargaining** as a key tool to improve the working conditions of persons performing platform work, irrespective of their employment status, which should be encouraged by the European Commission and Member States. On 2 **February 2023**, the Parliament's plenary confirmed the EMPL committee's decision to enter into interinstitutional negotiations with the Commission and the Council ('trilogue') based on the report.

36 It is hardly surprising that the **European Parliament** was the **most progressive force** in the negotiations on the Directive. This is evident not only from the **voting behaviour of MEPs** in Parliament, where the Directive was supported by a broad coalition of the Left, S&D, Greens, EPP and Renew[71], but also from the fact that, as described above, the Directive ultimately stems from an **initiative by Parliament**. It should also be mentioned that there was heavy and shady lobbying by the platform companies and other pressure groups.[72]

37 The **Council of the European Union** was the last of the relevant European players to adopt its position (a so-called 'general approach') on the proposed Directive on 12 **June 2023**.[73] The Council reverted to the European Commission's approach based on criteria to trigger the presumption, but it **split the original five criteria into seven**. In contrast to the Commission's proposal, the Council's version would have required three of these criteria to be fulfilled.

38 The final phase of the trilogue dragged on and showed how politically controversial the issue is. At the end of 2023, **a compromise** was negotiated under the **Spanish Council Presidency**. However, on 22 **December 2023**, this compromise did **not receive sufficient support** in the Council of the EU. Twelve countries, including France in particular, voted against it, while Germany abstained. This meant that the required approval of 55% of the states, representing at least 65% of the population, was not achieved.

39 **Another provisional agreement** between the Parliament and the Council was concluded on 8 **February 2024**, only for the Council to reject it once more on 16 February 2024.[74] Ultimately, the necessary qualified majority was achieved against a strong opposition from liberal, conservative and right wing governments under the **Belgian Council Presidency** on 11 March 2024. The governments of France and Germany

---

[70] Durri/Stylogiannis/Wouters in Sabato/Ghailani/Spasova, p. 81 (86).

[71] Howtheyvote.eu (Howtheyvote, 2024) <https://howtheyvote.eu/votes/168270> (last accessed: 11.12.2025).

[72] See for example Corporate Europe Observatory 2024; BBC News, 'Uber Files: Massive leak reveals how top politicians secretly helped Uber' (BBC, 2022), <https://www.bbc.com/news/business-62057321> (last accessed: 10.12.2025).

[73] Council of the European Union, Proposal for a Directive of the European Parliament and of the Council on improving working conditions in platform work – General approach, 7.6.2023, 10107/23 <https://data.consilium.europa.eu/doc/document/ST-10107-2023-INIT/en/pdf> (last accessed: 14.12.2025).

[74] European Parliament, Initiative to improve the working conditions of people working in the platform economy, In 'A Europe Fit for the Digital Age', Legislative train schedule 2025, <https://www.europarl.europa.eu/legislative-train/theme-a-europe-fit-for-the-digital-age/file-improving-working-conditions-of-platform-workers> (last accessed: 10.12.2025).

abstained, which is a first in European legislation. The short-term change of heart by the governments of Estonia and Greece ultimately broke the blocking minority that they had previously formed with Germany and France. In the **final text** of the Directive, **no predetermined legal criteria** were set for triggering the presumption. Instead, it can be activated when parties establish **facts indicating control and direction** in judicial or administrative proceedings. Therefore, the design of the presumption is shifted from being set at EU level (predetermined legal criteria) to becoming established at national level (relying on facts indicating direction and control). The **algorithmic management** chapter is based on the principles of **transparency, fairness and accountability** in algorithmic monitoring and decision-making systems. The compromise text **strengthens collective labour rights**, by promoting the right to collective bargaining, the creation of digital communication channels to enable it and establishing the right to information and consultation on important decisions which impact working conditions.

The Directive was then formally ratified by the Council and the plenary of the European Parliament on the penultimate day of the 2019–2024 legislative period.[75] The Member States have two years to transpose the legal act into their own national legal systems. The **new rules** will apply **from 2 December 2026.** 40

B. The Platform Work Directive – high and low lights

The Platform Work Directive serves a **dual purpose: improving working conditions and safeguarding personal data** in the context of platform work.[76] This reflects its reliance on **two legal bases** in the TFEU – Art. 16(1) on data protection and Art. 153(1)(b) on improving working conditions.[77] 41

The rights contained in the Directive have a **different scope of application**.[78] The Directive distinguishes between '**platform workers**' meaning 'persons performing platform work who have or are deemed to have an employment contract or employment relationship' and '**persons performing platform work**' – a broader category that includes everyone carrying out platform work, including the genuinely self-employed persons (Art. 2(1), (c) and (d)) (→ Art. 2 mn. 62).[79] While the algorithmic management provisions apply to all persons performing platform work, certain provisions remain exclusively applicable to employees, such as health and safety rules (→ Art. 12 mn. 4). 42

The **rebuttable presumption of employment** (→ Art. 5 mn. 5) represents the most politically controversial part of the Directive. Because the final text no longer contains specific legal criteria for activating the presumption, Member States now have considerable leeway in implementing it.[80] This outcome reflects the compromise required to reach an agreement at the European level after years of challenging negotiations. Impor- 43

---

[75] Directive (EU) 2024/2831 of the European Parliament and of the Council of 23 October 2024 on improving working conditions in platform work, PE/89/2024/REV/1, OJ L, 2024/2831, 11.11.2024.

[76] Art. 1 and recital 16 Platform Work Directive.

[77] Durri OSE Paper 2025, p. 7.

[78] Countouris/Prassl, Beyond bogus self-employment: the EU Platform Work Directive's presumption of employment, and its implications for the future of employment rights in the gig economy (Oxford Human Rights Hub, 2024) <https://ohrh.law.ox.ac.uk/beyond-bogus-self-employment-the-eu-platform-work-directives-presumption-of-employment-and-its-implications-for-the-future-of-employment-rights-in-the-gig-economy/> (last accessed: 10.12.2025).

[79] European Commission, Report Expert Group – Transposition of the Directive (EU) 2024/2831 on improving working conditions in platform work (12.1.2026), 17.

[80] For example, it was important for Austria that the 'independent contractor' remains as a form of contract; Austria has also issued a so-called protocol declaration on this issue (Österreichisches Parlament, 2024).

tantly, the Directive emphasises the importance of the facts relating to the performance of work, over the parties' own characterisation of the relationship ('primacy of facts') (→ Art. 4 mn. 27).

44 The Directive provides, for the first time, a regulatory framework for the use of algorithmic management (→ Preliminary remarks to Arts. 7–12 mn. 31) which provides safeguards against **automated monitoring and decision-making systems** to all persons performing platform work. This broad scope is based on the idea that automated monitoring and decision-making systems have a similar impact on the working conditions of genuinely self-employed persons as they do on platform workers.

45 The Directive explicitly forbids the **processing of certain personal data** and biometric information, including data on a person's emotional state, those relating to private conversations, or data used to predict the exercise of fundamental rights (→ Art. 7 mn. 2). Furthermore, digital labour platforms must carry out an **impact assessment** on how automated systems used for the processing of personal data affect the protection of personal data of persons performing platform work (→ Art. 8). Beyond data protection, the Directive seeks to enhance transparency, fairness, and accountability in algorithmic management within platform work. In light of **transparency** (→ Art. 9 mn. 2), all persons performing platform work should be informed about essential aspects of their work, such as the use of automated systems, the grounds and categories of decisions taken or supported by automated decision-making systems, etc. **Fairness** requires platforms to put in place human resources to monitor and evaluate automated systems, in view of the risks they pose, including potential discriminatory effects (→ Art. 10 mn. 1). To strengthen **accountability**, the Directive grants persons performing platform work the right to obtain explanation about decisions made and to challenge those decisions when the explanations provided are unsatisfactory (→ Art. 11 mn. 3).

46 In addition, the Directive sets out rules to protect the **health and safety** of **platform workers** (→ Art. 12 mn. 1). Platforms are therefore required to evaluate the risks that automated monitoring or decision-making systems may pose to workers' safety and health, assess whether adequate safeguards are in place and implement appropriate preventive and protective measures.

47 The Directive sets out important **collective labour rights** such as the right to information and consultation and the right to collective bargaining.[81] These rights are explicitly acknowledged as fundamental rights (Art. 7(1)(d)). With the exception of restrictions applicable to representatives of persons performing platform work, these rights apply to all persons performing platform work. Representatives of platform workers, such as trade unions, have platform-specific rights to **information and consultation** (→ Arts. 13 and 14) in connection with the use of or significant changes to automated monitoring and decision-making systems. In the absence of workers' representatives, platforms must directly inform platform workers (Art. 14, recital 53). Platform workers' representatives may consult experts for the analysis and evaluation of these systems, with the costs to be borne by the platform companies under certain circumstances (Art. 13(3)).

48 The Directive expressly embeds the **promotion of collective bargaining** in platform work within its final provisions (Art. 25). With a view to enable collective bargaining, platforms are required to create internal **communication channels** (→ Art. 20 mn. 8). Recital 62 explains that these channels are necessary due to a lack of common workplaces. The channels must be set up in such a way that all persons performing platform

---

[81] Gruber-Risak/Warter RdA 2024, 267 (268); Berger/Gogola in Raschauer/Tomaschek p. 97 (103 et seq.).

work can communicate with each other and/or their representatives, without surveillance or influence from the platform.

Finally, the Directive introduces **transparency requirements** for platform operators, obliging them to report platform work to the authorities of the Member State in which the work is performed (→ Arts. 16–17). Accordingly, platform companies must supply national authorities and representatives of persons performing platform work with relevant information, including data on the number of platform workers, their contractual status, the applicable terms and conditions, etc. **49**

C. Guidelines on collective agreements regarding the working conditions of self-employed persons

In **September 2022**, the European Commission also adopted a Communication regarding **antitrust guidelines**[82] for solo self-employed persons, particularly those performing platform work.[83] **50**

In addition to and complementary with the Directive, these guidelines refer to genuinely solo self-employed yet economically dependent persons who provide services personally.[84] **51**

They provide indications for compliance with Art. 101 TFEU, for persons who are solo self-employed and perform collective action and agreements as associations of undertakings, if they are in a comparable situation to employees, in particular those who work via digital labour platforms. This strengthens the **constitutionally recognised freedom of association of economically dependent self-employed persons** (Art. 28 of the Charter of Fundamental Rights of the EU), increases legal certainty and 'may provide an important means to improve the working conditions'[85] for this group. **52**

According to the Guidelines, the European Commission considers collective agreements between solo self-employed persons and a counterparty with a certain level of economic strength to be an effective means of **tackling power imbalances**; therefore competition law does not apply to solo self-employed persons that are in a **situation comparable to workers** (→ mn. 56) and the European Commission will not enforce EU competition rules against collective agreements made by solo self-employed persons who are in a **weak negotiating position** (→ mn. 59).[86] **53**

The guidelines are primarily intended to provide clarification considering economic developments and business trends (like subcontracting, outsourcing, spread of solo self-employment in general), academic debates on the scope of EU competition law in this context[87] and the certain relevant case law of the European Court of Justice.[88] In cases **54**

---

[82] Guidelines are a common, non-binding instrument in the European Commission's competition law practice, in which it sets out how it interprets and applies European law. This is a voluntary commitment by the Commission, guidelines do not establish rights or responsibilities. However, as the Commission has exclusive enforcement powers in the area of competition policy, its guidelines are of crucial importance for enforcement by Member States. A final judgement on the legal situation is therefore always the responsibility of the courts of the EU. See also Gramano in Hiessl, p. 1195 (1199 et seq.).

[83] European Commission communication, 'Guidelines on the application of Union competition law to collective agreements regarding the working conditions of solo self-employed persons' (2022/C 374/02), OJ C 374/2, 30.9.2022, hereinafter referred to as 'Guidelines'.

[84] Gramano in Hiessl, p. 1195 (1207).

[85] Guidelines, Paragraph 8.

[86] Guidelines, Paragraph 33.

[87] See for example Seifert, p. 55 et seqq.

[88] ECJ 3.7.1986 – case C-66/85, ECLI:EU:C:1986:284 – Deborah Lawrie-Blum / Land Baden-Württemberg; ECJ 21.9.1999 – case C-67/96, ECLI:EU:C:1999:28 – Albany International BV / Stichting Bedrijf-

where collective agreements extend beyond the regulation of labour relations, the prohibition of agreements restricting competition laid down in Art. 101(1) TFEU applies.[89] In *Albany*, the CJEU concluded that agreements entered into within the framework of collective bargaining, negotiated between employers' associations and an organisation of self-employed persons (rather than an employees' association), aimed at improving working conditions, fall outside the scope of European competition law.[90] In *FNV Kunsten*, the CJEU ruled that 'a provision of a collective labour agreement, in so far as it sets minimum fees for service providers who are 'false self-employed', cannot, by reason of its nature and purpose, be subject to the scope of Art. 101(1) TFEU'.[91] Following this, it was unclear whether the CJEU was referring to false self-employed persons or self-employed persons who are in a situation comparable to that of employees (employee-like self-employed persons).[92]

55 Against this background, the new guidelines define **three categories** of solo self-employed persons **who are in situation comparable to workers** that can negotiate collective agreements concerning working conditions[93] in compliance with EU Competition law:

56 **1) Economically dependent solo self-employed persons**, i.e. solo self-employed persons who receive on average more than half of their income from the same client over a period of one or two years.[94] The Guidelines therefore recognise that solo self-employed persons who provide services solely or primarily to one client are economically dependent on that client. Such contractual partners are more likely to be in a position to control and determine their working conditions.[95]

57 **2)** Solo self-employed persons who work **'side by side'** with real employees, e.g. self-employed temporary musicians who provide the same services as employed musicians.[96] Whether or not a functional 'side-by-side' relationship constitutes an employment relationship is left to national legislators to decide, but collective agreements which encompass both solo self-employed and employed persons are not prohibited by EU competition law.[97]

58 **3) Solo self-employed persons who work via digital labour platforms**,[98] i.e. classic cases of human labour in the gig economy such as driving services or food delivery

---

spensioenfonds Textielindustrie; ECJ 4.12.2014 – case C-413/13, ECLI:EU:C:2014:2411 – FNV Kunsten Informatie en Media / Staat der Nederlanden.

[89] Workers are excluded by legal definition from EU competition law, which applies to economic entities (‚undertakings'). Nevertheless, collective agreements inevitably have certain effects on competition, the social policy objectives pursued by such agreements would be seriously jeopardised if the social partners were always subject to Art. 101 TFEU when seeking measures to improve employment and working conditions.

[90] ECJ 21.9.1999 – case C-67/96, ECLI:EU:C:1999:28 – Albany International BV / Stichting Bedrijfspensioenfonds Textielindustrie.

[91] ECJ 4.12.2014 – case C-413/13, ECLI:EU:C:2014:2411 – FNV Kunsten Informatie en Media / Staat der Nederlanden, 41.

[92] Deinert/Maksimek/Sutterer-Kipping 2020, p. 375 seqq; Seifert, p. 82; Gramano in Hiessl, p. 77 (88).

[93] The term working conditions refers to 'remuneration, rewards and bonuses, working time and working patterns, holiday, leave, physical spaces where work takes place, health and safety, insurance and social security, and conditions under which solo self-employed persons are entitled to cease providing their services or under which the counterparty is entitled to cease using their services' (Guidelines, Section 2 (15)).

[94] Guidelines, Section 3.1.

[95] See also Gramano in Hiessl, p. 1195 (1213).

[96] Guidelines, Section 3.2.

[97] See also Gramano in Hiessl, p. 1195 (1213 et seq.).

[98] The term 'digital labour platform' is defined in accordance with the Platform Work Directive, see Guidelines, Section 1 (2), Foodnote 2.

services.[99] The term 'digital labour platform' is defined in accordance with the Platform Work Directive. The Guidelines recognise that solo self-employed persons performing platform work who find themselves in a situation comparable to that of platform workers vis-à-vis the digital labour platforms through or to which they provide their labour have little or no scope to negotiate their working conditions. The absolute bargaining power of digital platforms and their 'take it or leave it' approach toward contractual partners with regard to work offers are addressed in the Guidelines.[100]

Finally, the European Commission, acting as the European competition authority, will not enforce EU competition law against collective agreements made by self-employed persons in a **weak negotiating position**. However, these agreements are still subject to competition law under Art. 101 TFEU, but will not be given enforcement priority. The European Commission has assumed that, while these solo self-employed persons are not in a situation comparable to that of workers, they still have insufficient bargaining power to influence their working conditions. In this context, the Commission views collective agreements as a legitimate means of redressing the imbalance in bargaining power between the two parties.[101] **59**

The European Commission's clarifications are useful considering relevant decisions of the CJEU, which only **created legal certainty** on exemptions from EU competition law only for a limited number of cases. The guidelines cover a comprehensive range of issues and not just the area of the platform economy. The guidelines recognise the **de facto superiority** of large players in contract markets instead of pretending that self-employed micro-entrepreneurs are on an equal footing with global corporations or large agencies.[102] Nevertheless, there are still gaps in protection, for example for self-employed persons who receive less than 50% of their income from a client and are not covered by one of the other categories.[103] **60**

D. Conclusion

The Platform Work Directive emerged in response to the rapid growth of platform work, which despite offering flexibility and swift access to services, also raised concerns about (platform) worker misclassification and (correct) employment status, precarious working conditions, algorithmic control and limited access to social protection. The proclamation of the European Pillar of Social Rights in 2017, along with the explicit political mandate of President *von der Leyen* in 2019, elevated platform work as a **priority area for social policy reform**. At the same time, fragmented national case law and diverse legislative approaches highlighted the insufficiency of relying solely on Member State action. EU institutions increasingly recognised that platform work is inherently cross-border, and that national regulatory gaps enabled platforms to arbitrage between legal systems, undermining (platform) workers' rights and legal certainty across the **61**

[99] Guidelines, Section 3.3.

[100] See also Gramano in Hiessl, p. 1195 (1214).

[101] Guidelines, Section 3.1.

[102] Even in cases where solo self-employed persons are not in a situation comparable to that of employees, they may have a structurally weak negotiating position vis-à-vis their counterpart, for example when there is an imbalance in bargaining power in negotiations with economically stronger counterparts. In such cases, the European Commission will not enforce EU competition law (Guidelines, Section 4.(32)), see also Gramano in Hiessl, p. 1195 (1218).

[103] Schusta/Berger, 'Ein wichtiger Paradigmenwechsel: Ausnahme von kollektiven Verträgen vom EU-Kartellrecht zur Schaffung von Marktgegenmacht' (A&W-Blog 2023) <https://www.awblog.at/Arbeit/ausnahmen-vom-eu-kartellrecht> (last accessed: 11.12.2025).

Union. A Directive at the EU level was therefore necessary to establish some **minimum standards**, ensure **fair competition** across Member States, and improve **enforceability of labour and social protection** rules.

62 The negotiations revealed **substantial divergences** among institutional actors. The **European Parliament** emerged as the strongest advocate for expansive protections, proposing a presumption of employment without criteria for triggering it and enhanced algorithmic safeguards. The **Council,** by contrast, pushed for greater national flexibility, ultimately leading to a compromise where the presumption is triggered by facts indicating control and subordination rather than fixed EU-level criteria. The **European Commission**, having conducted extensive social partner consultations, positioned itself between these poles, while also issuing complementary **Guidelines** enabling economically dependent solo self-employed persons—including platform workers—to engage in collective bargaining without infringing EU antitrust rules.

63 **Social partners** played a central but divided role. **Trade unions** consistently demanded strong intervention by the EU and platform specific European labour law, emphasising misclassification, algorithmic exploitation, and the need for collective bargaining rights. **Employer organisations** insisted on preserving flexibility and cautioned against rigid rules that might restrict genuine self-employment. As these positions proved irreconcilable, Art. 155 TFEU route toward a negotiated agreement failed, compelling the European Commission to advance legislation independently.

64 The Directive's **core safeguards** include a rebuttable presumption of employment to counter widespread misclassification; algorithmic transparency, human oversight and accountability obligations that apply to all persons performing platform work; and strengthened collective labour rights, including information and consultation as well as collective bargaining. The Directive's approach to activate the presumption through evidence of control and subordination—rather than pred-determined EU-wide criteria—provides Member States with flexibility. Yet this very flexibility risks perpetuating **a fragmented regulatory landscape**, where rights and protections vary significantly across the single market. Unlike the rebuttable presumption of employment, the **national implementation** of the provisions on algorithmic management and transparency is unlikely to encounter any particular hurdles, as the Directive's requirements in these areas are already relatively detailed.

65 Overall, the Directive marks a **significant progress in European labour law**, aiming to rebalance power in the platform economy and to provide clarity, transparency, and fundamental protections for millions of platform workers. Yet its impact will depend heavily on **national transposition**, **effective enforcement**, and the **continued involvement of social partners**. While it sets a European floor of rights, it leaves space for Member States to adopt more ambitious solutions,[104] which are crucial for shaping fair and sustainable digital labour markets in the years ahead. The next years will be decisive in determining whether Europe can live up to its social ambitions in the digital age.

[104] See also recital 68 Platform Work Directive: 'This Directive lays down minimum requirements, thus leaving untouched the Member States' prerogative to introduce and maintain provisions which are more favourable to persons performing platform work Rights acquired under the existing legal framework should continue to apply, including as regards mechanisms to ascertain the existence of an employment relationship, unless more favourable provisions are introduced by this Directive [...]'.

Chapter II
Interaction between the P2B Regulation and the Directive on Platform Work

Literature: Adams-Prassl, 'Regulating Algorithms at Work: Lessons for a 'European Approach to Artificial Intelligence', ELLJ 2022, 30; Arncken, 'Scope of application § 15' in Steinrötter/Heinze/Dega (eds), EU Platform Law, Baden Baden Munich Oxford 2025, p. 433; Berberich, 'Due diligence obligations, content moderation and procedural fairness § 5' in Steinrötter/Heinze/Denga (eds), EU Platform Law, Baden Baden Munich Oxford 2025, p. 101; Busch, 'Mehr Fairness und Transparenz in der Plattformökonomie? Die neue P2B Verordnung im Überblick', GRUR 2019, 788; Busch, 'Small and medium-sized enterprises in the platform economy, more fairness for SMEs in digital markets', WISO Diskurs, Bonn 2020; Busch/Mak, 'Putting the Digital Services Act into Context: Bridging the gap between EU Consumer Law and Platform Regulation', European Legal Studies Insitute Osnabrück, Osnabrück 2021; Busch (ed), 'Verordnung (EU) 2019/1150 zur Förderung von Fairness und Transparenz für gewerbliche Nutzer von Online Vermittlungsdiensten (P2B V0)', Munich 2022; Busch, 'Platform regulation beyond DAS and DMA: Which role fort he P2B Regulation?', Journal of Antitrust Enforcement 2024, 201; Hofmann/Raue, Digital Services Act, Article by Article Commentary, Baden Baden Munich Oxford 2025; Höppner/Schulz, 'Die EU-Verordnung 2019/1150 für Fairness und Transparenz von Online-Vermittlungsdiensten ('P2B-Verordnung')', Zeitschrift für Wirtschaftsrecht 2019, 2329; Köhler/Feddersen (eds), Gesetz gegen den unlauteren Wettbewerb, Munich 2026; König, 'Obligations for gatekeepers § 12' in Steinrötter/Heinze/Denga (eds), EU Platform Law, Baden Baden Munich Oxford 2025, p. 342; Legner, 'Der Digital Services Act – Ein neuer Grundstein der Digitalregulierung', ZUM 2024, 99; Louven, 'Requirements for terms and conditions and market conduct § 16' in Steinrötter/Heinze/Denga (eds), EU Platform Law, Baden Baden Munich Oxford 2025, p. 449; Nolteernsting, 'The European Regulatory Framework of Ranking Transparency on Platform Markets – P2B + P2C = P2U', IIC 2025, 1359 (1360); Podszun, 'Verhandlungen des 73. Deutschen Juristentages, Band 1: Gutachten / Teil F: Empfiehlt sich eine stärkere Regulierung von Online-Plattformen und anderen Digitalunternehmen?', Munich 2020; Prassl/Risak, 'The Legal Protection of Crowdworkers: Four Avenues for Workers' Rights in the Virtual Realm' in: Meil/Kirov (eds), Policy Implications of Virtual Work, Heidelberg 2017, p. 273; Podszun/Bongartz/Langenstein, The Digital Markets Act: Moving from Competition Law to Regulation for Large Gatekeepers, EuCML 2021, 60; Schweitzer, 'Digitale Plattformen als private Gesetzgeber: Eine Perspektivwechsel für die europäische "Plattfom-Regulierung"', ZEuP 2019, 1; Steinrötter/Schauer, 'Scope of application § 2' in Steinrötter/Heinze/Denga (eds), EU Platform Law, Baden Baden Munich Oxford 2025, p. 12; Tribess, 'Complaint-handling, mediation, enforcement and monitoring § 17' in Steinrötter/Heinze/Dega (eds), EU Platform Law, Baden Baden Munich Oxford 2025, p. 482; Verhuyck, 'The Achilles heel of the Platform-to-Business Regulation: no Unfair Term Protection for platform workers?', Journal of Law, Market and Innovation 2024, 260; Wielsch, 'Wettbewerbsrecht zweiter Ordnung: Der DMA als Teil einer digitalen Medienverfassung', ZUM 2023, 153; Wilman/Kalėda/Loewenthal (eds), 'The EU Digital Services Act', Oxford 2024; Kersting/Meyer-Lindemann/Podszun, Kommentar zum Deutschen und Europäischen Kartellrecht, Munich 2025.

A. Introduction

1 The legal debate surrounding platform work centres on the precarious employment of bogus self-employed persons and on determining their correct employment status. This chapter, instead, examines how genuine solo self-employed persons in the platform economy are protected, as they are traditionally excluded from labour and social protection law, yet they may face similar challenges in terms of dependency towards digital platforms. For the purposes of this chapter, 'solo self-employed persons' refer to all those who do not qualify as workers under the EU worker concept or employment relationship as defined in Art. 45 TFEU,[1] and who rely primarily on their own personal labour to provide the relevant services.[2]

2 Both the **Platform Work Directive** and the **Platform-to-Business Regulation** (hereinafter P2B Regulation) offer instruments to protect solo self-employed, provided that they offer their services via a digital platform. Digital platforms enable solo self-employed persons to expand their distribution channels and tap into new markets. At the same time, as digital intermediaries between providers of goods and services and customers, digital platforms also pose the risk of providers becoming dependent on platforms which control the access to customers.

3 This chapter addresses the following questions: What challenges do solo self-employed persons face when offering their services to customers via digital platforms? What instruments are available to them at European level, and how do these instruments interact with each other? The chapter focuses on the P2B Regulation and the Platform Work Directive. First, the P2B Regulation is outlined, followed by an examination of how it interacts with the Platform Work Directive.

---

[1] ECJ 3.7.1986 – case C-66/85, ECLI:EU:C:1986:284 – Deborah Lawrie Blum v Land Baden-Württemberg: at the time of the case, Art. 48 TFEU was still Art. 48 of the EEC Treaty and the term 'Community meaning' was used instead of the current 'EU meaning'; ECJ 19.3.1964 – case 75/63, ECLI:EU:C:1964:19 – Hoekstra (née Unger) v. Bestuur der Bedrijfsvereniging voor Detailhandel en Ambachten; ECJ 14.10.2010 – case C-428/09, ECLI:EU:C:2010:612 – Union Syndicale Solidaires Isère v Premier ministre and Others; ECJ 9.7.2015 – case C-229/14, ECLI:EU:C:2015:455 – Ender Balkaya v Kiesel Abbruch- und Recycling Technik GmbH; ECJ 4.12.2014 – case C-413/13, ECLI:EU:C:2014:2411 – FNV Kunsten Informatie en Media v Staat der Nederlanden; ECJ 17.11.2016 – case C-216/15, ECLI:EU:C:2016:883 – Betriebsrat der Ruhrlandklinik gGmbH v Ruhrlandklinik gGmbH.

[2] The term refers to the definition of self-employed person under 2(a) of the Guideslines from the Commission on the application of Union competition law to ollecitve argreements regarding the working conditions for solo-self-employed (2022/C 374/02) EUR-Lex – 52022XC0930(02) – EN – EUR-Lex> (last accessed 12.2.2026).

B. Digital platforms: opportunities and challenges for solo self-employed persons

The rapid growth of the platform economy has transformed market structures and 4
the conditions for competition in the digital marketplace. Digital platforms have become the most important players in the digital economy, bringing together potential businesses and consumers (B2C) or businesses and businesses (B2B). At their core, digital platforms offer connecting services. They act as **information intermediaries** between supply and demand. Their role is to coordinate various parties and reduce their search and information costs (**transaction costs**) and they address the **issue of trust** in online marketplaces, where suppliers and customers usually do not know each other personally. The use of data and matching algorithms is necessary to accomplish this task. A wide range of data is collected and evaluated, including both personal and non-personal data. The spectrum of data encompasses transaction and payment data, address data, and **reputation data derived from customer rating systems**. This data is used in various ways to control supply and demand decisions, for example through pre-settings, a limited selection or guidance towards specific contractual partners. A typical means of controlling economic decisions is the ranking of search results.[3] As customers tend to choose among the first options displayed, those at the top of the rankings are more likely to be awarded the contract. These ranking systems and practices are generally not transparent to customers or businesses. Without information about the ranking mechanism, competition on platforms and between platforms is limited.

The structure of digital platform markets is characterised by the fact that the digital 5
platform acts as an intermediary between different user groups within a multi-sided market. Its attractiveness to users on one side of the platform increases as the number of users on the other side of the platform grows (**indirect network effects**). The more suppliers use the digital platform to list their products or services, the more attractive the service becomes to potential customers. Similarly, it is beneficial for suppliers if as many potential customers as possible use the platform, as this increases the likelihood of successful transactions.[4] As a result, customers and suppliers tend to use the largest platform, which becomes more dominant and wins the market competition.[5]

Each additional user incurs only marginal costs for the digital platform in relation to the considerable initial investment (known as **economies of scale**), resulting from a market used by several competing suppliers to a highly concentrated market or even monopolistic market. This creates 'winner-takes-it-all' markets with high barriers to entry.[6] Digital platforms are not just passive (digital) marketplaces, but also grant the platform economic control over the success or failure of other businesses.[7] By doing so, digital platforms are increasingly assuming the role of a 'private legislator', establishing the rules for participation in this new, technology-driven, centrally controlled economy.[8]

---

[3] According to studies cited by the European Commission in the Google Shopping case, the first ten search results receive around 95% of all clicks from Google users. European Commission, press release dated 27 June 2017, Antitrust: Commission fines Google € 2.42 billion for abusing its dominant position as a search engine by giving preferential treatment to its own price comparison service, available at <http://europa.eu/rapid/press-release_MEMO-17-1785_en.htm> (last accessed 12.2.2026).

[4] Alexander in Köhler/Feddersen P2B Regulation Introduction mn. 17.

[5] Nolteernsting IIC 2025, 1359 (1362).

[6] Podszun/Bongartz/Langenstein, EUCML 2021, 60 (61).

[7] Podszun, Gutachten F zum 73. Deutschen Juristentag: Empfiehlt sich eine stärkere Regulierung von Online-Plattformen und anderen Digitalunternehmen?, 2020, p. F10 et seqq.

[8] Schweitzer ZEuP 2019, 1 (8); Busch, p. 6.

6 Another complicating factor is the risk of '**self-preferencing**' when digital platforms act as intermediaries between supply and demand and also offer goods or services themselves, thereby competing with active suppliers on the platform (hybrid digital platforms). A well-known example of a hybrid digital platform is *Amazon*, where customers can purchase goods from *Amazon* itself via Amazon.com, as well as from third-party businesses via the *Amazon* Marketplace.[9]

7 For self-employed persons, the platform economy presents **opportunities and risks.** Digital platforms act as intermediaries between suppliers and customers, thereby expanding the distribution channels and markets available to the self-employed. However, there is a risk that suppliers may become dependent on these platforms, which control market access and set the rules of the marketplace.

8 In the recitals of the P2B Regulation, European legislators have described this trend accurately:

> 'Online intermediation services can be crucial for the commercial success of undertakings who use such services to reach consumers. To fully exploit the benefits of the online platform economy, it is therefore important that undertakings can trust online intermediation services with which they enter into commercial relationships. This is important mainly because the growing intermediation of transactions through online intermediation services, fuelled by strong data-driven indirect network effects, leads to an increased dependence of such business users, particularly micro, small and medium-sized enterprises (SMEs), on those services in order for them to reach consumers.'[10]

9 The P2B Regulation continues by stating the following:

> 'Given that increasing dependence, the providers of those services often have superior bargaining power, which enables them to, in effect, behave unilaterally in a way that can be unfair and that can be harmful to the legitimate interests of their businesses users and, indirectly, also of consumers in the Union. For instance, they might unilaterally impose on business users practices which grossly deviate from good commercial conduct, or are contrary to good faith and fair dealing.'

10 A study initiated by the European Commission in April 2018 on contractual relationships between platforms and business users confirms these unfair practices. The study found that almost half (46%) of the business users experienced problems in their business relationship with online platforms. These problems include: Potentially harmful trading practices such as sudden **unexplained changes in terms and conditions unilaterally** imposed by platforms **without prior notice or delisting** of products, services or businesses or suspension of accounts **without clear statement of reasons** and a lack of effective redress.[11]

---

[9] Busch, p. 7.

[10] Recital 2 P2B Regulation.

[11] European Commission, 'Proposal for a Regulation of the European Parliament and of the Council on promoting fairness and transparency for business users of online intermediation services Commission Staff Working Document, Impact Assessment', 26.4.2018, SWD(2018) 138 final, Part 1/2, Brussels, 11 et seqq.

C. Legal instruments at EU level to strengthen the rights of self-employed towards digital platforms: P2B Regulation and Platform Work Directive

I. P2B Regulation as a first building block

In order to counteract the imbalance of bargaining power in the platform economy caused by the loss of direct customer interaction and the increasing data power of digital platforms, the EU addressed the issue of platform regulation in 2015, announcing various measures to adapt the legal framework to the evolving conditions of the platform economy.[12] In a 2016 communication entitled 'Online Platforms in the Digital Single Market: Opportunities and Challenges', the European Commission addressed the question of whether, beyond the application of competition policy, EU-level action is needed to ensure the fairness of business-to-business (B2B) relations for the first time, and announced a targeted fact-finding exercise on B2B practices in the online platform environment.[13] Around the same time, the European Commission published its communication entitled 'European Agenda for the Collaborative Economy', which outlined key points for regulating 'collaborative platforms'.[14] 11

In April 2018, the Commission published a proposal for a regulation to promote fairness and transparency for business users of online intermediation services. The proposal resulted in the adoption of the P2B Regulation which **came into force on 12 July 2020** and is directly applicable in all Member States. Only about three months later, the Commission announced a legislative initiative on improving the working conditions in platform work in its work programme for 2021 (see for the legal background of the Platform Work Directive → Chapter I mn. 29).[15] 12

Although the P2B Regulation was the **first general legal framework for online intermediation services**[16], it has largely gone unnoticed. This may be because it came into force in July 2020, at **the height of the global pandemic.** At that time, digital platforms were widely regarded as the solution to many problems, given that much of our lives had shifted online. However, it may also be because the P2B Regulation was **overshadowed by the EU Commission's proposals for a Digital Markets Act (DMA) and a Digital Services Act (DSA).** Just six months after the P2B Regulation came into force, the Commission proposed the DMA, which sets out specific obligations for undertakings that provide core platform services, such as online intermediation services, and that act as gatekeepers in the digital economy. Around the same time, the Commission also proposed the DSA, which sets out specific liability privileges and special due diligence obligations for intermediation services.[17] 13

---

[12] European Commission, 'A Digital Market Strategy for Europe', 6.5.2025, COM(2015) 192 final.

[13] European Commission, 'Communication from the Commission to the European Parliament, the Council, the European Economic and Social Committee and the Committee of the regions, online platforms and the Digital Single Market Opportunities and Challenges for Europe', 25.5.2016, COM(2016) 288 final, 13.

[14] European Commission, 'Communication from the Commission to the European Parliament, the Council, the European Economic and Social Committee and the Committee of the Regions, a European agenda for the collaborative economy', 2.6.2016, COM(2016) 356 final, 2.

[15] European Commission, 'Communication from the Commission to the European Parliament, the Council, the European Economic and Social Committee and the Committee of the Regions Commission Work Programme 2021, A Union of vitality in a world of fragility', 19.10.2020, COM(2020) 690 final, Brussels, 4.

[16] Critical Höppner/Schulz, Zeitschrift für Wirtschaftsrecht 2019, 2329 et seq.

[17] Busch Journal of Antitrust Enforcement 2024, 201.

14 This chapter will firstly provide an overview of the P2B Regulation, including its objectives, scope and key provisions. Building on this, the P2B Regulation's interaction with the Platform Work Directive is examined.

1. Objective of the P2B Regulation

15 As the title of the P2B Regulation suggests, the **objective of this Regulation** is to create transparency and fairness as well as effective redress possibilities for business users of online intermediation services or corporate website users in relation to online search engines (i.e. digital platforms). The P2B Regulation aims to ensure a fair, predictable, sustainable and trusted online business environment within the internal market and a competitive, fair and transparent online ecosystem where companies act responsibly (recitals 7 and 3).

16 In its operative part, the P2B Regulation sets out the rules of fairness and transparency that providers of online intermediation services and online search engines must adhere to when dealing with business users.[18]

The P2B Regulation addresses three main topics: (1) the prohibition of certain unfair practices, such as **unannounced blocking of user accounts** and **changes to terms and conditions** without **prior notice** (Arts. 3, 8 P2B Regulation); (2) transparency with regard to **rankings**, certain business practices (such as data collection and use) and preferential treatment of own products, as well as 'best price clauses' (Arts. 5, 7 and 9); (3) effective dispute resolution measures, such as the establishment of complaint management systems and mediation (Arts. 11–13 P2B Regulation).

17 The P2B Regulation, for example, stipulates that digital platforms must outline the main parameters that determine ranking in order to improve predictability (Art. 5(1) P2B Regulation) and provide a description of how they treat their own services preferentially (Art. 7 P2B Regulation). However, the **Regulation does not prohibit self-preferencing** for hybrid platforms; it merely requires any advantages granted by the digital platform to its own products to be disclosed (see also → mn. 51). With regard to **best-price clauses and the issue of data access**, the P2B Regulation is also limited to transparency requirements (see also → mn. 55).[19]

2. Personal and substantive scope of P2B Regulation

a) Personal Scope

18 The P2B Regulation protects two specific groups of businesses: '**business users of online intermediation services**' and '**corporate website users of online search engines**'. The question is whether self-employed persons offering goods or services via a platform are considered 'business users of online intermediation services' and therefore fall within the scope of the P2B Regulation.

19 The term 'business user' is legally defined in Art. 2(1) P2B Regulation and means '**any private individual** acting in a commercial or professional capacity who, **or any legal person** which, through online intermediation services offers goods or services to consumers for purposes relating to its trade, business, craft or profession'. The term 'legal person' should be interpreted broadly. From an EU legal perspective, partnerships and other associations that can hold rights and obligations should also be classified as legal

[18] Busch in Busch P2B Regulation Art. 1 mn. 1.

[19] Busch, p. 11; Busch in Busch P2B Regulation Introduction mn. 14; Podszun in Busch P2B Regulation Art. 9 mn. 128 et seqq.

persons.[20] The decisive factor is whether the online intermediation service is used in connection with the user's ongoing commercial or professional activities, rather than occasionally. Therefore, activities such as employees selling used work clothes on *eBay* or travelling salespersons offering lifts via a ridesharing app (e.g. *blabla car*) do not qualify the acting party as a business user.[21] However, the circle of persons covered by the P2B Regulation remains **very broad**, as it depends neither on size – even though the initial focus was on small and medium sized enterprises – nor on the field of activity.[22]

The P2B Regulation also protects **corporate website users** who sell goods or services to consumers via their company website and therefore depend on online search engines (such as Google, Bing) or comparison platforms (such as Tripadvisor) in order to be found by customers, including consumers. Conversely to business users of online intermediation services, a **contractual relationship** between the corporate website user and the provider of the online search engine **is not required** (recital 26). Self-employed persons become corporate website users of the online search engine simply by placing their company website on the internet in such a way that it can be found by the search engine.[23] As the definition of 'platform work' in the Platform Work Directive (Art. 2 (1)(b)) requires the existence of a contractual relationship between the digital labour platform and the person performing platform work, the group of 'business users' is of particular interest with regard to interaction between the P2B Regulation and the Platform Work Directive. The subsequent analysis therefore **focuses on 'business users'**. 20

In conclusion, unlike the Platform Work Directive, which only applies to **private individuals performing platform work,** irrespective of the nature of the contractual relationship or the designation of that relationship by the parties involved (see also → Art. 2 mn. 21), the P2B Regulation applies to both **private individuals acting in a commercial** or **professional capacity and legal persons**. However, employees are not considered to be business users.[24] 21

b) Substantive Scope

The substantive scope complements the personal scope by defining the addressees of the P2B Regulation. The P2B Regulation applies to a specific type of platform activity that is facilitated by purely **online intermediation services**. According to Art. 2(2)(a) to (c) P2B Regulation, **online intermediation services** are **information society services** that enable business users to offer goods or services to consumers by **facilitating direct transactions** between **business users** and **consumers**, regardless of whether these transactions are actually concluded (recital 10). This excludes **online search engines** and **pure business-to-business intermediation services** from the scope of application of the P2B Regulation. 22

The requirements for the term 'consumer' are not too demanding; it is sufficient for consumers to be among the recipients of the service. This is met if such services are generally accessible (recital 11). Platforms on which business users sell goods and services to both consumers and non-consumers are therefore covered by the P2B Regulation.[25] The 23

---

[20] Alexander in Köhler/Feddersen P2B Regulation Art. 2 mn. 2.

[21] Arncken in Steinrötter/Heinze/Denga § 15 mn. 9.

[22] Alexander in Köhler/Feddersen P2B Regulation Art. 2 mn. 5; Naumann/Rodhausen ZEUP 2020, 769 (777).

[23] Schulte-Nölke in Busch P2B Regulation Art. 2 mn. 78.

[24] Alexander in Köhler/Feddersen P2B Regulation Art. 2 mn. 5a.

[25] Schulte-Nölke in Busch P2B Regulation Art. 2 mn. 57.

application of the P2B Regulation furthermore requires that information society services are provided **on the basis of a contractual relationship** with business users.[26]

24 Important examples of online intermediation services are named in recital 11. These includes online e-commerce marketplaces, online software applications services (e.g. app stores) and online social media services, irrespective of the technology used to provide such services. This refers to platforms such as *Amazon* Marketplace. An increasing number of customers are using the *Amazon* marketplace as a direct search engine for goods. To reach this growing customer group, providers need to have a presence on the platform. From the customers' perspective, individual sellers of goods are thus reduced to mere suppliers of the platform. This is the case even though, legally speaking, they are the customers' direct contractual partners.[27]

25 At the same time, not all types of **online intermediation services** fall within the personal scope of the P2B Regulation. In particular, digital platforms such as *Uber* or *Deliveroo*, which offer not only pure online intermediation services but also offer their own service (e.g. transport service or delivery service) do not fall within the scope of the P2B Regulation according to the case law of the CJEU.

26 In the case *Elite Taxi*, the CJEU ruled that the intermediation service provided by ***Uber*** must be regarded as 'forming an integral part of an overall service whose main component is a transport service' and therefore must be classified as '**a service in the field of transport**' rather than an '**an information society service**'.[28] The CJEU based its decision on the fact that both drivers and passengers were dependent on *Uber*'s app to provide and use the transport service. In addition, the CJEU pointed out that *Uber* has significant influence over the conditions under which these drivers provide their services given that *Uber* exercises a certain degree of control over the quality of the vehicles, the drivers and their conduct, which can result in their exclusion.[29]

27 This decision made **algorithmic control a key factor** in distinguishing between digital platforms that act as 'pure' intermediaries of online services and those that are closely involved in providing the underlying service, including the setting of prices and access. Consequently, the P2B regulation does not cover self-employed persons offering their services via platforms exercising decisive algorithmic control over the conditions under which those services are provided.[30] Conversely, the more dependent and vulnerable a self-employed person is on a digital platform, the less likely they are to be covered by the P2B Regulation.[31]

28 By contrast, in the case *Airbnb Ireland*[32], the CJEU ruled that *Airbnb* does not provide a service that is an integral part of the accommodation rental service. The service essentially consists of providing a tool for presenting and finding accommodation for rent, thereby facilitating the conclusion of future rental agreements. The CJEU pointed out that, unlike the intermedation service in the case *Elite Taxi*, neither the intermediation service nor the ancillary services (such as a format for setting out the content of their offer or civil liability insurance) offered by *Airbnb Ireland* make it possible to establish the existence of a decisive influence excercised by that company over the accommodation service to which its acitivity relates. This absence of control can be observed in relation

---

[26] Schulte-Nölke in Busch P2B Regulation Art. 2 mn. 37.

[27] Busch, p. 7.

[28] ECJ 20.12.2017 – case C-434/15, ECLI:EU:C:2017:981 – Asociación Profesional Elite Taxi mn. 40.

[29] ECJ 20.12.2017 – case C-434/15, ECLI:EU:C:2017:981 – Asociación Profesional Elite Taxi mn. 39; reaffirmed in ECJ 19.12.2019 – case C-390/18, ECLI:EU:C:2019:1112 – Airbnb Ireland UC. Critical Verhuyck Journal of Law, Market & Innovation 2024, 260 (277).

[30] Adams-Prassl ELLJ 2022, 30 (45).

[31] Adams-Prassl ELLJ 2022, 30 (45); Verhuyck Journal of Law, Market & Innovation 2024, 260 (277).

[32] ECJ 19.12.2019 – case C-390/18, ECLI:EU:C:2019:1112 – Airbnb Ireland UC.

to the rental prices charged and the selection of hosts or accommodation available on its platform. Therefore, *Airbnb* does qualify as a provider of an information society service.[33]

The Platform Work Directive has now closed this protection gap towards digital platforms that offer their own integral service, as it refers to digital labour platforms that use automated monitoring systems or automated decision-making systems (algorithmic management see for the definition → Art. 2 mn. 25 et seqq. and → Preliminary remarks to Articles 7–12 mn. 8) to **organise platform work**. 'Organising work performed by self-employed persons' involves at a minimum a significant role in matching the demand for the service with the supply of work of a person who is in a contractual relationship with the digital labour platform and is available to perform a specific task (recital 20 Platform Work Directive). However, the requirement to 'organise work' does not mean that the digital labour platform directs and controls the work in a way that would qualify the person as an employee. As the Platform Work Directive also applies to **genuinely self-employed persons**, the organisation of such work may also include other activities such as processing payments. At the same time, recital 20 of the Platform Work Directive clarifies that it does not apply to digital labour platforms that merely provide the means for service providers to reach end users (pure intermediation services) without the platform being further involved. Digital platforms such as '*Airbnb*' are even explicitly excluded from the scope of the Platform Work Directive (see also → Art. 2 mn. 54). **29**

In conclusion, digital platforms such as *Uber*, *Deliveroo* and others that offer an underlying service (e.g. a transport, delivery or cleaning service) in addition to pure online intermediation services do not fall within the scope of the P2B Regulation. They are now covered by the Platform Work Directive which **strengthens the rights of genuine solo self-employed persons**. The rights set out in Arts. 7–11, 17 and Chapter V are extended to 'persons performing platform work' who are not in an employment relationship. The examples demonstrate that, in many cases, the scopes of application of the P2B Regulation, on the one hand, and the Platform Work Directive, on the other hand, are mutually exclusive. A solo self-employed can either be a business user of an online intermediation service, or a person performing platform work via a digital labour platform. **30**

However, it cannot be ruled out that certain digital platforms are less involved in the underlying service, meaning they function as both 'online intermediation services' under the P2B Regulation and 'digital labour platforms' under the Platform Work Directive. The distinction between pure intermediation services and the organisation of platform work is **blurred**, and must be determined on a case-by-case basis in functional terms. In borderline cases, both legal instruments may apply to the contractual relationship between the digital platform and the self-employed person. This raises the question of how the P2B Regulation and the Platform Work Directive interact with each other: where are the overlaps, and which provision takes precedence? Firstly, the most important provisions of the P2B Regulation will be outlined, followed by a discussion of their interaction with the Platform Work Directive. **31**

3. Provisions of the P2B Regulation: Comparison between the P2B Regulation and the Platform Work Directive

Although the P2B Regulation does not directly address the working conditions and social protection of self-employed persons, its provisions affect their 'contractual relationship' with digital platforms providing online intermediation services. The P2B **32**

[33] ECJ 19.12.2019 – case C-390/18, ECLI:EU:C:2019:1112 – Airbnb Ireland UC mn. 68.

Regulation contains provisions relating to standard terms and conditions (Arts. 3, 8), sets out transparency requirements for **rankings** and **bestprice clauses** (Arts. 5, 7, 10), and introduces complaint and mediation procedures (Arts. 4, 11). Therefore, the P2B Regulation is a cross-cutting issue. It cannot be classified under a single area of law, but instead regulates elements of **contract law, competition law, and procedural law**.

a) Requirements for the terms and conditions of providers of online intermediation services (Art. 3 P2B Regulation)

33 Both legal instruments, the P2B Regulation and the Platform Work Directive, contain transparency requirements to counteract the unilateral distribution of control over data between digital platforms and self-employed (whether performing platform work or acting as business users) and to ensure predictability. While the P2B Regulation uses the term 'general terms and conditions', the Platform Work Directive lists the types of information that must be provided when digital labour platforms make use of automated monitoring or decision-making systems or when they are in the process of being introduced (see for the details → Art. 9 mn. 3).

aa) General transparency requirements

34 As the contractual relationship between digital platforms and business users is characterised by information asymmetries, it is important that the terms and conditions provided by the digital platforms towards their business users are clear and transparent. Digital **platforms can exploit this imbalance to their own advantage**, and business users may have no choice but to accept the terms and conditions due to their increasing dependency on platforms to reach a larger customer base.[34] Therefore, it is crucial that business users have access to clear, detailed information about the conditions that apply to their contractual relationship, to ensure fair, predictable business relations.[35] Transparent terms and conditions also enable business users to compare conditions between platforms more effectively, allowing them to make informed business choices.

35 Providers of online intermediation services must have 'terms and conditions' that are formulated in a **clear and comprehensible manner**, and that are **easily accessible to business users at all stages of their commercial relationship**, including the pre-contractual phase (Art. 3(1)(a)–(b) P2B Regulation). In order to enable business users to determine the commercial conditions for the use, termination and suspension of online intermediation services, the terms and conditions must be written in plain, intelligible language. This gives business users a reasonable degree of **predictability** regarding the most important aspects of the contractual relationship (recital 15 P2B Regulation).

36 According to Art. 3(1)(c) P2B Regulation the terms and conditions implemented by the digital platform must state **the grounds for decisions to suspend, terminate or impose any other kind of restriction upon the provision of the online services** to the

---

[34] European Commission, Directorate-General for Internal Market, Industry, Entrepreneurship and SMEs, Open Evidence and PPMI, 'Study on evaluation of the Regulation (EU) 2019/1150 on promoting fairness and transparency for business users of online intermediation services (the P2B Regulation)', Final report, 2023, 27 <Study on evaluation of the Regulation (EU) 2019/1150 on promoting fairness and transparency for business users of online intermediation services (the P2B Regulation) – Publications Office of the EU> (last accessed 10.2.2026).

[35] According to a 2017 study, one of the main problematic practices identified was very short notice, or a lack of notice, about changes to platform terms and conditions see for more details European Commission, 'Business-to-Business relations in the online platform environment', 22.5.2017, FWC ENTR/300/PP/2013/FC-WIFO, Final report, 35 <Business-to-business relations in the online platform environment – Publications Office of the EU> (last accessed 12.2.2025).

business user. This, however, is also a matter of particular relevance for persons performing platform work who are confronted with various forms of account termination such as access denials prior to the start of the co-operation, (temporary) suspension or closures of accounts and reduced access to work assignments during the cooperation, and indefinite termination of the accounts. The obligation to provide concrete reasons for restriction, suspension or termination is regulated in Art. 4 P2B Regulation (→ mn. 40).

bb) Amendment of the terms and conditions

The providers of online intermediation services must inform their users of any proposed change to their terms and conditions on a durable medium at least 15 days before the date at which the changes are to be undertaken (Art. 3(2) P2B Regulation). Changes can only be applied once the notification period has expired. Any terms and conditions that **do not comply with the requirements of Art. 3(1) P2B Regulation, or which contravene Art. 3(2) P2B Regulation, are considered ex tunc and erga omnes void**. The notification period can even be longer when this is necessary, to allow the business users to make technical or commercial adaptations to comply with the changes. Business user have the right to terminate the contract without consequences during the notification period. In other words, the P2B Regulation ensures that changes to the contractual relationship are being notified to business users in advance, hence allowing each business user to react. Art. 8(a) P2B Regulation clarifies that **retroactive changes to the general terms and conditions are not possible** unless they are advantageous to business users. 37

The Platform Work Directive sets out the type of information that digital labour platforms must provide on their use of automated monitoring and decision-making systems as well as the form and timing of this information (Art. 9 Platform Work Directive). According to Art. 9(1)(b) Platform Work Directive, digital labour platforms must **inform** persons performing platform work about the use or introduction of such systems, the categories of decisions made by these systems and the categories of data and the main parameters taken into account by them, as well as the grounds for any decision relating to the restriction, suspension or termination of their account, or any equivalent decision with detrimental effect.[36] Art. 9(1)(b) Platform Work Directive only applies if these decisions are taken or supported by automated decision-making systems. This information must be provided automatically, at the latest on the first working day, and before any relevant changes are made. However, this does not apply to the reasons for a specific decision, which are subject to ex post review under Art. 11 Platform Work Directive. 38

To conclude, Art. 3 P2B Regulation ensures that **general terms and conditions** unilaterally determined by providers of online intermediation services are **comprehensible and predictable**, thereby preventing providers from engaging in unfair conduct to the detriment of business users. To a certain degree, the P2B Regulation can be regarded as the counterpart to the **Directive on transparent and predictable working conditions (TPWC)**, as it addresses issues such as the provision of obligatory information regarding relevant aspects of the employment relationship (Arts. 3 and 4 TPWC). Art. 9(1) (b)(iii) Platform Work Directive, on the other hand, requires digital labour platforms to explain the **internal functioning of their automated decision-making systems**. The right to information covers the following questions: what categories of decisions are made by such 39

---

[36] According to the Commission services' view, this also includes contractual changes to the applicable law, the amount of remuneration and the duration of the contract, see European Commission, 'Report Expert Group Transposition of Directive (EU) 2024/2831 on improving working conditions in platform work', January 2026, 49.

systems and for what reasons; what data is taken into account; and to what extent does the behaviour of persons performing platform work influence these decisions. This information is intended to shed light on the 'black box' of algorithms. It is designed to highlight the risks typically associated with the use of algorithmic systems, such as constant monitoring and control, information asymmetry, susceptibility to discrimination and algorithmic bias, whilst also assisting persons performing platform work with enforcement of law (see for the risks also → Preliminary remarks to Articles. 7–12 mn. 34).

This shows that the two provisions have different regulatory objectives and consequently, the P2B Regulation and the Platform Work Directive do not exclude, but complement each other and **remain applicable alongside**.

b) Restriction, suspension and termination (Arts. 4, 11 P2B Regulation)

40 Many business users depend on being able to offer their goods or services via platforms, which constitute their main – and sometimes their only – channel for providing sales or services. Sudden restrictions, suspension or termination of users accounts may deprive these business users of important, or even their main, sources of income.[37] Art. 4 P2B Regulation sets out the conditions under which providers of online intermediation services may restrict, suspend or terminate their services. 'Restriction' includes **downgrading in rankings** and other limitations on the business user's visibility on the platform ('**dimming**' recital 22).[38]

aa) Obligation to state reasons

41 Any provider of online intermediation services that restricts, suspends or terminates the provision of its services must inform affected business users of **the reasons for the decision** via a durable medium (e.g. an email) at the latest at the same time when the restriction takes effect. These statements of reasons must explain the specific circumstances of the case and state why the restriction, suspension or termination is being imposed (Art. 4(5) P2B Regulation).

bb) Time requirements

42 In the case where providers of online intermediation services decide to terminate a business user's account, they must provide a statement of reason at least **30 days in advance** (Art. 4(2) P2B Regulation). The P2B Regulation requires providers of online intermediation services to have an internal complaint-handling system pursuant to Art. 11 P2B Regulation. This **internal complaint management system** must be **easily accessible** and **free of charge for business users**, and it must ensure that complaints are processed 'within a reasonable timeframe'.[39] However, the Regulation does not provide **any further details on the maximum duration or structure of the complaint procedure**. Art. 11(2) P2B Regulation is limited to a few vague phrases, such as 'careful examination' and 'prompt and effective handling'.[40]

---

[37] European Commission, Directorate-General for Internal Market, Industry, Entrepreneurship and SMEs, Open Evidence and PPMI, 'Study on evaluation of the Regulation (EU) 2019/1150 on promoting fairness and transparency for business users of online intermediation services (the P2B Regulation)', Final report, 2023, 40 et seq. <Study on evaluation of the Regulation (EU) 2019/1150 on promoting fairness and transparency for business users of online intermediation services (the P2B Regulation) – Publications Office of the EU> (last accessed 10.2.2026).

[38] Busch GRUR 2019, 788 (791).

[39] Tribess in Steinrötter/Heinze/Denga § 17 mn. 37.

[40] Busch GRUR 2019, 788 (795); Busch in Busch P2B Regulation Art. 11 mn. 27; Tribess in Steinrötter/Heinze/Denga § 17 mn. 38.

Also the Platform Work Directive addresses situations involving the restriction, suspension or termination of a contractual relationship or account, or any other decision with equivalent adverse effects. It also introduces certain decision-making standards (→ Art. 10 mn. 4) and minimum requirements for filing internal complaints with the digital labour platform (→ Art. 11 mn. 3). **43**

However, to avoid overlap with the P2B Regulation and multiple standards being applied, the relevant provisions of the Platform Work Directive regarding Art. 11 do not apply to persons performing platform work if they also fall under the definition of business users in Art. 2(1) P2B Regulation (→ mn. 18), provided that the digital labour platform is a provider of online intermediation services as defined in Art. 2(3) P2B Regulation (→ mn. 22). In this case, Arts. 4 and 11 P2B Regulation prevail over Art. 11 Platform Work Directive. Otherwise, only the Platform Work Directive applies.[41] **44**

c) Ranking (Art. 5 P2B Regulation)

Art. 5 P2B Regulation covers various aspects of ranking. The P2B Regulation defines the term 'ranking' in Art. 2(8) P2B Regulation as 'the relative prominence given to goods or services offered through online intermediation services, as presented, organised or communicated by providers of such services, irrespective of the technological means used for presentation, organisation or communication'. This can include the use of algorithmic sequencing, rating or review mechanisms, visual highlights or other saliency tools, or combinations thereof (see recital 27). The Ranking of goods and services is crucial for the success of online intermediation services and business users offering goods or services via these platforms. The way in which digital platforms rank goods and services significantly impacts consumers' choices and, consequently, the economic success of business users offering those goods and services to consumers (see recitals 25 and 26). Market participants, including business users and consumers, are usually unaware of the main parameters that determine ranking and how these are weighted.[42] Without information about the ranking mechanism, competition on platforms and between platforms is limited. This strengthens the **indirect network effect** (→ mn. 5). **45**

aa) Transparency requirements for online intermediation services

Art. 5(1) P2B Regulation is based on the **principle of predictability**. This principle requires providers of online intermediation services to determine rankings in a non-arbitrary manner. The P2B Regulation therefore requires such providers to set out the main parameters that determine ranking and the reasons for their relative weighting compared to others in their general terms and conditions. The aim is to improve predictability for business users by enabling them to better understand how the ranking mechanism works and to compare the ranking practices of various providers. **46**

According to Art. 5(3) P2B Regulation the description of the main parameters should also include an explanation of any possibility for a business user to actively influence the ranking in exchange for remuneration, as well as an explanation of the relative effects thereof. Ranking can be influenced by direct or indirect remuneration paid by business users. Indirect remuneration includes, for example, the use of additional services or pre-

[41] See als the explanation of the Commission services European Commission, Report Expert Group – Transposition of the Directive (EU) 2024/2831 on improving working conditions in platform work (12.1.2026), 59.

[42] Busch GRUR 2019, 788 (792).

mium features. A comprehensive list of examples is set out in Annex II to the Guidelines[43] pursuant to Art. 5(7) P2B Regulation.

bb) Specification of transparency requirements

47 Art. 5(5) P2B Regulation outlines the requirements for the descriptions referred to Arts. 5(1) and (3) P2B Regulation. According to Art. (5)(a) P2P Regulation, providers of online intermediation services must present this information in a way that enables business users to understand how and to what extent, the ranking mechanism considers the characteristics of the goods and services offered to consumers. It therefore concerns **product-related aspects** of the offer that business users can influence, such as price, availability and the number and quality of images.[44] According to Art. 5(5)(b) P2B Regulation, providers of online intermediation services must also provide information of the relevance of those characterics for those consumers (**consumer-related factors**), such as consumer search behaviour and intent (purchase and search history and the time of the search).[45] The intention is to provide a reasonable understanding of the most important ranking parameters (product-related aspects of the offer and the relevance of the features for consumers) and enable users to compare the ranking practices of different providers (recital 24 P2B Regulation).[46]

At the same time, providers of online intermediation services are not required to disclose the detailed functioning of their ranking methods — including the algorithms. Art. 5(6) P2B Regulation limits the transparency obligations. This is intended to ensure that their ability to act against the manipulation of rankings by third parties acting in bad faith — which also serves consumers' interests — is not compromised. Providing a general description of the main parameters used for ranking is meant to protect these interests while giving business users an adequate understanding of how ranking works in the context of their use of specific online intermediation services.[47]

48 The Platform Work Directive also requires the disclosure of how automated monitoring and automated decision-making systems work, including automated monitoring systems by which clients evaluate work performance (Art. 9(1)(ii) Platform Work Directive). The digital labour platform must inform persons performing platform work about the use or introduction of such automated systems, the categories of data and action monitored, supervised or evaluated by automated monitoring systems or the categories of decisions taken or supported by these systems, and the categories of data and the main parameters taken into account by automated decision-making systems, as well as the relative importance of these parameters in automated decision-making (in other words the digital labour platform must explain the **internal functioning** of their automated decision-making system) Art. 9(1)(b)(iii) Platform Work Directive. This includes how the personal data or behaviour of the person performing platform work influence the decisions. The information obligation is intended to mitigate the aforementioned risks associated with the use of algorithms (see → mn. 39).

49 Both sets of provisions are based on the principle that transparency requirements counter the risk of algorithms operating like a 'black box'. However, the two sets of pro-

---

[43] Commission Notice Guidelines on ranking transparency pursuant to Regulation (EU) 2019/1150 of the European Parliament and of the Council 2020/C 424/01, 8.12.2020, OJ C 424.

[44] Busch in Busch P2B Regulation Art. 5 mn. 66.

[45] Busch in Busch P2B Regulation Art. 5 mn. 67.

[46] See also Art. 5(5) P2B Regulation and the Guidelines of the European Commission, 'Guidelines on ranking transparency pursuant to Regulation (EU) 2019/1150 of the European Parliament and of the Council, 8.12.2020, (2020/C 424/01).

[47] Alexander in Köhler/Feddersen P2B Regulation Art. 5 mn. 29.

visions serve different objectives. The aim of Art. 5 P2B Regulation is to ensure **predictability**, so that providers of online intermediation services cannot determine rankings arbitrarily, and so that business users can improve the presentation of their goods or services, as well as compare ranking practices between providers.[48] The intention is to **optimise their ranking position** while minimising indirect network effects.

Art. 9 Platform Directive is not intended to create predictability in order to help business users improve the presentation of their goods and services ('ranking optimisation'). Instead, its aim is to ensure transparency regarding the internal functioning of automated monitoring and decision-making systems. The objective is to disclose the specific risks to which persons performing platform work are exposed when offering services via digital labour platforms, such as constant monitoring and control, information asymmetry, susceptibility to discrimination, and algorithmic bias. This disclosure will make it easier for them to assert their rights under the Directive. **50**

Consequently, Arts. 5 and 9(1) P2B Regulation apply alongside each other.

d) *Differentiated treatment (Art. 7 P2B Regulation)*

Differentiation is an inherent characteristic of online platforms that use ranking systems. For example, online platforms can differentiate between business users based on price or consumer ratings in order to provide consumers with the best offers.[49] However, differentiated treatment can distort competition in particular when digital platforms act as intermediaries for the supply of third parties and also offer goods or services themselves. These so-called hybrid platforms act as both providers and competitors to business users, and are therefore vertically integrated.[50] In this dual role, online platforms can give **preferential treatment** to their own goods and services compared with those of other business users (self-preferencing). **51**

Art. 7 P2B Regulation requires providers of online intermediat services to explain in their terms and conditions the so-called differentiated treatment of their own and third-party products or services. The Explanation should contain the main economic commercial or legal consideration for such differentiated treatment. Unlike the Digital Markets Act (see → mn. 58), the P2B Regulation does **not prohibit self-preferencing**, but only requires transparency. Art. 7 P2B Regulation does not have a counterpart in the Platform Work Directive, possibly because this provision has its background in competition law. The intention is to protect fair competition (recital 30). If persons performing platform work are covered by the P2B Regulation, Art. 7 P2B Regulation applies to them in addition to the Platform Work Directive. **52**

e) *Data access (Art. 9 P2B Regulation)*

Providers of online intermediation services collect large amounts of data on transactions, payment processes, and customer preferences as a by-product of their intermediation activities (see → mn. 4).[51] Privileged access to large amounts of data can give digital platforms particular market power. Art. 9 P2B Regulation addresses this issue under the **53**

---

[48] Busch in Busch P2B Regulation Art. 5 mn. 3; Busch GRUR 2019, 788 (793).

[49] European Commission, Directorate-General for Internal Market, Industry, Entrepreneurship and SMEs, Open Evidence and PPMI, 'Study on evaluation of the Regulation (EU) 2019/1150 on promoting fairness and transparency for business users of online intermediation services (the P2B Regulation)', Final report, 2023, 73 et seq. <Study on evaluation of the Regulation (EU) 2019/1150 on promoting fairness and transparency for business users of online intermediation services (the P2B Regulation) – Publications Office of the EU> (last accessed 10.2.2026).

[50] Podszun in Busch P2B Regulation Art. 7 mn. 2.

[51] Busch GRUR 2019, 788 (794).

titel 'data access'. According to Art. 9(1) P2B Regulation, providers of online intermediation services must be transparent about how they handle data. Providers of online intermediation services must include in their general terms and conditions on how business users can access data generated through their activities and transactions on the platform, as well as those of consumers. While the Digital Market Act introduces the right of business users to access data generated by the gatekeeper platforms on which they operate (see mn. 62), the P2B Regulation does not grant business users their own right of access; it is limited to a **mere transparency requirement**.[52]

54 The Platform Work Directive contains provisions on data access that go **beyond** the transparency obligations of providers of online intermediation services. Art. 9(6) Platform Work Directive grants persons performing platform work the right to data portability. Persons performing platform work have the right to receive any personal data generated through their work in the context of a digital labour platform's automated monitoring or decision-making systems, including ratings and reviews, in a structured, commonly used and machine-readable format, without hindrance, and to transmit it or have it transmitted to a third party, including another digital labour platform (recital 45 Platform Work Directive). If a provider of online intermediation services is also a digital labour platform, and if the business user performs platform work as defined in the Platform Work Directive, Art. 9 of the Directive applies alongside Art. 9 P2B Regulation.

f) Best price clauses (Art. 10 P2B Regulation)

55 Art. 10 P2B Regulation addresses restriction to offer the same goods and services to consumers under different conditions through other 'distribution channels'. Such clauses are often referred to as '**parity**', '**best price**' or '**most favoured nation**' clauses.[53] If the restriction only applies to the business user's own direct distribution channels, it is referred to as a 'narrow' best price clause.[54] However, if the restriction covers all distribution channels, it is referred to as a 'broad' best price clause. Art. 10 P2B Regulation covers all forms of most-favoured-nation/best price clauses.[55]

56 According to Art. 10 P2B Regulation, providers of online intermediation services must state the reasons for such restrictions in their terms and conditions. Art. 10 P2B Regulation does not constitute a prohibition. In terms of regulatory intensity, Art. 10 P2B Regulation is consistent with the other transparency obligations of the P2B Regulation, such as Arts. 5 and 7 P2B Regulation.[56]

57 The Platform Work Directive does not contain a corresponding provision. Art. 10 P2B Regulation also applies to those performing platform work, provided that they are covered by the P2B Regulation.

g) Judicial proceeding by representative organisation or associations Art. 14 P2B Regulation

58 Unlike Art. 19 Platform Work Directive, which grants representatives and legal entities 'the right to act on behalf of or in support of persons performing platform work', Art. 14 P2B Regulation expressly grants representative organisations and associations, as well as public bodies with a legitimate interest in representing business users, the right to take **legal action** to prevent or stop non-compliance with the P2B Regulation's provi-

[52] Podszun in Busch P2B Regulation Art. 9 mn. 128 et seqq.
[53] Louven in Steinrötter/Heinze/Denga § 16 mn. 66.
[54] Höppner/Wick in Busch P2B Regulation Art. 10 mn. 1 et seqq.
[55] Höppner/Wick in Busch P2B Regulation Art. 10 mn. 15.
[56] Höppner/Wick in Busch P2B Regulation Art. 10 mn. 6.

sions. In other words, these organisations are acting **in their own name**, not on behalf of or in support of business users. This strengthens private enforcement and ensures the Regulation's provisions are effectively applied. Experience has shown that individuals affected by a breach of the law often fail to assert their rights for various reasons. These reasons include a lack of financial resources, reluctance, and the time-consuming and costly risks of litigation (recital 44).[57] Furthermore, due to their dependency on digital platforms, business users may be concerned about retaliation or disadvantage at the hands of these platforms. The introduction of the **collective action**, brought by a representative organisation or associations, is intended to address these obstacles. The risk of litigation is transferred to the representative organisation or association bringing the action, leaving individual business relationships unaffected by the dispute (recital 44). Indirectly, Art. 14 P2B Regulation also serves to realise the right to effective legal protection enshrined in Art. 47 of the Charter of Fundamental Rights (recital 52), strengthening the effectiveness of the Regulation by putting pressure on digital platforms to implement it.[58]

II. P2B Regulation and the Digital Services Act Package

1. P2B Regulation and Digital Market Act (DMA)

The DMA came into force on 2 November 2021 and has been applicable throughout the European Union since 2 May 2023. Unlike the P2B Regulation, the DMA is an **asymmetric regulation**, meaning that the rules only apply to a new category of undertakings. These so called 'gatekeepers' are digital platforms that have a significant impact on the internal market, providing gateways for a large number of business users to reach end users (recital 6 DMA). Unlike competition law, the DMA does not focus on an undertaking's position in a specific market to assess market dominance, but rather on its function as a gatekeeper for users on different sides of the platform.[59] **58a**

According to the DMA, gatekeepers are undertakings which provide core platform services and must be designated as gatekeepers in accordance with Art. Art. 3 DMA by the European Commission before the specific oligations of the DMA apply to them.[60] The designation as a gatekeeper require that three conditions are met cumulatively (Art. 3(1) DMA): (a) the undertaking has a significant impact on the internal market; (b) it provides a core platform service which is an important gateway for business users to reach end users; and (c) it enjoys an entrenched and durable position in its operations, or it is foreseeable that it will enjoy such a position in the near future. **59**

Unlike the P2B Regulation, the DMA does not merely stipulate transparency obligations; it also imposes stringent self-exuciting requirements and prohibitions. At the same time, however, **its personal scope of application is narrower**. Its provisions are aimed **only at a small group of addressees who play a central role as 'gatekeepers'**.[61] **60**

Arts. 5–7 DMA are particularly relevant for gatekeepers' providing online marketplaces and app stores (*Amazon* Marketplace, *Facebook* Marketplace and *Apple* or *Google* **61**

---

[57] Höppner/Wick in Busch P2B Regulation Art. 14 Rn. 1.

[58] Höppner/Wick in Busch P2B Regulation Art. 14 mn. 2.

[59] Dietrich/Jung in Kersting/Meyer-Lindemann/Podszun DMA Art. 1 mn. 6; Wielsch, ZUM 2023, 153 (157).

[60] Six gatekeepers were designated by the Commission in September 2023 <Digital Markets Act: Commission designates six gatekeepers> (last accessed 16.1.2026).

[61] See for the reason of this narrow definition of the personal scope of application König in Steinrötter/Heinze/Denga § 10 mn. 31.

App Stores). For example, Art. 5(3) DMA prohibits so called '**most favoured nation clauses**', i.e. clauses that prevent business users from offering the same products or services to end users through third-party online intermediation services or through their own direct online sales channel at prices or conditions that are different from those offered through the online intermediation services of gatekeepers (see also → mn. 55). This addresses, for example **bestprice clauses**, which have been reviewed by competition authorities in relation to hotel booking platforms[62] and the distribution of e-books[63] (Art. 5(3) DMA).[64]

62 The DMA also addresses the issue of **self-preferencing**. According to Art. 6(5) DMA, a gatekeeper must not treat its own services and products more favourably than those of a third party in terms of ranking, indexing and crawling. The Commission's first major antitrust case against Google concerned this prohibition on self-preferencing.[65] According to Art. 6(10) gatekeepers shall provide **business users** 'with effective, high-quality, continuous and real-time access' to data provided for or generated in the context of the use of a core platform service by those business users or their customers.

2. P2B Regulation and Digital Service Act (DSA)

63 The DSA aims at contributing to the proper functioning of the internal market (harmonisation objective) and ensuring a safe, predictable, and trusted online enviromnement (protective objective).[66] The DSA primarily seeks to mitigate the social risks that have arisen from the increasing importance of platforms, particularly for public discourse and democratic decision-making. Accordingly, the DSA aims to prevent the dissemination of illegal content and targeted disinformation in order to protect the decision-making and determination of online users and to ensure the protection of consumers' fundamental rights in the platform environment.[67] To this end, the DSA relies on a variety of different regulatory instruments. In addition to behaviour control through liability privileges (Arts. 4–9 DSA) and information and transparency obligations (Arts. 15, 24, 26, 27, 39, 42 DSA), elements of cooperation between intermediaries and government authorities are provided for in order to mitigate systemic risks (Art. 33 DSA). Unlike the P2B Regulation, which primarily aims to promote fairness and transparency in the relationship between platforms and business users, the DSA thus pursues a different protective objective.

64 The DSA's overarching regulatory concept is based on a risk-based approach. The obligations imposed on providers of intermediary services **vary according to their role, size, and impact on the online environment**.[68] According to Art. 2(1) DSA, the Regulation applies to intermediary services as defined in Art. 3(g) DSA, i.e. information society services. These are categorised into three different forms. The first category is the mere transmission of information to another communications network, known as a '**mere conduit**' service.[69] If this transmission results in temporary caching to improve access efficiency, it is referred to as a 'caching service' (second category).[70] The third cat-

[62] European Commission Decision 4.5.2017 – AT.40153 – Amazon (eBooks).
[63] Bundeskartellamt Decision of 22.12.2015 – B9 – 121/13 – Booking; Decision 20.12.2013 – B9 – 66/10 – HRS; Decision 26.11.2013 – B6 – 46/12 – Amazon.
[64] König in Steinrötter/Heinze/Denga § 12 mn. 28.
[65] European Commission Decision 27.6.2017 – AT.39740 – Google Search Shopping.
[66] Hofmann in Hofmann/Raue Art. 1 DSA mn. 11; Wilman/Kalėda/ Loewenthal, The EU Digital Services Act Art. 1 mn. 12.
[67] Legner ZUM 2024, 99 (100); Hofmann in Hofmann/Raue Art. 1 DSA mn. 14.
[68] Hofmann in Hofmann/Raue Art. 1 DSA mn. 20.
[69] Steigenrötter/Schauer in Steinrötter/Heinze/Denga § 2 mn. 26.
[70] Steigenrötter/Schauer in Steinrötter/Heinze/Denga § 2 mn. 32.

egory form is a 'hosting service', which involves permanently storing information provided by the user (e.g. on social media). Hosting services include platform and search engine services. Depending on the intermediary service type, providers of intermediary services benefit from different liability privileges (Arts. 4 to 10 DSA) and are subject to varying due diligence obligations (Arts. 11 to 48 DSA).

The central provisions of the DSA are divided into four successive levels of regulation, known as 'four-level regulation'. Staring from the general provisions of the first chapter (Arts. 1–3 DSA), the requirements become stricter and apply to a smaller group of addressees at each level. **65**

The provisions of the lowest and at the same time weakest regulatory level (first level), apply to **all providers of 'intermediary services'** (Arts. 4–15 of the DSA).[71] In Arts. 4–5, the DSA retains the general liability privileges from Arts. 12–14 of the E-Commerce Directive with minor adjustments. In principle, online intermediary services are not liable for content, goods or services distributed by users. However, this only applies if the services process content automatically and neutrally without modifying or moderating it. Providers of intermediary services are not obliged to actively review content (Art. 8 DSA). Nevertheless, providers of intermediary services must take action as soon as they become aware of illegal content (notice-and-takedown procedure). Under Art. 14 DSA, providers of intermediary services must disclose any restrictions they impose on user-provided information in their terms and conditions. This includes details of all guidelines, procedures, measures and tools used to moderate content, such as algorithmic decision-making and human review, as well as the rules governing their internal complaints procedure. **66**

The scope of application of Arts. 16–18 DSA (level 2) refers to intermediary services that meet the personal requirements for **hosting services, including online platforms** that store and publicly disseminate information on behalf of users (such as online marketplaces, app stores, social media platforms).[72] According to Art. 17 DSA, any restrictive measures affecting user-provided content, such as its visibility or monetisation, the service itself, or users' accounts ('restrictions', 'suspensions', or 'terminations'), must be disclosed to the users concerned when such measures are taken. This disclosure must be accompanied by a clear and specific statement of the reasons for the measures (Art. 17(2) and (3) DSA)).[73] Art. 4(1) P2B Regulation goes one step further when it comes to terminating a user account, requiring the reasons to be communicated to the business user 30 days before the termination takes effect. Accordingly, Art. 4(2) P2B Regulation is considered to be a lex specialis to Art. 17 DSA.[74] **67**

Arts. 19–32 DSA (level 3) stipulate various **additional or stricter requirements** for providers of 'online platforms' and, in some cases, 'online search engines'. Art. 27 DSA requires 'large platforms' to disclose the main parameters used in their 'recommender systems'. The broad definition of recommender systems in Art. 3(s) DSA also covers automated product rankings and lists of search results displayed by a search engine, as defined in Art. 2(8) P2B Regulation.[75] Unlike Art. 27 DSA, however, Art. 5 P2B Regulation **explicitly addresses the economically relevant ranking of goods and services in a marketplace context**. Providers of online intermediation services or online search engines must explain how and to what extent their ranking mechanism considers the characteristics of the goods and services offered to consumers and the relevance of these **68**

---

[71] Hofmann in Hofmann/Raue Art. 1 DSA mn. 21.
[72] Steinrötter/Schauer in Steinrötter/Heinze/Denga § 2 mn. 40.
[73] Berberich in Steinrötter/Heinze/Denga § 5 mn. 28.
[74] Busch Journal of Antitrust Enforcement 2024, 201 (204).
[75] Grisse in Hoffmann/Raue Art. 27 mn. 14.

characteristics to those consumers. With regard to online search engines, they must also explain how the design of the website used by corporate users affects the ranking. The more specific and detailed provisions of the P2B Regulation should therefore take precedence over the DSA (Art. 2(4)(e) DSA).[76]

69 The **most regulatory-intensive** 'level 4' addresses online platforms or online search engines that exceed certain thresholds and are therefore classified by the European Commission as 'very large online platforms'[77] and 'very large online search engines'[78]. Arts. 33–48 DSA contain, among other things, regulations regarding risk assessments and mitigations, crisis response mechanisms, and increased transparency obligations.[79]

70 The P2B Regulation and the DSA have different **regultatory objectives. These different regulatory objectives are** reflected in their respective provisions. For example, some of these provisions of the P2B Regulation contain more specific and detailed rules tailored to business users offering goods or services via online intermediation services. Furthermore, the P2B Regulation has a **broader scope** than the DMA and DSA, as it is **not limited to gatekeepers**, and applies consistently to platforms **of all sizes or types.**[80]

III. Outlook

71 The future of the P2B Regulation is uncertain. The European Commission has announced in its **Digital Omnibus Package** ('the Omnibus') on 19 November 2025 to repeal the P2B Regulation in two stages.[81] The Commission argues that the provisions of the P2B Regulation are largely covered by the DMA and DSA. However, the Commission seems to overlook the fact that the P2B Regulation plays an important complementary and supplementary role to ensure a minimum level of fairness and transparency on all platforms who offer their services in the EU (not just gatekeepers).[82]

72 The Commission's initiative is all the more surprising given the important role that the P2B Regulation will play alongside the Platform Work Directive in the future. For example, the P2B Regulation supplements the Platform Work Directive by introducing transparency obligations concerning the differential treatment of online platforms' own products or third-party products, and addresses issues such as 'best price clauses'. It also closes remaining gaps by introducing transparency obligations concerning the terms and conditions of the commercial relationship between providers of online intermediation services and business users, acting as a counterpart to the TPWC.

---

[76] Busch in Busch P2B Regulation Art. 5 mn. 5; Busch/Mak, p. 12 et seq; Wilman/Kalėda/ Loewenthal, The EU Digital Services Act Art. 1 mn. 17.

[77] European Commission, 'Supervision of the designated very large online platforms and search engines under DSA | Shaping Europe's digital future', https://digital-strategy.ec.europa.eu/en/policies/list-designated-vlops-and-vloses#ecl-inpage-lqfbha7w (last accessed 20.1.2026).

[78] European Commission, 'Supervision of the designated very large online platforms and search engines under DSA | Shaping Europe's digital future', https://digital-strategy.ec.europa.eu/en/policies/list-designated-vlops-and-vloses#ecl-inpage-lqfbha7w (last accessed 20.1.2026).

[79] Steinrötter/Schauer in Steinrötter/Heinze/Denga § 2 mn. 23.

[80] Busch Journal of Antitrust Enforcement 2024, 201 (202).

[81] European Commission, 'Commission staff working document, accompanying the documents Proposal for a regulation of the European Parliament and of the Council, amending regulations (EU) 2016/679, (EU) 2018/1724, (EU) 2018/1725, (EU) 2023/2854 and Directives 2002/58/EC, (EU) 2022/2555 and (EU) 2022/2557 as regards the simplification of the digital legislative framework, and repealing Regulations (EU) 2018/1807, (EU) 2019/1150, (EU) 2022/868, and Directive (EU) 2019/1024 (Digital Omnibus) Amending Regulations (EU) 2024/1689 and (EU) 2018/1139 as regards the simplification of the implementation of harmonised rules on artificial intelligence (Digital Omnibus on AI), 19.11.2025 COM(2025) 837 final – COM(2025) 836 final, 83 et seqq.

[82] Busch in Busch P2B Regulation Introduction mn. 17.

D. Conclusion

The provisions of the Platform Work Directive demonstrate that the P2B Regulation served as a model in many respects. This is particularly evident in the provisions on algorithmic management (Arts. 9 and 11 Platform Work Directive), which are based on Arts. 4, 11 and 5 P2B Regulation. 73

Both legal instruments strengthen the position of solo self-employed by promoting greater transparency and fairness in digital platforms' control and management systems. For the first time, the Platform Work Directive introduces a regulatory framework for the use of automated monitoring and decision-making systems, which are designed to address the specific risks associated with algorithmic management. The P2B Regulation was designed to ensure that business users with limited bargaining power, relative to online platforms, are able to conduct business in a predictable manner (by relying on transparency regarding rankings and notification delays for termination of business accounts). The P2B Regulation protects business users from unfair practices by digital platforms. 74

Despite the fact that both legal instruments contain similar provisions regarding digital platforms (digital labour platforms or information society services) and their contractual relationships with solo self-employed (persons performing platform work and/or business users), closer examination reveals that they have different regulatory objectives. This results in a complementary relationship between the provisions of the P2B Regulation and the Platform Work Directive. 75

With regard to improving working conditions for solo self-employed, particularly with respect to health and safety issues, the P2B Regulation and the Platform Work Directive provide only limited assistance (see also → Art. 12 mn. 4). In this case, strengthening collective agreements for solo self-employed persons could provide a remedy. 76

However, the general consensus remains that collective agreements are primarily intended to protect employees. For two decades now, it has been recognised at EU level, in accordance with the established case law of the CJEU, that whilst collective agreements inevitably have certain anti-competitive effects, these are legitimate and do not fall within the scope of Art. 101(1) TFEU in so far as they serve to improve employment and working conditions, provided that they have been concluded between social partner organisations representing employers and employees.[83] This case law relates to collective agreements, which govern the terms of employment contracts, and are therefore linked to the status of the relevant person to be protected as an employee. In the case *FNV Kunsten*[84], the CJEU ruled that 'false self-employed' are also included within the personal scope of collective bargaining autonomy. However, the CJEU did not explicitly state whether 'false self-employed' refers to employees or to solo self-employed persons who find themselves in a situation comparable to that of employees (employee-like workers). Thus, it remains unclear whether this exemption under competition law also applies to economically dependent self-employed persons.[85] Against this background, the Euro-

---

[83] ECJ 21.9.1999 – case C-67/96, ECLI:EU:C:1999:28 – Albany; ECJ 21.9.1999 – case C-115/97, ECLI:EU:C:1999:434 – Brentjens'/Stichting; ECJ 21.9.1999 – case C-219/97, ECLI:EU:C:1999:437 – Maatschappij Drijvende Bokken; Prassl/Risak in Meil/Kirov 273 (285).

[84] ECJ 4.12.2014 – case C-413/13, ECLI:EU:C:2014:2411 – FNV Kunsten Informatie en Media / Staat der Nederlanden.

[85] To extend the exemption to include the solo self-employed persons who find themselves in a situation comparable to that of employees see Bayreuther SR 2019, 4 (5); Kocher SR 2022 125 (133); for the opposite view see Höffner EuZA 2024, 243; Goldmann EuZA 2015, 509 (514).

pean Commission's guidelines[86] are an important and appropriate step, even though they are not legally binding. The guidelines clarify that collective agreements for solo self-employed in a situation comparable to that of employees are not subject to Art. 101 TFEU, and are therefore exempt from competition law. Furthermore, the European Commission clarified that it will not take action against agreements if the solo self employed concerned are in a bargaining position that is too weak to influence their working conditions individually (see for more details → Chapter I mn. 50).

77 Just as there is no one-size-fits-all solution for solo self-employed, there is not one directive or regulation that suits all. Due to the heterogeneity of this category of individuals, different instruments are required for different subgroups. One instrument that could contribute to improving working conditions and taking different needs into account is collective agreements for solo self-employed.

Chapter III
Platform economy and collective bargaining – the Nordic approach

Literature: Arbetsmarknadsdepartementet, A2026/00012, Remiss av betänkandet Genomförandet av plattformsdirektivet (SOU 2026:3); Arbetsmarknadsekonomiska Rådet, Arbetsmarknadsekonomisk rapport – Olika vägar till jobb Stockholm 2018, AER; Adlercreutz/Nyström, Labour Law in Sweden, Alphen aan den Rijn 2024; Berg, Bemanningsarbete, flexibilitet och likabehandling: En studie av svensk rätt och kollektivavtalsreglering med komparativa inslag, Lund 2008; Dølvik/Jesnes, Nordic labour markets and the sharing economy – Report from a pilot project, Nordic Council of Ministers, Copenhagen 2018; Hartzén, 6.2. 'Fixed-Term Work Directive (1999/70/EC)' in Hiessl (ed.), EU Labour Law – A Commentary, Alphen an den Rijn 2025, p. 649; Hartzén, 'In-Work Poverty in Sweden' in Ratti (ed.), In-Work Poverty in Europe: Vulnerable and Under-Represented Persons in a Comparative Perspective, Bulletin of Comparative Labour Relations, Alphen aan den Rijn 2022, p. 277; Hartzén, 'Plattformsarbetares multipla otrygghet på arbetsmarknaden – anställning och sjukersättning i samklang?' in Förvaltningsrättslig tidskrift 1(2025), 31; Herzfeld Olsson, 'Den svenska modellen i en ny era' in Selberg/Sjödin (eds), Anställningsskydd i utveckling, Uppsala 2022, p. 127; Ilsøe, 'Digital rights as collective rights: The new Hilfr2 agreement on artificial intelligence ensures both the managerial prerogative and workers' rights to unionize', Tijdschrift Recht en Arbeid (TRA), 2025(1), Article TRA 2025/9; Ljunglöf, Collective agreement coverage and the labour market organisations 2024, Swedish National Mediation Office, Stockholm 2024; Nyström, EU och arbetsrätten, Stockholm 2021; SOU 2026:3, Genomförande av plattformsdirektivet; Svenska Taxiförbundet, Remissvar -betänkandet Genomförandet av plattformsdirektivet (SOU 2026:3) (A2026/00012); Söderqvist/Bernhardtz, Labor Platforms with Unions: Discussing the Law and Economics of a Swedish collective bargaining framework used to regulate gig work, Working paper 2019, Swedish Entrepreneurship Forum; Taxiunionen, Remissvar diarienummer A2026/00012 – Genomförande av Plattformsdirektivet (SOU 2026:3); Uppdragsarbetarförbundet, Remissvar över betänkandet SOU 2026:3; Weidenstedt/Geissinger/Lougui, Varför gigga som matkurir? – Förutsättningar och förväntningar bakom okvalificerat gig-arbete, Stockholm 2020; Westregård, Digitala daglönare i gig-ekonomin – En rättsvetenskaplig studie av arbetstagarbegreppet, IFAU, Rapport 2025:1, Uppsala 2025; Westregård, 'Digital collaborative platforms: A challenge for social partners in the Nordic model', in Nordic Journal of Commercial Law (NJCL), 1(2018), 89; Westregård, Plattformsarbetare och egenanställda i svenska rätt: En analys av arbetstagarbegreppet, Stockholm 2024; Westregård, Protection of platform workers in Sweden – Part 2 Country report, Nordic future of work project 2017–2020: Working paper 12. Pillar VI; Westregård, 'The Notion of 'employee' in Swedish and European Union Law. An exercise in Harmony or Disharmony?' in Carlson/Edström/Nyström (eds.) Globalisation, Fragmentation, Labour and Employment Law: a Swedish Perspective, Uppsala 2016, 187.

[86] European Commission communication, 'Guidelines on the application of Union competition law to collective agreements regarding the working conditions of solo self-employed persons' (2022/C 374/02), 30.9.2020, OJ C 374/2.

A. Introduction

The Nordic model for regulating employment and working conditions is well-known for its high degree of self-regulation with collective agreements as the main source for regulation. This model has been highlighted as successful in promoting decent working conditions and wages, with minimum wages well above the poverty threshold.[1] The model as such is characterised by a spirit of cooperation between trade unions and employers and employers' organisations where both parties acknowledge that successful enterprises and decent working conditions go hand in hand. Historically, when new sectors contributing to a more flexible labour market have emerged, trade unions and employers' organisations have also seen the need to assure strong collective bargaining coverage. This was for example the case when the temporary agency work sector started to develop in Sweden and the sectoral social partners joined forces to assure protection for the workers and good quality jobs in the sector in order to improve the reputation of the sector and allow companies to grow.[2] This led the temporary agency sector to become the sector with the highest rate of collective agreement coverage outside the public sector in Sweden in 2017, at 97 percent.[3] Whether similar developments could be the case also for the platform economy is at this stage too early to say. 1

However, some indications concerning platform work may be identified through recent developments and court cases. This chapter aims to provide some insights into the more recent developments concerning the regulation of platform workers employment and working conditions in a Nordic perspective, as exemplified by the Swedish labour market. The chapter will start by providing an overall and introductory explication of the concept of the Swedish model and then a similar introduction concerning the legal status of platform workers. These sections aim to highlight the structures of importance to understand the challenges that are found in the platform economy as concerns both the development of collective bargaining and to briefly explain the challenges these workers face from a labour law perspective. This will be followed by an explication of specific developments relating to collective bargaining and recent court cases of relevance for platform work. Finally, the chapter relates these developments to the initiated 2

[1] The positive aspects of strong collective bargaining systems in relation to wage levels and decent working conditions are highlighted in the Commission proposal for the Adequate Minimum Wage Directive and even highlighted in the preamble of that Directive. See European Commission, 'Proposal for a Directive of the European Parliament and of the Council on adequate minimum wages in the European Union', 28.10.2020, COM(2020) 682 final and Directive (EU) 2022/2041 on adequate minimum wages in the European Union.

[2] Concerning platform work see Söderqvist/Bernhardtz, Labor Platforms with Unions: Discussing the Law and Economics of a Swedish collective bargaining framework used to regulate gig work, Working paper 2019, p. 57; or for a brief discussion Hartzén in Ratti, p. 277 (310). Concerning the history of temporary agency work in Sweden see Berg, Bemanningsarbete, flexibilitet och likabehandling: En studie av svensk rätt och kollektivavtalsreglering med komparativa inslag, Juristförlaget i Lund, pp. 254–256.

[3] Arbetsmarknadsekonomiska Rådet, Arbetsmarknadsekonomisk rapport – Olika vägar till jobb Stockholm 2018, AER, 67.

process of implementing the Platform Work Directive in Sweden. The Swedish case will be in focus in order to exemplify the Nordic model, but a brief example from Denmark will be provided in relation to the issue of collective bargaining. The Danish example serves to highlight some overarching differences in relation to approach and themes of importance in the collective bargaining processes in Sweden and Denmark. In this chapter, the term 'platform worker' is employed in a broad sense to refer to all persons who perform work via a platform, and it should be noted that this does not strictly align with the legal definition set out in Art. 2 of the Platform Work Directive.

I. Concept of the Swedish model

3 The basic premises of the Swedish model for collective bargaining is set out in the Co-determination in the Workplace Act (CDA), where definitions of trade unions, employers organisations, collective agreements and bargaining rights are regulated. The definition of a trade union is that it shall be an organisation which has as its purpose to protect the interests of its members in relation to their employers. For employers' organisations the same applies from the other side of the employment relationship.[4] The right for trade unions and employers' organisations to bargain collectively on behalf of their members in matters concerning employment conditions and employment relationships also clearly refers to the role of the members as employees or employers. Worth clarifying is that trade unions' right to negotiate on behalf of their members also applies when an employment relationship has ended, enabling them to support members who have had an employment contract terminated on potential unjust grounds.[5] There is also a legal definition of a collective agreement whereby any agreement that fulfils the three criteria will be legally classified as a collective agreement. The three criteria included are: that the parties shall be a trade union on the one side and an employer or an employers' organisation on the other side; the agreement shall be in writing; and that the contents shall relate to employment conditions, relation or the relationship between employer and employees in general.[6] The overarching principle is in other words that the collective bargaining structures require a trade union to negotiate for employees, whereas employers may negotiate as a sole employer or be represented by an employers' organisation. Individual employees can neither on their own nor as a group not established as a trade union exercise these rights.[7] For the employer side it is natural that only companies that consider themselves employers will be likely to participate in collective bargaining.

4 The **unionisation rate in Sweden is rather high**, from an international perspective, but varies between different groups of workers. In general, workers with more flexible forms of employment are less frequently unionised.[8] Due to the organisation of platform work with fixed-term employments or work as an assignment taker, it is reasonable to assume that platform workers are less likely to be unionised. Despite the rate of unionisation being high, it is still lower than the actual **coverage rate of collective**

---

[4] Art. 6 CDA.

[5] Art. 10 CDA defines the general right to negotiate, which applies for all trade unions, employers and employers' organisations.

[6] Art. 23 CDA.

[7] For a more in-depth explication of the Swedish collective bargaining system in English see Adlercreutz/Nyström, p. 200 et seqq.

[8] Ljunglöf, Collective agreement coverage and the labour market organisations 2024 (available at https://www.mi.se/publikationer/collective-agreement-coverage-and-the-labour-market-organisations-2024/ (last visited 27.08.2025)).

agreements. The reason for this is that employers in Sweden tend to be organised to a high degree and through their membership in an employers' organisation they become bound by the collective agreement for the sector.[9] In general, larger companies are well organised, whereas small companies to a greater extent tend not to be organised. For the public sector collective agreement coverage is 100 percent. For the private sector it is lower at about 82 percent, but the coverage rate also varies between sectors.[10] There are no mechanisms in Sweden for declaring collective agreements generally applicable erga omnes, as is the case in for example Finland. Therefore, collective agreements in Sweden have been considered insufficient for implementing EU law, because the only way to assure that all workers are covered by the protection from EU law is to implement it through legislation.[11]

Even though the CDA in principle would allow collective agreements to be applied also for **dependent contractors**, i.e. someone performing work without being employed, but under such circumstances as being essentially dependent on the employer in similar terms as an employee, this is not really used in practice.[12] One reason for this is that there are challenges with such an application of collective agreements in relation to EU competition law since the term dependent contractor most likely covers a broader scope of persons conducting work than the term false self-employed used in EU competition law. Even though trade unions are opening up for self-employed to become members and access some services such as advice and insurances, they are not actively seeking to conclude collective agreements on behalf of this group.[13] The inclusion of dependent contractors in the CDA has served the function of assuring space for limiting risks of social dumping, but it has not led to any established practices of broadening the application of collective agreements to dependent contractors as a general practice.[14] In this sense, collective agreements generally do not regulate employment status as such. Instead, it is most often stated that the collective agreement is to be applied for employees conducting the form of work regulated by the collective agreement for the employer. Therefore, the application of a collective agreement for someone conducting work in a specific workplace will generally require that person to be an employee. 5

II. Legal status and challenges for platform workers in Sweden

As mentioned in the introduction, platform work in Sweden is still a small part of the labour market. The size of the sector is difficult to assess since the yearly Labour Force Study conducted by Statistics Sweden does not provide statistical data that allows for separating data on work organised through digital platforms.[15] What can be said is that platform work is a marginal part of the labour market in Sweden and that very few of those taking up platform work do so with the intention of having platform work as the 6

---

[9] Adlercreutz/Nyström, p. 200 et seq.

[10] Ljunglöf, Collective agreement coverage and the labour market organisations 2024 (available at https://www.mi.se/publikationer/collective-agreement-coverage-and-the-labour-market-organisations-2024/ (last visited 14.10.2025)).

[11] Nyström, p. 67 et seqq.

[12] Westregård, Protection of platform workers in Sweden – Part 2 Country report, Nordic future of work project 2017–2020: Working paper 12. Pillar VI, 2020, p. 16 et seqq.

[13] Westregård in Carlson/Edström/Nyström, p. 187 et seqq.

[14] Westregård, Protection of platform workers in Sweden – Part 2 Country report, Nordic future of work project 2017–2020: Working paper 12. Pillar VI 2020, p. 16 et seqq.

[15] Arbetsmarknadsekonomiska Rådet, Arbetsmarknadsekonomisk rapport – Olika vägar till jobb Stockholm 2018, AER, 37 et seq.

main income.[16] As for other countries, many of the platform companies claim that they are not employers and that they merely provide a platform connecting those in need of a specific service with those willing to perform that service. This poses a challenge both for platform workers wishing to gain the status of employee and for trade unions in seeking a counterpart on the employer side for collective bargaining. In this respect **umbrella companies** differ quite a lot. Even though these companies are not necessarily platform companies they have received specific attention and are an important aspect of the Swedish platform economy. The idea of umbrella companies implies a certain degree of independence from the worker through a set up where the worker decides which assignments to take on and then contacts the umbrella company to have someone acting as employer, taking care of invoicing, payment of taxes and social fees as well as payment of salary, during the time that the assignment is carried out.[17] The construction where umbrella companies become the employer for platform workers that carry out work through the use of a digital platform could likely render such umbrella companies to be classified as **intermediaries** in accordance with Art. 2(e)(i) of the Platform Work Directive.

7 As for the legal status of the **platform workers**, they are by no means a specific legal category on the Swedish labour market. Swedish labour law distinguishes between workers or employees[18] and independent contractors, i.e. those that are to be considered as self-employed, in a binary system. The classification is based on an overall assessment of the situation of the person performing work where factors such as the regularity of work, renumeration, responsibility for suitable equipment, direction and control over the work, etc. are important aspects. A platform worker can therefore be either self-employed, falling outside the scope of labour law, or an employee where the platform or the umbrella company is the employer.[19] Worth noting though is that Swedish labour law is very **flexible** in terms of **fixed-term employments** and being considered an employee in labour law in not the same as having a stable position on the labour market. Instead, the platform worker may be in a situation where every assignment is a new employment contract.[20] This means that a platform worker will have little to no employment protection as long as he/she has not reached the thresholds of time in employment required to qualify for having the contract converted to a permanent contract.[21] Before reaching the qualification threshold the platform worker may simply find that assignments from the digital platform suddenly ends. It is thus the scattering of assignments with irregular work conducted under short temporary contracts that are the main challenges for platform workers and this insecurity is also applicable for

---

[16] Weidenstedt/Geissinger/Lougui, p. 21 et seqq. (available at https://ratio.se/en/publications/varfor-gigga-som-matkurir-forutsattningar-och-forvantningar-bakom-okvalificerat-gig-arbete (last visited 14.10.2025)); Dølvik/Jesnes, p. 46 et seqq. (available under: https://norden.diva-portal.org/smash/get/diva2:1182946/FULLTEXT01.pdf (last visited 14.10.2025)).

[17] See for example Westregård, NJCL 1(2018), 89 et seqq. (available at https://journals.aau.dk/index.php/NJCL/article/view/2486 (last vsited 14.10.2025)).

[18] In Swedish labour law there is no difference between a worker and an employee, the binary system means that both these terms can be used for someone conducting work within the framework of an employment contract. However, in this text the term employee is predominantly used to contrast with the term platform worker which is used in a broad sense for anyone conducting work through a platform.

[19] Westregård, Plattformsarbetare och egenanställda i svenska rätt: En analys av arbetstagarbegreppet 2024, p. 49 et seqq.

[20] Section 5 of the Employment Protection Act (EPA) allows for temproary employment without a minimum length of the contract.

[21] Section 5 a EPA contains rules on conversion of fixed-term employment contracts where the most flexible form of fixed-term employment shall be converted to a permanent employment when reaching 12 months of fixed-term employment during specified time periods.

those being self-employed. The irregular and short-term work contracts also generate additional challenges for the platform workers with difficulties qualifying for social security benefits or getting very low financial support from the social security system.[22] In this sense platform workers are subject to multiple insecurities on the Swedish labour market.[23]

The situation for platform workers is resembling that of temporary agency workers at the early phase of the development of the temporary work agency sector. As already mentioned, the sectoral social partners managed to conclude collective agreements that assured the temporary agency workers good working conditions and better protection with high collective bargaining coverage. This has rendered the temporary agency work sector a higher degree of acceptance and the workers of the sector a stronger position on the labour market with improved employment conditions and access to social security structures.[24] Whether such a development will be the case also for the gig economy and digital platform work sector in Sweden remains to be seen. **8**

B. Collective bargaining developments in the gig-sector

The **first collective agreement** for the gig economy to be signed in the Nordic countries was the *Danish Hilfr1* agreement, between the Danish cleaning platform *Hilfr* and the *United Federation of Danish Workers* (3F) in 2018. This agreement allowed workers to be either employees or self-employed, but the agreement was subject to a verdict from **Danish Competition authorities** in 2020 and a renegotiated agreement came into place in 2024 whereby all cleaning assistants of *Hilfr* are considered employees. This agreement can be considered well adapted for the platform economy in the sense that it contains regulations on socially responsible use of artificial intelligence as well as collective digital rights of value for both employees' rights to freedom of association and the employer's managerial rights.[25] Even though this collective agreement is only applicable for one single gig-economy company on the Danish labour market it does indicate that the Danish trade union movement has the capability of adapting demands and building trust between the labour market parties within the gig economy. **9**

To what extent are similar developments visible within the Swedish trade union movement and are companies active in the platform work economy in Sweden adhering to the **Swedish model** of collective bargaining by signing collective agreements? The first collective agreement for platform workers in Sweden was signed between the transport workers federation and the food delivery platform *Foodora* in 2021. The agreement is not a specific platform economy agreement, instead it consist of the **transport sector agreement for delivery drivers**, with an add-on for delivery riders by bike.[26] In this sense it can be considered as intended mainly for the delivery riders using bikes as mode of transportation. In principle it also covers delivery riders using mopeds or cars, but its practical relevance for those workers depends on whether *Foodora* employs those delivery riders directly or engages them through a temporary work agency or umbrella **10**

---

[22] Westregård, Plattformsarbetare och egenanställda i svenska rätt: En analys av arbetstagarbegreppet, 2024, p. 122 et seqq.

[23] Hartzén FT 1/2025, 31 et seqq.

[24] Berg, p. 254–256.

[25] Ilsøe TRA 2025/9.

[26] Westregård, Plattformsarbetare och egenanställda i svenska rätt: En analys av arbetstagarbegreppet, 2024, p. 65 et seqq.

company.[27] The agreement recognises the delivery riders as employees of *Foodora*, with permanent employment being the main form of employment. It further stipulates working conditions and hourly salary as well as salary additions for each delivery.[28] The agreement can be considered a step forward for the Transport workers' federation which has been active in seeking to organise platform company delivery riders and establish the view that these workers are no different from other delivery riders. In other words, the fact that these workers sign up for deliveries using an app does not make them less dependent on the delivery services company than delivery riders employed by traditional transportation companies. So far this is the only collective agreement signed by a digital platform company in Sweden.[29] However, it is not the only collective agreement of relevance for platform workers. To understand collective bargaining structures for platform work in Sweden we need to consider the developments in relation to umbrella companies.

11 As already mentioned, **umbrella companies** have become more common on the Swedish labour market, not least in relation to the gig economy. Initially created to assist freelancers wishing to avoid the administrative practices of bookkeeping and other responsibilities related to running your own business, the use of umbrella companies required a certain degree of independence from its users. Early on a couple of the umbrella companies sought to establish themselves as respectable employers, which is a concept generally perceived as employers who sign collective agreements in respect of the Swedish labour market model. For these umbrella companies the sectoral agreements most closely connected to their business was the **temporary work agency** sectoral agreements and therefore they signed these agreements. However, the idea of umbrella companies where the employment relationship is initiated when the worker finds an assignment instead of the umbrella company finding work for the employee caused difficulties with the application of the clauses on forms of employment allowed in these collective agreements.[30] When the worker, not the employer, is the one responsible for finding assignments, then there are challenges for the employer to offer a permanent employment. One point that has been made in the past in relation to this is that one of the important factors when defining someone as a worker is that the person conducts work on the basis of what the employer requests, i.e. work that the employer needs to have done.[31] Is it then possible to be an employer if the employer does not in its own terms identify work that needs to be done, but instead is dependent on the assignments that the employees take on and could possibly take on as self-employed instead? The question has not been legally assessed in depth in any court cases and the legal status of umbrella companies will be discussed below. As already mentioned, these companies are likely to be considered as intermediaries in accordance with Art. 2(e)(i) of the Platform Work Directive, when they act as employers for platform workers conducting work through the use of digital platforms.

---

[27] As was discussed in relation to the *Foodora* case above where the delivery rider switched employer from *Foodora* to a temporary work agency when switching from bike to moped as mode of delivery (see Swedish Labour Court case No. 45 from 2022). The Swedish labour court concluded that the intermediary was to be considered a temporary work agency and did not say anything about the legal status of umbrella companies as employers in that case.

[28] Westregård, Plattformsarbetare och egenanställda i svenska rätt: En analys av arbetstagarbegreppet, 2024, p. 65.

[29] As far as the author's research has shown at the end of 2024.

[30] Söderqvist/Bernhardtz, p. 57.

[31] Focusing on the concept of worker the aspects of the employer exerting direction and control is discussed in relation to platform work in Westregård, Plattformsarbetare och egenanställda i svenska rätt: En analys av arbetstagarbegreppet, 2024, p. 42 et seqq.

However, with the growing platform economy umbrella companies are nowadays also taking on the role of employers for workers conducting work through the use of digital platforms, what these companies themselves call workforce management.[32] In other words, umbrella companies seem to employ workers that may be dependent on the digital platform in order to find work and as such may not be as independent as the original idea of umbrella companies would indicate. This may call for another assessment of the legal status of umbrella companies, since these situations most likely involve an agreement between the umbrella company and the digital platform concerning the provision of workers. 12

The **umbrella companies' employers' organisation** (*EAFA*) and its president are actively seeking to establish these companies as a specific sector, separate from the temporary work agency sector. To improve the reputation of the sector they seek to conclude collective agreements. So far there are two collective agreements for the umbrella company sector. The first collective agreement was signed with a trade union called *Säljarnas* (Swedish for 'the sellers/salesmen'), which is a free-standing trade union not part of the traditional central organisations of *LO*, *TCO* or *SACO*.[33] *Säljarnas* and the collective agreement cover the more independent umbrella company workers, generally freelancers who are in a situation to negotiate assignments and pay in a manner similar to self-employed workers. The collective agreement regulates working conditions, including minimum pay levels, and abolishes the semi-compulsory[34] right to conversion of fixed-term contracts to a contract of indefinite duration.[35] This is an important point for the established trade unions, causing tension and difficulties for further negotiations on collective agreements. The traditional trade unions refuse to erode the employment protection offered through the right to conversion of fixed-term employment contracts into permanent employment.[36] Abolishing that right completely in the sense that this collective agreement does in accordance with the demands from *EAFA* will thus make it very difficult to find any progress in collective bargaining with the traditional trade unions. However, *Säljarnas* have now also resigned from the collective agreement. They 13

[32] Julius, Arbetsgivare bakom nytt fack för gig-jobbare: 'Vi vill ha hållbara villkor' in Arbetet, published 24 February 2025 at https://arbetet.se/2025/02/24/arbetsgivare-bakom-nytt-fack-for-gig-jobbare-vi-vill-ha-hallbara-villkor/ (last visited 6 March 2025).

[33] Westregård, Plattformsarbetare och egenanställda i svenska rätt: En analys av arbetstagarbegreppet, 2024, p. 56 et seqq.

[34] Swedish labour law is designed in order to allow the social partners room for manoeuvre to adapt employment conditions to the needs of the sector and workplace. When a section of the law is semi-compulsory, it is possible to deviate from it through collective agreements and such deviation may also be done in pejus.

[35] Clause 2 of Säljarnas (2021) Kollektivavtal för egenanställda (Collective agreement for umbrella company workers).

[36] Nevertheless, there are collective agreements concluded by trade unions part of the centralised organisations where clauses opening for deviations from the right to conversion also exist. See for example Art. 3, Section 6 in the collective agreement for elderly care between Almega Vårdföretagarna on the employer side and the trade union organisations Akademikerförbunden, part of SACO, and Vision, Part of TCO, in force between 1 June 2023 and 31 May 2025 for Vision and from 1 July 2023 onwards for Akademikerförbunden. For a brief earlier discussion see Hartzén in Ratti, p. 277 (299). These agreements, however, do not contain a general abolishment of the right to conversion. Instead, they are formulated in terms of allowing the employer and the worker to make an agreement whereby the worker declines the right to conversion for six months, if this agreement is initiated by the worker. Such agreements may also be extended at the initiative of the workers. Even though these collective agreements do not abolish the right to conversion fully, they still open up for potential abuse, which undermines the credibility of the traditional trade unions' critique towards the umbrella company agreement.

gave notice of termination of the collective agreement in April 2025 since they did not get enough members to motivate an agreement.[37]

14 Therefore, the employers' organisation representing umbrella companies, *EAFA*, and its president are seeking other ways forward. Currently, a new free-standing trade union has been set up to represent platform workers using digital platforms to find their assignments.[38] The new trade union is called ***Uppdragsarbetarförbundet***, abbreviated *UAF*, which in English translates to assignment workers' federation. In their manifest they proclaim to work for the securing good working conditions and access to social security and competence development protection for assignment workers and the correct classification of platform workers as employees.[39] Interestingly it is also clearly stated that the federation shall seek to assure that working conditions are regulated by the social partners through collective agreements without permanent employment as a norm. Instead, they define a specific form of safety to strive for through a minimum of six months foreseeable income, which shall be achieved by employers' contribution to a fund for competence development.[40] It must be pointed out that it is highly controversial that a trade union states in their founding documents that the general norm of permanent employment is to be set aside. After all, this is a principle that it established and acknowledged since a long time both nationally and internationally.[41] Of course, this is not done without criticism.

15 Already at the outset, when *UAF* was starting up the president of *EAFA* welcomed the setting up of the trade union and expressed hopes of being able to conclude a collective agreement with them.[42] A collective agreement has now been signed between *UAF* and *EAFA* and as for the previous agreement with *Säljarnas* this also holds a clause whereby the general form of employment is set to be specific fixed-term employment and **the right to conversion into a permanent employment is abolished.**[43] The developments both in terms of the collective agreement signed and the setting up of this trade union is criticised from the traditional trade unions. They highlight the fact that *UAF* was registered less than a month before the collective agreement was signed, that *UAF* has no members except for the board of the organisation and that they are financed by contributions from employers. The traditional trade unions claim that *UAF* is a yellow union, i.e. a union controlled by the employer, but the president of *EAFA* denies that. However, the board members are employed by one of the umbrella companies where the president of *EAFA* is also the CEO and which has decided to make financial contributions to

[37] Green, 'Nytt avtal med pinfärskt fack väcker frågor – "Ett helt gult fack"' in Arbetsvärlden, published 19.08.2025 at https://www.arbetsvarlden.se/nytt-avtal-med-pinfarskt-fack-vacker-fragor-ett-helt-gult-fack/ (last visited 28.08.2025).

[38] Green, 'Nytt avtal med pinfärskt fack väcker frågor – "Ett helt gult fack"' in Arbetsvärlden, published 19.08.2025 at https://www.arbetsvarlden.se/nytt-avtal-med-pinfarskt-fack-vacker-fragor-ett-helt-gult-fack/ (last visited 28.08.2025).

[39] UAF manifest available at https://www.uppdragsarbetarforbundet.se/om-oss (last visited 28.08.2025).

[40] Point 5 UAF manifest available at https://www.uppdragsarbetarforbundet.se/om-oss (last visited 28.08.2025).

[41] At EU level this principle is highlighted in the Fixed-Term Work Directive and its importance has been highlighted by the CJEU in numerous cases concenrning the misuse of successive fixed-term employments. For further discussion see Hartzén in Hiessl, p. 649 et seqq.

[42] Julius, *Arbetsgivare bakom nytt fack för gig-jobbare: "Vi vill ha hållbara villkor"* in Arbetet, published 24 February 2025 at https://arbetet.se/2025/02/24/arbetsgivare-bakom-nytt-fack-for-gig-jobbare-vi-vill-ha-hallbara-villkor/ (last visited 6 March 2025).

[43] Clause 2.1 in the collective agreement for umbrella company employees, signed on 05.08.2025, valid from 06.08.2025 – 31.3.2027 between UAF and EAFA.

UAF.[44] It remains to be seen whether this new collective agreement and newly established trade union will stand a chance of becoming recognised as part of the Swedish model. There can be reasons to question the legality of the collective agreement if *UAF* is also judged to be a yellow union, but the question is how to get a judgement from the Swedish labour court on this. Another issue with the collective agreement is the total abolishment of the right to conversion of fixed-term employments into permanent employment. Such a deviation, when there is no other means to prevent misuse of successive fixed-term contracts, is questionable in the light of the CJEU case law on Art. 5 FTWD concerning the prevention of abuse of successive fixed-term employments.[45] It would indeed be interesting to see what a preliminary ruling from the CJEU would state in relation to potential objective reasons for unlimited use of fixed-term contracts with umbrella companies.

It is interesting to note that whereas the platform company *Foodora* has entered into **16**
a collective agreement with one of the established trade unions, *EAFA* who represents companies that may rather act as intermediaries than actual platform companies is driving the **agenda to establish a new sector**, including new trade unions. The reason is quite likely the harsh stance from the established trade unions, whereby the issue of fixed-term contracts as a general norm with total abolishment of a right to conversion into permanent contracts has become a red flag. As long as that issue is not solved it seems unlikely that the *EAFA* will manage to conclude agreements with the established trade unions. Whether other platform companies will follow *Foodora* and conclude collective agreements remains to be seen. In comparison the Danish trade unions seem to initially have held a more pragmatic stance that opened for dialogue with platform companies. That might also be the reason that the Danish collective agreement *Hilfr2* has moved forward and solved issues concerning the specific aspects of platform work relating to the digitalised communication between the involved parties and algorithmic steering of the work performed.

The challenges for collective bargaining as a model for regulating platform work in the Swedish model is in other words manifold. Relations between the established trade unions and the employers' side are subject to disagreements on basic premises, making collective bargaining an unlikely option. This is partly due to the locked view from both sides on the issue of employment form and partly due to the limited rate of organisation amongst both workers and employers. As long as the established trade unions do not manage to organise platform workers and new trade unions fail in attracting members, then there will be a low degree of credibility for collective agreements signed with the few employers that are willing to organise and act as employers. In this sense, regulation by means of implementing the Platform Work Directive and the presumption of employment status will be necessary in order to assure a minimum level of protection for platform workers. The employment presumption may spur developments in court whereby platform companies are classified to be employers. Such caselaw development could trigger an incentive for platform companies to take part in collective bargaining to find solutions that are better adapted to the needs of the sector. Regardless, there have

[44] Green, 'Nytt avtal med pinfärskt fack väcker frågor – "Ett helt gult fack"' in Arbetsvärlden, published 19.08.2025 at https://www.arbetsvarlden.se/nytt-avtal-med-pinfarskt-fack-vacker-fragor-ett-helt-gult-fack/ (last visited (28.08.2025)).

[45] The possibility of using objective reasons for the renewal of fixed-term contracts is rather limited and the CJEU has been strict especially in relation to situations where objective reasons are used in a manner that opens for the use of successive fixed-term contracts for covering needs that are fixed and permanent. For futher discussion see Hartzén in Hiessl, p. 649 et seqq.

already been some initial developments in case law concerning employment status in the platform economy based on existing Swedish legislation and this serves to be discussed.

I. Case law developments in the gig-sector

17 How then have Swedish courts been dealing with these issues? Is there any indication that the umbrella company sector is recognised as an independent sector or are these companies classified in other terms by Swedish courts? The only labour law court case dealing with what could potentially have been considered an umbrella company so far is the ***Foodora* case from the Swedish labour court**.[46] In this case the delivery rider had first been employed by *Foodora* as a bike delivery rider. When he wanted to switch to do the deliveries by moped, he instead became employed by a company that had an agreement with *Foodora* on renting out staff for delivery services. After a short period as a moped delivery rider, he was cut off from the *Foodora* app. Since the worker was employed on fixed-term contracts for each assignment, he was not offered new employment when he could no longer sign up for deliveries through the *Foodora* app. The main question in the case was whether he should be considered to have been employed by *Foodora* and illegally dismissed by that company. In this case the Court concluded that the employer was a temporary work agency according to the Swedish legislation on temporary agency work. The court based its argument on the wording of the agreement between the temporary work agency and *Foodora*, but did not in any sense assess the facts of what party had the responsibility for assuring that the employee was provided with delivery assignments.[47] The question of what an umbrella company is in legal terms was as such not discussed in the case and whether such a definition exists legally is thus still unclear.

18 In relation to issues on **occupational health and safety** there are a few cases from administrative courts of relevance for the **concept of employer** within the gig economy so far. However, none of these cases have been decided in the Highest Administrative Court of Appeal[48] and therefore the cases merely provide an indication of how case law could be interpreted. Nevertheless, five cases are of interest to mention, four from the Administrative Court of Appeal in Gothenburg[49] and one from the Administrative Court of Appeal in Stockholm.[50] Since all these cases concern the issue of potential employer responsibility for occupational health and safety of platform workers it is worth noting what the basic premises for the assessment are. The assessment of whether such responsibility exists is based on the extent to which the potential employer exerts **control and direction over the work** to be conducted in such a manner as to be in control of the work environment. With due regard given to the assessment of the em-

[46] Swedish labour court case number 45 from 2022 (AD 2022:45).

[47] See Fritz/Hartzén/Westregård, AD borde ha beaktat EU-rätten in Lag&Avtal, 18.1.2023 available at https://www.lag-avtal.se/nyheter/forskare-om-foodora-malet-ad-borde-ha-beaktat-eu-ratten/1584864 (last visited 17.3.2025).

[48] For some of the cases there have been requests for a ruling from the Highest Administrative Court of Appeals, but those requests have been declined, see Westregård, Digitala daglönare i gig-ekonomin – En rättsvetenskaplig studie av arbetstagarbegreppet, IFAU, Rapport 2025:1, p. 20 et seqq. (available on IFAU (https://www.ifau.se/Forskning/Publikationer/Rapporter/2025/digitala-daglonare-i-gig-ekonomin-en-ratt svetenskaplig-studie-av-arbetstagarbegreppet/) (last visited 15.10.2025)).

[49] Case No. 4120–21 of 2021 (the Taskrunner-case), case No. 6394–21 of 2021 (the Tipptapp-case), case No. 3983–23 of 2024 (the Bolt-case) and case No. 7245–23 of 2024 (the *Wolt* -case) all from the Administrative Court of Appeals in Gothenburg.

[50] Case No. 5725–18 of 2019 from the Administrative Court of Appeals in Stockholm (the Cool Company-case).

ployee concept in labour law, but focusing mainly on the extent of direction and control that the platform has exerted over the work conducted, the Administrative Court of Appeal of Gothenburg provides differing conclusions in relation to the **business model** and structures **for** the various **platform companies**. Two of the platform companies, *Taskrunner AB* and *Tipptapp AB*, were considered to not exert the degree of direction and control over the work conducted required to be considered in charge of the work environment. In both these cases the person wishing to have work conducted and the platform worker agreed on terms and conditions for the work without any interference of the platform company. Therefore, the platform company could not be considered to be in a position to influence the work environment in any way.[51]

In the third case concerning *Bolt AB*, through a similar reasoning, the Court concluded that the platform company could not be considered as the employer of the delivery riders due to the very low **degree of direction and control** over the work conducted. Interesting in this case was that the Court also had to assess whether the platform company could be considered as a user company renting workers form the transportation companies and as such subject to work environment responsibility for the platform workers. In its reasoning the Court compared the situation at hand with the situation in the *Foodora* case and concluded that *Bolt* was far from exerting the form of direction and control over the delivery riders that *Foodora* was. The main arguments were that *Foodora* also had its own employees for which it evidently was in charge over the work environment, which *Bolt* did not. In addition, *Bolt* did not exert the form of direction and control over the work required to be considered an employer in charge of the work environment. The conditions that *Bolt* had set up for deliveries did not include requirements in terms of a minimum number of deliveries, nor downgrading of a delivery rider in case of rejection of a suggested assignment and nor did they involve prohibitions to conduct deliveries for competing platforms. Therefore, *Bolt* could not be considered a user company either.[52] 19

In the fourth case, concerning *Wolt AB*, the Court came to a differing opinion. In this case the delivery riders were conducting work either as self-employed or as employed by the umbrella company *Invoicery Business AB*. In this case the Court concluded that the delivery riders who were conducting work as **self-employed were not independent enough** and should instead be considered as employed by *Wolt*. The reasons were amongst others that, the agreement between *Wolt* and these delivery riders required the delivery riders to take on deliveries on an ongoing basis, the work was clearly directed through algorithms within the *Wolt* digital platform, including the price for the delivery, and the possibility for the delivery riders to hand over a delivery to someone else was subject to approval from *Wolt*.[53] What can be concluded is that not only the business model of the platform matters when assessing the relationship between the platform company and those conducting the work. For a proper legal assessment, it is important to understand how the service provided through the platform is regulated by means of the agreements between the platform and the various parties using the platform. 20

As for the delivery riders that were employed by *Invoicery* the Court merely concluded that the agreement between *Invoicery* and *Wolt* clarified that these delivery riders were to be considered as **temporary agency workers**. In this sense *Wolt* was therefore to be held responsible for investigating, risk assessing, planning necessary action, control and assure the necessary routines for future control of the occupational health and safety 21

[51] Case No. 4120–21 of 2021 (the Taskrunner-case) and case No. 6394–21 of 2021 (the Tipptapp-case) from the Administrative Court of Appeals in Gothenburg.
[52] Case No. 3983–23 of 2024 from the Administrative Court of Appeals in Gothenburg, the *Bolt*-case.
[53] Case No. 7245–23 of 2024 from the Administrative Court of Appeals in Gothenburg (the *Wolt*-case).

of the delivery riders, both for those being employed directly by *Wolt*, i.e. those having worked under false self-employment, and for those rented out to *Wolt* from *Invoicery*. As concerns the workers employed through *Invoicery*, the Courts decision in the case is in line with the Swedish Labour Court's judgement in the *Foodora* case,[54] i.e. the company placed in between the platform worker and the digital platform company, thus providing an employer for the workers and providing workers to the digital platform, shall be considered as a temporary work agency. This is especially interesting considering the fact that *Invoicery Business AB* is a company within the umbrella company sphere, part of the group where the president of the umbrella companies' employer organisation is CEO and the main owner. Even though *Invoicery* is not listed as one of the members of the umbrella companies' employers' organisation,[55] *Invoicery* had signed the collective agreement with the free-standing trade union organisations *Säljarnas*.[56] The agreement that the president of the umbrella companies' employers' organisation exclaimed to be the sectoral agreement for umbrella companies,[57] before *Säljarnas* decided to terminate the agreement. It is interesting to note the **legal classification of an umbrella company as a temporary work agency**. Even if this is not a judgement from the Highest Administrative Court of Appeals, it indicates that the umbrella companies' employers' organisation is up for somewhat of a struggle in establishing umbrella companies as a sector on its own. The scepticism from the traditional trade unions as concerns adapting collective agreements and allowing for never-ending chains of fixed-term employment contracts is thus likely to remain. After all, the traditional trade unions and the employers' organisation of the temporary work agency sector have put in a lot of effort to improve the reputation of the temporary work agency sector. They have succeeded in this through regulations of amongst other things the use of fixed-term employment, and thereby assuring a high degree of collective agreement coverage.

22 However, the **status of umbrella companies** in terms of being classified as temporary work agencies is also dependent of the business model of the umbrella company and the circumstances of the specific case at hand. This is evident when considering the outcome of the fifth case, the one from the Administrative Court of Appeals in Stockholm concerning *Cool Company*.[58] In this case the question concerned the responsibility for safety measures during work conducted on a roof, a work with risks for falling. The Court expressed that in situations concerning umbrella companies and their workers, there may be reasons to specifically assess the relationship even when the worker and the umbrella company had stated to be in an employment relationship. In this specific case the worker had been in contact with the customer concerning the work to be conducted and the work had been initiated before *Cool Company* was contacted. When the Swedish Work Environment Authority inspected the workplace there was no contract in place between *Cool Company* and the customer, nor was there a contract of employment

---

[54] Swedish Labour Court case No. 45 of 2022.

[55] The Umbrella Companies' Employers' organisation provides information on its members on its webpage. See https://www.egenanstallning.org/medlemmar/?_gl=1*14nraia*_up*MQ..*_gs*MQ..&gclid=CjwKCAjwvr--BhB5EiwAd5YbXrdWxeuJPPJ6ZzL9gun65dM_p0RaHGX6grASqR-MXF31Iv39htpe4hoCfQcQAvD_BwE&gbraid=0AAAAAqc6Js0rGzqiCWIzzvLgnECJUVVyO (last visited 11 March 2025).

[56] This information is found on the webpage of *Invoicery Business* (see https://www.invoicerybusiness.se last visited 11.3.2025), where it is also clearly stated that *Invoicery Business* is closely connected to Frilans Finans which is listed as a member of the umbrella companies' employers' organisation and whose CEO is also the president of that employers' organisation.

[57] Stephen Schad participated in a seminar, at Lund University on 10 May 2023, concerning the *Foodora*-case, where he explicitly mentioned this collective agreement in terms of a sectoral agreement.

[58] Case No. 5725–18 of 2019 from the Administrative Court of Appeals in Stockholm (the Cool Company-case).

in place between *Cool Company* and the worker. Instead, it was clear that it was the **single person carrying out the work** who had taken the initiative for the work to be conducted. The fact that *Cool Company* after that took care of the invoicing, payment of salary and some other issues did not suffice to classify *Cool Company* as an employer and therefore the company could not be held responsible for the lack of safety installations.[59] The lack of initial contact between the customer and the umbrella company and the worker's initiative being essential for any of the contractual relationships to occur did in other words disqualify the umbrella company as an employer. Umbrella companies operating under these terms can as such hardly be considered employers and will face difficulties being recognised as such. However, with more strict processes concerning the conclusion of agreements assuring that no work will be conducted before the necessary contracts between the umbrella company, the customer and the worker are set up, the assessment could possibly provide another result. In such a case the umbrella company could be considered a temporary work agency depending on how the contract with the customer is designed. It is thus still too early to clearly state that umbrella companies are either temporary work agencies, and thus employers, or not employers at all. In addition, the coming implementation of the Platform Work Directive may affect the future legal developments.

II. The coming implementation of the Platform Work Directive in Sweden

Currently, the **process of implementing the Platform Work Directive** in Sweden is underway, with a legal inquiry providing legislative proposals presented at the beginning of 2026. *Jonas Malmberg*, Justice of the Supreme Court and previously professor of labour law, has been in charge of the work with the legal inquiry. The **inquiry was guided by Government directives** including requirements concerning the legal analysis of the inquiry as well as specific objectives and restrictions for the proposals that the inquiry presents. As concerns the employee presumption, the inquiry was tasked to analyse for what court proceedings and administrative processes the presumption shall apply and specifically assess whether such administrative processes involve the inspection work of the Swedish work environment authority. In addition, the analysis should assess what authorities and public bodies are to be considered competent authorities in accordance with the Directive as well as whether complementary legislation is required to fulfil the Directive requirements on data protection. In developing the legislative proposals necessary the inquiry committee was bound to protect the Swedish concept of worker and take the Swedish model of collective bargaining as a starting point. In doing this, possibilities for derogations through collective agreements should be allowed if suitable and as far the Platform Work Directive allows. Innovative capacity and competitiveness for Swedish enterprises has also been compulsory to consider in the design of the legislative proposals. The inquiry was not allowed to give legislative proposals that will lead to the presumption of employment being applied in procedures relating to tax law, criminal law or social protection (i.e. outside the scope of labour law), nor to propose legislation other than what is essential for implementing the Directive.[60] 23

[59] Case No. 5725–18 of 2019 from the Administrative Court of Appeals in Stockholm (the Cool Company-case).

[60] Governmental committee Directive 2024:116 on the implementation of the EU Platform Work Directive (Dir. 2024:116, Kommittédirektiv, Genomförande av EU-direktivet om förbättrade arbetsvillkor för plattformsarbete).

The result of the inquirey should in other words be a proposal that **provides minimal effects on the regulatory structures** for the Swedish labour market.

24 To assure this the inquiry proposes a new law, entitled the platform work act, in principle mirroring the structure of the Directive. The reasons for this are to assure that the requirements of the Directive can be fulfilled, whilst at the same time assuring that the scope of these requirements will not spill over to other businesses or other legal fields than those specifically targeted in the Directive. A separate legal act for platform work is simply assessed as the best solution to assure that there is no risk for misinterpretations affecting labour law or data protection in a broader sense. To further assure coherence with the Platform Work Directive the proposed legal act is structured and worded in very similar terms as the Directive.[61] The proposed legal act is divided in eight chapters where background, definitions and scope of application are found in the first chapter. The second chapter concerns the legal classification of those performing platform work including a presumption of employment. The third chapter governs data protection in relation to algorithmic management and the fourth information and consultaion rights in relation to algorithmic management. Chapter five regulates platform companies' duties concerning information to relevant authorities and organisations representing workers. Chapter six is focused on the communication channels that platform companies are obliged to ensure for those performing platform work and their representatives. The seventh chapter concern control and sanctions and the last chapter deal with procedural issues.[62] This is only the first stage proposal, which is now followed by a consultation process that may very well change the proposed legislation before the Governement Bill is presented. Therefore, there is little use of providing a detailed analysis of the proposal. However, a few remarks relating to the Swedish model and some of the actors relevant for the platform economy in Sweden are of interest.

25 In relation to the importance of collective agreements as a regulatory instrument for the Swedish labour market it is worth noting that only two sections of the proposed act are specifically addressed as allowing for deviations through collective agreements. One is a section concerning information and consultation and the other is a section on limitation period for bringing legal actions. Whilst the section on information and consultation implements requirements from the Directive on the same issue,[63] the section on limitation period is inserted to adopt the general Swedish rules on this to the specific situation of platform work.[64] Both sections are of a protective character for platform workers and regulating the possibility to use central collective agreements to deviate from that protection also in pejus as long as the overall protection of the Directive is respected is a traditional Swedish solution.

26 As concerns the general possibility to introduce more specific regulations through collective agreements, i.e. not deviate from protective clauses but rather specify how for example information and consultation is to be conducted, this is according ot the investigator applicable, nonetheless. The investigstor finds it unsuitable to introduce a specific section listing which parts of the act that can be subject to more specific regulations in collective agreements. It is highlighted that there is a risk that such a regulation could be interpreted as limiting the scope for negotiations to nothing else than the issues specifically mentioned and that such limitations can be counterproductive in terms of promoting collective bargaining. Since the general legal possibility for adopting more specific

---

[61] SOU 2026:3, Genomförande av plattformsdirektivet, p. 75 et seqq.
[62] SOU 2026:3, Genomförande av plattformsdirektivet, p. 41 et seqq.
[63] SOU 2026:3, Genomförande av plattformsdirektivet, p. 75 et seqq.
[64] SOU 2026:3, Genomförande av plattformsdirektivet, p. 336 et seqq.

regulations thorugh collective agreements is part of the Swedish tradition and specific regulations in collective agreements are referred to in Art. 28 of the Directive, the investigator suggests that this shall be reiterated in the preparatory works but not specifically addressed in the legal act as to assure the aim of promoting collective bargaining for platform work.[65] The difference between deviations from protective legislation by means of collective agreements and using collective agreements for more specific regulations than the law prescribes may not be entirely clear. There is a risk for a misconception that it is only the two sections specifically mentioned as dispostive that can be adapted in collective agreements.

In relation to this, it is worth noting that during the work with the proposal, continu- 27
ous dialogue has been held with a reference group involving representatives from the traditional and established social partner organisations. Within this reference group suggestions and draft proposals for legislation have been discussed. The investigators have also met with representatives from *Foodora*, *Bolt*, *Uber* and *Wolt* as well as The Council for Umbrella Company Employees which is the predecessor of *UAF* and the *Taxiunion* which is an organisation for both taxi drivers and companies.[66] Interestingly the umbrella companies' organisation *EAFA* was not listed amongst the parties with whom the investigator has sought dialogue, nor have they been listed amongst the organisations specifically requested to provide opinions on the proposal during the consultation phase.[67] Whether this is an indication that the legislator does not consider this organisation a recognised part of the labour market parties remains unsaid. What it is clear is that *EAFA* does not have a similar status as the established employer organistations have in relation to the legislator.[68] It may simply be that intermediaries have not been considered necessary to consult during the process. The similarity between intermediaries and temporary work agencies is highlighted in the investigation as well as the commentary to the proposed definition of intermediaries. It is clearly stated that intermediaries may very well be temporary work agencies, albeit it is not stated that they necessarily shall be classified as such.[69] Regardless of this the employers' organisation representing temporary work agencies has not been consulted neitheir during the investigation, nor during the consultation process following the legislative proposal.[70] Chosing to exclude both *EAFA* and the employers organisation for temporary work agencies indicates that intermediaries have not been found specifically relevant to consult in the work with preparing the legislation. Since these companies are not merely a marginal phenomenon within the Swedish gig-economy, this is somewhat remarkable.

The consultation process closed for opinions on 31 March 2026 and amongst the 28
opinions so far it is possible to see more critical voices from some of the actors more affected by or more involved in the gig-economy.[71] *UAF* is for example highly critical of the lack of flexibility and narrow margin for collective bargaining due to only two

---

[65] SOU 2026:3, Genomförande av plattformsdirektivet, p. 79 et seqq and 340.

[66] SOU 2026:3, Genomförande av plattformsdirektivet, p. 60.

[67] Arbetsmarknadsdepartementet, A2026/00012, Remiss av betänkandet Genomförandet av plattformsdirektivet (SOU 2026:3).

[68] For a discussion on the relation between the legislator anad the established social partners see for example Herzfeld Olsson in Selberg/Sjödin, p. 127 et seqq.

[69] SOU 2026:3, Genomförande av plattformsdirektivet, p. 114 et seqq. and p. 419.

[70] SOU 2026:3, Genomförande av plattformsdirektivet, p. 60; Arbetsmarknadsdepartementet, A2026/00012, Remiss av betänkandet Genomförandet av plattformsdirektivet (SOU 2026:3).

[71] The Swedish Government publishes the opinions from the consulted organisations on its website, see https://www.regeringen.se/remisser/2026/01/remiss-av-sou-20263-genomforande-av-plattformsdirektivet/ (last visited 1 April 2026).

sections being dispositive through collective agreements.[72] Organisations from the taxi sector are critical since the proposal does not sufficiently address the specificities of this sector where platform companies to a high degree are present and collective bargaining is an exception. They also highlight the problem of intermediaries that lack control over the algorithmic management of the work and requests a stronger responsibility for platform companies also when intermediaries are used.[73] Whether these opinions will be considered for the Govermnment Bill to come remains to be seen. To what extent the challenges for the platform economy in Sweden and the possibilities for regulation through collective agreements may be affected by legal developments once the implementation of the Directive is in place, is also for the future to tell. There is a gap between the Swedish model with its traditional actors, not least the established social partner organisations and the stance taken by some of the actors within the gig-economy. This gap seems to decrease the possibilities for platform eonomy actors and traditional social partners to build trust enough for reaching agreements. Gig-economy actors may therefore continue to seek alternative solutions unless legal proceedings would bring results classifying platform workers as employees to such a degree that platform companies would deem it more favourable to seek specific soultions for their company through collective agreements. However, if the current situation persists where umbrella companies are taking on the employer status for those performing platform work, then legal cases on employment classification will be less likely. This means that it is questionable whether the implementation of the Directive will provide changes or impeteus for change in this regard.

C. Concluding remarks

29 As has been discussed above some challenges persist concerning the regulation of platform work, especially in Sweden. Whereas the issue of algorithmic management has been included in the Danish collective agreement *Hilfr2*, the Swedish discussion on regulation of platform work, especially in collective agreements, has been more focused on the issue of employment status and forms of employment contracts. This may very well be related to the involvement of umbrella companies within the Swedish gig-economy. Inserting an umbrella company as the employer shifts the focus from the platform as employer and thereby the possible algorithmic management issue is curtailed. The implementation of the Platform Work Directive may be of importance for Swedish platform workers and may also contribute to opening up the discussion between the labour market parties on this.

30 Considering the case law developments from Swedish courts in relation to the status of platform companies as employers the assessment is closely linked to the degree of direction and control that the platform company exercises over the platform worker. In addition, umbrella companies are seeking to establish themselves as employers in between the digital platform company and the worker. This decreases the importance of the employment status in the regulation of the Swedish platform economy, because when a platform worker already has an employer the question of the platform company as potential employer will be less likely to be addressed in courts or administrative processes. Therefore, the implementation of a presumption of employment will probably

---

[72] Uppdragsarbetarförbundet, Remissvar över betänkandet SOU 2026:3.

[73] Svenska Taxiförbundet, Remissvar -betänkandet Genomförandet av plattformsdirektivet (SOU 2026:3) (A2026/00012) and Taxiunionen, Remissvar diarienummer A2026/00012 – Genomförande av Plattformsdirektivet (SOU 2026:3).

not generate vast changes to the Swedish labour market practices concerning platform work. Instead, legal developments concerning umbrella companies' status as employers and/or temporary work agencies will more likely be of importance for platform workers protection in Sweden. In relation to this it is noteworthy that the legislator so far has not recognised *EAFA* as an actor of relevance to consult, neither during the investigation for the legsialtive proposal, nor during the consultation process once it was presented. This may indicate a position that these companies are viewed more as temporary work agencies than a specific sector on their own. Possible future cases concerning the role of intermediaries may clarify this, especially if the final legislation maintain the highlighted similarity between intermediaries and temporary work agencies as found in the current proposal.

At this stage the implementation of the Platform Work Directive is nevertheless necessary for the Swedish labour market. Seeking solutions through collective bargaining at this stage would not result in a sufficient protection for platform workers. The low degree of willingness amongst platform companies to take on the role of employer is one obstacle since such willingness is necessary for providing the basis of an employers' side in collective bargaining. Another obstacle is the complete locked situation as concerns collective bargaining between the umbrella companies' employers' organisation *EAFA* and the established trade unions. Unless there is an opening for discussing alternatives to the idea of fixed-term employment as the only form of employment in that sector any further developments are unlikely. The efforts of establishing the umbrella company sector as its own sector including the setting up of its own trade union also seems to be a path towards a dead end. After all, if there is little to no interest from the actual workers to set up a specific trade union in the sector, then the membership base is very limited. The lack of credibility for a collective agreement signed by a trade union with no members need not to be pointed out. For the Swedish model to work in this sector there is a need for clarity concerning the employment status of platform workers and initiatives that can generate a more cooperative dialogue between platform and umbrella companies on the one hand and established trade unions on the other. For this to occur the presumption of employment, the status of intermediaries and the division of responsabilities between platform companies and intermediares following the implementation of the Platform Work Directive may work as a catalyst. **31**

This potential effect of the presumption of employment may be more interesting than the actual legal effects relating to the employee concept as such in Sweden. However, this is not to say that the Platform Work Directive will not provide interesting legal changes. The focus on employment status in the Swedish debate has to some extent overshadowed other important aspects of platform work such as algorithmic management. In these aspects it will therefore be highly interesting to follow the developments both in terms of the legislative implementation and coming debate within the Swedish collective bargaining system. As mentioned before, the Danish social partners are already dealing with these issues, possibly due to them having overcome the issue of employment status earlier on and having a lower degree of involvement of umbrella companies in the platform economy. Considering the obstacles and challenges for the Nordic model within the platform economy the Platform Work Directive may thus provide some important incentives for the actors within the platform economy to take further steps towards improved collective bargaining structures. Regulation through collective agreements only would not be sufficient for implementing EU legislation due to the importance of guaranteeing that all workers are covered by the protection required from EU law. Instead, the Platform Work Directive may be a catalyst for better and more successful collective bargaining within the sector. Maybe it will generate an impetus for improving **32** the image of the sector also amongst the potential employers leading to similar developments as we have seen previously for the temporary agency work sector. Nevertheless, the importance of collective bargaining and collective agreements for regulating work in the Nordic model will remain fairly firm, as the platform company sector is too small to pose a credible threat to this model.

PART II
COMMENTARY OF THE DIRECTIVE

CHAPTER I
GENERAL PROVISIONS

Article 1
Subject matter and scope

1. The purpose of this Directive is to improve working conditions and the protection of personal data in platform work by:
- **introducing measures to facilitate the determination of the correct employment status of persons performing platform work;**
- **promoting transparency, fairness, human oversight, safety and accountability in algorithmic management in platform work; and**
- **improving transparency with regard to platform work, including in cross-border situations.**

2. This Directive lays down minimum rights that apply to every person performing platform work in the Union who has or who, on the basis of an assessment of the facts, is deemed to have an employment contract or employment relationship as defined by the law, collective agreements or practice in force in the Member States with consideration to the case-law of the Court of Justice.

This Directive also lays down rules to improve the protection of natural persons in relation to the processing of their personal data by providing measures on algorithmic management applicable to persons performing platform work in the Union, including those who do not have an employment contract or employment relationship.

3. This Directive applies to digital labour platforms organising platform work performed in the Union, irrespective of their place of establishment or of the law otherwise applicable.

Recital (16) This Directive aims to improve the working conditions of platform workers and to protect the personal data of persons performing platform work. Both objectives are pursued simultaneously and, while mutually reinforcing and inseparably linked, one is not secondary to the other. As regards Article 153(1), point (b), TFEU, this Directive sets out rules aiming to support the determination of the correct employment status of persons performing platform work and to improve working conditions and transparency with regard to platform work, including in cross-border situations, as well as to protect workers in the context of algorithmic management. As regards Article 16 TFEU, this Directive establishes rules to improve the protection of persons performing platform work with regard to the processing of their personal data by increasing the transparency, fairness, human oversight, safety and accountability of relevant algorithmic management procedures in platform work.

Recital (38) While Regulation (EU) 2016/679 establishes the general framework for the protection of natural persons with regard to the processing of personal data, it is necessary to lay down specific rules addressing the concerns that are related to the processing of personal data by means of automated monitoring systems or automated decision-making systems in the context of platform work. Article 88 of Regulation (EU) 2016/679 already provides that Member States may, by law or by means of collective agreements, provide for more specific rules to ensure the protection of the rights and freedoms in respect of the processing of employees' personal data in the employment context. This Directive provides for more specific safeguards concerning the processing of personal data by means of automated systems in the context of platform work, thereby providing for a higher level of protection of the personal data of persons performing platform work. In particular, this Directive establishes more specific rules in relation to Regulation (EU) 2016/679 concerning the use of and transparency with regard to automated decision-making. This Directive also establishes additional measures in relation to Regulation (EU) 2016/679 in the context of platform work to safeguard the protection of the personal data of persons

performing platform work, in particular where decisions are taken or supported by the automated processing of personal data. Terms relating to the protection of personal data in this Directive should be understood in light of the definitions set out in Regulation (EU) 2016/679.
Recital (64) Given that this Directive provides for more specific rules and additional rules in relation to Regulation (EU) 2016/679 in the context of platform work to ensure the protection of personal data of persons performing platform work, the supervisory authorities provided for pursuant to Article 51 of Regulation (EU) 2016/679 should be competent to monitor the application of those safeguards. The procedural framework of Regulation (EU) 2016/679, in particular Chapters VI, VII and VIII thereof, should apply for the enforcement of the more specific and additional rules of this Directive, in particular as regards supervision, cooperation and consistency mechanisms, remedies, liability and penalties, including the competence to impose administrative fines up to the amounts referred to in Article 83(5) of that Regulation.

Reference to other provisions:

Article 88 GDPR Processing in the context of employment

1. Member States may, by law or by collective agreements, provide for more specific rules to ensure the protection of the rights and freedoms in respect of the processing of employees' personal data in the employment context, in particular for the purposes of the recruitment, the performance of the contract of employment, including discharge of obligations laid down by law or by collective agreements, management, planning and organisation of work, equality and diversity in the workplace, health and safety at work, protection of employer's or customer's property and for the purposes of the exercise and enjoyment, on an individual or collective basis, of rights and benefits related to employment, and for the purpose of the termination of the employment relationship.
2. Those rules shall include suitable and specific measures to safeguard the data subject's human dignity, legitimate interests and fundamental rights, with particular regard to the transparency of processing, the transfer of personal data within a group of undertakings, or a group of enterprises engaged in a joint economic activity and monitoring systems at the work place. [...]

Article 22 GDPR Automated individual decision-making, including profiling

1. The data subject shall have the right not to be subject to a decision based solely on automated processing, including profiling, which produces legal effects concerning him or her or similarly significantly affects him or her.
2. Paragraph 1 shall not apply if the decision:
(a) is necessary for entering into, or performance of, a contract between the data subject and a data controller;
(b) is authorised by Union or Member State law to which the controller is subject and which also lays down suitable measures to safeguard the data subject's rights and freedoms and legitimate interests; or
(c) is based on the data subject's explicit consent.
3. In the cases referred to in points (a) and (c) of paragraph 2, the data controller shall implement suitable measures to safeguard the data subject's rights and freedoms and legitimate interests, at least the right to obtain human intervention on the part of the controller, to express his or her point of view and to contest the decision.
4. Decisions referred to in paragraph 2 shall not be based on special categories of personal data referred to in Article 9(1), unless point (a) or (g) of Article 9(2) applies and suitable measures to safeguard the data subject's rights and freedoms and legitimate interests are in place.

Literature: Abraha, 'A Pragmaic Comromise? The Role of Article 88 GDPR in upholding privacy in the workplace', International Data Privacy Law (IDPL) 2022/12, 276; Abraha, 'Regulating Algorithmic Employment Decisions through Data Protection Law', ELLJ 2023, 172; Adams-Prassl, 'Der Algorithmus im Personalmanagement', DRdA 2022, 195; Adams-Prassl/Laulom/Vázquez, 'The Role of National Courts in Protecting Platform Workers: A Comparative Analysis', in Miranda Boto/Brameshuber (eds), Collective Bargaining and the Gig Economy, Oxford/London/New York/New Dehli/Sydney 2022 p. 75; Adams-Prassl/Abraha/Kelly-Lyth/Silberman/Rakshita, 'Regulating algorithmic management: A blueprint', ELLJ 2023, 124; Aloisi, 'Regulating Algorithmic Management at Work in the European Union: Data Protection, Non-discrimination and Collective Rights', The International Journal of Comparative Labour Law and Industrial Relations 2024, 37; Aloisi/De Stefano, Your Boss Is an Algorithm. Artificial Intelligencem Platform Work and Labour, Oxford/London/New York/New Delhi/Sidney, 2022; Aloisi/Joppe/Abraha, From 'General' to 'Context-Specific' Data Protection For Workers: Insights From the EU Rules on Platforms, Algorithmic Management and AI Systems, ELLJ 2025, 538; Bérastégui, Exposure to psychosocial risk factors in the gig economy: a systematic review – ETUI Report, Brussels 2021; De Groen /Kilhoffer/Westhoff/ Postica/Shamsfakhr, Digital labour platforms in the EU, Mapping and business models, Final Report European Commission Luxembourg 2021; De Stefano, "Negotiating the Algorithm': Automation, Artificial Intelligence and Labour Protection', Comparative Labor Law & Policy Journal 2019, 15; Frank/Heine, 'Algorithmisches Management unter der Plattformarbeitsrichtlinie', NZA 2024, 865; Frank/Heine, 'Plattformarbeit zwischen Erfurt und Brüssel', NUA 2022, 543; Gräf, 'Algorithmisches Management in der Plattformarbeit – Richtlinienvorgaben und nationale Umsetzung', SR 2025, 14; Gräf, 'Der Richtlinienentwurf zur Plattformarbeit – Analyse, Umsetzungsperspektiven und Alternativen', ZFA 2023, 209; Gruber-Risak, 'Die neue lattformarbeitsrichtlinie: Was kommt auf uns zu?', ARD 6953/3/2025; Gruber-Risak/Warter, 'Die EU-Richtlinie zur Verbesserung der Arbeitsbedingungen in der Plattformarbeit', DRdA 2024, 267; Gruber-Risak/Warter, 'What's Union law got to do with it? Rechtliche Ansätze auf EU-Ebene zur Verbesserung der Arbeitsbedingungen von Plattformbeschäftigten', in Haas/Klas/Lamura (eds), Plattformarbeit: Herausforderungen im deutschsprachigen Kontext, Weinheim Basel 2024, p. 185; Hießl, 'Case Law on the Classification of Platform Workers: Cross-European Comparative Analysis and Tentative Conclusions', Comparative Labour Law & Policy Journal 2024, 465; Hiessl, 'Multiparty relationships in platform work: Cross-European case law developments and points of departure for (supranational) regulation', ELLJ 2023, 514; Hießl, 'The legal status of platform workers: regulatory approaches and prospects of a European solution', Italian Labour Law E-Journal, 2022/15, 13; Hiessl (ed), EU Labour Law, Alphen aan Rijn 2025; Krause, 'Auf dem Weg zur unionsrechtlichen Regelung von Plattformtätigkeiten', NZA 2022, 521; Kilhoffer/De Groen/Lenaerts/Smits/Hauben/Waeyaert/Giacumacatos/Lhernould/Robin-Olivier, 'Study to gather evidence on the working conditions of platform workers', Final Report European Commission Luxembourg 2020; Lelley/Bruck, 'Stresstest für die Plattformwirtschaft?', RdA 2023, 257; Lutz/Gruber-Risak, 'Gute Arbeitsbedingungen in der Gig Economy – was tun?' in Lutz/Gruber-Risak (ed), Arbeit in der Gig-Economy, Wien 2017, p. 353; Mateescu/Nguyen, 'Explainer Algorithmic Management in the Workplace', Data & Society 2019; Nogarede, No digitalization without representation, FEPS Policy Study, Brussels 2021; Pionteck/Warter, 'Zur Reichweite betrieblicher Regelungsmacht im Lichte des Unionsrechts', AuR 2025, 296; Ratti, 'A Long Road Towards the Regulation of Platform Work in the EU', in Miranda Boto/Brameshuber (eds), Collective Bargaining and the Gig Economy, Oxford/London/New York/New Dehli/Sydney 2022, p. 39; Rosin/Parviainen, Improving the transparency of algorithmic management in platform work: The role of the Platform Work Directive, ELLJ 2025, 472; Samant, The promises and perils of the platform economy: occupational health and safety challenges, and the opportunities for labour inspections, ILO Article 2019; Simitis, Schutz von Arbeitnehmerdaten: Regelungsdefizite – Lösungsvorschläge, Bonn 1980; Stöhr, 'Der arbeitsrechtliche Status von Plattformtätigen nach dem Richtlinienentwurf – Eine kritische Analyse', EuZA 2022, 413; Veale/Silberman/Binns, Fortifying the algorithmic management provisions in the proposed Platform Work Directive, ELLJ 2023, 308; Waas, 'Verbesserung der Arbeitsbedingungen von Plattformbeschäftigten', ZRP 2022, 105; Wank, 'Der persönliche Geltungsbereich der Plattformarbeits-Richtlinie', EuZW 2023, 747.

A. General remarks

1 Art. 1 defines the subject matter and objectives of the Platform Work Directive (→ mn. 25 et seqq.), as well as its personal and territorial scope of application (→ mn. 44 et seqq.). As a standard provision at the outset of EU legislative acts, it establishes the regulatory context and frames the Directive's provisions within the broader aims of EU labour and social policy.

2 Art. 1(1) serves as the guiding provision of the Directive, setting out its **two overarching objectives**: to improve working conditions in platform work and the protection of personal data in platform work. As explicitly stated, both main objectives are pursued simultaneously and, while mutually reinforcing and inseparably linked, one is not secondary to the other.[1]

3 The objectives of the Directive are to be achieved through **three subordinate purposes**: facilitating the determination of the correct employment status; promoting transparency, fairness, human oversight, safety and accountability in algorithmic management; and improving transparency with regard to platform work, including in cross-border situations.

I. Competence under EU Law and fundamental rights

4 Reflecting the two overarching objectives, the provisions of the Platform Work Directive are based on both Art. 153(2)(b) and Art. 16 TFEU.[2] This broad legal basis is necessary because the Directive contains not only labour law provisions, but also data protection provisions, which apply to all persons performing platform work, **regardless of their employment status.**

5 Gaps in competences may arise in situations where the Platform Work Directive provides protective measures for self-employed persons performing platform work that are not directly linked to the processing of personal data. Art. 153 TFEU only covers workers (in the sense of Union law), and potentially dependent self-employed persons or quasi-employees, but not other self-employed persons.[3] The final version of the Directive takes into account such concerns: Arts. 12 and 14 of the Directive, which deal with labour law issues, only apply to platform workers.[4]

6 It is questionable whether any existing gaps can be closed by invoking the residual competence under Art. 352 TFEU. This is unlikely, since Art. 352 TFEU constitutes a special legislative procedure requiring unanimity in the Council.[5] A possible recourse to the internal market competence under Art. 114 TFEU is not precluded by the exemption in Art. 114(2) TFEU, as this applies only to 'employed persons'.[6] At least recitals 6, 14, 28 and 56 refer to the need to ensure fair conditions of competition. Alternatively, gaps of the Directive addressing the situation of genuine self-employed persons working

[1] Recital 16. European Commission, Report Expert Group – Transposition of the Directive (EU) 2024/2831 on improving working conditions in platform work (12.1.2026), 9.

[2] Recital 16.

[3] Regarding the Comission's proposal Gräf ZFA 2023, 225; Krause NZA 2022, 526; Aloisi/Potocka-Sionek Ital. LLeJ 2022, 30 (36); with a different view Hiessl in Hiessl, p. 88 (92 et seqq).

[4] Gräf SR 2025, 21.

[5] Gräf ZFA 2023, 226; with a different view Krause NZA 2022, 523; European Commission, 'Commission staff working document impact assessment report accompanying the document Proposal for a Directive of the European Parliament and of the Council on improving working conditions in platform work', 9.12.2021 SWD(2021) 396 final/2, 16.

[6] Gräf ZFA 2023, 226.

through platforms as business actors could be based on Art. 53(1) TFUE, which empowers the EU to issue directives coordinating national provisions concerning the uptake and pursuit of activities as self-employed persons.[7] However, none of Arts. 53, 114 or 352 TFEU were cited as a legal basis.

According to recitals 2 and 3, the provisions of the Platform Work Directive are based on Art. 8 (Protection of personal data), Art. 12 (Freedom of assembly and of association), Art. 16 (Freedom to conduct a business), Art. 27 (Workers' right to information and consultation within the undertaking) and Art. 31 (Fair and just working conditions) of the CFR as well as on Principle 5 (Secure and adaptable employment), Principle 7 (Information about employment conditions and protection in case of dismissals) and Principle 10 (Healthy, safe and well-adapted work environment and data protection) of the European Pillar of Social Rights.[8] Recital 49 also refers to the right to non-discrimination, as set out in Art. 21 CFR. The Directive must be interpreted together with the relevant provisions of the Charter of Fundamental Rights of the European Union and the European Pillar of Social Rights.[9] 7

The Platform Work Directive also gives effect to additional fundamental rights, such as Art. 7 CFR (Respect for private and family life).[10] This is reflected, for instance, in Art. 7 of the Directive, which prohibits the processing of any personal data in relation to private conversations. Similarly, Art. 3 of the Charter of Fundamental Rights (Right to the integrity of the person) is engaged (alongside Art. 31 CFR) where Art. 12(3) of the Directive prohibits the use of automated monitoring or decision-making systems that put undue pressure on platform workers or otherwise puts at risk their safety and physical or mental health. 8

II. Concept of protection

An analysis of the provisions of the Platform Work Directive reveals a particular emphasis on **collective protection mechanisms.**[11] This is especially evident in the data protection provisions of Chapter III. In the employment context, the individualistic protection afforded by the GDPR is often criticised.[12] It is argued that the GDPR, as an 'omnibus' regulation, does not sufficiently address the specific characteristics of employment relationships, which differ from other typical data protection constellations: these include the fact that employees as data subjects are embedded within the organisation of their employers, who also provide the work equipment and exercise managerial authority. There is a multitude of (fundamental rights-based) legitimate interests, and the general imbalance of power inherent in employment relationships.[13] As a result, 9

[7] European Commission, 'Commission staff working document impact assessment report accompanying the document Proposal for a Directive of the European Parliament and of the Council on improving working conditions in platform work', 9.12.2021 SWD(2021) 396 final/2, 16.

[8] For more on the pillar of social rights as a driving force behind the Platform Work Directive, see Krause NZA 2022, 522; Gräf ZFA 2023, 215.

[9] See also European Commission, Report Expert Group – Transposition of the Directive (EU) 2024/2831 on improving working conditions in platform work (12.1.2026), 9.

[10] Recital 4 mentions the right to privacy.

[11] Gruber-Risak/Warter DRdA 2024, 267 et seqq.; Waas ZRP 2022, 105 (108).

[12] De Stefano, Comparative Labor Law & Policy Journal 2019, 15; Nogarede, p. 27 et seqq.; Aloisi/De Stefano, p. 155; Abraha, International Data Privacy Law 2022/12, 276 (286 et seqq.); Abraha, ELLJ 2023, 172 (184 et seqq.); Aloisi, International Journal of Comparative Labour Law and Industrial Relations 2024, 37 et seqq.; in this sense already Simitis, p. 10 et seqq.

[13] Abraha, International Data Privacy Law 2022/12, 276.

affected employees are typically disadvantaged in two respects: they are subject both to informational (power) asymmetries and, by definition, to personal dependence.[14]

10 For this reason, numerous scholars have called for additional collective protection mechanisms, arguing that collective action is a necessary corrective to the difficulty – if not impossibility – for employees to assert their interests given their inherent (dual) dependence.[15] In addition to establishing individual rights for persons performing platform work, the Directive also provides for various collective protection measures. For example, it includes information and consultation rights[16] as well as elements of collective enforcement.[17] Art. 25 of the Directive explicitly requires Member States to take appropriate measures to promote the role of the social partners and to encourage the exercise of the right to collective bargaining in platform work.

11 This collective dimension is also reflected in the historical development of the Directive. As early as the initial attempt in 2021, the European Commission's focus was not solely on a legislative instrument but also on promoting self-organisation and collective bargaining by persons performing platform work, regardless of their legal status. This was demonstrated by the publication of the EC Guidelines on the application of Union competition law to collective agreements regarding the working conditions of solo self-employed persons.[18] These guidelines clarify, inter alia, that collective agreements concluded by self-employed platform workers do not infringe European competition law if they provide services primarily through their own personal labour ('solo self-employed')[19]

III. Relation to other legal acts

12 The provisions of the Platform Work Directive complement an extensive body of existing legal instruments, including the GDPR[20], the P2B Regulation[21], the OSH Framework Directive[22], the General Framework Directive on Information and Consultation[23], the Temporary Agency Work Directive[24], and the Artificial Intelligence Act[25], to name a few.[26]

13 As these instruments overlap in some areas, it is necessary to coordinate their content. Essentially, the relevant provisions apply alongside the others.[27] However, the

[14] See for instance Abraha, International Data Privacy Law 2022/12, 276 (279) with further evidence.

[15] See again, for example, De Stefano, Comparative Labor Law & Policy Journal 2019, 15; Nogarede, p. 19; Aloisi/De Stefano, p. 155; Abraha, International Data Privacy Law 2022, 276 (286 et seqq.); Abraha, ELLJ 2023, 172 (184 et seqq.); Aloisi, International Journal of Comparative Labour Law and Industrial Relations 2024, 37 et seqq.; in this sense already Simitis, p. 10 et seqq.

[16] See, for example Art. 8(1); Art. 9(4); Art. 10(4); Art. 13(2); Art. 15; Art. 17(1).

[17] See Art. 11(2); Art. 19.

[18] Guidelines on the application of Union competition law to collective agreements regarding the working conditions of solo self-employed persons, 2022/C 374/02, ABl 2022/C 374/02.

[19] On this point, see for example Gramano in Hiessl, p. 1214; Gruber-Risak/Warter DRdA 2024/3, 267 (268) et seqq.; Gräf SR 2025, 14 (15), each with further evidence.

[20] Regulation (EU) 2016/679.

[21] Regulation (EU) 2019/1150.

[22] Directive 89/391/EEC.

[23] Directive 2002/14/EC.

[24] Directive 2008/104/EC.

[25] Regulation (EU) 2024/1689.

[26] See recital 10; for further points of contact with EU law, see Krause, NZA 2022, 521 (523).

[27] For example, Art. 12 and 13 state that the Platform Work Directive is without prejudice to Directive 89/391/EEC and related directives in the field of safety and health at work, nor Directive 89/391/EEC, 2002/14/EC or 2009/38/EC.

Platform Work Directive sets out specific rules for resolving conflicts relating to certain legal acts. Some of these rules are found in the legally binding text, while others are found in the recitals.

1. Temporary Agency Work Directive (2008/104/EC)

14 Regarding the Temporary Agency Work Directive (2008/104/EC), the Platform Work Directive provides in recital 26 for the **primacy** of the Temporary Agency Work Directive. This means that where a party is found to be an employer and fulfils the conditions for being a temporary-work agency under Directive 2008/104/EC, the obligations laid down in that Directive shall apply (→ Art. 3 mn. 17).

2. P2B Regulation (EU 2019/1150)

15 With regard to human review of automated decisions (Art. 11), the Platform Work Directive states that Art. 11 shall **not apply** to persons performing platform work who are **also business users**, as defined in Art. 2(1) of the P2B Regulation (EU 2019/1150). The specific provisions of the P2B Regulation should **prevail** in respect of business users (→ Chap. II mn. 11 et seqq.).[28] P2B Regulation is to some extent comparable with Directive on Transparent and predictable working conditions (TPWC), covering as the title of the P2B Regulation suggests, issues between the platform and the business users, such as obligatory information provision, the right to notice in case of contract revision, and restructions on dismal or equalvalent measures. In personal scope P2B Regulation applies to business users, self-employed persons who exchange services or goods with end consumer or clients via an online intermediary service, which does not include all types of platforms through which work is allocated and organised.[29] Before the Directive came into force, it was possible for genuinely self-employed platform workers to fall outside the scope of the P2B Regulation. This could happen if the platform was not classified as an online intermediation service provider. As they were genuinely self-employed, they were also not covered by the TPWC.[30] The Platform Work Directive now appears to close this protection gap.[31]

3. AI Act

16 The Platform Work Directive does not expressly mention the relationship to the **AI Act**[32], However, the provisions of the AI Act should not affect those of the Platform Work Directive. It is more likely that in practice the two pieces of legislation will **complement and support each other** (→ Preliminiary remarks to Articles 7–12 mn. 55).[33]

4. GDPR

17 In relation to the GDPR, recitals 38 and 64 point out that the provisions of the Platform Work Directive constitute, especially regarding Chapter III, more specific rules and additional rules within the meaning of Art. 88(1) GDPR. These rules derogate from the

---

[28] See Art. 11(5) and recital 49.

[29] Recital 54; Veale/Silberman/Binns ELLJ 2023, 308 (322); Kilhoffer et al., p. 176 seq., 269.

[30] Cf. Adams-Prassl ELLJ 2022, 30 (45).

[31] Rosin/Parviainen ELLJ 2025, 472 (480).

[32] Regulation (EU) 2024/1689.

[33] Warter, Zwischen Code und Kontrolle – Arbeitnehmer:innenrechte und der AI-Act (forthcoming); Gräf SR 2025, 14 (18), also for further information on overlaps.

general provisions, in particular Art. 22 GDPR, in the context of platform work ensuring the protection of personal data of persons performing platform work.

18 This is surprising given that Art. 88(1) of the GDPR primarily permits Member States to provide for more specific rules, whereas the regulatory provisions in question originate from the European Union level.[34] Moreover, this is also problematic, since Art. 88(1) GDPR provides an opening clause only in the context of employment, but not to self-employed persons.[35] Yet most of the provisions in Chapter III apply to all persons performing platform work, irrespective of their employment status.

19 For these reasons, some scholars are **sceptical** about Art. 88 GDPR being used as a legal basis for data protection-related provisions in the Directive. They argue that the provisions of the Directive are *lex specialis* in relation to the GDPR, meaning that the laws are not linked to Art. 88 and will therefore not be subject to the requirements set out in Art. 88(2) of the GDPR.[36]

20 However, the explicit doctrinal anchoring set out in the two (!) recitals cannot be disregarded. Nor is the argument convincing that Art. 88(1) GDPR merely allows Member States to adopt more specific provisions but does not oblige them to do so.[37] The obligation to implement such rules does not arise from Art. 88 GDPR itself, but from Art. 288(3) TFEU. As the relevant provisions of the Directive must be transformed into national law, it can be argued that they fall under Art. 88(1) GDPR. This interpretation is supported by the fact that Member States still have some discretion, particularly since the Platform Work Directive, pursuant to Art. 26(2), only sets minimum standards and allows Member States to adopt more favourable provisions for platform workers and Art. 28 provides an opening clause regarding the processing of personal data of persons performing platform work.[38] Accordingly, national laws that implement the Platform Work Directive ('national implementing measures') constitute 'more specific rules' under Art. 88 GDPR, since they govern the processing of personal data in an employment context. Consequently, these national implementing measures must comply with the requirements set out in Art. 88(2) of the GDPR, even if the Platform Work Directive itself is regarded as lex specialis (see also → Preliminiary remarks to Articles 7–12 mn. 39 et seqq.).

21 Considering the opening clause in Art. 88(1) GDPR, which permits the adoption of more specific provisions only with regard to employees[39], the legal foundation of the Directive remains unclear regarding self-employed persons.[40] In this regard, the provisions of the Directive are independent rules based on Art. 16 TFEU. In the event of conflicting provisions, the general principle applies that the more specific provisions of the Platform Work Directive take precedence over the general rules of the GDPR (*lex specialis derogat legi generali*) for areas not covered by the material scope of the opening clause of Art. 88(1) of the GDPR. This interpretation is supported by recital 38, fifth sentence,

---

[34] Frank/Heine NZA 2024, 267.

[35] For the term employee in Art. 88 GDPR, reference can be made to the case law of the CJEU on the concept of worker (ECJ 30.03.2023 – case C-34/21, ECLI:EU:C:2023:270 para. 39 seq. – Hauptpersonalrat der Lehrerinnen und Lehrer). Consequently, Rosin/Parviainen ELLJ 2025, 472 (478).

[36] Gräf SR 2025, 14 (17); Daum in Giesen/Junker/Rieble, p. 91 (104 seq.); Frank/Heine NZA 2024, 267); Aloisi/Joppe/Abraha ELLJ 2025, 538 (549).

[37] In this sense arguing Frank/Heine NZA 2024, 267.

[38] See Gruber-Risak/Warter DRdA 2024/3, 267 (275).

[39] For the term employee, reference can be made to the case law of the CJEU on the concept of worker (ECJ 30.03.2023 – case C-34/21, ECLI:EU:C:2023:270 para. 39 seq. – Hauptpersonalrat der Lehrerinnen und Lehrer).

[40] Art. 88(1) of the GDPR explicitly refers to employees' personal data in an employment context. Cf. Gräf SR 2025, 14 (17).

which may be understood to suggest that regarding self-employed persons performing platform work the Directive establishes 'additional measures in relation to Regulation (EU) 2016/679 in the context of platform work to safeguard the protection of the personal data of persons performing platform work'.

However, the argument that the Directive's doctrinal foundation can be derived from Art. 88(1) GDPR faces another legal obstacle. While it has been clear since the CJEU judgment in C-34/21, that additional, stricter or derogating national rules may be adopted on the basis of Art. 88(1) GDPR,[41] the Court in the cases (C-34/21 and C-65/23) emphasized, that even where more specific provisions are adopted under Art. 88(1) GDPR, all processing of personal data must comply with the provisions of Chapters II and III of the GDPR.[42] In light of this, the doctrinal grounding of the Platform Work Directive on Art. 88(1) GDPR is contradicting these decisions, since Art. 22 GDPR on automated data processing and profiling forms part of Chapter III GDPR. This apparent conflict can be resolved by recognising that Art. 22 GDPR, contrary to its wording and systematic placement, does not establish a data subject right as such, but rather constitutes a prohibition.[43] Art. 22 GDPR does not provide a legal basis for processing either. Rather, it governs whether and how the outcome of a (lawful) processing operation may be used.[44] Moreover, the Platform Work Directive itself asserts that it not only provides appropriate safeguards for the processing of personal data but in fact ensures a higher level of protection of the personal data of persons performing platform work.[45] Accordingly, this reasoning is also compatible with the minimum harmonisation approach adopted by the CJEU in C-65/23. Finally, it should be noted that Art. 22(2)(b) GDPR expressly allows for exceptions of Art. 22 GDPR, if the decision is authorised by Union or Member State law to which the controller is subject and which also lays down suitable measures to safeguard the data subject's rights and freedoms and legitimate interests.[46] 22

In summary, it can be stated that, in relation to the GDPR, a **distinction must be made** between platform workers and self-employed persons performing platform work. With regard to **platform workers**, the Directive is based on Art. 88(1) GDPR and is therefore bound by the limits set out in Art. 88(1) and (2) GDPR.[47] This is arguably permissible, even though both the GDPR and the Platform Work Directive are secondary Union law acts of equal hierarchical status within the EU legal order.[48] **For other persons performing platform work**, this does not apply. In their case, the relevant provisions constitute additional measures (see recital 38), which, according to the lex specialis principle, take precedence over the GDPR. Outside the scope of the Directive, however, only the provisions of the GDPR apply to both employees and self-employed persons alike. 23

The practically decisive consequence of this seemingly academic debate – in both cases, the provisions of the Directive take precedence over those of the GDPR[49] – is not on- 24

[41] ECJ 30.3.2023 – case C-34/21, ECLI:EU:C:2023:270 para. 78 – Hauptpersonalrat der Lehrerinnen und Lehrer.

[42] ECJ 30.3.2023 – case C-34/21, ECLI:EU:C:2023:270, para. 68 et seqq. – Hauptpersonalrat der Lehrerinnen und Lehrer; 19.12.2024 – case C-65/23, ECLI:EU:C:2024:1051, para. 45 et seqq. – K-GmbH.

[43] ECJ 7.12.2023 – case C-634/21, ECLI:EU:C:2023:957, para. 52 – Schufa Holding.

[44] ECJ 7.12.2023 – case C-634/21, ECLI:EU:C:2023:957, para. 67 – Schufa Holding.

[45] Recital 38.

[46] See Pionteck/Warter AuR 2025/7, 296; Gruber-Risak/Warter DRdA 2024/3, 267 (275).

[47] The provisions of the Platform Work Directive that are not based on Art. 88(1) of the GDPR are not subject to its restrictions.

[48] Regarding the equality of regulations and directives, see Ruffert in Calliess/Ruffert (ed.), EUV/AEUV (2022) Art 288 AEUV para. 14.

[49] Cf. Gräf SR 2025, 14 (17).

ly that specifications of from Art. 22 GDPR can be made on the basis of Art. 88(1) GDPR, but also that the Directive provides a blueprint for the necessary, appropriate, and specific safeguards required under Art. 88(2) and Art. 22(3) GDPR.[50] Consequently, collective agreements at company level based on Art. 88(1) GDPR are possible and mirror the provisions of Chapter III of the Directive (such as German *Betriebsvereinbarungen* or work agreements). This would extend the scope of the regulatory framework for algorithmic management to situations not covered by the Platform Work Directive. If the special data protection provisions are based on Art. 88(1) of the GDPR, works agreements incorporating the provisions of Chapter III of the Platform Work Directive would then also be possible for workers not employed via a platform (for instance, in Amazon's warehouse logistics). Under the general provisions of Art. 22 GDPR, this would not be possible as the conditions for justification set out in Art. 22(2) GDPR are usually not met. The only question is then whether the existing national provisions on co-determination permit this, or if specific new provisions need to be created.[51] However, a company-level extension of Chapter III of the Directive to self-employed persons who are not performing platform work is *de lege lata* not possible, as they do not fall within the scope of Art. 88(1) GDPR or the opening clause of Art. 28 of the Directive (→ mn. 21).[52]

B. Subject matter and objectives of the Platform Work Directive

I. Primary objectives and subordinate purposes of the Platform Work Directive

25 Art. 1(1) serves as the guiding provision of the Platform Work Directive, setting forth its two primary objectives: the improvement of working conditions and the protection of personal data in the context of platform work.

26 In addition to these two main objectives, the original Commission draft also stated that the Platform Work Directive should support the conditions for the **sustainable growth of digital labour platforms** in the European Union.[53] The explanatory memorandum state that digital work platforms promote innovative services and new business models and create many opportunities for consumers and businesses.[54] This indicates that, at the draft stage, the Directive's provisions were intended not only to regulate platform work but also to foster its sustainable growth. However, the goal of sustainable growth is omitted from the final text. This shift likely reflects a deliberate narrowing of the Directive's focus towards the social protection of platform workers, prioritising the fundamental rights of persons performing platform work over market expansion. Including sustainable growth as an explicit objective could have created interpretational tensions between economic promotion and social safeguards, which are now resolved

[50] As already Gruber-Risak/Warter DRdA 2024, 267 (276).

[51] See Pionteck/Warter AuR 2025, 296. In Germany, § 26(4) of the Federal Data Protection Act (BDSG) allows works councils and employers to create specific rules on data processing.

[52] Gräf SR 2025, 23.

[53] See Art. 1(1) of the proposal of the European Commission, 'Proposal for a Directive of the European Parliament and of the Council on improving working conditions in platform work', 9.12.2021, COM(2021) 762 final.

[54] See the Explanatory Memorandum under 1. Context of the proposal, Reasons for and objectives of the proposal of the European Commission, 'Proposal for a Directive of the European Parliament and of the Council on improving working conditions in platform work', 9.12.2021, COM(2021) 762 final.

in favour of the latter. Sustainable growth is now mentioned as an objective only in recital 14, but no longer in the legally binding part.[55]

27 These overarching aims are further specified through three subordinate goals, namely: facilitating the determination of the correct employment status; promoting transparency, fairness, human oversight, safety, and accountability in algorithmic management; and enhancing overall transparency within platform work, including in cross-border situations.

1. Facilitating the determination of the correct employment status

28 Despite the existing regulatory framework, particularly in labour law and data protection law, the phenomenon of platform work necessitates specific protective provisions in the view of the Union legislator.[56] This need arises primarily from the issue of **bogus self-employment**. Court cases[57] in several Member States have revealed that digital labour platforms often incorrectly classify persons performing platform work as self-employed or 'independent contractors', despite exercising de facto direction and control over them. This is particularly prevalent in sectors where these platforms integrate such persons into their core business activities. These courts have therefore reclassified individuals who were previously considered self-employed as employees of the platforms.[58] This problem is exacerbated by the fact that platforms often only make minor adjustments to their practices after court proceedings have concluded, thereby exposing platform workers to renewed litigation risks.

29 Since there is no clear-cut legal distinction between employees and self-employed persons a high degree of legal uncertainty exists, which is sometimes systematically exploited by platform operators. A false declaration of self-employment is often made to avoid certain legal or fiscal obligations, minimum standards, or to create a competitive advantage compared to law-abiding undertakings.[59]

30 A further challenge inherent in the digital structuring of work processes on platforms is that the criteria for establishing an employment contract are often difficult to prove. This is particularly true in the platform economy, where persons performing platform work are confronted with an app that organises and manages their work, without them knowing how offers or instructions are generated or on which criteria they are based (lack of transparency). They are effectively faced with a digital black box, resulting in an evidential deficit that makes it nearly impossible for them to prove the existence of personal subordination.[60] This is an unsatisfactory situation, as such concealed misclassification creates a strong incentive to categorise platform workers incorrectly and thereby circumvent the application of labour law.[61]

31 The different legal statuses of platform workers result in significant disparities for all concerned, since only employees are covered by full labour law protection. For platforms, this primarily results in lower costs, as minimum wage regulations, paid leave and sick pay usually do not apply to the self-employed. In its proposal for the Platform

---

[55] Similar Gräf SR 2025, 14 (15).

[56] Recital 14.

[57] Recital 7; see Hiessl Comparative Labour Law & Policy Journal 2024, 465 et seqq.; Hiessl ELLJ 2023, 514; Hiessl Italian Labour Law E-Journal, 2022/15, 13.

[58] Recital 7; see for example Hießl, Comparative Labour Law & Policy Journal 2024, 465 et seqq.; Hiessl, European Labour Law Journal 2023/14, 514; Hiessl, Italian Labour Law E-Journal, 2022/15, 13; Adams-Prassl/Laulom/Vázquez in Miranda Boto/Brameshuber, p. 75 et seqq.

[59] Recital 28.

[60] See recital 30. Cf. for example Lutz/Gruber-Risak, Arbeit in der Gig-Economy, 353.

[61] Gruber-Risak/Warter in Haas/Klaus/Lamura, p. 185 (190).

Work Directive, the European Commission stated that up to 5.5 million of the estimated 28 million people working via digital labour platforms are 'bogus self-employed'.[62]

32 Therefore, the Platform Work Directive aims to improve legal certainty and to achieve a level playing field between digital labour platforms and offline providers of services.[63] To this end, Member States should have appropriate procedures in place to prevent and address the misclassification of the employment status of platform workers (→ Art. 4 mn. 7 et seqq.).[64]

2. Promoting transparency, fairness, human oversight, safety, and accountability in algorithmic management

33 The second purpose of the Platform Work Directive is to promote transparency, fairness, human oversight, safety and accountability in algorithmic management in platform work. In comparison to the Commission's proposal, the text of the Directive now also includes human oversight as a separate objective.

34 The term **'algorithmic management'** is not introduced as a legal term in the Directive. It only appears in the programmatic heading to Chapter III and in the general objective in Art. 1 (→ Preliminary remarks to Articles 7–12 mn. 1 et seqq.).[65] Algorithmic management refers to the increasingly prevalent practice whereby decisions traditionally made by employers are now fully automated or at least predominantly based on algorithmic calculations.[66] This includes, for example, the assignment of tasks, the evaluation of performance, and the modification of contractual status.[67] Algorithmic management enables platform operators to organise and administer the services provided via the platform with a high degree of efficiency.[68] Central to this development are the use of automated monitoring systems and automated decision-making systems (→ Art. 2 mn. 25 et seqq.).[69]

35 The background to these provisions of the Directive lies in the risks arising from the unregulated use of automated monitoring and decision-making systems, which can lead to technology-enabled surveillance, increase power imbalances and opacity about decision-making, and entail risks for decent working conditions, for the health and safety at work, for equal treatment and for the right to privacy.[70] In concrete terms, the use of such systems can lead to work intensification, pervasive monitoring, and insecurity, which in turn may cause stress, anxiety, exhaustion, and depression, thereby adversely affecting the physical and mental health, safety, and overall well-being of persons performing platform work.[71] These negative impacts are particularly pronounced among persons performing low-skilled, on-location tasks.[72]

---

[62] Cf. European Commission, 'Proposal for a Directive of the European Parliament and of the Council on improving working conditions in platform work', 9.12.2021, COM(2021) 762 final, 5; De Groen et al., p. 11 et seqq.

[63] Recital 14.

[64] Recital 25.

[65] Gräf SR 2025, 14 (15 et seq).

[66] Cf. recital 8; Adams-Prassl DRdA 2022, 195; Aloisi/De Stefano, p. 49 et seqq. A similar definition can be found in Mateescu/Nguyen, p. 3.

[67] Recitals 8 and 45.

[68] Recital 8.

[69] Recital 8; Frank/Heine NZA 2024, 865.

[70] See recitals 4 and 50.

[71] Bérastégui, p. 85 et seqq.; Mateescu/Nguyen, p. 13 et seqq.; in summary EU-OSHA, Occupational Safety and Health in Digital Platform Work, p. 5 with further evidence (available under: https://osha.europa.eu/sites/default/files/2022-02/Digital_platform_work_Review_policies_initiatives.pdf).

[72] EU-OSHA, Occupational Safety and Health in Digital Platform Work, p. 5 with further evidence.

36 At first glance, it may appear surprising that it is the Platform Work Directive that (for the first time) establishes specific regulations on algorithmic management. However, this is less surprising upon closer examination, given that the emergence of algorithmic management is closely connected with the rise of the gig economy.[73] In many cases, algorithmic management is not just a feature, but a structural prerequisite of the platform economy. It enables the platform business model to function, as coordinating and matching a large number of people performing platform work (the crowd) with a similarly large and dispersed number of service recipients (the crowdsourcers) would be unmanageable using traditional manual methods.[74]

37 This link between platform work and algorithmic management is reflected in the Directive's scope of application. The provisions apply exclusively to those platforms where the services are organised with the use of automated monitoring or decision-making systems. In other words, the use of algorithmic management constitutes a defining prerequisite for a digital labour platform to fall within the scope of the Platform Work Directive (→ Art. 2 mn. 25).[75]

38 Unlike the GDPR or the AI-Act, the provisions of the Platform Work Directive are specifically tailored to employment contexts, enabling them to address the realities of work more effectively.[76] However, such regulations are not entirely novel. Spain's Riders Law[77], for instance, introduced information rights relating to the use of algorithmic management as far back as 2021 although only for the delivery sector and not for platform work in general (→ see report Spain mn. 4 et seqq.).[78]

39 The fact that algorithmic management is now subject to regulatory oversight constitutes a 'pioneering achievement' of considerable significance.[79] In contrast to the rebuttable presumption of employment status, the provisions on algorithmic management were relatively uncontroversial during the legislative process, yet they are particularly innovative. They may pave the way for further rights and protective measures in the employment context, the development of which has already begun.[80]

3. Enhancing overall transparency within platform work, including in cross-border situations

40 The third objective of the Platform Work Directive is improving transparency with regard to platform work, including in cross-border situations. In this respect, Chapter IV of the Directive sets out specific transparency obligations, including requirements for the declaration of platform work and access to relevant information concerning platform work.

41 This objective is based on the insight that many of the existing digital labour platforms are international business actors that carry out activities and deploy business

---

[73] Adams-Prassl et al. ELLJ 2023, 124 with further evidence; in this sense also recital 4.

[74] Gräf SR 2025, 14 (16).

[75] See Art. 2(1)(a)(iv).

[76] Abraha, International Data Privacy Law 2022/12, 276; see also Aloisi/De Stefano, 'Gig' workers in Europe (available under: 'Gig' workers in Europe: the new platform of rights).

[77] Real Decreto-ley 9/2021.

[78] For their role model function, see Council of the European Union, Proposal for a Directive on improving working conditions in platform work, 10107/23, 6; Aloisi/De Stefano, 'Gig' workers in Europe (available under: 'Gig' workers in Europe: the new platform of rights).

[79] In this sense also Waas ZRP 2022/4, 105 (107).

[80] See the mission letter from the President of the European Commission, Ursula von der Leyen, an Roxana Mînzatu from 17th September 2024 available under: https://commission.europa.eu/document/download/27ac73de-6b5c-430d-8504-a76b634d5f2d_en?filename=Mission%20letter%20-%20MINZATU.pdf).

models in several Member States or across borders.[81] When platforms operate in several Member States or across borders, it is often unclear where the platform work is performed and by whom, especially as regards online platform work. Furthermore, national competent authorities do not have easy access to data on digital labour platforms, including the number of persons performing platform work, their employment status, and their working conditions. This complicates the enforcement of applicable rules.[82] In order to enable national competent authorities to ensure that digital labour platforms comply with labour legislation and regulations, in particular if they are established in a Member State other than the Member State in which the platform worker is performing work or in a third country, digital labour platforms have to declare work performed by platform workers to the competent authorities of the Member State in which the work is performed.[83]

II. Structure of the Directive

42 The Platform Work Directive does not provide a comprehensive regulation of platform work; rather, it focuses on three key areas that correspond to its stated objectives and purposes. This focus is reflected in the Directive's structure, where the three main purposes of the Directive are grouped into distinct chapters:

- Measures to address the issue of disguised self-employment, particularly by facilitating the determination of the correct employment status of persons performing platform work, through the introduction of the legal presumption of an employment relationship to the platform (Chapter II, Art. 4–6).
- Regulation of algorithmic management, including red lines, specific provisions on human agency and on information and consultation rights of persons peroforming platform work (Chapter III, Art. 7–15);
- Enhancement of transparency in platform work through the registration of platforms and access to relevant information (Chapter IV, Art. 16–17);
- Also included are detailed rules on enforcement mechanisms (Chapter V, Art. 18–24).

III. Normative relevance

43 Art. 1(1) does not impose directly binding normative obligations on Member States. However, it is to be understood as an **interpretation guidance** for all provisions of the Platform Work Directive, especially the various indeterminate legal terms. This also applies to the provisions enacted in the member states based on the opening clause set out in the Platform Work Directive.

---

81 Recital 5.

82 Recital 9.

83 Recital 56.

C. Scope of the Platform Work Directive

I. Personal scope of application (Article 1(2))

Art. 1(2) of the Platform Work Directive sets out the personal scope of application. The Directive distinguishes between **two groups** of persons it protects: **44**

On the one hand, the Directive lays down minimum rights that apply to every person performing platform work in the Union who has or who is deemed to have an employment contract or employment relationship as defined by the law, collective agreements or practice in force in the Member States with consideration to the case-law of the Court of Justice. Art. 1(2) of the Directive explicitly emphasises that this qualification should be based on an assessment of the facts. These persons are referred to as **platform workers** (see for more details → Art. 2 mn. 64 et seqq.). **45**

On the other hand, the Directive lays down rules to improve the protection of natural persons in relation to the processing of their personal data by providing measures on algorithmic management applicable to persons performing platform work in the Union, including those who do not have an employment contract or employment relationship. These are referred to in the Directive as **persons performing platform work** (see for more details → Art. 2 mn. 62). **46**

II. Territorial Scope (Article 1(3))

The territorial scope of the Directive is determined by the definition of platform work in Art. 1(3), which refers to work performed within the Union. According to recital 19, the Directive applies to all digital labour platforms regardless of their place of establishment and irrespective of the law otherwise applicable to their operations. Thus, the decisive factor is solely the physical location of the person performing platform work during the provision of their services.[84] **47**

This provision is of particular importance given that digital labour platforms are often international business actors operating and deploying their business models across multiple Member States or beyond Union borders.[85] Where platforms operate in several Member States or cross-border contexts, Art. 1(3) clarifies that the rules of the Directive apply whenever the person performing platform work is physically located within a Member State. Conversely, the Directive does not cover digital labour platforms established in the EU that organise platform work performed outside the EU.[86] **48**

Legal scholarship highlights the dual nature of the provision. With regard to public law norms, it is classified as part of public international law, giving concrete expression to the principle of territoriality. With regard to private law relations, however, it constitutes a rule of private international law.[87] **49**

From the perspective of private international law, the national implementing provisions of the Platform Work Directive are to be regarded as overriding mandatory provi- **50**

[84] Gruber-Risak ARD 6953/3/2025.

[85] Recital 5.

[86] See also European Commission, Report Expert Group – Transposition of the Directive (EU) 2024/2831 on improving working conditions in platform work (12.1.2026), 11.

[87] Cf. Gräf ZFA 2023, 209 (227). See also European Commission, Report Expert Group – Transposition of the Directive (EU) 2024/2831 on improving working conditions in platform work (12.1.2026), 11.

sions within the meaning of Art. 9 of the Rome I Regulation[88]. Therefore, the provisions of the Platform Work Directive take precedence over the law chosen by the parties.[89]

51 This primarily benefits persons performing platform work, whose contractual relationship would otherwise be subject to unrestricted private autonomy from a conflict-of-laws perspective.[90] Employees, and potentially employee-like individuals, are also subject to private autonomy under Art. 8 of the Rome I Regulation. However, such a choice of law may not deprive employees of the protection they are afforded under the law of the country in which or from which they habitually carry out their work.[91] However, the country where the work is habitually carried out shall not be deemed to have changed if the employee is working temporarily in another country.[92]

Article 2
Definitions

1. For the purposes of this Directive, the following definitions apply:

(a) 'digital labour platform' means a natural or legal person providing a service which meets all of the following requirements:
- **(i) it is provided, at least in part, at a distance by electronic means, such as by means of a website or a mobile application;**
- **(ii) it is provided at the request of a recipient of the service;**
- **(iii) it involves, as a necessary and essential component, the organisation of work performed by individuals in return for payment, irrespective of whether that work is performed online or in a certain location;**
- **(iv) it involves the use of automated monitoring systems or automated decision-making systems;**

(b) 'platform work' means work organised through a digital labour platform and performed in the Union by an individual on the basis of a contractual relationship between the digital labour platform or an intermediary, and the individual, irrespective of whether there is a contractual relationship between the individual or an intermediary and the recipient of the service;

(c) 'person performing platform work' means an individual performing platform work, irrespective of the nature of the contractual relationship or the designation of that relationship by the parties involved;

(d) 'platform worker' means any person performing platform work who has or is deemed to have an employment contract or an employment relationship as defined by the law, collective agreements or practice in force in the Member States with consideration to the case-law of the Court of Justice;

(e) 'intermediary' means a natural or legal person that, for the purpose of making platform work available to or through a digital labour platform:

---

[88] Regulation (EC) 293/2008.

[89] Cf. Krause NZA 2022, 527; Sutterer-Kipping in Hiessl, p. 714; with a different view Gräf (ZFA 2023, 228), who qualifies Art. 1(3) itself as a unilateral conflict rule which, as a lex specialis, takes precedence over the otherwise applicable conflict rules, in particular Arts. 3 and 8 (with regard to employees) and Arts. 3 and 4(1)(b) (with regard to self-employed persons) of the Rome I Regulation.

[90] Gräf ZFA 2023, 209 (228), with further evidence.

[91] Art. 8(1) Rome I Regulation.

[92] Art. 8(2) Rome I Regulation.

(i) establishes a contractual relationship with that digital labour platform and a contractual relationship with the person performing platform work; or
(ii) is in a subcontracting chain between that digital labour platform and the person performing platform work;

(f) 'workers' representatives' means representatives of platform workers, such as trade unions and representatives who are freely elected by the platform workers in accordance with national law and practice;

(g) 'representatives of persons performing platform work' means workers' representatives and, insofar as provided for in national law and practice,

(h) 'automated monitoring systems' means systems which are used for or which support monitoring, supervising or evaluating, by electronic means, the work performance of persons performing platform work or the activities carried out within the work environment, including by collecting personal data;

(i) 'automated decision-making systems' means systems which are used to take or support, by electronic means, decisions that significantly affect persons performing platform work, including the working conditions of platform workers, in particular decisions affecting their recruitment, their access to and the organisation of work assignments, their earnings, including the pricing of individual assignments, their safety and health, their working time, their access to training, their promotion or its equivalent, and their contractual status including the restriction, suspension or termination of their account.

2. The definition of 'digital labour platform' laid down in point (a) of paragraph 1 does not include providers of a service whose primary purpose is to exploit or share assets or by means of which individuals who are not professionals can resell goods.

Recital (19) Digital labour platforms differ from other online platforms in that they use automated monitoring systems or automated decision-making systems to organise work performed by individuals at the request, one-off or repeated, of the recipient of a service provided by the platform. Automated monitoring systems and automated decision-making systems process personal data of persons performing platform work and take or support decisions that affect, inter alia, working conditions. Those features make digital labour platforms a distinct form of organising the service provision by professionals compared to more traditional forms of organising service provision, such as traditional forms of ride hailing or transport service dispatch. Furthermore, the increased complexity in the structural organisation of digital labour platforms goes hand in hand with their fast-paced evolution, often creating systems with a variable geometry in the organisation of work. For instance, there could be cases where digital labour platforms provide a service whose recipient is the digital labour platform itself or a distinct business entity within the same group of undertakings, or organise work in such a way that it blurs the traditional patterns which are typically recognisable in the systems of provision of services. This might also be the case for microwork or crowdwork platforms, which are a type of online digital labour platform that provide businesses and other clients with access to a large and flexible workforce for the completion of small tasks that can be performed remotely using a computer and internet connection, such as tagging. Tasks are split up and distributed to a large number of individuals (the crowd) who can complete them asynchronously.

Recital (20) Organising work performed by individuals should involve at a minimum a significant role in matching the demand for the service with the supply of work by an individual who has a contractual relationship with the digital labour platform or an intermediary, regardless of its formal designation by the parties or of its nature, and who is available to perform a specific task. Organising such work can include other activities, such as processing payments. Online platforms which do not organise the work performed by individuals, but merely provide the means by which service providers can reach the end-user, without any further involvement of the platform, for instance by advertising offers or requests for services or aggregating and displaying available service providers in a specific area, should not be considered to be digital labour platforms. The definition of digital labour platforms should not include providers of a service whose primary purpose is to exploit or share assets, such as short-term rental of accommodation, or by means of which individuals who are not professionals can resell goods, nor those who organise the activities of volunteers. The definition should be limited to providers of a service for which the organisation of work performed by the individual, such as transport of persons or goods or

cleaning, constitutes a necessary and essential component, and not merely a minor and purely ancillary component.
Recital (55) The obligations of digital labour platforms, including with regard to information and consultation in respect of automated monitoring systems and automated decision-making systems, apply irrespective of whether such systems are managed by the digital labour platform itself or by an external service provider which carries out data processing on behalf of the digital labour platform.

Literature: Aloisi/Potocka-Sionek,'De-gigging the labour market? An analysis of the "algorithmic management" provisions in the proposed Platform Work Directive', Ital. Labour Law e-Journal 2022/15, 29; Aloisi/Joppe/Abraha, From 'General' to 'Context-Specific' Data Protection For Workers: Insights From the EU Rules on Platforms, Algorithmic Management and AI Systems, ELLJ 2025, 538; Brameshuber/Höllwarth, 'Die neue Plattformarbeitsrichtlinie – Ein Game Changer für das Arbeitsrecht?' ASoK 2024, 170; Daum, 'Richtlinienvorschlag Plattformarbeit: Algorithmisches Management und Überwachung durch automatisierte Systeme', in Giesen/Juncker/Rieble (eds), Arbeitsrechtsfragen bei Crowdworking und Plattformarbeit, München 2023, p. 91; Fischels/Sokoll, 'Die EU-Richtlinie zur Verbesserung der Arbeitsbedingungen in der Plattformarbeit', NZA 2024, 721; Frank/Heine, 'Algorithmisches Management von Plattformbeschäftigten', ZdiW 2022, 335; Frank/Heine, 'Algorithmisches Management unter der Plattformarbeitsrichtlinie', NZA 2024, 865; Gräf, 'Algorithmisches Management in der Plattformarbeit – Richtlinienvorgaben und nationale Umsetzung', SR 2025, 14; Gräf, 'Der Richtlinienentwurf zur Plattformarbeit – Analyse, Umsetzungsperspektiven und Alternativen', ZfA 2023, 209; Gruber-Risak, 'Die neue Plattformarbeitsrichtlinie: Was kommt auf uns zu?' ARD 6953/3/2025; Gruber-Risak/Obrecht, 'Under what conditions do volunteers escape being qualified as workers?', ELLJ 2024, 232; Gruber-Risak/Warter, 'Die EU-Richtlinie zur Verbesserung der Arbeitsbedingungen in der Plattformarbeit', DRdA 2024, 267; Krause, 'Auf dem Weg zur unionsrechtlichen Regelung von Plattformtätigkeiten', NZA 2022, 521; Franzen/Gallner/Oetker (eds), Kommentar zum europäischen Arbeitsrecht, München 2024; Kozak, 'Der Arbeitnehmerbegriff der Plattformarbeits-RL', in Auer-Mayer/Felten/Niksova/Pfeil/Schrattbauer/Warter (eds), Festschrift für Rudolf Mosler, Wien 2024, p. 213; Lelley/Bruck, 'Stresstest für die Plattformwirtschaft?', RdA 2023, 257; Rosin/Parviainen, Improving the transparency of algorithmic management in platform work: The role of the Platform Work Directive, ELLJ 2025, 472; Schmidt, Digital Labour Markets in the Platform Economy, FES 2017; Schöffmann, 'Die neue Transparenzrichtlinie', ZAS 2019, 244; Schubert, 'Arbeit in der Plattformökonomie', NZA-Beilage 2022, 5; Schwarz, Arbeitnehmerüberwachung und Mitbestimmung, Berlin 1982; Silberman, 'The Definition of 'Digital Labour Platform' in the Proposed Platform Work Directive', Verfassungsblog, 2023; Stöhr, 'Der arbeitsrechtliche Status von Plattformtätigen nach dem Richtlinienentwurf – Eine kritische Analyse', EuZA 2022, 413; Sutterer-Kipping, 'Platform Work Directive (2024/2831/EU)', in Hiessl (ed.), EU Labour Law: A Commentary, Alphen aan Rijn 2025, p. 704; Waas/Heerma van Voss, Restatement of Labour Law in Europe: Vol. I: The Concept of Employee, Oxford and Portland, Oregon 2017; Waas, 'Verbesserung der Arbeitsbedingungen von Plattformbeschäftigten', ZRP 2022, 105; Wank, 'Der persönliche Geltungsbereich der Plattformarbeits-Richtlinie', EuZW 2023, 747; Warter, 'The Legitimacy of Modern Data Processing in the Workplace', ELLJ 2025, 179; Wömpner, 'Let's get digital: Das digitale Zugangsrecht ist da!' AuR 2024, 378.

A. General remarks

Art. 2 of the Directive provides legal definitions for key terms. These legal definitions establish how particular terms are to be understood within the scope of the Directive. In this way, legal definitions are intended to ensure a uniform interpretation and application of the Directive. However, as the following analysis will demonstrate, this objective has been achieved more successfully for some terms than for others. 1

B. Material scope

I. Digital labour platform

Digital labour platforms are defined in Art. 2(1) as natural or legal persons providing a service that must meet four cumulative criteria (→ mn. 5 et seqq.). Art. 2(2) provides a negative definition of 'digital labour platform', describing the types of platforms that should be excluded from this definition (goods-related platforms, → mn. 53). 2

The term 'digital work platform' is the **key term** of the material scope of application, particularly for the presumption of Art. 5 of the Directive or the provisions on algorithmic management.[1] 3

The entity subject to the obligations is the natural or legal person that provides the services as defined by the criteria outlined below.[2] According to recital 55, this applies regardless of whether such systems are managed directly by the digital labour platform itself or by an external service provider processing data on its behalf.[3] 4

---

[1] Cf. Sutterer-Kipping in Hiessl, p. 704 (711); Gräf SR 2025, 14 (18); Fischels/Sokoll NZA 2024, 721 (723); Schubert NZA-Beilage 2022, 5 (11).

[2] From a legal perspective, it is important to distinguish between the platform and its operator as a legal entity (cf. Krause NZA 2022, 521, (524); Stöhr EuZA 2022, 413 (416).

[3] Cf. Gräf SR 2025, 14 (21).

1. Provided, at least in part, at a distance by electronic means

5 The requirement that a service be 'provided at a distance by electronic means' reflects the defining characteristic of the term 'digital' within the concept of a digital labour platform. It serves to distinguish platform-mediated work from purely analogue, non-digital forms of intermediation. The terms 'at a distance by electronic means' are to interpreted by analogy to their definiton in Art. 1(1)(b)(ii) of Directive (EU) 2015/1535. Therefore 'at a distance' means that the service is provided without the parties being simultaneously present. The terms 'by electronic means' means that the service is sent initially and received at its destination by means of electronic equipment for the processing (including digital compression) and storage of data, and entirely transmitted, conveyed and received by wire, by radio, by optical means or by other electromagnetic means. The criterion is met whenever the provision of services involves an electronic component, even if certain aspects of the service are carried out offline (see 'at least in part'). This serves to clarify that services involving on-location platform work are covered.[4] As a result, traditional notice boards or analogue means of matching supply and demand, such as physical bulletin boards or classified ads, fall outside the scope of the Directive.[5]

6 In practice, this requirement is met in almost all cases, since the platforms under consideration almost always operate via digital infrastructures.[6]

2. Provided at the request of a recipient – multi-party constellations

7 The service must be provided at the request of the recipient. In practice, this criterion does not present significant challenges as well, as it is highly unlikely that a platform operator would force a service on a recipient, or that platform work would be performed solely at the initiative of a person performing platform work.[7]

8 It is equally beyond doubt that the notion of a 'request' is not intended to imply the existence of any legal obligation on the part of the individual to perform the service. Such an (explicit) obligation is, in fact, often absent from platform work arrangements. Rather, the requirement merely ensures that the initiative to receive the service must originate from the recipient, i.e., from the demand side of the transaction.[8]

9 Since the Directive explicitly refers to the provision of a service at the request of recipients and other similar wordings of various provisions in Art. 2,[9] it is questionable if the scope is limited to **multi-party constellations**. In other words, does the Directive only apply to situations involving at least three distinct actors or groups of actors: the platform operator, the recipients of the service (recipients), and the natural person performing the actual work (person performing platform work including platform workers). If that would be the case, the Directive's provisions would not cover platforms without such a triangular relationship. This applies, for example, to **company-internal platforms** (internal crowdworking), if they are aimed exclusively at their own employees because, in this configuration, there would be no distinctive recipient for whom a service is provided apart from the platform.[10] By contrast, a triangular relationship exists

---

[4] European Commission, Report Expert Group – Transposition of the Directive (EU) 2024/2831 on improving working conditions in platform work (12.1.2026), 14.

[5] Cf. Sutterer-Kipping in Hiessl, p. 704 (713); Gräf SR 2025, 14 (19).

[6] Krause NZA 2022, 521 (525); Fischells/Sokoll NZA 2024, 721 (724).

[7] Cf. Krause NZA 2022, 521 (525); Fischells/Sokoll NZA 2024, 721 (724).

[8] Cf. Krause NZA 2022, 521 (525).

[9] See, for example, the terms 'natural or legal person providing a service' (Art. 2(1)(a)(iii); 'work performed by individuals' (Art. 2(1)(a)(iii); Art. 2(b); 'recipient of the service' (Art. 2(1)(a)(ii); Art. 2(b)).

[10] In this sense, based on the Commission draft Krause NZA 2022, 521 (524); Frank/Heine NZA 2024, 865 (867); sceptical Fischells/Sokoll NZA 2024, 721 (724); Gräf ZFA 2023, 209 (218).

when a group company operates a platform to allocate employees' work across different group entities.[11]

At first glance, this limitation of the Directive's scope would be unproblematic, since general labour law protections already apply to company-internal platforms. In this context, the presumption of employment status is irrelevant, given that the individuals concerned are employees[12]. However, general labour law does not provide any equivalent to the protective provisions on algorithmic management set out in Chapter III. This is particularly true for platforms that allocate tasks to both employees and self-employed persons. In these cases, there is no third-party recipient of services provided by the company acting as a platform operator, yet it is difficult to deny that self-employed persons, too, are in need of protection, particularly where the company deploys automated monitoring and decision-making systems in relation to this group (regarding the competence-related issues of extending Chapter III to self-employed persons, see → Art. 1 mn. 5 et seqq.).[13] **10**

However, the addition of the fifth sentence of recital 19 in its final version, which states that 'digital labour platforms provide a service whose recipient is the digital labour platform itself or a distinct business entity within the same group of undertakings', and the purposive interpretation of the Directive, indicate that the scope of the Directive should be interpreted broadly. There is, in particular, no rationale for providing a lower degree of protection to persons performing platform work engaged within the same corporate group than to those operating externally. Accordingly, the Directive should be interpreted as covering both internal and external platforms.[14] Nevertheless, work must be organised via a digital labour platform, even for internal crowdsourcing. This is why traditional work settings fall outside the scope of the Platform Work Directive.[15] **11**

3. Organisations of work performed by individuals in return for payment, irrespective of whether that work is performed online or in a certain location

The third criterion can be split up into four elements that will be treated separately in the following: **12**

a) the organisation of work,
b) performed by individuals,
c) in return for payment,
d) irrespective if the work is performed online or in a certain location.

a) Organisation of Work

The first necessary and essential criterion, as expressly stated in the Directive, is the organisation of work. In other words: The digital platform has to organise in some way the work performed by individuals to be regarded as a digital labour platform in the sense of the Directive. **13**

---

[11] Sutterer-Kipping in Hiessl, p. 704 (712); Gräf SR 2025, 18; Frank/Heine NZA 2024, 865 (867); based on the Commission draft Krause NZA 2022, 521 (524).

[12] Both terms are used for someone conducting work within the framework of an employment contract. Therefore, these terms will be used synonymously in this text.

[13] Krause NZA 2022, 521 (524).

[14] See convincingly Sutterer-Kipping in Hiessl, p. 704 (711); Gräf SR 2025, 14 (18). In this sense European Commission, Report Expert Group – Transposition of the Directive (EU) 2024/2831 on improving working conditions in platform work (12.1.2026), 14.

[15] Aloisi/Joppe/Abraha, ELLJ 2025, 539 (550).

14 While the criterion of 'organising work' initially served as the central distinguishing element in the original draft of the Platform Work Directive,[16] the structure became more complex when the fourth criterion was added: the use of automated monitoring and decision-making systems (→ mn. 25 et seqq.). A closer examination of the elements set out in Art. 2(1)(a) of the Directive reveals **conceptual overlap** between the 'organisation of work' requirement (subpoint iii) and the use of automated systems (subpoint iv).[17] This is primarily because, in the platform economy, work organisation typically happens through algorithmic management (→ Preliminary remarks to Articles 7–12 mn. 1 et seqq). These systems carry out organisation and control functions that have traditionally been performed by employers when organising work. Consequently, the use of automated systems often serves as the technical means through which the organisation of work is operationalised in platform-based business models.[18] Wherever algorithms are used to structure the performance of work tasks, this constitutes the organisation of work within the meaning of the Directive. The same applies to evaluation systems that determine access to future job opportunities or progression to higher pay categories based on the speed or quality of previous tasks completed. Due to their indirect steering effect, such systems often indicate the organisation of the work performed.[19]

15 Despite this overlap, the two are legally distinct criteria that must be assessed separately. They are also not identical in scope. Determining whether the platform is organising work in the sense of the Directive requires a case-by-case analysis of the specific business model in question.[20]

16 A central question in the context of Art. 2(1)(c) of the Platform Work Directive concerns the **threshold for determining** when a platform operator is deemed to **'organise' the work performed**, thereby qualifying the service as one provided by a digital labour platform.[21] In this regard, it must be emphasised that the concept of 'organisation of work' is to be interpreted broadly. Such an interpretation follows from a purposive reading of the Directive in light of the principle of *effet utile*: the protective purpose of the Directive set out in Art. 1 would be undermined if its scope of application were defined too narrowly (→ Art. 1 mn. 25 et seqq).

17 The requirement in question is not only fulfilled though where the platform organises work in a manner that would qualify the person performing platform work as an employee. This follows directly from the fact that the Directive explicitly applies to individuals performing platform work who do not qualify asemployees.[22] Similarly, the structure of the Directive makes it clear that direction or control, as set out in Art. 5(1), are not required for the Directive to apply.[23]

---

[16] Cf. Krause NZA 2022, 521 (525).

[17] This overlap is expressed in recital 19, which explicitly establishes the link.

[18] See recital 19: Digital labour platforms differ from other online platforms in that they use automated monitoring systems or automated decision-making systems to organise work performed by individuals. In this sense but regarding the Commission's proposal Krause, NZA 2022, 521 (525); Gräf, ZfA 2023, 209 (219 et seqq.); Frank/Heine focus solely on the significant role of matching demand for the service with the supply of work, NZA 2024, 865 (866).

[19] Krause NZA 2022, 521 (525).

[20] Once again Krause NZA 2022, 521 (526). Cf. European Commission, Report Expert Group – Transposition of the Directive (EU) 2024/2831 on improving working conditions in platform work (12.1.2026), 15.

[21] According to Gräf SR 2025, 14 (19), the question of what level of organisation is required is one of the most important and challenging issues in interpreting the Directive.

[22] convincingly Sutterer-Kipping in Hiessl, p. 704 (712); Frank/Heine NZA 2024, 865 (866); regarding the Commsions draft Krause NZA 2022, 521 (525).

[23] Gräf SR 2025, 14 (19).

18 According to recital 20, the organisation of work to a relevant extent may already be deemed to exist where the platform plays at a minimum a **significant role in matching the demand for the service with the supply of work by an individual**, which can include also other activities, such as **processing payments.**[24] The mere processing of payments though does not, in itself, constitute an organisation of work.[25] However, the situation is different when the platform controls the entire payment process, including price-setting. While these arrangements do not directly organise the work either, they nevertheless constitute an economic organisation of work, since a key element of entrepreneurial autonomy, i.e. negotiating for the price of work, is withheld from those performing platform work.[26]

19 By contrast, online platforms that only provide the means by which service providers can reach the end-user, without organising the work or any further involvement of the platform should not be considered digital labour platforms. This includes platforms that simply advertise service offers or requests, or that display available providers in a specific area without influencing the provision of the service at all.[27] Pure online marketplaces should therefore indeed fall outside the scope of the Directive when they merely list incoming tasks and make them freely accessible to all service providers, without exerting any influence over the distribution of tasks or the earning potential, and in particular without tracking which provider takes up which offer in order to use such data for future allocation decisions. Conversely, where a platform aggregates and displays offers in a particular manner, this may well constitute structuring access to and allocation of work opportunities. In such cases, the platform does not present both sides of the market with a full and equal overview; rather, it exerts significant influence over the matching process through sorting and selection mechanisms. This gatekeeping function allows the platform to play a decisive role in coordinating supply and demand, thus meeting the threshold of 'organising the work' as contemplated by the Directive.[28] This gatekeeper function shall not be confused with the term 'gatekeeper' as used in the Digital Markets Act (Regulation 2022/1925).[29]

20 This interpretation is supported by the CJEU's decision in the *Elite Taxi* case (C-434/15). While the Court did not address the employment status of *Uber* drivers in that case, it examined the company's platform-based business model. The Court concluded that *Uber* is not merely an intermediary connecting independent drivers with customers but rather provides a service itself with the help of its drivers. It combines intermediation and transport services into a single, integrated overall service, which has a significant influence on the conditions under which these drivers provide their services.[30]

---

[24] Recital 20; according to Frank/Heine, the central element to be fulfilled regarding organising work according to the Directive is the significant role in matching the demand for the service with the supply of work (NZA 2024, 866); also Silberman, The Definition of 'Digital Labour Platform' in the Proposed Platform Work Directive (available under: (https://verfassungsblog.de/the-definition-of-digital-labour-platform-in-the-proposed-platform-work-directive/); convincingly Sutterer-Kipping in Hiessl, p. 704 (712).

[25] Krause NZA 2022, 521 (525); Gräf SR 2025, 14 (19); with a different opinion Wömpner AuR 2024, 378.

[26] Krause NZA 2022, 521 (525); Gräf ZFA 2023, 209 (220).

[27] Recital 20; Krause NZA 2022, 521 (525); Frank/Heine NZA 2024, 865 (866 et seqq).

[28] Convincingly Krause NZA 2022, 521 (525 et seqq).

[29] Sutterer-Kipping in Hiessl, p. 704 (712).

[30] ECJ 20.12.2017 – case C-434/15, ECLI:EU:C:2017:981, para. 40 – Elite Taxi. In this sense see already Sutterer-Kipping in Hiessl, p. 704 (712).

b) Performed by individuals

21 The work must be carried out by individuals. This expressly clarifies that the scope of the Platform Work Directive is limited to activities carried out by individuals, thereby **excluding legal entities**, such as companies, from its scope. Crucially, it is irrelevant whether these individuals are employees or self-employed: the Directive's protective framework applies regardless of employment status.

c) In return for payment

22 According to the clear wording of the provision ('in return for payment'), the service of the persons performing platform work must be compensated. The organisation of voluntary work is not to be included.[31]

23 By contrast, the service provided by the platform operator does not have to be paid for. The Commission's original proposal required the platform operator's service to be commercial.[32] However, this requirement was omitted from the final version of the Directive. Consequently, platforms operated by public authorities or non-profit organisations may also fall within the Directive's scope.[33]

d) Offline and location-based platform work

24 A digital labour platform, as defined by the Directive, organises work performed by individuals in return for payment, regardless of whether the work is carried out online or at a specific physical location. This clarification ensures that the Directive is not limited to purely digital tasks but also covers location-based platform work.[34] By focusing on the organisational role of the platform, rather than the place of performance, the Directive prevents unduly narrow or restrictive interpretations, that would undermine its protective purpose.

4. Use of automated monitoring systems or automated decision-making systems

25 The fourth constitutive element of a digital labour platform is the **use of automated monitoring** or **decision-making systems**. This requirement was introduced during the legislative process, having not been included in the original Commission proposal.[35] Consequently, the use of these systems now forms an essential prerequisite for the Directive's scope of application (→ mn. 2 and 29 et seqq. for the definitions of these systems).

26 In practice there remains the problem that individuals performing platform work may first be required to demonstrate the use of automated systems in order to benefit from the rights granted under the Directive – an often difficult task, particularly given their lack of access to the platform's internal technical infrastructure.[36] From a systemic perspective, and in light of the principle of effectiveness (*effet utile*), scholarship has therefore proposed easing this evidentiary burden. One potential solution that has been

---

[31] Cf. recital 21; Gruber-Risak/Warter emphasise the need for protection also for volunteers (DRdA 2024, 267 (270); cf. Gruber-Risak/Obrecht ELLJ 2025, 232.

[32] Cf. Art. 2(1) of the Commissions' proposal, 'Proposal for a Directive of the European Parliament and of the Council on improving working conditions in platform work', 9.12.2021, COM(2021) 762 final.

[33] Gräf SR 2025, 14 (20).

[34] Cf. recital 5. Regarding the disctinction between online and location-based platform work see Schmidt, Digital Labour Markets in the Platform Economy (2017), 6.

[35] Cf. Art. 2(1)(a) of 2021/0414(COD).

[36] Cf. recital 8; cf. Aloisi/Joppe/Abraha, ELLJ 2025, 538 (550).

proposed is the introduction of a graduated allocation of the burden of proof.[37] Additionally, the Platform Work Directive itself provides specific measures to mitigate these difficulties, primarily through transparency obligations set out in Art. 9 (→ Art. 9 mn. 1 et seqq.), and a right of access to relevant evidence under Art. 21.

The alternative relationship ('or') makes it clear that also one form (either monitoring or decision-making) is sufficient for the platform to be considered a digital work platform under the Directive.[38] 27

The terms are defined in Art. 2(1)(h) and (i). 28

a) Automated monitoring systems

Art. 2(1)(h) provides a legal definition of automated monitoring systems. It defines automated monitoring systems as systems which are used for or which support monitoring, supervising or evaluating, by electronic means, the work performance of persons performing platform work or the activities carried out within the work environment, including by collecting personal data. 29

These systems are subject to special regulations because they potentially have a significant impact on the safety as well as the physical and mental health of platform workers.[39] As recital 50 explains 'algorithmic direction, evaluation, and discipline can intensify work effort by increasing monitoring, raising the pace required from workers, minimising gaps in workflow, and extending work activity beyond the conventional workplace and working hours'. The limited learning at work and the limited influence over tasks due to the use of non-transparent algorithms, work intensification and insecurity derived from the use of automated monitoring systems are likely to increase workforce's stress and anxiety.[40] 30

Automated monitoring systems may reinforce, amplify or support traditional managerial control and thereby intensify work. The Directive recognises the profound impact such systems may have not only on working conditions but also on the autonomy, dignity, and mental well-being of persons performing platform work, thus justifying their inclusion in the material scope of regulation.[41] 31

aa) By electronic means

The systems in question must operate by electronic means, meaning they must be driven by software, algorithms, or other digital technologies (→ mn. 5). Both the recitals and the title of Chapter III of the Directive explicitly refer to algorithms,[42] thereby underscoring the digital character of automated monitoring systems. 32

The system in question does not need to be particularly intelligent, or even self-learning (technology-neutral).[43] In practice, this requirement is unlikely to pose any difficulties in terms of applicability as it has to be understood widely and includes all systems that have an element of data processing even if this is combined with other forms of monitoring. Thus, the requirement of electronic operation excludes only genuine mechanical or analogue systems from the scope of application. 33

---

37 Gräf SR 2025, 14 (24).
38 Frank/Heine NZA 2024, 865; Wömpner AuR 2024, 378 (379); Gräf SR 2025, 14 (24).
39 Cf. Directive 89/391/EEC, which introduces measures to encourage improvements in the safety and health of workers at work. Therefore, Art. 12 only applies to platform workers.
40 Recital 50.
41 Recital 50.
42 See recital 8 and the heading of Chapter III, 'Algorithmic Management'.
43 Gräf SR 2025, 14 (24); Daum in Gießen/Junker/Rieble, p. 91 (106).

bb) Monitoring, supervising or evaluating the work performance or the activities carried out within the work environment

34 Automated monitoring systems fall within the scope of the Directive only where they are used for specific purposes: for monitoring, supervising, or evaluating the work performance or activities carried out within the work environment.

35 'Monitoring' refers to the (ongoing) observation, and review of work processes, or activities, involving their measurement or testing at intervals, especially for the purpose of regulation and control.[44] In the context of a platform work, this can include GPS tracking, app usage logs and real-time data collection on a person's movements and interactions, to name a few.[45]

36 'Supervising' involves overseeing and directing the execution of tasks and activities, as well as overseeing the work or conduct of employees or groups of employees.[46] Supervising can therefore relate to tasks and activities, but also to individuals or groups.

37 'Evaluating' refers to working out the value of work output and finding a numerical expression for quantitative facts or relations.[47] It is often based on structured criteria such as customer ratings, efficiency scores, task completion rates, or behavioural metrics.

38 These activities (monitoring, supervising and evaluating) must be carried out **in reference to work performance or activities within the work environment.** While the former relates clearly to the quality, efficiency and outcome of the tasks performed by the person performing platform work, the latter is significantly broader. Activities within the work environment are not limited to task-related conduct but can include any behaviour occurring in a professional setting, potentially even private or non-work-related activities as long it is monitored within the work environment.[48] This expansive notion highlights the potential intrusiveness of automated monitoring systems.

cc) Which are used for and which support those purposes

39 Platform work is characterised by extensive technological organisation and control, which is rarely exercised through a single core system for monitoring, supervising or evaluating performance or activities carried out within the work environment. Instead, it usually arises from the interaction of various digital tools. Data collected for specific

[44] Cf. Oxford English Dictionary, to monitor (https://www.oed.com/dictionary/monitor_v?tab=meaning_and_use#36265198, 2.9.2025). See also the definitions of monitoring and evaluation in ILO, Basic Principles of Monitoring and Evaluation (2015).

[45] See for instance the case studies by *Christl* on Surveillance and Digital Control at Work (https://crackedlabs.org/en/data-work, 2.9.2025). See also European Commission, Report Expert Group – Transposition of the Directive (EU) 2024/2831 on improving working conditions in platform work (12.1.2026), 20.

[46] Cf. Oxford English Dictionary, to supervise (https://www.oed.com/dictionary/supervise_v?tab=meaning_and_use#19700127, 2.9.2025).

[47] Cf. Oxford English Dictionary, to evaluate (https://www.oed.com/dictionary/evaluate_v?tab=meaning_and_use#5106424, 2.9.2025). See also the definitions of monitoring and evaluation in ILO, Basic Principles of Monitoring and Evaluation (2015).

[48] If a different interpretation were applied, systems processing personal data relating to private conversations, or collecting personal data from individuals performing platform work when they are not offering or performing such platform work, would fall outside the scope of the Directive; consequently, they would not be subject to the processing prohibitions set out in Art. 7; this would significantly undermine the Directive's protective purpose; Gräf takes a different view, referring to provisions of national labour constitution law (Gräf, SR 2025, 14 (24)).

business purposes can also be processed with different systems for other purposes, such as optimising work processes and the workforce.[49]

In this context, the clear wording of the provision defines that an automated monitoring system is present not only where systems are deployed directly for monitoring, supervision or evaluation of the work performance or activities carried out within the work environment, but also where these purposes are merely supported. A purposive interpretation further supports this finding, indicating that even a basic contribution to these functions is sufficient.[50] Therefore, the legal definition is much broader than the headline suggests. **40**

By covering systems that only play a supporting role, the provision prevents platforms from deliberately circumventing the scope of the Directive through strategic technical and organisational design. The interconnected use of various systems, including those not primarily intended for monitoring-, supervising- or evaluating-related purposes, may thus fall within the Directive's scope, provided they at least support such purposes. A restrictive interpretation would contradict the Directive's regulatory purpose, which explicitly seeks to capture asymmetric forms of control in the platform context.[51] **41**

The use of automated monitoring systems 'for or which support' specific purposes has led to significant discussion in the German scholarship, particularly concerning the requirement of a **specific intent to monitor**. The mere abstract capability of a system for monitoring purposes would not be sufficient.[52] From a doctrinal perspective, this view is derived from the word 'for' with a subjective element – 'an intention to observe' – being read into it. This interpretation is clearly influenced by the German (and Austrian) understanding of co-determination rights concerning the introduction and use of technical devices intended to monitor employees' conduct or performance (cf. § 87(1)(6) BetrVG; § 96(3) ArbVG).[53] **42**

Nonetheless, Art. 2(1)(h) must be interpreted **autonomously**.[54] What matters is neither the intent to monitor nor the abstract capability of a system for such purposes, but rather its actual '**use**' for specific purposes.[55] Equivalent terms are used in other languages, such as 'der Einsatz' in German, 'la utilización' in Spanish, 'l'uso' in Italian, 'l'utilisation' in French or 'gebruik' in Dutch, confirming the Directive's **functional approach**. Accordingly, the definition does not require any intention to monitor, supervise or eval- **43**

---

49 Consider, for example, the use of algorithms in Amazon's warehouses for managing operations. Scanner data is used to track the progress of products through the various stages of processing and distribution, as well as to measure workers' activity and performance (see Warter ELLJ 2025, 179 et seqq.).

50 Wömpner AuR 2024, 378 (380); Fischells/Sokoll NZA 2024, 721 (724). Rosin/Parvainen speak also of a rather broad notion ELLJ 2025, 472 (481); See also European Commission, Report Expert Group – Transposition of the Directive (EU) 2024/2831 on improving working conditions in platform work (12.1.2026), 20.

51 Cf. recital 30; in this direction also Wömpner AuR 2024, 378.

52 Frank/Heine NZA 2024, 865; already Frank/Heine NZA 2022, 543 (545).

53 Traditionally, a distinction is made between the subjective-final and the objective-final theory; according to the former, the works council's co-determination rights are only triggered where the employer intends to monitor and uses the system for this purpose; in contrast, the objective-final theory holds that the mere technical capability of a system to be used for monitoring purposes is sufficient to give rise to co-determination; the prevailing academic opinion and consistent case law have adopted the objective-final approach on teleological grounds (see Schwarz, Arbeitnehmerüberwachung und Mitbestimmung (1982), pp. 106 et seqq., and German Federal Labour Court 11.12.2018 – 1 ABR 13/17 or 8.3.2022 – 1 ABR 20/21).

54 Regarding a broad and autonomous nature of the definition see also European Commission, Report Expert Group – Transposition of the Directive (EU) 2024/2831 on improving working conditions in platform work (12.1.2026), 20.

55 The term 'use' is used in the legal definitions of digital work platforms (Art. 2(1)(a)), automated monitoring systems (Art. 2(1)(h)) and decision-making systems (Art. 2(1)(i)).

uate.[56] The decisive factor is whether the system is used to or supports the monitoring, supervising, or evaluating of performance or activities carried out within the work environment. As it is sufficient that the system merely supports monitoring, supervision, or evaluation, the wording of the Directive contradicts such an interpretation.[57] The threshold for what constitutes 'support' in this context has been set deliberately low.

dd) Including by collecting personal data

44 The precise meaning of the addition 'including by collecting personal data' is unclear. Notably, the term used is 'collecting', rather than 'processing'. This could suggest that processing personal data is not a prerequisite for applying the provision, as the reference to data collection appears merely illustrative.[58] However, it could also be interpreted to mean that the use of personal data is a necessary element, with the act of collection serving as an indicator thereof.[59] In practice, however, this distinction is of limited relevance since it is difficult to imagine any automated monitoring system that does not process personal data in some form.

b) Automated decision-making systems

45 In addition to automated monitoring systems, Art. 2(1)(g) provides a legal definition of automated decision-making systems for the purposes of the Directive. According to this definition, such systems must be used to take or support, by electronic means, decisions that significantly affect persons performing platform work.

aa) By electronic means

46 As with automated monitoring systems, the systems in question must be electronic, meaning they must be driven by software, algorithms, or other digital technologies. This criterion of the definition excludes genuine mechanical and analogue systems (→ mn. 5 and mn. 32).

bb) Used to take or support decisions

47 The system must be used to take or support decisions. Some scholars require that automatic decision-making systems must go beyond the mere monitoring, analysis and evaluation in order to be clearly distinguished from automated monitoring systems, and that these systems must at least make specific proposals for decisions.[60] Others argue that the protective purpose of the Platform Work Directive is only fulfilled when the system produces a distinct outcome.[61] However, both interpretations lack a basis in the text and overlook the **functional terminology** of the Platform Work Directive. Although alternative phrasing is frequently used when referring to the two categories (automated

---

[56] Wömpner AuR 2024, 378 (379); with a different opinion, however all referring to the German works constitution act (§ 87(1)(6) BetrVG): Gräf SR 2025, 14 (25); Frank/Heine NZA 2024, 865; Frank/Heine NZA 2022, 543 (545). According to Commission services (but without explanation and textual basis in the definition itself), a system is considered an automated monitoring system if it is intended or used to perform or support monitoring, supervision or evaluation (European Commission, Report Expert Group – Transposition of the Directive (EU) 2024/2831 on improving working conditions in platform work (12.1.2026), 20.

[57] In this sense already Sutterer-Kipping in Hiessl, p. 704 (713).

[58] Cf. Wömpner AuR 2024, 378.

[59] According to recital 19, automated monitoring and decision-making systems process personal data of persons performing platform work; in this sense Gräf SR 2025, 14 (24).

[60] Frank/Heine NZA 2024, 865 (866); Frank/Heine ZdiW 2022, 335 (336).

[61] In this sense Gräf SR 2025, (14) 25; Daum in Gießen/Junker/Rieble, p. 91 (108).

monitoring systems or automated decision-making systems) these functions often overlap in practice.[62] It is therefore possible that the same system collects data for monitoring or evaluating purposes which then is used to support or even make decisions. In other words, one and the same system may qualify as both, thereby simultaneously triggering the respective legal consequences under the Directive. The functional use is decisive. Accordingly, systems need not go beyond mere monitoring, analysis, and evaluation nor produce a specific output, such as a performance score, that determines a decision. It is sufficient that the data collected are used to make or support decisions. **The distinction is functional, not technical.** Therefore, the requirements are already met where, for instance, a system collects working time raw data which then is used as a basis for decision-making. As with the concept of automated monitoring systems, even a **merely supporting contribution** to the decision-making process **is sufficient**.

However, the definition contains an undefined 'significance threshold' applicable to the impact of the decisions supported by the system.[63] Unlike the case law of the CJEU on Art. 22 GDPR, it is not required that the decision-maker draws 'strongly' on the automated output in order for a system to qualify as an automated decision-making system under the Platform Work Directive.[64] If the EU legislator had intended this, they could have included such a requirement in the text of the Directive or mentioned it in the recitals. The Court's case law was already well known during the legislative process, and the term 'automated decision-making system' was introduced at a late stage of the process. **48**

This broad interpretation is based on a purposive reading of Art. 2(1)(i) of the Directive, which aims to ensure the effectiveness (*effet utile*) of Art. 1(2) and achieve its protective objectives (→ Art. 1 mn. 25 et seqq.). It is also consistent with the scope and the structure of the Directive, which links specific obligations, such as transparency and information duties[65], to the functions of a system. As is the case with automated monitoring systems, the legal definition is much broader than the headline suggests. **49**

cc) Significant affect for persons performing platform work

In order to fall within the scope of the definition under Art. 2(i) of the Platform Work Directive, the decision must significantly affect persons performing platform work. The legal definition offers a range of illustrative examples to clarify the threshold of significance. Automated decision-making systems, in this context, include those that make or support **status-related decisions** affecting their recruitment, their promotion or its equivalent, and their contractual status including the restriction, suspension or termination of their account. Moreover, the Directive explicitly includes automated decisions that are not status-related, but nonetheless materially **affect working conditions**. These include decisions concerning their access to and the organisation of work assignments, their earnings, including the pricing of individual assignments, their safety and health, their working time and their access to training.[66] It therefore suffices if a platform generates a price by algorithmic means even if the work process itself is not influenced otherwise by algorithmic management. **50**

---

62 In this sense Aloisi/Joppe/Abraha ELLJ 2025, 538 (550).

63 European Commission, Report Expert Group – Transposition of the Directive (EU) 2024/2831 on improving working conditions in platform work (12.1.2026), 21.

64 Cf. ECJ 7.12.2023 – case C-634/21, ECLI:EU:C:2023:957 – Schufa Holding.

65 For Instance, information regarding the use of such systems, the data the decisions rely on and the types of decisions supported by the collection of personal data.

66 Cf. Frank/Heine NZA 2024, 865 (866).

c) Conclusion

51 The use of automated monitoring or decision-making systems has led to significant discussion in the German legal literature, particularly concerning the requirement of a specific **intent to monitor** for the Directive to apply. The mere abstract capability of a system for monitoring purposes would not be sufficient.[67] From a doctrinal perspective, this view is derived from the word 'for' with a subjective element – 'an intention to observe' – being read into it. This interpretation is clearly influenced by the German (and Austrian) understanding of co-determination rights concerning the introduction and use of technical devices intended to monitor employees' conduct or performance (cf. § 87(1)(6) BetrVG; § 96(3) ArbVG).[68]

52 Nonetheless, Art. 2(1)(h) must be interpreted **autonomously**. What matters is neither the intent to monitor nor the abstract capability of a system for such purposes, but rather its actual '**use**'.[69] Equivalent terms are used in other languages, such as 'der Einsatz' in German, 'la utilización' in Spanish, 'l'uso' in Italian, 'l'utilisation' in French or 'gebruik' in Dutch. The Platform Working Directive is therefore based on a **functional concept**. In light of the broad definitions of automated monitoring and decision-making systems, such use is already established where these systems provide even basic support for monitoring, supervising or evaluating the work performance or the activities, or support for decisions (for automated monitoring systems → mn. 11; for automated decisions making systems → mn. 16).[70] Therefore, the use of automated monitoring and decision-making systems is to be read as a broad inclusive concept.[71]

II. Goods-related platforms

53 Finally, Art. 2(2) expressly states that the term 'digital labour platform' does not include providers of a service whose primary purpose is to exploit or share assets. The same applies to platforms where non-professional individuals can resell goods.

54 The definition is therefore limited to providers of a service for which the organisation of the work performed by the individual constitutes a necessary and essential component,[72] and not merely a minor and purely ancillary aspect. Accordingly, the definition covers platforms where the organisation of the individual's work is central to the service provided.[73] This is typically the case in sectors such as transporting persons or goods, or cleaning. In contrast, platforms that facilitate accommodation rentals, such as *Airbnb*, fall outside the scope of the definition because their primary focus is on providing furnished premises rather than organising preparatory work associated with that service,

---

[67] Frank/Heine NZA 2024, 865; Frank/Heine NZA 2022, 543 (545).

[68] Traditionally, a distinction is made between the subjective-final and the objective-final theory; according to the former, the works council's co-determination rights are only triggered where the employer intends to monitor and uses the system for this purpose; in contrast, the objective-final theory holds that the mere technical capability of a system to be used for monitoring purposes is sufficient to give rise to co-determination; the prevailing academic opinion and consistent case law have adopted the objective-final approach on teleological grounds (see Schwarz, Arbeitnehmerüberwachung und Mitbestimmung (1982), pp. 106 et seqq., and German Federal Labour Court 11.12.2018 – 1 ABR 13/17 or 8.3.2022 – 1 ABR 20/21).

[69] The term 'use' is used in the legal definitions of digital work platforms (Art. 2(1)(a)), automated monitoring systems (Art. 2(1)(h)) and decision-making systems (Art. 2(1)(i)).

[70] Fischells/Sokoll NZA 2024, 721 (724); in this sense Wömpner AuR 2024, 378 (379).

[71] Cf. Wömpner AuR 2024, 378; Fischells/Sokoll NZA 2024, 721 (724).

[72] See Art. 2(1)(a)(iii), which states that organisation of work must be a necessary and essential component.

[73] Argumentum 'Primary purpose'.

even if they are mathing demand with supply. The same applies to platforms where individuals can sell goods, such as *eBay*.[74]

C. Personal Scope

I. Platform work

Art. 2(1)(b) of the Directive defines platform work for the purposes of the Directive. This definition comprises several elements, many of which mirror criteria found in other legal definitions of Art. 2. 55

1. Work organised through a digital labour platform

The definition of platform work starts by stating that the work must be organised through a digital labour platform. However, this requirement is somewhat tautological, given that a digital labour platform must necessarily organise the work in order to qualify as a digital labour platform (on the organisation of work as a prerequisite for qualifying as a digital labour platform, see → mn. 13 et seqq.). 56

2. Performed in the Union

The territorial scope of the Directive is defined not only through the concept of platform work itself in Art. 2(1)(b) of the Directive, but is also explicitly clarified in Art. 1(3). Crucially, neither the place of establishment of the digital labour platform nor the applicable law is determinative. Instead, the only decisive criterion is the physical location of the person performing platform work when the service is provided (→ Art. 1 mn. 47 et seqq).[75] 57

3. By an individual

The work must be carried out by individuals. This clarifies that the scope of the Platform Work Directive only covers work performed by individuals, rather than companies. It is irrelevant whether they are employees or self-employed. It is irrelevant whether they are employees or self-employed; this wording is also found in the definition of a digital work platform (→ mn. 21). 58

4. On the basis of a contractual relationship between the digital labour platform or an intermediary, and the individual

The definition of platform work in Art. 2(1)(b) reflects the multi-party nature typical of work arrangements in platform work. It presupposes that the work is performed under a contractual relationship, either between the digital labour platform and the individual, or between an intermediary and the individual. This broad definition is particularly relevant in scenarios where there is no direct contractual relationship between those performing platform work and the digital labour platform itself. It is sufficient for individuals to provide their services under a contract with an intermediary that has a contractual relationship with the digital labour platform (→ Art. 3 mn. 1 et seqq.).[76] 59

---

[74] Cf. recital 20; Sutterer-Kipping in Hiessl, p. 704 (714); Gräf SR 2025, 14 (20); Gruber-Risak/Warter, DRdA 2024, 267 (269); Wömpner, AuR 2024, 378 (380); Krause NZA 2022, 521 (526).

[75] Recital 19; Gruber-Risak ARD 6953/3/2025.

[76] Recital 24; cf. Wömpner AuR 2024, 378 (380).

60 Concerns that this expansive definition might cover also professionals such as lawyers or tax advisers who run a website are not justified, as these 'platforms' do not organise work in the way envisaged by the Directive.[77] Therefore, the definition remains focused on genuine platform work relationships characterised by the organisation of work through digital labour platforms.

61 Furthermore, under Art. 2(1)(b), the existence of a contractual agreement with the recipient of the service is irrelevant.

II. Persons performing platform work

62 The provisions of the Platform Work Directive apply not only to platform workers (→ mn. 64), but to all individual performing platform work, irrespective of the nature of their contractual relationship or the designation of the relationship by the parties involved. Accordingly, wherever the Directive confers rights and obligations not solely on platform workers but instead refers more broadly to persons performing platform work, these provisions are equally applicable to self-employed persons and persons with third statuses that might exist at national level.[78]

63 This approach is consistent with the legal basis of the Directive and its framework of fundamental rights. Art. 16 TFEU permits the adoption of data protection measures for all natural persons, including self-employed individuals. Similarly, the Charter of Fundamental Rights of the European Union generally provides for a status-independent framework of protection. Only certain rights enshrined in Title IV of the Charter (Solidarity), such as in the context of the Platform Work Directive Art. 27 TFEU (Workers' right to information and consultation within the undertaking) and Art. 31 TFEU (Fair and just working conditions), are reserved for employees (for further discussion of the competence under EU Law and fundamental rights, see → Art. 1).

III. Platform worker

64 The Directive defines in Art. 2(1) the term 'platform worker'. This refers to any natural person performing platform work who has or is deemed to have an employment contract or an employment relationship as defined by the law, collective agreements or practice in force in the Member States with consideration to the case-law of the Court of Justice. This definition is not entirely free of contradictions,[79] as it refers to the national understanding of the term, while also requiring the consideration of the case law of the Court of Justice of the European Union. This reference to the Court of Justice's case law is, of course, far from new: the EU legislature uses similar formulations in all recent labour law related Directives.[80]

65 The definition of a platform worker must be interpreted in such a way that it include all individuals who, under the respective national legal concept, are considered to be in an employment relationship. The primary point of reference is therefore the definition of

---

[77] Fischells/Sokoll NZA 2024, 721 (724) express concerns in this regard; the application of the Directive in these cases rejecting Gräf SR 2025, (14) 20.

[78] See also European Commission, Report Expert Group – Transposition of the Directive (EU) 2024/2831 on improving working conditions in platform work (12.1.2026), 17.

[79] In this sense for example Gruber-Risak ARD 6953/3/2025.

[80] See for instance Art. 1(2) of Directive (EU) 2019/1152; Art. 2 of Directive (EU) 2019/1158; Art. 2(2) of Directive (EU) 2023/970) etc.; pointing this out Brameshuber/Höllwarth ASoK 2025, 170, (172).

'worker' under the law of the individual Member State.[81] This is made particularly clear not only in the wording of Art. 2(1)(b) but also in recital 17. However, the case law of the CJEU must also be taken into account, meaning that the EU law concept of 'worker' constitutes the outer limit of interpretation. Broader – and thus more favourable – definitions for persons performing platform work adopted by the Member States are not precluded.[82] Also the case law of the CJEU provides a certain degree of judicial oversight with regard to the principles of equivalence and effectiveness, as well as the prevention of abuse and arbitrary conduct.[83] In any case, the definition allows the Court of Justice to contribute to shaping the personal scope of application.[84]

The extension, in comparison to other Directives, whereby individuals are regarded as platform workers if they are 'deemed to have an employment contract or an employment relationship' is explained by the legal presumption set out in Art. 5 of the Platform Work Directive.[85] **66**

Although not included in the definitions of Art. 2(1)(d), Art. 1(2) of the Directive emphasises that the qualification should be based on an assessment of the facts. The **principle of primacy of facts,** meaning that the ascertainment of the existence of an employment relationship should be guided primarily by the facts relating to the actual performance of work.[86] This explicit statement is particularly relevant in the context of platform work, where the contractual arrangements often differ from the conditions in which the work is actually performed.[87] If the way in which the contract is carried out contradicts its written terms, the way in which it is actually executed takes precedence due to the mandatory nature of labour law provisions. The primacy of reality over contractual agreements is an essential principle of labour law, which is established in almost all Member States.[88] This principle can also be found in the jurisprudence of the CJEU.[89] Otherwise, the consequences of labour law would be arbitrary, and employers could avoid legal consequences by including relevant clauses in contracts. **67**

According to Art. 5(3), the Directive does not extend the legal presumption to tax, criminal or social security proceedings. Nevertheless, Member States remain free to implement corresponding mechanisms within the limits of their obligations under Union **68**

---

[81] Gruber-Risak/Warter DRdA 2024, 267 (270); Gruber-Risak, ARD 6953/3/2025; Fischels/Sokoll, NZA 2024, 721 (725 et seqq.); Wank, EuZW 2023, 747; Brameshuber/Höllwarth ASoK 2024, 170 (172 et seqq.).

[82] Cf. Krause NZA 2022, 521 (526); Kolbe in Franzen/Gallner/Oetker, Kommentar zum europäischen Arbeitsrecht (2024) RL (EU) 2019/1152 Art. 1 mn. 4.

[83] Fischels/Sokoll NZA 2024, 721 (726). In essence, the issue is ensuring the effectiveness of the provisions (effet utile), so that Member States cannot create arbitrary exceptions that would undermine the application of the Directive.

[84] In this sense see for example Schöffmann ZAS 2019, 244 (245 et seqq.); Kolbe in Franzen/Gallner/Oetker, Kommentar zum europäischen Arbeitsrecht (2024) RL (EU) 2019/1152 Art. 1 mn. 4.

[85] Gruber-Risak/Warter DRdA 2024, 267 (270); Gruber-Risak, ARD 6953/3/2025.

[86] See recital 27, which also refers explicitly to the ILO Employment Relationship Recommendation No. 198 (2006).

[87] Cf. recital 27; a striking example can be found in the reasoning of the Employment Tribunal London in the Uber case (Aslam v Uber, London Employment Tribunal, 28 October 2016, Case Nos: 2202550/2015 & Others); the Tribunal highlights the discrepancies between contractual arrangements and the actual lived realities of individuals performing platform work and refers, for instance, to the 'absurdity, which speaks for itself', describing the contractual terms as 'pure fiction', bearing 'no relation to the real dealings and relationships between the parties'; the Tribunal further characterises the contractual documents as 'an excellent illustration of the phenomenon of "armies of lawyers" contriving documents in their clients' interests which simply misrepresent the true rights and obligations on both sides' (see also Adams-Prassl, Uber BV v Aslam: '[W]ork relations … cannot safely be left to contractual regulation', Industrial Law Journal 2022/51(4) 955).

[88] See for instance, Waas/Heerma van Voss, Restatement of Labour Law in Europe, The Concept of Employee.

[89] Cf. ECJ 22.04.2020 – case C-692/19, ECLI:EU:C:2020:288 – Yodel Delivery Network.

law.[90] However, there is a debate about whether these areas of law are subject to an obligation of ensuring appropriate and effective procedures based on the primacy of facts according to Art. 4 (→ Art. 4 mn. 27 et seqq.).

69 The Platform Work Directive does not address the question of whether a person is an employee-like person or a home worker.[91] Therefore, it is possible that certain (additional) protective measures based on national provisions may also apply to non-platform workers.

IV. Intermediary

70 Art. 2(1)(e) defines the term 'intermediaries'. An intermediary is defined as a natural or legal person whose contract with a digital labour platform has the explicit purpose of making platform work available to or through the digital labour platform. The definition encompasses two scenarios where a intermediary existes between the digital labour platform and the person performing platform work or multiple intermediaries form a subcontracting chain. Contrary to what might be assumed at first glance, this provision does not refer to digital labour platforms acting as intermediaries themselves. Intermediaries do not need to comply with the definition of digital labour platforms.[92] Instead, the inclusion of intermediaries aims to extend the scope of the Directive to situations in which persons performing platform work are made available to digital labour platforms by a third party (the intermediary). This particularly concerns situations in which there is no direct contractual relationship between persons performing platform work and the digital labour platform. Digital labour platforms are then in a contractual relationship with the intermediary.[93] When an intermediary is involved, a fourth party is added to the standard three-party relationship (→ mn. 7 et seqq). The definition of intermediaries is intentionally broad to prevent digital Labour platforms from evading compliance by engaging third parties. The provision does not impose restrictions on the legal form of intermediaries.[94]

71 The background of the definition, which was not included in the Commission's proposal, is that the aim of the Platform Work Directive is to ensure that the protective provisions it introduces cannot be circumvented through complex contractual chains or intermediary arrangements. By explicitly including situations in which persons performing platform work are made available via intermediaries, the Directive closes a potential loophole that could otherwise be exploited to avoid responsibilities.[95] According to recital 24, persons performing platform work through intermediaries fall within the scope of the Platform Work Directive's protective provisions because they are exposed to the same risks related to the misclassification of their employment status and the use of algorithmic management systems as persons performing platform work directly for the digital labour platform.

72 In this sense, it is only consistent that the legal presumption may still be triggered even if the organising and control functions are split between the digital labour platform and the intermediaries.

---

90 Art. 5(3). Explicitly recital 32; for Austria recommending Kozak in Auer-Mayer et al., p. 213 et seqq.

91 Pointing this out Wank EuZW 2023, 747 (748).

92 See also European Commission, Report Expert Group – Transposition of the Directive (EU) 2024/2831 on improving working conditions in platform work (12.1.2026), 18.

93 Recital 24; cf. Wömpner AuR 2024, 378 (380); Gräf SR 2025, 14 (21).

94 Cf. European Commission, Report Expert Group – Transposition of the Directive (EU) 2024/2831 on improving working conditions in platform work (12.1.2026), 18.

95 Cf. recital 24.

All this reflects a broader goal of the Directive: to focus on the factual working relationship, rather than just the formal contractual structure, in order to protect persons performing platform work in practice (regarding the primacy of facts in context of the classification of platform workers → mn. 67). 73

V. Workers' representatives

Given that the Platform Work Directive sets out not only individual rights and obligations but also a collective protection framework (→ Art. 1 mn. 9 et seqq.), representatives of platform workers play a central role in effectuating this layer of protection. Art. 2(1)(f) provides a specific legal definition to determine who qualifies as a representative of platform workers. 74

The Directive **explicitly recognises trade unions as representatives of platform workers.** In addition to trade unions, other representative bodies may also qualify, provided they are freely elected by platform workers in accordance with national law and practice.[96] Notably, the requirement of free election applies only to non-union representatives.[97] 75

Informal collectives that have emerged in practice on some digital work platforms – not least due to failed attempts to establish a works council – are excluded if they are not in accordance with national law and practice.[98] 76

Unlike Directive 2002/14/EC on the information and consultation of employees,[99] the Platform Work Directive explicitly recognises trade unions, alongside elected representatives, as legitimate representatives of platform workers, regardless of their recognition under national law. The original proposal by the European Commission did not expressly mention trade unions.[100] At that stage, representatives were defined more generically as workers' organisations or representatives as provided for under national legislation or practice. This legislative modification clearly demonstrates the intention to give both trade unions and elected representatives equal standing within the Directive's framework for collective representation.[101] 77

In relation to the fulfilment of certain obligations set out in the Platform Work Directive, the question may arise as to which representative body such obligations must be addressed to, where multiple bodies exist. In this context, recital 22, which refers to ILO Convention No. 135, is particularly relevant for interpretation purposes. The convention states that the existence of elected representatives within the same undertaking should not be used to undermine the position of the relevant trade unions or their 78

[96] This would be the case for workers' councils (Betriebsräte) in Austria and Germany; cf. Wömpner AuR 2024, 378 (381); Gräf SR 2025, 14 (22); Krause NZA 2022, footnote 102; informal collectives that have emerged in practice on some digital work platforms – not least due to failed attempts to establish a works council – are excluded if they are not in accordance with national law and practice (cf. Gräf SR 2025, 14 (22)). See also European Commission, Report Expert Group – Transposition of the Directive (EU) 2024/2831 on improving working conditions in platform work (12.1.2026), 19.

[97] In this context, see Art. 3 of ILO Convention No. 135, to which recital 22 expressly refers; cf. Wömpner AuR 2024, 378 (381).

[98] Cf. Gräf SR 2025, 14 (22).

[99] See Art. 2(e) of Directive 2002/14/EC : 'employees' representatives' means the employees' representatives provided for by national aws and/or practices'.

[100] Art. 2(1)(5) of the Commission's Proposal, the European Commission, 'Proposal for a Directive of the European Parliament and of the Council on improving working conditions in platform work', 9.12.2021 COM(2021) 762 final.

[101] Cf. Wömpner AuR 2024, 378 (381).

representatives.[102] This supports the apparent intention of the **Directive to establish a coexistence model that combines trade union and elected worker representation.**[103] Consequently, obligations under the Directive must be fulfilled with regard to both categories of representative, if they exist in within the same undertaking.

VI. Representatives of persons performing platform work

79 In addition to representatives of platform workers, the Platform Work Directive establishes rights and obligations for 'representatives of persons performing platform work' who do not qualify as platform workers because they are self-employed rather than employees. This raises the question of who may act as their representatives.

80 According to the wording of the Directive, these representatives include the same categories as those for platform workers, namely trade unions and other bodies that are freely elected by platform workers (→ mn. 75). Additionally, organisations that specifically represent self-employed persons may qualify, provided they are recognised under national law and practice.

D. Concluding Remarks

81 The scope of the Directive encompasses a variety of criteria, some of which were only introduced in the final draft. This shows that the precise scope of the Directive and the definition of key terms were still being discussed until the end of the legislative process. However, as the foregoing analysis suggests, there are numerous indications that many of the Directive's definitions require a broad, purposive interpretation in line with its underlying objectives and protective rationale.

82 Given the substantial number of criteria and ambiguous legal terms, as well as the considerable terminological complexity, it is likely that future litigation will frequently focus on the scope of the Directive and, in particular, on what constitutes a 'digital labour platform'. Disputes are likely to arise concerning the organisational element of platforms, the use of automated monitoring and decision-making systems, and the extent to which internal platform work is covered by the Directive.

83 National legislators have limited opportunities to provide clarification of the Directive, as any national divergence would risk immediate conflict with Union law. Ultimately, the Court of Justice of the European Union will have interpretative authority and will determine the scope of the Directive's key concepts in light of its text and underlying objectives. Therefore, it is foreseeable that the Court's case law will play a decisive role in shaping the future interpretation of digital labour platforms within the EU legal order.

Article 3
Intermediaries

Member States shall take appropriate measures to ensure that, where a digital labour platform makes use of intermediaries, persons performing platform work who have a contractual relationship with an intermediary enjoy the same level of protection pursuant to this Directive as those who have a direct contractual relationship with

[102] Cf. Art. 3 of ILO Convention No. 135.
[103] Cf. Wömpner AuR 2024, 378 (381).

a digital labour platform. To that end, Member States shall take measures, in accordance with national law and practice, to establish appropriate mechanisms, which shall include, where appropriate, joint and several liability systems.

Recital (24) In some cases, persons performing platform work do not have a direct contractual relationship with the digital labour platform, but are in a relationship with an intermediary through which they perform platform work. This way of organising platform work often results in a vast array of different and complex multi-party relationships, including subcontracting chains, as well as in blurred responsibilities between the digital labour platform and the intermediaries. Persons performing platform work through intermediaries are exposed to the same risks related to the misclassification of their employment status and the use of automated monitoring systems or automated decision-making systems as persons performing platform work directly for the digital labour platform. Member States should therefore establish appropriate measures in order to ensure that, under this Directive, persons performing platform work working through intermediaries enjoy the same level of protection as persons performing platform work who have a direct contractual relationship with the digital labour platform. Member States should establish appropriate mechanisms, including, where appropriate, through joint and several liability systems.
Recital (26) Where a party is found to be an employer and fulfils the conditions of being a temporary-work agency in accordance with Directive 2008/104/EC, the obligations under that Directive apply.

Literature: Biasi, 'Beyond Employment: the Protection of Platform Workers in a Holistic Perspective', in Lo Faro (ed.), New Technology and Labour Law. Selected Topics, Giappichelli 2022, p. 139; Hiessl, 'Multi-party relationships in platform work: Cross-European case law developments and points of departure for (supranational) regulation', ELLJ 2023, 514; Kocher/Bronowicka, 'A blunt tool for women* in platform work? A feminist perspective on the Platform Work Directive', ELLJ 2025, 565; Perulli, 'A new category within European Union Law: Personal Work', ELLJ 2024, 184; Rainone/Aloisi, 'The EU Platform Work Directive: What's New, What's Missing, What's Next' ETUI Policy Brief 2024.06, Brussels 2024; Rainone, 'The collective rights dimension of the Platform Work Directive: Assessing regulatory effectiveness in the digital labour context', ELLJ 2025, 494; Ratti, 'Online platforms as labour market intermediaries', in Lo Faro (ed.), New Technology and Labour Law. Selected Topics, Giappichelli 2022, p. 89; Sanders, 'Article 3 in the Platform Work Directive on intermediaries: Joint liability or joint employment?' ELLJ 2025, 452.

A. Policy background

The Commission's initial proposal of the Platform Work Directive[1] did not entail any references to the legal issues arising from multiparty relationships in the platform economy. The initiative to include a specific provision on subcontracting was taken by the European Parliament's rapporteur. Her report of May 2022 suggested the insertion of an extensive Art. 12b, which was included with minor amendments in the European Parliament's starting position.[2] As discussed elsewhere,[3] the provision would have introduced a system of mandatory liability of platforms for wages and social security contributions not paid by their subcontractors, based on the structure of existing subcontractor liabili- 1

[1] European Commission, 'Proposal for a Directive of the European Parliament and of the Council on improving working conditions in platform work', 9.12.2021, COM(2021) 762 final, (https://eur-lex.europa.eu/legal-content/EN/TXT/PDF/?uri=CELEX:52021PC0762).

[2] European Parliament, 'Report on the proposal for a Directive of the European Parliament and of the Council on improving working conditions in platform work', 21.12. 2022, (COM(2021)0762 – C9-0454/2021 – 2021/0414(COD)), (https://www.europarl.europa.eu/doceo/document/A-9-2022-0301_EN.html). For details, see Sanders ELLJ 2025, 453 et seqq.

[3] Hiessl ELLJ 2023, 535 et seqq.

ty schemes in EU law,[4] but stricter than those – notably as it did not envisage a 'due diligence defence', so that platforms would have had no chance to avoid liability by taking proactive measures.

2 While the co-legislators agreed about the practical importance of the matter, the Council's starting position[5] considered a simple anti-circumvention provision ('Art. 2a: Member States shall ensure that the use of intermediaries does not lead to a reduction in the protection afforded by this Directive') sufficient. The eventual wording of Art. 3 of the Directive is much closer to this less specific version,[6] but additionally includes a reference to 'appropriate mechanisms' as discussed infra at – → mn. 14 et seqq.

3 No explanatory memorandum is available on the provision, and even the prior version of the European Parliament was not dealt with in the rapporteur's explanatory statement – leaving little but the text itself and a single recital 24 as a basis for interpretation.

B. Main elements

I. Intermediaries

4 Art. 3 speaks of 'intermediaries', thereby not specifically placing the third party in terms of the terminology generally used for liability provisions (the three 'su' levels – subsidiary, subcontractor, supplier). This seems appropriate, as the eventual provision does not entail any form of mandatory liability of the platform for the third party. Therefore, the provision is as such broadly applicable to every situation in which the person performing platform work has a **contractual relationship concerning this work performance with a third party** irrespective of whether the situation amounts to subcontracting in the legal sense, or whether it has the status of a temporary work agency, umbrella company[7] etc.[8]

5 This should arguably include also situations in which a person performing platform work has a contractual relationship with both the platform and an intermediary, e.g. because they have some form of personal account on the platform while working as part of the intermediary's workforce. The question is whether Art. 3 also covers situations where there is no contractual relationship between the platform and the third party. An example would be fleet managing companies that provide vehicles to drivers under 'rental contracts' that oblige the driver to use the vehicle for ride-hailing activities under a personal platform account, with (part of) the profit going to the company. As evident from litigation arising in these contexts,[9] such arrangements pose particularly difficult questions in terms of allocating potential employer responsibilities between the platform and the intermediary. A purposive interpretation might thus suggest that they should be included under the scope of Art. 3, so that Member States would be obliged to ensure the 'same level of protection' as discussed in the next section also in the relationship between

[4] Art. 8 of the Employer Sanctions Directive 2009/52/EC and Art. 12 of the Posting of Workers Enforcement Directive 2014/67/EU.

[5] Council, 'Proposal for a Directive of the European Parliament and of the Council on improving working conditions in platform work – General approach', 7.7.2023, 2021/0414(COD), 10107/23 (https://data.consilium.europa.eu/doc/document/ST-10107-2023-INIT/en/pdf).

[6] See Rainone/Aloisi, p. 4–5.

[7] Which have been discussed e.g. in the Swedish context: see → Chap. III mn. 6 on Sweden).

[8] See also Sanders ELLJ 2025, 458 and European Commission, Report Expert Group – Transposition of the Directive (EU) 2024/2831 on improving working conditions in platform work (12.1.2026), 23.

[9] Hiessl ELLJ 2023, 519 et seqq.

the individual and the intermediary. At the same time, such an interpretation would arguably go beyond the ordinary meaning of the provision's text ('where a digital labour platform *makes use* of intermediaries'). The latter would also seem to apply to a situations in which an individual creates a platform account and sublets it to another individual – which may happen without the platform's knowledge or consent.[10]

In any event, it is for the national lawmaker to consider potential further differentiations, e.g. by introducing a certain degree of liability of the platform only for proper subcontractors and taking more limited measures for other types of intermediaries. **6**

II. Same level of protection

The pertinent literature[11] leaves no doubt about the fact that intermediaries – e.g. 'fleet partners' that provide both vehicles and drivers to work via ride-hailing or delivery platforms – play an important and potentially growing role in practice. The idea that persons working in such a multiparty relationship should enjoy the 'same level of protection' as those in a bilateral relationship with a platform company is significantly less straightforward than it may seem at first sight. **7**

First, it should be stressed that, in accordance with the definitions in → Art. 2(1)(b-d), neither the status of a 'person performing platform work'[12] nor that of a 'platform worker' depend on a contractual relationship with the platform undertaking itself (Art. 2 (1)(b): 'platform work' means work organised through a digital labour platform and performed [...] by an individual on the basis of a contractual relationship between the digital labour platform **or an intermediary**, and the individual [...]). Thus, as soon as a platform is 'organising' the work of individuals in the sense of → Art. 2(1)a(iii), the **platform** is subject to the responsitilities laid down in the Directive in respect of those individuals – **even if it has no direct contractual relationship with them**. Thus, for instance, the limits and preconditions for the platform's algorithmic management activities as set out in → Arts. 7 et seqq. apply in full, and the wording of provisions such as → Art. 9 ('digital labour platforms [are required] to inform persons performing platform work') or → Art. 11 ('persons performing platform work have the right to obtain an [...] explanation *from the digital labour platform*') basically leaves no doubt that these duties exist immediately between the platform and the individual, irrespective of the potential interposition of one or even several intermediaries. This results from a simple textual interpretation for which Art. 3 is not even needed. **8**

The same effectively applies to → Art. 5, which clearly requires the presumption of a 'contractual relationship *between a digital labour platform and a person performing platform work*'. Member States can obviously introduce legal presumptions also in the relationship between the individual and the intermediary (→ Art. 26), but this can only come on top and never instead of the presumption applying to the platform. By contrast, → **Art. 4** requires effective procedures and primacy of facts whenever the determination of the employment status of persons performing platform work is at issue. Therefore, these preconditions need to be ensured **both in relation to the platform and the inter-** **9**

[10] Such 'clandestine intermediaries' have in some cases been identified as employers by national courts, as described in Hiessl ELLJ 2023, 521 et seq., 531 et seq. According to the Commission services as cited in the Expert Group Report (Transposition of the Directive (EU) 2024/2831 on improving working conditions in platform work (12.1.2026), 18), it is not excluded that subletting is covered by the Directive's concept of intermediaries.

[11] Cf. Ratti in Lo Faro, 89 et seqq., and the literature cited.

[12] See Perulli ELLJ 2024, 206.

mediary. This is also supported by the reference to the 'party *or parties*' responsible for employer obligations in → Art. 4(3).

10 This option for the individual to rely at least on → Art. 4 – with its potentially meaningful minimum standards (see → Art. 4 mn. 22 et seqq.) – also when opting to claim recognition as an employee of the intermediary[13] effectively raises additional questions of interpretation. An interesting role may e.g. be played by Art. 21, which is clearly applicable to all 'proceedings concerning the provisions of this Directive'. In other words, even based on a purely textual interpretation, it seems that platforms must be obliged to disclose any relevant evidence also in proceedings between person performing platform work and intermediaries. This could e.g. ensure insight into the degree to which the platform enabled the intermediary to take part in algorithmic monitoring.[14] More questions may arise in relation to Arts. 22–23. Both are basically formulated in a broad manner, indicating that also intermediaries might be prohibited from subjecting an individual to adverse treatment or contract termination for attempting to claim an employment relationship with the intermediary (including a reversal of the burden of proof). More than that, the formulation would basically suggest protection also in cases where a person performing platform work relies on their direct rights vis-à-vis the platform (e.g. regarding algorithmic management) and is subsequently subject to adverse treatment *by the intermediary* (who may act on request or pressure by the platform). The only counter-indication in the text is the phrase in Art. 23(2), according to which '[only] *the digital labour platform* [must] provide duly substantiated grounds for the dismissal, the termination of the contract or any equivalent action'. This is effectively where Art. 3 could become relevant: arguably, the same level of protection is only guaranteed when also those working via intermediaries are guaranteed protection against termination of the contract based on which they perform platform work. Consequently, one concrete conclusion to be derived from Art. 3 should be comprehensive protection from retaliation by the intermediary.

11 The Directive's text is less clear when it comes to obligations specifically for employees, i.e. 'platform workers'. Among those, notably → Art. 12 on health and safety is actually formulated in a manner that indicates that the platform's OSH assessment should include all platform workers, and also the prohibition of undue pressure in Art. 12(3) would seem to apply in relation to all of them – i.e. including those employed by an intermediary. By contrast, information and consultation duties under Art. 12(2) apply 'in accordance with Arts. 10 and 11 of Directive 89/391/EEC' – a directive which establishes duties only for employers with regard to their own employees. Similarly, → Art. 13 refers repeatedly to Directive 2002/14/EC, which entails information and consultation duties exclusively for employers. It thus seems that at least the aspects of **information and consultation** that go beyond algorithmic transparency and review can basically be limited to the platform's *own* employees.

12 Here, it will **depend entirely on the interpretation of Art. 3** whether platform workers employed by an indermediary are considered to enjoy the 'same' level of protection because they or their representatives have information and consultation rights in relation to their contractual employer. Arguably, the intermediary may not even be informed about 'decisions likely to lead to the introduction of or to substantial changes in the use of automated monitoring systems or automated decision-making systems' in the sense of → Art. 13 – and even then, a right to consultation at the level of the intermedi-

[13] Note that, depending on the circumstances of the case, such claims may be considerably more likely to succeed than those alleging a direct employment relationship with the platform: Hiessl ELLJ 2023, 519 et seqq.

[14] Hiessl ELLJ 2023, 524 et seqq.

ary may not be comparable to direct consultation with the platform as the one ultimately making these decisions. Therefore, a strict understanding of the 'same' level of protection might mean that Member States would need to ensure some form of access of subcontracted workers' representatives to the platform itself. Needless to say, this may be a very novel approach for countries whose systems of worker representation basically focus on the company level.

Finally, with a view to the many potential disadvantages of being employed by an intermediary rather than the platform itself,[15] it needs to be stressed that Art. 3 only guarantees the same level of protection '**pursuant to this Directive**' – and not full equal treatment in every respect. As the Directive does not contain a right to be recognised as an employee of the platform under any specific conditions, Art. 3 cannot be construed as meaning that a worker who is correctly classified as an employee of an intermediary (potentially with the help of → Art. 4) must as a result have access to exactly the same employment-related rights as if they were a direct employee of the platform. 13

III. Appropriate mechanisms

Finally, the most nebulous part of Art. 3 is the requirement of 'appropriate mechanisms'. The introductory phrase 'to that end' would basically indicate that mechanisms are only required to achieve the aim mentioned in the previous sentence – i.e. the 'same level of protection pursuant to this Directive'. As such, this would only reiterate the duties as discussed in the previous section. 14

Such a narrow interpretation would, however, seem to be contradicted by the addition that appropriate mechanisms 'shall include, where appropriate, joint and several liability systems'. Clearly, joint liability – classically understood as the platform's liability for (financial) obligations of the intermediary as an employer – would *not* concern the level of protection 'pursuant to this directive'. Rather, it addresses one of the differences in the general level of protection that go beyond the provisions of the Directive, having to do with the practically greater risk run by the employee of a subcontractor that their claims against the direct employer may be unenforceable. In other words, Art. 3 seems to require Member States to take also **measures that go beyond the rights ensured by the Directive itself, at least where this would seem 'appropriate'**. 15

This obviously begs the question under what circumstances such measures might be mandatory. In this respect, it should be cautioned that, where the English version uses 'where appropriate' in Art. 3, numerous language versions[16] actually use exactly the same phrase as in Art. 10(1) of the Maternity Directive.[17] On that provision, the CJEU has already found that the phrase ('where applicable' in the English version) has effectively no normative value at all.[18] Also those language versions that do not employ exactly the 16

---

[15] Including in terms of the enforceability of claims against the employer (incl. for reasons of solvency), the applicable collective agreement, workers' rights dependent on company size, the bargaining power of employees at company level, seniority (where the same worker keeps working for the same platform via different subcontractors), the applicability of collective redundancy legislation when dismissing workers working for the same platform via different intermediaries, or the justification of a redundancy when the platform gives the contract to a different subcontractor. See Hiessl ELLJ 2023, 531 et seqq. Cf. also Biasi in Lo Faro, 148; Rainone ELLJ 2025, 498.

[16] French, German, Italian, Spanish etc.

[17] 'Member States shall take the necessary measures to prohibit the dismissal [...], save in exceptional cases not connected with their condition which are permitted under national legislation and/or practice and, where applicable, provided that the competent authority has given its consent; [...].'

[18] In the sense that there was no duty for Member States to introduce dismissal procedures requiring the consent of a competent authority.

same phrase as in the Maternity Directive usually do not use terms referring to a standard of 'appropriateness'. Additionally, also the 'imperative' formulation of Art. 3 in its English version ('shall') does not seem to be reflected in any of the other language versions.[19] In other words, while the English version would suggest a positive duty to take measures going beyond equal protection under the Directive itself, and that their necessity would be assessed based on an objectifiable standard of 'appropriateness', this conclusion is not necessarily supported by any of the other versions.[20] As a result, it seems somewhat questionable whether even a decidedly purposive interpretation would find that under certain circumstances (e.g. where subcontractors with unsustainable business models regularly end up insolvent, pushing the damage on workers and guarantee funds[21]) it would be 'appropriate' – and thus, mandatory – for the Member State at issue to introduce subcontractor liability or equivalent measures.[22]

17 In any event, as recital 26 recalls, a situation in which an intermediary 'manages' the workforce (hiring, firing, wage payment etc.), but the platform is in charge of instructions and control regarding work performance, the situation is likely to fulfil the conditions of a **temporary agency work relationship** under Directive 2008/104/EC. This triggers, at the very least, the obligations under the Directive (whereby notably the equal treatment obligation under Art. 5 may, however, be worth little if the platform has no own comparable employees), and regularly the platform's health and safety obligations under Directive 91/383/EEC. National law may of course entail much more powerful consequences in case of temporary agency work, including joint or subsidiary liability or even a shift of employer status in case of unlawful agency work.[23]

CHAPTER II
EMPLOYMENT STATUS

Article 4
Determination of correct employment status

1. Member States shall have appropriate and effective procedures in place to verify and ensure the determination of the correct employment status of persons performing platform work, with a view to ascertaining the existence of an employment relationship as defined by the law, collective agreements or practice in force in the Member States, with consideration to the case-law of the Court of Justice, including through the application of the legal presumption of an employment relationship pursuant to Article 5.

---

[19] Virtually all of them are effectively equivalent to the French formulation ('À cette fin, les États membres prennent des mesures, conformément au droit national et à la pratique nationale, pour mettre en place des mécanismes appropriés, qui comprennent, le cas échéant, des systèmes de responsabilité solidaire.').

[20] Debating the question whether the English version should be given special relevance in the interpretation where the co-legislators have in fact worked with this version when agreeing their positions would go beyond the scope of the present commentary.

[21] Cf. the Employer Insolvency Directive 2008/94/EC.

[22] Note that the Commission (as cited in the Report of the Expert Group – Transposition of the Directive (EU) 2024/2831 on improving working conditions in platform work (12.1.2026), 22 et seq.) appears to focus mostly on the reverse form of 'liability', repeatedly suggesting that national law might give persons performing platform work the option of turning the intermediary rather than the platform e.g. with requests concerning algorithmic management.

[23] See also Kocher/Bronowicka ELLJ 2025, 574.

2. The ascertainment of the existence of an employment relationship shall be guided primarily by the facts relating to the actual performance of work, including the use of automated monitoring systems or automated decision-making systems in the organisation of platform work, irrespective of how the relationship is designated in any contractual arrangement that may have been agreed between the parties involved.
3. Where the existence of an employment relationship is established, the party or parties responsible for the obligations of the employer shall be clearly identified in accordance with national legal systems.

Recital (27) The principle of primacy of facts, meaning that the ascertainment of the existence of an employment relationship should be guided primarily by the facts relating to the actual performance of work, including the remuneration for the work, and not by the parties' description of the relationship, in accordance with the ILO Employment Relationship Recommendation No 198 (2006), is particularly relevant in the case of platform work where contractual conditions are often unilaterally determined by one party.
Recital (28) The abuse of the status of self-employed persons, either at national level or in cross-border situations, is a form of falsely declared work that is frequently associated with undeclared work. False self-employment occurs when a person is declared to be self-employed while fulfilling the conditions characteristic of an employment relationship. A false declaration of self-employment is often made to avoid certain legal or fiscal obligations or to create a competitive advantage compared to law-abiding undertakings. In a number of judgments (12), the Court of Justice has ruled that the classification of a self-employed person under national law does not prevent that person from being classified as a worker within the meaning of Union law if that person's independence is merely notional, thereby disguising an employment relationship.

Literature: Barrio Jacqueson, 'The social security relevance of the Platform Directive', ELLJ 2025, 516; Février, 'The Concept of 'worker' in the free movement of workers and the social policy directives: Perspectives from the case law of the Court of Justice', ELLJ 2020, 177; Hiessl, 'Case Law on the Classification of Platform Workers: Cross-European Comparative Analysis and Tentative Conclusions' (ECE Report, 2024; update 2026 forthcoming under same link) <http://dx.doi.org/10.2139/ssrn.3839603/>; Hiessl, 'General Concepts', in Hiessl (ed.), EU Labour Law: A Commentary, Alphen aan Rijn 2025, p. 5; Hiessl, 'Multiparty relationships in platform work: Cross-European case law developments and points of departure for (supranational) regulation', ELLJ 2023, 514; Hiessl/Steiert, 'EU Charter of Fundamental Rights: Arts 47 and 51', in Hiessl (ed.), EU Labour Law: A Commentary, Alphen aan Rijn 2025, p. 155; Holé, 'The procedural autonomy of the MSs and the principles of equivalence and effectiveness', RE 2022, 285; Menegatti, 'Taking EU labour law beyond the employment contract: The role played by the European Court of Justice', ELLJ 2020, 26; Sutterer-Kipping, 'Platform Work Directive (2024/2831/EU)', in Hiessl (ed.), EU Labour Law: A Commentary, Alphen aan Rijn 2025, p. 704.

A. Policy background

I. Proposal of the European Commission

1 In the **Explanatory Memorandum** to its Proposal,[1] the European Commission pointed out the benefits of digital labour platforms in promoting innovative services and new business models and creating many opportunities for consumers and businessess. Still, as digital labour platforms introduce new forms of work organisation, they also challenge existing rights and obligations related to labour law and social protection. The Commission notes that many experience subordination to and varying degrees of control by platforms, for instance as regards pay levels or working conditions. It cites estimates according to which up to five and a half million people working through digital labour platforms could be at risk of employment status misclassification. Those people are especially likely to experience poor working conditions and inadequate access to social protection.[2]

2 The Proposal, with its general objective to improve the working conditions and social rights of people working through platforms, including with the view to support the conditions for the sustainable growth of digital labour platforms in the European Union, includes three specific objectives. One of them is to ensure that people working through platforms have – or can obtain – the correct employment status in light of their actual relationship with the digital labour platform and gain access to the applicable labour and social protection rights.[3] This first specific objective shall be attained by establishing a comprehensive framework to tackle misclassification in platform work – including appropriate procedures to ensure correct status determination, in line with the principle of primacy of facts, as well as a rebuttable presumption of employment relationship. This aim is again stressed in the 'Detailed explanation of the specific provisions in the proposal'.[4]

3 According to the **impact assessment**,[5] the chosen combination of measures put forward in the Proposal was considered the most effective, efficient and coherent, indicating an expected substantial improvement in the working conditions and access to social protection for people working through platforms. Those who, as a result of correct determination of their employment status, will be recognised as employees would enjoy improved working conditions. Conversely, genuine self-employed people working through platforms would indirectly benefit from more autonomy and independence, as a result of digital labour platforms adapting their practices to avoid any risk of reclassification. Digital labour platforms would also gain from increased legal certainty, including with respect to potential court challenges, in line with the EU's social model. As a spillover effect, other businesses competing with digital labour platforms would

[1] European Commission, 'Proposal for a Directive of the European Parliament and of the Council on improving working conditions in platform work', 9.12.2021, COM(2021) 762 final, 1 et seq. (https://eur-lex.europa.eu/legal-content/EN/TXT/PDF/?uri=CELEX:52021PC0762).

[2] See European Commission, 'Proposal for a Directive of the European Parliament and of the Council, On improving working conditions in platform workaccompanying impact assessment', 9.12.2021, SWD(2021) 396 final, Section 2.1.

[3] European Commission, 'Proposal for a Directive of the European Parliament and of the Council on improving working conditions in platform work', 9.12.2021, COM(2021) 762 final, 3 et seq.

[4] European Commission, 'Proposal for a Directive of the European Parliament and of the Council on improving working conditions in platform work', 9.12.2021, COM(2021) 762 final, 15.

[5] SWD(2021) 396; European Commission, 'Proposal for a Directive of the European Parliament and of the Council on improving working conditions in platform work', 9.12.2021, COM(2021) 762 final, 12 et seq.

benefit from a newly levelled playing field as regards the cost of social protection contributions. Member States would enjoy increased revenues in the form of additional tax and social protection contributions.[6]

In the impact assessment it was estimated that as a result of actions to address the risk of misclassification, between 1.72 and 4.1 million people would be reclassified as employees (circa 2.35 million on-location and 1.75 million online considering the higher estimation figures). People currently paid below the minimum wage would enjoy increased annual earnings of up to EUR 484 million, as statutory laws and/or industry-wide collective agreements would cover them. In-work poverty and precariousness would decrease; income stability and predictability would improve. Up to 3.8 million people would receive confirmation of their self-employment status and, as a result of actions by platforms aimed at relinquishing control to avoid reclassification as employers, they would enjoy more autonomy and flexibility.[7] It has to be pointed out though that this assessment was done for the legal presumption in the Proposal (→ Art. 5 mn. 2), which has been significantly altered in the final version by giving the Member States more leeway. Therefore, the effects just mentioned above may be more or less than expected, depending on the design of the presumption in different Member States. **4**

The policy background of the provisions concerning the employment status is finally reflected in recitals 25–37, which will be treated in the given context. **5**

II. Genesis of the provision

Contrary to Art. 5 (→ Art. 5 mn. 2 et seq.), Art. 4 underwent few noteworthy changes in the legislation process. A certainly helpful addition with a view to the interpretation of the final version of Art. 4(1) is that the procedures need to be not only appropriate but also *effective*,[8] as discussed below in → mn. 22 et seqq. Another interesting detail is that the new Art. 4(3) expressly refers to the 'party *or parties* responsible for the obligations of the employer', thus supporting the view expressed supra (→ Art. 3 mn. 9), according to which the provision is also relevant in multiparty relationships. **6**

B. Main elements

I. Procedures ascertaining the existence of an employment relationship

Chapter II on *employment status* is not just about defining the Directive's personal scope for those provisions that are limited to employees (i.e. 'platform workers' in the sense of → Art. 2(1)d such as Arts. 12 or 13). Much rather, Arts. 4–6 Platform Work Directive are effectively the first provisions in EU law establishing standards for the **determination of employment status under national law**. The clear goal is to increase legal certainty in typical cases of litigation on the status of platform workers – which virtually **7**

[6] European Commission, 'Proposal for a Directive of the European Parliament and of the Council on improving working conditions in platform work', 9.12.2021, COM(2021) 762 final, 12.

[7] European Commission, 'Proposal for a Directive of the European Parliament and of the Council on improving working conditions in platform work', 9.12.2021, COM(2021) 762 final, 12.

[8] This is a result of an amendment proposed by the EP's rapporteur (see → Art. 3 mn. 1). Most of the other changes proposed by that report have eventually not been incorporated in the final text.

never focus on rights under EU law, but mostly on dismissal protection, minimum wages, overtime compensation and social security.[9]

8 This new construct of setting EU-level standards for procedures aimed at answering questions of national law necessarily entails a number of legal questions and uncertainties. The most pressing of these will be briefly discussed in the following subsections.

1. Procedures covered by Art. 4

9 One key question concerns the scope of procedures targeted by Art. 4. Most notably: are its requirements (notably effectiveness and primacy of facts, as described below) also applicable to procedures in the area of **tax, criminal or social security matters**? Clearly, these areas have been exempt from the scope of Art. 5 (→ Art. 5 mn. 24) due to concerns about the **limitation of the EU's competence** when acting on the basis of Art. 153(1)(b) TFEU, based on a qualified majority in the Council. *If* one assumes that thoses concerns were well-founded, in the sense that the current competence rules would prevent the EU from introducing the specific procedural rules under Art. 5 for litigation on tax, criminal or social security issues (as many observers appear to assume[10]), there would seem to be no logical way of construing the EU as competent to include those areas under the – equally procedural – rules under Art. 4.

10 In other words, when assuming such a limitation of EU competences, Art. 4 would need to be interpreted restrictively as not covering tax, criminal or social security-related litigation. As neither the restrictive interpretation of a general rule of EU law, nor the extensive interpretation of an exception (Art. 5(5)) beyond its clearly limited wording are in line with the CJEU's general approach,[11] it seems imperative to examine whether the delimitation of the EU's competences actually makes such an exceptional approach necessary.

11 In this regard, it may first be observed that at least criminal law provisions are expressly allowed in directives on other matters if they are 'essential to ensure the effective implementation of a Union policy', even when adopted under the ordinary legislative procedure, based on a qualified majority in the Council (Art. 83(2) TFEU).[12] This, however, applies only to 'the definition of criminal offences and sanctions', so that the establishment of procedural rules may seem questionable. For social security, Art. 153(1)(c) and (2)(b) contain a clear unanimity requirement in the Council. The same is true for tax provisions, whereby specifically matters of income tax – as the practically most relevant issue when litigating on the status of platform workers[13] – would not seem to be eligible for EU regulation even by unanimous decision (see Arts. 110 et seqq. TFEU).

12 At the same time, as pointed out by Barrio and Jacqueson,[14] CJEU case law has confirmed countless times that, when legislating on one matter, the EU may 'indirectly interfere' with other matters – including those that are exempt from harmonisation or

---

[9] For an overview of national-level case law see Hiessl, 'Case Law on the Classification of Platform Workers: Cross-European Comparative Analysis and Tentative Conclusions' (ECE Report, 2024) <http://dx.doi.org/10.2139/ssrn.3839603>.

[10] See Sutterer-Kipping in Hiessl, p. 704 (720), and literature cited.

[11] See e.g. ECJ 4.12.1974 – case C-41/74, ECLI:EU:C:1974:133 – Van Duyn, ECJ 12.12.1974 – case C-36/74, ECLI:EU:C:1974:140 – Walrave, ECJ 15.12.1995 – case C-415/93, ECLI:EU:C:1995:463 – Bosman, or ECJ 7.5.1998 – case C-350/96, ECLI:EU:C:1998:205 – Clean Car Autoservice.

[12] This has also been done in some labour law-related provisions, e.g. Art. 9 Employer Sanctions Directive (2009/52/EC).

[13] See Hiessl, p. 13, 27 et seq.

[14] Barrio/Jacqueson ELLJ 2025, 520.

would require different majorities for adoption. They point to classic precedents,[15] but also labour law-related evidence of this principle.[16] More recently, the Court has for the first time applied this principle to a Directive based on Art. 153(1)(b) TFEU, finding that Art. 4 of the Adequate Minimum Wages Directive (on the promotion of collective bargaining), despite including a 'distinct purpose or component in the field of "representation and collective defence of the interests of workers and employers"', was still 'merely ancillary to the main purpose' of improving working conditions.[17] Consequently, the entire Directive could be based on Art. 153(1)(b) TFEU (working conditions), without a need to include Art. 153(1)(f) TFEU (representation and collective defence of the interests of workers and employers) as an additional legal basis. The CJEU also stressed, with reference to prior case law, that '[i]t is only exceptionally that an EU measure must be founded simultaneously on several legal bases'.[18]

Specifically with respect to social security, it is also true that the CJEU has repeatedly found non-discrimination claims (relating to gender, part-time work, fixed-term work, parental leave etc.) to fall outside the scope of EU law, if the discrimination at issue concerned social security issues.[19] However, all these judgments were basically motivated by an interpretation of the concept of 'working conditions' in the area of equal treatment law, which has been viewed as excluding (state) social security in settled case law – starting with the *Defrenne* saga in the 1970s, i.e. long before the TFEU even contained a social chapter. Those rulings generally do not deal with the EU's competences, and they certainly cannot be interpreted as excluding rules affecting social security in a directive based on Art. 153(1)(b) TFEU, as long as those are an ancillary means to the main purpose of improving working conditions, as described above. 13

As for the question whether appropriate and effective procedures in the areas of tax, criminal and social security law could reasonably be considered a valuable ancillary tool to achieve the main goal (improving working conditions by ensuring correct classification), the practical development so far indicates that the answer should be a resounding 'yes'. In practice, the 'big cases', aiming at a collective reclassification of many or all employees of a particular platform, have sometimes been brought by labour inspections or trade unions[20] (meaning they would quite clearly be covered by Art. 4), but often also by tax authorities or public prosecutors, and in the great majority of cases by social security institutions (see also → Art. 5 mn. 24)).[21] 14

All in all, there are good reasons to assume that Art. 4 should not be interpreted restrictively, so that also litigation under tax, criminal and social security law are subject to an obligation of ensuring appropriate and effective procedures, based on the primacy of facts. 15

---

[15] Such as ECJ 5.10.2000 – case 376/98, ECLI:EU:C:2000:54 – Germany v Parliament and Council (Tobacco Advertising case).

[16] Such as the Court's confirmation of the adoption of the Posting of Workers Amendment Directive (2014/67/EU) exclusively on the competence basis relating to the free movement of services, despite the central role of working conditions for both the Directive's aim and its practical consequences. See ECJ 8.12.2020 – case C-620/18, ECLI:EU:C:2020:1001 para. 82 – Hungary v EP and Council.

[17] ECJ 11.11.2025 – case C-19/23, ECLI:EU:C:2025:865 para. 136 – Denmark v EP and Council.

[18] ECJ 11.11.2025 – case C-19/23, ECLI:EU:C:2025:865 para 132.

[19] E.g. cases ECJ 28.9.1994 – case C-7/93, ECLI:EU:C:1994:350 – Beune; ECJ 6.12.2012 – case C-124/11, C-125/11 and C-143/11, ECLI:EU:C:2012:771 – Dittrich; ECJ 22.10.2009 – case C-116/08, ECLI:EU:C:2009:645 – Meerts; ECJ 8.5.2019 – case C-486/18, ECLI:EU:C:2019:379 – Praxair or ECJ 8.5.2025 – case C- C-212/24, C-226/24 und C-227/24, ECLI:EU:C:2025:341 – L.T.

[20] Whereby unions regularly appear as claimants in their own right only in the Netherlands. Hiessl, p. 32 et seqq.

[21] See notably Hiessl, p. 14, 39 et seqq., 48 et seqq.

2. The concept of 'employment relationship'

16 The formulation 'an employment relationship as defined by the law, collective agreements or practice in force in the Member States, **with consideration to the case-law of the Court of Justice**' in Art. 4(1) has given rise to some discussion as to whether it might contain a hidden duty for the Member States to reinterpret their national employee concept in cases concerning platform workers.

17 Most notably, the formulation chosen here is effectively identical to the one used in the EU's most recent labour law directives[22] to deliminate their respective personal scope. As described in detail elsewhere,[23] the CJEU has regularly found that the effet utile[24] of EU law requires the application of various EU directives also to individuals whom national law does not recognise as employees. What's more, recital 28 to the Platform Work Directive stresses that 'the Court of Justice has ruled that the classification of a self-employed person under national law does not prevent that person from being classified as a worker within the meaning of Union law'.

18 Nonetheless, a systematic and purposive interpretation of the provision implies that the 'employment relationship' in Arts. 4–6 Platform Work Directive is not the same concept as in the just mentioned identically formulated other provisions, but effectively refers exclusively to the **concept of employee as defined under national law**. The reason is that the rationale of the CJEU's general effet utile approach for directives with harmonised minimum standards of protection is that Member States should not be able to arbitrarily exclude workers from those minimum standards. Accordingly, Member States need to include e.g. public servants and judges even under directives that refer exclusively to the national definition of employee.[25] This argumentation does not apply to Chapter II of the Platform Work Directive, which does not envisage any harmonisation but just wants platform workers to actually enjoy whatever protection national law reserves for employees, provided they fulfil the conditions that the same national law has established for their enjoyment. This interpretation is effectively shared by most authors commenting on Chapter II.[26]

19 Consequently, the phrase 'with consideration to the case-law of the Court of Justice' in Art. 4(1) should be read as containing an implicit 'where relevant'. Thus, for instance, if a person performing platform work intends to rely on national working time provisions, effective procedures will also need to be ensured in respect of the consideration of the considerable body of CJEU jurisprudence on the scope of the Working Time Direc-

---

[22] Transparent and Predictable Working Conditions Directive 2019/1152/EU, Work-Life Balance Directive 2019/1158/EU, Adequate Minimum Wages Directive 2022/2041/EU, Pay Transparency Directive (EU) 2023/970.

[23] See Hiessl in Hiessl, p. 16 et seqq.; Février ELLJ 2020, 177 et seqq.; Menegatti ELLJ 2020, 26 et seqq.

[24] Menegatti ELLJ 2020, 21 et seq.

[25] See e.g. judgments in ECJ 13.9.2007 – case C-307/05, ECLI:EU:C:2007:509 – Del Cerro Alonso v Osakidetza-Servicio Vasco de Salud, ECJ 22.12.2010 – joined cases C-444/09 and C-456/09, ECLI:EU:C:2010:819 – Rosa María Gavieiro Gavieiro and Ana María Iglesias Torres v Consellería de Educación e Ordenación Universitaria de la Xunta de Galicia, ECJ 16.9.2010 – case C-149/10, ECLI:EU:C:2010:534 – Zoi Chatzi v Ypourgos Oikonomikon, or ECJ 1.3.2012 – case C-393/10, ECLI:EU:C:2012:110 – Dermod Patrick O'Brien v Ministry of Justice, formerly Department for Constitutional Affairs. The 2016 Ruhrklinik judgment (ECJ 17.11.2016 – case C-216/15, ECLI:EU:C:2016:883 – Betriebsrat der Ruhrlandklinik gGmbH v Ruhrlandklinik gGmbH – on the inclusion of nurses working based on membership agreements under the protection of the Temporary Agency Work Directive 2008/104/EC) finally became the first to explicitly quote the Lawrie-Blum formula (Art. 5 → mn. 16), indicating that the CJEU's autonomous concept of employee is actually the benchmark also for those directives that refer exclusively to the definition under national law.

[26] See Sutterer-Kipping in Hiessl, p. 704 (720), and literature cited.

tive. This may obviously have an impact on how the personal scope of national working time legislation is interpreted.

20 This is not to argue that the CJEU's general effet utile approach as mentioned in → mn. 17 would be of no relevance for the Platform Work Directive. Most notably, it seems likely that this approach is still valid for the definition of 'platform workers' under Art. 2, which is the basis of the applicability of the Directive's minimum standards for employees – such as e.g. OSH provisions under Art. 12, or I&C provisions under → Art. 13. By contrast, Arts. 4–6 clearly relate to the correct classification for purposes of national law, rather than the harmonisation of any minimum standards, so that CJEU's general personal scope-related reasoning cannot logically apply to them.

21 A final question might be whether the term 'existence of an employment relationship' implies that Art. 4 is limited to those proceedings in which at least one party pleads for the classification of persons performing platform work as *employees*. This question is of immediate practical relevance, considering that notably a number of higher-level court rulings in certain countries have featured exclusively the distinction between 'pure' self-employment and another status that ensured the rights claimed by the plaintiffs, but is not equivalent to employee status.[27] Given that the insistence on procedures on the 'existence of an employment relationship' is repeated in all three paragraphs of Art. 4, a literal interpretation would seem strongly opposed to an extension of its scope to procedures such as those just described. The exact opposite would seem indicated from a teleological perspective: after all, these procedures have precisely the same aim (determining the correct categorisation of persons performing platform work, enabling them to enjoy the corresponding rights), and are sometimes even a continuation of procedures that still considered employee status among the options in the lower instances. There would seem to be no reason to exempt them from the requirements of effective procedures and primacy of facts. Considering that **third or intermediate categories** exist in a number of Member States,[28] one may wonder why this point was never addressed in the lengthy legislative procedure.

II. Appropriate and effective procedures

22 While the concept of 'appropriate and effective procedures' is as such new and reasonably vague, it connects both to the right to an effective remedy in Art. 47 CFREU and to the effectiveness requirements that the CJEU has developed for national procedural law under its test of 'equivalence and effectiveness' when assessing a directive's implementation. Both standards apply only when the Member States are implementing EU law (cf. Art. 51 CFREU[29]), so they would not normally be relevant for procedures ascertaining employment status under national law. Consequently, even if the concept 'appropriate and effective procedures' were to contain no specific novel requirements as such, the very fact that it makes those two powerful **principles of EU law applicable to the establishment of employment status under national law** is as such a potentially very meaningful achievement.

23 First, the potential of **Art. 47 CFREU** for labour rights and their enforcement is certainly still underexplored,[30] but notably recent case law has seen the CJEU derive some

[27] This notably concerns Italy (see e.g. Cassation Court 31.10.2025, 14002/2022) and the UK (see e.g. Uber BV v Aslam [2021] UKSC 5).
[28] See Sutterer-Kipping in Hiessl, p. 704 (717).
[29] See Hiessl/Steiert in Hiessl, p. 156 et seq.
[30] See Hiessl/Steiert in Hiessl, p. 155 et seq.

very concrete conclusions from this fundamental right. One interesting recent finding is that Art. 47 CFREU entails a right for workers to obtain basic information needed to assess whether their rights have been violated – in casu[31] a right to know the reasons for the preliminary termination of a fixed-term contract. In the context of determining the employment status of platform workers, this might potentially imply a right to be informed of practices indicative of direction and control – e.g. a policy of removing, blocking or de-prioritising workers after complaints by customers, even when this is done 'manually' and would thus fall outside the duty of algorithmic transparency under → Art. 9.

24 The **principle of effectiveness** – meaning that the exercise of rights conferred by EU law be neither made 'impossible in practice' nor 'excessively difficult' – has emerged as a particularly fruitful basis for the development of concrete minimum standards for procedures, remedies and sanctions in relation to (claimed) violations of EU law, including labour law directives.[32] For instance, the CJEU's findings on reasonable periods for bringing complaints,[33] on the burden of proof,[34] on the form of compensation (incl. the amount of damages)[35] and requirements for 'effective, proportionate and dissuasive' sanctions[36] might all be of relevance in cases on employment status.

25 A particularly interesting conclusion derived from both the effectiveness principle and Art. 47 CFREU is that the fact that claimants did not initially object to arrangements (such as a working time scheme in violation of the WTD[37] or a potentially unlawful

[31] ECJ 20.2.2024 – case C-715/20, ECLI:EU:C:2024:139 – K.L. v X sp. z o.o., Absence de motifs de résiliation.

[32] For details, see Hiessl in Hiessl, p. 27 et seqq.; Holé RE 2022, 285 et seqq.

[33] See e.g. cases ECJ 16.7.2009 – case C-69/08 – Visciano, ECJ 29.10.2009 – case C-63/08, ECLI:EU:C:2009:666 – Virginie Pontin v T-Comalux SA, ECJ 8.7.2010 – case C-246/09, ECLI:EU:C:2010:418 – Susanne Bulicke v Deutsche Büro Service GmbH, ECJ 8.9.2011 – case C-177/10, ECLI:EU:C:2011:557 – Francisco Javier Rosado Santana v Consejería de Justicia y Administración Pública de la Junta de Andalucía, ECJ 16.1.2014 – case C-429/12, ECLI:EU:C:2014:12 – Siegfried Pohl v ÖBB Infrastruktur AG, ECJ 27.2.2020 – joined cases C-773/18 to C-775/18, ECLI:EU:C:2020:125 – TK and Others v Land Sachsen-Anhalt, ECJ 16.2.2023 – joined cases C-524/21 and C-525/21, ECLI:EU:C:2023:100 – IG and Agenţia Municipală pentru Ocuparea Forţei de Muncă Bucureşti v Agenţia Judeţeană de Ocupare a Forţei de Muncă Ilfov and IM, or ECJ 27.6.2024 – case C-284/23, ECLI:EU:C:2024:558 – TC v Firma Haus Jacobus Alten- und Altenpflegeheim gGmbH.

[34] See e.g. cases ECJ 3.10.2006 – case C-17/05, ECLI:EU:C:2006:633 – B. F. Cadman v Health & Safety Executive, ECJ 19.4.2012 – case C-415/10, ECLI:EU:C:2012:217 – Galina Meister v Speech Design Carrier Systems GmbH, ECJ 19.10.2017 – case C-531/15, ECLI:EU:C:2017:789 – Elda Otero Ramos v Servicio Galego de Saúde and Instituto Nacional de la Seguridad Social, or ECJ 19.9.2018 – case C-41/17, ECLI:EU:C:2018:736 – Isabel González Castro v Mutua Umivale and Others.

[35] See e.g. cases ECJ 10.4.1984 – case C-14/83, ECLI:EU:C:1984:153 – Von Colson and Kamann v Land Nordrhein-Westfalen, ECJ 7.9.2006 – case C-53/04, ECLI:EU:C:2006:517 – Marrosu and Sardino v Azienda Ospedaliera Ospedale San Martino di Genova e Cliniche Universitarie Convenzionate, ECJ 8.3.2012 – case C-251/11, ECLI:EU:C:2012:133 – Huet v Université de Bretagne occidentale, ECJ 3.7.2014 – joined cases C-362/13, C-363/13 and C-407/13, ECLI:EU:C:2014:2044 – Fiamingo and Others v Rete Ferroviaria Italiana SpA, ECJ 26.11.2014 – joined cases C-22/13, C-61/13 to C-63/13 and C-418/13, ECLI:EU:C:2014:2401 – Mascolo and Others v Ministero dell'Istruzione, dell'Università e della Ricerca and Comune di Napoli, ECJ 7.3.2018 – case C-494/16, ECLI:EU:C:2018:166 – Santoro, ECJ 8.5.2019 – case C-494/17, ECLI:EU:C:2019:387 – MIUR v Rossato and Conservatorio di Musica F.A. Bonporti or ECJ 3.6.2021 – case C-103/19, ECLI:EU:C:2021:460 – SUSH.

[36] See e.g. cases ECJ 10.7.1990 – case C-326/88, ECLI:EU:C:1990:291 – Anklagemyndigheden v Hansen & Soen I/S, ECJ 8.6.1994 – case C-383/92, ECLI:EU:C:1994:234 -COM v. UK, ECJ 10.7.2008 – case C-54/07, ECLI:EU:C:2008:397 – Centrum voor gelijkheid van kansen en voor racismebestrijding v Firma Feryn NV, ECJ 25.4.2013 – case C-81/12, ECLI:EU:C:2013:275 – Asociaţia Accept v Consiliul Naţional pentru Combaterea Discriminării, or ECJ 7.3.2018 – case C-494/16, ECLI:EU:C:2018:166 – Giuseppa Santoro v Comune di Valderice and Presidenza del Consiglio dei Ministri.

[37] ECJ 25.11.2010 – case C-429/09, ECLI:EU:C:2010:717 – Günter Fuß v Stadt Halle.

fixed-term contract[38]) must not lead to a loss of rights. Applied to the context of the assessment of employment status in the platform economy, this might make judicial practices of attaching relevance to the worker's (initial) complicity in presenting their work as self-employed questionable. As discussed (→ mn. 28), such practices are in fact widespread and might also be in conflict with the concept of the primacy of facts.

26 Finally, it should be stressed that the idea of effective procedures is partly subject to concretisations in the Platform Work Directive itself – notably in Arts. 18–24. Notably, platforms must grant access to all relevant evidence at least to the court once procedures have been brought, including confidential information (→ Art. 21), and claimants must be protected against adverse treatment (→ Art. 22) or dismissal (→ Art. 23) as a form of retaliation when lodging a complaint – including a conditional reversal of the burden of proof. More generally, in line with similar formulations in most contemporary directives, Art. 18 requires 'access to timely, effective and impartial dispute resolution and a right to redress, including adequate compensation for the damage sustained, in the case of infringements of their rights arising from this Directive'.

III. Primacy of facts

27 A particularly intriguing element of Art. 4(2) is that it establishes a principle of primacy of facts, which incorporates almost literally the formulation of Point 9 of the ILO's Employment Relationship Recommendation No 198 (2006; see also recital 27). More specifically, it requires the ascertainment of the existence of an employment relationship to be guided 'primarily by the facts relating to the actual performance of work [...], ***irrespective*** **of how the relationship is designated in any contractual arrangement**.' This effectively indicates that EU law might require national law and its implementation to follow the model of an ***absolute*** **primacy of facts**, which attaches no importance whatsoever to the intentions of the parties. As mentioned above (→ mn. 25), such an interpretation would be supported by the CJEU's case law on the principle of effectiveness, which finds that – given the power relations between a company and a worker or jobseeker – no relevance can be attached to the worker's initial complicity in a contract design suggested by the employer.

28 If Art. 4 is assumed to contain a requirement of following a concept of absolute primacy of facts, this could have a substantial impact on the assessment of employee status in a number of countries. As explored in more detail elsewhere,[39] the existing case law on the status of platform workers entails various examples of courts taking the parties' intentions into account in their assessment – be it in the form of a formal core criterion for assessing employee status (Belgium – see also → Benelux mn. 7), as an 'additional factor' to support the interpretation of the main criteria (Denmark[40]), as the ultimately decisive element in an 'aut aut case' (Germany[41]), as the basis for a presumption of correctness (Luxembourg – see also → Benelux mn. 10) or a repeated insistence on the employee's awareness of and complicity in the contractual construct, without clarifying whether and how this influenced the eventual finding in favour of self-employed status

[38] GC 27.6.2017 – case T-233/16 P, ECLI:EU:T:2017:435 – José Luis Ruiz Molina v European Union Intellectual Property Office (EUIPO).

[39] Hiessl, p. 58.

[40] Competition Council of 26 August 2020 (Konkurrenceràdsafgørelse) on Hilfr and Happy Helpers.

[41] Hessisches LAG 14.2.2019 – 10 Ta 350/18, NZA-RR 2019, 505. Note that this decision concerned the competence of the labour court for the case, which is based on a cursory review of employee status.

(Hungary[42] and Turkey[43]). The same assumption of relevance of the parties' intentions underlies the rebuttable presumption of self-employment under French law,[44] which applies if the working individual is entered as self-employed in a business register (which is typically a requirement stipulated by platforms for anyone wanting to work for them). This presumption has been relied on by French courts in hundreds of cases on the claimed employer status of platforms like *Uber*, *Kapten*, *Stuart*, *Bolt* and *LeCab*.[45]

29 Needless to say, all of the examples just mentioned seem difficult to reconcile with an absolute understanding of the primacy of facts, which would imply that only the actual features of the contractual relationship (including the degree of direction and control factually exercised) should determine the assessment, and not what the parties believe or want the contract to be, nor any actions they take due to such considerations. While this may often not necessitate legislative amendments (except in countries like Belgium – see Benelux chapter → mn. 34), it might require courts in various countries to interpret the national principle of primacy of facts in a more absolute way to ensure conformity with EU law. As a result, quite contrary to the negligible attention devoted to Art. 4 in the legislative process, this provision might well turn out to have a **decisive impact on national systems for assessing employment status.** In some countries, this impact may effectively be more pronounced than that of Art. 5 (which only adds a presumption, but does not alter the eventually decisive assessment as such: see → Art. 5 mn. 4).

IV. Clear identification of employer and employer's obligations

30 Finally, in line with the preeminent importance of multiparty relationships in platform work (see Art. 3 → mn. 7), Art. 4(3) stipulates that, '[w]here the existence of an employment relationship is established, the party or **parties responsible for the obligations of the employer shall be clearly identified** in accordance with national legal systems'.

31 The practical effect of this provision may be doubtful. After all, where a claim for the recognition of employee status is brought against several defendants (platforms, intermediaries, clients etc.) in the first place, it is clear that the decision-making body will need to decide which (if any) of them is considered the employer – so Art. 4(3) would not really add anything relevant. By contrast, if the claim is originally brought against only one defendant, does Art. 4(3) imply that the court would need to **assess the role of relevant other actors ex officio** – potentially including cases in which those parties might be 'responsible for the obligations of the employer' in the sense of subcontractor liability (→ Art. 3 mn. 15 et seq.) or similar?

32 If interpreted this way, Art. 4(3) could indeed require a substantial revision of procedural law and practice across the Member States. As explored in more detail elsewhere,[46] there have been several instances in various countries of platform workers claiming the employer status or liability of a single defendant (platform or intermediary) and courts effectively answering in terms of 'at least not *this* defendant'. In this sense, a court's duty to include other potential souces of direction and control could be a useful tool that avoids cases from failing simply because the claimant was reasonably unable to comprehend where the decision-making power was actually located in a multiparty relationship.

[42] Hungarian Supreme Court 13.12.2023 – Mfv.VIII.10.091/2023/7.
[43] Istanbul Court of Appeal 20.4.2022 – 2022/934 E.
[44] Art. L. 8221-6 of the Labour Code.
[45] Hiessl, p. 16 et seqq.
[46] Hiessl ELLJ 2023, 525 et seqq.

At the same time, such a duty would raise a number of practical questions, especially when the role of other parties could only be properly assessed by adding them to the proceedings as defendants. If this results in a potentially substantial increase in the number of parties involved,[47] it might effectively lead to a significant increase in litigation costs for the claimant, who might even be liable to pay the costs of all 'non-employers' when they are successfully recognised as employed by *one* of those defendants. The resulting deterring effect would quite clearly be contrary to the central aims of the Directive. It thus seems highly unclear if Art. 4(3) should rather be interpreted narrowly (as excluding a duty of adding defendants ex officio), or rather particularly widely – as entailing such a duty *and* an additional obligation to avoid negative side effects (potentially based on the *effet utile* principle).[48]

Article 5
Legal presumption

1. The contractual relationship between a digital labour platform and a person performing platform work through that platform shall be legally presumed to be an employment relationship where facts indicating direction and control, in accordance with national law, collective agreements or practice in force in the Member States and with consideration to the case-law of the Court of Justice, are found. Where the digital labour platform seeks to rebut the legal presumption, it shall be for the digital labour platform to prove that the contractual relationship in question is not an employment relationship as defined by the law, collective agreements or practice in force in the Member States, with consideration to the case-law of the Court of Justice.

2. For the purposes of paragraph 1, Member States shall establish an effective rebuttable legal presumption of an employment relationship that constitutes a procedural facilitation for the benefit of persons performing platform work. Moreover, Member States shall ensure that the legal presumption does not have the effect of increasing the burden of requirements on persons performing platform work or their representatives in proceedings to determine their correct employment status.

3. The legal presumption provided for in this Article shall apply in all relevant administrative or judicial proceedings where the determination of the correct employment status of person performing platform work is at issue. The legal presumption shall not apply to proceedings which concern tax, criminal or social security matters. However, Member States may apply the legal presumption in such proceedings as a matter of national law.

4. Persons performing platform work and, in accordance with national law and practice, their representatives shall have the right to initiate the proceedings referred to in the first subparagraph of paragraph 3 to determine the correct employment status of the person performing platform work.

5. Where a national competent authority considers that a person performing platform work might be wrongly classified, it shall initiate appropriate actions or pro-

---

47 Note that there have been cases with up to sixteen defendants (cf. Catalonia Appeals Court 15.12.2021 – 6609/2021), including platform companies (with or without their parent companies and/or strategic business partners), subcontractors, temporary work agencies, liquidators and guarantee institutions in the sense of Art. 3 of the Employer Insolvency Directive 2008/94/EC (EID). See ibid., 515 et seq.

48 The Commission's brief statement on this requirement (in the Report of the Expert Group – Transposition of the Directive (EU) 2024/2831 on improving working conditions in platform work (12.1.2026), 27) unfortunately does not allow for any conclusions in this respect.

ceedings, in accordance with national law and practice, in order to determine the correct employment status of that person.
6. With regard to contractual relationships entered into before and ongoing on 2 December 2026, the legal presumption provided for in this Article shall apply only to the period starting from that date.

Recital (30) Direction and control can take different forms in concrete cases, considering that the platform economy model is constantly evolving. For instance, the digital labour platform might exert direction and control not only by direct means, but also by applying punitive measures or other forms of adverse treatment or pressure. In the context of platform work, it is often difficult for the persons performing platform work to have appropriate access to the tools and information required to assert before a competent authority the actual nature of their contractual relationship and the rights derived therefrom. In addition, the management of persons performing platform work through automated monitoring systems or automated decision-making systems is characterised by a lack of transparency on the part of the digital labour platform. Those features of platform work perpetuate the phenomenon of misclassification as false self-employment, thus hindering the determination of the correct employment status of persons performing platform work and the access to decent living and working conditions by platform workers. Member States should therefore lay down measures providing for effective procedural facilitation for persons performing platform work when determining their correct employment status. In that context, a legal presumption of an employment relationship in favour of persons performing platform work is an effective instrument which greatly contributes to the improvement of living and working conditions of platform workers. Therefore, a contractual relationship should be legally presumed to be an employment relationship as defined by the law, collective agreements or practice in force in the Member States with consideration to the case-law of the Court of Justice, where facts indicating direction and control are found.
Recital (31) An effective legal presumption requires that national law effectively make it easy for the persons performing platform work to benefit from the presumption. The requirements under the legal presumption should not be burdensome and should ease the difficulties of persons performing platform work in providing evidence indicating the existence of an employment relationship in a situation in which there is a power imbalance vis-à-vis the digital labour platform. The purpose of the legal presumption is to effectively address and correct the power imbalance between the persons performing platform work and the digital labour platform. The modalities of the legal presumption should be laid down by the Member States, provided that those modalities ensure the establishment of an effective rebuttable legal presumption of employment that constitutes a procedural facilitation for the benefit of persons performing platform work, and that they do not have the effect of increasing the burden of requirements on persons performing platform work or their representatives in proceedings to determine the correct employment status of such persons. The application of the legal presumption should not automatically lead to the reclassification of persons performing platform work. Where the digital labour platform seeks to rebut the legal presumption, it should be for the digital labour platform to prove that the contractual relationship in question is not an employment relationship as defined by the law, collective agreements or practice in force in the Member States, with consideration to the case-law of the Court of Justice.
Recital (34) The relationship between a person performing platform work and a digital labour platform may not meet the requirements of an employment relationship in accordance with the definition laid down by the law, collective agreements or practice in force of the relevant Member State, with consideration to the case-law of the Court of Justice. Member States should ensure that it is possible to rebut the legal presumption by proving, on the basis of that definition, that the relationship in question is not an employment relationship. Digital labour platforms have a complete overview of all factual elements determining the legal nature of the relationship, in particular the algorithms through which they manage their operations. Digital labour platforms should therefore have the burden of proof where they argue that the contractual relationship in question is not an employment relationship. A successful rebuttal of the legal presumption in judicial or administrative proceedings should not preclude the application of the legal presumption in subsequent judicial proceedings or appeals, in accordance with national procedural law.

Literature: Aloisi/Rainone/Countouris, An unfinished task? Matching the Platform Work Directive with the EU and international "social acquis", ILO Working Paper 101, Geneva 2023; Brameshuber/Höllwarth, 'Die EU-Plattformarbeitsrichtlinie: Ein Gamechanger für das Arbeitsrecht?', ASoK 2024, 170; Countouris/De Stefano, 'Not the usual gig: The personal scope(s) of application of Directive 2024/2831 on improving working conditions in platform work', ELLJ 2025, 432; Hiessl, 'Case Law on the Classification of Platform Workers: Cross-European Comparative Analysis and Tentative Conclusions' (ECE Report, 2024; update 2026 forthcoming under same link) <http://dx.doi.org/10.2139/ssrn.3839603/>; Hiessl,

'General Concepts', in Hiessl (ed), EU Labour Law: A Commentary, Alphen aan Rijn 2025, p. 5; Kocher/Bronowicka, 'A blunt tool for women* in platform work? A feminist perspective on the Platform Work Directive', ELLJ 2025, 565; Mangold, 'Platform work and traditional employee protection: The need for alternative legal approaches', ELLJ 2024, 726; Perulli, 'La présomption de subordination dans la directive européenne sur le travail des plateformes et l'ABC test californien: une comparaison', RDT 2024, 716; Ringelheim, 'The Burden of Proof in Antidiscrimination Proceedings. A Focus on Belgium, France and Ireland', EELR 2019, 49; Sutterer-Kipping, 'Platform Work Directive (2024/2831/EU)' in Hiessl (ed), EU Labour Law: A Commentary, Alphen aan Rijn 2025, p. 704; Vieira/Mendonça, 'The times, are they changing? Examining platform companies' chameleonic labour process as a response to the Spanish Rey Rider', SER 2025, 877.

A. Policy background

1 For the general policy background of the **Commission's choice** for a rebuttable presumption as one of the Directive's core provisions, see → Art. 4 mn. 1 et seqq.

2 As for the **drafting history**, no other provision has been subject to quite as much debate and as many proposals for amendment as the rebuttable presumption of employee status. The Commission's original proposal suggested that an employment relationship should be presumed in case of indications that the platform *controlled* the performance of work. Such an indication concretely required that at least two out of five enumerated criteria be met: (a) effective determination or upper limits for the level of remuneration; (b) a requirement that person performing platform work respect specific binding rules with regard to appearance, conduct towards the recipient of the service or performance of the work; (c) supervision of the performance of work or verification of the quality of the results of the work, including by electronic means; (d) effective restriction of the freedom, including through sanctions, to organise one's work, in particular the discretion to choose one's working hours or periods of absence, to accept or to refuse tasks or to use subcontractors or substitutes; and (e) effective restriction of the possibility to build a client base or to perform work for any third party.

3 Subsequently, major changes were proposed in effectively every single European Parliament resolution and all compromise texts established by the various Council presidencies. One particularly remarkable suggestion by the Parliament[1] was to keep the idea of a concrete enumeration of criteria, but to move them to the rebuttal stage. As a result, an employment relationship would generally be presumed in all cases between platforms and their workers, and that presumption could only be rebutted based on an exhaustive list of criteria to be proven by the platform. While several observers[2] expressed a preference for that version, referring to the much more pronounced shift in the burden of proof, it needs to be emphasised that, more than anything, adopting that version would have amounted to a quantum leap in terms of harmonisation. After all, it would have

[1] European Parliament 2022, Report on the proposal for a Directive on improving working conditions in platform work, A9-0301/2022 (2022).

[2] E.g. Aloisi/Rainone/Countouris, p. 15 et seq.; Perulli RDT 2024, 716 (718).

come down to a *full harmonisation* of the classification of platform workers as employees – as the platform could have avoided being classified as an employer only by reliance on criteria established by the directive, irrespective of national law. The ensuing unequal treatment between workers in the platform vs. the conventional economy might also have incentivised Member States to generally adapt their national employee concept to that of the EU. Such an unprecedented step towards the EU-wide harmonisation of labour law was – perhaps unsurprisingly – not acceptable for the Council, whose eventual suggestion of abolishing the list of criteria altogether laid the groundwork for the final compromise that became Art. 5 of the Directive. This abandonment of any attempt of concretisation has both been criticised for giving excessive leeway to national legislators[3] and welcomed for avoiding rigidities that might have risked to perpetuate outdated concepts and exacerbate rather than alleviate the burden of proof on the claimant.[4]

B. Main elements

4 Art. 5 is systematically connected to Art. 4. A rebuttable presumption must be included 'in all relevant administrative or judicial proceedings where the determination of the correct employment status of person performing platform work is at issue', which seems fully equivalent with procedures 'ascertaining the existence of an employment relationship' in the sense of Art. 4(1) – which also refers to the need of a rebuttable presumption. Consequently, for all questions on the **scope of Art. 5,** reference can be made to → Art. 4 mn. 7 et seqq. The commentary in this section will exclusively focus on the features of the rebuttable presumption.

I. Rebuttable legal presumption

5 The eventual text of Art. 5 does not contain many concrete requirements for the rebuttalbe presumption of an employment relationship between platforms and those who work for or through them. Art. 5(2) clarifies that the presumption must be '**effective**', thereby implicitly (and, arguably, superfluously) inviting the CJEU to scrutinise any national implementation for its compliance with effet utile considerations. The one clear red line drawn by the same paragraph (and repeatedly emphasised in recital 31) is that the legal presumption must never have the effect of ***increasing* the burden** for claimants.[5]

6 The difficulty of establishing whether a particularly designed presumption is actually helpful for claimants or rather an unnecessary additional complication may well be illustrated when referring to the **existing presumptions in the few countries where those are already in force** at the time of writing. As described in more detail in this volume (→ Benelux mn. 7, 14–15, 19), the Belgian experience shows how a multi-criteria presumption with 8–9 elements, few of which are genuinely easy to assess in the individual case, can increase the complexity of the legal assessment very significantly. The 6-criteria assessment in Portugal[6] has been assessed so erratically by dozens of court

---

[3] E.g. Brameshuber/Höllwarth ASoK 2024, 170 (175), and literature cited; Loiseau in this volume (→ France mn. 1 et seq.).

[4] E.g. Sutterer-Kipping in Hiessl, p. 704 (719), and literature cited.

[5] This also appeared as a key concern for trade unions in the stakeholder discussion as referenced in European Commission, Report Expert Group – Transposition of the Directive (EU) 2024/2831 on improving working conditions in platform work (12.1.2026), 32.

[6] See Hiessl, p. 37.

rulings in respect of the very same platforms that its potential to bring about more effective correct determination of employment status is doubtful at the very least. At the same time, in both countries, the practical tendency goes towards the recognition of an employment relationship in typical cases of on-location platform work. Thereby, notably the Portuguese Supreme Court's reasoning[7] seems to make it rather clear that its decision in this sense was decisively inspired by the *existence* of a legal presumption, seen as evidence of the will of the legislator to let the courts tilt the balance in favour of employee status where the existing national definition allows for some leeway. Pretty much the same seems to be happening in Belgium, where the (so far) highest-level court decisions are bending the national employee concept almost contra legem in order to achieve a categorisation of platforms as employers (→ Benelux mn. 19, 36). Arguably, this effect of encouraging courts to fill in possible grey areas in the national employee definition in favour of employee status could have been achieved much more easily, without forcing parties and courts to devote considerable time, energy and paperwork to the assessment of lists of criteria. Nonetheless, if the outcome is 'net positive' for the claimants, it would not seem that the prohibition of increasing their burden would be violated in these examples.

Similar considerations might apply to Spain, where it is also doubtful whether the much-hailed[8] Riders' Law[9] improved the situation for the claimants. Note that Spain already had a very broad and claimant-friendy presumption of employee status in place for all employees, and among the roughly onehundred court decisions on platform workers' status rendered before the Riders' Law, not a single one ever raised doubts about its applicability to typical situations of on-location platform work.[10] By 'confirming' that this presumption is also applicable to persons delivering consumer products for a platform that exercises powers of organisation, direction and control through algorithmic management, the Riders' Law not only seems to establish more demanding criteria for platform riders than for employees in general,[11] but might even create legal uncertainties for those working through non-delivery platforms on whether they should – a contrario – not be covered under the same conditions (→ Spain mn. 3). Still, in practice, it is clear that the provision sent a strong political message, which finally convinced platforms to stop fighting senseless legal battles (which, at least in the delivery sector, had been lost by the platforms virtually without exception ever since late 2019). Also, no actual negative side effects for other sectors of the platform economy could be discerned – to the contrary, Spain recently became the first country where both a caregiving and a cleaning platform[12] were reclassified as employers. Thus, again, the effect of sending a political message could potentially have been achieved also without introducing additional uncertainties, but still the result was effectively net positive for workers. 7

To this date, Malta seems to be the only country that introduced a 'zero-burden' presumption, in the sense that the law in question[13] generally shifts the burden of prove to the platform, so that both parties (and the court or authority) can fully and simply focus 8

[7] Portuguese Supreme Court 28.5.2025 – 29923/23.7T8LSB.L1.S1.

[8] See Mangold ELLJ 2024, 726 (733 et seq.); Vieira/Mendonça SER 2025, 877 (878).

[9] Real Decreto 9/2021, BOE-A-2021-7840.

[10] See Hiessl, p. 38 et seq.

[11] As the general presumption only requires the provision of services on behalf of and within the scope of the organisation and management of the contracting party in return for remuneration – and not direction or control. This is also remarked e.g. by Perulli RDT 2024, 717.

[12] Both already in second instance: see Catalonia Appeals Court 4.5.2023 – 2789/2023, Catalonia Appeals Court) 13.2.2025 – 1775/2025. See also Kocher/Bronowicka ELLJ 2025, 565 (569 et seq.).

[13] Legal Notice 268 of 2022 (Digital Platform Delivery Wages Council Wage Regulation Order).

on the actually determining criteria for establishing employee status. In theory, and without any practical application in the Maltese practice to date, this may seem a groundbreaking advantage for platform workers or even an excessively claimant-friendly setup. Note, however, that practice has shown, in the countries that have used some form of legal presumptions of employee status for a long time,[14] that the actual legal advantage for claimants in typical constellations of litigation in the platform economy is very limited anyway. Crucially, as has been noted elsewhere,[15] legal presumptions tend to be a gamechanger when they apply to facts that would otherwise be difficult to prove for the claimants. The presumption as intended in Art. 5, by contrast, relates to a legal question – namely, whether the facts, as they appear based on the abundant information that typically exists in platform-related cases,[16] are sufficient to indicate an employment relationship under national law. Accordingly, in the countries with a significant number of cases to which a presumption was applicable, there are in fact many decisions that find the presumption successfully rebutted,[17] and even more decisions that do not even mention a basically applicable presumption.[18] The latter may be evidence of the fact that, especially where legal presumptions have existed for a long time, courts tend to regard it more as an additional formality which does not change anything about the outcome anyway. This effect might be even more pronounced if and when → Art. 9 on algorithmic transparency and → Art. 21 on the disclosure of evidence are effectively implemented, thus ensuring that courts have effective and complete insight into all the facts that determine the relationship between the parties. This might enable courts to make a decision on coverage by the national concept of employee, without any room left for the consideration of a legal presumption.

9 In this regard, it should be mentioned that, paradoxically, the 'most successful' presumption in Europe to date, which has been referred to by courts as a decisive element in many hundreds of decisions, is the aforementioned French **presumption of self-employment** for persons entered in a business register. The way in which most courts give relevance to this provision is by stating that, in light of the presumption, any elements pointing towards an employment relationship would need to be particularly pronounced.[19] Thus, effectively, courts recognise the existence of a grey area in which a categorisation as an employed or self-employed relationship would both seem justifiable, and within which there is space to adapt the eventual decision to what is suggested by the presumption. By means of generalisation, one might expect legal presumptions to be potentially impactful in those countries where courts are willing to see such 'grey areas' in the existing national employee concept.

10 For countries with such existing presumptions of self-employed status, an effective implementation of Art. 5 might also require a clarification of the relationship between the two contradictory presumptions, and perhaps effectively a resolution that ensures that the presumption of employee status prevails in litigation that involves platforms.[20]

---

[14] See Sutterer-Kipping in Hiessl, p. 704 (718); Mangold ELLJ 2024, 733 et seq.

[15] Hiessl, p. 79 et seq.

[16] Due to the uniform application of contractual terms to a large number of workers, and the extensive documentation based on data collection and (algorithmic) monitoring.

[17] Notably in Belgium and Portugal.

[18] As the great majority of court decisions in Spain.

[19] Hiessl, p. 18 et seqq.

[20] Cf. the Commission's remark that different presumptions might co-exist 'as long as they are not contradictory' (Report of the Expert Group – Transposition of the Directive (EU) 2024/2831 on improving working conditions in platform work (12.1.2026), 32).

II. Facts indicating direction and control

11 The formulation of Art. 5 is, once again, modelled based on Recommendation 2006 (No. 198) – which in Point 11(b) suggests that states provide for 'a legal presumption that an employment relationship exists where one or more relevant indicators is [sic] present'. The relevant indicator chosen by the European lawmaker is that 'facts indicating direction and control' are established by the claimant.[21]

1. Margin for concretisation by the Member States

12 With a view to Art. 26, which stipulates that the Directive 'shall not affect the Member States' prerogative to apply or to introduce laws, regulations or administrative provisions which are **more favourable to platform workers**', it seems clear that **broader presumptions** that do not require any facts to be proven by the claimant – such as the Maltese one mentioned supra at → mn. 8 – should definitely be in line with the Directive.

13 More questions could arise in respect of countries which choose for an **exhaustive catalogue of criteria**, perhaps with a rigid 'fulfilling x out of n'-type formula for considering the presumption as established – similar to the original proposal of the Commission (→ mn. 2) and the current regulation in Belgium and Portugal (→ mn. 6). Arguably, this may lead to a situation in which the presumption is not triggered despite demonstrable elements of direction and control, simply because the 'type' of control differs from what was anticipated by the legislator. In a dynamic sector such as the platform economy, this scenario may not be entirely unrealistic. In such a case, the assessment of compliance with EU law seems particularly difficult because there is a lack of relevant case law also on similar existing provisions. Notably, it seems that most Member States transpose EU law provisions requiring a shift of the burden of proof in non-discrimination law[22] literally, leaving it to the courts to determine whether circumstances as referred to by claimants are sufficient 'facts from which it may be presumed that there has been discrimination'.[23] Thus, the CJEU has never had the opportunity to assess whether Member States could legally implement such provisions by establishing concrete criteria for the 'facts' that the claimant needs to establish – thereby likely increasing legal certainty (and potentially encouraging victims of discrimination to bring claims), but also risking to exclude forms of potentially relevant prima facie proof. Ultimately, the very fact that the CJEU has made some very concrete statements about a shift of the burden of proof being required in individual cases[24] indicates that it does not necessarily consider Member States to have any leeway in the implementation. If the Court were to take a similar approach to Art. 5 Platform Work Directive, in the sense that it would find that concrete individual situations require a triggering of the presumption based on *effet utile* considerations, then any approach based on an exhaustive list or similar rigidities runs the risk of being found in violation of Art. 5.[25]

14 Consequently, where legislators prefer to operate with particular criteria – e.g. to increase the system's predictability[26] – it may be wise to design the enumeration as open,

---

21 See Countouris/De Stefano ELLJ 2025, 432 (442).

22 E.g. Art. 19 Recast Directive 2006/54/EC, Art. 8 Race Equality Directive 2000/43/EC, Art. 13 Employment Equality Directive 2000/78/EC etc.

23 Ringelheim EELR 2019, 49 (51 et seqq.).

24 E.g. cases Brunnhofer (C-381/99), CHEZ RB (C-83/14).

25 Note that the Commission seems to elegantly evade the question in the discussion with stakeholders (see Report Expert Group – Transposition of the Directive (EU) 2024/2831 on improving working conditions in platform work (12.1.2026), 30 et seq.).

26 Cf. Brameshuber/Höllwarth ASoK 2024, 170 (175).

for instance by adding a flexible criterion including 'comparable other forms of direction and control', or similar.[27]

2. The relevance of CJEU case law

15 Next, just as with Art. 4, there is the question of what the 'consideration to the case-law of the Court of Justice' should be considered to imply for the implementation of Art. 5.

16 Given that Art. 5 Platform Work Directive is the first of its kind, there is no existing case law of the CJEU on how to interpret 'facts indicating direction and control' in the context of a legal presumption. Yet, given the overlap in formulation with the third 'Lawrie-Blum' criterion, i.e. the key criterion to distinguish workers/employees from self-employed/undertakings under the autonomous concept of EU law,[28] it would seem that case law on this criterion should be relevant for interpreting Art. 5(1). More specifically: if CJEU case law has identified certain elements as amounting to '**direction and control**', to the degree that the individual in the case at issue was found to be a worker for purposes of EU law, then the presence of the same or comparable elements in platform work should in any event be sufficient to trigger a *presumption* of employment for purposes of the applicable national law.

17 As discussed in more depth elsewhere,[29] concrete statements by the CJEU's on the concept of 'direction and control' have in fact been much less common than one would expect, and many of the pertinent cases leave room for speculation on their precise consequences. The 2004 *Allonby* ruling[30] seems to have been the first in which the question whether direction and control was present was both disputed and actually mattered for the outcome. It specified that direction and control must in particular be seen in '**any limitation on [the worker's] freedom to choose their timetable, and the place and content of their work**', and that the worker's claimed **independence must not be 'merely notional**, thereby disguising an employment relationship'. Both axioms have, with minor variation, been retained in the case law that followed.

18 Needless to say, these criteria are as such difficult to interpret. After all, also genuinely self-employed entrepreneurs, including those hiring own employees, may often work based on a prior agreement on the content of their work – so that the establishment of direction and control may effectively be a question of degree rather than a simple yes/no question. In any event, translated to the context of Art. 5, this implies that the presumption must be triggered whenever the platform either formally interferes (significantly) with the time, place or content of work, or exercises indirect pressure (including via algorithms) with the effect of making the worker's freedom in this regard seem 'merely notional'. As recital 30 recalls, 'the digital labour platform might exert direction and control not only by direct means, but also by applying punitive measures or other forms of adverse treatment or pressure'.

19 Particular attention may also need to be paid to the CJEU's rulings on managerial staff starting with *Danosa*[31] in 2010, which evidenced that the Court is satisfied with

---

[27] Cf. also the considerations on this in the chapter on → Germany mn. 30.

[28] Hiessl in Hiessl, p. 8 et seqq.

[29] Hiessl in Hiessl, p. 10 et seqq.

[30] ECJ 13.1.2004 – case C-256/01, ECLI:EU:C:2004:18 – Debra Allonby v Accrington & Rossendale College and Others.

[31] ECJ 11.11.2010 – case C-232/09, ECLI:EU:C:2010:674 – Dita Danosa v LKB Līzings SIA. See also cases ECJ 13.2.2014 – case C-596/12, ECLI:EU:C:2014:77 – European Commission v Italian Republic, ECJ 9.7.2015 – case C-229/14, ECLI:EU:C:2015:455 – Ender Balkaya v Kiesel Abbruch- und Recycling Technik GmbH, ECJ 10.9.2015 – case C-47/14, ECLI:EU:C:2015:574 – Holterman Ferho Exploitatie BV

the *possibility* of the employer to issue instructions on these aspects of work, to control compliance and to unilaterally remove the worker from their position – notably if the worker is an 'integral part of the company'. Rulings considering e.g. judges to be workers[32] confirm, in turn, that even substantial (inherent) limitations of the employer's possibility to issue content-related instructions cannot prevent a classification as an employment relationship – indicating that the limitations need not concern all three elements (time, place, content), and a sufficiently significant limitations of only one them may be enough to establish direction and control.

20 A final particularly relevant aspect for the platform context is that the judgments in *Raulin*[33] and *Allonby* clarify that the lack of an **obligation to accept work assignments** does not exclude employee status. However, the *Yodel* ruling[34] expressly identifies the lack of a duty to work as one indication of self-employment, at least when combined with three more elements: the worker's possibility to use substitutes or subcontractors, the freedom to work for the principal's competitors, and the free determination of working time. A contrario, it might be assumed that a significant limitation of any one of those four freedoms in the platform work context should be seen as a fact indicating direction and control, and accordingly trigger a presumption of employment.

III. Rebutting the legal presumption

21 Art. 5(1) stipulates that the platform can rebut the legal presumption by proving 'that the contractual relationship in question is not an employment relationship as defined by the law, collective agreements or practice in force in the Member States, with consideration to the case-law of the Court of Justice'.

22 Regarding this formulation, reference can be made entirely to the considerations on → Art. 4 mn. 19: the platform will have to prove the absence of an employment relationship **under national law,** based on the criteria established by said national law. The reference to the case law of the CJEU should, once again, be read as containing an implicit 'where relevant'.

23 Interestingly, recital 34 states that 'Member States should *ensure* that it is possible to rebut the legal presumption'. This interpretation, which finds no clear support in the binding text of the Directive (nor, arguably, in the aims of the Directive as set out in → Art. 1), may be questionable, as Art. 26 clearly allows provisions that are more favourable to platform workers. There would seem to be no reason to assume that such a more favourable provision should not be able to introduce a non-rebuttable presumption for (certain forms of) platform work – similar to what labour law in some countries already stipulates for certain groups that would otherwise be difficult to classify.[35]

---

and Others v F.L.F. Spies von Büllesheim and ECJ 10.9.2014 – case C-270/13, ECLI:EU:C:2014:2185 – Iraklis Haralambidis v Calogero Casilli.

[32] E.g. ECJ 16.7.2020 – case C-658/18, ECLI:EU:C:2020:572 – UX v Governo della Repubblica italiana, ECJ 7.4.2022 – case C-236/20, ECLI:EU:C:2022:263 – PG v Ministero della Giustizia and Others.

[33] ECJ 26.2.1992 – case C-357/89, ECLI:EU:C:1992:87 – V. J. M. Raulin v Minister van Onderwijs en Wetenschappen.

[34] ECJ 22.4.2020 – case C-692/19, ECLI:EU:C:2020:288 – B v Yodel Delivery Network Ltd. Note that this decision is not a judgment but an order.

[35] Cf. e.g. Part VII of the French labour code, which declares that certain categories of workers (including journalists, entertainment professionals, sales representatives etc.) are subject to labour law, with no option to rebut this classification based on the general criteria for an employment relationship. See → France, mn. 6.

IV. Administrative or judicial proceedings

24 The legal presumption of employee status must apply in all judicial and administrative proceedings, with the only **exception** of the three types expressly enumerated in Art. 5(3) (**tax, criminal** or **social security**). These exceptions, which – as discussed at → Art. 4 mn. 9 et seqq. – were based notably on concerns about the limits of EU competences, can be considered a very significant limitation of the Directive's potential effectiveness. After all, practice has shown that countries where institutional actors, and especially social security institutions (e.g. Finland, Spain, Switzerland), tax authorities (e.g. Denmark, Ireland) or public prosecutors (e.g. France, Italy, and notably Portugal)[36] have actively brought proceedings targeting platforms, litigation can happen in a much more targeted manner, involve much larger groups of employees and overcome the reluctance of marginalised workers to bring individual lawsuits. Member states using the option ('may') of including the three exempt areas may thus expect a substantial boost in the effectiveness of their legal presumption.[37] In any event, the exception applies only when the proceedings concern exclusively tax, criminal and/or social security matters.[38]

25 While persons performing platform work are given a **right to initiate proceedings** under Art. 5(4), the rights of representatives are made dependent on national law and practice. Accordingly, EU law does not force Member States to enable representation structures for those who are not (yet) recognised as employees and admit them as representatives in court.

26 For national competent authorities, Art. 5(5) stipulates a **duty** ('shall') **to initiate 'appropriate actions'** whenever they consider that a person performing platform work might be wrongly classified.[39] This will reasonably need to include legal proceedings if other actions (recommendations, warnings) do not result in the putative misclassification being addressed. The most important authorities clearly covered by this duty to act may in practice be labour inspections[40] – which have already emerged as key actors in relation to classification in the platform economy in Belgium, and even more pronouncedly in Spain and Sweden.[41] More doubts may exist regarding tax authorities, public prosecutors and social security institutions, given the exclusion of the relevant areas of law from the presumption as described above (→ mn. 24). However, interestingly, unlike para. 4, para. 5 does not refer to Art. 5(3) and is generally formulated like an independent duty of (all relevant) competent institutions – irrespective of whether the presumption applies. Thus, even though a systematic interpretation might indicate otherwise, both a purely textual reading and, arguably, the purpose of the provision suggest that the 'competent authorities' covered by Art. 5(5) include all those for whose work the question of employment status is of relevance.[42]

27 In practice, the effectiveness of this duty to act will crucially depend on its interpretation. Arguably, in order to *consider* that a particular platform misclassifies its workers,

---

[36] See Hiessl, p. 13 et seq., 22, 27 et seqq., 37 et seqq., 48 et seqq.

[37] Cf. also → France mn. 21.

[38] European Commission, Report Expert Group – Transposition of the Directive (EU) 2024/2831 on improving working conditions in platform work (12.1.2026), 33.

[39] As confirmed also by the Commission (Report Expert Group – Transposition of the Directive (EU) 2024/2831 on improving working conditions in platform work (12.1.2026), 36), this does not require the consent of the person performing platform work. In practice, numerous cases have been brought by various authorities even against the declared wish of the workers concerned to remain classified as self-employed.

[40] See also European Commission, Report Expert Group – Transposition of the Directive (EU) 2024/2831 on improving working conditions in platform work (12.1.2026), 34.

[41] Hiessl, 8 et seqq., 39 et seqq., 45 et seqq.

[42] For the question of compatibility with the limits of the Directive's competence basis, see → Art. 4 mn. 9 et seqq.

the authority in question would first need to conduct investigations, in order to come up with such an opinion. A literal interpretation would thus suggest that labour inspectorates could avoid the duty to act by not even starting investigations that could lead to a consideration of misclassification. As such an interpretation could result in the provision achieving the opposite of what it clearly seeks to achieve (as understaffed and/or overburdened labour inspections might be reluctant to even initiate investigations that might eventually result in a duty to get involved in a lengthy legal battle with the platform), it would seem at odds with *effet utile* considerations. Consequently, it seems realistic that the CJEU will consider authorities obliged to investigate or monitor at least those platforms that provide work to a significant number of people.

V. Non-retroactivity

Art. 5(6) helpfully clarifies that the presumption should self-evidently not apply retroactively (which would likely be at odds with general principles of EU law[43]), but also that contractual relationships established before the deadline's transposition deadline (2 December 2026) are not exempted from the application as from that date. **28**

Article 6
Framework of supporting measures

Member States shall establish a framework of supporting measures in order to ensure the effective implementation of and compliance with the legal presumption. In particular, they shall:

(a) develop appropriate guidance, including in the form of concrete and practical recommendations, in order for digital labour platforms, persons performing platform work and the social partners to understand and implement the legal presumption, including the procedures regarding its rebuttal;
(b) develop guidance and establish appropriate procedures for national competent authorities in accordance with national law and practice, including on cooperation between national competent authorities, in order to proactively identify, target and pursue digital labour platforms which do not comply with rules applicable to the determination of the correct employment status of persons performing platform work;
(c) provide for effective controls and inspections conducted by national competent authorities, in accordance with national law or practice and, in particular, provide, where appropriate, for controls and inspections on specific digital labour platforms where the existence of an employment relationship between such a platform and a person performing platform work has been ascertained by a national competent authority, while ensuring that such controls and inspections are proportionate and non-discriminatory;
(d) provide for appropriate training for national competent authorities and provide for the availability of technical expertise in the field of algorithmic management, to enable such authorities to carry out the tasks referred to under point (b).

[not commented] **1**

[43] Notably the principle of legal certainty, and the resulting protection of legitimate expectations. See Hiessl in Hiessl, p. 32 et seq.

CHAPTER III
ALGORITHMIC MANAGEMENT

Preliminary remarks to Articles 7–12

Literature: Abraha, 'Hauptpersonalrat der Lehrerinnen: Article 88 GDPR and the Interplay between EU and Member State Employee Data Protection Rules', MLR 2024, 484; Abraha, 'Regulating algorithmic employment decisions through data protection law', ELLJ 2023, 172; Abraha, Navigating workers' data rights in the digital age: a historical, current, and future perspective on workers' data protection, Geneva 2025; Adams-Prassl, 'What if your boss was an algorithm? Economic incentives, legal challenges, and the rise of artificial intelligence at work', CLLPJ 2019, 123; Adams-Prassl/Abraha/Kelly-Lyth/Silberman/Rakshita, 'Regulating algorithmic management: A blueprint', ELLJ 2023, 124; Agosti/Bronowicka/Polidoro/Priori, Exercising workers' rights in algorithmic management systems, Etui Report 2023.11, Brussels 2023; Alexander/Song/Hickman/Joo Shin, 'Sourcing algorithms: Rethinking fairness in hiring in the era of algorithmic recruitment,' Int. J. Sel. Asses. 2025, 1; Aloisi, 'Regulating Algorithmic Management at Work in the European Union: Data Protection, Non-discrimination and Collective Rights', Int. J. Comp. Labour Law Ind. Relat. 2024, 37; Aloisi/De Stefano, 'Between risk mitigation and labour rights enforcement: Assessing the transatlantic race to govern AI-driven decision-making through a comparative lens', ELLJ 2023, 283; Aloisi/De Stefano, Your Boss Is an Algorithm: Artificial Intelligence, Platform Work and Labour, Oxford 2022; Aloisi/Gramano, 'Artificial intelligence is watching you at work: Digital surveillance, employee monitoring, and regulatory issues in the EU context', Comparative Labor Law & Policy Journal 2019, 95; Aloisi/Potocka-Sionek/Ratti, 'Straddling two horses: digital or social regulation? behind, within and beyond the eu platform work directive', CML Rev. 2025, 1407; Bernhardt/Kresge/Suleiman, 'Data and Algorithms at Work: The Case for Worker Technology Rights' (UC Berkeley Labor Center 2021); Bernhardt/Kresge/Suleiman, 'The Data-Driven Workplace and the Case for Worker Technology Rights', ILR Review 2023, 3; Brameshuber/Höllwarth, 'Die EU-Plattformarbeitsrichtlinie Ein Game-Changer für das Arbeitsrecht?, ASoK 2024, 170; Clacci/Stein,' From access to understanding: Collective data governance for workers', ELLJ 2023, 1; Däubler, Gläserne Belegschaften – Das Handbuch zum Beschäftigtendatenschutz, 10th edn, Frankfurt a.M. 2025; Daum, 'Algoritmisches Management und Überwachung durch automatisierte Systeme' in Giesen/Junker/Rieble (eds), Arbeitsrechtsfragen bei Crowdworking und Plattformarbeit, Munich 2023, p. 91; De Stefano, "Negotiating the Algorithm': Automation, Artificial Intelligence and Labour Protection', CLLPJ 2019, 1; De Stefano, 'Negotiating the algorithm: Automation, artificial intelligence and labour protection', Comparative Labor Law & Policy Journal 2019, 15; Dubal, 'On Algorithmic Wage Discrimination', Columbia Law Rev. 2023, 1929; Frank/Heine, 'Algorithmisches Management unter der Plattformarbeitsrichtlinie', NZA 2024, 865; Franzen/Gallner/Oetker (eds), Kommentar zum europäischen Arbeitsrecht, 5th edn, Munich 2024; Gräf, 'Algorithmisches Management in der Plattformarbeit – Richtlinienvorgaben und nationale Umsetzung', SR 2025, 14; Gruber-Risak/Warter, 'Die EU-Richtlinie zur Verbesserung der Arbeitsbedingungen in der Plattformarbeit', DRdA 2024, 267; Hendrickx/Mangan, 'Privacy and Data Protection' in Hiessl, EU Labour Law, Alphen aan den Rijn 2025, p. 1034; Imana/Korolova/Heidemann, 'Auditing for Discrimination in Algorithms Delivering Job Ads' in ACM (ed), Proceedings of ACM Web Conference 2021, Ljubljana 2021; Irani, 'The cultural work of microwork', New Media & Society 2015, 720; Jarrahi/Newlands/Lee/Wolf/Kinder/Sutherland, 'Algorithmic management in a work context', Big Data & Society 2021, 1; Kaminski and Malgieri, 'The right to explanation in the AI Act', University of Colorado Law Legal Studies Research Paper 2025 No. 25-9; Kilhoffer/De Groen/Lenaerts/Smits/Hauben/Waeyaert/Giacumacatos/Lhernould/Robin-Olivier, Study to gather evidence on the working conditions of platform workers, Publications Office of the European Union, Luxembourg 2019; Krause, 'Auf dem Weg zur unionsrechtlichen Regelung von Plattformtätigkeiten, die Kommissionsinitiave zur Plattformarbeit', NZA 2022, 521; Kocher, Digital Work Platforms at the Interface of Labour Law: Regulating Market Organisers, Oxford 2022; Lee/Kusbit/Metsky/Dabbish, 'Working with machines: The impact of algorithmic, data-driven management on human workers' in ACM (ed), Proceedings of the 33rd Annual ACM SIGCHI Conference, Seoul, South Korea 2015, p. 1603; Li/Toh, 'Data Subject Rights as a Tool for Platform Worker Resistance: Lessons from the Uber/Ola Judgments', CPDP 2022, 1; Lynn/Kim/Gao/Schneider/Pandya/Kyung Lee, 'Regulating Algorithmic Management: A Multi-Stakeholder Study of Challenges in Aligning Software and the Law for Workplace Scheduling' FAccT '25: Proceedings of the 2025 Association for Computing Machinery (ACM) Conference on Fairness, Accountability, and Transparency, New York 2025, p. 547; Martini/Wendehorst, KI-VO: Verordnung über künstliche Intelligenz, München 2024; Mateescu/Nguyen, 'Explainer Algorithmic Management in the Workplace', Data & Society 2019; Minotakis, 'Regulating AI in the workplace: A critique of the EU AI act and the platform work directive through a worker-centred lens' Platforms & Society 2025, 1; Möhlmann/Zalmanson/Henfridsson/Gregory, 'Algorithmic Management of Work on Online Labor Platforms: When Matching Meets Control', MIS Quarterly 2021,1999; Nogarede, No Digitalisation without Representation:

An Analysis of Policies to Empower Labour in the Digital Workplace, Brussels 2021; Peters-Lange, 'Die Richtlinie 2024/2831 zur Verbesserung der Arbeitsbedingungen in der Plattformarbeit', ZESAR 2025, 266; Prassl, Humans as a Service: The Promise and Perils of Work in the Gig Economy, Oxford 2018; Rainone/Aloisi, 'The EU Platform Work Directive, What's new, what's missing, what's next?', etui Policy Brief 2024.06, Brussels 2024; Rhea/Markey/D'Arinzo/Schellmann/Sloane/Squires/Stoyanovich, 'Resume Format, LinkedIn URLs and Other Unexpected Influences on AI Personality Prediction in Hiring: Results of an Audit', AIES '22: Proceedings of the 2022 AAAI/ACM Conference on AI, Ethics, and Society, p. 572; Rosenblat/Stark, 'Algorithmic Labor and Information Asymmetries: A Case Study of Uber's Drivers', IJoC 2016, 3758; Schellmann, The Algorithm: How AI Can Hijack Your Career and Steal Your Future, London 2024; Schneider/Harknett, 'Hard Times: Routine Schedule Unpredictability and Material Hardship among Service Sector Workers', Social Forces 2021, 1682; Scloetzer/Yoshinaga, 'Algorithmic Hiring Systems: Implications and Recommendations for Organisations and Policymakers' in Gill-Pedro/ Moberg (eds), YSEC Yearbook of Socio-Economic Constitutions 2023: Law and the Governance of Artificial Intelligence, Switzerland 2013, p. 213; Sloane, 'Boolean Clashes: Discretionary Decision Making in AI-Driven Recruiting', Communications of the ACM 2025, p. 24; Struna/ Reese, 'Automation and the surveillance driven warehouse in inland southern California' in Wilson/Reese (eds) The Cost of Free Shipping: Amazon in the Global Economy, London 2020, p. 85; Teachout, 'Algorithmic personalized wages', Politics and Society 2023, 436; Wood, Algorithmic management consequences for work organisation and working conditions, Seville 2021.

A. What is meant by Algorithmic Management?

I. Legal definitions of algorithmic management and related terms in the Platform Work Directive

Algorithmic Management is an umbrella term covering several uses of electronic and/or algorithmic technologies and practices to manage work and workers[1].[2] The term is not defined in the Platform Work Directive (the 'Directive') but only appears prominently in the text of the Directive as the title of Chapter III and in Art. 1. Instead, the 1

[1] This chapter uses the term 'worker' in the broader sense, including also self-employed workers. When a distinction according to legal classification is intended, the terms 'employee' and 'self-employed (worker)' will be used, respectively.

[2] Aloisi Int. J. Comp. Labour Law Ind. Relat. 2024, 37 (40).

terms 'automated monitoring' and 'automated decision-making systems' are introduced as legal terms, and defined in detail.[3]

2 In the Directive, the term 'algorithmic management' is used to refer to 'automated monitoring systems and automated decision-making systems powered by algorithms' that perform 'functions that managers [have historically] usually perform[ed] in businesses, such as allocating tasks, pricing individual assignments, determining working schedules, giving instructions, evaluating the work performed, providing incentives or applying adverse treatment' (recital 8).

3 The verb 'manage' is not used in a specific or decisive manner; other verbs that are sometimes used in its place, or to complement it, include 'organise' (see e.g. recital 8, recital 20), 'enable,' or 'facilitate.' Conceptually, 'algorithmic management' can therefore be understood as **the practice of using algorithmic or electronic systems in managing work and workers** (cf. recital 8, sentence 2).

II. Definitions in scholarship

4 In legal scholarship, the term 'algorithmic management' is often interpreted in a similar manner:

5 *Adams-Prassl* et al. define 'algorithmic management systems' to include: the collection or creation of any information (whether identifiable or not) with a view to organising, monitoring, supervising, or evaluating work performance or behaviour; and/or the use of that information to support, augment, or fully automate decisions that affect working conditions, including access to work, earnings, occupational safety and health, working time, promotion and contractual status, and disciplinary as well as termination procedures.[4]

6 *Bernhardt* et al. describe 'algorithmic management' as the use of 'digital' or 'data-driven technologies' for functions such 'as workforce scheduling, coordination, and direction of worker activities'.[5] They describe algorithmic management as part of a cluster of practices – the others being 'worker data collection' and 'electronic monitoring' – that constitute the 'data-driven workplace'.[6]

7 These relatively recent definitions from policy and legal scholarship are also consistent with usages from earlier empirical research in social science and human-computer interaction. For example, *Irani* described 'automated management' strategies used in managing online platform work, wherein pre-programmed 'algorithmic systems' evalute work, release payment, and screen workers for access to different tasks.[7] *Lee* et al. used 'algorithmic management' to refer to 'software algorithms that assume managerial functions' – such as 'allocat[ing], optimiz[ing], and evaluat[ing] work' – 'and [the] surrounding institutional devices that support algorithms in practice'.[8]

---

[3] Gräf SR 2024, 14 (16).
[4] Adams-Prassl et al. ELLJ 2023, 124 (125).
[5] Bernhardt/Kresge/Suleiman ILR Review 2023, 3 (7).
[6] Bernhardt/Kresge/Suleiman ILR Review 2023, 3 et seqq.
[7] Irani New Media & Society 2015, 720 (727).
[8] Lee et al. in ACM, p. 1603.

III. Meaning of the terms 'algorithm'; 'automated monitoring systems', and 'automated decision-making systems'

8 The term 'algorithmic' refers to systems that use data and rules to inform or make decisions. The 'rules' may be explicitly programmed by human programmers, or they may be 'learned'; thus, the term 'algorithmic systems' includes both systems incorporating explicit domain-specific rules and all forms of 'artificial intelligence.'

9 Legally, however, the application of the 'algorithmic management' provisions of Chapter III does not depend on whether or not a particular system or practice constitutes, or is 'to be considered as,' an instance of 'algorithmic management' – as this term is not legally defined. Rather, the provisions apply to '**automated monitoring systems**' and '**automated decision-making systems**.' These are the **decisive legal concepts and terms for the application** of the Chapter III provisions.

1. Automated monitoring systems and automated decision-making systems

10 The Platform Work Directive defines 'automated monitoring systems' and 'automated decision-making systems' as follows (Art. 2(1)(h–i)):

11 'automated monitoring systems' means systems which are used for or which support monitoring, supervising or evaluating, by electronic means, the work performance of persons performing platform work or the activities carried out within the work environment, including by collecting personal data;

12 'automated decision-making systems' means systems which are used to take or support, by electronic means, decisions that **significantly** affect persons performing platform work, including the working conditions of platform workers, in particular decisions affecting their recruitment, their access to and the organisation of work assignments, their earnings, including the pricing of individual assignments, their safety and health, their working time, their access to training, their promotion or its equivalent, and their contractual status including the restriction, suspension or termination of their account.

13 Although the two legal terms are defined separately, they are **not mutually exclusive**. A particular system may be both an 'automated monitoring system' and an 'automated decision-making system.' For example, consider a rating system that collects customer satisfaction information and uses it to allocate work to specific workers (with higher ratings) and suspend or deactivate those with lower ratings. Such a system 'evaluates' work performance, and is therefore an 'automated monitoring system.' However, it also takes decisions and is therefore also an 'automated decision-making system.' One common feature and one difference between decision-making and monitoring systems should be highlighted. As with monitoring systems, even a merely supporting contribution to the decision-making process is sufficient (→ Art. 2 mn. 47). Conversely, the distinction lies in the incorporation of a so-called '**significance threshold**' (→ Art. 2 mn. 50). This means that the decision-making process must 'significantly affect persons performing platform work.' This significance threshold is invariably met when the examples included in Art. 2(1)(i) are demonstrated in the context of the given case.[9]

14 The Directive does not define the term 'automated.' As with the undefined term 'algorithmic,' this omission is not operationally relevant. Rather, the **decisive criterion** in the definitions set out in Art. 2(1)(h–i) **is whether or not a system carries out the relevant function** (i.e., 'monitoring, supervising or evaluating,' in the case of automated moni-

[9] Compare European Commission, Report Expert Group – Transposition of the Directive (EU) 2024/2831 on improving working conditions in platform work (12.1.2026), 21.

toring systems, or 'tak[ing] or support[ing] [...] decisions', in the case of automated decision-making systems) '**by electronic means**.' In defining the terms in this way, the European legislators have opted for a technology-neutral, functional approach that aligns with the views expressed by legal and policy scholars (→ mn. 5 et seqq.).

15 This means that uncertainties or arguments about whether a system is, for example, 'automated' or not, 'fully automated' or merely 'partially automated', or 'algorithmic' are not relevant. If a system **fulfils the functions** set out ('monitoring, supervising or evaluating', or taking or supporting decisions) '**by electronic means**,' the Chapter III provisions apply.[10]

2. Chapter III and the GDPR have different scopes of application

16 The fact that the decisive criterion for the scope of application of the Chapter III provisions is whether or not a system fulfils the relevant functions 'by electronic means' has the result that the scope of application of the Chapter III provisions is both narrower and wider than the scope of application of GDPR in terms of the types of system and data to which they apply, respectively.

17 While the Chapter III provisions apply only to systems carrying out their functions 'by electronic means', the GDPR applies to all processing of personal data regardless of physical medium, so long as the data are incorporated into (or intended to be incorporated into) a 'filing system' (Art. 2(1) GDPR, Art. 4(6) GDPR).[11] A 'filing system' may be electronic or (for example) paper-based; the GDPR applies in either case. The Chapter III provisions, in contrast, apply only to electronic systems.[12]

18 Notably, however, unlike GDPR, applicability of the Chapter III provisions are not dependent on the processing of 'personal data' in the systems in question. Art. 2(1)(h) of the Directive, for example, notes that 'automated monitoring systems' may 'includ[e]' 'collecti[on of] personal data'– but a system need not collect personal data to be considered an 'automated monitoring system'.

B. Algorithmic Management in the Workplace

19 Algorithmic management systems and practices are used to substitute or complement a wide range of managerial activities, including for example **recruiting and hiring, organisation and allocation of work, payment processing, evaluation of work and workers, monitoring and oversight, promotion, discipline**, and **termination.**[13] The following section provides several practical examples to clarify the roles of 'data' and 'personal data' in algorithmic management in the workplace.

---

[10] The European Commission, Report Expert Group – Transposition of the Directive (EU) 2024/2831 on improving working conditions in platform work (12.1.2026), 20. The Commission services explicitly supports the view that the notion of automated monitoring and decision-making systems should be understood as 'broad and autonomous', confirming a functional understanding of these legal terms. Doubts about the effects of a broad functional understanding are being mitigated by the fact that the Directive only applies to digital labour platforms.

[11] Hendrickx/Mangan in Hiessl, p. 1034 (1040).

[12] The European Commission, Report Expert Group – Transposition of the Directive (EU) 2024/2831 on improving working conditions in platform work (12.1.2026), 40.

[13] Rosenblat/Stark IJoC 2016, 3758; see further generally Abraha, p. 10 et seqq.; Adams-Prassl et al. ELLJ 2023, 124 (128 et seqq.); Aloisi/De Stefano 2022, p. 23 et seqq.; Jarrahi et al. Big Data and Society 2021, 1 (2 et seqq.), who see algorithmic management as a sociotechnical concept in the general work context; for a detailed overview of the wide range of managerial functions that algorithmic, data-driven systems can undertake, see Bernhardt/Kresge/Suleiman ILR Review 2023, 3 (5 et seqq.).

In recruiting, algorithmic targeting systems (for example, on social media platforms and digital job boards) may be used to decide who sees what job ads. These systems typically use the personal data of platform users to show them job ads they are expected to be interested in.[14] 20

In hiring, 'applicant tracking systems' and CV screening software are used to decide – in some cases fully automatically – which applicants will 'advance' to later stages of job application and hiring processes. Video-based interviewing software is increasingly used to 'interview' job applicants. In some cases, videos are reviewed by a human hiring manager; in other cases, machine learning or 'artificial intelligence' systems are used automatically to evaluate applicants based on the videos they have submitted.[15] 21

In **work organisation**, shift planning software is commonly used in the service, retail, healthcare, and logistics sectors to allocate shifts to workers – in some cases on a fully automated basis.[16] 22

In **location-based platform work**, especially in transportation and delivery, algorithmic systems automatically 'decide' which workers will be offered jobs based on workers' real-time location and other attributes (many of which are 'personal data').[17] 23

Algorithmic systems relying on quantitative ratings provided by customers and/or colleagues are used to **evaluate worker performance in many sectors**, including in 'white-collar' workplaces where workers are employees; in service-sector work where workers may be employed under 'precarious' (e.g., zero-hours or fixed-term) contracts; and in platform work (both location-based and online) where workers are nominally self-employed. 24

Worker ratings and other criteria are often used by digital labour platforms (especially 'online freelance' platforms) in order to rank workers' profiles when those profiles are displayed as results to potential clients' searches. These ranking and ordering algorithms rely on workers' personal data and directly affect their access to work.[18] 25

Employers may install software on workers' computers, phones, or other electronic devices to **oversee their activity**, for example by monitoring their mouse movement 26

---

[14] Imana/Korolova/Heidemann in ACM, p. 3767–3778; Alexander et al. Int. J. Sel. Asses. 2025, 1; See also for the Netherlands: 'Meta Platforms Ireland Ltd. maakt verboden onderscheid op grond van geslacht bij het tonen van advertenties voor vacatures aan gebruikers van Facebook in Nederland' (mensenrechten 2025) Meta Platforms Ireland Ltd. verbietet Diskriminierung aufgrund des Geschlechts bei der Anzeige von Jobanzeigen an Facebook-Nutzer in den Niederlanden | Niederländisches Institut für Menschenrechte (last accessed: 16.12.2025); for the United States of America see also United States District court for the Northern District of California San Francisco Division 30.7.2020 – case 3:19-cv-07185, Opiotennione v. Facebook, Collection of documents <https://www.courtlistener.com/docket/16408797/opiotennione-v-facebook-inc/> Main complaint <https://storage.courtlistener.com/recap/gov.uscourts.cand.350804/gov.uscourts.cand.350804.1.0.pdf> Amicus brief from Lawyers' Committee for Civil Rights <https://lawyerscommittee.org/wp-content/uploads/2020/07/Opiotennione-v-Facebook-Amicus-Brief-7-10-20.pdf> (all last accessed: 16.12.2025). Compare news coverage of the same issue (various countries): Dotto, 'Facebook enables gender discrimination in job ads, European human rights body rules' (CNN 2025) <https://edition.cnn.com/2025/02/28/tech/facebook-gender-discrimination-europe-ruling-asequals-intl> (last accessed: 16.12.2025); Global Witness, 'How Facebook's ad targeting may be in breach of UK equality and data protection laws' – includes link to EHRC submission (globalwitness 2025) <https://globalwitness.org/en/campaigns/digital-threats/how-facebooks-ad-targeting-may-be-in-breach-of-uk-equality-and-data-protection-laws/> (last accessed: 16.12.2025); Duffy and Dotto, 'People are missing out on job opportunities on Facebook because of gender, research suggests' (CNN 2023) <https://edition.cnn.com/2023/06/12/tech/facebook-job-ads-gender-discrimination-asequals-intl-cmd/index.html> (last accessed: 16.12.2025).

[15] Rhea et al. in ACM, p. 572 et seqq.; Scloetzer/Yoshinaga in Gill-Pedro/ Moberg, p. 213 et seqq.; Schellmann, p. 17 et seqq.; Alexander et al. Int. J. Sel. Asses. 2025, 1; Sloane, p. 24 et seqq.

[16] Schneider/Harknett Social Forces 2021, 1682; Lynn et al., p. 547 et seqq.

[17] Lee et al. in ACM, p. 1603 et seqq.; Adams-Prassl CLLPJ 2019, 123 (129 et seqq., 139 et seqq.); see also Kocher, p. 87 et seqq.

[18] De Stefano Comparative Labor Law & Policy Journal 2019, 15 (24).

or keystroke activity, taking screenshots of their desktop, or recording photos or video through their webcams. The data recorded through this employee monitoring or surveillance software – sometimes called 'bossware' – can be used for a wide range of purposes, including combating fraud and theft or monitoring worker performance. The data can be used to initiate worker 'performance improvement initiatives' or more significant disciplinary action.[19]

27 In warehouses and other physical, in-person work, digital devices may be used to track worker productivity in 'real time' and enforce work quotas and 'pace,' including by warning workers when they have been 'inactive' for 'too long.' The data collected by these devices can be used automatically to **deduct workers' pay or impose other disciplinary measures**, up to and including **termination of the employment contract**.[20]

28 It is important to note that despite the Directive's focus, algorithmic management systems and practices are not limited to the 'gig economy'.[21] They are used increasingly across all sectors of the economy and in all types of work – including low- and high-pay work from service and retail to healthcare and engineering; 'blue-collar' and 'white-collar' work (i.e., manual and 'knowledge' work); in both private and public sectors; and in diverse contractual relationships (i.e., workers under algorithmic management may be employees, self-employed, or in a 'third' or 'intermediate' category such as 'employee-like person' in Germany or 'worker' in the UK).

29 These algorithmic systems and practices in the workplace, while complex in their operation, are generally composed of a **few key features** that work together to direct and control labour:

30 Typically, such systems rely on the **constant data collection** and **surveillance** of workers by technological means; the collected data is then utilised to make decisions without direct human input (**automated or semi-automated decision-making**). This can range from the automatic assignment of the next task to a worker to the deactivation of their account due to the non-achievement of certain performance indicators. The performance of workers is frequently evaluated through the utilisation of simple quantitative metrics, such as the average star rating or the number of tasks completed per hour. These metrics subsequently serve as the primary basis for evaluation (**transfer of performance to rating systems or other metrics**). The systems use subtle incentives and disincentives to influence the behaviour of workers. These could include a modest bonus for working during peak hours or a temporary suspension for declining too many assignments (**behavioural nudges and penalties**).[22]

C. Objectives of Chapter III Algorithmic Management

31 The Platform Work Directive can be seen as having the main goal of **ensuring that digital labour platforms and persons performing platform work are correctly incorporated into existing and novel regulatory frameworks** – especially employment

[19] Aloisi/Gramano Comparative Labor Law & Policy Journal 2019, 95 (105 et seq).

[20] De Stefano Comparative Labor Law & Policy Journal 2019, 15 (23 et seqq.) with further references. Amazon's fulfilment centres are one example of this. Employees' movements are continuously tracked there, and algorithms evaluate errors and primarily enforce increasingly unattainable productivity targets see also Struna/Reese in Wilson, p. 85 et seqq; Minotakis Platforms & Society 2025, 1 (5).

[21] Abraha, p. 10. Algorithmic management is relevant not only to platform work, but also to the wider working context. However, Jarrahi et al. Big Data and Society 2021, 1 (10) argue that the unique characteristics of gig work limit the transferability of current findings on algorithmic management to traditional work settings.

[22] Mateescu/Nguyen, p. 3; Jarrahi et al. Big Data and Society 2021, 1 (4 et seq.).

and labour laws, data protection law, tax and social security, and social dialogue. The Directive recitals themselves set out that the Directive has a 'twofold objective,' 'namely the improvement of working conditions and the protection of personal data' (recital 67).

These correspond to the Directive's two legal bases: the EU's competence to pass legislation relating to the improvement of working conditions (Art. 153 TFEU), and its competence to pass legislation relating to the protection of personal data (Art. 16 TFEU). 32

From a policy rather than purely constitutional perspective, however, the Directive can be seen as having three main goals: 33

- reducing false self-employment in platform work (Chapter II);
- establishing a regulatory framework for algorithmic management in platform work (Chapter III), including improving transparency and human oversight of automated decision-making, and incorporating digital labour platforms into existing frameworks for ensuring occupational health and safety and information and consultation of worker representatives; and
- establishing rights of access to information for relevant authorities, as well as remedies and enforcement procedures (Chapters IV-V).

In the context of the three main goals of the Directive, the objective of Chapter III is to address the **specific risks associated with the use of automated monitoring and decision-making systems in the workplace**. Constant monitoring, evaluation, and analysis of the behaviour of persons performing platform work poses significant **risks to the mental and physical health of** persons performing platform work (Art. 3 ECHR).[23] Persons performing platform work often lack information about how automated systems work, what personal data is being used, and how their behaviour influences the decisions made by automated systems ('**risk of undermining informational self-determination**' Arts. 7, 8 ECHR). This one-sided distribution of control over data exacerbates the **information asymmetry** inherent in the employment relationship. This is compounded by well-documented biases in automated monitoring and decision-making systems.[24] The problem is exacerbated by the tendency of humans to favour the suggestions of automated decision-making systems and to ignore contradictory information from non-automated sources, even if it is correct ('**automation bias**').[25] 34

Chapter III responds to these risks by establishing a regulatory framework for algorithmic management, understood concretely as comprising the two (legally defined) categories of 'automated monitoring' and 'automated decision-making.' 35

Chapter III of the Directive can be seen as having **four main goals**: 36

- To establish **prohibitions** on the collection of certain kinds of data, and certain kinds of data processing (Art. 7, Art. 10(5)).
- To establish **rights to information, data access, and review** for workers and worker representatives:
  - regarding automated monitoring and decision-making systems **generally** (e.g., Art. 9, Art. 14, Art. 15), including a right to data portability (Art. 9(6)); as well as
  - regarding **specific individual decisions**, including a right to explanations for decisions taken or supported by automated systems (Art. 11).
- To establish human **oversight procedures** for automated monitoring and decision-making (e.g., Art. 8, Art. 10), including:

23 Kilhoffer et al., p. 60 et seqq.
24 Kilhoffer et al., p. 272.
25 De Stefano CLLPJ 2019, 1 (14 et seq.).

- data protection impact assessments (Art. 8);
- 'responsible persons', analogous to data protection officers, within platform operating entities, protected from retaliation (Art. 10(2)); and
- involvement of worker representatives (Art. 8(2), Art. 9(4), Art. 10(1), Art. 10(4)).

37 Finally

– To **integrate platform work, and in particular algorithmic management, into existing regulatory frameworks** for:
  - managing and mitigating occupational safety and health risks (Art. 12), and
  - information and consultation of workers' representatives regarding 'substantial changes' (Art. 13).

D. Relation of Chapter III of the Platform Work Directive to the GDPR and AI Act

38 The obligations imposed on digital labour platforms by Chapter III of the Directive interact with the obligations imposed on them by two other important pieces of EU legislation: the GDPR and the AI Act. However, Chapter III relates to these two pieces of legislation in different ways.

I. Chapter III: Algorithmic Management and GDPR

39 While the GDPR establishes a general framework for the protection of natural persons with regard to the processing of their personal data, the Directive lays down specific rules addressing the concerns that are related to the processing of personal data by means of automated monitoring systems or automated decision-making systems in the context of platform work (recital 38).

40 The GDPR can be understood as establishing a 'floor' of personal data protection rights for all 'data subjects.' These rights are realised by imposing certain obligations on the entity who undertakes the processing of the personal data in question. This entity is called the 'controller.' Obligations imposed include a requirement that processing of personal data be fair, accurate, and transparent; a requirement to inform data subjects about personal data being processed and the purposes of that processing; and a requirement to grant certain rights to data subjects, including the right of access to the personal data processed; the right to rectify inaccurate personal data; and the right to obtain human intervention in the event of automated decision-making producing legal or 'similarly significant' effects.

41 The GDPR applies to all processing of personal data, including the processing of personal data of persons performing platform work, irrespective of the nature of the contractual relationship between the platform and the person performing platform work (i.e., irrespective of whether that person is employed or self-employed). In the context of digital labour platforms, persons performing platform work will generally be 'data subjects' and the platform will be the 'controller.' This means that the rights established by the GDPR for all personal data processing apply to algorithmic management in digital labour platforms, at least insofar as the data being processed in that context are 'personal data' in the sense of the GDPR.

42 Data processing in the context of algorithmic management of persons performing platform work will generally concern 'personal data' of those persons in the sense of the

GDPR, as even if it does not 'relate to' those persons in the sense of being 'about' them (i.e., it does not relate to them by virtue of its 'content'), it will likely relate to them by virtue of the purpose or 'impact' or 'effect' of the processing.[26]

43 Despite establishing a 'floor' of data protection rights, the GDPR leaves some situations ambiguous. For example, the meanings of some requirements set out in Arts. 5–6, such as the requirement that personal data be processed 'fairly' (Art. 5(1)(a)), or the meaning of the term 'legitimate' in the 'legitimate interests' legal basis (Art. 6(1)(f)), have been discussed by legal scholars and policymakers as potentially ambiguous, especially in work-related contexts. While Chapter III of the Directive does not clarify all of these ambiguities in the context of platform work, it effectively constitutes a collection of 'more specific rules' for the processing of personal data in the context of platform work (recital 38). Chapter III of the Directive contains supplementary provisions that complement or specify the GDPR.[27] In particular, the Directive establishes more **specific rules** in relation to the GDPR concerning the use of and transparency with regard to automated decision-making (recital 38).[28] The Directive also establishes **additional measures** (i.e., beyond those established by the GDPR) in the context of platform work to safeguard the protection of the personal data of **persons performing platform work**, in particular where decisions are taken or supported by the automated processing of personal data (recital 38).[29]

44 The Directive's precise relation to Art. 88 GDPR, on the other hand, remains disputed. Art. 88 GDPR provides that Member States may, by law or by means of collective agreements, implement more specific rules to ensure the protection of the rights and freedoms in respect of the processing of employees' personal data in the context of employment. The question arises as to whether the provisions of the Directive, insofar as it falls within the scope of the GDPR, constitute 'more specific rules' within the meaning of Art. 88 GDPR or whether the provisions of the Directive are *lex specialis* to the GDPR (see also → Art. 1 mn. 17 et seqq.).

45 Scholars have different views on this point:

46 Some scholars interpret recital 38 as meaning that the provisions of the Directive, and consequently the corresponding national implementation acts, are to be understood as 'specific rules' within the meaning of Art. 88(1) GDPR. As a consequence, the provisions of the Directive would have to be assessed under and in light of Art. 88 GDPR (see also → Art. 1 mn. 17 et seqq.).[30]

47 Others argue that the provisions of the Directive are *lex specialis* in relation to the GDPR and therefore also in relation to Art. 88 GDPR.[31] This would have the consequence that the national implementing acts would only be measured against the provisions of the Directive and not against Art. 88 GDPR. While the terms 'specific rules' and

---

[26] See ECJ 20.12.2017 – case C-434/16, ECLI:EU:C:2017:994 para 34–35 – Nowak v. Data Protection Commissioner; further Art. 29 Working Party Opinion 4/2007 on the concept of personal data, pp. 9–12; Hendrickx/Mangan in Hiessl, p. 1034 (1040).

[27] See also European Commission, Report Expert Group – Transposition of the Directive (EU) 2024/2831 on improving working conditions in platform work (12.1.2026), 39.

[28] See also European Commission, Report Expert Group – Transposition of the Directive (EU) 2024/2831 on improving working conditions in platform work (12.1.2026), 40.

[29] See also European Commission, Report Expert Group – Transposition of the Directive (EU) 2024/2831 on improving working conditions in platform work (12.1.2026), 41: The European Commission explained 'The GDPR already allows Member States to maintain or introduce more specific rules in the employment context, and the Directive does that for the platform economy, and even goes beyond, as it introduces such rules at Union level and extends their scope to include PPPW who are not workers.'

[30] Gruber-Risak/Warter DRdA 2024, 267 (274); also Brameshuber/Höllwarth ASoK 2024, 170 (178); Frank/Heine NZA 2024, 865 (867).

[31] Gräf SR 2025, 14 (17); Daum in Giesen/Junker/Rieble, p. 91 (104 et seq.).

'lex specialis' have the same linguistic meaning, in the context of the Directive, the discussion essentially concerns a question of legal basis or competence, and consequently, a question of the dependency of the Directive's provisions on Art. 88(1) GDPR. If the Directive, and consequently a national implementation act, were based on Art. 88(1) GDPR, each such law would be limited to, and interpreted in the context of, the implementation of more specific rules to ensure the protection of rights and freedoms with regard to the processing of employees' personal data in the context of employment. Instead, a 'true lex specialis' understanding would mean that the rules of the Directive are independent of the GDPR and override the GDPR provisions where they are more specific and conclusive. The rules of the GDPR would only apply where the Directive refers to the GDPR or where a question is not specifically regulated in the Directive (for a detailed discussion see → Art. 1 mn. 17 et seqq.).

48 Regardless of which scholarly interpretation is adopted, the following applies:

49 The rules set out in Art. 7 of the Directive, establishing prohibitions on the processing of some types of personal data of persons performing platform work, and on some processing purposes, can be understood as '**more specific rules**' relating to the matters covered by Art. 9 GDPR, which establishes '**special categories of personal data**' and prohibits processing of data in those categories except under specific circumstances (see also → Art. 7 mn. 2 et seq.).

50 Art. 8 (see also recital 43) establishes that personal data processing in the context of algorithmic management in digital labour platforms is to be considered as posing 'a high risk to the rights and freedoms of persons performing platform work' and therefore to require a data protection impact assessment as set out in Art. 35 GDPR.

51 It additionally 'establishes **more specific rules**' regarding the consultation of persons performing platform work and their representatives in the context of data-protection impact assessments' (recital 43). Similarly:

52 Art. 9(1–5) can be understood as setting out '**more specific rules**' relating to the matters addressed in Art. 12–15 GDPR[32] (see also → Art. 9 mn. 3 et seqq.); namely, information to be provided regarding the data processing in general, as well as access to copies of personal data undergoing processing;

53 Art. 9(6) can be understood as setting out '**more specific rules**' relating to the matters addressed in Art. 20 GDPR (see also → Art. 9 mn. 9); namely, while Art. 20 GDPR sets out rules regarding the portability (i.e., the right to receive machine-readable copies) of personal data generally (specifically, the right to portability of personal data 'provided' by the data subject), Art. 9(6) establishes that persons performing platform work have a right to portability of all personal data 'generated through their performance of work' in the context of a platform's algorithmic management systems (not only those they have 'provided'); and

54 Art. 10(5) and Art. 11 can be understood as setting out '**more specific rules**' relating to the matters addressed in Art. 22 GDPR (see also → Art. 10 mn. 4; → Art. 11 mn. 6); namely, limitations on legally or economically significant automated decision-making, and rights to explanation and human review of automated decisions if they are taken.

II. Chapter III Algorithmic Management and AI Act

55 The AI Act aims to 'promote the uptake of human-centric and trustworthy artificial intelligence (AI)' systems, while ensuring that the deployment and use of those systems

---

[32] Compare European Commission, Report Expert Group – Transposition of the Directive (EU) 2024/2831 on improving working conditions in platform work (12.1.2026), 49.

respects and protects 'health, safety, [and] fundamental rights' (Art. 1 AI Act). To this end, the AI Act establishes obligations on a wide range of actors in the 'supply chain' of AI systems, including 'provider[s]', 'deployer[s]', and 'operator[s]' (Art. 3 AI Act).

56 The AI Act defines 'AI system' broadly – namely, as:

> 'a machine-based system that is designed to operate with varying levels of autonomy and that may exhibit adaptiveness after deployment, and that, for explicit or implicit objectives, infers, from the input it receives, how to generate outputs such as predictions, content, recommendations, or decisions that can influence physical or virtual environments' (Art. 3(1)).

57 Under this definition, 'algorithmic management' systems, including those in digital labour platforms, are likely to be considered 'AI systems.'[33]

58 The obligations established by the Act on providers, deployers, and operators of AI systems include absolute prohibitions on certain practices, including:

- 'subliminal' or 'purposefully manipulative or deceptive techniques' that impair someone's ability to 'make an informed decision' and that thereby lead to 'significant harm' (Art. 5(1)(a));
- 'exploit[ing] any of the vulnerabilities of a natural person or a specific group of persons due to their age, disability or a specific social or economic situation' in a manner that 'materially distort[s]' their behaviour and leads to 'significant harm' (Art. 5(1)(b);
- 'social scor[ing]' systems (Art. 5(1)(c));
- AI-generated 'risk assessments' of the risk that a person will commit a criminal offence based on characteristics other than 'objective and verifiable facts directly linked to a criminal activity' (Art. 5(1)(d));
- **AI systems for emotion inference in workplaces** or education institutions (Art. 5(1)(f)); and
- AI systems that use biometric data to infer sensitive personal data as defined in Art. 9 GDPR (Art. 5(1)(g)).

59 Empirical research indicates that some of these practices may be in use in some digital labour platforms. The legal scholar and ethnographer *Veena Dubal*, for example, documents 'algorithmic wage discrimination,' in which some platform operators in the United States use algorithmic systems, apparently including profiling techniques, to offer different amounts of pay to different persons performing tasks through digital labour platforms – even when the tasks they perform are substantially similar.[34] Computer scientist and ethnographer *Lilly Irani* documents use by digital labour platforms of error-prone algorithmic systems that suspend workers' accounts on suspicion of fraud (where procedures for establishing 'suspicion' are defined unilaterally by the platform), even in cases where no 'objective and verifiable acts' linked to criminal activity are present (indeed because no criminal activity has occurred).[35] Under the AI Act such practices would likely be prohibited in the EU.

60 Chapter III Section 2 of the AI Act establishes specific requirements for 'high-risk AI systems.' A 'high-risk AI system' is defined as an AI system that is either:

---

[33] See also European Commission, Report Expert Group – Transposition of the Directive (EU) 2024/2831 on improving working conditions in platform work (12.1.2026), 42.

[34] Dubal Columbia Law Rev. 2023, 1929 et seqq. See additionally Teachout Politics and Society 2023, 436.

[35] Irani in Nyabola/Owen/Tworek, 'When managers rely on algorithms of suspicion: fraud logics and their fallouts' (Centre for international Governance Innovation 2022) https://www.cigionline.org/articles/when-managers-rely-on-algorithms-of-suspicion-fraud-logics-and-their-fallouts/ (last accessed: 16.12.2025).

- 'intended to be used as a safety component of a product,' or 'is itself a product', and is subject to existing EU product safety legislation (Art. 6(1) AI Act)[36]; or
- listed in Annex III of the Act (Art. 6(2) AI Act).

61 Annex III High-Risk systems referred to in Art. 6(2) of the AI Act lists systems making use of specific types of data (biometrics, Annex III, 1) as well as systems in different areas that could be described as 'application domains' for AI systems, including 'critical infrastructure,' education and training, and – most relevant in considering the relationship between the AI Act and the Directive – 'employment, workers' management and access to self-employment' (Annex III 4). These are primarily AI systems intended to be used 'for the recruitment or selection' (Annex III, 4(a) of the AI Act), for 'making decisions on promotion and termination, as well as for task allocation, monitoring or evaluation of persons in work-related contractual relationships' (Annex III, point 4(b) of the AI Act).

62 Annex III 4 means that any algorithmic management system considered an 'AI system' is also likely to be considered 'high-risk.' This includes but is not limited to algorithmic management systems in the context of digital labour platforms. Such systems are likely to be considered 'high-risk' regardless of the nature of the employment or self-employment relationship between the worker (or 'person performing work') and the employer or platform. The requirements for 'high-risk AI systems' established in Chapter III Section 2 of the AI Act will therefore apply to such systems in almost all cases.[37]

63 Most relevant for algorithmic management systems in digital labour platforms may be the requirements to:

- provide for human oversight of high-risk AI systems, with the purpose of 'aim[ing] to prevent or minimise the risks to health, safety or fundamental rights that may emerge when a high-risk AI system is used in accordance with its intended purpose or under conditions of reasonably foreseeable misuse' (Art. 14 AI Act);
- ensure that high-risk AI systems 'achieve an appropriate level of accuracy, robustness, and cybersecurity' (Art. 15 AI Act) – where of particular interest in the context of algorithmic management systems is the question of accuracy, as such systems may make inappropriate or even unlawfully discriminatory decisions based on inaccurate or incomplete data or logic;
- before putting a high-risk AI system into service or using it in the workplace, inform workers' representatives and the affected employees that they will be subject to the use of the high-risk AI system (Art. 26(7) AI Act) (applicable to deployers who are employers); and
- where outputs of high-risk AI systems are used in decision-making, provide 'clear and meaningful explanations of the role of the AI system in the decision-making procedure and the main elements of the decision taken' to persons adversely affected by the decision (Art. 86 AI Act).[38] However it should be noted that this article **only applies to the 'affected person' and does not extend to workers' representatives**.[39]

[36] For example, toys. Installing an AI system as a safety component automatically results in a high-risk system.

[37] Minotakis Platforms & Society 2025, 1 (4).

[38] Critical Kaminski and Malgieri, The right to explanation in the AI Act. University of Colorado Law Legal Studies Research Paper No. 25-9, p. 8 et seqq.

[39] Minotakis Platforms & Society 2025, 1 (4).

Chapter III Section 2 of the AI Act also establishes obligations regarding the production and management of technical documentation relating to high-risk AI systems (Arts. 10, 11, 12 AI Act); cooperation with responsible authorities (Arts. 21, 77 AI Act); and the establishment of risk and quality management systems (Arts. 9, 17 AI Act), including ongoing 'test and validation procedures' (Art. 17(1)(d) AI Act). 64

These requirements and obligations attach primarily to AI system 'providers' (Art. 16 AI Act). However, other entities – 'distributor[s], importer[s], deployer[s] or other third-part[ies]' – are considered to be providers for the purposes of compliance with the obligations under certain circumstances (Art. 25 AI Act). Additionally, these other entities are also explicitly subject to specific obligations, even if they are not considered providers (Arts. 23, 24, 26 AI Act). 65

Taken collectively, these requirements and obligations create a system or network of interlocking rights and procedural checks that can be understood as aiming to reduce the risk that an AI system will be used in a way that adversely impacts the fundamental rights of natural persons, including in workplace or self-employment contexts such as digital labour platforms. 66

These requirements, obligations, rights, and checks overlap to some extent with those set out in Chapter III of the Directive. 67

Recital 9 clarifies that the AI Act 'should not affect the provisions aiming to improve working conditions in platform work laid down in a Directive of the European Parliament and of the Council on improving working conditions in platform work'. The relationship with the Directive is governed by Art. 2(11) of the AI Act, which allows Member States to provide for more favourable legislation in favour of employees in relation to the use of AI systems. In the event of any overlap, the more favourable provisions apply.[40] 68

For example, the prohibition on emotion inference in workplace and educational contexts established by Art. 5(1)(f) AI Act can be understood as overlapping with the prohibition on processing personal data on the 'emotional or psychological state of a person performing platform work', established in Art. 7(1)(a), and the prohibition of drawing conclusions about a person's emotional or psychological state, established in Art. 7(1)(e) of the Directive.[41] Since the Directive does not allow for exceptions, in particular for medical or safety reasons, it goes beyond Art. 5(1)(f) AI Act. Furthermore, Art. 7(1)(b), (c), (d) and (f) of the Directive contain further restrictions on the collection and processing of personal data by digital labour platforms (see also → Art. 7 mn. 2 et seqq.). As the Directive must be implemented into national law, these implementation acts are to be regarded in accordance with the principle of Art. 2(11) AI Act as additional restrictions under Art. 5 AI Act.[42] 69

Similarly, the information rights set out in Art. 9 of the Platform Work Directive are much more wide-reaching than those in Art. 26(7) AI Act. For instance, Art. 9(1) gives persons performing platform work and their representatives the right to access information about automated monitoring and decision-making systems. This includes details such as categories of monitored data and actions, the aim of the monitoring, categories of decisions taken, categories of data and main parameters considered by such automated systems, and the grounds for decisions to restrict, suspend, or terminate the account of a person performing platform work. Additionally, Art. 11(1) grants persons perform- 70

[40] Peters-Lange ZESAR 2025, 266 (273).
[41] Aloisi/Potocka-Sionek/Ratti CML Rev. 2025, 1407 (1440).
[42] Däubler, mn. 250za; Wendehorst in Wendehorst/Martini KI-Verordnung Art. 5 mn. 104.

ing platform work the right to discuss any decision made or supported by an automated system.[43]

71 Although at first glance Art. 14 AI Act appears to set out similar requirements to Art. 10(1) and (3), Art. 10 of the Platform Work Directive is more worker-centred. In contrast to Art. 14 AI Act, it explicitly involves employee representatives in the supervisory process.

72 Overlaps are also possible with regard to the right to an explanation of the decision-making process in individual cases under Art. 86(1) AI Act and the right to human review under Art. 11 of the Directive. However, Art. 86(3) AI Act clarifies that rights to an explanation are subsidiary to provisions in other Union legal acts. Accordingly, in the platform context Art. 86 AI Act must be read subject to Art. 11(1) and (2) of the Directive.[44]

73 Considered as a whole, however, the prohibitions and rights set out in Chapter III of the Directive focus largely (although not entirely) on prohibitions and rights regarding the processing of personal data of persons performing platform work, while the prohibitions and requirements established by the AI Act apply to AI systems and the entities that provide and deploy them.

74 Consequently Art. 86 AI Act creates a general right to an explanation for individual decisions produced by high-risk AI systems regardless of the role of 'personal data'.

75 The prohibitions and requirements established by the AI Act can be read as being informed by a more profound alertness on the part of the co-legislators of the sophistication of AI systems (e.g., the possibility for subliminal techniques to erode natural persons' ability to make informed decisions) and the possibility for sophisticated AI techniques to pose serious risks to fundamental rights.

76 These differences can be explained by the fact that the AI Act was drafted subsequent to the Directive, after the capabilities of increasingly sophisticated AI systems – and the risks to fundamental rights posed by such systems – had become clearer in public and policy discourse.

77 The definition of 'AI system,' however, may not be completely unambiguous. While unlikely, it is conceivable that some algorithmic management systems in digital labour platforms could be successfully argued not to constitute 'AI systems.' If a system is not an 'AI system', none of the provisions of the AI Act apply, even if the system produces or influences decisions taken in a 'high-risk' domain such as employment or access to self-employment.[45] The protections set out by Chapter III of the Directive should therefore not be understood as a simple subset of those established by the AI Act.[46]

78 Finally and importantly, the Directive has a different orientation than the AI Act. The AI Act is fundamentally a piece of product safety legislation; it aims to promote the adoption within the EU market of new technology while ensuring it is 'safe'.[47] The Directive, in contrast, is a piece of legislation concerned primarily with the protection of the

[43] Minotakis Platforms & Society 2025, 1 (6).

[44] Gräf SR 2025, 14 (33).

[45] Wendehorst in Wendehorst/Martini KI-Verordnung Art. 3 mn. 4.

[46] See European Commission, Report Expert Group – Transposition of the Directive (EU) 2024/2831 on improving working conditions in platform work (12.1.2026), 42.

[47] Compare European Commission, Report Expert Group – Transposition of the Directive (EU) 2024/2831 on improving working conditions in platform work (12.1.2026), 42: 'The Commission services explained that the AI Act sets standards for the safety of AI technology developed and deployed in the EU economy, including in the platform economy, and the Platform Work Directive provides specific protections in relation to how the deployed systems, going beyond AI systems, are then used by DLPs in the platform work environment.'

fundamental rights of persons performing platform work.[48] Put shortly, the Directive is a human rights instrument, while the AI Act is focused on product safety. While some scholars have criticised the AI Act on this ground, it seems possible that in practice – provided appropriate and full development of the 'harmonised standards' and other mechanisms foreseen in the AI Act (see e.g. Art. 40), and an effective enforcement regime – the two pieces of legislation will **complement and support** each other.

E. Conclusion

The Platform Work Directive provides a detailed regulatory framework for algorithmic management. In this regard, Chapter III of the Directive sets out four main policy objectives. First, to prohibit the collection of certain types of data and data processing that have been deemed by the legislators to pose the greatest risk to the fundamental rights of persons performing platform work and that cannot plausibly serve a legitimate interest of the digital labour platform. Even if such an interest were present, it could not outweigh the risks to the fundamental rights of persons performing platform work. These prohibitions are primarily set out in Art. 7 and Art. 10(5), as well as (for 'platform workers' only) Art. 12(3). Secondly, it sets out rights to information, data access and review for persons performing platform work and their representatives regarding algorithmic management systems in general and specific individual decisions. Thirdly, procedures for the human oversight of the design, deployment and operation of algorithmic management systems must be established. Finally, the objective is to integrate platform work, particularly algorithmic management, into existing regulatory frameworks, especially those concerning occupational safety and health, as well as information and consultation. 79

On paper at least, the provisions of Chapter III appear to achieve the major policy objectives, with only one potentially significant exception. The use of algorithmic management systems by digital labour platforms that impose 'undue pressure' leading to health and safety risks is prohibited, but this only applies to 'platform workers' – i.e. persons performing work in the context of an employment relationship (see Art. 2(1)(d)), not to all 'persons performing platform work', due to the legal basis (→ Art. 1 mn. 4 et seqq.). 80

However, the Directive does not prevent Member States from providing similar protections for persons performing platform work who are, or may be, genuinely self-employed. From a policy perspective, a strong argument can be made that Member States should apply the Art. 12(3) prohibition to all persons performing platform work, regardless of their employment status. This would prevent perverse incentives for digital labour platforms and ensure a 'level playing field' for all platform workers. 81

At the same time, the Platform Work Directive creates an 'uneven playing field', providing different levels of protection with respect to algorithmic management for persons performing platform work compared to other types of working persons, especially as algorithmic management practices have grown beyond platform work into the wider economy. The limitation of the Chapter III provisions arises from the specific scope of application of the Directive itself – namely, platform work. This is a historical or 'path dependent' outcome of the evolution of the research and policy discourses around both platform work and algorithmic management. Researchers and some research-active policymakers were already in 2017 aware that algorithmic management was expanding beyond the platform economy. However, it was not until the middle of the Covid 82

[48] See further Aloisi/De Stefano ELLJ 2023, 283 et seq.

pandemic that the phenomenon grew very significantly and attained broader visibility both to policymakers and the general public; and by this time, political momentum at EU level had already accumulated around a Directive specific to platform work which would include provisions relating to algorithmic management. However, Member States are not constrained in the same way and have the opportunity to establish sensible, reasonably-balanced protections around algorithmic management across the entire labour market simply by extending the provisions of Chapter III to all working persons.

83 Finally, the provisions of Chapter III address some ambiguities relating to application of GDPR in the workplace context. While Art. 88 GDPR establishes that Member States may set out 'more specific rules' relating to processing of personal data in the workplace, few have done so – and those that have struggled to do so correctly.[49] In some countries, including Germany, significant political interest has developed in creating 'workplace data protection rules' according to Art. 88 GDPR – and in Germany in particular the matter has even been inscribed in governing coalition agreements. However, this apparent political will has not yet been translated into consensus and legislative action. Applying the provisions of Chapter III to 'all working persons' could thus achieve a significant level of protection without protracted legal and political negotiation on the finer points of workplace data protection.

Article 7
Limitations on the processing of personal data by means of automated monitoring systems or automated decision-making systems

1. Digital labour platforms shall not, by means of automated monitoring systems or automated decision-making systems:

(a) process any personal data on the emotional or psychological state of a person performing platform work;
(b) process any personal data in relation to private conversations, including exchanges with other persons performing platform work and the representatives of persons performing platform work;
(c) collect any personal data of a person performing platform work while that person is not offering or performing platform work;
(d) process personal data to predict the exercise of fundamental rights, including the freedom of association, the right of collective bargaining and action or the right to information and consultation as laid down in the Charter;
(e) process any personal data to infer the racial or ethnic origin, migration status, political opinions, religious or philosophical beliefs, disability, state of health, including chronic disease or HIV status, emotional or psychological state, trade union membership, sex life or sexual orientation;
(f) process any biometric data, as defined in Article 4, point (14), of Regulation (EU) 2016/679, of a person performing platform work to establish that person's identity by comparing that data to stored biometric data of natural persons in a database.

2. This Article shall apply to all persons performing platform work from the start of the recruitment or selection procedure.

[49] Abraha MLR 2024, 484 et seqq.

3. In addition to automated monitoring systems and automated decision-making systems, this Article shall also apply where digital labour platforms use automated systems taking or supporting decisions that affect persons performing platform work in any manner.

Recital (8) Automated monitoring systems and automated decision-making systems powered by algorithms increasingly replace functions that managers usually perform in businesses, such as allocating tasks, pricing individual assignments, determining working schedules, giving instructions, evaluating the work performed, providing incentives or applying adverse treatment. Digital labour platforms, in particular, use such algorithmic systems as a standard way of organising and managing platform work through their infrastructure. Persons performing platform work subject to such algorithmic management often do not have access to information on how the algorithms work, which personal data are used or how the behaviour of those persons affects decisions taken by automated systems. Furthermore, workers' representatives, other representatives of persons performing platform work, labour inspectorates and other competent authorities do not have access to such information. Moreover, persons performing platform work often do not know the reasons for decisions taken or supported by automated systems and are not able to obtain an explanation for those decisions, to discuss those decisions with a human contact person, to contest those decisions or to seek rectification or, where relevant, redress.
Recital (38) While Regulation (EU) 2016/679 establishes the general framework for the protection of natural persons with regard to the processing of personal data, it is necessary to lay down specific rules addressing the concerns that are related to the processing of personal data by means of automated monitoring systems or automated decision-making systems in the context of platform work. Article 88 of Regulation (EU) 2016/679 already provides that Member States may, by law or by means of collective agreements, provide for more specific rules to ensure the protection of the rights and freedoms in respect of the processing of employees' personal data in the employment context. This OJ L, 11.11.2024 EN ELI: http://data.europa.eu/eli/dir/2024/2831/oj 7/26 Directive provides for more specific safeguards concerning the processing of personal data by means of automated systems in the context of platform work, thereby providing for a higher level of protection of the personal data of persons performing platform work. In particular, this Directive establishes more specific rules in relation to Regulation (EU) 2016/679 concerning the use of and transparency with regard to automated decision-making. This Directive also establishes additional measures in relation to Regulation (EU) 2016/679 in the context of platform work to safeguard the protection of the personal data of persons performing platform work, in particular where decisions are taken or supported by the automated processing of personal data. Terms relating to the protection of personal data in this Directive should be understood in light of the definitions set out in Regulation (EU) 2016/679.
Recital (39) Articles 5, 6 and 9 of Regulation (EU) 2016/679 require that personal data be processed in a lawful, fair and transparent manner. This implies certain restrictions on the manner in which digital labour platforms are able to process personal data by means of automated monitoring systems or automated decision-making systems. Nonetheless, in the particular case of platform work, the consent of persons performing platform work to the processing of their personal data cannot be assumed to be freely given. Persons performing platform work often do not have a genuine free choice or are not able to refuse or withdraw consent without detriment to their contractual relationship, given the power imbalance between the person performing platform work and the digital labour platform. Therefore, digital labour platforms should not process the personal data of persons performing platform work on the basis that a person performing platform work has given consent to the processing of his or her personal data.

The Directive prohibits the processing of certain personal data by means of automated monitoring or automated decision-making systems which pose a high risk to the privacy of persons performing platform work.[1] Non-personal data, such as fully anonymised data, can be processed. Other means of processing (non-electronic processing) remain permissible if authorised under the GDPR.[2] 1

Art. 7(1)(a)-(f) of the Directive addresses these privacy risks by **prohibiting** the processing of certain types of personal data from the start of the recruitment or selection procedure, including any personal data relating to private conversations, health, and 2

[1] Adams-Prassl et al. ELLJ 2023, 124 (130).
[2] European Commission, Report Expert Group – Transposition of the Directive (EU) 2024/2831 on improving working conditions in platform work (12.1.2026), 40.

psychological or emotional state, and any personal data collected while the person is not performing or offering platform work. This provision not only creates legal certainty, but also limits the scope of argumentation for platforms that would otherwise arise from the general clauses of the GDPR. It furthermore ensures technological neutrality by shifting from a focus on categories of data alone to the purposes for which processing takes place.

3 While the GDPR also prohibits the processing of these categories of personal data, such as the processing of personal data revealing trade union membership (Art. 9(1) GDPR), it also provides a catalogue of exceptions in its Art. 9(2). For example, Art. 9(2) (a) GDPR establishes a prohibition regarding the processing of special categories of personal data, unless the data subject has given explicit consent. The Directive, in contrast, **excludes the possibility of consent** in recital 39. The reason given is that it cannot be assumed that the consent of persons performing platform work to the processing of their personal data is freely given.[3] Persons performing platform work often do not have a real choice or are unable to refuse or withdraw their consent without affecting their contractual relationship due to the power imbalance between the person performing platform work and the digital labour platform.[4] Therefore, digital labour platforms must not process the personal data of persons performing platform work on the basis that the latter have consented to the processing of their personal data.[5]

4 Art. 7(1)(a) prohibits the use by digital labour platforms of automated monitoring or decision-making systems to process any personal data on the emotional or psychological state of a person performing platform work.

5 Art. 7(1)(b) prohibits digital labour platforms from processing personal data relating to **private conversations** on the digital devices of persons performing platform work, including exchanges with other persons performing platform work and their representatives. Art. 7(1)(b) must be strictly distinguished from Art. 20. Private communication channels cannot simultaneously be subject to automated monitoring or decision-making systems (→ Art. 20 mn. 65). When digital labour platforms provide communication channels via their own infrastructure, processing personal data in connection with exchanges between persons performing platform work and their representatives is unavoidable. However, Art. 20 concerns private communication channels, which should not be subject to any automated monitoring or decision-making system.[6]

6 Art. 7(1)(c) prohibits digital labour platforms from collecting personal data of persons performing platform work while they are not offering or performing platform work (e.g., geolocalisation data of persons performing platform work to monitor whether they are attending protest activities, or at any time while not performing or offering work), meaning while persons performing platform work are not 'logged in' to the platform or application.[7] This prohibition gives rise to the question of the conditions under which digital labour platforms may proactively offer work assignments to inactive workers (e.g. 'push notifications'). In practice, actively offering work assignments should be permissible **as long as no personal data is collected**. This can be done, for example, by sending

[3] Adams-Prassl et al. ELLJ 2023, 124 (132).

[4] Eurofound, 'Employee Monitoring and Surveillance: The Challenges of Digitalisation', Research report (2020), 7.

[5] However, this issue remains unresolved in the report of the Expert Group. European Commission, Report Expert Group – Transposition of the Directive (EU) 2024/2831 on improving working conditions in platform work (12.1.2026), 41.

[6] European Commission, Report Expert Group – Transposition of the Directive (EU) 2024/2831 on improving working conditions in platform work (12.1.2026), 40.

[7] European Commission, Report Expert Group – Transposition of the Directive (EU) 2024/2831 on improving working conditions in platform work (12.1.2026), 40.

an email, text message or push notification to the employee's mobile phone via the platform app, provided that the worker has activated this function.

7 Conversely, this also means that as soon as the person performing platform work responds to the offer, they are once again performing or offering platform work and their personal data can be collected. Therefore, Art. 7(1)(c) does not prevent the mass collection of personal data for monitoring and evaluating the performance of persons performing platform worker **during working hours**, or for analysing their behaviour (for example, to measure their reaction time). This problem is addressed in Art. 12(3), which prohibits the use of automated monitoring and decision-making systems in a way that exerts 'undue pressure' on platform workers or otherwise puts their 'safety and physical and mental health' at risk (→ Art. 12 mn. 2). Accordingly, Art. 12(3) should also be considered part of the list of 'red lines,' or prohibitions, established by the Directive.[8]

8 Moreover, the Directive moves beyond a focus on special categories of data by prohibiting the processing of workers' data for the purpose of predicting the exercise of fundamental rights such as freedom of association and the right to collective bargaining under Arts. 12, 27 and 28 ECHR (Art. 7 (d)). While Art. 9(1) GDPR would apply in the case of an employer trying to determine current union membership, it may not apply to an employer trying to predict the likelihood of future union organising activity.[9] Art. 7(1)(e) of the Directive also goes beyond Art. 9 GDPR. The former adds the data categories of 'migration status' and 'emotional and psychological state', and prohibits not only the processing of such data, but also any processing of personal data that allows inferences to be drawn regarding 'racial or ethnic origin, migration status, political opinions, religious or philosophical beliefs, disability, state of health, including chronic illness or HIV infection, emotional or psychological state, trade union membership, [or] sexual life or sexual orientation.'[10] In other words, the Platform Work Directive not only prohibits the processing of the aforementioned special categories of data, but also any data processing aimed at drawing conclusions about them without consent.

9 Art. 7(1)(f) prohibits digital labour platforms from processing any biometric data. However, this does not prevent digital labour platforms from conducting biometric verification (recital 41). Recital 42 clarifies that biometric-based data constitutes personal data, but not biometric data. Accordingly, biometric-based data is subject to the prohibitions of Art. 7(1)(a)–(e), but not Art. 7(1)(f).[11]

10 According to Art. 7(2), the prohibitions outlined in Art. 7(1) apply from the start of the recruitment or selection procedure.

11 Art. 7(3) extends the material scope of the prohibitions to include automated monitoring and/or decision-making systems. This covers all automated systems that make or support decisions that impact persons performing platform work in 'any manner' (see also Arts. 9(1)(c) and 12(4)).[12]

---

[8] Aloisi/Potocka-Sionek/Rati CML Rev. 2025, 1407 (1424).

[9] Adams-Prassl et al. ELLJ 2023, 124 (131).

[10] Examples include the inference of trade union membership or health data from geolocation data (e.g. presence at trade union activities or at a hospital). See European Commission, Report Expert Group – Transposition of the Directive (EU) 2024/2831 on improving working conditions in platform work (12.1.2026), 40.

[11] See European Commission, Report Expert Group – Transposition of the Directive (EU) 2024/2831 on improving working conditions in platform work (12.1.2026), 40.

[12] See European Commission, Report Expert Group – Transposition of the Directive (EU) 2024/2831 on improving working conditions in platform work (12.1.2026), 41.

Article 8
Data-protection impact assessment

1. The processing of personal data by a digital labour platform by means of automated monitoring systems or automated decision-making systems is a type of processing which is likely to result in a high risk to the rights and freedoms of natural persons within the meaning of Article 35(1) of Regulation (EU) 2016/679. When carrying out, pursuant to that provision, the assessment of the impact of the processing of personal data by automated monitoring systems or automated decision-making systems on the protection of personal data of persons performing platform work, including on the limitations of processing pursuant to Article 7 of this Directive, digital labour platforms, acting as controllers as defined in Article 4, point (7), of Regulation (EU) 2016/679, shall seek the views of persons performing platform work and their representatives.
2. Digital labour platforms shall provide the assessment as referred to in paragraph 1 to workers' representatives.

Recital (43) The processing of personal data by automated monitoring systems or automated decision-making systems used by digital labour platforms is likely to result in a high risk to the rights and freedoms of persons performing platform work. Therefore, digital labour platforms should always carry out a data-protection impact assessment in accordance with the requirements laid down in Article 35 of Regulation (EU) 2016/679. Taking into account the effects that decisions taken by automated decision-making systems have on persons performing platform work, in particular platform workers, this Directive establishes more specific rules regarding the consultation of persons performing platform work and their representatives in the context of data-protection impact assessments.

1 According to Art. 8 of the Directive, there is an **irrebuttable presumption** that the processing of personal data by a digital labour platform using automated monitoring or decision-making systems is likely to result in a high risk to the rights and freedoms of the person performing platform work and therefore triggers the obligations of **digital labour platforms** to carry out a data protection impact assessment pursuant to Art. 35(1) GDPR (see also recital 43 sequence 2: 'digital labour platforms should **always** carry out a data-protection impact assessment').[1]

Digital labour platforms acting as controllers, as defined in Art. 4(7) GDPR, are obliged to 'seek the views of persons performing platform work and their representatives' during a data protection impact assessment for automated monitoring or decision-making systems. While the Directive does not specify exactly what this involvement entails, the Commission services clarified in the Report of the Expert Group that those performing platform work and their representatives must be actively involved in a way that enables them to contribute their own input (see for the term 'input' → Art. 15 mn. 33).[2]

2 According to Art. 8(2), digital labour platforms are obliged to provide the data protection impact assessment to workers' representatives, as well as to the representatives of the persons performing platform work (Art. 15). The Commission service confirmed that platform workers are initially excluded from receiving the data protection impact

[1] See in this regard, European Commission, Report Expert Group – Transposition of the Directive (EU) 2024/2831 on improving working conditions in platform work (2026), 43.
[2] See in this regard, European Commission, Report Expert Group – Transposition of the Directive (EU) 2024/2831 on improving working conditions in platform work (2026), 44.

assessment directly. However, the Commission service emphasised that the Directive sets minimum standards, and that Member States are free to extend these rights further.[3]

Art. 15 of the Directive establishes collective rights for representatives of persons performing platform work, which can be summarised as follows (see → Art. 15 mn. 30): First, representatives of persons performing platform work may initiate the procedure for determining the correct employment status in accordance with Art. 5(4) (right of initiative). Second, their views will be sought in the context of the data protection impact assessment pursuant to Art. 8(2) and Art. 8(1), and the assessments shall be made available to them. Third, pursuant to Art. 9(1) and Art. 9(4), they have the right to request at any time full and detailed information on the use of automated monitoring and decision-making systems. Fourth, they have the right to be informed about the evaluation of the impact of individual decisions taken or supported by automated monitoring systems and automated decision-making systems on persons performing platform work (Art. 10(4) and Art. 15). Fifth, according to Art. 11(2), they may request that automated decisions be reviewed by a human being (Art. 11(1)).[4] 3

Article 9
Transparency with regard to automated monitoring systems and automated decision-making systems

1. Member States shall require digital labour platforms to inform persons performing platform work, platform workers' representatives and, upon request, national competent authorities, of the use of automated monitoring systems or automated decision-making systems.
That information shall concern:

(a) as regards automated monitoring systems:
- **i. the fact that such systems are in use or are in the process of being introduced;**
- **ii. the categories of data and action monitored, supervised or evaluated by such systems, including evaluation by the recipient of the service;**
- **iii. the aim of the monitoring and how the system is to carry out that monitoring;**
- **iv. the recipients or categories of recipient of the personal data processed by such systems and any transmission or transfer of such personal data, including within a group of undertakings;**

(b) as regards automated decision-making systems:
- **i. the fact that such systems are in use or are in the process of being introduced;**
- **ii. the categories of decision that are taken or supported by such systems;**
- **iii. the categories of data and the main parameters that such systems take into account and the relative importance of those main parameters in the automated decision-making, including the way in which the personal data or behaviour of the person performing platform work influence the decisions;**
- **iv. the grounds for decisions to restrict, suspend or terminate the account of the person performing platform work, to refuse the payment for work**

[3] See in this regard, European Commission, Report Expert Group – Transposition of the Directive (EU) 2024/2831 on improving working conditions in platform work (2026), 44.

[4] See also Rainone/Aloisi, p. 7.

performed by them, as well as for decisions on their contractual status or any decision of equivalent or detrimental effect;

(c) all categories of decision taken or supported by automated systems that affect persons performing platform work in any manner.

2. Digital labour platforms shall provide the information referred to in paragraph 1 in the form of a written document, which may be in electronic form. The information shall be presented in a transparent, intelligible and easily accessible form, using clear and plain language.

3. Digital labour platforms shall provide persons performing platform work, in a concise form, with the information referred to in paragraph 1 with regard to the systems and their features that directly affect them, including, where applicable, their working conditions:

(a) at the latest on the first working day;

(b) prior to the introduction of changes affecting working conditions, the organisation of work or monitoring work performance; and

(c) at any time upon their request.

Upon the request of the persons performing platform work, digital labour platforms shall also provide them, in a comprehensive and detailed form, with the information referred to in paragraph 1 with regard to all relevant systems and their features.

4. Digital labour platforms shall provide workers' representatives, in a comprehensive and detailed form, with the information referred to in paragraph 1 with regard to all relevant systems and their features. They shall provide such information

(a) prior to the use of those systems,

(b) prior to the introduction of changes affecting working conditions, the organisation of work or monitoring work performance; and

(c) at any time upon their request.

Digital labour platforms shall provide national competent authorities, in a comprehensive and detailed form, with the information referred to in paragraph 1 at any time upon their request.

5. Digital labour platforms shall provide the information referred to in paragraph 1 to persons undergoing a recruitment or selection procedure. The information shall be provided in accordance with paragraph 2, shall be concise, shall concern only the automated monitoring systems or automated decision-making systems used in that procedure, and shall be provided before the start of the recruitment or selection procedure.

6. Persons performing platform work shall have the right to the portability of personal data generated through their performance of work in the context of a digital labour platform's automated monitoring systems or automated decision-making systems, including ratings and reviews, without adversely affecting the rights of the recipient of the service under Regulation (EU) 2016/679.

The digital labour platform shall provide persons performing platform work, free of charge, with tools to facilitate the effective exercise of their portability rights referred to in Article 20 of Regulation (EU) 2016/679 and in the first subparagraph of this paragraph. Where the person performing platform work so requests, the digital labour platform shall transmit such personal data directly to a third party.

Recital (44) In addition to the requirements laid down in Regulation (EU) 2016/679, digital labour platforms should be subject to transparency and information obligations in relation to automated

monitoring systems and automated systems which are used to take or support decisions that affect persons performing platform work, including the working conditions of platform workers, such as their recruitment, their access to and the organisation of work assignments, their earnings, their safety and health, their working time, their access to training, their promotion or its equivalent, and their contractual status, including the restriction, suspension or termination of their account. The type and form of information that is to be provided to persons performing platform work regarding such automated systems, as well as the timing of its provision, should be specified. Individual platform workers should receive that information in a concise, simple and understandable form, in so far as the systems and their features directly affect them and, where applicable, their working conditions, so that they are effectively informed. They should also have the right to request comprehensive and detailed information about all relevant systems. Comprehensive and detailed information regarding such automated systems should also be provided to representatives of persons performing platform work, as well as to national competent authorities upon their request, in order to enable them to exercise their functions.

While Arts. 13 and 14 of the Directive apply at the early stage of the introduction or 1 modification of automated systems and aim to ensure transparency in planning, Art. 9 **deals with transparency in the specific functioning of these systems**. In the context of judicial and administrative proceedings, Art. 9 is supplemented by Art. 21.

Art. 9 establishes that platforms must provide information to persons performing 2 platform work, representatives of persons performing platform work, and – on their request – national competent authorities. Although the text of Art. 9(1) refers only to representatives of platform workers, Art. 15 establishes that platforms must provide the same information to representatives of persons performing platform work who may not be 'platform workers' (see further recital 44).

In Art. 9, the Directive requires digital labour platforms to provide information on 3 the use or introduction of automated monitoring and decision-making systems. The information to be provided is listed in Art. 9(1) (see for automated monitoring systems (1)(a) and decision-making systems (1)(b)). The right to information goes beyond mere notification of the use or introduction of automated monitoring and decision-making systems. Art. 9 requires the digital labour platform to explain the internal functioning of such systems.

Regarding automated monitoring systems, it includes information on the categories of data and actions that are monitored, supervised or evaluated by such systems, including the recipient's evaluation of work performance (Art. 9(1)(a)(ii)), the monitoring aim and how the system carries out that monitoring (Art. 9(1)(a) (iii)). Regarding automated decision-making systems, it includes the categories of data and the main parameters that are taken into account by such systems, and their relative importance in the outcomes of automated decision making systems (Art. 9(1)(b)(iii)). The Commission service provided examples in the Expert Group report of the main parameters in the ride hailing sector. These main parameters may include the distance from clients, past reviews, vehicle type and size, and driving behaviour.[1]

Finally, Art. 9(1)(b)(iv) requires digital labour platforms to provide in advance information on the grounds for decisions to restrict, suspend or terminate the account of a person performing platform work, to refuse payment for work performed by them, as well as for any consequential decision that is taken or supported by automated decision-making systems. The term 'to restrict the account' is explained in recital 46 seq. 2 and is to be understood as any limitation imposed on that person's ability to perform platform work through the account, including restricting the access to the account or to work assignments.

---

[1] See in this regard, European Commission, Report Expert Group – Transposition of the Directive (EU) 2024/2831 on improving working conditions in platform work (2026), 49.

To conclude, Art. 9(b)(i-iv) requires digital labour platforms to provide information not only regarding the use or introduction of automated decision-making systems, but also to provide information on the logic involved, the significance and envisaged consequences of processing data relating to persons performing platform work.[2]

Art. 9(1)(c) serves a similar purpose to Art. 7(3) and Art. 12(4) insofar as Art. 9(1) expands the scope of the information obligation relating to automated decision-making systems to cover all categories of automated decision, including those that do not meet the significance threshold in the definition of automated decision-making systems. In other words, it covers automated systems that take or support decisions that impact persons performing platform work in 'any manner'. However, Art. 9(1)(c) is limited in scope, as it only covers categories of decisions, rather than the internal functioning of the systems ('main parameters').[3]

4 Art. 9(3) provides for a graduated system for the timing of the provision of information to persons performing platform work. In the first stage, only information on the system and its characteristics referred to in Art. 9(1) which **directly affect persons performing platform work or their working conditions** must be provided. This information must be provided in a '**concise form**'. This information must be provided at the latest on the first day of work (Art. 9(3)(a)) and 'prior to the introduction' of any changes affecting working conditions, the organisation of work, or the monitoring of work performance (Art. 9(3)(b)) and at any time upon request (Art. 9(a)(c)). The three possibilities in Art. 9(3)(a) to (c) are not optional for digital labour platforms; rather, information must be provided at any one of these times. Art. 9(3)(a) and (b) relate to moments at which digital labour platforms must proactively provide information, i.e. without being asked. While the term 'prior to the introduction' is not specified, a reasonable amount of time should be afforded to persons performing platform work to process and understand the information before the change takes effect.[4]

5 Only in a second step, at the request of the persons performing platform work, are digital labour platforms required to provide them with the full range of details referred to in Art. 9(1) with regard to all relevant systems and their features in **a comprehensive and detailed form**.

6 Other parties, on the other hand, shall be informed without any restriction on content. **Representatives of persons performing platform work** shall be provided with all detailed information referred to in Art. 9(1) with regard to all relevant systems and their features in a comprehensive and detailed form automatically before the first use of these systems and before any relevant change, as well as at any time upon their request (Art. 9(4)(a) to (c)). **National competent authorities** need only be informed upon their request (Art. 9(4)).

7 The situation of persons who are in a recruitment or selection process is regulated separately, in Art. 9(5). These persons must initially only be provided with information about the systems that are used in the recruitment or selection process.[5]

8 All information must be provided in a written document in accordance with Art. 9(2). The document need not be 'physical'; it may also be provided electronically (e.g., in a common format amenable for electronic storage or further processing such as

[2] See in this regard, European Commission, Report Expert Group – Transposition of the Directive (EU) 2024/2831 on improving working conditions in platform work (2026), 47.
[3] See in this regard, European Commission, Report Expert Group – Transposition of the Directive (EU) 2024/2831 on improving working conditions in platform work (2026), 47.
[4] See in this regard, European Commission, Report Expert Group – Transposition of the Directive (EU) 2024/2831 on improving working conditions in platform work (2026), 48.
[5] Gräf SR 2025, 14 (29).

PDF).[6] The information must be presented in a transparent, intelligible and easily accessible form, using clear and plain language.

According to Art. 9(6), persons performing platform work **have the right to transfer** 9 (e.g., to another platform, or to a worker- or union-operated 'data trust' for analysis along with other workers' data[7]) personal data **generated through their performance of work** within the automated monitoring and decision-making systems of a digital labour platform. Although persons performing platform work can also invoke Art. 20 GDPR, Art. 20 GDPR only covers the transfer of data provided by the data subject to a controller; it does not cover data that is generated by the controller.[8] Furthermore, the term 'personal data generated through their performance of work' is much broader than 'provided' data, as it explicitly includes ratings or reviews by clients. This must be provided in a way that does not affect the data protection rights of other data subjects (e.g., clients who provide reviews or other persons performing platform work). This can be achieved by anonymising their data or obtaining their consent.[9]

Furthermore, digital labour platforms must provide persons performing platform 10 work, free of charge, with 'tools to facilitate' the effective exercise of their portability rights. Recital 45 specifies that the personal data must be provided in a structured, commonly used and machine-readable format. The Commission services clarified the exact nature of tools is not specified, and that the facilitation could be achieved through technical interfaces within the app or website of the digital labour platform, enabling the data to be easily downloaded or transferred.[10]

Article 10
Human oversight of automated monitoring systems and automated decision-making systems

1. Member States shall ensure that digital labour platforms oversee and, with the involvement of workers' representatives, regularly and in any event every two years, carry out an evaluation of the impact of individual decisions taken or supported by automated monitoring systems and automated decision-making systems on persons performing platform work, including, where applicable, on their working conditions and equal treatment at work.

2. Member States shall require digital labour platforms to ensure sufficient human resources for the effective oversight and evaluation of the impact of individual decisions taken or supported by automated monitoring systems or automated decision-making systems. The persons charged by the digital labour platform with the function of oversight and evaluation shall have the competence, training and authority necessary to exercise that function, including for overriding automated decisions. Those persons shall enjoy protection from dismissal or its equivalent, disciplinary measures and other adverse treatment where they exercise their functions.

3. Where the oversight or the evaluation referred to in paragraph 1 identifies a high risk of discrimination at work in the use of automated monitoring systems

---

[6] See in this regard, European Commission, Report Expert Group – Transposition of the Directive (EU) 2024/2831 on improving working conditions in platform work (2026), 48.

[7] On the latter, see e.g. Li/Toh CPDP 2022; Calacci/Stein ELLJ 2023.

[8] Gräf SR 2025, 14 (34).

[9] See in this regard, European Commission, Report Expert Group – Transposition of the Directive (EU) 2024/2831 on improving working conditions in platform work (2026), 48, 51.

[10] See in this regard, European Commission, Report Expert Group – Transposition of the Directive (EU) 2024/2831 on improving working conditions in platform work (2026), 51.

or automated decision-making systems or finds that individual decisions taken or supported by automated monitoring systems or automated decision-making systems have infringed the rights of a person performing platform work, the digital labour platform shall take the steps necessary, including, if appropriate, the modification of the automated monitoring system or the automated decision-making system or the discontinuation of its use, in order to avoid such decisions in the future.
4. Information on the evaluation pursuant to paragraph 1 shall be transmitted to platform workers' representatives. Digital labour platforms shall also make that information available to persons performing platform work and the national competent authorities upon their request.
5. Any decision to restrict, suspend or terminate the contractual relationship or the account of a person performing platform work or any other decision of equivalent detriment shall be taken by a human being.

1 According to Art. 10(1), digital labour platforms must **continuously and proactively oversee** automated decision-making systems and, with the involvement of workers' representatives, **periodically evaluate** the impact of decisions taken or supported by these systems on persons performing platform work, including their working conditions and equal treatment at work, at least every two years. The information on the evaluation shall be **promptly** communicated to the representatives of the persons performing platform work without request, and made available to the persons performing platform work themselves and provided to the national competent authorities upon request (Art. 10(4); see also → Art. 15).

2 According to Art. 10(2), digital labour platforms must provide sufficient human resources to ensure effective oversight and evaluation. This means that the person charged by the digital labour platform with functions of oversight and evaluation must have the necessary competence, training, and authority – including the ability to override automated decisions. They are protected from dismissal, disciplinary measures, or other forms of adverse treatment where they excercise their functions (recital 47). Art. 10(3) should be read in reference to Arts. 22 and 23, and aims to grant autonomy to those responsible for human oversight, encouraging them to carefully interrogate such decisions.[1] Accordingly, as the purpose of the provision is to protect those exercising their function, it makes no difference whether the person in charge is employed by the digital labour platform or has been mandated to perform an external oversight function. The Commission service confirmed that both would have to be protected from termination of contract.[2]

3 Where an evaluation identifies a high risk of discrimination or infringement of the rights of persons performing platform work by automated decision-making systems, digital labour platforms must take corrective action, such as modifying or discontinuing the systems, to prevent risks from materialising (Art. 10(3)). In this context, 'high risk' means either a high chance of materialising or the likelihood of serious harm if the risk materialises. Regarding infringement, a single instance suffices.[3]

4 According to Art. 10(5), decisions to restrict, suspend, or terminate the contractual relationship or the account of a person performing platform work, or any decision which

---

[1] See in this regard, European Commission, Report Expert Group – Transposition of the Directive (EU) 2024/2831 on improving working conditions in platform work (2026), 53.

[2] European Commission, Report Expert Group – Transposition of the Directive (EU) 2024/2831 on improving working conditions in platform work (2026), 54.

[3] See in this regard, European Commission, Report Expert Group – Transposition of the Directive (EU) 2024/2831 on improving working conditions in platform work (2026), 53.

has a particularly adverse effect on persons performing platform work **must be taken by a human being, not an automated system**. The Commission service clarified that this prohibition only concerns **fully automated decisions**. Automated decision-making systems can still be used to support such decisions (later taken by humans), e.g. by making recommendations.[4] However, according to Art. 9(1)(b)(iv), grounds for decisions to restrict, suspend or terminate the contractual relationship or the account still need to be provided (see for more details → Art. 9 mn. 3).

Art. 10(5) goes beyond Art. 22(1) GDPR. Unlike Art. 22(1) GDPR, Art. 10 of the Directive does not require that the decision 'significantly affects the data subject'; it entirely prohibits certain types of decisions from being made in an automated manner. It furthermore does not provide for any of the exceptions foreseen in Art. 22(2) GDPR.[5] 5

Article 11
Human review

1. Member States shall ensure that persons performing platform work have the right to obtain an oral or written explanation from the digital labour platform for any decision taken or supported by an automated decision-making system without undue delay. The explanation shall be provided in a transparent and intelligible manner, using clear and plain language. Member States shall ensure that digital labour platforms provide persons performing platform work with access to a contact person designated by the digital labour platform to discuss and to clarify the facts, circumstances and reasons having led to the decision. Digital labour platforms shall ensure that such contact persons have the competence, training and authority necessary to exercise that function.

Digital labour platforms shall provide the person performing platform work with a written statement of the reasons for any decision taken or supported by an automated decision-making system to restrict, suspend or terminate the account of the person performing platform work, any decision to refuse the payment for work performed by the person performing platform work, any decision on the contractual status of the person performing platform work, any decision with similar effects or any other decision affecting the essential aspects of the employment or other contractual relationships, without undue delay and at the latest on the date on which it takes effect.

2. Persons performing platform work and, in accordance with national law or practice, representatives of persons performing platform work acting on their behalf shall have the right to request the digital labour platform to review the decisions referred to in paragraph 1. The digital labour platform shall respond to such request by providing the person performing platform work with a sufficiently precise and adequately substantiated reply in the form of a written document, which may be in electronic form, without undue delay and in any event within two weeks of receipt of the request.

3. Where the decision referred to in paragraph 1 infringes the rights of a person performing platform work, the digital labour platform shall rectify that decision without delay and in any case within two weeks of the adoption of the decision. Where such rectification is not possible, the digital labour platform shall offer

---

[4] See in this regard, European Commission, Report Expert Group – Transposition of the Directive (EU) 2024/2831 on improving working conditions in platform work (2026), 55.

[5] Gräf SR 2025, 14 (32).

adequate compensation for the damage sustained. In any event, the digital labour platform shall take the steps necessary, including, if appropriate, the modification of the automated decision-making system or the discontinuation of its use, in order to avoid such decisions in the future.
4. This Article does not affect disciplinary and dismissal procedures laid down in national law, collective agreements and practice.
5. This Article shall not apply to persons performing platform work who are also business users as defined in Article 2, point (1), of Regulation (EU) 2019/1150.

1 Art. 11 deals with the review of individual automated decisions, whereas Art. 10 concerns monitoring the impact of automated decision-making systems at a broader level. While Art. 9 ensures ex-ante and abstract information, Art. 11 requires explanations to be provided after a decision has been taken in a specific case.[1]

As regards human review, the Directive draws a distinction between two categories of decisions. According to Art. 11(1) subparagraph 2, first, digital labour platforms must provide the person performing platform work with a **written statement of the reasons** for **any decision** taken or supported by an automated decision-making system to restrict, suspend or terminate the account of the person performing platform work, **any decision** to refuse payment for work performed by the person performing platform work, any decision on the contractual status of the person performing platform work, and **any decision** with similar effects or any other decision affecting the essential aspects of the employment or other contractual relationships, **without undue delay** and **at the latest on the date on which it takes effect**. The term 'any decision' refers to 'a decision, the lack of a decision or a set of decisions' (recital 49).[2]

2 For all other decisions made or supported by automated decision-making systems as referred to in Art 11(1), **an oral or written explanation** must be provided by the digital labour platform **only** on the initiative of the persons performing platform work (see the wording in Art. 11(1): 'have the right to obtain').

3 Regardless of the type of decision (here paragraph 1 or subparagraph 2), persons performing platform work enjoy not only the right to an explanation of decisions taken or supported by an automated system, but also the right to a 'human interface', meaning a human contact person with the necessary competence to discuss and clarify the facts, circumstances and reasons that led to certain decisions, such as restriction, suspension or termination of the conctractual relationship or the account (Art. 11(1)). The person reviewing the decision does not have to be the same person who made it (Art. 10(5)). What needs to be clarified is whether a human manager would have made the same decision.[3] The Commission service clarified that the review must provide reasoning to demonstrate why the decision was well-founded and should not merely confirm it.

The requirements for those contact persons are the same as for Art. 10 ('competence, training and authority necessary to exercise that function').[4]

4 Furthermore, the Directive affords persons performing platform work the right to request a review of a decision that has been taken. In such instances, the digital labour

[1] See in this regard, European Commission, Report Expert Group – Transposition of the Directive (EU) 2024/2831 on improving working conditions in platform work (2026), 56.
[2] See in this regard, European Commission, Report Expert Group – Transposition of the Directive (EU) 2024/2831 on improving working conditions in platform work (2026), 57.
[3] So explicitly stated by Commission services, European Commission, Report Expert Group – Transposition of the Directive (EU) 2024/2831 on improving working conditions in platform work (2026), 58.
[4] See in this regard, European Commission, Report Expert Group – Transposition of the Directive (EU) 2024/2831 on improving working conditions in platform work (2026), 57.

platform is obliged to provide the person performing platform work with a reasoned reply without delay and at the latest within two weeks (Art. 11(2)). Representatives of persons performing platform work may also request a review of the decision on behalf of the person concerned (see Art. 15).

In the event that the automated decision has infringed the rights of the person performing platform work and this infringement cannot be rectified, the digital labour platform is obliged to offer the person concerned adequate compensation for the damage sustained (Art. 11(3)). One potential example of this would be the compensation of lost earnings due to the automated blocking of an account based on discriminatory ratings. It is, however, unclear whether appropriate compensation could also cover non-monetary damages (such as discrimination), although the wording of Art. 11 suggests that it might.[5] **5**

Art. 11 thus goes beyond the protection afforded by Art. 22 GDPR in several respects: First, Art. 11 also applies to decisions that are merely supported by an algorithmic system, whereas Art. 22, at least in its wording, only concerns decisions that are based exclusively on automation. Second, the procedural rights in Arts. 11(1) and (2) are significantly stronger and more precisely defined than the rights of intervention in Art. 22(3) GDPR.[6] **6**

Art. 11(5) contains a conflict rule to clarify the interplay between the Directive and the P2B Regulation. If a digital labour platform is also a provider of online intermediation services as defined in the P2B Regulation and the person performing platform work a business user within the meaning of the P2B Regulation, the provisions of the P2B Regulation prevail over Art. 11 (→ Chap. II mn. 44). **7**

The following example of the Commission service is intended to illustrate the interaction between Arts. 9(1)(b)(iv), 10(5) and 11(1) subparagraph 2.[7] **8**

Firstly, under Art. 10(5), an automated decision-making system that automatically blocks accounts as soon as it detects fraud is prohibited. Nevertheless, the system may support human operators in other ways. However, if the system detects fraud and recommends suspension to a human operator, who then makes the final decision following a reasonable investigation, this constitutes a partly automated decision and would be permissible under Art. 10(5). In this case, the digital labour platform must specify the possible grounds in accordance with Art. 9(1)(b)(iv) and provide a written statement of reasons in accordance with Art. 11(1) subparagraph 2. Not only must the digital labour platform inform platform workers about the use of such systems, it must also inform them in advance, *in abstracto*, of the grounds for decisions to restrict, suspend or terminate their account (e.g. that their account may be suspended or terminated if fraud is detected). The explanation *ex post* should be more specific, stating what type of fraud is suspected or has been detected and on what evidence this is based. **9**

Article 12
Safety and health

1. Without prejudice to Directive 89/391/EEC and related directives in the field of safety and health at work, with regard to platform workers, digital labour platforms shall:

[5] Krause NZA 2022, 521 (530); see also Gräf SR 2025, 14 (34).

[6] Gräf SR 2025, 14 (33).

[7] See in this regard, European Commission, Report Expert Group – Transposition of the Directive (EU) 2024/2831 on improving working conditions in platform work (2026), 58.

(a) evaluate the risks of automated monitoring systems and automated decision-making systems to their safety and health, in particular as regards possible risks of work-related accidents, psychosocial and ergonomic risks;
(b) assess whether the safeguards of those systems are appropriate for the risks identified in view of the specific characteristics of the work environment;
(c) introduce appropriate preventive and protective measures.

2. In relation to the requirements laid down in paragraph 1 of this Article, digital labour platforms shall ensure effective information and consultation and the participation of platform workers and/or their representatives in accordance with Articles 10 and 11 of Directive 89/391/EEC.
3. Digital labour platforms shall not use automated monitoring systems or automated decision-making systems in a manner that puts undue pressure on platform workers or otherwise puts at risk the safety and physical and mental health of platform workers.
4. In addition to automated decision-making systems, this Article shall also apply where digital labour platforms use automated systems taking or supporting decisions that affect platform workers in any manner.
5. In order to ensure the safety and health of platform workers, including from violence and harassment, Member States shall ensure that digital labour platforms take preventive measures, including providing for effective reporting channels.

1 Art. 12 of the Directive addresses the health and safety risks posed by automated systems by setting out occupational safety measures, such as risk assessments, and providing an additional ban on practices where platform workers are concerned.

2 Additional health and safety risks arise also from digital labour platforms' use of incentive, ranking or penalty systems similar to those identified in the Crowdworker decision of the German Federal Labour Court (BAG)[1] in 2020. Although platform workers were not obliged to accept orders, the organisational structure was such that they could only improve their status and receive more lucrative orders by accepting a certain number of orders. While this may initially seem motivating, it simultaneously **puts pressure on platform workers, increases stress and potentially leads to accidents**. A prime example of this are riders who travel at high speeds on their bikes in large cities in order to complete orders quickly and receive better orders. **Art. 12(3) is an important provision in counteracting these dynamics**, as it prohibits digital labour platforms from using automated monitoring and decision-making systems 'in a way that puts undue pressure on platform workers or otherwise puts at risk the[ir] safety [or] physical and mental health'.[2]

3 Art. 12(5) requires Member States to ensure that digital labour platforms adopt preventive measures, including effective reporting channels, to ensure the health and safety of platform workers, and to protect them against violence and harassment. However, Art. 12 and Art. 7 must be read together when introducing preventive and protective measures. The Commission services emphasised that digital labour platforms cannot process platform workers' personal data via automated monitoring or decision-making systems in a way that is prohibited under Art. 7.

4 Art. 12 addresses the specific risks of violence and harassment. This violence and harassment may not only result from the digital labour platform itself, but also from the recipient of the service, particularly in the context of on-location platform work (e.g. do-

[1] BAG 01.12.2020 – 9 AZR 102/20, NZA 2021, 552.
[2] Minotakis Platforms & Society 2025, 1 (3).

mestic services). Digital labour platforms are therefore also obliged to protect their workers from violence and harassment by third parties.

5 At the same time it should be noted that Art. 12 applies only to platform workers in line with the personal scope of the Framework Directive on Occupational Safety and only includes their representatives (Art. 12(2)). It does not apply to other persons performing platform work.[3]

Article 13
Information and consultation

This Directive is without prejudice to Directive 89/391/EEC as regards information and consultation and to Directives 2002/14/EC or 2009/38/EC of the European Parliament and of the Council [1].
Member States shall ensure that information and consultation, as defined in Article 2, points (f) and (g), of Directive 2002/14/EC, of workers' representatives by digital labour platforms also covers decisions likely to lead to the introduction of or to substantial changes in the use of automated monitoring systems or automated decision-making systems. For the purposes of this paragraph, information and consultation of workers' representatives shall be carried out under the same arrangements concerning the exercise of information and consultation rights as those laid down in Directive 2002/14/EC.
The platform workers' representatives may be assisted by an expert of their choice, in so far as this is necessary for them to examine the matter that is the subject of information and consultation and formulate an opinion. Where a digital labour platform has more than 250 workers in the Member State concerned, the expenses of the expert shall be borne by the digital labour platform, provided that they are proportionate. Member States may determine the frequency of requests for an expert, while ensuring the effectiveness of the assistance.

Article 14
Provision of information to workers

Where there are no representatives of platform workers, Member States shall ensure that digital labour platforms directly inform the platform workers concerned of decisions likely to lead to the introduction of or to substantial changes in the use of automated monitoring systems or automated decision-making systems. The information shall be provided in the form of a written document which may be in electronic form. It shall be provided in a transparent, intelligible and easily accessible form, using clear and plain language.
Article 15 Specific arrangements for representatives of persons performing platform work other than platform workers' representatives
Representatives of persons performing platform work other than workers' representatives shall be able to exercise the rights provided to workers' representatives under

---

[3] European Commission, Report Expert Group – Transposition of the Directive (EU) 2024/2831 on improving working conditions in platform work (12.1.2026), 62.

[1] Directive 2009/38/EC of the European Parliament and of the Council of 6 May 2009 on the establishment of a European Works Council or a procedure in Community-scale undertakings and Community-scale groups of undertakings for the purposes of informing and consulting employees (OJ L 122, 16.5.2009, p. 28).

Article 8(2), Article 9(1) and (4), Article 10(4) and Article 11(2) only insofar as they are acting on behalf of persons performing platform work who are not platform workers, with regard to the protection of their personal data.

Article 15
Specific arrangements for representatives of persons performing platform work other than platform workers' representatives

Representatives of persons performing platform work other than workers' representatives shall be able to exercise the rights provided to workers' representatives under Article 8(2), Article 9(1) and (4), Article 10(4) and Article 11(2) only insofar as they are acting on behalf of persons performing platform work who are not platform workers, with regard to the protection of their personal data.

Recital (21) Arrangements and processes of workers' representation vary between Member States, reflecting their respective histories, institutions, and economic and political situations. Among the enabling conditions for a well-functioning social dialogue are the existence of strong, independent trade unions and employers' organisations, with access to relevant information necessary to participate in social dialogue, and respect for the fundamental rights of the freedom of association and of collective bargaining.
Recital (22) According to the International Labour Organization (ILO) Workers' Representatives Convention No 135 (1971), currently ratified by 24 Member States, worker representatives can be persons who are recognised as such under national law or practice, whether they are trade union representatives, namely representatives designated or elected by trade unions or by members of such unions, or elected representatives, namely, representatives who are freely elected by the workers of the undertaking in accordance with provisions of national laws or regulations or of collective agreements and whose functions do not include activities which are recognised as the exclusive prerogative of trade unions in the country concerned. That Convention states that, where both trade union representatives and elected representatives exist in the same undertaking, such representation is not to be used to undermine the positions of the trade unions concerned or of their representatives, and that cooperation between the elected representatives and the trade unions concerned or their representatives is to be encouraged.
Recital (23) The Member States have ratified the ILO Right to Organise and Collective Bargaining Convention No 98 (1949), which provides that acts which are designed to promote the establishment of workers' organisations under the domination of employers or employers' organisations, or to support workers' organisations by financial or other means, with the object of placing such organisations under the control of employers or employers' organisations, are to be deemed to constitute acts of interference, against which ILO Member States need to protect workers' organisations. It is important for such acts to be addressed in order to ensure that, when defining or implementing practical arrangements for information and consultation pursuant to this Directive, employers and the workers' representatives work in a spirit of cooperation with due regard to their reciprocal rights and obligations, taking into account the interests both of the undertaking or establishment and of the workers.
Recital (52) Information and consultation of workers' representatives, which are regulated at Union level pursuant to Directive 2002/14/EC, are key to fostering effective social dialogue. As the introduction of or substantial changes in the use of automated monitoring systems and automated decision-making systems by digital labour platforms have direct impacts on the work organisation and individual working conditions of platform workers, additional measures are necessary to ensure that digital labour platforms inform and effectively consult platform workers' representatives before such decisions are taken, at the appropriate level. Given the technical complexity of algorithmic management systems, information should be given in due time to enable platform workers' representatives to prepare for consultation, with the assistance of an expert chosen by the platform workers or their representatives in a concerted manner where needed. The information and consultation measures provided for in Directive 2002/14/EC remain unaffected by this Directive.
Recital (53) Representatives of persons performing platform work should be able, in accordance with national law and practice, to represent one or several persons performing platform work in any judicial or administrative proceedings to enforce any of the rights or obligations arising from this Directive. Bringing claims on behalf of or supporting several persons performing platform work is a way to facilitate proceedings that would not have been brought otherwise because of procedural and financial barriers or a fear of reprisals.

Recital (61) In the absence of workers' representatives, it should be possible for the workers to be directly informed by the digital labour platform of the introduction of or substantial changes in the use of automated monitoring systems and automated decision-making systems.

Literature: Aloisi/De Stefano, 'AI at work, algorithmic bosses, and the ambivalence of automation' in Biasi (ed), Artificial Intelligence and Labour Law, forthcoming; Aloisi/Joppe/Abraha, 'From 'general' to 'context-specific' data protection for workers: insights from the EU rules on platforms, algorithmic management and AI systems', Eur. Labour Law J. 2025, forthcoming; Aloisi/Potocka-Sionek, 'De-Gigging the Labour Market? An Analysis of the Algorithmic Management Provisions in the Proposed Platform Work Directive', Ital. Labour Law e-J. 2022, 29; Aloisi/Rainone/Countouris, 'An unfinished task? Matching the Platform Work Directive with the EU and international 'social acquis'', ILO Working Paper 101, Geneva 2023; Barrio/Jacqueson, 'The social security relevance of the Platform Directive', Eur. Labour Law J. 2025, 516; Miranda Boto, 'La Contrattazione Collettiva per i Lavoratori Autonomi e Nella Gig Economy: Incontri e Incomprensioni', LavoroDirittiEuropa 2023; Borelli,' Subcontracting: exploitation by design tackling the business model for social dumping', The Left, Brussels 2022; Cardo/Alonso, 'Multiparty work relationships in Spain: Legal provisions and emerging trends', ELLJ 2022, 492; Cefaliello, 'An occupational health and safety perspective on EU initiatives to regulate platform work: Patching up gaps or structural game changers?', J. Work Health Saf. Regul. 2023, 117; Cherry, 'Lost in a crowd: how crowdworkers are denied their rights at work', ILAW Taken for a Ride Series (3) 2025; Collins/Atkinson, 'Worker voice and algorithmic management in post-Brexit Britain', Transfer 2023, 37; Cremers/Houwerzijl, 'Subcontracting and social liability', ETUC 2021; De Stefano/Durri/Stylogiannis/Wouters, 'Platform Work and the Employment Relationship', ILO Working Paper 27, Geneva 2021; Donini, 'Il luogo per l'esercizio dei diritti sindacali: l'unità produttiva nell'impresa frammentata', Labour and Law Issues 2019, 99; Dube/Jacobs/Naidu/Suri, 'Monopsony in online labour markets', Am. Econ. Rev. 2020, 33; Durri/Stylogianis/Wouters, 'The Platform Work Directive: a milestone or a nothingburger?' in Sabato/Ghailani/Spasova (eds), Social policy in the European Union: state of play 2024, Brussels 2025, p. 81; ETUC, 'Platform Reps Austria: Country Report 2022', 2022; Fairwork, 'Cloudwork Ratings 2025: Advancing standards in digital labour and AI supply chain governance', 2025; Ferrari/Bertolini/Borkert/Graham, 'The German Platform Economy: Strict Regulations but Unfair Standards?', Digital Geography and Society 2024, 5; Ferrari/Bertolini/Borkert/Graham, 'The German Platform Economy: Strict Regulations but Unfair Standards?', Digital Geography and Society 2024, 5; Fredman/Du Toit/Bertolini/Valente/Graham, 'Fair work for platform workers: lessons from the EU Directive and beyond', Industrail Law Journal (Ind. Law J.) 2025, 425; Friedrich-Ebert-Stiftung, 'Collection of Factsheets on Online Platforms and Platform Work in Selected Countries', Brussels 2023; Fulton, 'Trade Unions Protecting Self-Employed Workers', ETUC Brussels 2018; Gaudio, 'Litigating the Algorithmic Boss in the EU: A (Legally) Feasible and (Strategically) Attractive Option for Trade Unions?', Int. J. Comp. Labour Law Ind. Relat. 2024, 95; Geyer/Vandaele/Prinz, 'Riding Together? Why App-Mediated Food Delivery Couriers Join Trade Unions in Austria', Econ. Ind. Dem. 2023, 835; Griesser/Plank/Vogel/Risak/Herr/Ustek/Steward/Graham, 'Fairwork Austria Ratings 2022: Labour Standards in the Platform Economy', Fairwork Annual Report 2022, Oxford Berlin 2022; Gyulavári, 'Collective rights of platform workers: the role of EU law', Maastricht J. Eur. Comp. Law 2020, 406; Hadwiger, 'Realizing the Opportunities of the Platform Economy through Freedom of Association and Collective Bargaining', ILO, Geneva 2022; Herr, 'Riding in the gig economy: An in-depth study of a branch in the app-based on-demand food delivery sector', Working Paper-Reihe AK Wien Vol. 169, Wien 2017; Hießl, 'Case Law on Algorithmic Management at the Workplace: Cross-European Comparative Analysis and Tentative Conclusions', 2025; Hießl, 'Multiparty relationships in platform work: Cross-European case law developments and points of departure for (supranational) regulation', ELLJ 2023, 514; Hießl, 'National approaches to collective bargaining for the self-employed: common trends, innovative potential and unresolved problems' in Hießl/Waas (eds), Collective bargaining for self-employed workers in Europe, Alphen aan den Rijn 2021; Hießl, 'The classification of platform workers in case law: a cross-European comparative analysis', CLLPJ 2021, 465; Hossein Jarrahi/Sutherland, 'Algorithmic Management and Algorithmic Competencies: Understanding and Appropriating Algorithms in Gig Work' in Greene Taylor/Christian-Lamb/Martin/Nardi (eds), Information in Contemporary Society, Washington 2019; Jesnes/Neumann/Trappmann/Becdelièvre, 'The Role of Worker Collectives among App-Based Food Delivery Couriers in France, Germany and Norway: All the Same or Different?' in Drahokoupil/Vandaele (eds), A Modern Guide to Labour and the Platform Economy, Edward Elgar Publishing 2021, p. 258; Krämer/Cazes, 'Shaping the transition: Artificial intelligence and social dialogue', OECD Social, Employment and Migration Working Papers n. 279, Paris 2022; Lamannis, 'Collective bargaining in the platform economy: a mapping exercise of existing initiatives', ETUI Report 2023.02, Brussels , 2023; Morgan/van Zoonen/ter Hoeven, 'Lost in the crowd? An investigation into where microwork is conducted and classifying worker types', Eur. J. Ind. Rel. 2023, 301; Neumann, 'Platform Labour Protest in Germany', Leeds Index of Platform Labour Protests 2023, 3; Otto, 'A step towards digital self- & co-determination in the context of algorithmic management systems', Ital. Labour Law e-J. 2022, 51; Pignot, 'Who is pulling the strings in the platform economy? Accounting for the dark and unexpected sides of algorithmic control', Organization 2021, Vol. 30 Issue 1, 140; Ponce Del Castillo/Naranjo, 'Regulating algorithmic management: An assessment of the EC's draft Directive on improving working conditions in platform work', ETUI Policy Brief 2022.08, Brussels 2022; Potocka-Sionek/Aloisi, 'The Spillover Effect of Algorithmic Management and How (Not) to Tame It' in Vandaele/Rainone (eds), The Elgar companion to regulating platform work: Insights from the food delivery sector, Edward Elgar Publishing 2025, p. 251; Pupeter/Lukas/Bertazolli, 'Safeguarding the Right to Collective Bargaining in the Face of Precarious Self-Employment – Gaps in Protection in Austria and Germany and Obligations under European Law', ELLJ 2026, 47; Rainone, 'Collective rights dimension of the Platform Work Directive: assessing regulatory effectiveness in the digital labour context', Eur. Labour Law J. 2025, 494; Rainone, 'Digital and remote work: pushing EU labour law beyond its limits' in Countouris/De Stefano/Piasna/Rainone (eds), The future of remote work, ETUI Brussels 2023, p. 163; Rainone, 'Rethinking the concept of the employer in the digital economy: corporate fragmentation and power dynamics through labour law and competition law lenses', CLLPJ 2025, 147; Rainone/Aloisi, 'The EU Platform Work Directive: What's new, what's missing, what's next', ETUI Policy Brief 2024.06, 2024; Rainone/Hießl, 'Judicial creativity in the platform economy: Normative insights for broadening the scope of labour law' in Vandaele/Rainone (eds), The Elgar companion to regulating platform work: Insights from the food delivery sector, Cheltenham UK 2025, p. 171; Rani/Pulignano/Gobel/Muszyński, 'Challenging boundaries: exploring pricing strategies, and unpaid labour time to explain earning disparities in online labour markets', New Political Economy 2025, 342; Risi/Pronzato, 'Smart working is not so smart – Always-on lives and the dark side of platformisation', Work Organ. Labour Glob. 2021, 107; Rosin, 'Towards a European employment status: The EU proposal for a Directive on improving working conditions in platform work', Ind. Law J. 2022, 478; Schreyer, 'Algorithmic Work Coordination and Workers' Voice in the COVID-19 Pandemic: The Case of Foodora/Lieferando', Work Organ. Labour Glob. 2021, 69; Schwertner, 'Kollektivverträge für freie Dienstnehmer. Ein Etappensieg?', ASoK 2025, 314; Vandaele, 'Will trade unions survive the platform economy? Emerging patterns of platform workers' collective voice and representation in Europe', ETUI Working Paper 2018.05, Brussels 2018; Vandaele, 'Inevitable, Vulnerable, Unprofitable: An Inquiry into Food Delivery Platforms in Europe', ETUI Working Paper 2024.10, 2024; Vandaele, 'Inevitable, Vulnerable, Unprofitable: An Inquiry into Food Delivery Platforms in Europe', ETUI Working Paper 2024.10, Brussels 2024; Vandaele/Piasna/Zwysen, 'Are platform workers willing to unionize? Exploring survey evidence from 14 European countries', ILO Working Paper Geneva 2024; Weil, 'Understanding the present and future of work in the fissured workplace context', RSF J. Social Sciences 2019, 147; Wray, 'Is sub-contracting becoming the new normal in the platform economy?', Brave New Europe, 22 April 2021; Wyputta, 'Lieferando Torpediert Betriebsratswahl Ausgelieferte Mitarbeiter', taz.de, 2020.

A. Introduction

1 This chapter explores **the role of worker representatives** within the framework of the Platform Work Directive. It provides an overview of the newly established prerogatives as well as the remaining challenges that may hinder the effectiveness of the Directive's collective rights dimension if not addressed during national implementation.

2 Although the Platform Work Directive is often presented as a landmark instrument for its introduction of a presumption of employment and its explicit address of the

impact of digital technology on working conditions,[1] its contribution also lies in the advancement of collective labour rights. Chapter III of the Platform Work Directive on algorithmic management (hereinafter also referred to as 'AM') complements key data-related, transparency, and automated decision-making rights with a range of information and consultation prerogatives, some of which are also accessible to workers beyond traditional employment relationships. As a result, the Directive intervenes in the EU collective rights framework by (partially) expanding its personal scope to include self-employed platform workers and by creating a new set of participatory rights related to the use of algorithmic technologies.

The presence of a collective dimension in the Platform Work Directive represents a promising step for EU labour lawmaking as it acknowledges the importance of comprehensive forms of workplace democracy in contexts such as the platform economy, where employment status is often blurred and statutory labour norms fail to have effective reach.[2] It thus sets an important precedent for the integration of robust collective rights in future national and EU legislation regulating artificial intelligence (AI) and AM at work. 3

At the same time, structural gaps risk weakening the actual impact of the Platform Work Directive on platform workers' collective rights. A first set of limitations stems from its own wording and structure, while other obstacles relate to broader, non-platform-specific issues–such as the limited access of self-employed workers to collective bargaining rights and the disruptive implications of digitalisation for the applicability of existing collective rights regimes. These challenges are addressed in sections 2 and 3. 4

Against this backdrop, the chapter reflects on constructive ways forward. Drawing on empirical analysis, Section 4 identifies examples from different jurisdictions where strategic litigation and the establishment of stable representation structures (e.g. works councils) can complement the Directive and help address some of its shortcomings. Ultimately, the chapter argues that much will depend on how national regulatory and industrial relations frameworks respond to the transformations introduced by the platform economy–a process that will unfold during the Directive's transposition phase. 5

As a **final introductory note**, it is important to clarify that, unless otherwise specified, this chapter does not adopt the Directive's technical terminology distinguishing between 'persons performing platform work' (self-employed individuals) and 'platform workers' (employees). In what follows, **the term 'workers' is used more broadly** to refer to all individuals engaged through digital labour platforms, regardless of their employment status. 6

B. The collective dimension of the Platform Work Directive: which rights and for whom?

This section outlines the **collective rights dimension** of the Platform Work Directive, focusing on the newly established prerogatives of workers' representatives in two areas: the algorithmic management rights set out in Chapter III (Section 2.1); and the enforcement mechanisms mainly developed in Chapter IV (Section 2.2). It then reflects on the limited competences of representatives of self-employed workers and the resulting risks for the coherence of the legal and industrial relations framework (Section 2.3). 7

[1] Rosin Ind. Law J. 2022, 478; Aloisi/Rainone/Countouris, ILO Working Paper 101 2023; Durri/Stylogianis/Wouters in Sabato/Ghailani/Spasova, p. 81 et seqq.

[2] Hießl CLLPJ 2021, 465.

I. Collective rights and algorithmic management

8 Chapter III of the Platform Work Directive on 'Algorithmic Management' has rightly been described as one of the most innovative aspects of the Directive as it transposes key GDPR safeguards into the workplace context and overcomes some of their limitations.[3] It includes provisions prohibiting the processing of specific types of data (Art. 7(1)), introduces robust transparency rights (Art. 9), requires human oversight (Art. 10) and review of automated systems (Art. 11), and puts forward the stronger involvement of workers' representatives in relation to the impact of automated monitoring systems (AMS) and automated decision-making systems (ADMS) on health and safety (Art. 12) and, more broadly, on working conditions (Art. 13). Embedded in this regulatory architecture, the Platform Work Directive envisages an active role for workers' representatives throughout the algorithmic management governance process. Art. 8, on 'Data Protection Impact Assessment', requires the involvement of representatives in the impact assessments that platforms must carry out pursuant to Art. 35(1) GDPR. In particular, platforms are required to 'seek the views of persons performing platform work and their representatives' and to provide them with the final assessment.

9 Art. 9 establishes transparency duties,[4] obliging platforms to inform, inter alia, workers' representatives of the use of AMS or ADMS and of 'all categories of decisions taken or supported by automated systems that affect persons performing platform work in any manner.' The Directive details that the content of such information should include: the categories of data being monitored; the purpose of the monitoring and its modalities; the recipients of the processed data; the categories of the decisions taken or supported by ADMS; the data and parameters feeding into these systems; and the grounds for decisions to restrict, suspend, or terminate a worker's account.[5] Paragraph 2 further specifies that the information must be provided in writing (which may be electronic) and in a 'transparent, intelligible and easily accessible form, using clear and plain language.' Communication with workers' representatives should take place 'prior to the use of AMS and ADMS,' 'prior to the introduction of changes affecting working conditions, the organisation of work or monitoring work performance,' and, in any case, 'at any time upon their request.'

10 Art. 10 introduces safeguards related to the human oversight of AMS and ADMS, where workers' representatives are again involved. They must be consulted in the periodic evaluation of the impact of individual decisions taken or supported by AMS and ADMS on working conditions and equal treatment. Once the evaluation is completed, it must be shared with them.

11 Art. 11 outlines the 'human review' principle, according to which workers have the right to obtain an explanation from the platform for any decisions taken or supported by ADMS.[6] More stringent obligations apply where decisions affect essential aspects of the employment or contractual relationship, such as account suspension or termination, refusal of payment, or determinations regarding contractual status. In such cases, workers may request the platform to review the decision, and may ask their representatives to submit this request on their behalf.

---

[3] Aloisi/Joppe/Abraha ELLJ 2025, forthcoming; Potocka-Sionek/Aloisi in Vandaele/Rainone, p. 251–270; Bronowicka, 'How the Platform Work Directive Protects Workers' Data' (Verfassungsblog 2023) How the Platform Work Directive Protects Workers' Data (last accessed: 15.12.2025).

[4] Otto Ital. Labour Law e-J. 2022, 51 et seqq.

[5] Aloisi/Potocka-Sionek Ital. Labour Law e-J. 2022, 29 (30).

[6] Aloisi/Potocka-Sionek Ital. Labour Law e-J. 2022, 29 (40); Ponce Del Castillo/Naranjo, ETUI Policy Brief, 2022.08.

Art. 12 concerns health and safety obligations. Platforms must evaluate risks, assess whether adequate safeguards are in place, and implement appropriate preventive and protective measures. In this context, platforms are also required to engage with workers' representatives. Paragraph 2 specifies that, when carrying out such assessments, platforms must observe the information and consultation prerogatives set out in Arts. 10 and 11 of Directive 89/391/EEC on the introduction of measures to encourage improvements in the safety and health of workers at work.[7] 12

A cross-reference to existing EU collective rights instruments is also present in Art. 13, which reaffirms that the platform economy is not exempt from the application of Directive 2009/38/EC on European Works Councils and Directive 2002/14/EC establishing a general framework for informing and consulting employees.[8] In particular, it clarifies that, where applicable, the participatory practices set out in Directive 2002/14/EC should be triggered in relation to managerial decisions likely to result in 'the introduction of or substantial changes in the use' of AMS and ADMS. The Commission has, however, clarified that the mere implementation of Directive 2002/14/EC does not, in itself, satisfy Art. 13: in their national transposition, Member States must expand its provisions and make them explicit as regards the obligation to inform and consult on decisions likely to introduce, or substantially change, the use of AMS and ADMS.[9] Paragraph 4 further stipulates that workers' representatives may be assisted by an expert of their own choosing to support them in the technical aspects of algorithmic management, and that related expenses must be borne by the platform – provided it employs more than 250 workers (including not only platform workers, but also other staff)[10] in the Member State concerned. 13

Overall, these provisions offer substantial guarantees for timely exchanges on key features of algorithmic management systems–ranging from monitoring and data processing to automated decision-making–creating genuine opportunities for the engagement of workers' representatives. Moreover, going further in the promotion of social dialogue principles, the EU legislator has laid the groundwork for a regulatory framework in which collective bargaining may complement statutory norms as a standard-setting instrument.[11] In addition to stressing that the Directive must be implemented in line with the principles of ILO Convention No. 98 (1949) on the Right to Organise and Collective Bargaining (recital 23), the Platform Work Directive also includes a final provision on the 'promotion of collective bargaining in platform work' (Art. 25). Emphatically, it requires Member States to 'take adequate measures to promote the role of the social partners and encourage the exercise of the right to collective bargaining in platform work.' 14

Additional protections against managerial interference with collective rights are found in Arts. 7(1)(b) and 7(1)(d) which prohibit platforms from processing personal data related to private communications–including with workers' representatives – or any data that could be used to predict the exercise of freedom of association, collective bargaining and action, or the right to information and consultation. Similarly, Art. 20 requires the creation of channels through which workers can communicate with each oth- 15

[7] Cefaliello, Work Health Saf. Regul. 2023, 117et seqq.

[8] Rainone, 'More than formal recognition? Collective labour rights in the Platform Work Directive', (Verfassungsblog 2023) More than Formal Recognition? (last accessed: 15.12.2025).

[9] European Commission, Report Expert Group – Transposition of the Directive (EU) 2024/2831 on improving working conditions in platform work (12.1.2026), 64.

[10] European Commission, Report Expert Group – Transposition of the Directive (EU) 2024/2831 on improving working conditions in platform work (12.1.2026), 64.

[11] For an overview of the state of collective bargaining initiatives in the platform economy, see Lamannis, ETUI Report, 2023.

er and with their representatives, without the possibility for platforms to access or monitor those communications.[12]

16 At the same time, certain **weaknesses may undermine the effectiveness of the Directive's collective rights dimension**. First, while the Platform Work Directive refers to various forms of collective engagement–information, consultation, participation, and collective bargaining – it is notable that most of the Platform Work Directive prerogatives concern information and to a lesser extent consultation rights, with only residual space being left for more meaningful forms of involvement.

17 It is only in the context of the application of OSH Directive 89/391/EEC – which prescribes that workers' representatives be accorded 'balanced participation in accordance with national law and/or practices' on all the questions relating to safety and health at work mentioned in Art. 12 – that the Platform Work Directive requires potentially more intense commitments. Art. 25, while emphasising the importance of collective bargaining in regulating the platform economy, has limited impact on the actual competences of workers' representatives as its language lacks prescriptive force.[13] The obligation to engage is even weaker when representatives are elected by self-employed platform workers, as further discussed in Section 2.3. With workers' representatives conceived primarily as interlocutors – rather than counterparts – the Directive largely reflects a model in which collective rights serve more to facilitate managerial transitions than to make substantive improvements in the terms and conditions of work.[14] It thus remains doubtful whether the Directive will promote the creation of stable and effective structures for negotiating algorithmic management systems, ultimately leading to collective agreements.

18 This leads to a further critical point concerning the collective rights framework established in the Platform Work Directive: by focusing narrowly on the data processing aspect of algorithmic management, the Directive avoids making explicit connections between ADMS and core working conditions.[15] Aside from introducing safeguards against arbitrary account suspension and termination, the Directive does not address the implications of algorithmic systems for essential issues such as wage setting and working time.[16] Rather than treating AMS and ADMS as modern expressions of managerial prerogatives, the Directive frames them primarily as technical HR tools for monitoring and disciplining workers. This approach risks downplaying the broader implications of algorithmic systems for the organisation of work as a whole, thereby weakening the reach and effectiveness of collective negotiation processes and their outcomes.

---

[12] Ebenhö/Hampel/Loschert/Silberman/Prassl/Höller, "Implementing Article 20 of the EU Platform Work Directive: " Communication channels" (Global Workplace Law & Policy 2025) < Implementing Article 20 of the EU Platform Work Directive: 'Communication channels' | Global Workplace Law & Policy>(last accessed: 15.12.2025).

[13] Rainone ELLJ 2025, 494-515.

[14] Such an approach reflects a broader institutional trend. See: Krämer/Cazes, OECD Social, Employment and Migration Working Papers, n. 279, 2022. The European Commission Communication on 'Strengthening social dialogue in the European Union: harnessing its full potential for managing fair transitions,' COM(2023)40final, Brussels, 25 January 2023, states that 'Social partners have a vital role to play in helping to anticipate, change and address, through dialogue, negotiation and joint action where relevant, the employment and social consequences of the challenges of economic restructuring and the ongoing twin transitions.'

[15] Fredman/Du Toit/Bertolini/Valente/Graham Ind. Law J. 2025, https://doi.org/10.1093/indlaw/dwaf018; Aloisi/De Stefano in Biasi, forthcoming; Rainone ELLJ 2025, 494-515.

[16] On the widespread phenomenon of unpaid labour in the platform economy, see: Rani/Pulignano/Gobel/Muszyński New Pol. Econ. 2025, 342–358.

II. Collective rights and enforcement

19 The Platform Work Directive contains a **solid enforcement dimension** where workers' representatives are recognised as having a potentially significant role.[17] The framework set out by the Directive can be described as resting on three main pillars: ad hoc provisions on the activation of the presumption of employment (Arts. 5(4), 5(5), and 6); transparency obligations towards public authorities and other stakeholders (Arts. 16 and 17(1)); and provisions on access to justice and the coordination of competent authorities within the justice system (Arts. 18 to 24). As Table 1 illustrates, the Directive grants important prerogatives to workers' representatives across all three pillars, although a broad margin of discretion is left to national legislation with regard to certain procedural aspects.

Table 1: Enforcement-related measures in the Platform Work Directive. 20

Article	Enforcement-related provisions	Room for workers' representatives	Scope for national variability
Art. 5(4)	Persons performing platform work and their representatives shall have the right to initiate proceedings for ascertaining correct employment status	✓	In accordance with national law and practice
Art. 5(5)	Competent national authorities can initiate actions or proceedings in order to ascertain employment status		In accordance with national law and practice
Art. 6	Member States shall establish supporting measures to ensure effective implementation of the legal presumption	✓	
Art. 16	Platforms shall declare work performed by platform workers to the competent authorities		
Art. 17(1)	Platforms shall provide a series of information, including the n. of persons working through the platform, their employment situation, and the use of intermediaries	✓	
Art. 18	Access to dispute resolution and right to redress		
Art. 19	Representatives of persons performing platform work may engage in judicial or administrative procedures to enforce rights or obligations arising from the directive	✓	They may act on behalf of or support one or several persons performing platform work, in accordance with national law and practice
Art. 20	Secure communication channels, on platforms' own digital infrastructure or by similarly effective means	✓	

[17] Rainone/Aloisi, ETUI Policy Brief, 2024.

Article	Enforcement-related provisions	Room for workers' representatives	Scope for national variability
Art. 21	Access to evidence and the possibility for national courts to disclose confidential information if relevant for the proceedings		
Art. 22	Protection from adverse treatment resulting from enforcing the rights established in the Platform Work Directive	✓	
Art. 23	Protection from dismissal as adverse treatment (specification of Art. 22)		
Art. 24	Specific areas of competence for the supervisory authorities responsible for monitoring the application of the GDPR		

Source: Authors' own elaboration

21 In the context of Chapter I on the presumption of employment, the Platform Work Directive ensures that workers' representatives can initiate judicial and administrative proceedings for the determination of employment status (Art. 5(4)). Furthermore, pursuant to Art. 6, the social partners–including workers' representatives–are entitled to receive guidance from the national government on the practical functioning of the presumption mechanism.[18] The Directive thus establishes broad *locus standi* rights (i.e. the procedural legitimacy to bring an action before an enforcement authority), recognising the importance of allowing third parties (such as trade unions) to provide legal and representational support.[19] At the same time, the operationalisation of this provision must be done 'in accordance with national law and practice,' reflecting a broad interpretation of the principle of procedural autonomy which limits the EU's competence to regulate domestic enforcement systems. Whether representatives will be able merely to support workers' individual reclassification claims or act fully on their behalf will ultimately depend on national rules.

22 Beyond the provisions related to the presumption of employment, Arts. 16 and 17 introduce general transparency obligations that are key for the effective enforcement of the Directive. While Art. 16 focuses on ensuring that platforms officially declare the employment of workers to the appropriate public authorities, Art. 17(1) requires that the competent authorities, as well as workers' representatives, be provided with a series of statistical and aggregated data on the platform's work organisation.[20] This includes information on the composition of the workforce, applicable terms and conditions, average weekly working hours and corresponding income, and information about the intermediaries with whom the platform has contractual relationships. These data are crucial for comparing business models across platforms, identifying potential violations (e.g., in the case of food delivery, rules prohibiting pay-per-delivery schemes), and informing litigation strategies.

23 Chapter V of the Platform Work Directive (Arts. 18 to 24) is specifically dedicated to enforcement and establishes a set of rights and guarantees applicable to the entire regulatory framework introduced by the Directive. From the perspective of workers' repre-

[18] ETUC, "Platform Work Directive: a milestone towards innovation that delivers for all", Press Release, 29 March 2024.
[19] Rainone ELLJ 2025, 494-515.
[20] Barrio/Jacqueson ELLJ 2025, 516-537.

sentatives, these provisions are particularly important as they integrate a collective dimension into the Directive's compliance and remedies architecture. Art. 19 reiterates the *locus standi* prerogatives introduced in Art. 5(4) in the context of employment status: representatives must be able to 'act on behalf of or in support of one or several persons performing platform work in the case of the infringement of any right or obligation arising from this Directive, in accordance with national law and practice.' Again, the wording leaves significant room for national variability, meaning that the actual role of workers' representatives in judicial or administrative proceedings will vary across Member States.

Art. 20 ensures that platform workers–regardless of their employment status–are able to exchange among themselves and with their representatives through ad hoc channels provided by the digital labour platform 'in its infrastructure, or by similarly effective means'. The Directive emphasises that these communications need to be secure, without any form of interference or monitoring from the platform. In choosing to locate this provision on the right to private communication in the Platform Work Directive Chapter dedicated to enforcement, EU lawmakers are conferring on these 'channels' the function of key, potentially structural forums in which workers' representatives can act as enforcement 'facilitators'. Not only workers can reach out to them with individual complaints, but workers' representatives may also use these 'digital spaces' to collect data, conduct surveys, and build strategic litigation or mobilisation campaigns.[21] 24

Finally, Art. 22 introduces essential safeguards to ensure that workers' representatives can carry out their functions without fear of retaliation.[22] Member States must guarantee protection against 'any adverse treatment [...] and any adverse consequences resulting from a complaint lodged with the digital labour platform or resulting from any proceedings initiated with the aim of enforcing compliance with the rights provided for in this Directive.' 25

Overall, the Platform Work Directive grants a solid set of prerogatives enabling workers' representatives to play an active role in fostering compliance with the rights conferred. Ultimately, the transposition of this framework into national systems will test the preparedness of trade unions and worker representation structures to mobilise legal frameworks, particularly in the context of strategic litigation. 26

III. Workers' representatives

Having outlined the prerogatives that the Platform Work Directive confers on workers' representatives, a crucial issue remains to be clarified: who does the Directive actually refer to when it uses the term 'workers' representatives'? Art. 2 provides a dual definition, reflecting the personal scope of application of the Directive, which distinguishes 'platform workers' – essentially used as a synonym for platform employees – from 'persons performing platform work,' a broader notion that also includes individuals engaged under self-employment arrangements.[23] Art. 2(1)f then defines 'workers' representatives' as 'representatives of platform workers, such as trade unions and representatives who are freely elected by the platform workers in accordance with national law and 27

[21] See Vandaele/Piasna/Zwysen, ILO Working Paper, 2024; Risi/Pronzato Work Organ. Labour Glob. 2021, 107–125.

[22] Pignot Organization 2021, 140–167.

[23] Aloisi/Potocka-Sionek Ital. Labour Law e-J. 2022, 29–50.

practice'.[24] In contrast, 'representatives of persons performing platform work' are defined in Art. 2(1)(g) as 'workers' representatives and, insofar as provided for in national law and practice, the representatives of persons performing platform work other than platform workers.'[25]

28 It is therefore clear that the latter definition is broader, as it includes representatives elected not only by platform employees but also by workers with a different employment status. This distinction reflects that the Directive does not grant self-employed workers the same collective rights afforded to employees.[26] This is particularly evident in the provisions on algorithmic management, whereas the enforcement provisions apply to all workers regardless of status. In Chapter III, the Directive thus refers to 'workers' representatives' or 'representatives of persons performing platform work' depending on whether the relevant provision also applies to those without employee status. Further complicating the picture, Art. 15 introduces an umbrella clause which extends the applicability of certain provisions referring exclusively to 'workers' representatives' to include in addition representatives of persons performing platform work, provided the prerogatives are exercised solely for the protection of personal data. This is because the rights extended under Art. 15 are based on Art. 16 TFEU on data protection, rather than on Art. 153 TFEU on social policy.[27]

29 **Table 2: Collective labour rights for self-employed workers in Chapter III of the Platform Work Directive**

Article	Collective rights for workers' representatives	Inclusion of representatives of self-employed workers
Art. 8(2)	Information on data protection impact assessment	✓
Art. 9(1)	Information on the use of automated monitoring and decision-making	✓
Art. 9(4)	Information on automated monitoring and decision-making and its features, use and changes affecting working conditions	✓
Art. 10(1)	Oversight of the impact of individual decisions taken or supported by automated monitoring and decision-making	
Art. 10(4)	Information concerning evaluation of the impact of ADMS	✓
Art. 11(2)	Right to ask for a review of the decisions taken or supported by ADMS	✓

[24] European Commission, Report Expert Group – Transposition of the Directive (EU) 2024/2831 on improving working conditions in platform work (12.1.2026), 18–19, clarifying that the qualifier 'freely elected' attaches to the representatives rather than to trade unions, that no minimum size threshold or bargaining capacity is required, and that works councils may qualify under the definition.

[25] This definition is drawn from the French version of the Directive, as the corresponding English version is presently incomplete.

[26] Rainone/Aloisi, ETUI policy brief, 2024.

[27] European Commission, Report Expert Group – Transposition of the Directive (EU) 2024/2831 on improving working conditions in platform work (12.1.2026), 66.

Article	Collective rights for workers' representatives	Inclusion of representatives of self-employed workers
Art. 12(2)	Information, consultation and participation rights in relation to occupational safety and health (OSH) risk assessment and introduction of preventive measures	
Art. 13	Information and consultation rights on decisions that are likely to lead to the introduction of or substantial changes in ADMS	

Source: S. Rainone and A. Aloisi, 'The EU Platform Work Directive: What's new, what's missing, what's next', ETUI Policy Brief, 2024.06, 2024.

Note: Arts. 8(2), 9(1), 9(4), and 10(4) apply to representatives of self-employed workers by effect of the umbrella provision in Art. 15, and thus apply only with regard to the protection of personal data.

Table 2 offers an overview of the scope of application of the collective rights established in Chapter III, indicating which provisions also apply to representatives of self-employed workers. What emerges is that the Directive requires platforms to engage in **consultation practices only with representatives of employees**, while representatives of self-employed workers are granted access only to information rights. The sole possible exception is Art. 8(1), which requires platforms to 'seek the views of persons performing platform work and their representatives' when conducting the data protection impact assessment. However, the phrasing ('seek the views') does not appear to create clear, enforceable obligations and is open to flexible interpretation–both narrow and broad–and has therefore been excluded from Table 2. It could be understood either as a general invitation to provide input or as an actual consultation duty. 30

As elaborated elsewhere,[28] the Directive establishes a status-based, multi-tiered system, raising questions about its practical application in situations where the platform workforce includes both employees and self-employed workers. First, Art. 2 seems to suggest that the composition of representation structures may differ based on the employment status of the workers represented, as it refers to 'trade unions' only in letter (f), when defining 'workers' representatives'. Theoretically, this could lead to the establishment of two separate representative bodies within the same undertaking–a rather impractical solution.[29] Conversely, if all information and consultation practices are channeled through a single body representing all workers regardless of status, those representatives would be expected to exercise certain prerogatives solely in the interest of those who are employees. This would be difficult to implement in practice, particularly given the nuance introduced by Art. 15 which limits the applicability of Arts. 8(2), 9(1), 9(4), and 10(4) to representatives of self-employed workers only insofar as the rights are exercised 'with regard to the protection of their personal data'. 31

Another unresolved issue concerns the implementation of rules on workplace representation–such as determining jurisdiction, election procedures, and the functioning 32

[28] Rainone ELLJ 2025, 494-515.

[29] On the challenges of coordinating collective representation in the platform economy, see: Vandaele, ETUI Working Paper, 2018.

of representative bodies–in cases of cloud work.[30] Dispersed across various countries, often engaged on a self-employed basis, and working for platforms (or subcontractors) established in different jurisdictions, these workers face more than just organisational barriers in exercising their collective rights.[31]

33 A similar **challenge arises in cases where the workforce is not directly employed by the platform** – or not entirely – but instead hired through one or more intermediaries.[32] Multiparty relationships are common in the platform economy, allowing platforms to retain control over the work process via algorithmic management while externalising labour, tax, and social security responsibilities to the contractor or intermediary.[33] Art. 3 establishes that workers who have a contractual relationship with an intermediary should enjoy the same level of protection as those directly hired by the platform. This could be interpreted to mean that workers hired by intermediaries should not face weaker collective rights or diminished opportunities to elect representatives. However, this equal treatment could be undermined if the constituency for electing representatives is not interpreted as encompassing the platform's entire workforce – regardless of contractual links to intermediaries – but as instead fragmented into smaller groups based on ties to individual subcontractors.[34]

34 Both EU and national laws on company-based collective rights often require a minimum threshold (i.e. a certain number of workers being employed within an undertaking or establishment) to allow for the election of representatives.[35] This is the case, for instance, under Art. 3 of Directive 2002/14/EC on information and consultation practices, which is explicitly referred to in Art. 13 of the Platform Work Directive. To comply with the 'same level of protection' principle in Art. 3 and prevent contractual fragmentation from undermining collective rights, it would be necessary to adopt a functional interpretation of workplace representation rules–one that bypasses intermediaries when defining workers' representative constituency. This concern was partially addressed by the Expert Group on the transposition of the Directive, in which the Commission clarified that the company-size thresholds set out in Art. 3 of Directive 2002/14/EC do not apply to information and consultation rights concerning ASM and ADMS.[36] The Commission's guidelines, however, lack binding force, and platforms are likely to resist such an interpretation in favour of a more textual reading of the obligations contained in the EU and national acquis. Moreover, while this reading could help circumvent formalistic barriers to the effective enjoyment of collective rights under Art. 13, it does not go so far as to promote a broader and more unitary notion of the workforce, encompassing workers engaged through subcontracting structures.

35 Lastly, it is worth noting that the Directive does not establish an obligation to create channels or structures for worker representation. Art. 14 provides that: 'Where there are no representatives of platform workers, Member States shall ensure that digital labour platforms directly inform the platform workers concerned of decisions likely to lead to the introduction of or to substantial changes in the use of AMS or ADMS'. In other

[30] Donini Labour and Law Issues 2019, 99–114; Rainone in Countouris/De Stefano/Piasna/Rainone, p. 163–185.

[31] Morgan/van Zoonen/ter Hoeven Eur. J. Ind. Rel. 2023, 301–322; Fairwork, "Cloudwork Ratings 2025: Advancing standards in digital labour and AI supply chain governance", 2025.

[32] Wray, "Is sub-contracting becoming the new normal in the platform economy?", Brave New Europe, 22 April 2021.

[33] Hießl ELLJ 2023, 514–540.

[34] Rainone CLLPJ 2025, 147–174.

[35] Another example can be found in Art. 1(1) Directive 98/59/EC.

[36] European Commission, Report Expert Group – Transposition of the Directive (EU) 2024/2831 on improving working conditions in platform work (12.1.2026), 64.

words, only individual information duties are imposed, and only in relation to platform employees. This softer regime is thus likely to deter platforms from cooperating in the creation of mechanisms for collective representation and, in turn, place pressure on trade unions and grassroots organisations to mobilise workers and establish an effective presence in the workplace.[37]

C. Exogenous barriers to the exercise of collective labour rights

The Directive's gaps and inconsistencies are not the only obstacle between platform workers and the full enjoyment of their collective rights. This section discusses other **structural barriers that are inherent to EU and national legal and industrial relations systems** which, despite not being specific to the platform economy, risk significantly eroding the Platform Work Directive's gains. **36**

A first, serious challenge relates to the scope of application of general labour law frameworks, including the rules defining collective labour rights. While under ILO conventions No. 98 and No. 87 the rights to collective bargaining and trade union membership should be accessible to all workers regardless of their status, many countries have structured their laws so that only employees are allowed to join unions, organise, and bargain collectively.[38] Studies demonstrate that several European jurisdictions (e.g., Estonia, Romania, Slovakia, Bulgaria, Malta, Latvia) have legislation that either prevents most self-employed workers from joining trade unions or fails to guarantee this right.[39] In some cases, legal obstacles arise from self-employed individuals being mandatorily members of business associations. For instance, in Austria, unions report obstacles to unionisation for platform workers as they can only be represented by the Economic Chamber, which represents business interests, and not by the Chamber of Labour, which negotiates on behalf of workers.[40] These legal frameworks reflect outdated models of work organisation and are poorly suited to the platform economy where a significant share of workers operate outside traditional employment relationships. **37**

The Directive engages with this gap in Art. 2(1)(g), though not without controversy. The qualifier 'insofar as provided for in national law and practice' in the definition of 'representatives of persons performing platform work' was contested within the expert group on the transposition of the Directive. Trade unions objected that the right to join a trade union is protected by ILO Conventions and cannot be left to national arrangements. The Commission services replied that the qualifier only limits the scope of representation under the Directive itself: where national law does not already provide for the representation of self-employed workers, the Directive does not require Member States to introduce it, though it leaves them free to do so. recital 23 nonetheless stresses that the Directive must be implemented in line with ILO Convention No. 98 (1949) on the Right

[37] For an overview of social dialogue initiatives and the main challenges encountered in the absence of a clear legislative framework supporting the creation of collective representation bodies, see: Lamannis, ETUI Report 2023.02, 2023.

[38] Cherry, 'Lost in a crowd: how crowdworkers are denied their rights at work', ILAW Taken for a Ride Series (3), 2025.

[39] Fulton, 'Trade Unions Protecting Self-Employed Workers', ETUC 2018; Eurofound, 'Exploring self-employment in the European Union', 2017; Eurofound, 'Regulating minimum wages and other forms of pay for the self-employed', 2020.

[40] ETUC, 'Platform Reps Austria: Country Report 2022', 2022, at p. 7.

to Organise and Collective Bargaining, which may caution against an overly restrictive reading.[41]

38 This dichotomous approach creates challenges that extend beyond collective bargaining. Self-employed workers are also excluded from statutory frameworks regulating information and consultation practices, as well as the rules on the composition and functioning of workplace representation structures. For example, in Germany, only employees have the right to establish a works council.[42] In the context of platform work, Miranda Boto has framed this issue as a key challenge for both self-employed and gig workers, particularly in relation to the training and selection of representatives:[43] who can speak for them, within or beyond traditional trade union structures?

39 Still linked to the personal scope of labour law norms, another structural limitation that may hinder the exercise of collective rights in the platform economy is the difficulty of extending those rights beyond the corporate veil.[44] Labour laws are generally designed to create rights and obligations between the parties to a contractual relationship, and the prerogatives of workers' representatives are meant to be exercised primarily–if not exclusively–vis-à-vis the direct employer (or contractor, in self-employment arrangements). This becomes problematic in situations where workers are hired by intermediaries and have no contractual ties with the leading firm/platform which ultimately defines the terms and conditions of service provision.[45] The result is that information and consultation practices risk being reduced to ineffective outcomes or complex triangulations between the contractual employer and the platform, particularly when the intermediary is not actively involved in managing work operations.[46]

40 The Directive only partially addresses this issue, having established in Art. 3 that workers hired by intermediaries should enjoy the same level of protection as those directly hired by the platform. This implies that, where worker representation bodies exist, the intermediary must be able to comply with the information and consultation obligations laid out in the Platform Work Directive and, arguably, cannot justify violations by claiming that the platform refused to provide the necessary information. In Art. 8, the Directive also recognises that digital labour platforms are to be considered data controllers for the purposes of data protection impact assessments. It is therefore logical to infer that platforms remain bound by the transparency and disclosure obligations concerning the functioning of algorithmic management systems, even where intermediaries are involved. This has also been confirmed by the European Commission in the context of the Expert Group on the transposition of the Directive, where it clarified that responsibility for complying with the obligations set out in Arts. 7 to 11 should rest with the entity running and managing the algorithmic management system.[47]

41 At the same time–as discussed in Section 2.3–the Platform Work Directive offers limited guidance to national legislators on how to operationalise this multi-layered framework. It is unlikely that platforms will establish specific communication channels

---

[41] European Commission, Report Expert Group – Transposition of the Directive (EU) 2024/2831 on improving working conditions in platform work (12.1.2026), 19–20.

[42] Ferrari/Bertolini/Borkert/Graham Digital Geography and Society 2024, 5.

[43] Boto, 'La Contrattazione Collettiva per i Lavoratori Autonomi e Nella Gig Economy: Incontri e Incomprensioni', LavoroDirittiEuropa (3) 2023.

[44] Weil RSF J. Social Sciences 2019, 147–165.

[45] On the implications of subcontracting for employer accountability see, among others: Borelli, "Subcontracting: exploitation by design tackling the business model for social dumping', The Left, Brussels 2022.

[46] For examples from the Spanish context: Cardo/Alonso ELLJ 2022, 492–514.

[47] European Commission, Report Expert Group – Transposition of the Directive (EU) 2024/2831 on improving working conditions in platform work (12.1.2026), 23.

with workers who are formally managed by subcontractors, and equally doubtful that workers will have the resources to approach platforms directly. To avoid a situation in which corporate fragmentation leaves some workers less informed or less involved, a **clear duty of cooperation between platforms and their subcontractors** is essential. This interpretation reflects the position of the European Commission, which recognised that it would place an excessive burden on a person performing platform work to exercise the rights set out in Chapter III of the Directive against a digital labour platform with which they have no contractual relationship.[48] Yet here too the Platform Work Directive falls short, limiting mandatory guarantees to a general obligation on Member States to 'establish appropriate mechanisms, which shall include, where appropriate, joint and several liability systems'.[49]

Beyond the challenges related to the establishment of effective representation struc- 42
tures and communication channels, another potentially concerning aspect relates to the *quid* of collective engagement. The opacity of digital technologies – and of algorithmic management in particular – exacerbates the power imbalance between workers and firms.[50] As long as the inner workings of algorithms remain opaque to workers, their representatives, and trade unions, information asymmetries will undermine the ability to negotiate and assert control over working conditions. Accordingly, understanding and engaging with algorithms has become a key demand among workers across sectors (not only in platform work), prompting calls for rapid regulatory solutions to improve the intelligibility of digital-intensive management systems.[51]

A combined reading of the Platform Work Directive and the GDPR provides impor- 43
tant guarantees, compelling digital companies to disclose the data they collect and how data processing affects automated decision-making and disciplinary practices.[52] However, data-related safeguards alone are insufficient. To allow workers' representatives to negotiate on core working conditions, a comprehensive understanding of how algorithms govern those conditions–particularly wage setting – is essential.[53] The Platform Work Directive's silence on this point underscores the centrality of algorithmic competence and AI literacy for the effective exercise of information and consultation rights.[54] Art. 13(3) acknowledges the need for technical support, allowing workers' representatives to be assisted by an expert of their choice. However, this possibility is limited to the exercise of information and consultation rights under Directive 2002/14/EC–which only applies to workers in an employment relationship – and is further restricted to platforms employing more than 250 workers in a given Member State.

Overall, these broader challenges show that regulating platform work cannot be 44
detached from the deeper structural transformations which are reshaping the world of work and weakening workers' bargaining autonomy. The two-year transposition period for implementing the Platform Work Directive has offered a window of opportunity to consider how national legislative and industrial relations systems could be adapted to address these critical issues. The next section explores constructive avenues through which both policymakers and non-regulatory actors – such as workers' representatives,

[48] European Commission, Report Expert Group – Transposition of the Directive (EU) 2024/2831 on improving working conditions in platform work (12.1.2026), 23.
[49] Art. 3 Platform Work Directive.
[50] Collins/Atkinson Transfer 2023, 37–52.
[51] Hossein Jarrahi/Sutherland in Greene Taylor/Christian-Lamb/Martin/Nardi 2019.
[52] Rosin Ind. Law J. 2022, 478–493.
[53] Aloisi/De Stefano in Biasi, forthcoming.
[54] Otto Ital. Labour Law e-J. 2022, 51–64.

unions, lawyers, and judges – can further advance the Directive's protective function and reduce the regulatory gaps in the wider collective rights framework.

D. Regulatory, organising and judicial synergies for a stronger framework

45 Sections 2 and 3 identified a series of shortcomings relating both to the way the Directive was conceived and to the structural gaps in general labour law frameworks–now aggravated by the integration of algorithmic management at the workplace. Such limitations carry risks for the implementation phase, which could lead to weak results unless national regulatory and industrial relations structures succeed in absorbing (some of) the highlighted blind spots.

46 This section explores different **constructive avenues** which national systems could approach in view of integrating the novelties introduced by the Platform Work Directive into a coherent framework while minimising the limitations of the Directive.

I. Overarching regulatory reforms

47 The first key area for intervention is regulatory. As discussed in previous sections, several structural limitations risk weakening the Platform Work Directive's collective rights framework. **Legislative reforms** at national level with the transposition of the Directive in view should therefore focus on enabling access to representation for self-employed workers, streamlining representation structures across fragmented workforces, and clarifying the roles and obligations of platforms and intermediaries.

48 Looking at the first aspect, a central task for lawmakers is to go beyond platform-specific norms and consider whether the existing framework on collective rights is sufficiently conducive to representing workers – regardless of their status – in the platform economy.[55] This would, first and foremost, require ensuring that the applicable rules governing workplace representation and collective bargaining allow for the inclusion of self-employed workers, and that they do so without resulting in complex or burdensome duplication of representation structures.[56] Austria offers an interesting recent development in this regard. The October 2025 revision of § 1 ArbVG, which entered into force in January 2026, extended the scope of collective bargaining to *freie Dienstnehmer* – a category of contractually self-employed persons working under freelance arrangements that are economically close to employment.[57] While the reform stops short of covering all self-employed – a limitation that has drawn criticism in the scholarship –[58] it illustrates how an existing collective bargaining framework can be incrementally opened up to non-employees.

49 It will also be necessary to clarify the rules governing the creation and functioning of representative bodies in contexts marked by high levels of fragmentation – characteristics that, in the platform economy, primarily stem from extensive subcontracting practices and the absence of fixed (or physical) workplaces.[59] This implies providing new

---

[55] Gyulavári Maastricht J. Eur. Comp. Law 2020, 406–424.

[56] Hießl in Hießl/Waas, p. 278.

[57] Pupeter/Lukas/Bertazolli ELLJ 2026, 47 (51–52).

[58] Schwertner ASoK 2025, 314 (316).

[59] Borelli, 'Subcontracting and algorithmic management in e-commerce are turning the logistic sector into a laboratory for labour abuses', interview in Equal Times, 29 August 2025, https://www.equaltimes.org/subcontracting-and-algorithmic?lang=en.

guidance on how existing norms may be applied in ways that could help re-establish unity.[60] Such reinterpretative efforts should, in particular, address the rules determining the legal thresholds for the election of workers' representatives and for the applicability of information and consultation rights, and ultimately provide an inclusive definition of the representation base.

Furthermore, it is important to assess whether existing systems include sufficient safeguards to ensure the active engagement and accountability of digital labour platforms in cases of collective rights violations occurring along the subcontracting chain.[61] While joint liability systems may assist workers in claiming compensatory measures, representatives must also be in a position to negotiate working conditions – regardless of whether governance of the algorithmic management system lies directly with the platform or with the intermediaries who formally employ the workers. Similarly, appropriate channels should be in place to ensure compliance with the information obligations relating to data use and processing in cases where the data controller – typically the platform – is not the same entity as the contractual employer, i.e. the intermediary. 50

II. Enhancing the preparedness of collective representation systems

To be effective, these proposed regulatory revisions should go hand-in-hand with **complementary innovations in national industrial relations frameworks** and, specifically, in the internal organisation of trade unions and workers' representation bodies. 51

A first critical aspect requiring prompt action is the information asymmetry regarding the functioning of algorithmic management systems.[62] Only partially addressed by the Directive, the difficulty in obtaining a clear picture of the platform's work organisation and the rationale behind managerial decisions ultimately aggravates workers' weak bargaining position.[63] This calls for extensive capacity-building programmes, along with adequate resources and support, to enable workers' representatives and unions meaningfully to engage with the technical aspects that the regulation of platform work inevitably entails. A fuller understanding of how algorithms function would place workers' representatives in a stronger position during consultation processes,[64] increasing the likelihood that these will lead to the negotiation of collective agreements also covering core working conditions, such as wage setting or working time. 52

An important channel through which workers could strengthen their literacy on algorithmic management and artificial intelligence is the establishment of **stable representation structures, such as works councils**, which are arguably better positioned to access knowledge and resources than less formal and organised forms of worker representation.[65] Cross-European analysis, however, reveals that the creation of such bodies in the platform economy remains exceptional, with initiatives identified only in Austria and Germany. Even in these two countries, the reported experiences are not without difficulties and present an uneven and fragmented picture, highlighting the importance of strong trade union and institutional support. 53

The Austrian context provides clear examples of how platform opposition and resistance can pose obstacles to the effective functioning of elected bodies. The first works 54

---

60 Rainone CLLPJ 2025, 147–174.

61 For an overview of different regulatory options, see: Cremers/Houwerzijl, 'Subcontracting and social liability', 2021, ETUC.

62 Dube/Jacobs/Naidu/Suri Am. Econ. Rev. 2020, 33–46.

63 Gaudio Int. J. Comp. Labour Law Ind. Rel. 2024, 95–96.

64 Hießl 2025, p. 60.

65 Vandaele, p. 17.

council in the platform economy was formed by *Foodora* workers, with the primary aim of negotiating a collective agreement. However, Eurofound sources report that the bargaining process took nearly 2.5 years, even though representatives were supported by crucial legal and technical advice from the Austrian Transportation and Service Union.[66] Moreover, the agreement applies only to employees, who make up around 10% of a workforce predominantly composed of self-employed riders.[67]

55 Subsequently, a works council was established at *Lieferando* in 2019,[68] but the legitimacy of the initiative was immediately challenged in court by the platform, which argued that its operations fell outside the territorial scope of the legislation governing works councils since no legal entity was established in Austria and all the servers operating the app were located abroad.[69] At the time of writing, the council continues to operate amid ongoing legal proceedings.[70]

56 Attempts to set up works councils have also been suppressed by platforms through targeted disciplinary sanctions and dismissals. This was the case for couriers working for *Veloce*, a food delivery platform that had reportedly prevented the formation of a works council from 2004 onward by dismissing those who sought to organise their colleagues.[71] Eventually, the couriers succeeded in establishing a works council in 2020, but only after taking legal action to challenge the platform's conduct.

57 Platforms in Austria have also been reported to obstruct the functioning of works councils by failing to respond to inquiries, providing inaccurate information, and making consultation processes so time-consuming and frustrating that representatives have, at times, withdrawn from their roles.[72]

58 Turning to the German context, the overall picture is characterised by several successful initiatives. For instance, 11 works councils had been formed at *Lieferando* (formerly *Foodora*) by January 2023,[73] with the earliest initiatives dating back to 2017.[74] In some cases, platforms and workers' representatives have established a structured negotiation routine, occasionally mirroring the protocols typical of German industrial relations.[75] Nevertheless, efforts to establish works councils in Germany have also met with significant resistance.[76]

---

[66] Griesser/Plank/Vogel/Risak/Herr/Ustek/Steward/Graham, 'Fairwork Austria Ratings 2022: Labour Standards in the Platform Economy', Fairwork, 2022, p. 11; Eurofound 'Works council Foodora Austria (Initiative), Record number 3008', Platform Economy Database, 2021.

[67] Griesser/Plank/Vogel/Risak/Herr/Ustek/Steward/Graham, 'Fairwork Austria Ratings 2022: Labour Standards in the Platform Economy', Fairwork, 2022, p. 11; Geyer/Vandaele/Prinz Econ. Ind. Dem. 2023, 835–858; Eurofound, 'Works council Foodora Austria (Initiative), Record number 3008', Platform Economy Database, 2021.

[68] Herr, Working Paper-Reihe der AK Wien Vol. 169, 2017.

[69] Friedrich-Ebert-Stiftung, 'Collection of Factsheets on Online Platforms and Platform Work in Selected Countries', 2023, p. 7.

[70] ETUC, 'Platform Reps Austria: Country Report 2022', 2022, p. 7.

[71] Eurofound, 'Lieferando, Mjam and Veloce establish works council (Initiative), Record number 2430', Platform Economy Database, 2020.

[72] ETUC, 'Platform Reps Austria: Country Report 2022', 2022, p. 6.

[73] Neumann Leeds Index of Platform Labour Protests 2023, 3.

[74] Schreyer Work Organ. Labour Glob. 2021, 69 (71); Jesnes/Neumann/Trappmann/Becdelièvre in Drahokoupil/Vandaele, p. 269; Eurofound, 'Works Council *Foodora* Cologne and Hamburg; Works Council Lieferando Cologne and Frankfurt (Initiative), Record number 2977', Platform Economy Database, 2021; Eurofound, 'Works Council Deliveroo Cologne, Germany (Initiative), Record number 2978', Platform Economy Database, 2021.

[75] Neumann Leeds Index of Platform Labour Protests 2023, 3; Jesnes/Neumann/Trappmann/Becdelièvre in Drahokoupil/Vandaele, p. 269; Eurofound, 'Establishment of works councils by riders for Foodora and Lieferando (Initiative), Record number 2977', Platform Economy Database, 2021.

[76] See e.g., Eurofound, 'Establishment of works councils by riders for Foodora and Lieferando (Initiative), Record number 2977', Platform Economy Database, 2021; Wyputta, 'Lieferando Torpediert Betrieb-

At *Lieferando*, *Gorillas*, and *Flink*, the legitimacy of works council elections has been – and in some cases still is – contested in court.[77] Platforms have also exploited the limited statutory protections afforded to self-employed workers to avoid the creation of elected bodies. This was the case with *Deliveroo*, which changed the contractual status of its employees to independent contractors, effectively dissolving the works council.[78] The German experience illustrates further that works councils may be dismantled following corporate takeovers – an occurrence not uncommon in the platform economy. Schreyer reports that, following the acquisition of *Foodora*, *Lieferando* attempted to persuade couriers to accept revised contracts in exchange for waiving their previously acquired collective rights.[79] **59**

Germany is also home to the only example of a European Works Council (EWC) so far identified in the platform economy. Its creation followed a tortuous process which clearly illustrates the pressure that platforms can exert to suppress or weaken workers' representation structures. The initiative began when riders at *Foodora* requested that the parent company, *Delivery Hero* (*DH*), establish a company-wide works council across all German sites. Following *DH*'s opposition – which led to legal proceedings – the company was required to install employee representatives on its supervisory board. To avoid that, *DH* converted its legal business form to a Societas Europea (SE).[80] The platform states that this change was meant to express its 'self-image as an internationally oriented company with European roots,' yet its motives are probably less poetic in practice: SE status is often sought by German companies to circumvent stricter national rules on board-level employee representation.[81] **60**

Eventually, this change in legal form gave rise to a pioneering EWC, established in April 2018 with an agreement signed in Berlin with the German union *NGG*, the Italian Federation of Commerce, Hotels and Service Workers, and the European Federation of Food, Agriculture and Tourism.[82] The main strengths of the initiative lie in creating an international network of riders who exchange practices and ideas, and in facilitating exchanges between workers' representatives and management,[83] in a sector where the transnational presence of platform companies has challenged nationally oriented industrial relations structures. EWCs have, however, only limited capacity to improve working conditions directly. Compared to national works councils, cooperation takes place at a more abstract level and relies less on concrete, actionable measures.[84] **61**

The reported experiences show that, while platform workers still see traditional forms of collective representation as a viable vehicle to strengthen their bargaining position, additional safeguards are required to protect against platforms' antagonistic behaviours. In particular, there is a need for more robust and enforceable protections against retali- **62**

---

sratswahl Ausgelieferte Mitarbeiter', taz.de, 2020; Ferrari/Bertolini/Borkert/Graham Digital Geography and Society 2024, 5.

[77] Neumann Leeds Index of Platform Labour Protests 2023, 3.

[78] Jesnes/Neumann/Trappmann/Becdelièvre in Drahokoupil/Vandaele, p. 269; Eurofound, 'Works Council Deliveroo Cologne, Germany (Initiative), Record number 2978', Platform Economy Database, 2021.

[79] Schreyer Work Organ. Labour Glob. 2021, 69–84 (75).

[80] Eurofound, 'Establishment of works councils by riders for Foodora and Lieferando (Initiative), Record number 2977', Platform Economy Database, 2021.

[81] Vandaele, p. 17.

[82] Eurofound, 'SE (Societas Europaea, European Company) Works Council Delivery Hero (Initiative), Record number 3009', Platform Economy Database, 2021.

[83] Eurofound, 'SE (Societas Europaea, European Company) Works Council Delivery Hero (Initiative), Record number 3009', Platform Economy Database, 2021.

[84] Eurofound, 'SE (Societas Europaea, European Company) Works Council Delivery Hero (Initiative), Record number 3009', Platform Economy Database, 2021.

ation and union-busting practices. Moreover, opposition from platforms stresses the importance of better integrating self-employed workers into existing collective structures: the broader the representation base, the greater the capacity for mobilisation in the face of hostile or uncooperative employers.

63 Platforms' resistance also underscores the potential for constructive synergies between workplace representation structures and local trade unions–not only to reinforce workers' bargaining position but also to facilitate knowledge sharing and harmonise negotiating efforts and practices. Finally, safeguards should be put in place to ensure that transnational initiatives are in synergy with the ways of working of national workers' representatives and trade unions and, above all, that they do not substitute more meaningful forms of collective representation rooted in national law.

III. Mobilising litigation channels

64 Besides advocating legal reforms or pushing for a renewal of the rules and practices governing workplace representation, collective actors could also pursue a third avenue to promote compliance with the Platform Work Directive's collective rights framework: judicial enforcement.

65 An analysis of the (fast-growing) body of case law on the platform economy shows that, in some jurisdictions in particular, trade unions have relied heavily on judicial proceedings to challenge platforms' abusive practices and degrading working conditions.[85] While the focus of such proceedings has predominantly been on employment reclassification, trade unions are increasingly turning to the courts to **enforce platform workers' access to information and consultation rights**.[86] Two different judicial approaches can be identified across EU jurisdictions.

66 The first is the mobilisation of the existing data rights framework – primarily the GDPR – to address violations of platforms' duties to disclose details about algorithmic management processes and automated decision-making. In the absence of dedicated labour law provisions applicable to self-employed workers, the broad personal scope of data rights – which extend to all individuals regardless of employment status – has provided alternative juridical avenues for establishing safeguards against exploitative platform practices. Although not part of the EU's collective labour rights acquis, data rights are designed to reduce information asymmetries, and their successful mobilisation in case law demonstrates their potential as a complement to labour rights in strengthening workers' bargaining position.[87]

67 Italy offers a notable example. Food delivery platforms *Foodinho* and *Deliveroo* were fined for violating couriers' information rights under the GDPR.[88] In addition, two rulings by the Tribunal of Palermo found *Uber Eats*[89] and *Glovo*[90] in breach of their obligation to disclose information about the functioning of their algorithmic management systems. GDPR-related cases have also emerged in Dutch jurisprudence. The Amsterdam

[85] See e.g., Hießl CLLPJ 2021; Leeds Index of Platform Labour Protest, 'A Global Database of Platform Worker Protest Actions', 2023; Lamannis, ETUI Report 2023.02, 2023; De Stefano/Durri/Stylogiannis/Wouters, ILO Working Paper 27, 2021; Hadwiger, ILO 2022.

[86] Rainone/Hießl in Vandaele/Rainone, p. 171–189; Gaudio Int. J. Comp. Labour Law Ind. Rel. 2024, 95–96.

[87] Potocka-Sionek/Aloisi in Vandaele/Rainone, p. 251 (260).

[88] Injunction against *Foodinho* srl – 10 June 2021 [9675440] and injunction order against *Deliveroo* Italy srl – 22 July 2021 [9685994].

[89] Judgment of 31 March 2023, RG 645/2023.

[90] Palermo Civil Court, 20 June 2023.

Court of Appeal has ruled on three cases brought against ride-hailing platforms *Uber* and *Ola*.[91] In each case, the platforms were found to have violated Art. 15(1) GDPR by withholding comprehensive information, failing to provide supplementary information on the personal data processed, and deactivating drivers' accounts via automated systems.[92] Additional cases have been reported in Germany[93] and Luxembourg,[94] where judges have confirmed several breaches of transparency obligations in the context of algorithmic data processing.[95]

The transposition of the Directive into national law will strengthen the applicable data rights framework by further embedding it in the labour context and, arguably, making it easier to enforce within labour relations. In this respect, the existing body of jurisprudence is promising as it indicates that, at least in some Member States, the judiciary is already attuned to the potential of data rights provisions as a means of enhancing understanding of organisational models and limiting the expansion of employers' discretion – suggesting that further litigation in this area can be expected. **68**

The second judicial approach emerging from national case law is the use of litigation to compel platforms to comply with existing labour law provisions on information and consultation rights.[96] While, to date, proceedings based on collective labour law are fewer than those based on data rights, this avenue is both strategic and forward-looking: it requires courts to reinterpret 'classical' labour law norms in light of new business models and work organisation patterns. Trade unions and labour advocates can thereby support–and help steer–regulatory adaptation efforts to ensure that collective labour law retains its protective function and remains resilient in the face of disruptive employer practices such as those seen in the platform economy. **69**

A recent significant example can be found in Spain, where a violation of consultation rights relating to collective dismissals led to a Supreme Court decision.[97] In this case, the unions *UGT* and *CCOO* brought a lawsuit against *Uber Eats*, arguing that the deactivation of couriers' accounts following the implementation of the Rider Law should be considered a collective redundancy and should have been preceded by mandatory consultation with workers' representatives. The unions asked to be recognised as the most representative in the sector and claimed that, had the proper procedure been followed, they should have been invited to form an ad hoc consultation committee. The case thus raised two key questions: to what extent can automatic account deactivations be equated with collective redundancies; and who is entitled to exercise the prerogatives of a 'representative' in the absence of established workplace representation structures? The Supreme Court ultimately upheld the applicability of the collective dismissals framework and ruled that, in the absence of internal worker representation, *UGT* and *CCOO* were entitled to represent the workforce in the consultation process, as they were deemed the most representative unions in the platform's sector of activity. **70**

This case shows that, by developing litigation strategies grounded in the collective labour law acquis, lawyers and unions can help reposition platform work within the disciplinary boundaries of labour law, reopening access to protective frameworks that platforms have systematically sought to circumvent. **71**

---

[91] Amsterdam Appeals Court, 4 April 2023: [ECLI:NL:GHAMS:2023:796, ECLI:NL:GHAMS:2023:804, ECLI:NL:GHAMS:2023:793].

[92] Hießl 2025, p. 16–23.

[93] Hanover Administrative Court, 9 February 2023 [10 A 6199/20].

[94] Hießl 2025, p. 15.

[95] Hießl 2025, p. 30.

[96] Rainone/Hießl in Vandaele/Rainone p. 171–189.

[97] Spanish Supreme Court 20.07.2022 – STS 684/2022.

E. Concluding remarks

72 This chapter explored the collective rights framework established in the Platform Work Directive and outlined the prerogatives attributed to workers' representatives, distinguishing their reach and depth with reference to the employment status of workers.

73 The Platform Work Directive introduces important innovations both from a normative perspective (by recognising that the bargaining inequality inherent in platform work requires stronger involvement of collective actors) and from a more technical one (by establishing clear transparency and engagement obligations regarding the functioning of algorithmic management systems). At the same time, the analysis showed that a number of gaps and obstacles may hinder the full enjoyment of the Directive's collective rights.

74 A first set of limitations stems from the Directive's own regulatory architecture. The Platform Work Directive fails to explicitly link collective rights to aspects of algorithmic management beyond data processing, AMS, and automated decisions leading to account suspension or termination; it thereby overlooks their impact on other core working conditions–such as wage setting and working time–thus falling short of laying the foundation for meaningful collective negotiations on these issues. Furthermore, while the enforcement framework allows for the potentially strong involvement of workers' representatives, the Directive leaves ample room for national discretion which may result in fragmentation in the level of protection afforded to platform workers across the EU. A closer look at how the Platform Work Directive defines 'representatives' reveals a dual regime: representatives of self-employed workers enjoy fewer and less meaningful prerogatives than those elected by platform employees. Here, too, there is a risk of fragmented and uneven information and consultation practices, potentially leading to a two-tier system of workers' representation with overlapping competences.

75 A second set relates to broader, non-platform-specific obstacles that may significantly weaken the Platform Work Directive's innovative potential. First, legal barriers at national level continue to prevent many self-employed individuals from accessing structures of worker representation – such as trade unions and works councils – or from being covered by collective bargaining rights. Therefore, even if the Platform Work Directive formally grants self-employed platform workers non-negligible collective rights, they may still struggle to find suitable structures through which to exercise them. Second, digitalisation has enabled new business models that disrupt the application of existing legal frameworks. The spread of subcontracting and the opacity of algorithmic decision-making further complicate the role of representatives in exercising their functions effectively, highlighting the need for stronger technical support.

76 Against this backdrop, the **transposition of the Platform Work Directive** into national legal systems presents both a **challenge and an opportunity**. It offers Member States the chance to address structural inconsistencies and blind spots in the personal and material scope of collective rights, and to ensure that the implementation of the Directive does not reproduce or deepen existing exclusions. This chapter outlined three main avenues through which domestic actors could support this process. The first – and most obvious – is regulatory. Lawmakers now have a window of opportunity to revise or help reinterpret existing collective labour laws to ensure that the Platform Work Directive's innovations–first and foremost, the extension of rights to self-employed workers – can be given effect within national systems. The second avenue concerns collective actors themselves and the industrial relations frameworks in which they operate. Stable structures of worker representation struggle to emerge in the platform economy and, when they do, they often face strong resistance due to the overt antagonism of platforms. This highlights the need for a more strategic integration of trade unions into

workplace representation so that workers can more effectively rely on their support and resources. The third avenue is litigation, which has emerged as a powerful tool for leveraging existing instruments – such as the GDPR or rules on collective redundancies – to challenge platforms' arbitrary conduct and secure workers' rights to information and consultation.

Overall, what emerges is that only through a purposive and inclusive implementation 77
can the Platform Work Directive contribute meaningfully to re-embedding collective representation in the platform economy and reaffirming the relevance of collective labour rights in the evolving digital world of work.

CHAPTER IV
TRANSPARENCY WITH REGARD TO PLATFORM WORK

Article 16
Declaration of platform work

Member States shall require digital labour platforms to declare work performed by platform workers to the competent authorities of the Member State in which the work is performed, in accordance with the rules and procedures laid down in the law of the Member States concerned.
This Article is without prejudice to specific obligations under Union law pursuant to which work is to be declared to relevant bodies of the Member State in cross-border situations.

Article 17
Access to relevant information on platform work

1. Member States shall ensure that digital labour platforms make the following information available to competent authorities and to representatives of persons performing platform work:

(a) the number of persons performing platform work through the digital labour platform concerned, disaggregated by level of activity, and their contractual or employment status;
(b) the general terms and conditions determined by the digital labour platform and applicable to those contractual relationships;
(c) the average duration of activity, the average weekly number of hours worked per person and the average income from activity of persons performing platform work on a regular basis through the digital labour platform concerned;
(d) the intermediaries with which the digital labour platform has a contractual relationship.

2. Member States shall ensure that digital labour platforms provide information on work performed by persons performing platform work and their employment status to competent authorities.
3. The information referred to in paragraph 1 shall be provided for each Member State in which persons are performing platform work through the digital labour platform concerned. As regards point (c) of paragraph 1, the information shall be provided only upon request.

4. The information referred to in paragraph 1 shall be updated at least every six months, and, as regards point (b) of paragraph 1 each time the terms and conditions are modified in substance.
Notwithstanding the first subparagraph, with regard to digital labour platforms which are SMEs, including microenterprises, Member States may provide that the information referred to in paragraph 1 is to be updated at least once every year.
5. The competent authorities and representatives of persons performing platform work shall have the right to ask digital labour platforms for additional clarifications and details regarding any of the information provided, including details regarding the employment contract. The digital labour platforms shall respond to such request by providing a substantiated reply without undue delay.

CHAPTER V
REMEDIES AND ENFORCEMENT

Article 18
Right to redress

Without prejudice to Articles 79 and 82 of Regulation (EU) 2016/679, Member States shall ensure that persons performing platform work, including those whose employment or other contractual relationship has ended, have access to timely, effective and impartial dispute resolution and a right to redress, including adequate compensation for the damage sustained, in the case of infringements of their rights arising from this Directive.

1 [not commented]

Article 19
Procedures on behalf or in support of persons performing platform work

Without prejudice to Article 80 of Regulation (EU) 2016/679, Member States shall ensure that representatives of persons performing platform work and legal entities which have, in accordance with national law or practice, a legitimate interest in defending the rights of persons performing platform work are able to engage in any judicial or administrative procedure to enforce any of the rights or obligations arising from this Directive. Member States shall ensure that such representatives and legal entities are able to act on behalf or in support of one or several persons performing platform work in the case of the infringement of any right or obligation arising from this Directive, in accordance with national law and practice.

1 See comments to → Art. 13 et seqq.

Article 20
Communication channels for persons performing platform work

Member States shall take the measures necessary to ensure that digital labour platforms provide persons performing platform work, by means of the digital labour

platforms' digital infrastructure or by similarly effective means, with the possibility to contact and communicate privately and securely with each other, and to contact or be contacted by representatives of persons performing platform work, while complying with Regulation (EU) 2016/679. Member States shall require digital labour platforms to refrain from accessing or monitoring those contacts and communications.

Recital (51) Persons performing platform work are exposed, in particular in on-location platform work, to a risk of violence and harassment, without having a physical workplace where they are able to address complaints. Harassment and sexual harassment are liable to have a negative impact on the health and safety of platform workers. Member States should therefore provide for preventive measures, including the setting up of effective reporting channels. Member States are also encouraged to support effective measures to combat violence and harassment in platform work and, in particular, include appropriate reporting channels for persons performing platform work who do not have an employment relationship.
Recital (62) Platform work is characterised by the lack of a common workplace where persons performing platform work can get to know and communicate with each other and with their representatives, also with a view of defending their interests with regard to the digital labour platform. It is therefore necessary to create digital communication channels, in line with the digital labour platforms' work organisation, where persons performing platform work can exchange privately and securely with each other and can be contacted by their representatives. Digital labour platforms should create such communication channels within their digital infrastructure or through similarly effective means, while respecting the protection of personal data and refraining from accessing or monitoring those communications.

Reference to other provisions:

Article 12 CFR Freedom of assembly and of association

1. Everyone has the right to freedom of peaceful assembly and to freedom of association at all levels, in particular in political, trade union and civic matters, which implies the right of everyone to form and to join trade unions for the protection of his or her interests.
2. Political parties at Union level contribute to expressing the political will of the citizens of the Union.

Article 28 CFR Right of collective bargaining and action

Workers and employers, or their respective organisations, have, in accordance with Union law and national laws and practices, the right to negotiate and conclude collective agreements at the appropriate levels and, in cases of conflicts of interest, to take collective action to defend their interests, including strike action.

Literature: Albicker, Gewerkschaften im Plattformkapitalismus, Arbeitskämpfe und gewerkschaftliche Organisierung in der Lieferbranche, Baden-Baden 2023; Aloisi/Rainone/Countouris, An unfinished task? Matching the Platform Work Directive with the EU and international 'social acquis', Geneva 2023; Barcevičius/Gineikytė-Kanclerė/ Klimavičiūtė/Martin, Study to support the impact assessment of an EU initiative to improve the working conditions in platform work, Final Report European Commisson 2021; Boecken/Düwell/Diller/Hanau (eds), Gesamtes Arbeitsrecht, 2nd edn, Baden-Baden 2023; Cini, 'Resisting algorithmic control: Understanding the rise and variety of platform worker mobilisations', New Technology, Work and Employment 2023, 125; Däubler, Interessenvertretung durch Betriebsrat und Gewerkschaft im digitalen Betrieb, Frankfurt am Main 2022; De Groen/Kilhoffer/Westhoff/Postica/Shamsfakhr, Digital labour platforms in the EU, Mapping and business models, Luxembourg 2021; Degner/Kocher, 'Arbeitskämpfe in der "Gig-Economy"? Die Protestbewegungen der Foodora- und Deliveroo- Riders und Rechtsfragen ihrer kollektiven Selbstorganisation', KJ 2018, 247; Ebenhöh/Hampel/Loschert, 'Sichere Kommunikationskanäle für Plattformarbeiter*innen', Berlin 2024; Franzen/Gallner/Oetker (eds), Kommentar zum europäischen Arbeitsrecht, 6th edn München 2024; Gärtner, 'Koalitionsfreiheit und Crowdwork, Zur Kollektivierung der Beschäftigteninteressen soloselbstständiger Crowdworker', Berlin 2020; Graham/Hjorth/Lehdonvirta, Transfer 2017, 135; Greef, de, '"Riders unite!", Arbeitskämpfe bei Essenslieferdiensten in der Gig-Economy – das Beispiel Berlin', 2nd edn, Berlin 2022; Gruber-Risak/Warter, 'Die EU-Richtlinie zur Verbesserung der Arbeitsbedingungen in der Plattformarbeit', DRdA 2024, 267; Gruszka/Pillinger/Gerold/Theine, '(In)visible by Design: An Analysis of a Domestic Labor Platform', Critical Sociology 2024, 1; Halefom, '"Hauptpersonalrat der Lehrerinnen": Article 88 GDPR and the Interplay between EU and Member State Employee Data Protection Rules', Modern Law Review 2024, 484; Hampel/Loschert, 'Anforderungen und Umsetzungsformen für wirksame digitale Kommunikationskanäle', DIAS 2026, 19; Heiland/Schaupp, 'Digitale Atomisierung oder neue Arbeitskämpfe? Widerständige Solidaritätskulturen in der plattformvermittelten Kurierarbeit', Momentum Quarterly 2020, 50; Heselhaus/Nowak (ed.), Handbuch der Europäischen Grundrechte, 2nd edn, München 2020; Honneth, Der arbeitende Souverän, Frankfurt am Main 2023; Kiess/Schmidt, 'Schützt demokratische Selbstwirksamkeit im Betrieb gegen Rechtsextremismus? Ein Vergleich zwischen Ost und West sowie 2020 und 2024', WSI-Mitt. 2025, 253; Kilhoffer/DeGroen/Lenaerts/Smits/Hauben/Waeyaert/Giacumacatos/Lhernould/Robin-Olivier, Study to gather evidence on the working conditions of platform workers, Luxembourg 2019; Kocher/Bronowicka, 'Blunt Tool for Women* in Platform Work? A Feminist Perspective on the Platform Work Directive', ELLJ 2025, 565; Krause, 'Auf dem Weg zur unionsrechtlichen Regelung von Plattformtätigkeiten, Die Kommissionsinitiative zur Plattformarbeit', NZA 2022, 521; Kühling, Die Kommunikationsfreiheit als europäisches Gemeinschaftsgrundrecht, Berlin 1999; LaPlante/Silberman, 'Building Trust in Crowd Worker Forums, Worker Ownership, Governance, and Work Outcomes', Proceedings of WebSci16. ACM 2016, 35; Lörcher/Bruun/Ribeiro (eds.), 'The International Covenant on Economic, Social and Cultural Rights and the employment relation', Oxford 2025; Mamerow, 'Digitales Zugangsrecht der Gewerkschaft', DIAS 2026, 3; Moore/Woodcock (eds), 'Augmented Exploitation: Artificial Intelligence, Automation and Work', London 2021; Niebler/Animento, 'Organising fragmented labour: the case of migrant workers at Helpling in Berlin', The Economic and Labour Relations Review, 2023, 689; Orth/Baum, 'Researching Care Platforms: Methodological and Ethical Considerations in the Broad Field of Domestic Platform Labour', Critical Sociology 2024, 1; Pechstein/Nowak/Häde (eds), Frankfurter Kommentar EUV/GRC/AEUV, 2nd edn, Tübingen 2023; Poblete/Kocher (eds) 'Digital intermediaries in the care and domestic work sector', London 2026 (forthcoming); Salehi/Irani/Bernstein/Alkhatib/Ogbe/Milland/Clickhappier, 'We Are Dynamo', in Begole/Kim/Inkpen/Woo (eds), Proceedings of the 33rd Annual ACM Conference on Human Factors in Computing Systems, Seoul 2015, 1621; Specht, 'Die Umsetzung des Art. 20 der EU-Plattformarbeitsrichtlinie', DIAS 2026, 14; Vaele/Silberman/Binns, 'Fortifying the algorithmic management provisions in the proposed Platform Work Directive', European Labour Law Journal 2023, 308; Warter, 'Datenschutzrechtliche Fragen zum digitalen Zugangsrecht', DIAS 2026, 9; Wömpner, 'Das digitale Zugangsrecht ist da!, Let's get digital', AuR 2024, 378.

A. Background and objectives

I. Background

Art. 20 calls for Member States to ensure that digital labour platforms provide persons performing platform work with **communication channels.** It forms part of Chapter V which is dedicated to remedies and enforcement and from the assumption that without effective means for communication, persons performing platform work will have difficulty in organising collectively, a difficulty which would, among other issues, hamper an effective enforcement not only of their fundamental collective labour rights. 1

A version of Art. 20 was already present in the **Commission's proposal** of 2021, then as Art. 15.[1] It went rather undisputed in the following discussions around the proposal, with a minor clarification in the wording of the recital which, in the Commission's proposal had referred to persons performing platform work defending their interests towards the 'employer' instead of the platform. It deserves to be mentioned that while what is now Art. 2(1)(f) was amended and now explicitly mentions 'trade unions' as workers' representatives, this concretisation has not been added to Art. 20.[2] 2

In the drafting process, there were several attempts at **formulating** in which way the channels should enable communication between persons performing platform work and their representatives. While the Commission proposal said these persons should be able to 'be contacted by' representatives, the Council proposed 'to contact and communicate with' representatives.[3] How the Directive's formula ('to contact or be contacted by') will have to be understood on these premises, will be discussed below (→ mn. 55 et seqq.). 3

In addition, Parliament had proposed several amendments, which were prepared by the Committee on Transport and Tourism for the Committee on Employment and Social Affairs. Part of these were intended to add **more specificities** to the recital and the article, when describing the digital communication channels.[4] 4

Parliament also unsuccessfully sought to make the close connection of this provision to the **right to organise in trade unions and to collective bargaining** clearer, proposing an additional article, calling for Member States to 'promote collective bargaining in platform work and ensure that workers' representatives have the right to access platform 5

[1] European Commission, 'Proposal for a Directive of the European Parliament and of the Council on improving working conditions in platform work', 9.12.2021, COM(2021) 762 final.

[2] Cf. Wömpner AuR 2024, 378 (384).

[3] Council, Permanent Representatives Committee, 'Proposal for a Directive of the European Parliament and of the Council on improving working conditions in platform work – General approach' General approach on the PWD' 7.6.2023, 10107/23, <https://eur-lex.europa.eu/legal-content/EN/TXT/PDF/?uri=CONSIL:ST_10107_2023_INIT> (last accessed 15.12.2025).

[4] European Parliament, 'Report on the plenary sitting on the proposal for a directive of the European Parliament and of the Council on improving working conditions in platform work', 22.12.2023, A9–0301/2022, <https://www.europarl.europa.eu/RegData/seance_pleniere/textes_deposes/rapports/2022/0301/P9_A(2022)0301_EN.pdf>, (Amendment 61 Proposal for a directive recital 45); see also the Committee on Transport an Tourism for the Committee on Employment and Social Affairs, 5.10.22 <https://www.europarl.europa.eu/RegData/seance_pleniere/textes_deposes/rapports/2022/0301/P9_A(2022)0301_EN.pdf> from Page 116) (last accessed: 15.12.2025) (Amendment 28 Proposal for a directive recital 45).

workers, including through digital access, for the purpose of organising their representation'.[5] It also proposed an amendment to what is now Art. 22 of the Directive (then Art. 17), reminding digital labour platforms of their duties to refrain from directly or indirectly undermining the right of association or the right of collective bargaining and action.[6] This initiative resulted in the addition of Art. 25 (promotion of collective bargaining in platform work → mn. 22).

6 Next to communication channels, the European Parliament also unsuccessfully proposed establishing **reporting channels**,[7] as a mechanism to 'safeguard persons performing platform work from violence, including gender-based violence and harassment'. It notes that persons performing platform work can be exposed to an increased risk of violence, including gender-based violence and harassment.[8] On this background, it proposed calling for Member States to ensure that digital labour platforms develop policies against violence and harassment and take preventative measures, including effective reporting channels, as well as address reports being received through these channels.

7 Although this proposal has not been accepted in the Trilogue negotiations, its concerns were included as recital 51 in the Platform Work Directive. It is a reminder of the challenges that the enforcement of rights on digital labour platform poses. Directive (EU) 2019/1937 of the European Parliament and of the Council of 23 October 2019 on the protection of persons who report breaches of Union law (**Whistleblowing Directive**) contains minimum standards for internal reporting channels (Arts. 7–9) and external reporting channels (Arts. 10–14) which also apply to digital labour platforms.

II. Legal context: Enforcement

8 Art. 20 is part of Chapter V of the Directive, regulating remedies and enforcement. As it does not say anything about remedies in the strict sense, the provision is rather directed towards **enforcement**, albeit indirectly. It recognises that, in view of the power imbalance between platforms and persons performing platform work, collective organisation is paramount for effective rights enforcement. Art. 25 confirms this assumption, by strongly linking collective organisation, collective bargaining and the exercise of rights (here: the rights related to algorithmic management). Art. 20 aims to address and compensate for the shortcomings persons performing platform work face when organising collectively, due to their lack of a common physical workplace.

[5] European Parliament, 'Report on the plenary sitting on the proposal for a directive of the European Parliament and of the Council on improving working conditions in platform work' ', 22.12.2023, A9-0301/2022, <https://www.europarl.europa.eu/RegData/seance_pleniere/textes_deposes/rapports/2022/0301/P9_A(2022)0301_EN.pdf> In the EP Mandate for the Trilogue, it was proposed as Art. 10a <(https://data.consilium.europa.eu/doc/document/ST-10758-2023-INIT/en/pdf> (last accessed: 15.12.2025).

[6] European Parliament, 'Report on the plenary sitting on the proposal for a directive of the European Parliament and of the Council on improving working conditions in platform work', 22.12.2023, A9-0301/2022, 107 <https://www.europarl.europa.eu/RegData/seance_pleniere/textes_deposes/rapports/2022/0301/P9_A(2022)0301_EN.pdf> (last accessed: 15.12.2025).

[7] European Parliament, 'Report on the plenary sitting on the proposal for a directive of the European Parliament and of the Council on improving working conditions in platform work', 22.12.2023, A9-0301/2022, <https://www.europarl.europa.eu/RegData/seance_pleniere/textes_deposes/rapports/2022/0301/P9_A(2022)0301_EN.pdf> (last accessed: 15.12.2025), (Amendment 61 Proposal for a directive recital 45).

[8] Kilhoffer et al., p. 88 et seqq.

III. Objectives: Compensating for the lack of a common workplace

By compensating for the lack of a common workplace, the communication channels Art. 20 of the Directive regulates are supposed to **enable processes of getting to know and communicating**, i.e. to offer opportunities that can be used for a variety of purposes (recital 62). At a physical workplace, daily acts of communication can create social and emotional connections between colleagues. Means of digital communication also hold this promise, without being able to guarantee its fulfilment. That's why regulation is necessary. 9

1. Enabling trust

The primary objective of Art. 20 is to compensate for the lack of opportunities for persons performing platform work to get to know and communicate with each other (recital 62). In this respect, digital labour platforms are required to provide means to **combat isolation**, i.e. to meet the fundamental human need for social interaction. The opportunity to communicate has intrinsic value. As social beings, humans need it for personal development;[9] workplace isolation can negatively impact on the well-being of persons performing platform work.[10] 10

Communication, i.e. exchanging opinions with others is also essential for democratic processes at workplaces, but also in the **political system**.[11] By providing experiences of self-efficacy, communication at the workplace encourages and enables voters to also effectively participate in democratic decision-making.[12] 11

Processes that enable persons to get to know each other are key to **building trust**, i.e. the conviction that one can rely on other persons. The problem of the trust deficit in digital communication and its negative impact on potential self-organisation is well known, as it is a fundamental issue of digital communication that is not limited to the field of digital labour relations.[13] It is also a fundamental requisite for collective organisation and collective action.[14] 12

Digital means will not be able to compensate the trust-building function of physical workplaces completely: persons performing online platform worker without the possibility of analogue contact have been shown to have greater problems building trust than persons performing location-bound platform work.[15] Research on platform work conflicts has analysed how communication is constitutive for the establishment of social connections and that **analogue communication (face to face) leads to faster and stronger social connections** than purely digital communication.[16] 13

2. Enabling solidarity

Recital 62 addresses the second objective of Art. 20, highlighting the importance of **defending common interests** in relation to digital labour platform. Due to the power imbalances between employees and employers, workplaces as social places have always 14

---

[9] Kühling in Heselhaus/Nowak EU-Grundrechte-HdB § 27 mn. 5 et seqq.; Kühling, p. 89 et seqq.

[10] De Groen et al., p. 11.; Kilhoffer et al., p. 88 et seqq, 155.

[11] Kühling in Heselhaus/Nowak EU-Grundrechte-HdB § 27 mn. 8 et seqq.

[12] Kühling, p. 91 et seqq.; cf. Kiess/Schmidt WSI-Mitt. 2025, 253 et seqq.; Honneth 2023, p. 300 et seqq.

[13] LaPlante/Silberman Proceedings of WebSci16. ACM 2016, 35.

[14] For more information on the topic of 'trust in platform work' see: Salehi/Irani et al. in Begole/Kim/Inkpen/Woo, p. 1621 (1624 et seq.); LaPlante/Silberman, p. 1 et seq.

[15] Cini New Technol Work Employ 2023, 125 (139).

[16] Cini New Technol Work Employ 2023, 125 (139), see also: Heiland/Schaupp Momentum Quarterly 2020, 50 (60 et seq.); Albicker, p. 80.

been places of collective self-organisation and collective resistance.[17] By referring to 'common interest', the Platform Work Directive addresses this aspect of collectivity.

15 **Organising collectively** in the workplace requires a relationship of trust that is built on personal interaction.[18] This enables problems in the workplace to be recognised and addressed collectively as common issues. In this context, communication and trust, are intended to facilitate collective self-organisation,[19] and should be designed accordingly (→ mn. 81 et seqq).

16 With the formula 'defending common interests with regard to the digital labour platform', recital 62 makes it clear that collective organisation of persons performing platform work must be thought of as potentially **conflictive**, as conflicts of interest are inherent in the relationship between digital labour platforms and persons performing platform work. Confrontational communication should therefore also be made possible; Art. 20 acknowledges this implicitly when it requires the communication channels to be protected from employers' control.

17 **Analyse of conflicts in platform work** have shown[20] that disputes require a particularly strong basis of trust. For online gig work, however, the situation is complex. Persons who perform platform work fully online and rarely meet face-to-face find it more challenging to establish trust and organise collectively.[21] The same can be said for platform work provided in isolated offline spaces such as private households.[22] Persons who perform these types of platform work have therefore tended to favour less confrontational approaches, in contrast to food-delivery workers, for example.[23] The means to be provided by Art. 20 will most probably not be able to completely compensate for this barrier, but it may **facilitate** its overcoming.

18 The Platform Work Directive is the result of years of academic, legal and political discussion on the basis of empirical insights into specific forms of platform work – mainly crowdworking, food delivery and transport. This is partly due to the fact that the latter groups in particular made themselves heard and seen, through collective action, protest and social media. However, the knowledge on which the Directive is based ended up with a gendered bias:[24] **Care and domestic work platforms**, which are often mentioned as examples of on-location work,[25] are rarely discussed in detail – partly due to the difficulty of access for researchers.[26] Still, the research done until now

---

[17] The German Federal Labour Court acknowledged this already in 1967: 'Working life takes place on the company premises, and it is there that the services are performed for which the employees are remunerated under collective agreements. It is there that questions arise from the cooperation between employer and employee and from the cooperation between employees themselves. Therefore, informing their members and recruiting new members, including and especially in the workplace, is part of the core area of freedom of advertising and information granted to coalitions under constitutional law. The principle of relevance applies', see BAG 14.2.1967 – 1 AZR 494/65, NJW 1967, 843 (845); AuR 2024, 378.

[18] Wömpner AuR 2024, 378.

[19] There are more issues that need to be addressed to enable effective collective organisation at digital workplaces; see Aloisi/Rainone/Countouris, p. 21.

[20] Cini New Technol Work Employ. 2023, 125 (139 et seqq.); Albicker, p. 102 et seqq.

[21] Cini New Technol Work Employ. 2023, 125 (139 et seqq.); Gärtner, p. 218 et seqq.; Graham/Hjorth/Lehdonvirta, Transfer 2017, 135 (155).

[22] Niebler/Animento ELRR 2023, 689 (695); Gruszka/Pillinger/Gerold/Theine Critical Sociology 2024 1 (15).

[23] For examples see Degner/Kocher KJ 2018, 247 seqq.; Cini New Technol Work Employ. 2023, 125 (139 et seq.).

[24] Discussed in detail by Kocher/Bronowicka ELLJ 2025, 565.

[25] Kilhoffer et al., p. 15; Barcevičius et al., p. 34, De Groen et al., p. 18. On empirical evidence see also the contributions in Poblete/Kocher (ed.), Digital intermediaries in the care and domestic work sector (forthcoming 2026).

[26] Orth/Baum Critical Sociology 2024, 1 et seqq.

on these on-location platforms shows the greater need for communication channels as these persons are almost as invisible to the public as persons performing online platform work, and nearly as isolated. Research on social media interaction for these persons shows the dynamics of trust and solidarity these are able to engender nevertheless.[27]

B. Legal bases

I. EU competence

The Platform Work Directive is based on Art. 153(1)(b) TFEU which enables the EU to support and complement the activities of the Member States in the field of **working conditions**. In particular, it also covers working conditions of persons performing platform work who are not employees in the strict sense (discussed in → Art. 1 mn. 4–6).[28] **19**

Although the creation of digital communication channels does not directly confer working conditions, it does relate indirectly to working conditions, insofar as it affects enforcement. If one of several components of a Directive is identifiable as the main or predominant purpose, whereas the other is merely incidental, the Directive must (and can) be based on the legal basis required by the predominant purpose or component.[29] Such is the case for the remedies and enforcement section of this and other Directives based on Art. 153 TFEU. In the context of the Platform Work Directive, these are **ancillary** to the main provisions of the Directive,[30] and therefore partake of the competence conferred upon the EU by Art. 153(1)(b) TFEU. **20**

II. Giving specific form to fundamental rights

According to Art. 51 (1) CFR, with the entry-into-force of the Directive, all provisions of the Charter become **applicable** as far as the Platform Work Directive and the Member States' implementation are concerned.[31] **21**

Recital 2 of the Platform Work Directive refers to Art. 12 CFR, as **legal context** for the Directive. With Art. 13 and 14 in mind, it also mentions Art. 27 CFR. Still, given the close connection of Art. 20 to collective organisation and collective bargaining (→ mn. 9 et seqq.), **Art. 28 CFR** also has to be considered relevant legal context of the Platform Work Directive. **22**

With its view towards the defense of collective interests vis-à-vis the digital labour platform, Art. 20 gives specific form to the fundamental rights established by Art. 12 and Art. 28 CFR and must, therefore, be interpreted in the light of the latter.[32] **23**

---

[27] Cini New Technol Work Employ 2023, 125 (133).

[28] This legal construct is discussed in Krause NZA 2022, 521 (523).

[29] Kocher in Pechstein/Nowak/Häde AEUV Art. 153 mn. 8; see ECJ 10. 1. 2006 – case C-94/03, ECLI:EU:C:2006:2 para. 34 et seqq. – Commission v Council; ECJ 30.1.2001 – case C-36/98, ECLI:EU:C:2001:64 para. 59 – Spain v Council; ECJ 11.9.2003 – case C-211/01, ECLI:EU:C:2003:452 para. 39 – Commission v Council; ECJ 29.4.2004 – case C-338/01, ECLI:EU:C:2004:253 para. 55 – Commission v Council.

[30] Cf. recently ECJ 11. 11. 2025 – case C-19/23, ECLI:EU:C:2025:865 para. 136 – Denmark v Parliament and Council (Minimum Wage Directive).

[31] ECJ 26.2.2013 – case C-617/10, ECLI:EU:C:2013:105 – Åkerberg Fransson.

[32] For the concept of concretisation of fundamental rights through secondary EU law, see ECJ 17.4.2018 – case C-414/16, ECLI:EU:C:2018:257 – Egenberger (referring to Art. 21(1) CFR), and ECJ 6.11.2018 – joined cases C-569/16 and C-570/16, ECLI:EU:C:2018:871 – Bauer und Broßonn, as well as ECJ 14.5.2019 – case C-55/18, ECLI:EU:C:2019:402 para. 31 – Comisiones Obreras, CCOO, (both referring to Art. 31(2) CFR).

1. Art. 12 CFR

24 Art. 12(1) CFR establishes, among other rights, the **right to freedom of association, in particular in trade union matters**, implying the right of everyone to form and to join trade unions for the protection of his or her interests. The provision is designed after Art. 11 of the European Convention of Human Rights,[33] the meaning and scope of which define, according to Art. 52(3) CFR, a minimum standard for the interpretation of Art. 12(1) CFR.

25 When interpreting Art. 11 ECHR, **international standards** have to be considered.[34] There are numerous legal sources on international level establishing the right to freedom of association, in particular trade union matters, most importantly ILO Conventions 87 and 98, which have been established as fundamental labour rights already in 1998[35] and therefore as international *ius cogens*.[36] Art. 8 of the International Covenant on Economic, Social and Cultural Rights also has to be mentioned in this context.[37]

26 Another important additional reference for Art. 12(1) CFR is the right to organise as enshrined in **Art. 5 of the (Revised) European Social Charter (ESC)** of 1961/1996, according to which national laws of the signatories of the Charter 'shall not be such as to impair, not shall it be applied as to impair' the 'freedom of workers and employers to form local, national or international organisations for the protection of their economic and social interests and to join those organisations.' Most importantly, Art. 5 (R)ESC gives the explicit perspective of 'ensuring or promoting' the right to organise in mind. The fact that not all EU Member States have ratified the ESC is not a barrier for this interpretation of Art. 12 CFR, as it does not create any direct obligations.[38]

27 In lack of a physical workplace, the **establishment of digital communication channels** is therefore part of the Members States duty to protect the fundamental right established by Art. 12 (1) CFR.

2. Art. 28 CFR

28 Art. 28 CFR establishes the **right to collective bargaining and collective action** and guarantees the rights of workers and employers, or their respective organisations, in accordance with Union law and national laws and practices, to negotiate and conclude collective agreements at the appropriate levels. In cases of conflicts of interest, the right to take collective action to defend common interests, including strike action, is also encompassed. Similarly to Art. 12 CFR, Art. 28 CFR has been designed according to Art. 11

---

[33] ECtHR 12. 11. 2008 – App. No. 34503/97 – Demir and Baykara v Turkey; ECtHR 21. 4. 2009 – App. No. 68959/01 – Enerji Yapi-Yol Sen v Turkey; ECtHR 5.7.2022 – App Nos. 815/18, 3278/18, 12380/18, 12693/18, 14883/18 – Association of civil servants and union for collective Bargaining and others v Germany; ECtHR 14.12.2023, App Nos. 59433/18, 59477/18, 59481/18, 59494/18 – Humpert and others v Germany.

[34] Cf. ECtHR 12. 11. 2008 – App. No. 34503/97, para. 147, 166 – Demir and Baykara v Turkey; ECtHR 21. 4. 2009 – App. No. 68959/01, para. 40 et seq. – Enerji Yapi-Yol Sen v Turkey; ECtHR 5.7.2022 – App Nos. 815/18, 3278/18, 12380/18, 12693/18, 14883/18 – Association of civil servants and union for collective Bargaining and others v Germany, mn. 32 seqq.; ECtHR 14.12.2023, App Nos. 59433/18, 59477/18, 59481/18, 59494/18 – Humpert and others v Germany, mn. 52 seqq.

[35] ILO 1998 Declaration on Fundamental Principles and Rights at Work and its Follow-up, https://www.ilo.org/sites/default/files/2024-04/ILO_1998_Declaration_EN.pdf (last accessed: 15.12.2025).

[36] Heuschmid in Boecken/Düwell/Diller/Hanau GRCh Art. 12 mn. 2.

[37] Lörcher/Bruun/Ribeiro (eds), 'The International Covenant on Economic, Social and Cultural Rights and the employment relation', Oxford 2025.

[38] For the expectations of the European Committee of Social Rights that the ECJ would handle this in this way, see ECtHR 3. 7. 2013 – App. No. 85/2012 – LO and TCO v Schweden, mn. 121 (on Art. 6 (4) ESC).

ECHR, and Art. 6 (R)ESC, but also No. 12–14 of the Community Charter of the Fundamental Social Rights of Workers from 1989.[39]

29 Insofar as Art. 20 of the Directive envisages the conflictive defence of common interests with regard to digital labour platforms (→ mn. 9 et seqq.), it specifies the infrastructure of collective communication among persons performing platform work that is an indispensable **preliminary stage of collective bargaining and collective action**.

30 Art. 28 CFR is a fundamental right which cannot be directly specified by the European Union, due to the competence barrier Art. 153(5) TFEU has put up. Only in ancillary provisions to Directives such as the Platform Work Directive can this right be promoted by the EU. This makes the fundamental right particularly relevant. It is for this reason – and others – that Art. 28 CFR has to be interpreted as establishing an **enforceable right** for employees and employers as well as their representatives.[40]

III. Relationship to Art. 25

31 The relevance of Art. 28 CFR for improving working conditions in platform work is confirmed by **Art. 25** which calls for the Member States to promote the role of the social partners and encourage the exercise of the right to collective bargaining in platform work.[41] While Art. 25 specifies this obligation in relation to the determination of the correct employment status of platform workers and the exercise of rights related to algorithmic management, Art. 20 complements the obligation to provide for the material conditions (i.e. communication) that are a precondition of collective self-organisation.

C. Obligations of the Member States

I. Regulate obligations for digital labour platforms

32 According to Art. 20, Member States have to 'take the measures necessary to ensure that digital labour platforms provide' persons performing platform work with certain possibilities, in other words: Member States must require platforms to put digital communication channels in place. They have to create a legally enforceable **obligation of digital labour platforms**.

33 The wording of Art. 20 does not directly require the Member States to provide an **enforceable right** for persons performing platform work or their representatives. In fact, the wording of the Directive ('provide the possibility'; 'die Möglichkeit bieten'; 'que faciliten la posibilidad', 'la possibilité de') only speaks about options and does not imply rights. However, depending on the design of the implementation, the demands of effective implementation can require the establishment of rights for persons performing platform work, or – more likely – the establishment of rights for representatives of persons performing platform work.

34 The fact that Art. 20 **specifies the fundamental rights** established by Art. 12 and 28 CFR (→ mn. 21 et seqq.), is a strong argument for the existence of a right to the establishment of digital communication channels, enforceable by individual persons performing platform work as well as by their representatives.

---

[39] Explanations relating to the Charter of Fundamental Rights 14. 12. 2007, OJ 2007 C 303/17, 26.
[40] Kocher in Pechstein/Nowak/Häde GRC Art. 28 mn. 7.
[41] This collective focus of the directive is welcomed by Gruber-Risak/Warter, DRdA 2024, 267 (267).

35 In addition, the **principle of effectiveness** in the context of a specific institutional design of rights enforcement can make it necessary to create individually enforceable rights, for persons performing platform work, as well as for their representatives. The principle is essentially enshrined in Art. 47 CFR, a provision which however presupposes the existence of an individual right. More important still, in the context of implementation of a EU Directive, is Art. 288(3) TFEU the wording of which says that a Directive shall be binding, 'as to the result to be achieved'. This has to be understood as an obligation for Member States to make the implementation effective in national law.

36 The Platform Work Directive itself specifies minimum standards of effectiveness, in Art. 24(5), according to which '**penalties**, applicable to infringements of national provisions adopted pursuant to provisions of this Directive [...] shall be effective, dissuasive and proportionate to the nature, gravity and duration of the undertaking's infringement and to the number of workers affected'.

37 Art. 26(1) establishes the **principle of non-regression**: Existing and acquired rights should continue to apply, insofar they are at least as favourable to persons performing platform work or workers' representatives as Art. 20. As is clear from the wording of Art. 28 which does not refer to Art. 20, not even the social partners can be allowed to maintain, negotiate, conclude and enforce collective agreements which **deviate** from Art. 20 to the disadvantage of persons performing platform work and their **representatives**. In accordance with Art. 153(4) TFEU, Art. 26(2) of the Directive allows for **more favourable provisions**.

38 Depending on the institutional framework of rights enforcement in the Member States' national systems, effectiveness may only be achieved in some cases by establishing **rights for representatives** to enforce Art. 20, beyond the support of members or other individuals that Art. 19 guarantees.

39 Recital 70 calls to mind that the Member States should, when implementing the Directive, avoid imposing 'unnecessary administrative, financial and legal constraints in a way which would hold back the creation and development of **small and medium-sized enterprises** (SMEs)'. The text of the Directive does not reproduce this idea, with good reason: Art. 153(2)(b) TFEU regulates that the Directive itself should avoid imposing such constraints; Member States must therefore depart from the assumption that the Directive has already taken care of the concerns of SMEs. However, in case of doubt, the Directive has to be interpreted in a way as to avoid unnecessary constraints that could hamper the development of SMEs.

II. Role of social partners

40 Art. 29(3) of the Platform Work Directive also calls for Member States to take adequate measures to ensure that the **social partners are effectively involved in the implementation** of the Directive, in accordance with national law and practice. The Member States may even entrust the social partners with the implementation of this Directive, where the social partners jointly request to do so (Art. 29(4) of the Platform Work Directive in line with Art. 153(3) TFEU). The Directive clearly places the focus on social dialogue here; unilateral Codes of Conduct and similar instruments by platform organisations would not be in line with this provision.

41 However, even in the event of the social partners implementing the Directive, it **remains up to the Member State** to ensure that the results sought under the Directive can at all times be guaranteed. It is also a duty of the Member State to ensure that, no later than the date on which the Directive must be transposed or implemented, social part-

ners have introduced the necessary measures by agreement (Art. 153(3) subpara 2 TFEU).[42]

III. Direct application?

Art. 20 of the Directive creates an obligation by the Member States in the sense of Art. 288(3) TFEU. However, if a Member State has not implemented the provision until the transposition and implementation deadline of 2 December 2026 (Art. 29(1)), the question arises as to the **direct applicability** of Art. 20. Insofar as Art. 20 creates an enforceable right to have digital communication channels established (→ mn. 32 et seqq.), this right will be direct applicable once implementation deadlines have expired. **42**

According to Art. 24(1) of the Directive, and contrary to the ideas the European Parliament had for them,[43] the **data protection authorities** responsible for monitoring the application of the GDPR (=Regulation (EU) 2016/679) will not necessarily be also competent for the enforcement of Art. 20 of the Platform Work Directive. However, Member States can regulate this differently and extend their competence. **43**

D. Scope of application

I. Digital labour platforms

According to Art. 20, Member States are called on to pose obligations in relation to communication channels on **all digital labour platform** as defined by Art. 2(1)(a) of the Directive (→ Art. 2 mn. 2 seqq.). **44**

Member States also have to make sure that persons performing platform work who have a contractual relationship with an intermediary (Art. 2(1)(e)) enjoy the same level of protection, also as regards communication channels (Art. 3 and recital 24). **45**

II. Persons performing platform work

Art. 20 applies to **all persons performing platform work**, 'irrespective of the nature of the contractual relationship or the designation of that relationship by the parties involved' (Art. 2 (1)(c)) (→ Art. 2 mn. 62/63). The definition includes platform workers with out an employment contract or in an employment relationship (Art. 2 (1)(d)). This means that this right applies not only to employees but also to self-employed persons. **46**

---

[42] See ECJ 11. 2. 2010 – case C-405/08, ECLI:EU:C:2010:69 para. 35 et seqq. and para 45 (with regard to Art. 11(1) of Directive 2002/14/EC) – Ingeniørforeningen i Danmark; ECJ 18. 12. 20008 – case C-306/07, ECLI:EU:C:2008:743 para. 24 et seqq. (with regard to Art. 9 of Directive 91/533/EEC) – Ruben Andersen; ECJ 25. 10.1988 – case C-312/86, ECLI:EU:C:1988:485 – Commission v France; ECJ 30. 1.1985 – case C-143/83, ECLI:EU:C:1985:34 – Commission v Denmark; ECJ 10. 7.1986 – case C-235/84, ECLI:EU:C:1986:303 – Commission v Italy.

[43] European Parliament, 'Report on the plenary sitting on the proposal for a directive of the European Parliament and of the Council on improving working conditions in platform work', 22.12.2023, A9-0301/2022, <https://www.europarl.europa.eu/RegData/seance_pleniere/textes_deposes/rapports/2022/0301/P9_A(2022)0301_EN.pdf> (last accessed: 15.12.2025) (Amendment 63 Proposal for a directive recital 47).

III. Representatives

47 Art. 20 of the Directive not only requires Members States to enable persons performing platform work to contact and communicate with each other, but also to contact or be contacted by **representatives of persons performing platform work**. The term covers 'representatives of platform workers, such as trade unions and representatives who are freely elected by the platform workers in accordance with national law and practice' (Art. 2 (1)(g) (→ Art. 2 mn. 74–78), but also other representatives of any kind of persons performing platform work 'insofar as provided for in national law and practice' (Art. 2 (1)(g) (→ Art. 2 mn. 79/80)

48 As recital 21 of the Directive reminds us, the arrangements and processes for workers' representation vary between Member States. Often, the interests of persons performing platform work are represented by **more than one trade union or other type of representative institution,** such as Works Councils. Therefore, there may be (and often is) a coexistence not only between elected representatives and trade unions (recital 22, referring to ILO Workers' Representatives Convention 135 (1971)), but also between trade unions.

49 With regard to the rights set out in Art. 20, it is not necessary to choose between several representatives and thereby exclude some of them. To the contrary: In order to fulfil the functions of this communication (→ mn. 60 seqq), it is important that every person performing platform work is able to contact the representative with whom they feel most comfortable.

50 The possibility to contact persons performing platform work and be contacted by them is established **independently of the *locus* of workers' representation** if such a reference unit is legally regulated.[44]

E. Contact and communication

51 **Overview**: Art. 20 of the Platform Work Directive obliges Member States to enable communication between persons performing platform work (→ mn. 52 et seqq.) as well as contact to representatives (→ mn. 55 et seqq.). Further, in view of the provision's objective to support collective bargaining processes (→ mn. 9 seqq), the question arises whether communication with the digital labour platform itself also has to be facilitated (→ mn. 67).

I. Contact and communication among persons performing platform work

1. Possibility to contact each other

52 According to Art. 20, persons performing platform work have to be given the possibility to contact each other – a facility that can be described as the possibility to make a **personal and direct communicative connection**. Due to the lack of a physical workspace, the connection has to be provided through a digital infrastructure (→ mn. 69 et seqq.), for example via email, messengers, or social media messaging or collaboration tools. This does not necessarily mean that persons performing platform

[44] On the issue of establishing an adequate *locus*, see Aloisi/Rainone/Countouris, p. 23; for fundamentals on this topic see also: Däubler, 2022.

work need to be given each other's contact information (→ mn. 90). Communication via aliases is preferable. However, a mere group chatwould not suffice as communication between individuals has to be enabled.[45]

2. Possibility to communicate with each other

The next step after contact is communication, which is an exchange between two or more individuals. 'Communicating **'with each other'** encompasses both one-to-one communication and collective and group communication, such as group chats. Minimum standard is asynchronous communication in writing.[46] Simply providing a list of contacts is insufficient (and problematic under EU data protection rules).[47] Enabling communication via audio and video would be preferable.[48] 53

In view of the Directive's objective to enable the creation of trust, by any kind of work-related or other communication (→ mn. 9 et seqq.), **communication** has to be enabled independent of its content or goal.[49] 54

II. Contact and communication with representatives

1. Possibility to contact representatives

The digital infrastructure will also have to give persons performing platform work the possibility to **contact representatives**. Links to workers' representatives, representative organisations, or persons representing these organisations can enable this kind of contact.[50] Those performing platform work will also need information on the identity and organisational profile of existing workers' representatives and the kind of support they offer. This does not necessarily entail information on the persons representing the organisation. 55

Importantly, the possibility to contact representatives has to respect the fact that these organisations may be in competition with each other. Therefore, **separate** contact possibilities have to be provided for each representative or organisation. 56

In order to provide the possibility to contact representatives, the organisation hosting the communication channel (→ mn. 71 et seqq.) needs information on the representatives who wish to offer contact to persons performing platform work. Therefore, it needs to **be accessible for representatives** wishing to offer contact information to persons performing platform work. 57

2. Possibility to be contacted by representatives

Art. 20 also provides for representatives to **actively take up direct contact** to persons performing platform work. As a consequence, they need a similar kind of access as persons performing platform work (→ mn. 52 et seqq.). This does not necessarily mean that representatives need to be given contact information of persons performing plat- 58

---

[45] European Commission, Report Expert Group – Transposition of the Directive (EU) 2024/2831 on improving working conditions in platform work (12.1.2026), 76.

[46] Ebenhöh/Hampel/Loschert, p. 7.

[47] European Commission, Report Expert Group – Transposition of the Directive (EU) 2024/2831 on improving working conditions in platform work (12.1.2026), 76.

[48] Wömpner AuR 2024, 378 (382).

[49] Wömpner AuR 2024, 378 (382).

[50] See for example the 'Trade union bulletin board' set up by *Deliveroo* on its website <https://riders.deliveroo.it/en/bachecasindacale> (last accessed: 15.12.2025).

form work[51] (on the requirements of the GDPR → mn. 87 et seqq.). This requirement goes beyond enabling contact by persons performing platform work. Setting up a link to representatives' websites or informing persons performing platform work of representatives' contact addresses is not equivalent to active contact by representatives. In addition, representatives need access to a mailing list or similar they can use to send messages to all persons performing platform work.

59 With this possibility, Art. 20 expands the rights that Art. 15 of the Directive extends to **representatives of persons performing platform work other than workers' representatives**, beyond rights concerning data protection and automated monitoring or decision-making systems (→ Art. 15 mn. 8–18).

3. Possibility to communicate with representatives

60 The formula Art. 20 uses for communication between persons performing platform work, and for contact with representatives differ in an important aspect: While the Directive speaks of 'contact and communication' between persons performing platform work, the wording limits the minimum abilities in relation to representatives to 'contact or be contacted by'. The formula changed in the **drafting process**: While the Commission proposal only stated that persons performing platform work should be able to 'be contacted by' representatives,[52] the Council proposed the formula 'to contact and communicate with' representatives.[53]

61 The difference in wording suggests that representatives of persons performing platform work will have to be given access to those persons, but **do not have to be admitted as participants in communicative exchange** on the digital infrastructure the digital platform has to set up. We do not know the reasons behind the agreement on the final wording that was reached in the trilogue process. However, the consequences seem clear: If representatives of persons performing platform work want to communicate with these, they will have to use communication channels they set up by themselves, using the channels established on the basis of Art. 20 only to invite persons performing platform work on their own communication channel(s).[54]

62 This may look like a cumbersome procedure, and it is – the principle of effectiveness would be an argument against this interpretation of the Directive.

63 On the other hand, the reason why it could make sense to not obligate digital platforms to have representatives communicate with persons performing platform work on the channel established by the platform could be found in seen as reaching too far – at least further than what most employers are obligated to allow in physical workspaces. It is also prudent. Establishing an obligation for digital labour platforms to provide the means for communication between persons performing platform work and their representatives would create risks of platforms accessing this communication. Not establishing this obligation could serve as a form of prevention and risk management.

---

[51] On the requirements in German law, cf. BAG 28 Jan 2025, case 1 AZR 33/24; Mamerow AuR 2026, 3 seqq.

[52] European Commission, 'Proposal for a Directive of the European Parliament and of the Council on improving working conditions in platform work', 9.12.2021, COM(2021) 762 final, 40.

[53] Council, Permanent Representatives Committee, 'Proposal for a Directive of the European Parliament and of the Council on improving working conditions in platform work – General approach' 7.6.2023, 10107/23, 55 <https://eur-lex.europa.eu/legal-content/EN/TXT/PDF/?uri=CONSIL:ST_10107_2023_INIT> (last accessed: 15.12.2025).

[54] Different view: Wömpner AuR 2024, 378 (381) (she does however not give the reasons for her interpretation).

While Art. 20 does not directly obligate digital labour platforms to establish full access for worker representatives to communication with persons performing platform work, **an obligation may arise indirectly, in specific cases,** from the requirements of effectiveness under Art. 20 for the design of the communication channel (→ mn. 68 et seqq.). In particular, it is hard to imagine how representatives can be enabled to contact persons performing platform work (→ mn. 47 et seqq.) without, at the same time, enabling communication. **64**

The fact that Art. 20 does not demand communication channels enable continuous communication between persons performing platform work and their representatives does not mean that communication channels would not be **allowed to include this form of communication**. However, care would have to be taken that Art. 7(1)(b) is complied with and the processing of personal data by digital labour platforms, by limiting automated monitoring systems or automated decision-making systems 'in relation to [...] exchanges with other persons performing platform work and the representatives of persons performing platform work'. The Member States, when implementing this provision, will have to demand safeguards in this respect. **65**

Lastly, while digital labour platforms may not be required to enable communication, they are **banned from inhibiting this communication** in any way. Communication between persons performing platform work and their representatives is protected by Art. 12 and 28 CFR (→ mn. 21 et seqq.). **66**

III. Contact and communication with the digital labour platform

Contact and communication of persons performing platform work and/or their representatives vis-à-vis the digital labour platform is **not in the scope** of Art. 20. Arts. 11–15 of the Directive regulate some aspects of this communication. **67**

F. Means of contact and communication

Research on collective organisation by persons performing platform work has shown that the emergence and strength of social connections between these persons depends heavily on the specific **design of communication channels.**[55] It is therefore with good reason that Art. 20 mentions minimum standards the digital communication channels have to comply with. They concern the means of contact and communication (→ mn. 68 et seqq.) as well as the quality and modalities of contact and communication that have to be provided (→ mn. 81 et seqq.). **68**

I. Platforms' digital infrastructure

Art. 20 envisages establishing communication channels primarily 'by means of the digital **labour platforms' digital infrastructure**'. This refers to the fact that digital labour platforms have often integrated communication channels they use for organisational and work purposes. Establishing a second similar channel would therefore not on- **69**

---

[55] Ebenhöh/Hampel/Loschert p. 5 et seqq.; Ebenhöh/Hampel/Loschert/Silberman/Adams-Prassl/Höller, 'Implementing Article 20 of the EU Platform Work Directive: "Communication Channels"' 20.02.2025, <https://global-workplace-law-and-policy.kluwerlawonline.com/2025/02/20/implementing-article-20-of-the-eu-platform-work-directive-communication-channels/#respond> (last accessed: 15.12.2025).

ly be 'in line with [most] digital labour platforms' work organisation' (recital 62), but would also be an effective way of enabling communication between persons performing platform work.[56] Some platforms had already implemented such communication channels for employees.[57]

70 However, this second channel would not only have to be **protected** from access and monitoring by the platform (→ mn. 84 et seqq.). It also has to conform with the data protection principles of transparency, lawfulness and fairness (with regards to the requirements of the GDPR in relation to such communication channels (→ mn. 87 et seqq.)).

71 Art. 20 does not exclude establishing communication channels hosted by an **external service provider**, as long as the cost is borne by the digital labour platform.[58] In view of the requirements of independency from interference from the digital labour platforms, and in regard of the democratic objectives of the communication to be fostered, a non-profit service provider seems preferable; in particular, open source solutions are able to conform with requirements.[59]

72 As Art. 20 requires the Member States to create an obligation for the digital platforms themselves, in the case of an external service provider hosting the communication channel its requirements have to be regulated via a **contract** between the provider and the digital labour platform. In this case, the digital platform would be the controller (on the limits on control and monitoring → mn. 84 et seqq.), and the external service provider would become the processor of the data.

73 For the reasons mentioned in favour of an external non-profit service provider (→ mn. 71), a **trade union** can also be commissioned with establishing the communication channel,[60] via contract between the digital labour platform and the trade union.

II. Similarly effective means

74 With the formula 'similarly effective' means, Art. 20 implies that communication channels established on the platform's digital infrastructure has to be **effective**. Effectivity here refers to the usability for its purposes of contacting and communication.

75 As the communication channels are ultimately supposed to enable trust among persons performing platform work, standards for effective communication are high. A possibility of mere group chat is not sufficient.[61] In particular, this implies a minimum of content moderation. Digital communication has its pitfalls – in particular rapid escalations and low barriers for emotional communication, including discrimination and hate crimes. Effective communication that can form the basis of trust through digital communication can only thrive if a system of **content moderation** is set up.[62] For this end, guidelines for digital conduct have to clarify basic communication rules,

---

[56] For delivery platforms: Specht DIAS 2026, 14 (17).

[57] Heiland/Schaupp in Moore/Woodcock, p. 138 (141 et seq.); Heiland/Schaupp Momentum Quarterly 2020, 50 (60, 63 et seq.); De Greef, p. 62. They also show that these channels were often shut down after they ended up being used for collective organisation.

[58] Wömpner AuR 2024, 378 (382); Specht DIAS 2026, 14 (17).

[59] Ebenhöh/Hampel/Loschert/Silberman/Adams-Prassl/Höller, 'Implementing Article 20 of the EU Platform Work Directive: "Communication Channels"' 20.02.2025, <https://global-workplace-law-and-policy.kluwerlawonline.com/2025/02/20/implementing-article-20-of-the-eu-platform-work-directive-communication-channels/#respond> (last accessed: 15.12.2025).

[60] Ebenhöh/Hampel/Loschert, p. 3 et seq; Hampel/Loschert DIAS 2026, 19 (20) .

[61] European Commission, Report Expert Group – Transposition of the Directive (EU) 2024/2831 on improving work conditions in platform work (12.1.2026), 76.

[62] Hampel/Loschert DIAS 2026, 19 (20).

to protect data and personality rights of all participants. These guidelines need to be enforced (in particular, illegal and transgressive content has to be deleted).

In addition, however, in order to promote trust based on good communication, **community moderation** will also be necessary. This is due to typical problematic dynamics of self-organisation which is acerbated in digital communication among groups where trust has not yet been established. These problems have been described as 'friction' (never-ending discussions) and stalling (threads of discussion gradually dwindling).[63] Community moderation can keep them in check. Community moderation involves trained moderators with administrator rights structuring communication processes,[64] by for example grouping threads.[65] **76**

However, in the case of a communication channel being hosted by the digital labour platform, community moderation creates **additional risks** that the digital labour platform influence communication. Community moderation will therefore be most effective on communication channels hosted outside of the digital labour platform (→ mn. 71 et seqq.).[66] In any case, moderators need legal positions similar to that of data protection officers, i.e. act independently, without being subject to instructions, but bound by secrecy and confidentiality (cf. Art. 38(3)(1–2) and (5) GDPR). **77**

One of the requirements of effectivity concerns the question of **accessibility** and **connectivity**: Access should be at least as easy,[67] immediate, intuitive and user-friendly[68] as the digital labour platforms' general digital infrastructure. In particular, the channel has to be easily found, for example by linking it on the webpage the persons performing platform work need to regularly access. The channel has to be accessible to persons with disabilities, and designed in a way as to be operated by persons performing platform work with low technical skills and poor technical devices.[69] Other criteria of effectivity concern visibility,[70] high-speed wireless and fixed connectivity.[71] **78**

If the platform, for its own communication with persons performing platform work, offers communication in several **languages**, the same must apply to the means of contact and communication.[72] For languages the digital labour platform itself does not usually **79**

---

63 Salehi/Irani et al. in Begole/Kim/Inkpen/Woo, p. 1621 (1626 et seqq.).

64 On the possible powers of moderators: Salehi/Irani et al. in Begole/Kim/Inkpen/Woo, p. 1621 (1628 et seq.).

65 Wömpner AuR 2024, 378 (382); Heiland/Schaupp, Momentum Quarterly 2020, 50 (60, 63). See also European Commission, Report Expert Group – Transposition of the Directive (EU) 2024/2831 on improving working conditions in platform work (12.1.2026), 76, on the importance of content moderation in view of prevention of digital harassment and violence.

66 European Commission, Report Expert Group – Transposition of the Directive (EU) 2024/2831 on improving work conditions in platform work (12.1.2026), 76.

67 Ebenhöh/Hampel/Loschert, p. 6, Wömpner AuR 2024, 378 (382); Expert Group, Transposition of the Directive (EU) 2024/2831 on improving working conditions on digital platforms. Reports European Commission.

68 Wömpner AuR 2024, 378 (381), Vaele/Silberman/Binns, ELLJ 2023, 308 (327), Ebenhöh/Hampel/Loschert, p. 6 et seqq.

69 Ebenhöh/Hampel/Loschert, p. 7.

70 European Parliament, 'Report on the plenary sitting on the proposal for a directive of the European Parliament and of the Council on improving working conditions in platform work', 22.12.2023, A9–0301/2022, <https://www.europarl.europa.eu/RegData/seance_pleniere/textes_deposes/rapports/2022/0301/P9_A(2022)0301_EN.pdf> (last accessed: 15.12.2025), (Amendment 174 and 175 Proposal for a directive Article 15 – title).

71 The Parliament's Committee on Transport an Tourism (for the Committee on Employment and Social Affairs 9, 5.10.22 <https://www.europarl.europa.eu/RegData/seance_pleniere/textes_deposes/rapports/2022/0301/P9_A(2022)0301_EN.pdf> (last accessed: 15.12.2025) (Amendment 67 Proposal for a directive Article 15 – paragraph 1).

72 On language barriers: Ebenhöh/Hampel/Loschert, p. 7, Wömpner AuR 2024, 378 (382).

use, digital translation tools should be implemented.[73] In case of offline platform work such as on delivery platforms, the channel should be enable communication on a local level as well as on federal and European level.[74]

80 **Intuitive operation** could be facilitated with the help of pictograms and other visual design tools such as commonly used for organising content. Designing the tool based on well-known communication tools also supports effectivity.

G. Design requirements

I. Contact and communicate privately and securely

81 The most important design requirement refers to guaranteeing 'private and secure' contact and communication. '**Privately**' means that only persons who are participating in the communication on their own will be allowed to access it. Unauthorised persons include, in particular, representatives of the digital labour platform and its operators (→ mn. 84).

82 'Securely' refers to the **security of personal data** as regulated in Section 2 of the GDPR. According to Art. 32 GDPR, the controller and the processor shall implement appropriate technical and organisational measures to ensure a level of security appropriate to the risk, including inter alia as appropriate: the pseudonymisation and encryption of personal data (a);[75] the ability to ensure the ongoing confidentiality, integrity, availability and resilience of processing systems and services (b); the ability to restore the availability and access to personal data in a timely manner in the event of a physical or technical incident (c); a process for regularly testing, assessing and evaluating the effectiveness of technical and organisational measures for ensuring the security of the processing (d). These measures have to be implemented both by the digital labour platform as controller and the processor hosting the communication channel.

83 In a fundamental rights perspective (Art. 8 CFR, Art. 16 TFEU), user interfaces have to be designed in such a way to not only facilitate intuitive use, but also **promote responsible handling** of one's own data.

II. No access or monitoring by digital labour platforms

84 One of the most important requirements is the **prohibition for digital labour platforms to access or monitor** contacting and communication via the communication channel. Member States have to require digital labour platforms to refrain from accessing such channels other than for their functional maintenance. Art. 20 of the Directive insofar constitutes a collection of 'more specific rules' in relation to the GDPR's princi-

[73] Ebenhöh/Hampel/Loschert, p. 8, Wömpner AuR 2024, 378 (382). Translation tools may however not be required in every single case (European Commission, Report Expert Group – Transposition of the Directive (EU) 2024/2831 on improving working conditions in platform work (12.1.2026), 76, requirements therefore depending on the platforms' general practives.

[74] Specht DIAS 2026, 14 (18).

[75] European Parliament, 'Report on the plenary sitting on the proposal for a directive of the European Parliament and of the Council on improving working conditions in platform work', 22.12.2023, A9-0301/2022, <https://www.europarl.europa.eu/RegData/seance_pleniere/textes_deposes/rapports/2022/0301/P9_A(2022)0301_EN.pdf> (last accessed: 15.12.2025), (Amendment 61 Proposal for a directive recital 45).

ples of purpose limitation and data minimisation (→ mn. 88 and → Art. 1 mn. 17–24 regarding the relationship between the GDPR and the Platform Work Directive).

85 If the channel is not established on the platform's digital infrastructure itself, but by an external service provider, the ban on access and monitoring has to be **regulated contractually.**[76]

86 **Technical and organisational measures** need to be in place to prevent misuse of the data and of the channel (Art. 25 GDPR: data protection by design). A technical firewall between the platform's digital infrastructure and the communication channel is indispensable. Member States have to monitor compliance. An independent management of the channel by non-profit organisations or certified external providers would also be a design option.

III. Data Protection

87 Art. 20 reminds Member States to ensure compliance with the rules of Regulation (EU) 2016/679 (GDPR) when implementing the obligation on communication channels. First and foremost this refers to the requirements for the lawfulness of data processing as regulated in Art. 6 GDPR. Due to the requirements for lawful consent (Art. 7 GDPR[77]), a communication channel based on consent does not appear manageable. Data processing in the context of a communication channel will therefore have to be based on **Art. 6(1) (c) GDPR** which allows data processing if it is necessary for compliance with a legal obligation to which the controller is subject[78] (in this case it would be the obligation arising from the Member States' implementation of Art. 20 of the Platform Work Directive or Art. 20 directly (→ mn. 42 et seq.)). Purpose of the processing is the enabling of communication (→ mn. 51 et seqq.).

88 According to the principles of **purpose limitation**[79] and **data minimisation** (Art. 5(1)(b) and (c) GDPR), only those data may be processed that are relevant and necessary for the purposes for which they are processed. These will usually only be names of the person performing platform work and contact details. The platform may also not use metadata on the use of the channels for profiling or management purposes.

89 Processing of **special categories of personal data** such as trade union membership (Art. 9(1) GDPR), will usually not be covered by the purpose of the channel which only consists in enabling communication. However, in specific instances, the requirements of Art. 9(2) GDPR (processing necessary to fulfil 'obligations and exercising specific rights of the controller […] in the field of employment […] law' can become relevant.

90 In view of the requirement of data minimisation, the offer of **aliases** for persons performing platform work in the communication channels will in most cases be the only way to comply with data protection. Persons performing platform work wishing to communicate with each other need basic **contact information** of each other; however, communication can be conducted anonymously with the help of aliases.

91 The requirement of **transparency** (Art. 5(1)(b) and (c) GDPR) means that data processing has to be understandable and comprehensible to persons performing platform work.[80] They need to know without doubt which data are being processed, who can ac-

---

[76] Ebenhöh/Hampel/Loschert, p. 3.

[77] Basically, the consent has to be freely given, specific, informed and unambiguous. In order to be considered free, the person must have a real and meaningful choice.

[78] On the requirements in relation to trade unions' digital access see Warter DIAS 2026, 9 seq.

[79] Franzen in Franzen/Gallner/Oetker VO (EU) 2016/679 Art. 5 mn. 6.

[80] Franzen in Franzen/Gallner/Oetker VO (EU) 2016/679 Art. 5 mn. 3.

cess them, and when they will be deleted. Information has to be provided in a clear, intelligible and easily accessible way. After all, effective data protection requires that the data subject understands the functions that are offered and how rights can be exercised. In this respect, an intuitive user interface is not just a requirement of the channel's effectivity for communication (→ mn. 80), but also makes it easier for users to make independent decisions about their data processing.

92 These principles have to be established through technical and organisational measures (Art. 25 GDPR: **data protection by design**).

93 Member States implementing Art. 20 of the Platform Directive will inevitably 'provide for more specific rules to ensure the protection of the rights and freedoms in respect of the processing of employees' personal data in the employment context, in particular […] for the purposes of the exercise and enjoyment, on an individual or collective basis, of rights and benefits related to employment' (Art. 88 GDPR).[81] As far as persons performing platform work who are not employees are concerned, Art. 20 is lex specialis. For example, in order to establish a ban on the platform to access or monitor communication, rules with a specific normative content are needed, **beyond the GDPR**.

Articles 21 to 32 omitted

[81] On Art. 88 GDPR, see ECJ 30. 3. 2023 – case C-34/21, ECLI:EU:C:2023:270 – Hauptpersonalrat der Lehrerinnen und Lehrer; Halefom MLR 87 (2024), 484.

PART III
COUNTRY REPORTS

Austria

Literature: Piasna/Zwysen/Drahokoupil, 'The platform economy in Europe: Results from the second ETUI Internet and Platform Work Survey (IPWS)', in Working Paper 2022.05 ETUI Brussels 2022; Griesser/Plank/Vogel/Gruber-Risak/Herr/Ustek-Spilda/Steward/Graham, 'Fairwork Austria Ratings 2022: Labour Standards in the Platform Economy', Fairwork Oxford 2022; Gruber-Risak/Griesser/Plank, 'Arbeiten in der österreichischen Plattformwirtschaft – Ergebnisse der ersten österreichischen Fairwork-Studie und arbeitsrechtliche Einschätzungen', DRdA 2023, 3; Gruber-Risak/Warter, 'Die EU-Richtlinie zur Verbesserung der Arbeitsbedingungen in der Plattformarbeit', DRdA 2024, 267; Kozak, 'Der Arbeitnehmerbegriff der Plattform-RL', in Auer-Mayer/Felten/Niksova/Pfeil/Schrattbauer/Warter (eds), Festschrift Mosler, Wien 2024, p. 213; Balla, 'Transportdienstleistungen: Uber' in Lutz/Risak (eds), 'Arbeit in der Gig-Economy', Wien 2017, p. 106; Risak, 'New forms of employment', ZAS 2014, 40; Risak/Prassl, 'Uber, TaskRabbit, & Co: Platforms as Employers? Rethinking the legal analysis of crowdwork', Comparative Labor Law & Policy Journal 2016, 618; Warter, 'Anspruch des Betriebsrates auf Mitteilung von Arbeitnehmer:innendaten', DRdA 2025, 414.

A. Facts and figures on the phenomenon of platform work in Austria

Platform work is a phenomenon that has gained importance in recent years, both in economic systems worldwide and within the European Union (EU). Although one might not expect it, platform work is also widespread in Austria and has become increasingly relevant in the Austrian labour market. 1

A study conducted in 2022 on internet and platform work shows that although 5.1% of respondents working in Austria have performed platform work in the last 12 months, this activity does not represent their main source of income. Consequently, only a small proportion (0.6%) of respondents stated that they had generated 50% of their income through platform-based work, and only 0.3% worked at least 20 hours per week. Furthermore, it is surprising in this context that only 0.9% of respondents stated that platform work was their main activity. Compared to other EU member states, Austrian respondents nevertheless have more experience in platform-based work, namely 5.1% of Austrian respondents, compared to 4.3% of all respondents across the EU. In terms of securing a livelihood, there is also a difference in direct comparison with other EU countries: only 0.9% of those surveyed in Austria earn their living purely from platform work, while the European average is higher, at 1.1% of all respondents. While 0.7% of all respondents work at least 20 hours per week in platform work, the proportion in Austria is only 0.3%.[1] 2

[1] Cf. Piasna/Zwysen/Drahokoupil, p. 17.

3 In Austria, platform work is somewhat more widespread than the EU average; however, it is predominantly undertaken as a supplementary activity rather than a means of securing a livelihood, and Austrian platform workers tend to be engaged in it with comparatively low intensity.

4 A differentiation can also be made with regard to the various forms of platform work: In Austria, for example, 1.7% of respondents engaged in remote platform work, 1.0% performed transport- or delivery-related tasks, and 0.6% carried out on-location work. These figures refer to the minimum amount of work performed within a month. A gender-specific distribution can be observed across the different types of platform work: 64% of surveyed women were engaged in on-location platform work, while the remaining categories were predominantly male-dominated. In the delivery sector, 58% of workers were male and 45% were female. A similar pattern emerged in remote and professional platform activities, where 68% of workers were male and 32% were female. Transport services were clearly dominated by men, accounting for 82% compared to 18% of women. By contrast, on-location click work had a balanced gender representation.[2] The age structure of platform workers in Austria ranges, on average, between 35 and 40 years. From a demographic perspective, the study indicates that a high proportion of platform workers have a migration background: more than 35% were not born in Austria. Furthermore, the majority – 70% of those surveyed – reside in urban areas or their immediate surroundings.[3]

5 In terms of income levels, the study shows that persons performing platform worker earn an average of between 250 Euro and 300 Euro per month.[4] The results reveal significant heterogeneity within the Austrian platform economy, particularly with regard to on-location work.[5] These figures highlight the important role of platform work in the Austrian labour market.

6 Against this backdrop, Statistic Austria, national statistical office of Austria, is planning to conduct an ad hoc module on 'Employment on Digital Platforms' in 2026. The results of this module will be presented in 2027.[6]

B. State of regulation ('legal framework')

I. Case law on the status and temporary agency work of persons performing platform work

7 Unlike other Member States, Austria has **not yet produced a single supreme court** (OGH) decision addressing the status of persons performing platform work. As of late November 2025, only one higher-instance ruling concerning individual labour law aspects of the platform economy appears to exist. This case involved the transport platform *Uber* and addressed the question of whether the relationship constituted temporary employment, a finding that was affirmed by the Higher Regional Court of Vienna. Unlike in other countries, where the legal relationships surrounding platform work have already been addressed by the courts, this legal relationship in Austria is quadruple,

[2] Cf. Piasna/Zwysen/Drahokoupil, p. 9, 21 et seqq.
[3] Cf. Piasna/Zwysen/Drahokoupil, p. 26.
[4] Cf. Piasna/Zwysen/Drahokoupil, p. 47.
[5] Cf. Gruber-Risak/Griesser/Plank DRdA 2025, 3 (17); Plank et al., p. 4.
[6] Cf. Statistik Austria, Die Informationsmanager, 'Statistisches Arbeitsprogramm für das Jahr 2026, 2025', 44 <https://www.statistik.at/fileadmin/pages/534/Statistisches_Arbeitsprogramm_2026.pdf> (last accessed: 16.12.2025).

involving the driver, the transport platform, the customer and a rental car company. This case concerned the legal relationships between the transport platform, the rental company and its drivers. As argued by *Balla*,[7] the underlying relationship was classified under Austrian labour law as a **temporary employment arrangement**, thereby imposing the duties and obligations of an employer on the transport platform.[8] No supreme court decision has yet addressed social security law issues in this context either. However, on 10 July 2025, a major targeted operation was conducted to combat social security fraud. Based on detailed surveys and risk analyses carried out by the **Financial Police and the Austrian Social Insurance** (ÖGK), the operation focused specifically on delivery services, particularly food delivery platforms. These inspections were conducted in response to the increasing number of cases observed in recent months in which genuine employment relationships had been converted into independent service contracts. Preliminary investigations also revealed that a substantial proportion of these self-employed persons did not possess a business licence, had not reported their activities to the tax authorities, and had not made any social security contributions or notifications.[9] In this respect, the existing Austrian legal framework shows that introducing a rebuttable presumption of an employment relationship for persons performing platform work would be highly beneficial and that it would also be desirable to extend the presumption to tax and social security law.[10]

II. Establishment of works councils at delivery platforms

Austrian labour law places significant emphasis on a collective approach, particularly 8
at company level. Works councils have a wide range of information, consultation and participation rights, including co-determination. It is therefore not surprising that **the first works council in this sector** in Europe was established at the bicycle delivery service '*Foodora*' in Austria in spring 2017. Following the initiatives at '*Foodora*' and '*Pink Pedals*', a works council was subsequently elected and established at the food delivery company '*Lieferservice*', now operating under the name '*Lieferando*'.[11]

The establishment of these works councils was not free of friction. The works council 9
election was challenged multiple times by the employer. At the heart of the legal debate was the question of whether the individual 'hubs' could qualify as independent establishments within the meaning of § 34 of the Austrian Labour Constitution Act (ArbVG), given that managerial and decision-making authority was exercised centrally by the Country Manager and the Head of Human Resources. In fact, the Labour and Social Court of Vienna (ASG Wien) upheld the challenge; however, this proved largely inconsequential, as a subsequent nationwide works council election was held.[12]

---

[7] Cf Balla in Lutz/Risak, p. 106 (117).

[8] Vienna Higher Regional Court 23.11.2020, 10 Ra 59/20z, DRdA 2021, 203 (Gruber-Risak).

[9] See Bundesministerium Finanzen, 'Umfangreiche Kotrollmaßnahmen zu Sozialbetrug bei Essenszustellern' (Bundesministerium Finanzen, 11.6.2025) <https://www.bmf.gv.at/presse/pressemeldungen/2025/juli/sozialbetrug-essenszusteller.html> (last accessed: 4.12.2025).

[10] Cf. Kozak in Auer-Mayer et al., p. 213 et seqq.

[11] See 'Arbeitsbedingungen: Radzusteller gründen Betriebsrat bei Lieferservice' (Der Standard 4.6.2019) <https://www.derstandard.at/story/2000104328349/radzusteller-gruenden-betriebsrat-bei-lieferservice> (last accessed: 4.12.2025).

[12] Cf. Labour and Social Court Vienna Wien 4.7.2022, 11 Cga 135/20g; OGH 17.1.2025, 6 ObA 2/23x, DRdA 2025, 414 (note Warter).

10 In Austria, there is also an initiative known as the 'Riders Collective', which works between the riders and the trade union to educate the drivers about their rights and to foster solidarity among them, regardless of which delivery company they work for.[13]

III. Communication with works councils and trade unions

11 Also relevant in this context is the refusal of a delivery platform to provide the works council with the **employees' email addresses and phone numbers**, thereby preventing the council from engaging with the workforce. However, the Austrian Supreme Court (OGH) ruled that the **employer must disclose these contact details to the works council**. This right was derived from the Labour Constitution Act's overall framework, despite no specific rule explicitly addressing this. This is likely connected to the fact that, in this case, the matter concerned more than just contact information; it related to the core of the works council's activities: its ability to communicate effectively with the workforce.[14]

12 Correctly, the Austrian Supreme Court (OGH) also rejected the employer's 'offer' to provide the works council with a weekly-updated email distribution list of employees in which the individual email addresses were not visible. Such a list provided by the employer would not satisfy the requirements for effective employee representation enshrined in the Labour Constitution Act (ArbVG), as it would leave the works council's ability to communicate restricted in several respects: it could neither control the recipient group nor target specific groups or individual employees. The lack of transparency regarding the reach of its communications, coupled with the council's factual dependence on the employer's technical infrastructure and updates, is incompatible with the effective exercise of the tasks entrusted to the works council. Communication mediated in this manner would undermine the structural balance between employer and works council, which forms the foundation of the system of co-determination in Austrian labour law.[15]

13 Interestingly, however, the **Austrian Supreme Court** (OGH) ruled that the company had to provide the email addresses of the employees but **refused to disclose their phone numbers to the works council on data protection grounds**. This decision could be argued to be problematic as the ability to contact employees by phone is often essential, for example, when making time-sensitive statements or dealing with sensitive issues such as bullying, discrimination or conflicts with supervisors. Curiously, it was the employer who raised the data protection objection rather than the employees themselves. In this respect, it seems that the OGH has fallen into a data protection trap, as effective personal contact between the works council and the workforce strengthens the council's ability to mobilise and organise the workforce – an outcome that is not necessarily in the employer's interest.[16]

14 In this context, reference should be made to Art. 20 of the Platform Work Directive. This stipulates that Member States must take the necessary measures to ensure that digital work platforms offer persons performing platform work the opportunity to communicate with each other and their representatives via the platforms' digital infrastructure or similar effective means (→ Art. 20 mn. 55 et seqq.).

---

[13] See <https://www.riderscollective.at/> (last accessed: 4.12.2025).
[14] OGH 17.1.2025, 6 ObA 2/23x, DRdA 2025, 414 (Warter).
[15] Cf. Warter DRdA 2025, 414 (418 et seqq).
[16] Cf. Warter DRdA 2025, 414 (420).

IV. Collective Agreement for Bicycle Couriers

With effect from 1 January 2020, the collective agreement for bicycle couriers entered into force, applying to courier services as a sub-sector of the small transport trade. The trade union 'vida', which concluded the agreement, described it as the world's first collective agreement specifically for bicycle couriers, tailored predominantly to the logistics operations of food-delivery platforms active in Austria. Even in its original version, the collective agreement established significant entitlements, including a thirteenth and fourteenth monthly salary as well as a night-work supplement applicable from 10:00 p.m. In the years that followed, the agreement underwent substantial further development. This included the introduction of Sunday work supplements in 2022.[17] As of 2024, no agreement had been reached on further wage increases under the collective agreement, partly due to high inflation. This prompted platform workers to take industrial strike action. In response, the delivery platforms introduced internal pay rises. However, no new collective agreement has been reached since then. 15

Most recently, the delivery service Lieferando, which until then had employed all its suppliers under employment contracts, terminated all employment contracts and converted them into independent service contracts,[18] following a practice that is already common among competing providers. As a result, the collective agreement for 'bicycle couriers'[19] no longer applies, nor do statutory labour-law minimum standards linked to employee status, such as paid annual leave or continued remuneration in the event of sickness. On 30 September 2025, the relevant trade union, 'vida', formally terminated the collective agreement for bicycle couriers. For employment relationships commencing on or after 1 October 2025, only general labour law provisions apply. For employment relationships established up to and including 30 September 2025, the collective agreement continues to apply by virtue of its statutory survival clause (Nachwirkung) pursuant to § 13 ArbVG. 16

V. Inclusion of self-employed persons in collective agreements

Beyond platform-based work, it can generally be observed that contractual relationships traditionally executed as employment contracts are increasingly being structured as independent service contracts (freier Dienstvertrag). This trend is linked both to the technological and organisational changes in the world of work and to the fact that traditional mechanisms of personal dependence in work supervision play an increasingly minor role. However, when it comes to platform-based independent contracting, it is often reasonable to suspect the use of structures designed to circumvent labour law protections. 17

Since an independent service contract does not constitute an employment contract, labour law provisions designed to protect and secure employees, apart from a few exceptions,[20] do not apply to independent service providers. Only the general contractual pro- 18

[17] Meister, 'Weltweit erster KV für FahrradbotInnen' (OGB,13.09.2019) <https://www.oegb.at/themen/arbeitsrecht/kollektivvertrag/weltweit-erster-kv-fuer-fahrradbotinnen> (last accessed: 18.11.2025).

[18] Kainrath, 'Lieferando kündigt alle Rider und stellt gesamte Logistik auf freie Dienstverträge um' (Der Standard, 18.3.2025) <https://www.derstandard.de/consent/tcf/story/3000000261760/lieferando-kuendigt-alle-rider-und-stellt-gesamte-logistik-auf-freie-dienstvertraege-um> (last accessed: 8.11.2025).

[19] 'Kollektivvertrag für Fahrradboten Gültig ab 1.1.2023' (KollektivVertrag.at 2023) <https://www.kollektivvertrag.at/volltext?doc-set-id=SI-2936_de> (last accessed: 8.11.2025).

[20] For example, the provisions on legal enforcement before the labour and social courts, the eased liability rules under damages law, or the applicability of equal treatment law apply.

visions of the Austrian Civil Code (ABGB) apply. To address this situation by introducing minimum standards and making it less attractive to circumvent labour law provisions,[21] a statutory provision has been introduced that makes it possible to include 'independent service providers' within the meaning of § 4(4) ASVG in the scope of collective agreements or to conclude collective agreements specifically for such self-employed persons, which will come into force on 1 January 2026. Under § 4(4) ASVG, the term 'independent service providers' refers to those persons who, under independent service contracts, commit to providing services for a fixed or indefinite period in return for remuneration, perform the services essentially personally, and do not possess significant independent operational resources.

19 By limiting the applicability of collective agreements to 'independent service providers' within the meaning of § 4(4) ASVG – rather than extending it to all independent service providers – it is intended to ensure that only those self-employed persons who can be regarded as quasi-employees are covered.[22] However, the legislative explanations explicitly emphasise that the newly created possibility of collective regulation for independent service providers does not establish a new definition of 'employee' under the Labour Constitution Act (ArbVG), nor does it entail the inclusion of independent service providers in works agreements. Moreover, the parties to collective agreements **are not obliged** to take independent service providers within the meaning of § 4(4) ASVG into account when drafting collective agreements.[23]

20 With the new 'Guidelines on collective agreements regarding the working conditions of self-employed persons[24]' at least three groups of persons can have minimum labour standards set out in collective agreements (Chapter I Legal Background -> mn. 1 et seqq). This should increase the level of protection for (self-employed) persons, especially regarding platform work. Therefore, it can be assumed that including self-employed persons in the scope of application of collective agreements will also lead to significant improvements in the legal protection of platform workers in the future.

C. Status of implementation of the Directive

21 The EU Platform Work Directive must be transposed into national law by early December 2026. However, no implementing legislation has yet been presented at the national level and no draft bill has been released for consultation. This means that the specific content of the forthcoming national implementation remains unclear as of April 2025.

22 The core of the Directive undoubtedly lies in the obligation imposed on Member States to establish a rebuttable presumption of employee status for platform workers in their national legal systems. This concept is unfamiliar to Austrian labour law and represents a significant change to the current system. Under current legislation, it is the responsibility of the claimant to prove that a given contractual relationship constitutes an employment relationship. However, in its strategic programme aimed at combating bogus self-employment and the erosion of labour protections, the Austrian Trade Union

[21] Explanatory notes to the government bill 212 Number XVIII GP p. 1 et seqq.

[22] Explanatory notes to the government bill 212 Number XVIII GP p. 3.

[23] Explanatory notes to the government bill 212 Number XVIII GP p. 3 et seqq.

[24] European Commission communication, 'Guidelines on the application of Union competition law to collective agreements regarding the working conditions of solo self-employed persons' (2022/C 374/02), OJ C 374/2, 30.09.2022, hereinafter referred to as 'Guidelines'.

Federation (ÖGB) has called for the introduction of a statutory rebuttable presumption of employee status in the context of platform work.

While the introduction of a rebuttable presumption of employee status has already led to intense debate at a European level, similar controversies can be expected during the national legislative process. A key challenge in transposing Art. 5(1) of the Platform Work Directive into domestic law is likely to be the requirement for the rebuttable presumption to apply only where there are circumstances indicating 'direction and control' over the performance of work. As the Directive provides no further clarification of this notion, it remains highly open to interpretation. In this respect, further specification and explanatory guidance at the national level would be desirable. From an Austrian perspective, two aspects are decisive in this context: first, the substantive criteria as indicators of direction and control; and second, the fact that they only need to be made plausible ('Glaubhaftmachung'), without requiring full proof. As regards the substantive criteria, it would be preferable, on the one hand, for the Austrian legislature to refer to those already contained in the legislative drafts, such as determining, or setting upper limits for the level of remuneration, binding rules with regard to appearance, conduct towards the recipient of the service or performance of the work or restricting the possibility to build a client base or to perform work for any third party etc.[25] On the other hand, within the national framework it would also be conceivable to draw on the criteria developed in academic scholarship and case law concerning the contractual concept of the 'employee' under § 1151 of the Austrian Civil Code (ABGB), which place particular emphasis on personal dependence understood as 'organisational subordination'.[26] At the very least, the explanatory notes to the legislative text should therefore contain some clarifications as to what is meant by the terms 'direction' and 'control' within the meaning of the Platform Work Directive. This would make it easier for those applying the law, and in particular for the examining authorities and courts, to ensure effective implementation of the provisions transposing the Directive. 23

As other issues addressed in the Directive, such as algorithmic management, are comparatively detailed, it is more likely that the national implementing legislation will closely follow the Directive's provisions. However, given recent experiences and criticism from some government parties regarding the establishment of higher standards than those set out in EU Directives – commonly referred to as 'gold plating' – it is generally not expected that national implementation will exceed Directive requirements. 24

[25] In this sense Gruber-Risak/Warter DRdA 2024, 267 (271 et seqq.). For further criteria see for example Art 4 of the Commission's proposal European Commission, 'Proposal for a Directive of the European Parliament and of the Council on improving working conditions in platform work', 9.12.2021, COM(2021) 762 final, (https://eur-lex.europa.eu/legal-content/EN/TXT/PDF/?uri=CELEX:52021PC0762) or Art 4 of the Counicl's proposal Council, 'Proposal for a Directive of the European Parliament and of the Council on improving working conditions in platform work – General approach', 7.7.2023, 2021/0414(COD), 10107/23 (https://data.consilium.europa.eu/doc/document/ST-10107-2023-INIT/en/pdf).

[26] Cf. Rebhahn/Kietaibl in Neumayr/Reissner § 1151 ABGB para. 55 et seqq, with further evidence.

Benelux

Literature: Hießl, 'Case Law on the Classification of Platform Workers: Cross-European Comparative Analysis and Tentative Conclusions', Comparative Labour Law & Policy Journal (CLLPJ) 2024, 4; Franquet/Maisin, 'Chapter Belgium' in Waas/Hieß (eds), Collective Bargaining for Self-Employed Workers in Europe: Approaches to Reconcile Competition Law and Labour Rights, Bulletin of Comparative Labour Relations 109, Alphen aan den Rijn 2021, p. 73; Hiessl, 'Introduction: Special Issue on Income Support for Self-Employed Workers in the Wake of the Pandemic', International Journal of Comparative Labour Law and Industrial Relations 2022, 415; Hießl, 'Case Law on Algorithmic Management at the Workplace: Cross-European Comparative Analysis and Tentative Conclusions' 2021, (update 2025) p. 4; Machtelings, 'Een analyse van de Arbeidrelatiewet: Het belang van de wilsautonomie', Jura Falconis 2015–2016, 611.

A. Introduction: digital labour platforms in Benelux

1 The **Benelux** area has had a key role to play in the rise of the platform economy in Europe from the very start. Several of the most well-known US platform companies chose the region as their entry point to the continent (cf. *Amazon*'s European headquarters in Luxembourg and *Uber*'s in Amsterdam), and also some of the first 'genuinely European' platforms attaining cross-border significance originated there. This includes the Brussels food delivery startup *Take Eat Easy*, which in 2018 (almost two years after its insolvency) became subject to the first ever European last-instance decision on the status of platform workers,[1] handed down by the French cassation court.[2] Another prominent example is the Dutch platform *Just Eat Takeaway*, widely known as the first major delivery platform pledging to aim for employee status for its riders – a promise that was widely (but never fully) implemented and whose further development seems increasingly uncertain.[3] As evident from case law,[4] the contracts or terms and conditions that workers are required to sign regularly include a choice of law in favour of the platform's seat state, with the consequence that the Benelux countries' laws may

[1] Contrary to the terminology employed by the Platform Work Directive, this chapter uses the term 'platform worker' in the broader sense, including also self-employed workers. When a distinction according to legal classification is intended, the terms 'employee' and 'self-employed (worker)' will be used, respectively.

[2] Cour de cassation of 28.11.2018, Arrêt n°1737 (17–20.079).

[3] Cf. developments in Austria, where *Just Eat*'s national subsidiary recently terminated a collective agreement that had been in force for five years and dismissed all employees to offer them work as self-employed riders: Verena Kainrath, Lieferando kündigt alle Rider und stellt gesamte Logistik auf freie Dienstverträge um, in Der Standard of 18.3.2025, https://www.derstandard.at/story/3000000261760/lieferando-kuendigt-alle-rider-und-stellt-gesamte-logistik-auf-freie-dienstvertraege-um.

[4] For this and further references to general case law developments in Europe, cf. Christina Hießl, CLLPJ 2024.

be of relevance for platform workers across Europe, notably if they are classified as self-employed.[5]

2 Notwithstanding this clear significance that the region has long had in shaping developments and discussions across Europe, distinct conclusions about the regulatory environment and the related potential and challenges for the transposition of the Platform Work Directive are difficult to draw. This is linked to the substantial heterogeneity of the three national systems, the significant legal uncertainties concerning the status quo in all three countries, as well as the lack of a clear roadmap for the Platform Work Directive's transposition in any of them. Accordingly, the present chapter will essentially give a summary description of the relevant legal framework before zooming in on a number of particular developments expected to shape the future implementation of the Platform Work Directive, followed by a discussion of the major lessons of transnational relevance that could be learnt from these developments. To reflect the major issues addressed by the Platform Work Directive, the following sections will focus notably on questions of worker status and legal presumptions, on algorithmic management and on the collective representation of platform workers.

B. Existing legal framework and motions to transpose the Platform Work Directive

3 Before the European Commission published the proposal on which the Platform Work Directive is based back in December 2021, Belgium was the only Benelux country with some specific legislation in place to regulate platform work. Thereby, the goal was not to introduce protections for workers or make platforms responsible for their workforce, but rather to create a simple and affordable framework for the formalisation of 'peer-to-peer' work tasks among individuals whose supply and demand was matched via a platform. The 2016 'Lex de Croo'[6] introduced rules to facilitate small-scale[7] work in the 'sharing economy', essentially exempting it from social security contributions and subjecting it to a very low flat-rate tax. These rules have become exceptionally popular in practice – with estimates[8] considering that around 80% of platform riders have been operating under that statute in recent years, with the result that their level of social protection is even lower than that of the 'ordinary' self-employed. The introduction of the system has even been cited by the *Smart cooperative* – which formerly acted as an intermediary to provide employment contracts to *Deliveroo* and *Take Eat Easy* riders – as the key reason why the platforms quit that arrangement and forced riders into self-employment as from 2017.[9] As regards the present situation, results of investigative journal-

[5] Note that Art. 8 of the Rome I Regulation does not apply to the self-employed, making a choice of law under Art. 3 fully effective.

[6] Programmawet 2016021055 of 1 July 2016.

[7] Note that a further extension of these exemptions was enacted in 2018, but overruled by the Constitutional Court in Judgment no. 53/2020 of 23 April 2020 (see https://www.const-court.be/public/n/2020/2020-053n-info.pdf), confirming the claimant trade unions' plea that it violated the constitutional principle of equality and non-discrimination.

[8] See Sam Ooghe, 'De slaven van Deliveroo en Uber Eats' (De Morgen, 3.11.2021), <https://www.demorgen.be/nieuws/de-slaven-van-deliveroo-en-uber-eats-van-de-ene-dag-op-de-andere-was-ik-mijn-werk-kwijt-dat-had-het-algoritme-beslist~b2fbfc59/> (last accessed: 28.11.2025).

[9] See description at https://digitalplatformobservatory.org/initiative/smart/. On the former construct, see Franquet/Maisin in Waas/Christina Hießl, p. 73–102 (96 et seqq.).

ism[10] report that numerous riders circumvent the annual upper earnings threshold (EUR 7700 in 2025) by working under multiple accounts, and that there is even a 'market' where individuals offer their data to riders willing to work under their name. According to the Brussels Labour Appeals Court,[11] reliance on the system in these cases by a commercial food delivery platform is actually unlawful, most notably because the law expressly refers to 'non-professional' service provision between private individuals via a platform. Yet, so far, practice does not seem to have reacted to the judgment, with the Supreme Court's decision on the issue still pending (→ mn. 18).

Intriguingly, once the Commission's proposal of the Platform Work Directive was published, political actors in both Belgium and Luxembourg called for a '**transposition**' ahead of the directive's adoption. In Luxembourg, this resulted in a legislative bill filed by a small leftist opposition party in May 2022, which has so far not been debated in session.[12] As obvious from the text,[13] the bill would go (considerably) further than the Platform Work Directive in a number of respects. This includes the establishment of a rebuttable presumption of employment as soon as any single one out of eight criteria is fulfilled and a non-rebuttable(!) presumption in case of the fulfilment of at least three of those criteria;[14] as well as the prohibition of staple terms employed by various platforms, such as the prohibition of circumventing the platform by contracting directly with a client found through the platform.[15] In Belgium, the Commission's proposal's key provisions regarding the presumption of employee status were included in the 'Labour Deal' on which political agreement was reached in February 2022 and which was enacted[16] by October of the same year. Just like the bill in Luxembourg, it raises the number of criteria for presuming worker status to eight, with further specifications as explained (→ mn. 15). Beyond this presumption, the Labour Deal introduced a system of mandatory industrial accident insurance for platform workers irrespective of their status.[17] 4

Apart from this partial 'pre-transposition' in Belgium, none of the Benelux countries has published a concrete bill to implement the Platform Work Directive. 5

C. The status of platform workers: past litigation and status quo

I. Definition of employee status

All three Benelux countries depart from a binary concept of classification without any formally recognised intermediary groups between those qualified as employees or self-employed, respectively. The traditional definition of an employment contract is broad and open to interpretation in all three countries. The Belgian reference to an individual committing themselves to perform work for another in exchange for remuneration, cod- 6

[10] See e.g. Moors, 'Maaltijdkoeriers plegen identiteitsfraude om belastingen te ontduiken' (De Tijd 13.8.2024) <https://www.tijd.be/ondernemen/voeding-drank/maaltijdkoeriers-plegen-identiteitsfraude-om-belastingen-te-ontduiken/10557588.html> (last accessed: 28.11.2025).

[11] Cour du travail de Bruxelles of 21.12.2023, 2023/3153.

[12] See https://www.chd.lu/fr/dossier/8001 for the current progress of the bill.

[13] Available at https://wdocs-pub.chd.lu/docs/Dossiers_parlementaires/8001/20250514_Depôt.pdf.

[14] Proposed Art. L. 371–3 Labour Code.

[15] Proposed Art. L. 371–4 Labour Code.

[16] Wet houdende diverse arbeidsbepalingen of 3.10.2022.

[17] Note that, while Belgium generally covers the self-employed by mandatory social security in a rather comprehensive way, this does not apply to accident insurance.

ified in Arts. 2–3 Labour Contract Law,[18] is almost identical to the Art. 7:610 of the Dutch Civil Code,[19] which defines the employment contract as an agreement whereby an employee commits themselves to perform work in service of an employer in exchange for remuneration. By contrast, Luxembourg's law never codified the concept of employee. From the outset, it would thus seem that qualifying typical forms of platform work as an employment relationship would be easiest for the courts in Luxembourg, as they do not need to deal with the fact that a form of work which allows workers to freely accept or reject tasks is difficult to reconcile with an express legislative reference to a worker 'committing themselves' to perform work. As will be seen below, the exact opposite has so far emerged in practice – with decision-making bodies in Belgium and the Netherlands proving much more willing to adapt the traditional concept to 'modern forms of subordination' than in Luxembourg.

7 The only country to have taken legislative measures in the past to streamline the judicial interpretation of the broad traditional concept of the employment relationship is **Belgium**. The 2006 Labour Relations Law[20] introduces a test relying on four 'general criteria' for the existence of an employment relationship: 1) the will of the parties as expressed in their agreement; 2) the freedom to organise working time; 3) the freedom to organise work; and 4) the possibility of exercising hierarchical control (Art. 333 (1)). While this catalogue of criteria may be a useful tool to systematise the classification test, it is clearly based on a formalistic understanding of subordination, leaving little room to focus on forms of dependency other than contractual commitments and constraints. As will become evident below, this is in remarkable contrast to the legal presumption introduced by the same law, with its central reliance on criteria indicating organisational integration. As a result, ironically, a literal interpretation of these provisions would in most cases result in platform workers being presumed employed, just for this presumption to be immediately rebutted due to a lack of formal subordination.

8 In the Netherlands and **Luxembourg**, the concrete tests applied in practice are based exclusively on prior case law. In Luxembourg, unsurprisingly, the basic case law-based formula is again virtually identical to the statutory one in Belgium and the Netherlands as cited at → mn. 6, referring to an agreement in which one person agrees to make their activity available to another, under whose subordination they are placed, in return for remuneration.[21] This concept of subordination is subsequently assessed via a set of criteria relating i.a. to obligations regarding the time, place and modalities of work, but also the provision of tools and personal work performance.[22] There is no hierarchy between those elements; the eventual decision depends on the overall weighing of the criteria in the specific context. In the scarce case law concerning platform work so far (→ mn. 17), the courts have not seen a reason to reconsider or modify those criteria.

9 As opposed to this rather stable and possibly somewhat inflexible approach, which emerged in Luxembourg despite the interpretational freedom created by the lack of a statutory definition, the Dutch courts have traditionally applied a flexible and purposive approach to the Civil Code's concept of working 'in service' of an employer. To illustrate, already long before the first platform-related cases, the overall assessment of criteria conducted by the Dutch courts has included the consideration of economic depencence sensu stricto – which is expressly and categorically rejected by courts in most European

[18] Arbeidsovereenkomstenwet of 3.7.1978.
[19] Burgerlijk Wetboek.
[20] Programmawet of 27.12.2006.
[21] See e.g. Tribunal du Travail of 8.5.2025, 1549/25.
[22] Tribunal du Travail of 8.5.2025, 1549/25.

jurisdictions.[23] In the **Netherlands**, too, economic dependence is never decisive in itself, but may tilt the balance in favour of employee or self-employed status where the other criteria are not conclusive.[24]

Another remarkable demonstration of the flexible approach in the Netherlands is the Supreme Court's decision in the landmark case *X/Gemeente Amsterdam*[25] of November 2020, in which it expressly overturned its own earlier case law to find in favour of an absolute primacy of facts. In other words, when assessing the potential existence of an employment contract, the parties' intentions are not only less important than the factual execution of the contract but in fact *entirely irrelevant*. This could be said to have pre-empted the codification of an absolute primacy of facts in → Art. 4(2) Platform Work Directive ('irrespective of how the relationship is designated in any contractual arrangement that may have been agreed between the parties involved'). This actually raises attention to an aspect of the Directive that seems to have been largely overlooked by commentors so far – and probably also by a number of Member States which have traditionally departed only from a *relative* primacy of facts. This is nowhere as obvious as in Belgium, where, as mentioned (→ mn. 7), the will of the parties 'as expressed in their agreement' is even the first of the four 'general criteria' which the courts are statutorily obliged to apply. While Luxembourg's case law indicates an absolute understanding of the primacy of facts in line with Art. 4(2),[26] it sometimes seems to reintroduce its relevance 'through the backdoor'[27] and also treats the contractual designation as creating a presumption of correctness *as long as neither party in a judicial dispute challenges it* – which has already concretely prevented the assessment of platform workers' status in a judgment of 2021.[28] In other words, the transposition of the Platform Work Directive might actually require a revision of structural elements of the test of worker status – certainly in Belgium and potentially also in Luxembourg, depending on how Art. 4(2) is interpreted. 10

Finally, the Dutch Supreme Court used the occasion of the first of its (hitherto three, see → mn. 21) platform-related cases to specify and restructure the test to be applied by the courts. The new test takes a significant step away from a conventional understanding of subordination and requires and assessment of eight elements as to whether they point into the direction of subordination or rather self-employed work performance: 1) the nature and duration of work; 2) the determination of activities and working hours; 3) the integration of work and worker in the undertaking; 4) personal work performance; 5) the methods of contract conclusion; 6) remuneration and commercial risk; 7) entrepreneurship; and 8) other relevant circumstances. 11

II. Legal presumption of employee status

Both Dutch and Belgian law have required working individual to be (rebuttably) presumed employed under certain circumstances long before the adoption of the Platform Work Directive. 12

Under Dutch law, a legal **presumption of employment** is stipulated in Art. 7:610a Civil Code whenever work is performed to the extent of twenty or more hours per 13

[23] See Hießl, supra note 4, section 2.1.8.
[24] See Gerechtshof Amsterdam of 16.2.2021, ECLI:NL:GHAMS:2021:392.
[25] Hoge Raad of 6.11.2020, ECLI:NL:HR:2020:1746.
[26] See Tribunal du Travail of 8.5.2025, 1549/25.
[27] Notably when ascribing relevance to the fact that the worker was aware of his contractual classification as a self-employed.
[28] See description in fn. 31.

month over at least three months. Whereas this presumption, based on criteria that are very straightforward and comparatively easy to verify, could certainly be of use to platform workers when bringing individual claims, it has not had any relevance in the practical assessment to date since, as explained at → mn. 20, all cases so far have aimed as a collective reclassification of the workforce of a given platform, without distinction as to the extent of their work in the course of three months.

14 In Belgium, a very different, less straightforward type of legal presumption was introduced by the aforementioned 2006 Labour Relations Law (see Art. 337(2)). It effectively pre-empted the European Commission's approach of a multi-criteria presumption as included in the 2021 Proposal of the Platform Work Directive, with the difference that the Belgian concept is even considerably more complex. It stipulates that, in four 'sensitive' sectors (including notably the transport and logistics sector that became relevant in the *Uber* and *Deliveroo* cases, see → mn. 18) if at least half of the following eight criteria are fulfilled: a) lack of financial or economic risk (particularly no personal and substantial investment in the company or participation in its gains and losses); b) lack of responsibility and influence regarding the financial means of the company; c) lack of decision-making power concerning the company's purchasing policy; d) lack of decision-making power concerning its pricing policy; e) lack of an obligation of results concerning the agreed work; f) absence of own employees or substitution option; g) lack of appearance as a business or co-contractor vis-à-vis other persons; h) work in premises of with equipment owned, financed or guaranteed by the company. This presumption can be overturned based on an evaluation of the four 'general criteria' for the existence of an employment relationship (see → mn. 7). As discussed below, the presumption in this form played a crucial but also somewhat controversial role in the leading cases on the classification of platform workers.

15 The specific rebuttable presumption of employee status for platform workers, introduced as Art. 337(3) Employment Relations Law by the aforementioned (→ mn. 4) 'pre-transposition' of the Commission's proposal, follows a similar structure based on eight criteria (i.e. adding three to the five criteria proposed by the Commission): 1° the platform's possibility to demand exclusivity; 2° its use of a geolocation mechanism for purposes other than the proper functioning of its basic services; 3° its possibility to restrict the worker's freedom in how to perform work; 4° its possibility to limit the worker's income level, in particular by paying hourly rates and/or restricting the right to refuse job offers and/or determine the price of the service; its possibility to require the worker to comply with mandatory requirements regarding appearance, behaviour towards the recipient of the service, or work performance; 6° its possibility to determine the prioritisation of future job offers and/or the payment offered and/or the ranking by using information collected in particular by electronic means; 7° its possibility to restrict, including through sanctions, the worker's freedom to organise work, in particular to choose their working hours or periods of absence, accept or refuse tasks, or use subcontractors or substitutes; 8° its possibility to restrict the worker's ability to build a customer base outside the platform or work for a third party. The main difference compared to the 'old' presumption described in the last paragraph is that its establishment requires only three of these eight criteria to be fulfilled – even just two if both are among the last five of them.

III. Assessment of platform workers' status in case law

Coincidentally, in all Benelux countries, the first instance in which a competent public body made a formal decision about the status of a food delivery rider occurred in 2018. After that, events in the three countries took very different directions – in terms of the range of platform types to be assessed, the intensity of litigation, the speed at which the leading cases proceeded through the instances, the legal questions raised, and notably the outcomes of the assessment of worker status. 16

In **Luxembourg**, litigation on platform workers' status is essentially still in its infancy – with all three relevant decisions concerning the same food delivery platform (*WeDely*) and only the last of them – of May 2025[29] – even containing a reasoned decision on employment status.[30] In this recent judgment, the Luxembourg Labour Court rejected a claim brought by an individual delivery rider to demand compensation for unfair dismissal and the monetary entitlements that would have resulted from an employment relationship with the platform. The Court cited the above-mentioned (→ mn. 8) case law definition and found that, despite various indications of employment,[31] those were outweighed notably by the worker's free determination of his work hours and the lack of any exclusivity requirement. 17

In **Belgium**, all 14 decisions handed down so far (→ mn. 4) have focused on *Deliveroo* and *Uber*. Also here, the leading cases were originally brought by individual platform workers, who used the unique institution of the 'Administrative Commission for the Regulation of Labour Relations', which was – once again – installed by the 2006 Labour Relations Law (see → mn. 7). Whereas this commission decided in favour of employee status in relation to *Deliveroo* riders, *Uber* drivers and recently also *Uber Eats* riders,[32] both of the earlier decisions were overturned by the Brussels Labour Court (which considered all platform workers self-employed),[33] just to be later overturned again by the Brussels Labour Appeals Court.[34] As *Deliveroo* has already been reported to have brought an appeal before the Cassation Court and *Uber* may be expected to do the same, none of the cases have been closed so far. 18

What is striking in any event is that the applicability of the legal presumptions as described supra (→ mn. 14–15) in every single of the described decisions does not seem to have increased legal certainty – to the contrary, so far every judge that had the opportunity of overruling the assessment of another judge in the same case applying the very same presumption did exactly that. Thereby, it should be stressed that all decisions agreed that the legal presumption was established due to the fulfilment of a sufficient 19

---

[29] Tribunal du Travail of 8.5.2025, 1549/25.

[30] Earlier, the Labour Inspection in a non-published assessment conducted in 2018 discontinued its investigation of the platform as it saw no sufficient grounds for requalifying *WeDely*'s food delivery drivers as employees. This was briefly referenced in Luxembourg District Court decision 955/2021 of May 2021, as an obiter dictum when stating that there was no basis for the Court to check ex officio whether the classification of the deliverers as self-employed was actually correct. More importantly, an ex oficio investigation was precluded by the aforementioned (see → mn. 10) legal assumption of correctness of a contractual classification that is not disputed by either of the parties to the proceedings. The Court's decision fined WeDely for working with contractors who had not been registered as commercial delivery drivers.

[31] Which were actually more pronounced than in case of *Deliveroo* (→ mn. 18 et seqq.) in various respects – including notably the obligation of accepting all work offers within a self-chosen shift and the duty to wear a uniform.

[32] Commission Administrative de règlement de la relation de travail of 23.2.2018, 116 – FR – 20180209, of 9.3.2018, 113 – FR – 20180123, of 26.10.2020, and of 22.4.2024, 270 – FR – 2023/12/28.

[33] Tribunal du travail francophone de Bruxelles of 8.12.2021, 19/5070/A, and of 21.12.2022, 21/632/A.

[34] Cour du travail de Bruxelles of of 21.12.2023, 2022/AB/12, and of 13.6.2025, 2023/AB/119.

number of criteria,[35] but disagreed as to whether the presumption was rebutted. This illustrate the difficult task that courts are confronted with when a broad presumption focusing mainly on organisational integration is opposed to a definition of employee status that strongly focuses on subordination – and is of course eventually decisive for the outcome. Needless to say, situations like this may occur in more countries if → Art. 5 Platform Work Directive is implemented without reassessing the national notion of employee.

20 The **Netherlands** can quite clearly be identified as the country with the most advanced and most instructive case law developments so far. Not only have the 23 decisions (→ mn. 4), virtually all of which related to cases brought by trade union federations in relation to a platform's entire workforce, concerned four different platform types – delivery (*Deliveroo*), ride hailing (*Uber*), cleaning (*Helpling*), and hospitality (*Temper*) – they also included legal questions that went beyond the establishment of employee status in the individual case.

21 Thus, the *Deliveroo* case, in which the employee status of all riders was confirmed in last instance in 2023,[36] was used by the Supreme Court as an occasion to modernise and refocus the case law formula for assessing employee status on questions of dependency and organisational integration rather than formal subordination (see → mn. 11). The *Uber* proceedings were used by the second-instance court to expressly demand a clarification from the Supreme Court in cases where a taxi driver generally organising their activity as a genuine independent business uses the *Uber* app in a complementary fashion to fill gaps. This is a question that, despite its practical relevance, does not seem to have ever been expressly addressed in the many judgments on *Uber* in the different European countries – whereby all last-instance decisions effectively agreed that *Uber* is an employer (→ mn. 4). The Dutch Supreme Court's answer in 2025,[37] according to which such drivers could be seen as self-employed even if their colleagues working only for *Uber* were reclassified as employees, is controversial[38] and caused the government to amend a pending bill on self-employed work.[39] The *Helpling* case dealt with another key question otherwise unaddressed in the European case law so far, namely whether a temporary agency work construct could be used to characterise a platform as an employer when direction and control in relation to the individual work tasks are in fact exercised by the clients, i.e. the households using cleaning services. This solution, which required a reconsideration of past case law to consider private households as 'user undertakings', was confirmed by the Supreme Court in 2025.[40] Finally, the *Temper* case, only recently decided in first instance[41] (in favour of the platform) and currently pending before the Amsterdam Appeals Court, constitutes the first European lawsuit on a type of platform providing 'freelancers' to businesses for short assignments and thus operating in a way that differs in various respects from those that have widely been reclassified as employers (→ mn. 4).

---

[35] Although the assessment of the individual criteria varied widely, proving that these are themselves difficult to interpret and actually increase the complexity of the legal assessment, forcing the court to perform a detailed reasoning in relation to those eight criteria before even turning to the actual assessment of employee status.

[36] Hoge Raad of 24.3.2023, ECLI:NL:HR:2023:443.

[37] Hoge Raad of 21.2.2025, ECLI:NL:HR:2025:319.

[38] See the diametrically opposed findings of the Advocate General on 30.9.2024, ECLI:NL:PHR:2024:996.

[39] Tweede Kamer, Kamerbrief Zelfstandig ondernemerschap, vergaderjaar 2024–2025, 31 311, nr. 281, available at https://open.overheid.nl/documenten/1ee9a35b-b8a8-48b5-a3ff-79134b224647/file.

[40] Hoge Raad of 11.4.2025, ECLI:NL:HR:2025:543.

[41] Rechtbank Amsterdam of 10.7.2024, ECLI:NL:RBAMS:2024:3987.

IV. Platform work as a gamechanger?

22 If the preceding subsections have essentially identified the Netherlands as the probably most progressive in terms of opening up the national employee concept to new forms of dependency, whereas the opposite seems true in Luxembourg,[42] it may be important not to lose sight of reality. EU-level statistics[43] show that, over the last decade, the Netherlands have continuously featured one of the highest rates of persons classified as solo self-employed among the working population, whereas the Luxembourgish share has consistently been among the lowest in Europe. This may serve as a reminder that, in practice, the prevalence of bogus self-employment is not primarily influenced by the judicial interpretation of the complex and evolving concept of employee, whose details are rarely fully understood by the parties concluding a concrete contract, but crucially by elements such as the fiscal attractiveness and administrative ease of self-employment, the frequency of controls by authorities and the likelihood and severity of sanctions.[44] In this regard, it remains to be seen whether the case law on platform workers has the potential to act as a gamechanger in terms of mainstreaming developments in the interpretation of the concept of employee – with judgments effectively concerning large numbers of workers working under identical contracts for the same platform and also gaining significant attention in the public debate.

D. Algorithmic management

23 So far, none of the Benelux countries has legislative measures focusing specifically on **algorithmic management** in place.

24 In terms of case law, reference needs to be made to the famous rulings on *Uber* and *Ola* in the Netherlands – the first and so far only court rulings in Europe dealing in detail with the requirements of the GDPR for algorithmic transparency.[45] All of them were brought by drivers, who had worked for the platforms mostly in the UK. Two of the claims required general transparency about data processing and notably algorithmic decision-making by, respectively, *Uber* and *Ola*; a third claim targeting *Uber* specifically required an explanation for five drivers' removal from the platform, claiming they had been 'robo-fired' by an algorithm. The claimants were supported by an international collaboration of workers' associations, which specifically decided to launch the lawsuits at the platforms' seat in Amsterdam (see Art. 4 Brussels 1 bis Regulation 1215/2012), rather than in the jurisdiction of work performance – notably because the Dutch courts' practice of interpreting the GDPR appeared more favourable to the claimants.[46]

---

42 See also Jean-Luc Putz, Une première décision concernant les plateformes sur internet, commentaire sous TA Lux, 4 mai 2021, Revue pratique de droit social, N° 12, 2021.

43 Available at https://ec.europa.eu/eurostat/databrowser/view/tqoe4a3/default/line?lang=en&category=qoe.qoe_soe.

44 See Hiessl, International Journal of Comparative Labour Law and Industrial Relations 2022, 415 et seqq.

45 For an overview, see Hießl, Case Law on Algorithmic Management at the Workplace: Cross-European Comparative Analysis and Tentative Conclusions (update 2025), https://papers.ssrn.com/sol3/papers.cfm?abstract_id=3982735.

46 Information based on personal interaction with representatives of the claimant organisations, Feldkirch 21.11.2024.

25 All three cases were ruled on by the Amsterdam Civil Court in 2021,[47] then overruled by the Amsterdam Appeals Court in 2023.[48] The second-instance decisions upheld the key claims in all three lawsuits and ordered the platforms to provide detailded information on the functioning of their algorithms – including those deciding on the distribution of tasks to workers, the pricing of rides (and thus the remuneration of drivers), including deductions and penalties, and notably the establishment of 'fraud probability scores' and the suspension or deactivation of drivers' accounts.

26 The cases illustrate a number of difficulties and legal uncertainties that platform workers face when relying on Arts. 15 and 22 GDPR to demand algorithmic transparency. Thereby, they also demonstrate the potential impact of the Platform Work Directive on the chances and expected outcome of similar cases in future. This includes, for instance:

- an unconditional right to information about the use of algorithms: one of the aims not achieved in the Dutch cases was to obtain clarity whether the platforms used any additional algorithmic systems not already known by the workers. Whereas Art. 15(1)(h) GDPR ensures that, for *certain* forms of automated decision-making and/or profiling, the data subject has a comprehensive information right (incl. the existence of the algorithm, its underlying logic, significance and envisaged consequences), this is formulated as an all-or-nothing provision. Accordingly, an employer or principal using an algorithm outside the scope of Art. 15(1)(h) GDPR is not obliged to even inform the data subject of the algorithm's very existence. In line with the basic interpretation that effectively underlies the Dutch decisions in both instances (despite their very different outcomes), this includes notably algorithms not meeting the vague criteria formulated in Art. 22(1) GDPR of having legal or 'similarly significant' effects on the data subject. Needless to say, when a platform company conceals even the existence of an algorithm based on a perceived lack of 'significance', workers have nothing to go on in terms of questioning the decisions made by it. Note that the claimants tried also an 'indirect' avenue to achieve algorithmic transparency, requiring to be informed about all their personal data processed by the platforms and the respective purpose of those forms of processing. While this is clearly a legitimate request under Art. 15 GDPR, it was rejected by the first-instance court as too general, considering that recital 63 to the GDPR, which states that controllers processing 'a large quantity of information concerning the data subject' – which is clearly the case for platform companies – can require the data subject to 'specify the information or processing activities to which the request relates'. In light of all this difficulty and legal uncertainty, → Art. 9 Platform Work Directive achieves a significant improvement simply because, apart from an instructive list, it contains the catch-all information requirement on 'all categories of decision taken or supported by automated systems that affect persons performing platform work in any manner'.
- the labour law-specific identification of decisions requiring additional transparency: one major uncertainty in the Dutch cases was the question if the typical algorithms used by platforms, e.g. the ones assigning work tasks and determining pay levels, met the just mentioned threshold of affecting the data subject 'similarly significantly' as in case of a legal effect. The diametrically opposed view of the judges in different instances bears witness of this. By contrast, → Art. 9 Platform Work Directive

[47] Rechtbank Amsterdam of 11.3.2021, C/13/689705/HARK20–258, C/13/692003/HARK20–203 and C/13/687315/HARK20–207.

[48] Gerechtshof Amsterdam of 4.4.2023, 200.295.747/01, 200.295.806/01 and 200.295.742/01.

specifically refers to 'decisions to restrict, suspend or terminate the account of the person performing platform work, to refuse the payment for work performed by them, as well as for decisions on their contractual status or any decision of equivalent or detrimental effect' – thereby not only ensuring that those elements are included in the information provided by platforms, but also requiring that, for these particular algorithmic decisions, also their grounds must be explained.

At the same time, the Platform Work Directive does not alleviate the tedious task of balancing the right to algorithmic transparency with other rights and interests – which under the GDPR is done notably by reference to Arts. 5–6 and 23. Arguably, the unconditional formulation of → Art. 9 Platform Work Directive certainly underline the point already made by the Amsterdam Appeals Court based on recital 63 to the GDPR – namely that no conflicting interests could justify the denial of *any* information on automated decision-making that significantly affect platform workers. However, the devil may often be in the detail when it comes to the question of just how detailed the information can and must be. Interests that were in principle recognised as legitimate and thus justifying the omission of certain details under the GDPR in the Dutch cases included the protection of privacy of customers who trusted in the anonymity of the reviews they had given the drivers; the protection of business secrets in relation to the algorithm's precise way of working; and the maintenance of an effective fraud protection system, which may imply withholding certain information that could enable workers actually intending to commit fraud to circumvent the algorithmic detection system. How precisely these interests could be taken into account sufficiently while ensuring that workers obtain information that allows them effectively use and enforce their rights is still not entirely clear. 27

E. Collective organisation of platform workers

The Platform Work Directive has a key focus on **collective labour rights**, with → Art. 25 requiring the 'promotion of collective bargaining in platform work' and workers' representatives being given a clear role e.g. in terms of own information rights or of acting 'on behalf or in support of' platform workers in judicial and administrative procedures (→ Art. 19). To futher encourage collective bargaining, → Art. 28 even allows collective agreements to deviate from some of the Platform Work Directive's provisions. 28

While no precise numbers are generally communicated for any of the Benelux countries, unions generally confirm[49] that unionisation is not a widespread phenomenon among platform workers. This is not to deny that unions have emerged – in the Benelux region much more so than elsewhere – as a key driving force behind (largely successful) claims for the reclassification of platform workers. The Netherlands are, in fact, the only country where almost every single claim so far has been brought by unions in their own name – a claim setup virtually unknown in platform-related litigation in other European countries.[50] In Belgium, the unions have at least had a supporting role in all of the major proceedings. Yet, from a collective labour rights point of view, the pursuit of platform workers' reclassification as employees is just a first step to create better preconditions for those workers' possible future unionisation and collective bargaining. So far, the only cases actually brought by platform workers that were union members 29

[49] Interviews with trade union representatives, conducted by the author on 20.6.2025.
[50] Cf. Hießl, supra note 4.

were the Dutch *Uber* and *Ola* cases just described in the previous section – i.e. claims that concerned a UK-based union and drivers working mainly in the UK. By contrast, the established domestic unions in Benelux have so far litigated either as interveners next to non-affiliated individual platform workers (as in the Belgian *Deliveroo* case, see supra → mn. 18) or as claimants defending their own right to ensure the application of sectoral collective agreements to workers that should be recognised as employees – as in effectively all Dutch cases brought so far. In the latter constellation, the Dutch unions have even been accused of pursuing their interests to the detriment of platform workers.[51]

30 Apart from the route of strategic litigation, trade unions have been vocal in their demands for the sector, organising dozens of demonstrations and strikes, notably among riders and drivers in the major cities of Belgium and the Netherlands.[52] Ever since the first strikes organised against *Deliveroo* in early 2018[53] at the occasion of riders' loss of employee status, the unions have generally been in charge of channelling workers' demands, with few exceptions of actions organised by ad hoc gatherings of workers or alternative cooperations. At several occasions, union delegates in Brussels and/or Amsterdam acted as the driving force behind coordinated industrial action of a European dimension – including repeated rallies before the EU Parliament in relation to the adoption of the Platform Work Directive.[54]

31 So far the only noteworthy developments in terms of (attempts of) collective bargaining for platform workers in the Benelux region have taken place in Belgium. Above (→ mn. 3), reference has already been made to the *Smart cooperative*, which started off as an association of freelance workers in the cultural sector, but organised also platform riders between 2015 and 2017. In that capacity, it exercised a double role as an intermediary and employer of the riders on the one hand and a union-like representative organisation on the other, negotiating with *Deliveroo* and *Take Eat Easy* about the conditions under which its workers provided delivery services for the platforms.[55] As mentioned, this particular construct was only short-lived.

32 More recently, in October 2022, the transport section of one of Belgium's three relevant union federations (*ABVV-BTB*) concluded a framework agreement with *Uber*, in which the platform formally recognises the union as representing the interests of its workers (about 2,500 drivers and 3,000 riders), commits to providing it with facilities at its Brussels headquarters and to arrange a meeting once per quarter. The union thereby became the third national affiliate of the *International Transport Workers' Federation*

---

[51] Cf. the fact that *Uber* drivers wishing to stay self-employed intervened on *Uber*'s side in the court proceedings, and that the unions have been accused of orchestrating *Helpling*'s bankruptcy in the Netherlands Arets, 'Hoe het faillissement van Helpling de weeffouten van het platformdebat blootlegt' (ZiPconomy,16.1.2023) <https://www.zipconomy.nl/2023/01/hoe-het-faillissement-helpling-de-weeffouten-van-het-platformdebat-blootlegt> (last accessed: 28.11.2025).

[52] Information based on numerous press releases published in every year since 2018, with notably collective actions targeting *Uber* often organised repeatedly in the same year.

[53] See e.g. Belga, 'Des coursiers de Deliveroo feront grève ce samedi dans 5 villes belges' (Le Soir, 12.1.2018) <https://www.lesoir.be/133608/article/2018-01-12/des-coursiers-de-deliveroo-feront-greve-ce-samedi-dans-5-villes-belges> (last accessed: 28.11.2025); Redactie economie, 'Deliveroo bezorgers gaan weer staken' (Trouw, 2.1.2018) <https://www.trouw.nl/nieuws/deliveroo-bezorgers-gaan-weer-staken~b2f15023/?referrer=https%3A%2F%2Fwww.ecosia.org%2F> (last accessed: 28.11.2025).

[54] See e.g. Hertogs, 'Dinsdag nieuwe actie tegen Uber aan Europees Parlement' (HLN, 24.10.2022) <https://www.hln.be/brussel/dinsdag-nieuwe-actie-tegen-uber-aan-europees-parlement~a66473a5/?referrer=https%3A%2F%2Fwww.ecosia.org%2F> (last accessed: 28.11.2025); Philippe, 'Hinder in Brussel door betoging straattaxi's aan kantoren Uber en Brussels Parlement' (VRT News, 14.11.2024) <https://www.vrt.be/vrtnws/nl/2024/11/14/brusselse-straattaxi-s-betogen-aan-kantoren-uber-en-brussels-par/> (last accessed: 28.11.2025).

[55] See Franquet/Maisin in Waas/Hießl, p. 73 (96 et seqq).

(*ITWF*) to follow up on a Memorandum of Understanding with *Uber* concluded in 2022[56] – after the *British GMB* and the *Australian TWU*.[57] The move has been met with much controversy – with proponents describing it as a 'historic achievement', while sceptics (including notably the country's two other union federations) criticising *ABVV-BTB* for blindsiding the established social partner structures in the sector, for apparently committing to exempt wages and worker status from the topics on which it seeks dialogue with the platform, and the fact that details of the agreement were never published.[58] All in all, after the initial upheaval, no further developments in the collective relations between *Uber* and the union have been reported (not even among the union's own press releases), indicating that no noteworthy concrete agreements abour working conditions could be reached based on the framework agreement.

F. Conclusions

Drawing any general conclusions about the expected impacts of the Platform Work Directive in the Benelux is, in a certain sense, a pointless exercise, as the cooperation between these three countries has never involved labour law, leading to highly individual developments in each country that would probably each merit a separate assessment. However, in several instances, it is precisely the contrast between these national systems that throws certain aspects of the Platform Work Directive's provisions into sharper relief. 33

This includes, for instance, the contrasting approaches and developments relating to frequently overlooked question of the primacy of facts (→ mn. 10).[59] Considering that Belgium is by far not the only country with a tradition of an only *relative* primacy of facts which has already played a role in courts' rejection of employee status in platform-related cases,[60] one might expect controversy about → Art. 4(2) and its interpretation to emerge at some point. The preference for an absolute primacy of facts, in line with the ILO Employment Relationship Recommendation No 198 (2006), as cited in recital 27 to the Platform Work Directive, is clear and, in the eyes of the author, even implied by the very concept of labour law. Attaching any relevance to the 'will of the parties' risks to exclude precisely the most vulnerable, who lack the bargaining power to have any actual say in the contractual provisions. Needless to say, platform work is an excellent illustration of this issue, considering that precisely the most precarious forms are characterised by standardised and non-negotiable contracts that may be changed by the platform unilaterally at any time. At the same that, the fact that → Art. 4(2) seems to force Member States to adapt their national concept of determining employee status – which arguably goes much further than the introduction of a rebuttable presumption as a procedural tool – may be legally controversial, considering that employee status under national law affects various areas for which the EU lacks competence under Art. 153 TFEU. 34

[56] See ITWF, 'ITF signs agreement with *Uber* to begin social dialogue on working conditions for drivers and couriers' (ITWF, 17.2.2022) <https://www.itfglobal.org/en/news/itf-signs-agreement-uber-begin-social-dialogue-working-conditions-drivers-and-couriers> (last accessed: 28.11.2025).

[57] Moreels, 'BTB-ABVV tekent historisch akkoord met Uber' (De Nieuwe Werker, 25.10.2022) <https://denieuwewerker.be/btb-abvv-tekent-historisch-akkoord-met-uber/> (last accessed: 28.11.2025).

[58] See e.g. Michiels,'Waarom het 'akkoord om niet akkoord te gaan' tussen ABVV-BTB en UBER onmiddellijk verscheurd moet worden' (Vonk, 25.10.2022) <http://www.vonk.org/analyse/belgie/syndicaal/3936-waarom-het-akkoord-om-niet-akkoord-te-gaan-tussen-abvv-btb-en-uber-onmiddellijk-verscheurd-moet-worden.html> (last accessed: 28.11.2025).

[59] See Machtelings, Jura Falconis 2015–2016, 611 et seqq.

[60] See, for Germany, Landesarbeitsgericht Hessen of 14.2.2019, 10 Ta 350/18; for Hungary Kúria of 13.12.2023, Mfv.VIII.10.091/2023/7.

35 Another aspect illustratively emerging from the comparison concerns the gap between legal and case law developments and their practical implementation, as referred to at → mn. 22. This underlines both the crucial role of enforcement as addressed in → Art. 24 Platform Work Directive and notably fiscal incentives that exacerbate bogus self-employment – some of which may even be platform-specific, as exemplified in the regulation described at → mn. 3.

36 Several other interesting lessons of broader significance may be drawn from the experience in individual Benelux countries with platform work-related litigation. This certainly includes the Dutch cases on algorithmic management (→ mn. 25), which illustrate like no other precedent which important issues of legal uncertainty are effectively tackled by the Platform Work Directive and which open questions remain. The Belgian experience with legal presumptions (→ mn. 19) in turn confirms what might be indicated also by developments in other countries (→ mn. 4) – namely that legal presumptions do not necessarily make the decision-making bodies' assessment of worker status any less complex (rather the opposite), but they may be read by at least some judges as an indication that an interpretation in line with the legislator's will requires them to resolve uncertainties about workers' classification in favour of employee status. However, determining the point at which such uncertainties exist may again be very difficult and controversial, especially as platforms' terms and conditions are changing constantly and frequently in a manner that emphasises elements of workers' independence (→ mn. 4).

37 As for collective labour rights, the contrast between the three countries certainly illustrates the very considerable impact that active union involvement can have on the development of impactful strategic litigation on employee status. At the same time, the challenges of unionising platform workers are evident throughout the region. Finally, the main conclusion from the very limited experience of bargaining collectively with platform operators (→ mn. 31–32) may be that, eventually, it takes two to tango, and said tango may be highly unbalanced if one side lacks any effective leverage. The degree to which the obligation of promoting collective bargaining in → Art. 25 can stimulate innovative approaches in this regard remains to be seen.

France

Literature: Brihi, 'Quelle régulation pour les plateformes numériques?', Sem. soc. Lamy 2024, n° 2085, p.9; Gabroy, 'Premier décryptage de la Directive du 23 octobre 2024 sur le travail de plateforme : entre dualité des statuts et garanties communes', Lexbase Social 2024, n° 1003; Larrazet, 'Directive des plateformes numériques : derrière les ambitions abandonnées, une petite révolution en cours du droit du travail?', Dr. ouvrier 2024, 241; Loiseau, 'Un droit européen des travailleurs de plateformes', JCP S 2024, 735; Loiseau, 'Les contrats unissant les travailleurs aux plateformes', JCP S 2025, 1001; Lokiec, 'Le contrôle des algorithmes, Les avancées de la directive sur les travailleurs de plateformes', Bulletin Joly Travail (BJT) 3/2025, 49; Marzo, 'La proposition de directive relative à l'amélioration des conditions de travail dans le cadre du travail via une plateforme : une occasion de repenser les statuts et les droits des travailleurs de plateformes, RTD eur. 2022, 665', Perulli, 'Vers l'octroi d'une protection au-delà de la subordination : la voie de lutte contre la précarité', RDT 2024, 640; Vicente, 'La directive « plateformes » et la lutte contre la précarité des travailleurs : la portée d'une ambition', RDT 2024, 636.

A. Introduction

I. Employment Status of persons performing platform work: a regulation that the French authorities did not want

Transposing EU 2024/2831 of 23 October 2024 into French law will be challenging. 1
France is one of the EU Member States that have ensured that this legislation will fail. These manoeuvres certainly did not improve the legal text which had been laboriously adopted. Rather, they have weakened the impact of its content. The initial ambition, which was principally to establish a presumption of an employment relationship, was retained only at the cost of concessions that weakened the very meaning of a presumption. Whereas the presumption was to operate by operation of law on the basis of

predefined criteria,[1] it will now apply on the basis of facts demonstrating control and direction in accordance with national legislation, collective agreements or practices in force in the Member States and with regard to the case law of the Court of Justice. This is a regrettable step backwards, showing cruelly that some state authorities prioritise preserving the platforms' business model over enhancing the legal status of employment, despite the proven disadvantages of the 'platformisation of work' (social optimisation, distorted competition with traditional operators, etc.). However, it is significant that the legal presumption remains and, in this respect, it is a strong sign of labour law's vocation to constitute the model for organising employment relations, and of its predisposition to apply to workers[2] in grey areas who have the status of micro-entrepreneurs solely for the purpose of carrying out a paid activity, without truly being independent.

2 However, the extent of progress depends on the implementation of the principle of a legal presumption. Left partly to the Member States, the way it is formulated in national law risks reducing the presumption to nothing more than a deceptive mechanism. Implementing the presumption during the employment relationship would still give it an advantage over a judicial reclassification of the contract. Currently, this only takes place *ex-post*, after the contractual relationship has been terminated, in order to liquidate its effects. But a minimalist transposition would not send a positive message to those who view the Directive as a change in platform workers' status classification. However, this is to be feared, as the French legislator has been intent on defending the platform business model for nearly ten years. It has organised itself in such a way as to preserve the exclusive self-employed status of workers, even if it means embellishing it with the possibility of adjustments by means of collective agreements[3] . From this point of view, the transposition of the Directive will determine, for the future, the choice of a legal policy towards platforms and the workers they employ.

II. Algorithmic management: a more consensual aspect

3 The presumption of employment status, which is the text's flagship measure, is not the subject of the entire Directive. European legislation also takes a longer look at the algorithmic governance of workers, whether or not they are employees. On this aspect, the Directive aims to protect workers by regulating the application of automated decision-making systems and automated monitoring systems, by guaranteeing human intervention when decisions are taken or supported by an artificial intelligence system, and by prohibiting the processing of certain sensitive data. In this respect, it shares the philosophy of the regulation on the protection of personal data, which is to defend the fundamental rights and freedoms of the individual. Conversely, it distances itself from the liberal approach of the regulation on artificial intelligence, which deals with cases of use in employment relationships. Unlike the first part of the Directive, the second part sets a high level of harmonisation, leaving little scope for national legislators to transpose it. Overall, it should therefore adhere to the text's prescriptions, although a

---

[1] See Art. 4(2)(a)-(e) European Commission, Proposal for a Directive of the European Parliament and of the Council on improving working conditions in platform work, 9.12.2021, Com(2021) 762 final, 34 et seqq.

[2] The term 'worker' is used in this contribution to refer to self-employed persons. All platform workers have the status of self-employed in the French system.

[3] The French legislator has organised the possibility of concluding collective agreements at the level of the mobility platforms' sectors of activity, between platforms' representatives and workers' representatives (Labour Code, Arts. L. 7341-1 to L. 7143-59).

few adjustments are required. This could be an opportunity to consider the algorithmic governance of workers from a perspective that goes beyond platform operations alone.

III. Where do we stand?

While it is now virtually certain that the directive will not be transposed by the deadline, there is no way to predict when the transposition law will be adopted. On 26 February 2026, the government tasked a working group with an interministerial consultation mission to prepare for transposition. The results of their work are expected before the end of the third quarter of 2026. In a written question addressed in April to the Minister of the Economy, Finance, and Industrial, Energy, and Digital Sovereignty, a member of parliament raised concerns that no draft legislation had yet been drafted.[4] For their part, labour unions called on 24 April 2026 for a maximalist transposition of the directive.[5] 4

B. The Status of platform workers

I. The law: between legislation and case law

French law is afflicted by the strange malady of duplicating the same reality. On the one hand, legislation confines platform workers to a form of independence that is often artificial in order to protect an economic model that provides jobs. On the other hand, the Court of Cassation favours reclassifying the contracts of bogus self-employed workers as employment contracts, relying as much on indications of legal subordination as on the absence of any element that gives credibility to the status of self-employed worker[6]. Obliged by the Directive to evolve, national legislators are entitled to decide how to formulate the presumption. Without prejudging the outcome, the key issues to consider are the conditions for applying the presumption, the extent of its scope and how it will be implemented. 5

II. Conditions for applying the presumption of an employment contract

1. Determinants of the presumption

French law has a long tradition of presuming an employment contract. For many workers covered by Part Seven of the French Labour Code, such as entertainers, models and professional journalists, whose autonomy makes it difficult to establish a relationship of subordination, it is a means of accessing the status of employee and the associated benefits as soon as the contract is concluded. This useful stepping stone for workers on the edge of legal presumption of subordination could also obviously be useful for 6

[4] Written Question n° 14781 by Ms. Amiot, Transposing the Directive on Platform Workers by December 2026, Official Journal of 28 April 2026, page 3580.

[5] These are the CFDT, CGT, and SUD unions.

[6] This position has been that of the Labour Chamber of the Court of Cassation since 2018. It is now shared by the Commercial Chamber (Cass. com. 25.6.2025, n° 23–22.430, P; JCP S 2025, 1270, comment Coursier; D. 2025, p. 1824, comment Bettoni; Communication commerce électronique (hereinafter Comm. com. électr.) 2025, comm. 74, comment Loiseau).

persons performing platform work. On 9 December 2021[7], the European Commission proposed in its draft to make it easier to recognise an employment relationship on the basis of predefined criteria (at least two out of five) that make such a relationship likely. At the end of the day, the Directive leaves it up to each national law to devise the direction and control criteria for applying the presumption on the basis of facts that bring them out, taking into account the case law of the Court of Justice.

7 When conceived in this way, the legal presumption, at first glance, is not actually a presumption because, although it is based on facts 'indicating direction and control' in accordance with French law, it effectively establishes the conditions for an employment contract. Unlike a presumptive mechanism, it does not dispense with the need to prove legal subordination, at least with regard to the constituent elements of direction and control. The difference is striking when compared to the presumptions currently established by Part Seven of the French Labour Code for professional journalists, performing artists, or models[8]. As a legal presumption, the one set forth in Art. 5 of the Directive of 23 October 2024, appears rather as a simple 'procedural facilitation', as the Directive describes it.[9]

8 Although it will essentially apply to cases in which an employee could currently seek to have a service contract reclassified as an employment contract by the courts, the progress made is nonetheless significant. Under the conditions of the 'presumption', the courts will have to recognise an employment contract, whereas some lower courts currently refuse to do so in identical situations[10]. It may also be applied in relevant administrative procedures. Lastly, the legal presumption is intended to benefit employees during the performance of the contractual relationship, when disputes over the requalification only arise after the contract has been terminated.

2. A strengthening of the presumption mechanism

9 Although the legal presumption in the Directive is not technically a presumption, it can still come close. The implementation into national law opens up a wide range of possibilities, since the term 'evidence' in the phrase 'facts indicating direction and control' can have a more or less broad meaning. Interpreted broadly, it enables evidence of direction and control to be provided without having to prove that the digital labour platform exercises full power of direction and control. The expert group established by the European Commission to assist it in monitoring the transposition of the Directive – whose report was submitted on 12 January 2026 – shares this view, as it acknowledges that facts indicating direction and control could be factual elements that make legal subordination plausible or at least possible.[11] In the context of this work, the Commission's services have also acknowledged that the standard of proof required to trigger the presumption must be logically lower than full proof of the elements constituting an employment relationship.[12] The national laws implementing the Directive could therefore

[7] See Art. 4(2)(a)-(e) European Commission, Proposal for a Directive of the European Parliament and of the Council on improving working conditions in platform work, 9.12.2021, Com(2021) 762 final, 34 et seqq.

[8] Labour Code, Arts. L. 7112-1, L. 7121-3, and L. 7123-3.

[9] Art. 5(2) Platform Work Directive.

[10] See for examples CA Paris 11.5.2023, n° 22/08225; Comm. com. électr. 2023, comm. 51, comment G. Loiseau – CA Paris 19.12.2024, n° 24/05934.

[11] European Commission, Report of the Expert Group – Transposition of Directive (EU) 2024/2831 on improving working conditions in platform work (12.1.2026), 30 et seq.

[12] The Commission's services add that, while the terms of the legal presumption are set by the Member States, 'this discretion is limited by the requirements of effectiveness' and that the legal presumption 'does not require full proof, but only prima facie evidence of direction and control' (European Commission, Re-

express this by making the recognition of an employment contract conditional upon establishing factual elements that 'suggest the existence of direction and control' or, at least, 'make the existence of direction and control likely'. To emphasise this reduction in the burden of proof, in the absence of a genuine presumptive mechanism, another paragraph could state that the use of automated decision-making systems or automated monitoring systems may constitute a factual element making direction and control likely. Art. 4(2) of the Directive on determining the correct employment status of workers suggests this approach by stating that verification of the existence of an employment relationship is guided by the facts relating to the actual performance of work, including the use of automated monitoring systems or automated decision-making systems in the organisation of work.[13]

Another way to approach a presumption is to consider indications of direction and control, whether positive or negative. Negative indications are inferred from the absence of evidence that the activity is carried out on a self-employed basis – this is the current approach of the Cour de cassation. It would undoubtedly be difficult to codify this rule. However, it could be included in the explanatory memorandum of the national implementing legislation, which could help clarify the text's interpretation. 10

Of course, the opposition that would be aroused by such a strengthening of the mechanism – incorrectly described as presumptive – is easy to anticipate. Yet it is the only way to make the Directive's provisions coherent. As Art. 5 requires Member States to 'establish an effective rebuttable presumption of an employment relationship', so the fact that it is based on establishing facts, that make direction and control likely is the closest thing to a presumption. This approach also makes sense of the provision that the employment platform can rebut the legal presumption by proving that the contractual relationship is not an employment relationship under domestic law. If the employee had to prove facts establishing direction and control in order to trigger the presumption, it would be impossible to prove the contrary *a priori*. 11

3. Codification of the presumption

It is expected that the presumptive mechanism will be formalised in the Labour Code and, more specifically, in Part Seven of the Code, which covers atypical workers and already includes a section dedicated to platform workers.[14] However, the provisions of Art. L. 8221-6 of the French Labour Code would still need to be adapted accordingly. This article establishes a presumption of the absence of an employment contract for any natural person registered in the Trade and Companies Register, in the National Business Register as a business in the trades and crafts sector, in the Register of Commercial Agents, or with social security contribution collection agencies. The presumption of an employment contract applicable to individuals performing work via a digital work platform is, in fact, difficult to reconcile with this presumption of non-salaried status. This could likely be resolved: *specialia generalibus derogant*. However, it would be preferable to formalise this in Art. L. 8221-6 and provide that the presumption of non-salaried status applies except to individuals performing work via a digital work platform. Given 12

port of the Expert Group – Transposition of Directive (EU) 2024/2831 on improving working conditions in platform work (12.1. 2026), 31 et seq.

[13] During the expert group's work, the Commission's services agreed on the importance of taking into account the role of these systems in identifying elements of subordination. These systems are increasingly replacing the functions typically performed by managers in companies and can exercise direction and control (European Commission, Report of the Expert Group – Transposition of Directive (EU) 2024/2831 on improving working conditions in platform work (12.1.2026), 30 et seq.).

[14] Labour Code, Arts. L. 7341-1 to L. 7345-12.

the opportunity to expand the provisions of the Labour Code, the question may arise as to whether it would be appropriate to introduce a definition of the subordination relationship in the first part of the Code. The point now is less on refining the concept – with the criteria of direction and control having been consolidated – and more on defining self-employment in parallel, drawing on the criteria identified by the Court of Justice in relation to platform workers.[15] The location of the latter definition would need to be considered, but it would be advantageous to have it available in order to derive negative criteria for the purposes of applying the legal presumption.

13 Placed in the seventh part of the Code, the legal presumption should have a specific space of its own, formally distinguished from the provisions currently covering platform workers, in order to set them apart from employees in practical terms. The definition of self-employment could be positioned among the latter, in contrast to the rules organising the presumption of an employment contract.

III. The scope of the presumption of a contract of employment

1. The platforms concerned

14 Since the presumption of an employment relationship applies to the relationship between digital labour platforms and the persons performing work via these platforms, the definition of 'platform' may limit the scope of application. According to this definition, it is the use of automated monitoring systems or automated decision-making systems that could lead to discrimination: a platform that does not use either of these systems would therefore be outside the scope of the legislation. This possible restriction, which also applies to determining the correct employment status of workers,[16] is imposed on the Member States *a priori* and they cannot modify the legal definition of digital labour platforms. Due to the design of the platforms' digital infrastructure, they cannot broaden it by deleting the reference to automated systems, nor can they restrict it by substituting an 'and' for an 'or' with regard to the system's functionality.[17]

15 To this extent, it is the mobility platform that will be most affected by the application of the presumption. Since the Mobility Orientation Act of 24 December 2019[18] and the Orders of 21 April 2021 and 6 April 2022 came into effect, they have been subject special legislation designed to protect their business model, which relies on self-employed drivers in the chauffeur-driven car sector and in the delivery of goods using a two- or three-wheeled vehicle. Since 2018,[19] however, they have also been the subject of case law

[15] ECJ 22.4.2020 – case C-692/19, ECLI:EU:C:2020:288 – B. c/ Yodel Delivery Network Ltd; JCP S 2020, 2037, comment Loiseau.

[16] Art. 4(2) of the Platform Work Directive, which provides that the ascertainment of the existence of an employment relationship shall be guided primarily by the facts relating to the actual performance of work, including the use of automated monitoring systems or automated decision-making systems in the organisation of platform work.

[17] The European Commission's services have stated that the condition regarding the use of automated systems 'implies either the use of automated monitoring systems, or the use of automated decision-making systems, or the use of both' (European Commission, Report Expert Group – Transposition of the Directive (EU) 2024/2831 on improving working conditions in platform work (12.1.2026), 16).

[18] LOI n° 2019-1428 du 24 décembre 2019 d'orientation des mobilités.

[19] Cass. soc. 28.11.2018, n° 17-20.079, P; JCP S 2018, 1398, comment Loiseau; JCP S 2019, 1026, comment Anciaux; JCP G 2019, p. 103, comment Roche; JCP E 2019, 1031, comment Bossu.

from the Cour de cassation, which is favourable to the recognition of an employment contract: *Uber*[20], *Bolt*[21], *TokTokTok*[22] and others.

16 Conversely, the Directive will have little impact on *jobbing* platforms, that do not organise the work performed by individuals, but merely provide the means by which service provider can reach the end-user without the involvement of the platform, for instance by advertising offers or requests for services. These platforms offer services to private individuals (such as cleaning, DIY, gardening, etc.) for which the workers are not under the direction and control of the customer, and even less so of the platform that matches them with each other, and therefore the platform is merely acting as a gatekeeper.[23] It is also likely that *freelance* platforms will be affected little or not at all by the Directive, as workers who provide services that generally have a high added value (consultancy, graphics, design, etc.) have the profile of self-employed workers.

17 On the other hand, it is more difficult to predict what will happen to microwork or crowdwork platforms. They are identified by the Directive as a type of platform that either supplies businesses or is itself the beneficiary of a flexible workforce for the performance of small tasks that can be carried out remotely, such as tagging, with these tasks being divided up and distributed among a large number of people (the crowd) who can perform them asynchronously (recital 19 sentence 5). Depending on how they operate, it cannot be ruled out that the presumption of an employment relationship may apply in areas where visibility is still limited. At this stage, the Court of Cassation has only considered the activities of the *Clic and Walk* platform, which is being prosecuted for concealed work. Following the Social Division's opinion[24] that there was no subordinate relationship, the Criminal Division[25] also ruled out the existence of an employment relationship.

2. Arrangements specific to platforms for making workers available

18 These platforms (*Brigad*, *Staffme*, *Mediflash*, etc.) are known for providing user companies with micro-entrepreneur wokers to carry out short-term assignments, according to their needs. With the exception of a few structures that only act as intermediaries to place genuinely self-employed workers, the vast majority of them welcome all kinds of workers willing to adopt the status of self-employed to monetise their labour power in all kinds of sectors of activity, especially sectors in short supply: hotels, restaurants, construction, medical and medico-social services and so on. In this respect, these platforms are a crude copy of temporary employment agencies, but they are not subject to temporary employment regulations.

19 The situation here is more complex, since the user companies, to which the workers are made available for temporary assignments, mainly exercise management and control. Therefore, the presumption should apply to the relationship between the user company and the micro-entrepreneur. However, we cannot ignore the economic reality of the contractual operation as a whole, in which the platform is engaged in a temporary labour lending activity. In cases where a worker has requested a ruling on their employment status, the lower courts have accepted the existence of a contract of

[20] Cass. soc. 4.3.2020, n° 19–13.316, P; JCP S 2020, 1080, comment Loiseau; JCP G 2020, 601, comment Bossu; Dr. soc. 2020, p.374, comment Antonmattei; RDT 2020, p. 328, comment Willocx – Cass. soc. 25.1.2023, n° 21–11.273; Cass. soc., 5.3.2025, n° 23–18.430, n° 23–18.431.

[21] Cass. soc. 15.3.2023, n° 21–17.316.

[22] Cass. soc. 27.9.2023, n° 20–22.465, P; JCP S 2023, 1267, comment Loiseau.

[23] Cass. soc. 16.10. 2024, n° 23–17.574.

[24] Cass. soc. 15.12.2021, n° 21–70.017; JCP S 2022, 1039, comment Loiseau.

[25] Cass. crim. 5.4.2022, n° 20–81.775, P; BJT 5/2022, p.33, comment Casado.

employment both between the worker and the user company and, by ricochet, between the worker and the platform, after considering that the latter is in fact carrying out a temporary employment activity.[26] The implementation of the Directive should be used to clarify the rules. The Directive does not ignore platforms of this type, as recital 26 states that 'where a party is found to be an employer and fulfils the conditions of being a temporary-work agency in accordance with Directive 2008/104/EC, the obligations under that Directive apply'. Therefore, it would be inconceivable for the presumption not to apply to the relationship between workers and platforms that provide self-employed workers. As the general aim of the Directive is to correct the misclassification of workers' employment status in order to combat bogus self-employment (recital 25), the business model of these platforms, which is designed to avoid legal obligations and to create a competitive advantage over companies that comply with the law (recital 28), must be subject to the procedures that the Member States are required to implement in order to ensure that workers' employment status is correctly determined.

20 Special provisions would therefore be useful for operations involving the hiring out of workers to user undertakings. The presumption of employment status could apply to the relationship between the digital labour platform and the person performing platform work if there is evidence of both work organisation by the digital labour platform (e.g. selection of the worker, setting of the remuneration, and invoicing of the latter to the client company), and if the person performing platform work is made available to the user company to work temporarily under its supervision and direction. Where appropriate, it could be specified that the recognition of an employment relationship with one or more workers obliges the digital labour platform to submit to temporary work regulations. This effect would nevertheless be induced by the existence of an employment contract with at least some of the workers made available to client companies. This could even be sought, primarily, by workers' representatives.

IV. Application of the presumption of a contract of employment

1. Triggering the presumption: procedures.

21 The legal presumption is according to Art. 5(3) of the Directive applicable in all relevant administrative or judicial proceedings where the determination of the correct professional status of the person performing work via a digital labour platform is at stake. This requirement is binding on the Member States when transposing the Directive. On the other hand, they have the option to apply the presumption to proceedings relating to tax, criminal matters or social security. The stated aim of the Directive is to make it easier to determine the correct employment status of workers, which obviously supports the idea of increasing the number of contexts in which the presumption can be invoked. Moreover, given that the judicial route is impractical (due to reluctance to bring a case before the courts, especially during the performance of the contractual relationship and the time it takes to process the case,[27] although the summary procedure could be envisaged), alternative, non-contentious routes would optimise the establishment of the correct employment status. With this in mind, it would be appropriate to include social security procedures alongside administrative procedures.

---

[26] Cph Paris 9.1.2023, n° 20/05493; JCP S 2023, 1064, comment Loiseau; Cph Paris 19.12.2023, n° 21/03963; BJT 2/2024, p.3, comment Loiseau ; Cph Paris 4.4.2024, n° 21/04739; BJT 5/2024, p.8, comment Loiseau ; Cph Créteil 3.10.2024, n° 23/00710.

[27] The duration of the procedure is to be seen in relation to the duration of the activity, which is sometimes limited.

Appeal procedures would also need to be adapted. If the authority to which a request for the presumption to be applied is made does not act on it because it considers that the conditions have not been met, the worker should be able to appeal against the decision. If the initial procedure followed is not judicial, this appeal should fall within the remit of the employment contract judge – that is the industrial tribunal – unless provision is made for it to be brought directly before a court of appeal. 22

2. Triggering the presumption: individuals

The applicability of the presumption does not prejudge its implementation. In practical terms, workers who would be in a position to invoke the presumption should be able to choose to retain micro-entrepreneur status for professional reasons, such as taking advantage of greater flexibility in carrying out their activity (especially if it is a secondary activity), or for tax reasons. From the same point of view, recognising an employment contract for persons performing platform work who have requested should not effect the situation of other workers, even if their circumstances are identical. As a procedural facilitation for workers, the presumption should generally not be applied against the will of those concerned. 23

This raises the question of whether the Directive allows workers' representatives to initiate judicial or administrative proceedings to determine the correct employment status of the persons concerned.[28] It is inconceivable that a trade union could request the application of the presumption when the Court of Cassation quite rightly refuses to allow trade union organisations acting in the collective interest of the profession to submit requests which directly affect the individual situation of workers.[29] It is important to note, as this is a case law position, it might be useful to make it clear that action by organisations representing employees with a view to recognition of the status of salaried employee has no effect with regard to individual employees.[30] 24

So, what is the purpose of action by representatives? A trade union could be interested in ensuring that the conditions for applying the legal presumption are met for some or all persons performing platform work, to ensure compliance with employment legislation requirements. In particular, a trade union should be able to obtain recognition of the fact that a digital labour platform providing self-employed workers is actually a temporary employment agency. This would force them to comply with temporary employment regulations. The labour inspectorate should also be able to ascertain this, as the Directive requires Member States to provide for effective checks and inspections by competent authorities[31]. Other actors could join these, who would also have an interest in establishing employee status, such as the Urssaf in order to collect back social security contributions.[32] However, these third parties will likely be expected to establish, beyond the conditions for applying the presumption, the reality of salaried work. It is, moreover, 25

[28] Art. 5(4) of the Platform Work Directive.

[29] Last: Cass. soc. 22.1. 2025, n° 23–17.782, P; Cass. soc. 4.6.2025, n° 23–21.051, n° 23–22.856.

[30] During the work of the expert group established by the Commission, the Commission's services noted that workers' representatives may initiate proceedings on behalf of several workers 'where national law so provides' (European Commission, Report Expert Group – Transposition of the Directive (EU) 2024/2831 on improving working conditions in platform work (12.1.2026), 33).

[31] Art. 6(c) of the Platform Work Directive. The Commission's services have agreed that, in their capacity as national authorities with enforcement powers, labour inspectorates may initiate actions or proceedings (European Commission, Report Expert Group – Transposition of the Directive (EU) 2024/2831 on improving working conditions in platform work (12.1.2026), 34).

[32] In December 2024, Urssaf demanded that *Uber* pay the sum of 1.7 billion euros as part of a record-breaking tax adjustment.

from the perspective of 'determining the proper professional status'[33] that the Directive requires competent authorities to be able to verify the existence of an employment relationship and, where applicable, confirm the status of a self-employed worker for a person performing work through a platform.[34]

3. Triggering the presumption: effects

26 Assuming that the Directive is transposed in a minimalist, or even restrictive, manner, and that it applies primarily to cases in which a worker can currently seek judicial reclassification of a contract for services into an employment contract, there will nonetheless be noticeable progress. On the one hand, it will certainly be easier for workers seeking to obtain employee status to do so through an administrative procedure rather than having to bring a case before a court. On the other hand, when a case is brought before a court, the judge will be required to recognise an employment contract under the terms of the presumption, whereas, in identical situations, certain trial courts currently refuse to do so. Finally, the advantage of the presumption mechanism is that it applies to workers during the performance of the contract – that is, at a time when employee status is most beneficial to them – whereas disputes over contract reclassification generally occur only after the contractual relationship has ended. The direct effects of applying the presumption are predictable: the recognition of employment contracts for workers who invoke it, with the consequence, while the contractual relationship is ongoing, that workers with self-employed status and workers with employee status will coexist within the same organisation. Since the triggering of the presumption does not produce a collective effect with respect to all workers, even those in identical or comparable situations, the consequence of its application to some and not to others will be the coexistence within the same structure of workers with self-employed status and workers with employee status. Under current legislation, which includes specific rules for mobility platform workers, these workers will continue to be subject to those rules if they retain their status as self-employed, particularly with regard to the existence of a collective status. Those who have opted for employee status, however, will no longer be subject to these rules, even if they benefit from another collective status should one be established.

27 These potentially disruptive effects will probably encourage platforms that do not radically change their business model to pay all workers in order to protect themselves against the risk of the legal presumption being applied on a large scale. Platforms could put pressure on workers not to request a change of status, under the threat of terminating the contractual relationship, where appropriate, by bringing it to an end and bearing the financial cost of termination, once some workers have had their employee status recognised. For these reasons, it is essential to provide for monetary penalties on platforms that refuse to comply with a decision recognising employee status. The Directive allows the Member States to do so;[35] this is a matter of prophylaxis.

28 That said, even without waiting, the prospect of a legal presumption of an employment contract is already having unintended consequences, as many platforms are seeking to circumvent it by developing avoidance strategies. Operators are thus working to adapt their contractual models to protect themselves, today, against the risk of reclassification as an employment contract and, tomorrow, against the risk of widespread application of the presumption. Major platforms, such as *Uber*, have amended their

[33] Art. 4 of the Platform Work Directive.
[34] Art. 6 and recitals 35 and 36 of the Platform Work Directive.
[35] Art. 24(6) of the Platform Work Directive.

terms and conditions to highlight indicators of workers' independence and, correspondingly, obscure indicators of employee status. This strategy is beginning to bear fruit, since in two decisions handed down on 9 July 2025, the Social Chamber of the Cour de cassation dismissed appeals lodged against judgments that had refused to reclassify *Uber* drivers' contracts as employment contracts.[36] These decisions thus bring to an end a long line of cases which, since the *Take Eat Easy* judgment of 28 November 2018, had been favourable to the recognition of an employment contract for mobility platform workers. This shift, which appears to be taking hold,[37] is cause for concern as the transposition of the Directive approaches. It would be somewhat paradoxical if such platforms were to escape the application of the presumption, even though they were among the first to be considered by the European Parliament in its resolution of 16 September 2021 on fair working conditions, rights, and social protection for platform workers, which gave rise to the Draft Directive published a few months later by the European Commission.[38] Other platforms – including those whose business consists of making micro-entrepreneur workers available to client companies for temporary assignments – have, for their part, modified the structure of the contractual arrangement. Rather than framing it within an intermediation model that involves contracts between, on the one hand, the platform and the micro-entrepreneur service providers, and, on the other hand, between the latter and the client company to which they are made available, the client company is now offered the option of entering into a single service contract with the platform, for a lump-sum price covering all services, with the platform subcontracting the performance of the services to the workers in their capacity as micro-entrepreneurs.[39] This contractual arrangement, which relies on the mechanism of subcontracting for the performance of the services covered by the contract between the platform and the client company, thus diverges from the temporary staffing activity that platforms are, in fact, engaged in.

In these circumstances, the French legislature must remain vigilant regarding oppor- **29**
tunistic adjustments to the contractual model or the organisation of the contractual arrangement in an attempt to conceal the existence of an employment relationship that could give rise to a presumption of an employment contract. The platforms in question have not changed their business model, which still requires the use of micro-entrepreneurship to provide a service to a client, whether an individual or a user company. From this perspective, the examination of the contractual situation must be guided, beyond appearances, by the principle of the primacy of facts enshrined in Art. 4 of the Directive.[40] According to this text, 'the verification of the existence of an employment relationship is guided first and foremost by the facts relating to the actual performance of work, including the use of automated monitoring systems or automated decision-making systems in the organisation of work via a platform, regardless of the designation of the relationship in any contractual agreement that may have been concluded between the parties concerned'.

[36] Cass. soc. 9.7.2025, n° 24-13.504, n° 24-13.513; JCP S 2025, 1264, comment Loiseau; BJT 9/2025, p.21, comment Ranc.

[37] See CA Bordeaux 3.2.2026, n° 25/00917; Comm. com. électr. 2026, comm. 31, comment Loiseau – Cph Paris 6.2.2026, n° 22/08654.

[38] See Loiseau, Platform workers in the European Parliament, Comm. com. électr. 2021, comm. 80.

[39] This is notably the case with the Student Pop platform.

[40] It was observed during the work of the expert group established by the European Commission that the principle of the primacy of facts 'should be expressly reflected in the transposition measures' (European Commission, Report Expert Group – Transposition of the Directive (EU) 2024/2831 on improving working conditions in platform work (12.1.2026), 26).

C. Regulation of Algorithmic Management

I. Transposition of the law as it stands

30 Unlike the provisions relating to the status of workers, the provision relating to those working to protect them in a context of algorithmic management of work are more firmly and more precisely prescriptive. The national legislator's task here is therefore essentially to transpose the rules devised by European legislation. Only at the margins can we consider going beyond these rules.

II. Transcription of the rules

1. An area of maximum harmonisation

31 The standards for protecting workers are particularly stringent in terms of both the algorithmic direction and control of workers and the processing of personal data. These standards exceed the requirements of the regulation on artificial intelligence concerning high-risk artificial intelligence systems. Whether in terms of risk assessment, the imperative of transparency, human control, human review of decisions and the obligation to give reasons for certain decisions, the rules are more demanding, more detailed and stronger than those of the AI Act.[41] They also go beyond those of the General Data Protection Regulation (GDPR) by systematically requiring an impact assessment and by prohibiting, without exception, the processing of certain data, in particular data concerning workers' emotional or psychological state or their state of health. In contrast, the GDPR allows exceptions in certain cases.[42]

32 The Directive also organises the participation of workers' representatives by associating them with the review that digital labour platforms must carry out regularly, and in any event every two years, to assess the impact of automated decisions on workers and on their working conditions,[43] as well as with the impact assessments that digital labour platforms are required to carry out.[44] It further provides that they receive information on automated monitoring systems (the categories of data and actions monitored or assessed, the purpose of the monitoring, and so on) and on automated decision-making systems (the categories of decisions taken or supported by such systems, the categories of data and the main parameters taken into account, and so on). Workers' representatives must also be informed of the impact assessment and of the evaluation that platforms must carry out at least every two years. Finally, they must be consulted on projects to introduce automated monitoring systems, or automated decision-making systems, and on substantial changes in the use of such systems. In this context, they may be assisted by an expert of their choice to deliver an informed opinion. If the digital labour platform has more than 250 employees in the relevant Member State, the platform must cover the cost of the expert, provided the cost is proportionate.[45]

33 All of these provisions are presented as requiring maximum harmonisation, leaving Member States with little room for manoeuvre. They are intended to be included in the seventh part of the French Labour Code. The national laws implementing the Platform

[41] See Loiseau, A European Platform Workers' Rights, JCP S 2024, 735.
[42] Art. 9 GDPR.
[43] Art. 10(1) of the Platform Work Directive.
[44] Art. 8(1) of the Platform Work Directive.
[45] Art. 13(3) of the Platform Work Directive.

Work Directive must therefore transpose them faithfully, without attempting to alter them – even if this means justifying them with the less restrictive provisions of the European regulations. The latter expressly recognise the competence of the Member States to introduce more favourable legislative provisions for employees regarding the protection of their rights, including the processing of personal data[46] and the use of artificial intelligence systems by deployers/employers.[47]

2. A model

In many respects, the rules that the Directive requires Member States to transpose into their national law appear to set a standard for the protection of the rights of workers subject to automated decision-making systems and/or automated surveillance systems. As these systems correspond to artificial intelligence systems classified as high risk under Annex 3 of the Regulation on artificial intelligence, it is tempting to opt for the highest level of protection. Perhaps this is inspired the European Commission, which, in the guidelines published on 6 February 2025 relating to prohibited cases of use, extended the ban on using artificial intelligence systems to recognise emotions 'in the workplace' to include their use at the recruitment stage. This aligns with the Directive which prohibits any processing of data relating or deducing information about emotional states from the start of the recruitment procedure.[48] **34**

Designed for workers on digital labour platforms, the rules to be transposed into national law are in fact effective and useful for all workers exposed to the use of automated decision-making and/or surveillance systems that constitute high-risk systems. While it is unrealistic to expect an over-transposition of the Directive – which would extend the rules on algorithmic work management to all workers and not just those on platforms – some of these rules could be made applicable under domestic law, either through legislation – which is, however, unlikely[49] – or through collective bargaining, which is beginning to address issues related to artificial intelligence.[50] **35**

III. Accommodation of the regulation

1. Measures relating to the algorithmic management work

The Directive settles virtually all issues and leaves very little room for interpretation in its implementation. At most, the transposition law could provide clarifications on two points. **36**

The first concerns the risk assessment that must be carried out before automated systems are implemented. The Directive provides that, once informed of the outcome of this assessment, workers' representatives must be consulted on the measures taken in relation to health and safety.[51] It also states that they must likewise be consulted on **37**

[46] Regulation (UE) 2016/679 of 27 April 2016, Art. 88 GDPR.

[47] Regulation (UE) 2024/1689 of 13 June 2024, Art. 2, § 11.

[48] See Loiseau, First guidelines on the AI regulation – The ban on emotion recognition systems, JCP S 2025, 92.

[49] An information report was nevertheless prepared by the Economic Committee of the National Assembly regarding the effects of artificial intelligence on economic activity and the competitiveness of French companies. Submitted on 24 September 2025, it sets forth numerous recommendations for the attention of the legislature.

[50] See Loiseau, Artificial Intelligence and Technological Social Dialogue, BJT 3/2025, p. 55.

[51] Art. 11 of the Platform Work Directive.

substantial changes in the use of the systems,[52] from which it may be inferred that a new risk assessment should be carried out on that occasion. The obligation to assess risks is both *ex ante* and *ex post*, which the transposition law could usefully spell out.

38 The second point relates to the obligation imposed on digital labour platforms to ensure monitoring and assessment of the impact of individual decisions taken or supported by automated decision-making systems by assigning sufficient human resources to this monitoring. The persons entrusted with this task must have the necessary skills, training, and authority, including, importantly, the authority to override automated decisions.[53] It follows that this monitoring may lead to a change in the decision taken or even only supported by the automated system. The question may then arise as to whether the change of decision can be made of the platform's own motion by the person responsible for monitoring, or whether it presupposes that a request for review is submitted by the worker concerned. The first solution seems more consistent with the text, which provides for review in another provision.[54]

2. Involvement of workers' representatives and representatives of persons performing platform work

39 The Directive gives an important role to workers' representatives. But which representatives? In Art. 2(f) of the Directive, workers' representatives are defined as trade unions or representatives freely elected by platform workers in accordance with national law. If there are already employees working in the structure and/or if some of the self-employed workers are making use of the legal presumption in order to obtain employee status, a social and economic committee with eleven or more employees or, with extended powers, with fifty or more employees, will be set up to ensure that employees are represented. The committee must be provided with the compulsory information and, in certain legally defined cases, be consulted. The new cases requiring consultation should be formalised, not in the section of the French Labour Code concerning the consultative powers of the employee representative body, but alongside the other provisions addressing digital labour platforms, in Part Seven of the Code.[55]

40 If the digital labour platform has and maintains an activity with self-employed workers (whether they are bogus self-employed workers who do not make use of the legal presumption or genuine self-employed workers, to whom this part of the Directive applies without distinction), the question of their representation arises. While representatives already exist, as provided for in the French Labour Code, they are mainly concerned with negotiating collective agreements and only at the sector level of mobility platforms.[56] Currently, in the absence of representatives with the power to be informed and, where appropriate, consulted, the self-employed workers concerned would only need to be informed directly. However, it would be more appropriate to take legislative action to organise representation for self-employed workers using a digital labour platform. The duplication of labour law rules that have been used until now to set up sectoral social dialogue – such as the representation of self-employed workers

[52] Art. 13(2) of the Platform Work Directive. The concept of substantial modification is defined in Art. 3, § 23 of Regulation (UE) 2024/1689 of 13 June 2024.

[53] Art. 10(2) of the Platform Work Directive.

[54] Art. 12(2) of the Platform Work Directive.

[55] During the work of the expert group commissioned by the European Commission, the Commission's services emphasized that the obligation to inform and consult must be made explicit in the national transposition (European Commission, Report Expert Group – Transposition of the Directive (EU) 2024/2831 on improving working conditions in platform work (12.1.2026), 63 et seqq.).

[56] Labour Code, Arts. L. 7343–27 et seq.

and platforms, the appointment of representatives and collective bargaining – would simply have to be extended by creating an elected representation body, established at platform level and extended to all sectors of activity. There is already a chapter devoted to 'platform social dialogue' in the French Labour Code, but it is currently devoid of any provisions and is simply awaiting further legislative intervention.

In reality, it is unlikely that the national law transposing the Platform Work Directive 41
will be responsible for this enrichment, given the considerable amount of work involved. In the context of the work of the expert group established by the European Commission, the Commission's services have also indicated that the Directive does not require Member States to create new forms of representation.[57] There will therefore still be time to consider this, with a view to establishing individual and collective rights applicable to anyone performing work via a platform, a situation that will persist once the Directive has been transposed. In this regard, the Directive does require Member States to take appropriate measures to promote the role of social partners and encourage the exercise of the right to collective bargaining. However, the European Commission's services have clarified that Member States are not required to introduce collective bargaining rights for self-employed workers,[58] which is significant given that French law currently contains rules governing collective bargaining for self-employed platform workers only at sector level – not at the level of the platforms themselves – and solely with regard to mobility platforms.

[57] European Commission, Report Expert Group – Transposition of the Directive (EU) 2024/2831 on improving working conditions in platform work (12.1.2026), 19.

[58] European Commission, Report Expert Group – Transposition of the Directive (EU) 2024/2831 on improving working conditions in platform work (12.1.2026), 85.

Germany

Literature: Baethge/Boberach/Hoffmann/Wintermann, Plattformarbeit in Deutschland, Bertelsmann Stiftung, Gütersloh 2019; Berschtek/Ohnemus/Viete, Befragung zum sozioökonomischen Hintergrund und zu den Motiven von Crowdworkern, Zentrum für Europäische Wirtschaftsforschung, Mannheim 2015; Boes/Kämpf/Langes/Lühr, 'Landnahme im Informationsraum. Neukonstituierung gesellschaftlicher Arbeit in der "digitalen Gesellschaft"', WSI Mitteilungen 68 (2015), 77; Boes/Kämpf/Langes/Lühr/Steglich, Cloudworking und die Arbeit der Zukunft, Kassel 2014; Bonin/Rinne, Omnibusbefragung zur Verbesserung der Datenlage neuer Beschäftigungsformen, IZA Research Report No. 80, Kassel 2017; Brockmann, 'Freiwillige Selbstverpflichtungen als alternative Instrumente zur Standardsetzung? Das Beispiel des deutschen "Code of Conduct – Grundsätze für bezahltes Crowsourcing"' in Brameshuber/Brockmann/Marhold/Miranda Boto (eds), Kollektive Arbeitsbeziehungen in der Gig Economy, Vienna 2023, p. 141; Chandna-Hoppe, 'Who is a platform worker? Plattformarbeit im deutschen und englischen Recht sowie in der EU-Richtlinie zur Plattformarbeit', ZEuP 2025, 9; Däubler/Klebe, 'Crowdwork: Die neue Form der Arbeit – Arbeitgeber auf der Flucht?', NZA 2015, 1032; Degner/Kocher, 'Arbeitskämpfe in der "Gig-Economy"?', KJ 2018, 247; De Groen/Kilhoffer/Westhoff/Postica/Shamsfakhr, Digital labour platforms in the EU – Mapping and business models, Publications Office of the European Union, Luxembourg 2021; Deinert, 'Die heutige Bedeutung des Heimarbeitsgesetzes', RdA 2018, 359; Doherty, 'European Commission Guidelines on collective bargaining for solo self-employed persons: whose 'priorities' take priority?', ZVglRWiss 124 (2025), 28; Ellmer/Herr/Klaus/Gegenhuber, Platform workers centre stage! – Taking stock of current debates and approaches for improving the conditions of platform work in Europe, HBS-Working Paper Forschungsförderung No. 140, Dusseldorf 2019; Erdsiek/Ohnemus/Viete, Crowdworking in Deutschland 2018: Ergebnisse einer ZEW-Unternehmensbefragung, Zentrum für Europäische Wirtschaftsforschung, Mannheim 2018; Eurofound, Employment and working conditions of selected types of platform work, Publications Office of the European Union, Luxembourg 2018a; Eurofound, Platform work: Types and implications for work and employment – Literature review, Dublin 2018b; Eurofound, Mapping the contours of the platform economy, Dublin 2019; Fabo/Beblavý/Kilhoffer/Lenaerts, An overview of European Platforms: Scope and Business Models, Publications Office of the European Union, Luxembourg 2017; Fairwork, Labour Standards in the Platform Economy – Fairwork Germany Ratings 2025, Oxford, Berlin, 2025; Fischels/Sokoll, 'Der Arbeitnehmerbegriff – Entwicklungen und Impulse aus der Plattformarbeit – Arbeitsvertragsparagraf, Crowdworker-Entscheidung und Systematisierungsvorschlag', NZA 2024, 656; Funke/Picot, Platform work in a Coordinated Market Economy, IJR 52 (2021), 348; Gärtner, Koalitionsfreiheit und Crowdwork, Berlin 2020; Gerber, 'Crowdworker*innen zwischen Autonomie und Kontrolle', WSI Mitteilungen 73 (2020), 182; Gräf, 'Der Richtlinienentwurf zur Plattformarbeit – Analyse, Umsetzungsperspektiven und Alternativen', ZFA 2023, 209; Gramano, 'Collective Rights, Competition, and Self-Employed Workers in the EU: Recent Developments and Ongoing Problems', IJCLLIR 41 (2025), 135; Gruber-Risak/Warter, 'Die EU-Richtlinie zur Verbesserung der Arbeitsbedingungen in der Plattformarbeit', DRdA 2024, 267; Haipeter/Hoose, Interessenvertretung bei Crowd- und Gigwork, IAQ-Report 05 2019, 11; Haipeter/Hoose, Plattformökonomie in Deutschland, IAQ-Forschung 2023/04, Duisburg 2023; Heckelmann, 'Crowdworking – eine arbeitsrechtliche Bestandsaufnahme', NZA 2022, 73; Heiland, 'Plattformarbeit im Fokus', WSI Mitteilungen 72 (2019), 298; Heiland, 'Die Ombudsstelle Crowdwork – Entwicklung, Prozesse und Effekte', WSI Mitteilungen 75 (2022), 457; Heiland/Schaupp, 'Digitale Atomisierung oder neue Arbeitskämpfe? Widerständige Solidaritätskulturen in der plattformvermittelten Kurierarbeit', Momentum Quarterly – Zeitschrift für sozialen Fortschritt 9 (2) 2020, 50; Hensel/Koch/Kocher/Schwarz, 'Crowdworking als Phänomen der Koordination digitaler Erwerbsarbeit – Eine interdisziplinäre Perspektive', Industrielle Beziehungen 23 (2016), 162; Hießl, 'The classification of platform workers in case law: A cross-European comparative analysis', CLLPJ 42 (2022), 465; Hinck, 'Rider Captain unterwegs in den Aufsichtsrat', Mitbestimmung 2018 (3), 19; Hoose/Beckmann, 'Solidarität in atomisierten Arbeitsformen', AIS 17 (1) 2024, 8; Hoose/Beckmann/Topal/Glanz, 'Innovativer Wurf oder am Ziel vorbei? Die Bewertung der EU-Plattformrichtlinie durch deutsche Arbeitsmarktakteure', WSI Mitteilungen 78 (2025), 461; Huws/Spencer/Syrdal/Holts, Work in the European Gig Economy, FEPS/UNI Europa/University of Hertfordshire, Brussels 2017; Ivanova/Bronowicka/Kocher/Degner, Foodora and Deliveroo: The App as a Boss? Control and Autonomy in App Based Management – The Case of Food Delivery Riders, HBS-Working Paper Forschungsförderung No. 107, Dusseldorf 2018; Jäger/Reinbach, 'Mitbestimmung ohne Leitung? – Betriebsbegriff bei digitaler Plattformarbeit und KI-Einsatz', NZA 2025, 1299; Junker, 'Anmerkung', JZ 2021, 510; Kawalac/Menz, 'Die Verflüssigung von Arbeit. Crowdsourcing als unternehmerische Reorganisationsstrategie – das Beispiel IBM', AIS 6 (2) 2013, 5; Keller/Seifert, 'Atypische Beschäftigungsverhältnisse in der digitalisierten Arbeitswelt', WSI Mitteilungen 71 (2018), 278; Kirchner, 'Arbeiten in der Plattformökonomie: Grundlagen und Grenzen von "Cloudwork" und "Gigwork"', KZfSS 71 (2019), 3; Knop, Arbeitsrechtliche Fragen der Plattformarbeit, Berlin 2024; Kocher, 'Anwendungsbereich des Arbeitsrechts: Anpassungsbedarfe im deutschen Recht aus unionsrechtlicher Sicht', NZA-RR 2024, 449; Kocher/Bronowicka, 'Kampf und Offenheit – Wie muss eine Gewerkschaft im Rechtssinne organisiert sein?', KJ 2024, 504; Krause, Digitalisierung der Arbeitswelt – Herausforderungen und Regelungsbedarf, Gutachten B zum 71. Deutschen Juristentag Essen 2016, Munich 2016; Krause, 'Kollektivverträge für soloselbstständige Plattformbeschäftigte?' in Deinert/Klebe/Pieper/Schmidt/Wankel (eds), Festschrift für Michael Kittner zum 80. Geburtstag, Frankfurt 2021, p. 239; Krause, 'Betriebliche Mitbestimmung ohne Betrieb? – Zur Basis der betrieblichen Interessenvertretung bei digitalen Arbeitsstrukturen', KJ 2024, 466; Krause, 'Kollektive Rechte nach der Plattformarbeitsrichtlinie', in Bayer/Fleischer/Habersack/Klöhn/Leistner/Münch/Veil/Wiebe/Zech (eds), In Publica Commoda, Gedächtnisschrift für Gerald Spindler, Munich 2026, p. 423; Krause, 'Zur Bestimmung des Beschäftigungsstatus nach der Plattformarbeitsrichtlinie', in Chandna-Hoppe/Greiner/Ricken/Schlegel/Schmidt (eds), Arbeits- und Sozialrecht – Nachhaltig konzipiert, Festschrift für Raimund Waltermann, Munich 2026, P. 395; Kreß, Crowdwork, Berlin 2021; Kreßel, 'Sind Crowdworker Arbeitnehmer nach § 611a BGB?', DB 2021, 1671; Leimeister/Durward/Zogaj, Crowd Worker in Deutschland, Hans Böckler Stiftung, Dusseldorf 2016; Leimeister/Zogaj, Neue Arbeitsorganisation durch Crowdsourcing, Hans Böckler Stiftung, Dusseldorf 2013; Leimeister/Zogaj/Durward/Blohm, Systematisierung und Analyse von Crowd-Sourcing-Anbietern und Crowd-Work-Projekten, Hans Böckler Stiftung, Dusseldorf 2016; Leist/Hießl/Schlachter, Plattformökonomie – Eine Literaturauswertung, BMAS Forschungsbericht 499, 2017; Loritz, 'Die Entscheidung des BAG zu Crowd Working – Disruption der Arbeitsbeziehungen und ihre versuchte Verhinderung –', in Deckenbrock/Höpfner/Kilian/Markworth/Sittard (eds), Arbeit – Wirtschaft – Recht, Festschrift für Martin Henssler zum 70. Geburtstag, Munich 2023, p. 383; Maier/Viete, Plattformbasierte Erwerbsarbeit: Stand der empirischen Forschung, IZA Research Report No. 81, Mannheim 2017; Martina, 'Crowdworker: Arbeitnehmer, Heimarbeiter oder Solo-Selbstständige?', NZA 2021, 616; Mayr, Arbeitsrechtlicher Schutz Soloselbständiger am Beispiel der Plattformarbeit, Berlin 2021; Munkholm, 'Collective agreements regarding the working conditions of solo self-employed persons in Denmark', ZVglRWiss 122 (2023), 399; Pacha, Crowdwork. Arbeitsrechtlicher Schutz einer neuen Beschäftigungsform, Munich 2018; Palmer, 'Foodora & Co.: Die Revolte der neuen Dienstbotenklasse', Blätter für deutsche und internationale Politik 2017 (7), 32; Pesole/Urzi Brancati/Férnándes-Macias/Biagi/González Vázquez, Platform Workers in Europe (COLLEEM-I), Publications Office of the European Union, Luxembourg 2018; Pongratz, 'Plattformarbeit: Zwischenbilanz und Perspektiverweiterung', WSI Mitteilungen 76 (2023), 355; Pongratz/Bormann, 'Online-Arbeit auf Internet-Plattformen. Empirische Befunde zum "Crowdworking" in Deutschland', AIS 10 (2) 2017, 158; Rech, 'Die Entwicklung der Rechtsprechung zu Crowdworking und Plattformarbeit', ZFA 2023, 279; Riesenhuber, 'Arbeitnehmer(ähnlicher) Schutz von Crowd-Dienstleistern?', ZFA 2021, 5; Rolfs, Wen schützt das Arbeits- und Sozialversicherungsrecht? – Empfiehlt sich eine Neuausrichtung seines Anwendungsbereichs?, Gutachten B zum 74. Deutschen Juristentag Stuttgart 2024, Munich 2024; Schäfer, 'Crowdwork und Plattformarbeit in Deutschland', IW-Kurzbericht 79 (2019); Schliemann, 'Crowdworker – Arbeitnehmer? Gedanken zum Crowdworker-Urteil des BAG vom 1.12.2020 –', in Deckenbrock/Höpfner/Kilian/Markworth/Sittard (eds), Arbeit – Wirtschaft – Recht, Festschrift für Martin Henssler zum 70. Geburtstag, Munich 2023, p. 559; Schmidt, Arbeitsmärkte in der Plattformökonomie – Zur Funktionsweise und den Herausforderungen von Crowdwork und Gigwork, Friedrich-Ebert-Stiftung, Bonn 2016; Schneider-Dörr, Crowd Work und Plattformökonomie, Baden-Baden 2021; Schneider-Dörr, 'Von Arbeitnehmern und Plattformen', KJ 2024, 481; Schreyer/Feist, 'Brüchige Solidarität in der Gig Economy: Zwischen Zusammenhalt und Individualismus', AIS 17 (1) 2024, 23; Schreyer/Schrape, 'Algorithmische Arbeitskoordination in der plattformbasierten Gig Economy: Das Beispiel Foodora', AIS 11 (2) 2018, 262; Schubert, 'Arbeit in der Plattformökonomie', NZA Beilage 1/2022, 5; Schubert, 'Beschäftigung durch Online-Plattformen im Rechtsvergleich – Zur Rechtsstellung von Fahrern bei Fahr- und Kurierdiensten in Europa', ZVglRWiss 118 (2019), 341; Schubert, 'Guidelines on the application of Article 101 of the TFEU to collective agreements regarding the working conditions of solo self-employed persons – an analysis', ZVglRWiss 122 (2023), 363; Serfling, Crowdworking Monitor Nr. 1, Kleve 2018; Serfling, Crowdworking Monitor Nr. 2, Kleve 2019; Söller, 'Die Kraft des Faktischen – oder: Warum Crowdworker doch Arbeitnehmer sein können', NZA 2021, 997; Staab, Digitaler Kapitalismus, 2nd edn, Berlin 2020; Thüsing/Hütter-Brungs, 'Crowdworking: Lenkung statt Weisung – Was macht den Arbeitnehmer zum Arbeitnehmer?', NZA-RR 2021, 231; Umney/Stuart/Bessa/Joyce/Neumann/Trappmann, 'Platform Labour Unrest in a Global Perspective: How, Where and Why Do Platform Workers Protest?', Work, Employment and Society 38 (2024) (1), 3; Urzi Brancati/Pesole/Férnándes-Macias, New evidence on platform workers in Europe (COLLEEM-II), Publications Office of the European Union, Luxembourg 2020; Waas, 'Crowdwork in Germany' in Waas/Liebman/Lyubarsky/Kazuka (eds), Crowdwork – A Comparative Law Perspective, Frankfurt 2017, p. 142; Waltermann, 'Digitalisierung der Arbeitswelt – arbeits- und sozialrechtliche Fragen' in Kitaibl/Mosler/Pačić (eds), Gedenkschrift Robert Rebhahn, Vienna 2019, p. 634; Waltermann, 'Crowdworking – Arbeitsverhältnis ohne Arbeitspflicht', NJW 2022, 1129; Walzer, Der arbeitsrechtliche Schutz der Crowdworker, Baden-Baden 2019; Wank, 'Der Crowdworker als Arbeitnehmer oder als Arbeitnehmerähnlicher?', in Deckenbrock/Höpfner/Kilian/Markworth/Sittard (eds), Arbeit – Wirtschaft – Recht, Festschrift für Martin Henssler zum 70. Geburtstag, Munich 2023, p. 701; Warter, Crowdwork, Vienna 2016; Warter/Gruber-Risak, 'Kommentar', AuR 2021, 331; Wenckebach, 'BAG: Crowdwork ante portas! Von persönlicher Abhängigkeit in der digitalen Arbeitswelt', SR 2020, 165; Wisskirchen/Haupt, 'Crowdworker: Arbeitnehmer oder Selbstständiger?', RdA 2021, 355; Wisskirchen/Schwindling, 'Crowdworking im Lichte des Arbeitsrechts', ZESAR 2017, 318; Zander, 'Naturtalent der Mitbestimmung', Mitbestimmung 2018 (3), 16.

A. Introduction

1 As in many other countries, the digital economy ('digital capitalism')[1] has also given rise to a new type of employment in Germany: platform work. This refers to any form of work organisation in which supply and demand for paid work are matched via an internet-based platform, so that, at least at first glance, the platform operator only acts as an intermediary with varying degrees of control over the work performed. Although the political and economic conditions are less favourable than in the U.S., as the origin of platform work,[2] this type of work organisation has also become widespread in Germany in recent years. This applies to both German and international platform operators. An international study from 2021 lists 201 work platforms (out of a total of 516 platforms in the EU) that are active in Germany, 41 of which are based in the country.[3] Examples include *Clickworker*, *Crowdguru*, *99designs*, *Freelancer*, *Helpling*, *Lieferando*, *Streetspotr* and *Testbirds*.[4] Work-related platforms in Germany thus comprise both basic types, i.e. platforms for location-based (analogue) 'offline' activities (gig work, on-demand work) and for location-independent (virtual) 'online' activities.[5] *Uber* is also present in Germany with various business models. However, in 2015 it discontinued its most controversial service of arranging rides through unlicensed drivers (*UberPop*) due to a conflict with German public transportation law and a resulting violation of unfair

[1] For a comprehensive analysis, see Staab, 2020.
[2] See in detail Funke/Picot IJR 52 (2021), 348.
[3] De Groen et al., p. 31 et seq.
[4] Cf. Baethge et al., p. 14.
[5] For the distinction, see BT-Drs. 19/16886 and BT-Drs. 19/22122; Kirchner KZfSS 71 (2019), 3 (4 et seq.); Schmidt, p. 5 et seqq.; from an international perspective, see Eurofound, 2018a, p. 5 et seq.; ILO, 'World Employment and Social Outlook', 2021, p. 74 et seqq.; for the heterogeneity of platform work, see Pongratz WSI Mitteilungen 76 (2023), 355 (356 et seqq.).

competition law. Instead, since 2024, *Uber* has been presenting itself as a partner for all licensed taxi drivers and making its app available to them nationwide.[6]

2 For roughly a decade, the problems caused by platform work with regard to the social protection of platform workers have been the subject of intense debate at the political level in Germany. The main actor in this regard is the Federal Ministry of Labour and Social Affairs (*Bundesministerium für Arbeit und Soziales, BMAS*). Platform work was an important topic in the 'Working 4.0' (*Arbeiten 4.0*) discussion process, which dealt comprehensively with the digitalisation of the world of work. The issue was addressed in the 'Green Paper Working 4.0' ('Grünbuch Arbeiten 4.0') from 2015[7] and, even more intensively, in the subsequent 'White Paper 'Working 4.0' ('Weißbuch Arbeiten 4.0') from 2016.[8] Following this process, the *BMAS* established the *Denkfabrik Digitale Arbeitsgesellschaft*, a mixture of think tank and future lab, has since organised a series of workshops on platform work with relevant stakeholders, including a 'platform summit' in 2021,[9] and continues to focus on the platform economy.[10] Moreover, back in 2019, the *BMAS* and the Food, Beverages and Catering Union (*Nahrung-Genuss-Gaststätten, NGG*), which is competent for food delivery services, published a joint policy paper describing the problematic situation in this sector and calling for fair working conditions and social protection in the platform economy.[11] One year later, in 2020, the *BMAS* published a policy paper in which it also advocates fair working conditions in the platform economy.[12] In addition, against the backdrop of the coronavirus pandemic, the *Rat der Arbeitswelt* ('Council for the World of Work'), an expert committee set up by the *BMAS* in 2020 and active until 2024, also devoted its first report in particular to platform work, focusing on the legal classification of platform workers.[13] Furthermore, platform work has been a prominent topic in academic discourse for a number of years and was identified early on as a new work-related problem within both the sociology of work[14] and labour law[15].

3 This chapter on platform work in Germany begins by examining the empirical situation in greater detail (section B). Secondly, it addresses one of the most pressing issues, namely the classification of platform workers within traditional categories (section C). Thirdly, the chapter turns to previous political initiatives aimed at the legal regulation of platform work (section D). Forthly, it examines certain aspects of the forthcoming implemenation of the Pltaform Work Directive (section E) and, finally, activities of plat-

---

[6] Cf. https://www.uber.com/de/newsroom/uber-taxi-deutschland/ (last accessed: 22.5.2026).

[7] Cf. BMAS, 'Grünbuch Arbeiten 4.0', 2015, 15 et seq. and 66, also available in English: https://www.bmas.de/SharedDocs/Downloads/DE/Publikationen/arbeiten-4-0-green-paper.pdf;jsessionid=00CB0784C78F41A70D13A86A184E861D.delivery2-replication?__blob=publicationFile&v=1 (last accessed: 22.5.2026).

[8] BMAS, 'Weißbuch Arbeiten 4.0', 2016, 6, 9 et seq., 24, 42, 55 et seqq., 85 et seq., 100, 128 et seq., 133, 170 et seq., 176 and 193, also available in English: https://www.bmas.de/SharedDocs/Downloads/EN/PDF-Publikationen/a883-white-paper.pdf?__blob=publicationFile&v=1 (last accessed: 22.5.2026).

[9] For more details, see Haipeter/Hoose IAQ-Forschung 2023/04.

[10] https://www.denkfabrik-bmas.de/schwerpunkte/plattformoekonomie (last accessed: 22.5.2026).

[11] Available at: https://www.ngg.net/fileadmin-ngg.net/medien/2019/PDF/190206_Gemeinsames_Papier_NGG_BMAS_final.pdf (last accessed: 22.5.2026).

[12] Available at: https://www.denkfabrik-bmas.de/fileadmin/Downloads/eckpunkte-faire-plattformarbeit_1_.pdf (last accessed: 22.5.2026).

[13] Rat der Arbeitswelt, *Vielfältige Ressourcen stärken – Zukunft gestalten*, Berlin 2021, p. 86 et seqq.

[14] Among the first contributions are: Kawalac/Menz AIS 6 (2) 2013, 5; Leimeister/Zogaj, 2013; Boes et al., 2014; Boes et al. WSI Mitteilungen 68 (2015), 77. Interdisciplinary approach by Hensel et al. Industrielle Beziehungen 23 (2016), 162.

[15] Early contributions include: Klebe/Neugebauer AuR 2014, 4; Däubler/Klebe NZA 2015, 1032; Lingemann/Otte NZA 2015, 1042; Klebe NZA 2016, 277; Kocher/Hensel NZA 2016, 984; Krause, 2016, p. 99 et seqq. For an overview on the German and international literature, see Eurofound, 2018b; Leist/Hießl/Schlachter, 2017.

form operators, trade unions and the platform workers themselves to regulate platform work (section F).

B. Quantitative aspects of platform work

Obtaining a comprehensive picture of the prevalence of platform work and the working conditions of platform workers[16] in Germany is difficult, as no official statistics are available on this subject.[17] This gap is filled to a certain extent by a large number of German studies on various empirical aspects of platform work that have been published in recent years.[18] In addition, there are many international studies that also contain data on the situation in Germany.[19] However, the figures reported in these studies do not fully correspond, but in some cases differ considerably from one another. 4

The comprehensive COLLEEM-I study of 2018 cites the exceptionally high figure of 10.4% of the total adult population for Germany, when asked whether any activity has ever been performed offline or online following a digital matching process between provider and demander. When narrowed down to those platform workers who work more than 10 hours per week, the number is reduced to 6.6%. When further narrowed down to those who generate more than 50% of their total income from platform work, the number drops to 2.5%, although this is still very substantial.[20] The 2020 COLLEEM-II study differentiates among four groups of platform workers (sporadic, marginal, secondary and main). According to this study, the group of main platform workers (working hours of more than 20 hours per week or where income from platform work constitutes more than 50% of their total income) accounted for 1.5%, while secondary platform workers (working more than 10 hours per week or where income from platform work constitutes more than 25% of their total income) accounted for 4.2% of the total adult population in Germany.[21] Another international study estimated that 2.5% of the total working population in Germany, i.e. more than 1.4 million workers, earn at least half of their income from crowdwork.[22] According to a German study, one quarter of all active crowdworkers, representing 2.3% of the whole population, say their main income comes from platform work,[23] which would correspond to 450,000 platform workers reliant on this type of work. In contrast, other German studies cite significantly lower figures and estimate that only a few thousand workers receive their main income 5

[16] In this chapter, the term 'platform worker' is used in a broad sense to refer to all persons performing platform work, regardless of their employment status.

[17] Cf. BT-Drs. 19/6186, 2, and BT-Drs. 20/12276, 2.

[18] See Berschtek/Ohnemus/Viete, 2015; Leimeister/Durward/Zogaj, 2016; Leimeister et al., 2016; Bonin/Rinne, 2017; Maier/Viete, 2017; Pongratz/Bormann AIS 10 (2017), 158; Erdsiek/Ohnemus/Viete, 2018; Serfling, 2018; Baethge et al., 2019; Ellmer et al., 2019; Serfling, 2019. See also the BMAS 'Forschungsberichte' (Research Reports) on numerous aspects of platform work, nos. 462 (2016), 473 (2016), 490 (2017), 498 (2017), 499 (2017), 500 (2017), 508 (2018) and 525 (2018), available at: https://www.bmas.de/DE/Service/Publikationen/Forschungsberichte/forschungsberichte.html (last accessed: 22.5.2026).

[19] See European Parliament, Directorate-General for Internal Policies, *The Social Protection of Workers in the Platform Economy*, Brussels 2017; Fabo et al., 2017; Huws et al., 2017; Eurofound, 2018a; Pesole et al. (COLLEEM-I), 2018; Eurofound, 2019; Urzì Brancati/Pesole/Férnándes-Macias (COLLEEM-II), 2020; De Groen et al., 2021; ILO, *World Employment and Social Outlook*, Geneva 2021.

[20] Pesole et al., p. 14 et seqq.

[21] Urzì Brancati/Pesole/Férnándes-Macias, p. 15 et seq.

[22] Huws et al., p. 26.

[23] Serfling, 2019, p. 12 et seq.

from platform work.[24] This is consistent with an international study that estimates a total of only 35,000 people working in the entire collaborative economy.[25] According to recent data of the Institute for Labour Market and Occupational Research (*Institut für Arbeitsmarkt- und Berufsforschung, IAB*), which is affiliated with the Federal Labour Agency (*Bundesagentur für Arbeit*), the number of workers in the delivery services sector increased from 1,000 in 2012 to 38,000 in 2022, peaking at 50,000 during the coronavirus pandemic, most of them are younger than 30 years (61%), male (91%) and migrants.[26]

6 There is also a lack of clarity with regard to the wages earned by platform workers. According to a German study, average hourly wages vary from under EUR 20/h for the lowest 25% to a median of EUR 30/h and more than EUR 60/h for the top 25%,[27] which is much higher than the statutory minimum wage in Germany.[28] By contrast, the 2020 COLLEEM-II study indicates significantly lower average hourly wages, namely between EUR 6.60 and EUR 23.10, for different types of platform activities, but without differentiating between the Member States surveyed.[29] A German study concludes that only 13.2% of all crowdworkers are working more than three hours per week via platforms and only 6.4% are earning more than EUR 400 per month.[30] Another German study indicates that performing microtasks is the main source of income for only 6% of crowdworkers, whereas for 94% of workers, this type of work is only a secondary source of income, with monthly earnings ranging between EUR 150 and EUR 250 and working hours between 7 hours and 17 hours per week. In the area of so-called marketplaces, the share of full-time employees rises to 28%, with this group of people earning an average monthly salary of approximately EUR 1,560 with an average weekly working time of just below 32 hours.[31] According to the *IAB* full-time gig workers in the delivery sector earn around EUR 1,700 per month.[32]

7 Given these highly divergent figures, it remains difficult to accurately assess the significance of the phenomenon of platform work in Germany and, in particular, the extent of the social risks associated with this form of employment.

C. Legal status of platform workers

8 Due to the fundamental distinction between employed and self-employed work under German law, the legal status of platform workers has been at the centre of the discussion on platform work from the outset. Employment and social security law only applies if the worker is classified as an employee, whereas classification as self-employed generally results in a lack of any social protection. The system thus essentially follows

---

[24] Bonin/Rinne, p. 9 et seqq., 17 et seq.; Pongratz/Bormann, AIS 10 (2) 2017, 158 (164); see also Maier/Viete, p. 14 et seqq.; Schäfer, IW-Kurzbericht 79/2019.

[25] European Commission, Directorate-General for Internal Market, *Study to Monitor the Economic Development of the Collaborative Economy in the EU*, Brussels 2018, p. 91.

[26] See https://iab-forum.de/gig-work-bei-lieferdiensten-in-deutschland-beschaeftigung-hat-in-den-letzten-jahren-stark-zugenommen/ (last accessed: 22.5.2026).

[27] Serfling, 2019, p. 27 et seq.

[28] The statutory minimum wage was introduced in Germany only in 2015 and developed from EUR 8.50 (1.1.2015) to EUR 13.90 (1.1.2026), cf. https://www.destatis.de/DE/Themen/Arbeit/Verdienste/Mindestloehne/Tabellen/gesetzlicher-mindestlohn.html (last accessed: 22.5.2026).

[29] Urzì Brancati/Pesole/Férnándes-Macias, p. 37 et seq.

[30] Berschtek/Ohnemus/Viete, p. 35 and 38.

[31] Leimeister/Durward/Zogaj, p. 48 et seqq.

[32] See https://iab-forum.de/gig-work-bei-lieferdiensten-in-deutschland-beschaeftigung-hat-in-den-letzten-jahren-stark-zugenommen/ (last accessed: 22.5.2026).

an 'all or nothing' approach. This applies, for example, to the statutory minimum wage, continued payment of wages in the event of illness, protection against fixed-term employment contracts and protection against dismissal. Consequently, the attempt by many platform operators to circumvent the role of employer in order to avoid the financial and administrative burden of social protection laws has attracted a great deal of attention in the German debate. In addition to numerous articles, several dissertations on this topic have been published in recent years, discussing in detail the entire range of categories conceivable under German law. Besides the distinction between employees and self-employed persons, the law also provides for a third category of 'employee-like persons' (*arbeitnehmerähnliche Personen*) who benefit from a certain degree of social protection.[33]

However, it should be noted that some platform work providers, particularly in the delivery sector, do not attempt to circumvent the status of their workers as employees. Rather, in Germany, more and more gig workers are hired as part-time or even full-time employees.[34] This trend can be explained by the institutional framework, in particular the harsh legal consequences (back payment of social security contributions) for employers in the case of bogus self-employment.[35] For instance, *Deliveroo* drivers are generally hired on a self-employed basis, while *Foodora* drivers are engaged as employees.[36] However, this may change over time. For example, *Lieferando*, a subsidiary of the Dutch company *Just Eat Takeaway*, decided in 2025 to dismiss 2,000 employees nationwide, i.e. 20% of its total workforce, and to continue its business model in part with subcontractors.[37] 9

I. The triangular relationship between platform worker, platform operator and client

Determining the legal status of a platform worker is particular complex in situations where the platform operator has not clearly hired the worker as an employee but claims to act solely as an intermediary, as the business models of platform operators – and thus also the legal relationships – differ in many respects. In any case, there is a framework agreement between the platform operator and the individual platform worker. Such agreements often do not contain an obligation to accept an assigned task, but only ancillary duties (e.g. the duty to update personal data). 10

In addition, a separate framework agreement often exists between the platform work provider and the client who wishes to have a task performed by a worker in the future. This framework agreement must be distinguished from the contract covering the specific task. In this respect, direct contractual relationships between the platform worker and the client can arise in different ways. In some cases, the platform operator can act as a representative of the worker or the client and submit or accept contract offers itself. In other cases, the platform operator merely forwards contract offers or acceptances from the worker or the client. In this second scenario, the matching process may occur through individualised offers or via a competition in which several platform 11

[33] Pacha, 2018; Walzer, 2019; Gärtner, 2020; Kreß, 2021; Mayr, 2021; Schneider-Dörr, 2021; Knop, 2024; from an Austrian perspective, see Warter, 2016; cf. also Waas in Waas et al., p. 142 et seqq.

[34] Cf. https://iab-forum.de/gig-work-bei-lieferdiensten-in-deutschland-beschaeftigung-hat-in-den-letzt en-jahren-stark-zugenommen/ (last accessed: 22.5.2026).

[35] Funke/Picot IJR 52 (2021), 348 (358).

[36] Ivanova et al., p. 20 et seq.

[37] Cf. https://www.tagesschau.de/wirtschaft/lieferando-stellenabbau-100.html (last accessed: 22.5.2026).

workers submit the work, but the client only accepts and pays for the best work result. Furthermore, it is common for platform operators to forward the individual offer exclusively in their own name. In such cases, even with regard to the specific work task, only one contract is concluded between the platform and the client on the one hand and the platform and the worker on the other, meaning that there is only an indirect relationship between the client and the worker. The following sections do not address all these different possibilities but focus exclusively on the question of whether and under what conditions the legal relationship between the platform operator and the worker can be qualified in such a way that it leads to social protection under employment and social security law.

12 This does not preclude the possibility of an employment relationship arising directly between a platform worker and a client. Rather, this can happen if, for example, a domestic service (e.g. cleaning) is repeatedly provided by the same worker for the same client. Conversely, if the client changes constantly (e.g. driving services for different private individuals), an employment relationship is highly unlikely. Furthermore, this chapter excludes scenarios in which work tasks are allocated via internal company platforms to existing employees ('employer-led internal platforms'). Although this form of work organisation can also lead to employment law problems, in these cases the legal status of the workers as employees is clear and not open to debate.

II. Platform workers as employees

1. The general concept of an employee as a starting point

13 Since 2017, the general term 'employee' has been defined in German law in § 611a of the Civil Code (*Bürgerliches Gesetzbuch, BGB*). More specifically, this provision defines the term 'employment contract'. According to this definition, an employment contract exists when a person is obliged to perform work for another person in a relationship of personal dependence, being bound by instructions (subordination) and subject to external determination. With regard to the interpretation of this concept, it is most convincing to understand personal dependence as a generic term as opposed to personal independence (self-employment) and mere economic dependence.

14 The further terms 'bound by instructions' and 'external determination' serve to specify personal dependence. In this context, being bound by instructions is the narrower term characterising the normal case of an employment contract. It is irrelevant whether the employer constantly exercises the right to issue binding instructions or grants the employee considerable leeway. Rather, it is solely the existence of the right to issue instructions that matters. Given its unclear contours, external determination should not be understood from the outset as an equivalent alternative criterion. However, this criterion serves to classify a work relationship as an employment contract even in atypical constellations in which the right to issue instructions takes a back seat, preventing employment law protection from becoming meaningless in relation to new forms of work that give employees more formal freedom but still lead to work in a work environment that is controlled and monitored by another person. External determination is primarily expressed through integration into a work organisation created and controlled by the employer, which restricts the employee's conduct in a manner that is incompatible with genuine self-employment.

15 In enacting § 611a BGB, the legislator did not intend to create a new definition but merely to codify the established case law of the Federal Labour Court (*Bundesarbeits-*

gericht, BAG).[38] However, this intention of the legislator does not require the understanding of the term 'employee' to be frozen at the 2017 level. Rather, the legal framework can certainly be used in the manner described above, to accommodate newer forms of organisation of paid work, provided the interpretation remains consistent with the wording of § 611a BGB. A more far-reaching reinterpretation of the employment contract, for example in the sense that all persons who permanently provide personal services for another person on a contractual basis are to be classified as employees, would, in contrast, require a reform of the law.

2. The classification of platform workers

The usefulness of § 611a BGB in achieving appropriate results is illustrated by the only decision to date of the *BAG* on the classification of a crowdworker.[39] The case concerned a person who worked for a platform operator, the Dutch enterprise *Roamler*, that checked the proper presentation of branded products in retail shops and petrol stations on behalf of customers. The platform worker carried out this activity and achieved average monthly earnings of EUR 1,750 with a weekly working time of approximately 20 hours. In detail, the worker accepted a large number of micro-tasks (in this specific case, 2,978 micro-tasks within a period of eleven months) via the company's website and an app that he could download to his smartphone. Once a task was accepted, the 'basic agreement' concluded between the parties stipulated that this constituted an obligation to execute the task. However, the 'basic agreement' did not provide for a right on the part of the company to assign tasks to the platform worker, nor did it provide for an obligation on the part of the platform worker to accept certain tasks or even a certain number of tasks within a certain period of time. Furthermore, the worker was allowed to cancel an accepted task. At the same time, the working environment made the activity financially viable only if tasks were accepted on an ongoing basis. In particular, this enabled the platform worker to earn higher remuneration and increase his own earning potential. Over time, the platform worker reached 'Level 15', which allowed him to accept 15 tasks at the same time. When the platform operator announced that it would stop assigning tasks and deactivate the platform worker's account, the latter sued the company, arguing, among other things, that an indefinite employment relationship existed between the parties. 16

The court of first instance, the Munich Local Labour Court,[40] and the court of second instance, the Munich Regional Labour Court,[41] denied the existence of an employment contract. Both courts argued that, firstly, the 'basic agreement' did not establish a legal obligation to perform work, and, secondly, the employee was neither bound by instructions nor integrated into the organisation of the company with regard to the individual tasks.[42] In its own decision on this case, the *BAG* agreed with the first argument,[43] which is in line with its established case law that an agreement that does not contain a legal obligation to perform work cannot establish an employment relationship from the outset.[44] However, in its following reasoning, the *BAG* went a decisive step further 17

[38] Cf. BT-Drs. 18/9232, 31 et seq.

[39] BAG 1.12.2020 – 9 AZR 102/20, NZA 2021, 552.

[40] ArbG München 20.2.2019 – 19 Ca 6915/18, BeckRS 2019, 37646.

[41] LAG München 4.12.2019 – 8 Sa 146/19, NZA 2020, 316.

[42] This corresponds with LAG Hessen 14.2.2019 – 10 Ta 350/18, NZA-RR 2019, 505, denying the existence on an employment contract in an atypical form of platform work.

[43] BAG 1.12.2020 – 9 AZR 102/20, NZA 2021, 552, paras. 42, 52 et seqq.

[44] BAG 31.7.2002 – 7 AZR 181/01, AP TzBfG § 12 no. 1; BAG 16.4.2003 – 7 AZR 187/02, NZA 2004, 40; BAG 15.2.2012 – 10 AZR 111/11, NZA 2012, 733, para. 15; BAG 16.5.2012 – 5 AZR 268/11, NZA 2012,

and considered the individual tasks as having been performed in a state of personal dependence within a uniform employment relationship.[45] Essentially, the *BAG* put forward four arguments:[46] Firstly, once a task was accepted, the platform worker was obliged to carry out the work personally, i.e. he could not hire a substitute, for example.[47] Secondly, the tasks were simple and their content was specified by the company, so that the worker had minimal freedom in carrying out the tasks. Thirdly, even without specific instructions, the digital infrastructure created a kind of external determination, as it was designed to prompt the platform worker to continuously accept tasks in order to earn a reasonable wage and reach a higher level, which would lead to a more attractive manner of performing tasks. In other words: the app's function was not to assign micro-tasks to self-employed workers, but to solicit workers to work continuously via the platform and thereby to determine their behaviour. Fourthly, the continuous sequence of tasks should be regarded as forming a single employment relationship rather than a succession of fixed-term contracts.

18 The decision has sparked a heated debate in German academic circles. On the one hand, there were many critical comments that emphasised above all that, contrary to the normative requirement of § 611a BGB, the *BAG* had abandoned the principle that an employment contract, as a subcategory of a service contract, presupposes a legal obligation to work, which is precisely what is lacking in a pure incentive structure.[48] On the other hand, some authors support the *BAG*'s new approach on the grounds that the decision is in line with the times and aligns with emerging methods of managing and controlling workers in the digital age.[49]

19 However, it should be noted that the *BAG* only ruled on a specific case and its approach does not imply that platform workers will automatically be deemed employees under German law in future. Rather, it is a matter of applying the criteria of § 611a BGB appropriately in accordance with the respective digital structure of the platform operator, which amounts to a case-by-case approach. It is also noteworthy that, following the ruling, *Roamler* changed the incentive structure of the app in order to avoid the employee status of crowd workers in future.[50]

20 As far as is known, unlike in other European countries,[51] Germany has not seen further legal disputes regarding employee status as such. However, in another case where the employee status of the platform worker ('rider') was clear and undisputed, the *BAG* held that the employer is contractually obliged to provide the employee with the essential work equipment and may not leave this burden to the employee. Consequently,

---

974, para. 17; BAG 21.7.2015 – 9 AZR 484/14, NZA-RR 2016, 344, para. 25; BAG 21.5.2019 – 9 AZR 295/18, NZA 2019, 1411, para. 26.

[45] BAG 1.12.2020 – 9 AZR 102/20, NZA 2021, 552, para. 44.

[46] BAG 1.12.2020 – 9 AZR 102/20, NZA 2021, 552, paras. 45 et seqq. Detailed analysis of the BAG's reasoning by Rech ZFA 2023, 279 (286 et seqq.).

[47] The wording of the 'basic agreement' expressly provided otherwise, but was superseded by the prohibition on transferring the personal account.

[48] Fischels/Sokoll NZA 2024, 656 (661 et seqq.); Heckelmann NZA 2022, 73 (76 et seqq.); Knop, p. 124 et seqq.; Loritz in Deckenbrock et al., p. 383 (391 et seqq.); Söller NZA 2021, 997 (999 et seqq.); Thüsing/Hütter-Brungs NZA-RR 2021, 231 (233 et seqq.); Wisskirchen/Haupt RdA 2021, 355 (359 et seq.); also critical Kreßel DB 2021, 1671 (1678); Schliemann in Deckenbrock et al., p. 559 (574 et seqq.); Schubert NZA-Beilage 1/2022, 5 (7 et seqq.).

[49] Chandna-Hoppe ZEuP 2025, 9 (14 et seqq.); Junker JZ 2021, 519 (521 et seq.); Schneider-Dörr KJ 2024, 481 (484 et seqq.); Waltermann NJW 2022, 1129 (1130 et seqq.); Wank in Deckenbrock et al., p. 701 (712 et seqq.); Warter/Gruber-Risak AuR 2021, 331 (332 et seqq.).

[50] Cf. Rolfs, p. 18.

[51] Cf. Hießl CLLPJ 42 (2022), 465; see also Rech ZFA 2023, 279 (299 et seqq.); Schubert ZVglRWiss 118 (2019), 341.

the platform operator must provide the rider with a roadworthy bicycle and a fully functional smartphone.[52]

III. Platform workers as employee-like persons

21 As already indicated, the 'all-or-nothing' approach is mitigated by the legal concept of the 'employee-like person'. According to this concept, German law recognises a third category of workers between employees on the one hand and genuinely self-employed persons on the other, to whom certain employment law provisions apply. These include the prohibition of discrimination, the right to statutory minimum paid leave, inclusion in occupational safety and health, maternity protection and employee data protection. They also benefit from the restrictions on civil liability developed by case law in favour of employees.[53] In addition, disputes between employee-like persons and their principals fall within the jurisdiction of the labour courts, which are regarded as having greater understanding of social protection issues. However, important employment law provisions do not apply to employee-like persons, notably the statutory minimum wage,[54] as well as protection against fixed-term employment contracts and dismissal.

22 In contrast to the term 'employee', there is no generally applicable legal definition for the term 'employee-like person'. However, § 12a(1) of the Collective Bargaining Act (*Tarifvertragsgesetz, TVG*) provides a definition for collective bargaining purpose, which is also used by case law as a point of reference beyond this context.[55] According to this definition, a person is similar to an employee if, firstly, he or she is economically dependent on another person and, secondly, is in need of social protection comparable to that of an employee. Economic dependence exists where person relies on income from the activity for the contractual partner to secure his or her own livelihood, which presupposes a certain permanent relationship.[56] This will mostly constitute cases where the person works for only one client. However, the existence of several clients does not exclude the status of an employee-like person from the outset, provided that the activity for one of the clients predominates and the remuneration earned from it forms the main basis of existence.[57] With regard to comparable social protection needs, case law is based on whether there is a dependency that usually only occurs in the context of an employment relationship and where the services provided are comparable in sociological terms to those of an employee.[58] In all such cases, the decisive factor it is not the wording of the contractual agreement between the parties, but solely the actual circumstances.

23 Based on these criteria, it is again a question of the individual case whether a platform worker can be classified as an employee-like person.[59] Economic dependence can best be determined in cases where a worker only generates tasks via one or two platforms, which is statistically the most common situation.[60] In addition, the income generated from these jobs must be essential for securing the worker's own livelihood,

---

52 BAG 11.11.2021 – 5 AZR 3341/21, NZA 2022, 401.

53 Cf. LAG Hessen 2.4.2013 – 13 Sa 857/12, BeckRS 2013, 70404.

54 Cf. LAG Schleswig-Holstein 11.1.2016 – 1 Sa 224/15, NZA-RR 2016, 291, para. 38.

55 BAG 17.1.2006 – 9 AZR 61/05, NJOZ 2006, 3821, para. 13.

56 BAG 17.1.2006 – 9 AZR 61/05, NJOZ 2006, 3821, para. 14; BAG 21.2.2007 – 5 AZB 52/06, NZA 2007, 699, para. 11, BAG 21.12.2010 – 10 AZB 14/10, NZA 2011, 309, para. 8.

57 BAG 30.8.2000 – 5 AZB 12/00, NZA 2000, 1359 (1360).

58 BAG 2.10.1990 – 4 AZR 106/90, NZA 1991, 239 (240); BAG 17.1.2006 – 9 AZR 61/05, NJOZ 2006, 3821, para. 14.

59 Detailed analysis by Mayr, p. 254 et seqq.

60 Leimeister/Durward/Zogaj, p. 31.

which is relatively rare among platform workers, but certainly possible. Finally, comparable social protection needs among platform workers arise because platform workers typically lack independent market access and depend on the digital infrastructure of the platform operator. Furthermore, the status achieved through the rating and reputation systems on a particular platform is generally not transferable, creating a kind of 'lock-in effect' for platform workers, i.e. they do not have the 'exit option' typical of independent market participants. Where a platform worker is not an employee due to a lack of personal dependence, the conditions for classification as an employee-like person may still be met.[61] However, as already mentioned, the resulting protection under employment law remains limited.

IV. Platform workers as homeworkers

24 In some cases, it may be possible to classify platform workers as home workers within the meaning of the Home Work Act (*Heimarbeitsgesetz, HAG*). However, this is only conceivable for those platform workers who work from home without being tied to a specific location, which is a situation frequently found among crowdworkers.[62] while, for example, riders for food delivery companies who work in public spaces are excluded in this respect from the outset.

25 Classification as a home worker leads to the application of a separate protection regime. While this regime is significantly less comprehensive than general employment law protection, it is nevertheless more comprehensive than the legal protection afforded to (other) employee-like persons. For example, the *HAG* contains special provisions on the setting and enforcement of minimum wages, occupational safety and health protection, and (albeit limited) protection against dismissal. In addition, there are special provisions on continued payment of wages in the event of illness and provisions on paid leave. Finally, home workers fall within the scope of the Works Constitution Act (Betriebsverfassungsgesetz, BetrVG) if they perform their main activity for one establishment.

26 A decision by *BAG* in 2016 illustrates that the *HAG* is not outdated, but can also be applied to modern forms of work. The case concerned a programmer who, over an extended period of time, essentially programmed construction projects for a company from home and performed additional individual tasks at the request of the company's employees. In its ruling, the *BAG* rejected the existence of an employment relationship, based primarily on the fact that the worker was legally free to decide whether and to what extent he worked for the company.[63] Mere economic pressure to accept tasks and not to refuse them was expressly considered irrelevant.[64] Instead, the *BAG* classified the worker as a home worker within the meaning of the *HAG*.[65] In line with this decision, some academics assume that crowdworkers can also be classified as home workers, as the provisions of the *HAG* must be interpreted in accordance with the specific characteristics of digital work.[66] However, according to the majority of academics, the *HAG* is not tailored to the specific situation of crowdworkers, as the specific work tasks to be

---

[61] In the same vein, Pacha, p. 198 et seqq.
[62] Leimeister/Durward, p. 53 et seq.
[63] BAG 14.6.2016 – 9 AZR 305/15, NZA 2016, 1453, paras. 20 et seqq.
[64] Cf. BAG 14.6.2016 – 9 AZR 305/15, NZA 2016, 1453, para. 25.
[65] BAG 14.6.2016 – 9 AZR 305/15, NZA 2016, 1453, paras. 41 et seqq.
[66] In particular Pacha, p. 212 et seqq.; in the same vein, Martina NZA 2021, 616 (618 et seq.); Waltermann in Kitaibl/Mosler/Pačić, p. 634 (644); advocating a case-to-case approach Mayr, p. 216 et seqq.

performed are not assigned to the individual platform workers by the platform operator, but are choosen by crowdworkers themselves from available options.[67]

D. Political initiatives for legal regulations

27 Although the *BMAS* had already addressed the social problems of platform work in 2015, it was not until 2020 that it published its first proposals for specific regulation of this form of work in the policy paper mentioned at the beginning.[68] In this paper, the *BMAS* called for the enforcement of employees' rights to be made easier by proposing a burden of proof rule in favour of platform workers. Once the platform worker provides some evidence of an employment relationship with the platform operator, the burden of proof for the non-existence of an employment relationship would be placed on the platform operator. In addition, fair employment conditions for self-employed platform workers were also envisaged. These should include minimum notice periods to prevent immediate termination of the employment relationship by the platform operator ('digital cold dismissal'). Furthermore, regulations on paid leave, continued payment of wages in the event of illness and maternity protection were being considered. In addition, the *BMAS* announced a joint initiative with the Federal Ministry of Justice and Consumer Protection (*Bundesministerium der Justiz und für Verbraucherschutz, BMJV*) to make it easier for courts to review general terms and conditions that disadvantage platform workers. In the area of social security law, self-employed platform workers were to be included in the statutory pension insurance scheme, with platform operators contributing to the costs of this insurance. Platform operators should also be required to contribute to the health insurance costs of self-employed platform workers. With regard to location-based platform work (e.g. food delivery services), options for protection through statutory accident insurance should be examined.

28 Following the policy paper, the *Denkfabrik Digitale Arbeitsgesellschaft* developed a preliminary draft of a 'Platform Work Act' and discussed a number of proposals with experts[69] and stakeholders. The draft concerned the definition of platform work, the shift in the burden of proof regarding the existence of an employment relationship under certain circumstances, social rights for self-employed platform workers such as working hours, paid leave, continued payment of salary in the event of illness, health and safety (at least for gig workers such as riders) and social security (accidents, pensions). However, unlike in countries such as France, Italy or Spain, these efforts never led to legal regulations for platform work or at least to an official draft law. Possible explanations include lobbying efforts of both employers and trade unions in opposite directions on the issue of regulating platform work.[70] Another, and arguably more important, reason is likely to be the efforts to draw up regulations on platform work at European level, which led to a Commission proposal at the end of 2021[71] and which the *BMAS* wished to await without pre-empting it with hasty national legislation. It is noteworthy that the discussions within the *Denkfabrik Digitale Arbeitsgesellschaft* mainly revolve around

---

[67] Cf. Däubler/Klebe NZA 2015, 1032 (1036); Gärtner, p. 91 et seqq.; Krause, 2016, p. 105; Riesenhuber ZFA 2021, 5 (40 et seq.); Waas in Waas et al., p. 170 et seq.; Wisskirchen/Schwindling ZESAR 2017, 318 (325 et seq.); for other reasons sceptical Deinert RdA 2018, 359 (363).

[68] See above fn. 10.

[69] The author of this chapter was also involved in this process.

[70] Cf. on the one hand, Bundesvereinigung der Deutschen Arbeitgeberverbände (BDA), *Selbstständigkeit fördern, statt unnötig zu regulieren*, Opinion of 19.11.2020; on the other hand, Deutscher Gewerkschaftsbund (DGB), *DGB-Diskussionspapier zur Plattformarbeit, Regeln für Plattformarbeit*, 2019.

[71] Cf. COM(2021) 762 final.

the extension of traditional labour and social security law to self-employed platform workers, while protection against algorithmic management, which has received increasing attention in the international debate, apparently played no role.

29 The 2021 agreement between the governing parties envisaged a review of existing legal frameworks to achieve decent and fair working conditions for people working on digital platforms,[72] whereas the 2025 agreement between the current governing parties does not contain any explicit reference to digital labour platforms[73].

E. Implementation of the Platform Work Directive

30 Against this backdrop, the implementation of the European Platform Work Directive, which has been broadly welcomed by German stakeholders,[74] by 2 December 2026 poses various challenges for German legislators that are best addressed through a dedicated Platform Work Act. The focus here is on the long-debated question of employment status, including the legal presumption of an employment relationship, the issue of algorithmic management as a new topic that has hitherto received limited attention[75] and the topic of collective rights. In particular, legislators should establish a specific procedure to comply with Art. 4(3) Platform Work Directive, which stipulates that if an employment relationship is established, the party responsible for the employer's obligations must be clearly identified, since the existing procedure in German law covers only social security matters and does not permit the identification of a responsible third party in bilateral labour court proceedings.[76] With regard to the legal presumption provided for in Art. 5(1) Platform Work Directive, the German legislator may establish a set of indicators relating to direction and control. Alternatively, it is also possible to interpret the legal presumption broadly and, for this purpose, simply refer to the concept of a digital labour platform as defined in Art. 2(1)(a) Platform Work Directive as such[77] with further operational details specified in subordinate guidelines within the meaning of Art. 6(a) Platform Work Directive. This appears to be the (unofficial) view of the Commission as well, which notes that Art. 5 Platform Work Directive does not require Member States to lay down criteria in their transposition measures.[78] However, it should be noted that a low-threshold presumption is likely to result in a greater number of cases in which the platform operator can successfully rebut the legal presumption. With regard to algorithmic management, implementation should be used to assess whether at least certain core elements can be transferred to employment relationships outside platform work, given that forms of algorithmic management are not used exclusively on digital work platforms but also occur in other work environments. Finally, regarding collective rights, legislators must take into account the dual structure of German labour law, which consists, on the one hand, of membership-based trade unions and, on the other, of staff-

[72] Cf. Koalitionsvertrag zwischen SPD, BÜNDNIS 90/DIE GRÜNEN und FDP, 2021, p. 57, https://www.spd.de/fileadmin/Dokumente/Koalitionsvertrag/Koalitionsvertrag_2021-2025.pdf (last accessed: 22.5.2026).

[73] Cf. Koalitionsvertrag zwischen CDU, CSU und SPD, 2025, https://www.koalitionsvertrag2025.de/sites/www.koalitionsvertrag2025.de/files/koav_2025.pdf, (last accessed: 22.5.2026).

[74] See Hoose et al. WSI Mitteilungen 78 (2025), 461.

[75] For exceptions, see Gerber WSI Mitteilungen 73 (2020), 182; Schreyer/Schrape AIS 11 (2) 2018, 262; Wenckebach SR 2020, 165 (168 et seq.).

[76] See Gräf ZFA 2023, 209 (248 et seq.) for more details.

[77] Same opinion Gruber-Risak/Warter DRdA 2024, 267 (272); Kocher NZA-RR 2024, 449 (452). For more details, see Krause in Chandna-Hoppe et al., p. 395.

[78] Cf. European Commission, Report Expert Group – Transposition of Directive (EU) 2024/2821 on improving working conditions in platform work (12.1.2026), 30.

based works councils, both of which are regarded as legitimate workers' representatives under Art. 2(1)(f) with recital 22 Platform Work Directive.[79] As a rule of thumb rights aimed to support and promote individual interests of platform workers (e.g. Art. 5(4) Platform Work Directive) should be assigned to trade unions, while rights affecting the entire work platform staff (e.g. Art. 13 Platform Work Directive) should be assigned to the works councils.[80] At the time of writing of this chapter, however, not even a draft of the German legislation transposing the Platform Work Directive has been published, even though the *BMAS* had already organised a comprehensive dialogue with stakeholders back in October 2024 and has been working on this issue ever since.[81]

F. Activities of other actors

Other actors have also initiated various measures to regulate platform work and improve the situation of platform workers. Essentially, three groups of actors can be distinguished that have undertaken various activities relevant to the present context: first, platform operators; second, trade unions; and third, platform workers themselves. 31

I. Code of Conduct of platform operators

An important first step was the drafting of a Code of Conduct[82] as early as 2015 on the initiative of the German platform operator *Testbirds*.[83] This code was initially signed by seven German crowdsourcing companies and one British crowdsourcing company operating in Germany.[84] It was supported by the German Crowdsourcing Association and, as a result of cooperation in the following years, even by the trade union for metal workers (IG Metall).[85] In its latest press release on this topic, issued on the occasion of the French marketplace platform *ComeUp* joining the code in 2025, *Testbirds* stated that the Code of Conduct aims to complement the European Platform Work Directive by encouraging platforms to proactively shape fair working environments.[86] 32

The Code of Conduct contains ten principles for paid crowdwork. First and foremost, platform operators commit to offer only legally compliant tasks and to inform crowdworkers about legal issues. In addition, on the crucial aspect of payment, platform operators commit to calculate prices to the best of their knowledge and belief and to provide certain payment terms (e.g. payouts at least once a month). The other principles concern a friendly working environment, respectful interaction, clearly defined tasks and realistic time frames, preserving the freedom and flexibility of crowdworkers, constructive feedback, a regulated approval process including the opportunity for rework, and respect for the privacy of crowdworkers. 33

The general shortcomings of codes of conduct are well known. Firstly, they are merely unilateral regulations and not collective agreements with representatives of the 34

[79] See in this context also European Commission, Report Expert Group – Transposition of Directive (EU) 2024/2821 on improving working conditions in platform work (12.1.2026), 18 et seq.

[80] For more details, see Krause in Bayer et al., p. 423.

[81] Cf. BT-Drs. 21/5454, 2 et seq.

[82] See http://crowdsourcing-code.com/ (last accessed: 22.5.2026).

[83] Comprehensive analysis by Brockmann in Brameshuber et al., p. 141 et seqq.

[84] *Testbirds, Clickworker, Content, Crowdguru, Streetspotr, AppJobber, ShopScout and Bugfinders.*

[85] Currently (2025), the Code of Conduct has been signed by *Testbirds, Clickworker, Content, Crowdguru, AppJobber, Streetspotr, Digivante, Textbroker and ComeUp.*

[86] See https://crowdsourcing-code.com/assets/ComeUp-Joins-Crowdworking-Code-of-Conduct_20250820.pdf (last accessed: 22.5.2026).

crowdworkers concerned. Secondly, they are soft law, raising doubts about whether a crowdworker could effectively invoke these principles in legal proceedings. Thirdly and finally, many of these principles are vaguely worded. Nevertheless, the value of this initiative should not be underestimated, as these principles attempt to constructively address the main problems of crowdworkers' working conditions and propose solutions that represent a step toward improving working conditions in this sector.

II. Initiatives of trade unions

35 Since the emergence of platform work in Germany, trade unions quickly recognised the risks posed by this new form of work to employees by replacing regular jobs with poorly paid and insecure jobs.[87] As early as 2012, the trade union for service workers (*Vereinte Dienstleistungsgewerkschaft, ver.di*) published a position paper entitled 'Crowdsourcing and cloud working: dangers for society and workers'.[88] An important trigger for the trade union debate came in 2013 with the introduction of the 'Generation Open' programme by IBM, which apparently marked the first large-scale use of internal and external crowdworking in Germany. This prompted *IG Metall* to draw awareness to this new phenomenon and to develop counter-strategies.[89] In addition to the two trade unions *ver.di* and *IG Metall*, the aforementioned *NGG* trade union is also active in the field of platform work. It is no coincidence that these three trade unions, which are united under the umbrella of the German Trade Union Confederation (*Deutscher Gewerkschaftsbund, DGB*), have been intensively involved in platform work for many years, as the organisational areas of *IG Metall*, *ver.di* and *NGG* are most affected by this new phenomenon.

36 A key response to the spread of platform work is the amendment of trade union statutes. In 2015, *IG Metall* expanded its statutes to allow not only employees but also self-employed persons to become union members.[90] This includes platform workers who are not employees, but extends far beyond that. The same applies to *ver.di*,[91] *NGG*[92] and the trade union for building, agriculture and the environment (*IG Bauen-Agrar-Umwelt, IG BAU*).[93]

37 *IG Metall* stands out as the most active union in the field of platform work, due both to the personal commitment of key union officials and to the considerable resources of this largest and most powerful German union. *IG Metall* initially launched the 'crowdsourcing project' in 2015, which aims to improve working conditions on digital platforms. A milestone in this process was the 2016 'Frankfurt Paper on Platform Work', which was published by *IG Metall* in collaboration with the Austrian Chamber of Labour (*Arbeiterkammer*), the Austrian Trade Union Federation (*Österreichischer Gewerkschaftsbund, ÖGB*), the Danish Trade Union of Commercial and Clerical Employees (*HK*) and the Swedish trade union *Unionen*, as well as the US-Canadian trade unions *International Brotherhood of Teamsters Local 117* and *Service Employees International*

---

[87] For a concise summary of the specific risks of platform work, see Keller/Seifert WSI Mitteilungen 71 (2018), 278 (282).

[88] See https://innovation-gute-arbeit.verdi.de/++file++557583e5aa698e5a58000e47/download/verdi-Positionspapier_Cloudworking-Crowdsourcing.pdf (last accessed: 22.5.2026).

[89] See https://www.igmetall.de/download/docs_0195804_IGM_Crowdsourcing_Web_ec8e869de1e912d44199c2db810c5585eec9ce57.pdf (last accessed: 22.5.2026).

[90] See § 3 No. 1(5) statutes of IG Metall.

[91] See§ 6 No. 1(b) statutes of ver.di.

[92] See § 4 No. 1(2) statutes of NGG.

[93] See § 4 No. 2(c) statutes of IG BAU.

Union.[94] This policy paper set out numerous demands relating to compliance with national laws and international principles, clarification of the employment relationship, the right of association, pay, social security, issues of arbitration and transparency, and the continuous improvement of regulation.

An important outcome of this initiative was *IG Metall*'s involvement in the revision of the above-mentioned Code of Conduct for platform operators in 2017. This partly compensates for the fact that *IG Metall* has not yet concluded a collective agreement with the German Crowdsourcing Association or any individual platform operator. This could initially be attributed to legal concerns from the perspective of antitrust law under Art. 101 TFEU and the corresponding decision of the CJEU in the *FNV Kunsten* case.[95] However, even after the obstacles were removed by the European Commission's 2022 'Guidelines on the application of Union competition law to collective agreements on the working conditions of self-employed individual contractors',[96] *IG Metall* apparently made no attempts to reach a collective agreement for self-employed platform workers, unlike in Denmark where such agreements were concluded.[97] Some time ago it was reported that *ver.di* has been engaged in talks with several platform operators in Germany to establish long-term binding regulations for working conditions[98] and that collective agreements between platform operators and platform workers are already in place with the involvement of *ver.di* and other German trade unions,[99] but no reliable information is available on this. 38

Another result of *IG Metall*'s activities is the establishment of the '*Fair Crowd Work*' platform, which went online in 2017 with the primary goal to overcome the isolation of individual crowd workers and to enable them to effectively protect their own work-related interests.[100] A key instrument for achieving this goal is the creation of transparency across the various platforms by giving platform workers the opportunity to rate the platform operators themselves, thus establishing a reverse rating system.[101] Currently, there are 12 reviews of platforms on the *Fair Crowd Work* website, ranging from consistently positive to predominantly negative. The aim is to create an incentive for platform operators to continuously improve their working conditions in order to obtain a more positive rating and, if necessary, to prevent the exodus of qualified platform workers, especially to better-rated competing platforms. In theory, this mechanism is effective if platform operators value a positive reputation or even seriously expect that platform workers will choose to leave the platform in large numbers if it receives a negative rating in order to continue working on another platform, as this development would reduce the number of crowd workers working on the respective platform and thus the number of profitable transactions. However, whether this market-based approach actually produces measurable effects has not yet been empirically investigated. If the number of workers is large enough from the platform operators' point of view to ensure a constant supply 39

---

[94] See https://www.igmetall.de/download/20161214_Frankfurt_Paper_on_Platform_Based_Work_EN_b939ef89f7e5f3a639cd6a1a930feffd8f55cecb.pdf (last accessed: 22.5.2026).

[95] ECJ 4.12.2014 – case C-413/13, ECLI:EU:C:2014:2411 – FNV Kunsten Informatie en Media. For the German discussion, see Krause in Deinert et al., p. 239 with further references.

[96] OJ 2022, C 374/2. For details, see Doherty ZVglRWiss 124 (2025), 28; Gramano IJCLLIR 41 (2025) 135 (144 et seqq.); Schubert ZVglRWiss 122 (2023), 363.

[97] Cf. Eurofound, 2018a, p. 54; Munkholm ZVglRWiss 122 (2023), 399 (404).

[98] Haipeter/Hoose IAQ-Report 2019/05, p. 11 et seqq.

[99] Eurofound, 2018a, p. 54.

[100] See https://faircrowd.work (last accessed: 22.5.2026).

[101] This corresponds with the approach of the 'Fairwork' initiative, cf. Fairwork, Labour Standards in the Platform Economy – Fairwork Germany Ratings 2025, Oxford, Berlin 2025, available at: https://fair.work/wp-content/uploads/sites/17/2025/09/Fairwork-Germany-Report-2025-EN.pdf (last accessed: 22.5.2026).

of labour, the ratings given by platform workers are irrelevant from a purely economic perspective and therefore remain largely insignificant. Nevertheless, the fact that several German platform operators have signed the Code of Conduct even without without being legally or economically compelled to do so shows that at least some companies seek to maintain a positive image and smooth working relationships.

40 Another noteworthy development is the establishment of an Ombuds Office on the initiative of *IG Metall*. Referenced in the above-mentioned Code of Conduct, its task is to resolve individual disputes between crowdworkers and platform operators who have signed the code. The Ombuds Office began operating in 2017 and consists of five persons:[102] a neutral chairperson (currently a retired judge of the *BAG*), a representative of the German Crowdsourcing Association, a representative of the *DGB* or a trade union member, a representative of one of the platform operators who have signed the Code of Conduct, and a crowdworker registered on one of the platforms. This composition of the Ombuds Office is intended to take into account the different interests and experiences in the settlement of disputes, combining elements of conciliation and arbitration. The regularly published annual reports show that the Ombuds Office is definitely being used. In 2022, a total of 37 cases from 17 countries[103], in 2023 a total of 135 cases from 20 countries,[104], and in 2024 a total of 117 cases from 17 countries[105] were brought before the office, predominantly in English. Most disputes were settled amicably. In some cases, however, the Ombuds Office also interpreted the Code of Conduct or referred to other rights and obligations of the parties involved, for example on questions of when remuneration is earned and under what conditions a contractual relationship can be terminated by the platform operator on the basis of an opinion expressed or the disclosure of trade secrets by a platform worker. The Ombuds Office thus acts as a dispute resolution mechanism, but at the same time contributes to the development of a kind of 'platform law'. An empirical study concludes that the Ombuds Office effectively resolves conflicts regardless of national borders and contributes to social cohesion among the persons concerned, but at the same time constitutes only a weak form of regulation.[106]

41 Finally, it should be mentioned that *IG Metall* and the *YouTubers Union*, an internet movement founded in 2018 with almost 25,000 members, agreed in 2019 to collaborate under the title '*FairTube*' in order to achieve better working conditions in this area as well. In late 2020, the *FairTube e.V. association* was founded with the main goal of promoting fairness, transparency, accountability, dialogue, non-discrimination and democratic participation for all platform workers. *FairTube e.V.* went online in February 2021, although its current level of activity remains unclear.

---

[102] Cf. § 3 Crowdsourcing Code of Conduct, Ombuds Office, Rules (updated 21.09.2018), https://ombudsstelle.crowdwork-igmetall.de/rules.html (last accessed: 22.5.2026).

[103] Cf. https://ombudsstelle.crowdwork-igmetall.de/uploads/annual-report-ombuds-office-code-of-conduct-2022.pdf (last accessed: 22.5.2026).

[104] Cf. https://ombudsstelle.crowdwork-igmetall.de/uploads/annual-report-ombuds-office-crowdsourcing-code-of-conduct-2023.pdf (last accessed: 22.5.2026).

[105] Cf. https://ombudsstelle.crowdwork-igmetall.de/uploads/annual-report-ombuds-office-crowdsourcing-code-of-conduct-2024.pdf (last accessed: 22.5.2026).

[106] Heiland WSI Mitteilungen 75 (2022), 457.

III. Self-empowerment of platform workers

42 As part of the global platform labour unrest[107] platform workers in the food delivery sector ('riders') are also seeking to take their fate into their own hands in Germany as well. In accordance with the two-channel approach of German labour law, a distinction exists between strike action on the one hand and the use of the legal framework of institutional worker participation on the other. This corresponds roughly to the sociological distinction between distributional protests and regulatory protests, although in practice both paths and goals are sometimes intertwined.

43 From 2017 onwards, *Deliveroo* and *Foodora* 'riders' began staging public protests and demonstrations against their working conditions.[108] At the same time, they turned to the grassroots organisation Free Workers' Union (*Freie Arbeiter-Union, FAU*) to represent their interests. This movement led to some negotiations with *Foodora*, but no collective agreement. Furthermore, a regional labour court (in connection with an earlier labour dispute) ruled that the *FAU* is not a trade union within the meaning of German labour law and therefore cannot conclude a valid collective agreement.[109] In addition, the 'riders' of the German food delivery service *Gorillas* in Berlin organised themselves independently into a '*Gorillas Workers Collective*' and waged such a fierce battle against the platform operator in 2021 that even the Federal Minister of Labour and Social Affairs became involved in the conflict.[110] In this context, the Berlin Regional Labour Court ruled that the dismissal without notice of a 'rider' (who had been hired in 2021 as an employee with a one-year fixed-term contract) was valid on the grounds of her participation in a wildcat strike in 2021, which is according to established case law illegal under German labour law.[111] However, the most intense labour disputes concern *Lieferando*.[112] This company gained a virtual monopoly in the German delivery service sector following *Deliveroo*'s withdrawal from the market and the takeover of *Foodora* by *Lieferando*'s Dutch parent company in 2019. *Lieferando* therefore became the main target of the grassroots initiative '*Liefern am Limit*' (Delivering at the Limit), founded via social media in 2018. Due to the need for professionalisation, the autonomous initiative '*Liefern am Limit*' was integrated into the *NGG*'s increasing protests against precarious working conditions[113] at *Lieferando* in 2020. Finally, in 2023, the *NGG* officially called on *Lieferando* to conclude a collective agreement and accompanied this demand with repeated strike action. However, as the *NGG* was unable to maintain its pressure on *Lieferando* due to high staff turnover and a lack of solidarity,[114] the demand for a collective agreement ultimately failed.

44 Parallel to these developments, platform workers repeatedly attempted to establish works councils so as to be able to rely in future on the institutional rights granted to works councils. For example, in spring 2018, supported by the *NGG*, a works council was

---

[107] Cf. Umney et al. Work, Employment and Society 38 (2024), 3 et seqq., who count no fewer than 1,271 cases of platform labour unrest.

[108] Degner/Kocher KJ 2018, 247; Palmer Blätter für deutsche und internationale Politik 2017 (7), 32; see also Heiland/Schaupp Momentum Quarterly 9 (2) 2020, 50.

[109] LAG Berlin-Brandenburg 16.2.2010 – 19 SaGa 2480/09, BeckRS 2010, 68201. Critical Kocher/Bronowicka KJ 2024, 504 (506 ff.).

[110] Cf. https://www.tagesspiegel.de/berlin/streiks-bei-berliner-lieferdienst-arbeitsminister-heil-schaltet-sich-in-gorillas-streit-ein/27419858.html (last accessed: 22.5.2026).

[111] LAG Berlin-Brandenburg 25.4.2023 – 16 Sa 868/22; NZA-RR 2023, 584.

[112] For comprehensive details, see Schreyer/Feist AIS 17 (1) 2024, 23.

[113] The reality of platform work is aptly described from Heiland WSI Mitteilungen 72 (2019), 299 (301 et seqq.).

[114] For a detailed analysis on the issue of solidarity among self-employed platform workers, see Hoose/Beckmann AIS 17 (1) 2024, 8.

established at *Deliveroo*'s Cologne site. However, it ultimately had to cease operations when management did not renew the fixed-term employment contracts of the works council members.[115] At *Foodora*, the 'riders' were apparently more successful, at least temporarily, in establishing a works council at the Cologne site.[116] Here, too, the disputes at *Lieferando* are the most complex. After initial resistance, *Lieferando* accepted the election of works councils at its headquarters and its so-called 'hub', leading to the establishment of 19 works councils in 2023. However, with regard to the election of works councils in so-called 'remote cities', *Lieferando* contested the election on the grounds that 'riders' in a remote city do not constitute an establishment or at least a qualified part of a branch, which is required for a lawful works council election under the Works Constitution Act (*Betriebsverfassungsgesetz, BetrVG*). Several court cases are currently pending before German labour courts.[117] A local labour court dismissed the claim and considered a delivery area to be a qualified part of a branch, which is sufficient for the election of a local works council.[118] In fact, it can be argued that the concept of an establishment, which is not defined in the Works Constitution Act but has been developed through case law, is flexible enough to take into account the specificities of platform work in the delivery service sector.[119] However, all regional labour courts followed *Lieferando*'s argument and declared the works council elections to be unlawful on the grounds that there was no sufficiently separate local management structure as a prerequisite for the existence of an establishment or a qualified part of a branch.[120] In early 2026, the *BAG* upheld the decisions of the regional labour courts and ruled that a delivery area does not, in itself, constitute an establishment or a qualified part thereof, and that riders within that delivery area are therefore not entitled to elect their own local works council.[121]

45 This problem has now also been acknowledged at the political level. As part of the ongoing general discussion on the modernisation of the Works Constitution Act, the Federal Council ('*Bundesrat*') called on the Federal Government to pay particular attention to platform work and the need for a modern concept of establishment that enables platform workers to elect a local works council.[122] Even if the *BAG* adheres to the established concept of a works council, legislative intervention remains possible, potentially amending the Works Constitution Act in such a way that the options for electing works councils in the case of platform work are expanded.

46 In a sense, platform work has also reached the level of corporate governance, as illustrated by the example of *Delivery Hero*, a Berlin-based company that also operates in the food delivery sector. Following a ruling by the Berlin Civil Court,[123] *Delivery Hero* was required to apply the German Co-Determination Act (*Mitbestimmungsgesetz, MitbestG*), which stipulates equal co-determination on the supervisory board, due to its high number of employees. Following the conversion of the company into a European Company (SE), the supervisory board consists of six members, three of whom are

---

[115] Zander Mitbestimmung 2018 (3), 16 (17 et seq.).

[116] Haipeter/Hoose IAQ-Report 2019/05, p. 18.

[117] For an overview, see Jäger/Reinbach NZA 2025, 1299.

[118] ArbG Aachen 23.4.2024 – 2 BV 56/23, NZA-RR 2024, 422.

[119] Krause KJ 2024, 466 (474 et seqq.).

[120] LAG Niedersachsen 30.5.2024 – 5 TaBV 84/23, NZA-RR 2025, 38; LAG Schleswig-Holstein 7.8.2024 – 6 TaBV 20/23, BeckRS 2024, 29315; LAG Hamburg 21.11.2024 – 3 TaBV 1/24, BeckRS 2024, 45753; LAG Hessen 10.2.2025 – 16 TaBV 30/24, NZA-RR 2025, 325; LAG Köln 7.3.2025 – 9 TaBV 29/24, NZA 2025, 1342; LAG Hamm 8.4.2025 – 7 TaBV 41/24, BeckRS 2025, 14149.

[121] BAG 28.1.2026 – 7 ABR 23/24, Press release No. 2/26.

[122] Cf. BR-Drs. 239/25, 2.

[123] LG Berlin 9.3.2018 – 102 O 72/17 AktG, BeckRS 2018, 20202.

from the employee side, which originally also included a 'rider captain'.[124] However, according to *Delivery Hero* SE's 2019 annual corporate governance report, the person in question was only a member of the supervisory board from July 2018 to March 2019.[125] At present, equal co-determination remains in place on the *Delivery Hero* supervisory board, but the employee representatives (now four out of eight members) apparently come from higher-ranking employee groups.[126]

These developments show that workers of food delivery platforms who work location-based are more likely than their location-independent counterparts to join forces and take advantage of labour unrest. This difference can be attributed to the fact that 'riders' meet more often in public transport areas or at certain other locations than isolated platform workers. In addition, uniformly precarious working conditions foster a stronger sense of solidarity and a desire to improve their own working situation through joint action. 47

G. Concluding remarks

Platform work has become established in Germany in recent years, although its actual scale remains uncertain, with estimates ranging from a mere niche phenomenon to a significant share of the German labour market. To date, the labour courts have addressed the issue of a platform worker's status in only one case and, taking into account the circumstances of that particular case, recognised the individual as an employee. In most cases, however, platform workers will ultimately only have the status of self-employed persons. The European Platform Work Directive and its implementation in German law are certain to improve working conditions for all platform workers. However, it remains to be seen whether the German legislator will seize the opportunity to introduce additional social rights for self-employed platform workers. In any event, relying solely on legal regulations will not be sufficient. Additional initiatives are needed to bring about a real improvement in the working conditions of platform workers. Therefore, the activities of trade unions such as *IG Metall*, *ver.di* and *NGG*, but also the self-empowerment of platform workers, will remain indispensable in order to achieve fair and reasonable working conditions in the world of platform work. 48

---

[124] Hinck Mitbestimmung 2018 (3), 19 (20 et seqq.).

[125] Delivery Hero SE, Annual Report 2019, p. 45, https://ir.deliveryhero.com/media/document/76180021-64c4-4482-b6ab-638acaada132/assets/DE000A2E4K43-JA-2019-EQ-E-00.pdf?disposition=inline (last accessed: 22.5.2026).

[126] Cf. https://ir.deliveryhero.com/de/team (last accessed: 22.5.2026).

Greece

Literature: Adams-Prassl/Abraha/Kelly-Lyth/Silberman/Rakshita, 'Regulating algorithmic management: A blueprint', ELLJ 2023, 124; Aloisi, 'Time Is Running Out' The Yodel Order and Its Implications for Platform Work in the EU', ILLeJ 2020, 67; Aloisi/Potocka-Sionek/Ratti, 'Straddling Two Horses: Digital or Social Regulation? Behind, Within and Beyond the EU Platform Work Directive', CML Rev. 2025, 1407; Aloisi/Rainone/Countouris, 'An Unfinished Task? Matching the Platform Work Directive with the EU and International "Social Acquis" ', ILO Working Paper 101, Geneva 2023; Bernhardt/Kresge/Suleiman, 'The Data-Driven Workplace and the Case for Worker Technology Rights', ILR Review 2023, 3; Chandna-Hoppe, 'Who is a platform worker? Plattformarbeit im deutschen und englischen Recht sowie in der EU-Richtlinie zur Plattformarbeit', ZEuP 2025, 9; Collins, 'Is the contract of employment illiberal?' in Collins/Lester/Mantouvalou, Philosophical Foundations of Labour Law, Oxford 2018, p. 48; Collins, 'Market Power, Bureaucratic Power, and the Contract of Employment', Ind. L. J. 1986, 1; Countouris/De Stefano, '"Not the usual gig": The personal scope(s) of application of Directive 2024/2831 on improving working conditions in platform work', ELLJ 2025, 432 (437); Davidov, 'Setting Labour Law's Coverage: Between Universalism and Selectivity', OJLS 2014, 543; De Stefano, 'The EU Commission's proposal for a Directive on Platform Work: an overview', ILLe-J 2022, 1; Dimarellis, 'Προβληματισμοί σχετικά με την έννοια της εξάρτησης στη συνεργατική οικονομία' ('Reflections on the Concept of Subordination in the Collaborative Economy') in Aliprantis et al. (eds), Festschrift for Travlos-Tzanetatos, Athens – Thessaloniki 2020; Fischels/Sokoll, 'Die EU-Richtlinie zur Verbesserung der Arbeitsbedingungen in der Plattformarbeit', NZA 2024, 721; Fudge, 'Fragmenting Work and Fragmenting Organizations: The Contract of Employment and the Scope of Labour Regulation', Osgoode Hall L.J. 2006, 609; Georgiadis (ed), Σύντομη Ερμηνεία του Αστικού Κώδικα (Short Commentary on the Greek Civil Code) I Art. 1–947, Athens 2010; Giannakourou, 'Εργασία με πληθοπορισμό (crowdwork) και νέοι επαγγελματικοί κίνδυνοι: προκλήσεις για τον νομοθέτη' ('Crowdwork and New Occupational Risks: Challenges for the Legislator'), Epitheorisis Ergatikou Dikaiou (Review of Labour Law, EErgD) 2019, 1401; Giannakourou, 'Πίσω από τον αλγόριθμο της ψηφιακής πλατφόρμας: ανακαλύπτοντας τη σύγχρονη σχέση εξάρτησης' ('Behind the Algorithm of the Digital Platform: Discovering the Contemporary Relation of Subordination'), EErgD 2021, 983; Goulas, 'Η έννοια του εργοδότη στο εργατικό δίκαιο κατά την ελληνική νομολογία' ('The Notion of the Employer in Labour Law in Greek Case Law'), EErgD 2022, 1299; Gräf, 'Der Richtlinienentwurf zur Plattformarbeit – Analyse, Umsetzungsperspektiven und Alternativen', ZFA 2023, 209; Greiner/Baumann, 'Der Beschäftigungsstatus von Plattformtätigen und die Richtlinie zur Verbesserung der Arbeitsbedingungen in der Plattformarbeit', ZESAR 2023, 409; Hiessl, 'Statusfragen in der Plattformarbeit: Europäische Arbeitnehmer- und Arbeitgeberkonzepte auf dem Prüfstand', SR 2024, 128; Hießl, 'The legal status of platform workers', ILLe-J 2022, 13; Kaisari, 'Courier και Delivery: Επίκαιρα ζητήματα ενός επαγγέλματος που αναδείχθηκε την περίοδο της πανδημίας' ('Courier and Delivery: Current Issues of an Occupation that Emerged during the Pandemic'), EErgD 2021, 1079; Kazakos, 'Ο ψηφιακός εργαζόμενος, το άρθρο 69 ν. 4808/2021 και η διεύρυνση των νομικών εννοιών «εξαρτημένη εργασία» και «διευθυντικό δικαίωμα» – Κριτική δογματική ανάλυση' ('The Digital Worker, Article 69 of Law 4808/2021 and the Expansion of the Legal Concepts of "Dependent Employment" and "Managerial Prerogative" – A Critical Dogmatic Analysis'), EergD 2023, 369; Kazakos, 'Ο ψηφιακός εργαζόμενος, το άρθρο 69 ν. 4808/2021 και η διεύρυνση των νομικών εννοιών «εξαρτημένη εργασία» και «διευθυντικό δικαίωμα» – Κριτική δογματική ανάλυση' ('The Digital Worker, Article 69 of Law 4808/2021 and the Expansion of the Legal Concepts of "Dependent Employment" and "Managerial Prerogative" – A Critical Dogmatic Analysis') in Ladas/Papadimitriou (eds), Η εξάρτηση στις εργασιακές σχέσεις (Dependence in Employment Relations), Athens 2023, p. 85; Kocher, 'Anwendungsbereich des Arbeitsrechts, Anpassungsbedarfe im deutschen Recht aus unionsrechtlicher Sicht', NZA-RR 2024, 449; Kocher, 'Digitale Rechte am Arbeitsplatz: Das Arbeitsrecht im Wettbewerb der Diskurse' in Brose et al. (eds), Festschrift for Ulrich Preis, Munich 2021, p. 665; Kocher/Hensel, 'Herausforderungen des Arbeitsrechts durch digitale Plattformen – ein neuer Koordinationsmodus von Erwerbsarbeit', NZA 2016, 984; Koukiadis, 'Μεταρρύθμιση ή απορρύθμιση από τις ρυθμίσεις του ν. 4808/2021;' ('Reform or Deregulation through the Provisions of Law 4808/2021?'), Elliniki Dikaiosyni (Hellenic Justice, EllDni) 2021, 1601; Koukiadis, Ατομικό και συλλογικό εργατικό δίκαιο (Individual and collective labour law), 8th edn, Athens – Thessaloniki 2021; Koukiadis, Εργατικό Δίκαιο – Ατομικές εργασιακές σχέσεις και το δίκαιο της ευελιξίας της εργασίας (Labour Law – Individual Employment Relations and the Law of Labour Flexibility), 9th ed., Athens – Thessaloniki 2021; Krause, 'Auf dem Weg zur unionsrechtlichen Regelung von Plattformtätigkeiten', NZA 2022, 521; Kullmann, 'Platformisation of Work: An EU Perspective on Introducing a Legal Presumption', ELLJ 2022, 66; Ladas, 'Teleworking and Crowdworking in the Employment Relationship', EuZA 2025, 3; Ladas, 'Η προοπτική νομοθετικής ρύθμισης του Crowdworking' ('The Prospect of Legislative Regulation of Crowdworking'), Dikaio Epicheiriseon kai Etairion (Business and Company Law, DEE) 2021, 749; Lampropoulos, 'Εργασία μέσω ψηφιακής πλατφόρμας – Οι διατάξεις του Ν 4808/2021 και πρόσφατες Κοινοτικές κανονιστικές προτάσεις' ('Work through Digital Platforms: The Provisions of Law 4808/2021 and Recent EU Legislative Proposals'), DEE

2022, 1038; Leventis/Papadimitriou, Ατομικό εργατικό δίκαιο (Individual labour law), Athens 2011; Lixouriotis, 'Ψηφιακές πλατφόρμες: Μια νέα κατηγορία παροχής ανεξαρτήτων υπηρεσιών;' ('Digital Platforms: A New Category of Independent Service Provision?'), Efarmoges Dimosiou Dikaiou (Applications of Public Law, EfDD) 2021, 216; Menegatti, 'Taking EU Labor Law beyond the Employment Contract: The Role Played by the European Court of Justice', ELLJ 2020, 26; Minotakis, 'Regulating AI in the workplace: A critique of the EU AI act and the platform work directive through a worker-centred lens', Platforms & Society (2) 2025, 1; Miskedakis, 'Παρέμβαση' ('Intervention') in Papadimitriou (ed), Ο Νέος Εργασιακός Νόμος 4808/2021 (The New Labour Law 4808/2021), Athens 2023, p. 165; Mpakopoulos, 'Εργοδοτική ιδιότητα και ευθύνη' ('Employer status and liability'), Athens – Thessaloniki 2025; Orfanidis, 'Το τεκμήριο της εξάρτησης – δικονομική προσέγγιση' ('The Presumption of Subordination – A Procedural Approach') in Ladas/Papadimitriou (eds), Η εξάρτηση στις εργασιακές σχέσεις (Dependence in Employment Relations), Athens 2023, p. 197; Palli, 'Η παροχή μεταφορικών υπηρεσιών με τη διαμεσολάβηση πλατφόρμας σύμφωνα με τη γαλλική νομολογία και εμπειρία' ('The Provision of Transport Services through Platform Intermediation According to French Case Law and Experience'), EErgD 2021, 1015; Müller-Glöge/Preis/Gallner/Schmidt (eds), Erfurter Kommentar zum Arbeitsrecht, 25th edn, Munich 2025; Papadimitriou, 'The Concept of 'Employee': The Position in Greece' in Waas/van Voss (eds), Restatement of Labour Law in Europe: Vol I: The Concept of Employee, Oxford London Portland 2017, p. 275; Papadimitriou, 'Εργατικό δίκαιο και νέες τεχνολογίες' ('Labour Law and New Technologies') in University of Piraeus/Hellenic Court of Audit (UoP/HCoA, eds), Δίκαιο και Τεχνολογία (Law and Technology), Athens – Thessaloniki, 2019, p. 37; Patsourakis, 'Εργασία μέσω ψηφιακής πλατφόρμας – crowdwork και work on-demand' ('Work via Digital Platforms – Crowdwork and Work On-Demand') in Ladas (ed), Ευέλικτες μορφές εργασίας (Flexible Forms of Employment), Athens 2021, p. 189; Patsourakis, 'Η εργασία στον τομέα της gig-economy ενώπιον του ΔικΕΕ – Παρατηρήσεις επί της υποθέσεως C-692/19 Yodel Delivery Network' ('Work in the Gig-Economy Sector before the CJEU – Remarks on Case C-692/19 Yodel Delivery Network'), DEN 2020, 809; Preis, '§ 611 a BGB – Potenziale des Arbeitnehmerbegriffes', NZA 2018, 817; Preis, 'Überlegungen zum Begriff der Arbeit' in Gallner et al. (eds), Festschrift for Moll, Munich 2019, p. 539; Preis, 'Von der Antike zur digitalen Arbeitswelt', RdA 2019, 75; Rainone/Countouris, Collective Bargaining and Self-Employed Workers, ETUI Policy Brief 2021.11, Brussels 2021; Rolfs, 'Gutachten B zum 74. Deutschen Juristentag: Wen schützt das Arbeits- und Sozialversicherungsrecht? – Empfiehlt sich eine Neuausrichtung seines Anwendungsbereichs?' in Ständige Deputation des Deutschen Juristentages (ed), Verhandlungen des 74. Deutschen Juristentages I, Munich 2024; Rosin, 'Towards a European Employment Status: The EU Proposal for a Directive on Improving Working Conditions in Platform Work', Ind.L.J. 2022, 478; Sagan, 'Für wen gilt das Arbeitsrecht der EU – Rechtsprechung, Richtlinien, Rechtsweg', NZA-Beil. 2023, 51; Schubert, 'Richtlinienvorschlag Plattformarbeit: Anwendungsbereich und Beschäftigungsstatus', in Giesen/Junker/Rieble, Arbeitsrechtsfragen bei Crowdworking und Plattformarbeit, Munich 2023, p. 69; Simitis, S., 'Europäisierung oder Renationalisierung des Arbeitsrechts?' in Heinze (ed) Festschrift for Kissel, Munich 1994, p. 1097; Skandalis, 'Κριτική ανάλυση της οδηγίας 2024/2831 για τη βελτίωση των συνθηκών εργασίας των απασχολούμενων σε πλατφόρμες και οι εκτιμώμενες επιπτώσεις της στο ελληνικό δίκαιο' ('Critical Analysis of Directive 2024/2831 on the Improvement of Working Conditions of Platform Workers and its Estimated Impact on Greek Law'), DEE 2025, 450; Skandalis, 'Ο οικονομικά εξαρτημένος αυτοαπασχολούμενος' ('The Economically Dependent Self-Employed Worker') in Ladas/Papadimitriou (eds), Η εξάρτηση στις εργασιακές σχέσεις (Dependence in Employment Relations), Athens 2023, p. 225; Stone, From Widgets to Digits – Employment Regulation for the Changing Workplace, Cambridge 2004; Theodosis, 'Τεχνητή Νοημοσύνη και η συνταγματική προστασία της εργασίας' ('Artificial Intelligence and the Constitutional Protection of Labour' in Stylianidis (ed), Τεχνητή Νοημοσύνη (Artificial Intelligence), Athens 2025, 452; Travlos-Tzanetatos, 'Η εργασία στις ψηφιακές πλατφόρμες με αφορμή τις ρυθμίσεις του ν. 4808/2021' ('Work on Digital Platforms in Light of the Provisions of Law 4808/2021'), EllDni 2021, 1608; Travlos-Tzanetatos, 'Ψηφιακή επανάσταση και εργασία – Η πλατφόρμα crowdworking' ('Digital Revolution and Work – The Crowdworking Platform'), EErgD 2016, 1289; Travlos-Tzanetatos, Το εργατικό δίκαιο στην τέταρτη βιομηχανική επανάσταση (Labour Law in the Fourth Industrial Revolution), Athens 2019; Tzotzes, 'Εργαζόμενοι και ψηφιακές πλατφόρμες' ('Workers and Digital Platforms'), Athens 2024; Vergis, 'Gig Work και νομικός χαρακτηρισμός: το παράδειγμα του Ηνωμένου Βασιλείου και η χρησιμότητά του' ('Gig Work and Legal Classification: The Example of the United Kingdom and its Usefulness'), EErgD 2021, 1025; Vergis, 'Ψηφιοποιημένη εργασία και η αξία της συλλογικής αυτονομίας: Θεωρητικές προσεγγίσεις (με αναφορά στο ευρωπαϊκό εργατικό δίκαιο) ('Digitalised Work and the Value of Collective Autonomy: Theoretical Approaches (with Reference to European Labour Law)'), EErgD 2023, 717; Wank, 'Der persönliche Geltungsbereich der Plattformarbeits-Richtlinie', EuZW 2023, 747; Wank, 'Ο πάροχος υπηρεσιών σε ψηφιακή πλατφόρμα (crowdworker) ως εξαρτημένος εργαζόμενος; Σκέψεις με αφορμή μία απόφαση του Γερμανικού Εργατικού Ακυρωτικού' ('The Provider of Services on a Digital Platform (Crowdworker) as an Employee? Reflections on a Judgment of the German Federal Labour Court'), EErgD 2021, 999; Zerdelis, 'Απασχόληση μέσω ψηφιακών πλατφορμών και εργατικό δίκαιο' ('Employment through Digital Platforms and Labour Law' in Papadimitriou (ed), Ο Νέος

Εργασιακός Νόμος 4808/2021 (The New Labour Law 4808/2021), Athens 2023, p. 139; Zerdelis, 'Ζητήματα κατανομής του βάρους απόδειξης στις εργατικές διαφορές' ('Issues Concerning the Allocation of the Burden of Proof in Labour Disputes'), Epitheorisi Politikis Dikonomias (Review of Civil Procedure, EPolD) 2023, 487; Zerdelis, 'Η έννοια της εξαρτημένης εργασίας στη σύγχρονη ψηφιακή εποχή' ('The Concept of Dependent Employment in the Contemporary Digital Era') in Ladas/Papadimitriou (eds), Η εξάρτηση στις εργασιακές σχέσεις (Dependence in Employment Relations), Athens 2023, p. 47; Zerdelis, 'Η έννοια της εξάρτησης στην ψηφιακή εποχή του εργατικού δικαίου' ('The Concept of Subordination in the Digital Era of Labour Law'), EErgD 2023, 667; Zerdelis, Εργατικό Δίκαιο (Labour Law), 5th edn, Athens – Thessaloniki 2022; Zografidis, '«Το πρόβλημα των τριών τεκμηρίων»' ('The problem of the three presumptions'), EErgD 2025, 899.

A. Introduction

Art. 68–72 L. 4808/2021, established a legal framework of rights and duties regarding the provision of services via digital labour platforms in Greece. The legislator realised that service providers[1] could either be employees under a dependent employment contract or be self-employed.[2] Therefore, the Greek law provides a legal presumption regarding the classification of the contractual relationship between platforms and providers, and specifically against the existence of an employment contract in platform work. Moreover, it grants specific collective, health-and-safety and information rights[3] to self-employed persons carrying out platform work, recognising their partial need for protection under labour law despite the absence of an employment contract. It is evident that if a platform work relationship can be considered as an employment contract, then all Greek labour legislation is applicable. The absence of Greek case law on the subject means the stance of the Greek courts on platform work is unclear. This chapter, however, aims to highlight some of the key trends in Greek theory and regulation in this area. 1

[1] This chapter uses the term 'service provider' to indicate that no legal assumptions are being made regarding the classification of the contract or the employment status. The terms 'platform worker' and 'person performing platform work' are used in accordance with the Directive. According to the Directive, 'persons performing platform work' includes both self-employed individuals and those working under an employment contract, whereas 'platform worker' does not refer to genuine self-employed persons. See Countouris/De Stefano ELLJ 2025, 432 (437, 441).

[2] See very recently Ladas EuZA 2025, 3 (12).

[3] Collective rights (Art. 70), health and safety (Art. 71), and information rights and duties (Art. 72).

B. Digital labour platform

2 Art. 68 L. 4808/2021 defines a 'digital platform' as 'an undertaking that acts either directly or as an intermediary and that connects service providers, undertakings or third parties with users, clients or consumers through an online platform, facilitating transactions between them or transacting directly with them'. This provision defines the material scope of the relevant provisions in terms of the platforms covered. In terms of personal scope, the provisions apply to individuals who have a contractual relationship with a platform for the provision of services. The legislator recognises that this could be an employment contract (Art. 69(1)), in which case all labour legislation would – obviously – apply. What is worth noting is that the provisions refer to and cover independent contractors, who would not otherwise enjoy the collective (Art. 70), health and safety (Art. 71), and information rights (Art. 72) conferred through the law.

3 However, Greek scholarship has largely criticised the definition of a 'digital platform' as being **too broad**.[4] This definition could include even social networks or product marketplaces. The definition could also cover pure intermediary websites, which merely provide the means by which service providers can reach the end-user or client. The main defect is therefore that the definition does not focus on **digital labour platforms**, such as platforms through which work on demand or crowdwork is provided. The definition, in its current broad form, does not obviously exclude them,[5] but is not focused on them, even though they are primarily relevant to the regulation of working conditions.[6] To avoid possible implementation problems, the prevailing opinion in legal scholarship interprets the law's scope narrowly.[7] For teleological and systematic reasons, these provisions should apply to platforms that organise or mediate the provision of services or labour by individuals in exchange for remuneration, using algorithmic management tools.

4 The scope of the Greek legal framework, when read teleologically and systematically, approaches the narrower concept of a 'digital labour platform' set out in the Directive. Under Art. 2(1)(a) and (b) of the Directive the 'service' provided by a digital labour platform is – on the other side – the work performed by individuals for remuneration.[8] Organisation of work by the platform is therefore for the Directive a sine qua non (→ Art. 2 mn. 13 et seqq.).[9] Platforms that simply 'connect parties' or 'facilitate transactions', without organising the performance of work fall outside the notion of a digital labour platform (→ Art. 2 mn. 19). Notably, the term 'intermediary' is used differently in the Directive and in Greek law. Greek law refers to platforms acting 'as intermediaries', whereas the Directive locates intermediaries within chains between the platform and the

[4] Zerdelis in Papadimitriou, p. 139 (160); Kaisari EErgD 2021, 1079 (1113); Travlos-Tzanetatos, EllDni 2021, 1608 (1620); Patsourakis in Ladas, p. 639 (682). The breadth of Art. 68 L. 4808/2021 is explained by the explanatory memorandum to the law 4808/2021, which records that the definition was drawn from the Commission Communication 'A European agenda for the collaborative economy' COM(2016) 356 final, 2.6.2016. That horizontal, market-oriented approach is broader than – and not confined to – the labour-law relevant notion of a digital platform.

[5] Koukiadis, Labour Law, p. 420; see also Travlos-Tzanetatos EllDni 2021, 1608 (1620).

[6] Compare Lixouriotis EfDD 2021, 216 (217 et seq.).

[7] Zerdelis in Papadimitriou, p. 139 (160); Travlos-Tzanetatos EllDni 2021, 1608 (1620); Lixouriotis EfDD 2021, 216 (224 et seq.) (at the request of a final recipient of services); judging by the result of his argument Koukiadis, Labour Law, p. 420 also limits the scope; Kaisari EErgD 2021, 1079 (1113); Patsourakis in Ladas, p. 639 (682).

[8] Krause NZA 2022, 521 (524).

[9] Cf. recital 19 ('to organise work'); recital 20 ('Online platforms which do not organise the work performed by individuals [...] should not be considered to be digital labour platforms').

service provider.[10] In the Directive, the notion of 'intermediary' serves an anti-circumvention function (→ Art. 2 mn. 71). Where platform work is organised through intermediaries, Greek transposition must also ensure compliance with Art. 3 Platform Work Directive. Persons performing platform work who have a contractual relationship with an intermediary must enjoy the same level of protection pursuant to the Directive as those contracting directly with the platform[11] (→ Art. 3 mn. 7 et seqq., 14 et seqq.). Finally, the Directive – unlike domestic law – expressly excludes services whose primary purpose is the exploitation or sharing of assets or the non-professional resale of goods.

In conclusion, the Greek definition of 'digital platforms' (Art. 68 L. 4808/2021) does not depict the Directive-specific type of platform work organisation, although it does not preclude it. The Greek legislator should incorporate the **labour dimension** in a statutory definition of a digital platform. The labour dimension entails primarily providing work, which is organised by the platform through algorithmic management, in exchange for remuneration (→ Art. 2 mn. 2, 22, 25, 53). 5

C. Employment status

I. National law

The question of who is an employee under the law is different from the question of who should enjoy decent working standards.[12] The same applies to platform work.[13] This section addresses the former question. From the perspective of labour law, issues regarding platform work in Greece are still theoretical due to the lack of case law on the subject. However, scholars and the legislator have identified potential legal issues. Research has centred on categorising platform work relationships, while the legislature has introduced a rebuttable legal presumption **against** the existence of a contract of employment. 6

1. Dependence (or subordination) and platform work

Greek law does not offer a legal definition of an employment contract.[14] The concept of dependence is largely based on previous case law rather than a proper deliberation by the democratically legitimised legislator. **Greek case law** distinguishes contracts of employment through the concept of personal (or legal) dependence. For a relationship between a service provider and a digital labour platform to be characterised as a contract of employment, it must therefore fulfil the concept of personal dependence.[15] Tradition- 7

---

[10] Cf. recital 24 Platform Work Directive.

[11] European Commission, Report Expert Group – Transposition of the Directive (EU) 2024/2831 on improving working conditions in platform work (12.1.2026), 22–23.

[12] Preis NZA 2018, 817 (823 et seqq.) (Distinguishing between contract type assignment and vulnerability).

[13] Compare Aloisi/Rainone/Countouris, p. 7 (Classifying persons providing platform work as employees may not automatically solve the problem of precariousness in platform labour market, as labour regulation is based on other work models.); Kocher/Hensel NZA 2016, 984 (989) (With regard to the question whether there should be specific protection for specific needs, regardless of the type of contract); Kocher in Brose et al., p. 665 (Distinguishing between the question of employee status and the question of assigning specific rights and obligations to digital platforms).

[14] See Papadimitriou, in Waas/van Voss, p. 275 et seqq.

[15] For example Areios Pagos (Supreme Court of Greece, AP) 1411/1988, EErgD 1990, 13; AP 459/2004, EErgD 2005, 15; AP 821/2006, DEN 2007, 14; Zerdelis, Labour Law, p. 12; Zerdelis EErgD 2023, 667 (668); Koukiadis, Labour Law, p. 259.

ally, the prevailing view is that personal dependence derives contractually from the employee's submission to the employer's managerial prerogative.[16] Another criterion is the integration into the employer's organisational structure.[17] A purposive approach supports treating as relevant the absence of the assumption of entrepreneurial risk as well as the absence of the exploitation of entrepreneurial opportunities for one's own account.[18] This last criterion may seem similar to economic dependence. But the last one in itself, according to the prevailing opinion in Greece, is not enough to prove employee status,[19] because it focuses on economic facts (like relying on wages to live).[20] Greek case law holds that the decisive element of personal dependence does not hinge on the accumulation of numerous indicators, but rather on the quality of subordination.[21] In addition to this general framework, Greek law provides a **general rebuttable presumption in favour of the legal characterisation of a contract as one of employment,**[22] when work is performed personally and exclusively or predominantly for the same employer for nine consecutive months, shifting the burden to the employer.[23] Nevertheless, the employer could always prove that the personal dependence criteria are not met. It is therefore important to consider whether personal dependence under Greek case law could cover platform work.

8 Many aspects of platform work render traditional criteria, such as subordination under managerial prerogative and the employee's duty to adhere to instructions, inadequate for determining entitlement to the protection of labour law.[24] According to the prevailing opinion in Greek labour scholarship, the criteria for personal dependence should be adapted to the new conditions of platform work.[25] This involves reinterpreting

---

16 Leventis/Papadimitriou, p. 357; Zerdelis, Labour Law, p. 8; Koukiadis, Labour Law, p. 226.

17 Zerdelis EErgD 2023, 667 (670); Koukiadis, Labour Law, p. 225.

18 Zerdelis, Labour Law, p. 25 et seqq.; Zerdelis in Papadimitriou, p. 139 (154 et seq.); Zerdelis in Ladas/Papadimitriou, p. 47 (48).

19 Zerdelis, Labour Law, p. 5; Zerdelis EErgD 2023, 667 (668).

20 Koukiadis, Labour Law, p. 221; Kazakos EErgD 2023, 369 (377 et seqq.); Zerdelis in Papadimitriou, p. 139 (145); compare Skandalis in Ladas/Papadimitriou, p. 225 (227).

21 Areios Pagos (Supreme Court of Greece, AP) (Plenary) 28/2005, EErgD 2005, 1441. See also Koukiadis, Labour Law, p. 219; Kaisari EErgD 2021, 1079 (1103); Kazakos EErgD 2023, 369 (423).

22 Art. 1(1) L. 2639/1998 as substituted by Art. 1 L. 3846/2010 ('An agreement between an employer and a person engaged for the provision of services or the execution of result-based works, for a fixed or an indefinite term—in particular in cases of piece-rate remuneration, telework, or home-based work—shall be presumed to amount, in substance, to a contract of employment where the work is performed personally, exclusively or predominantly for the same employer for nine (9) consecutive months.').

23 Zerdelis, Labour Law, p. 36; Orfanidis, in Ladas/Papadimitriou, p. 197 (207); Koukiadis, Labour Law, p. 262, 289; Zerdelis in Papadimitriou, p. 139 (148); Skandalis in Ladas/Papadimitriou, p. 225 (238); Kazakos EErgD 2023, 369 (377 et seqq.); Kazakos in Ladas/Papadimitriou, p. 85 (97, 113 et seq.) (economic dependence as the decisive precondition for the application of labour law).

24 According to Aloisi/Potocka-Sionek/Ratti CML Rev. 2025, 1407 (1415) platform work is characterised by a combination of factors indicating both independence and subordination. Compare Kocher, 'A Timid Proposal: Employment Status in the Proposal for an EU Directive on Improving Working Conditions in Platform Work' (Verfassungsblog 18.7.2023) <https://verfassungsblog.de/a-timid-proposal/> (last accessed: 15.8.2025); The criterion of subordination was already criticised for not being effective because of changing employment realities even before platform work expanded: Fudge Osgoode Hall L. J. 2006, 609 (622) – and platform work makes matters worse. Compare Stone 2004, p. 6 (New ways of working are putting pressure on labour law because it was designed for an earlier era); Preis in Gallner et al., p. 539 (544) (The standard employment relationship is being replaced by increasingly flexible and digital forms of work).

25 Zerdelis in Papadimitriou, p. 139 (150 et seqq.); Koukiadis, Labour Law, p. 230, 419; Giannakourou EErgD 2021, 983 (996 et seq.); Kaisari EErgD 2021, 1079 (1103 et seqq.); Dimarellis in Festschrift for Travlos-Tzanetatos, p. 151 (163 et seqq.); Vergis EErgD 2021, 1025 (1040).

the personal dependence case law criteria in light of the protective purpose of labour law[26] and thus adjusting them to the new reality.[27]

9 The traditional understanding of Greek case law on personal dependence is based on the premise that the employee is legally obliged to undertake work as set out in the employment contract. However, typically, platform work relationships do not define the provider's obligation to undertake specific tasks, nor the platform's obligation to assign them. Platforms have access to a pool of individuals who can perform the required work. As a result, they no longer need to legally bind these individuals through an employment contract, as employers previously did. However, by focusing on the facts and circumstances under which the relationship is exercised by the parties, the algorithmic management of service providers and the organisation of labour on platforms can create a **factual commitment equivalent to a legal obligation** to provide dependent work,[28] in terms of Greek case law. Greek case law will in the future have to consider this factual commitment, because otherwise labour legislation would only apply if the platform drafting the contracts opted for it, which would contradict that Greek labour law operates irrespective of the parties' wishes. For example, some platforms' automated systems could impose sanctions on service providers who do not show up for work, are unable to work, or fail to complete a minimum workload. Presumably, this should be sufficient to convince the Greek courts that such a relationship is, in reality, dependent or subordinate, especially since these sanction mechanisms render a corresponding explicit contractual obligation unnecessary.

10 Nevertheless, this is not the only obstacle to establishing an employment contract. The criterion of **submitting to an employer's orders, directions and instructions** poses a particular challenge, as digital labour platforms typically do not provide orders of this kind. Instead, they exhaustively regulate the relationship and the service to be provided in advance. This exhaustive regulation once again renders the exercise of the platform's managerial prerogative unnecessary. If managerial prerogative had the final say, the application of labour law in the context of platform work would be called into question. This is why the prevailing opinion in Greece deems this traditional criterion to be ineffective and urges the adaptation of employment contract criteria to the new reality of platform work.

11 To address this issue, some scholars have sought to incorporate the alternative criterion of 'external determination' or '**hetero-determination of work**' into the concept of personal dependence.[29] In Germany, this same criterion of ***Fremdbestimmung*** is considered particularly important in cases where the traditional approach is less applicable, especially in the context of platform work (→ Germany mn. 13–15).[30] Greek labour law theory interprets this concept as broader than submission to the employer's managerial prerogative.[31] It is often understood as combining elements from other criteria, such as integration into the organisational structure of the platform, or economic dependence

---

[26] Travlos-Tzanetatos, p. 84 et seq.; Kazakos EErgD 2023, 369 (381, 423); Kazakos in Ladas/Papadimitriou, p. 85 (114).

[27] On changing reality causing a crisis of labour law see Davidov OJLS 2014, 543 (548, 560).

[28] Compare Wank EErgD 2021, 999 (1007).

[29] Zerdelis EErgD 2023, 667 (671); Giannakourou EErgD 2021, 983 (997); Kazakos in Ladas/Papadimitriou, p. 85 (158).

[30] See Preis in ErfK, BGB § 611a mn. 10 et seqq., 42 et seqq.; Kocher NZA-RR 2024, 449 et seq. This is evidenced by the Federal Labour Court judgment on the employee status of a crowdworker on 1 December 2020: BAG 1.12.2020 – 9 AZR 102/20; see further Greiner/Baumann ZESAR 2023, 409 (411 et seq.). While not yet recognised in Greek case law, adopting this theory in Greek scholarship further demonstrates the ongoing influence of German labour law doctrine. See Wank EErgD 2021, 999 (1010 et seq.).

[31] Zerdelis in Papadimitriou, p. 139 (150 et seq.); Zerdelis in Ladas/Papadimitriou, p. 55 et seqq.

elements, such as the fact that platform workers relinquish their entrepreneurial opportunities. On the one hand, the platform operator exerts hetero-determination over the service provider by means of organisational structures, especially algorithmic ones and, on the other hand, the platform worker relinquishes their entrepreneurial freedom. Accordingly, it is argued that the criterion of hetero-determination of work is better able to capture platform-organised service provision, where the exercise of managerial prerogative takes on new, atypical forms owing to new technologies, most notably algorithmic management.[32] The platform's organisational structures, which are largely algorithmic, give rise to commitments that conflict with the notion of a self-employed person operating in the market, assuming business risks and capitalising on business opportunities. According to Greek scholarship, these structures give rise to heterodetermination and influence the provider's performance, aligning it with the platform's objectives. Examples of hetero-determination include exhaustive work scheduling involving predetermined routes and narrow time windows for completing tasks, software that can direct work step by step, and algorithmic systems that can monitor and control work provision by taking regular screenshots, logging keystrokes and using geolocation systems.

2. Legal presumption against an employment relationship

12 In light of the challenges around classifying platform work relationships, Greece introduced a specific rebuttable legal presumption **against** the existence of an employment contract between service providers and platforms in 2021. Apart from a brief description of the provision introduced, the explanatory memorandum contains no further information that could clarify the legislator's motives in establishing this specific and negative rebuttable presumption. Reliable data on the extent of platform work in Greece remains scarce.[33] Nevertheless, platform work – especially in passenger transport and food delivery – is now a major socio-legal issue. In September 2021, Greece's dominant food delivery platform 'efood' reclassified its riders from salaried employees to zero-hour independent contractors under threat of dismissal. A four-hour strike, coordinated by the riders and two unions, coincided with a viral #cancel_efood campaign by users. Under this collective and reputational pressure, the company reversed the reclassification and offered permanent contracts to 2,000 riders.[34] Nevertheless, the criteria of the Greek negative legal presumption could be used to guide such reclassification intentions.

13 According to Art. 69(2) L. 4808/2021:

> 'The contract between a digital platform and a provider of services **is presumed not to be a contract of employment** where, under that contract, the provider is entitled, **cumulatively**:
>
> a) to use subcontractors or substitutes to provide the services which he or she has undertaken to supply. [...];
> b) to choose the various tasks which the digital platform proposes that he or she undertake, or unilaterally to set the maximum number of such tasks to be undertaken from time to time, which may vary, provided that it is always fixed unilaterally by the provider;
> c) to provide his or her independent services to any third party, or to perform tasks for any third party, including competitors of the digital platform; and
> d) to determine his or her own time of service provision, within given time frames, adjusting it to personal needs and not according to the interests of the digital platform.'

---

[32] Giannakourou EErgD 2019, 1401 (1405); Zerdelis in Papadimitriou, p. 139 (142 et seqq.); Zerdelis, Labour Law, p. 38; Travlos-Tzanetatos, p. 78, 132.

[33] See, for example, Tzotzes, p. 133.

[34] Tsardanidis, '#cancel_efood: Online solidarity to platform workers' (Futures of Work, 29.4.2024) <https://futuresofwork.co.uk/2024/04/29/cancel_efood-online-solidarity-to-platform-workers/> (last accessed: 15.08.2025).

A person performing platform work is presumed to be **self-employed** if, under the **terms of their contract**, they may **cumulatively** use subcontractors or substitutes, select tasks or set a maximum workload, provide services to third parties and determine working hours within set limits. This presumption reflects 'the criteria identified by the Court of Justice of the European Union in *Yodel Delivery* Network Ltd (C-692/19) for distinguishing between subordinate employment and the provision of independent services in the context of digital collaborative platforms'.[35] However, this order has been criticised for failing to consider the specific characteristics of platform work.[36] If the Greek legal presumption is based on that CJEU order, the criticisms levelled at *Yodel* automatically apply to the Greek legislator. Furthermore, in contrast to *Yodel*,[37] the Greek legislator has not considered the possibility that the four criteria may only be met in the contract – 'on paper' – and not in practice. However, the CJEU emphasised that these freedoms must not merely be notional.[38] It is possible that the Greek legislator has misinterpreted the CJEU's order, taking it to mean that the CJEU has classified service providers via a digital platform as self-employed.[39] 14

While Greek courts have not yet expressed their views on how they would apply it, legal literature has predominantly **criticised** the presumption.[40] Greek labour law theory is concerned that the presumption is tied to the formal contract terms rather than the actual performance of the services.[41] Including rights in a contract does not guarantee that they will be exercised in practice.[42] The prevailing view in Greece is that the presumption does not benefit the worker.[43] It has been argued that the presumption instructs platforms on how to draft their contracts to secure classification as a contract for independent services, thereby avoiding labour law.[44] Another opinion criticises that prescribing such a presumption may contravene constitutional provisions which reserve the legal characterisation of the relationship for the courts.[45] However, according to another perspective, the presumption does not put the worker at a disadvantage.[46] The worker's burden of proof remains the same here, regardless of the presumption. Instead, the platform's legal position becomes more difficult: To prove the contract for independent services, the platform must now demonstrate all four of the above criteria, whereas previously it could rely on some of them. Conversely, nothing prevents the service provider from demonstrating that these contractual entitlements only existed on paper and not in practice. 15

---

35 Explanatory Memorandum to L. 4808/2021, p. 257/250. While the Explanatory Memorandum relies on *Yodel*, the CJEU did not promulgate a four-limb test; it articulated context-specific indicia conditioned on genuine freedom in reality. The Greek law goes further by positivising those indicia as cumulative contractual rights. On this choice of the Greek legislator see Vergis EErgD 2021, 1025 (1069).

36 Aloisi ILLe-J 2020, 67 (76 et seq.). See further Hießl ILLe-J 2022, 13 (23).

37 Rosin Ind. L. J. 2022, 478 (485).

38 ECJ 22.04.2020 – case C-692/19, ECLI:EU:C:2020:288 para. 30,36 – B v Yodel; see Sagan NZA-Beil. 2023, 51(55); Rosin Ind. L. J. 2022, 478 (484); Aloisi ILLe-J 2020, 67 (73).

39 This is entirely wrong according to Aloisi ILLe-J 2020, 67 (77).

40 Vergis EErgD 2021, 1025 (1077): The introduction of the presumption in Art. 69(2) L. 4808/2021 contradicts international standards.

41 Zerdelis, Labour Law, p. 45; Zerdelis in Papadimitriou, p. 139 (161); Koukiadis, Labour Law, p. 421; Travlos-Tzanetatos, EllDni 2021, 1608 (1622); Kaisari EErgD 2021, 1079 (1116); Skandalis DEE 2025, 450 (454 et seq.); Kazakos in Ladas/Papadimitriou, p. 85 (134, 142); Orfanidis in Ladas/Papadimitriou, p. 197 (218).

42 Note Aloisi's ILLe-J 2020, 67 (78 et seqq.) concerns regarding a formalistic application of the law.

43 Ladas DEE 2021, 749 (756).

44 Kaisari EErgD 2021, 1079 (1116); Kazakos in Ladas/Papadimitriou, p. 85 (134).

45 Kazakos EErgD 2023, 369 (417); Kazakos in Ladas/Papadimitriou, p. 85 (137).

46 Lixouriotis EfDD 2021, 216 (226).

16 In formal procedural terms, the position of the service provider remains the same.[47] Even without this negative presumption, the platform worker would still have to prove the facts necessary to support their claim.[48] If the presumption is activated by the platform, the service provider still has to prove the contrary.[49] In other words, they have to satisfy the dependence criteria under Greek case law, because the presumption is formulated negatively, i.e. against the existence of a contract of employment.[50] Essentially, a person performing platform work is required to prove the criteria of personal dependence, regardless of the presumption.

17 However, as the evidential position remains formally unchanged, service providers continue to face evidential disadvantages, particularly with regard to how automated algorithmic management systems function. They usually lack access to the relevant facts in legal proceedings.[51] How, for example, can they demonstrate that, despite having discretion over their working hours, they cannot refuse assignments without jeopardising their position, or that they are subject to indirect monitoring and direction by the platform?[52] The usual function of a legal presumption in labour law – protecting the weaker party in the event of impaired contractual parity and information asymmetry – is not being fulfilled here.[53] The presumption could be perceived as adding evidential detail and complexity,[54] especially given the information imbalance[55] between providers and platforms, whereas against the backdrop of a typological concept of dependence – as perceived by Greek case law – involving fluid, gradable criteria (→ mn. 7 et seqq.), the absence of certain indicators does not necessarily preclude employee status. The increased volume and specificity of evidence caused by such a presumption may also explain why courts in France, which have a similar presumption in favour of self-employment, have been reluctant to reclassify the status of drivers engaged by platforms.[56]

18 Moreover, it is conceptually questionable to use a presumption based on criteria that mirror those of the applicable rule, since this would mean using the same criteria that define self-employment to presume it.[57] The same applies in reverse to a presumption in favour of a contract of employment.[58] If there is room for contrary proof, then this is only because the approach to defining personal dependence at the stage of the legal

[47] Kaisari EErgD 2021, 1079 (1114 et seq.); Orfanidis in Ladas/Papadimitriou, p. 197 (220); similarly, Patsourakis in Ladas, p. 639 (687).

[48] See Zerdelis EPolD 2023, 487 (487 et seq.).

[49] Lixouriotis EfDD 2021, 216 (226).

[50] Kaisari EErgD 2021, 1079 (1114 et seq.); Orfanidis in Ladas/Papadimitriou, p. 197 (220); similarly, Patsourakis in Ladas, p. 639 (687).

[51] Cf. recital 8 Platform Work Directive ('Persons performing platform work […] often do not have access to information […] do not know the reasons […] are not able to obtain an explanation […]'). See also Ladas DEE 2021, 749 (756); Kaisari EErgD 2021, 1079 (1116).

[52] On information asymmetry see Adams-Prassl et al. ELLJ 2023, 124 (128); for a detailed overview of the wide range of managerial activities that can be undertaken by opaque, data-driven, automated systems, refer to Bernhardt/Kresge/Suleiman ILR Review 2023, 3 (5 et seqq.); Minotakis Platforms & Society (2) 2025, 1 (2 et seqq.).

[53] Compare on this function Rosin Ind. L. J. 2022, 478 (486); Kullmann ELLJ 2022, 66 (68 et seq.).

[54] Similarly, Kazakos in Ladas/Papadimitriou, p. 85 (147).

[55] Cf. recital 8 Platform Work Directive ('Persons performing platform work […] often do not have access to information […] do not know the reasons […] are not able to obtain an explanation […]. See also Zerdelis in Papadimitriou, p. 139 (153).

[56] See Hiessl SR 2024, 128 (139).

[57] Similarly, Orfanidis in Ladas/Papadimitriou, p. 197 (219).

[58] For example, compare Kocher, 'A Timid Proposal: Employment Status in the Proposal for an EU Directive on Improving Working Conditions in Platform Work' (Verfassungsblog 18.07.2023) <https://verfassungsblog.de/a-timid-proposal/> (last accessed: 15.08.2025), who rightly thinks that such presumptions may operate differently as a burden of proof, guiding the weighing of the indicators of an employment relationship in the context of typological method.

characterisation of the contract is open-textured under Greek case law and should take into consideration the actual performance of the contract. However, assuming that the cumulative structure of the presumption makes it improbable that a relationship of personal dependence will coexist with all four contractual entitlements,[59] then, in effect, the presumption **defines self-employment in the context of platform work**. This indirectly and negatively defines the legal concept of a 'platform worker'. The term 'definition' is used here not to imply that the legislator provided an ex-lege legal characterisation of the relationship,[60] but rather to indicate that the court may have to consider the certain elements of this 'definition' in order to characterise the relationship. This 'definition' is indirect and negative, as it does not define who is a platform worker under Greek law; instead, it describes who is not. This is in contrast to the contractual rights said to attach to a self-employed person performing platform work. Moreover, if we assume that the presumption is only triggered when the contractual terms on which it is based are met in practice, i.e. during the performance of the contract,[61] then the presumption becomes an even stronger definition of self-employment, since it would be even more difficult to rebut in that scenario. In this case, this legal 'definition' fails to consider the particular features of algorithmically managed employment relationships at platform level.

In conclusion, the presumption does not shift the burden of proof in favour of platform workers. It fails to consider how the contract is performed in practice. There is a risk that it will become a negatively formulated definition of the legal concept of 'platform worker' and, consequently, of dependence in the context of the gig economy. In doing so, it fails to take into consideration central features of platform work, such as algorithmic management. Therefore, it is fair to say that the legal classification of the relationship, and consequently the application of labour law to platform work in Greece, may come to depend on standard terms imposed unilaterally by the platform operator.[62] Normally, this would be justification enough to shift the burden of proof onto the platform.[63] 19

II. EU legal influences

1. Primacy of facts

In contrast to focusing on the contractual wording, like the Greek legislator did, 20
Art. 4(2) provides that the existence of an employment relationship is determined by the facts of how work is actually performed, regardless of how it is designated in any contractual agreement. The EU legislature tackles the tension between factual reality and the content of the contract. When applied to platform work, the Directive's facts-first, label-indifferent approach aligns with a labour law perspective that starts from the specific social reality[64] that the written terms are drafted unilaterally by the platform and imposed on the service provider, who has limited autonomy or scope for negotiation in decision-

59 Lixouriotis EfDD 2021, 216 (226).

60 Kazakos in Papadimitriou/Ladas, p. 85 (143).

61 Zografidis EErgD 2025, (899) 917.

62 Compare Kaisari EErgD 2021, 1079 (1115 et seq.); Kazakos EErgD 2023, 369 (417); Kazakos in Ladas/Papadimitriou, p. 85 (99, 134); Miskedakis in Papadimitriou, p. 165 (167); Travlos-Tzanetatos, p. 129 et seq.; Travlos-Tzanetatos EllDni 2021, 1608 (1610).

63 Kullmann ELLJ 2022, 66 (70).

64 Compare Travlos-Tzanetatos, p. 140; Travlos-Tzanetatos EErgD 2016, 1289 (1300); Kazakos in Ladas/Papadimitriou, p. 85 (92); Koukiadis, Labour Law, p. 416; Vergis EErgD 2023, 717 (720).

making.[65] Contract theory primarily considers a contract that has been negotiated and concluded properly by the parties involved. This paradigm is far removed from the atypical contractual relationships of service providers in the platform economy. The principle of freedom of contract is not always able to fairly balance the power asymmetries between platforms and workers.[66] Contract designs that circumvent mandatory labour law standards should be avoided.[67] That is why the EU legislator decided to include the so-called 'principle of primacy of facts' in the Directive.[68]

21 If Art. 4(2) is to be understood as meaning that the true common intention of the parties to agree on the rights and duties of an employment contract is evident from the facts relating to the performance of the work itself, which leads to the legal classification of the contract, then Greek case law should already fulfil the requirements for the implementation of Art. 4(2).[69]

22 According to established case law,[70] the legal classification of a contract depends on its actual content, as evidenced by its wording and practical implementation. If these contradict each other, it is the practical implementation that is decisive. The practical implementation of contractual relationships is the best way to determine the rights and duties assumed by the contracting parties, i.e. what they actually intended. The prevailing opinion in scholarship is also consistent with the doctrine of taking into account the facts relating to the actual performance of work.[71] Greek case law and theory thereby capture the mandatory legal regime for the employment contract, which cannot be contracted out of by drafting or design, once a particular agreement is performed as a contract of employment. The parties' common intention is examined as manifested in the actual performance of the relationship to identify the mutual rights and obligations from which the contract's legal characterisation is derived.[72] This could not differ from a primacy of facts as set out in Art. 4(2), unless the EU legislator intended to establish an absolute primacy of facts, attaching no importance to the common intention or will of the parties involved[73] (→ Art. 4 mn. 27–29).

[65] Cf. recital 27 Platform Work Directive ('contractual conditions are often unilaterally determined by one party').

[66] This is not a recent development in the context of employment. See Preis RdA 2019, 75 (78); Collins Ind. L. J. 1986, 1 et seqq.; Collins in Collins/Lester/Mantouvalou, p. 48 et seqq.

[67] Compare Papadimitriou in UoP/HCoA, p. 37 (38) (New technologies increase the existing opportunities for circumventing labour law).

[68] Cf. recital 27 Platform Work Directive ('The principle of primacy of facts').

[69] The diagnosis of Aloisi/Potocka-Sionek/Ratti CML Rev. 2025, 1407 (1415) that 'this principle is already well embedded in national legal systems' can, from the perspective of Greek case law, only be confirmed, if it means that the true will of the parties becomes evident based on how the contract is implemented in practice. The same cannot be true if the Directive were intended to establish an absolute primacy of facts, attaching no importance to the common intentions or the will of the parties involved.

[70] Areios Pagos (Supreme Court of Greece, AP) 626/2023 (NOMOS database); AP 1532/2021 (NOMOS); AP 884/2017, EErgD 2018, 42, (44); AP 1006/2017 (NOMOS); AP 22/2014, EErgD 2014, 349 (351); AP 994/2013, EErgD 2014, 273 (275); AP 1672/2010, EErgD 2011, 366 (367); AP (Plenary) 28/2005, EErgD 2005, 1441.

[71] Mpakopoulos, p. 198 et seqq.; Goulas EErgD 2022, 1299 (1328 et seq.); Sideris in Georgiadis, p. 1215 (1216); Giannakourou EErgD 2021, 983 (986); Zerdelis, Labour Law, p. 12; Zerdelis in Papadimitriou, p. 139 (148); Kazakos in Ladas/Papadimitriou, p. 85 (111) speaking of 'principle of the primacy of facts'; Dimarellis in Festschrift for Travlos-Tzanetatos, p. 151 (169); Vergis, EErgD 2021, 1025 (1030, 1043).

[72] This is a significant issue also in German labour law doctrine: Rolfs 74. djt I/B 2024, p. 14 et seqq.

[73] See, however, European Commission, Report Expert Group – Transposition of the Directive (EU) 2024/2831 on improving working conditions in platform work (12.1.2026), 27: 'The Commission services highlighted that Art. 4(2) regards the ascertainment of the existence of an employment relationship and that for that purpose the consideration of the facts must always prevail over the will of the parties.'.

2. Legal presumption in favour of the employment relationship

The Directive does not require a new definition of the concept of 'employee', nor specifically for platform work.[74] This may be why the Directive cannot through a legal presumption fully eliminate classification problems relating to the employment status of platform workers. Presumptions are not a game changer when it comes to accessing employee rights.[75] Nevertheless, Art. 5(1) requires a legal presumption in favour of the existence of an employment relationship. Platform workers who benefit from this presumption do not need to prove the existence of an employment relationship, i.e. facts indicating personal dependence under Greek case law. Instead, they must prove the prerequisites of the presumption, i.e. facts indicating direction and control. However, it should be noted that the difference between facts indicating personal dependence under Greek case law, which already lead to the recognition of employee status, and facts indicating direction and control under Art. 5(1), which trigger the employment presumption, may be very thin. This will present a significant challenge to the Greek legislator in terms of transposition. Once these facts are established, the court must presume that an employment relationship exists. It is then for the opposing party to prove that the presumed employment relationship does not exist, but that another legal relationship does. At the stage of rebuttal, the platform will have to prove to the court that personal dependence of the platform worker, as defined by national case law (albeit with consideration of CJEU case law), is not present. 23

Perhaps this is why it has been suggested in Greece that the presumption will not effectively improve the position of service providers via digital platforms.[76] The reference to facts indicating direction and control may be insufficient, and the traditional concept of dependence will ultimately be decisive.[77] In any case, the Directive cannot reclassify everyone who performs platform work as an employee, and it does not do so.[78] Nevertheless, the prevailing scholarly opinion has welcomed the presumption, noting that it is moving in the right direction.[79] According to Greek scholars, the transposition of Art. 5 must therefore result in the elimination of the Greek legal presumption against the existence of an employment contract in the context of platform work. 24

It has also been suggested that the Greek legislator could formulate some of the indicators of the criterion of hetero-determination as constituent elements of the presumption required by the Directive.[80] The reasoning behind this choice is clear and comprehensible, given that the Directive refers to facts indicating direction and control, and the presumption should provide a plausible basis for the presumed legal characterisation. This approach reflects the Directive's legislative technique, as it establishes a presumption based on facts indicating direction and control.[81] Heterodetermination is a defining 25

[74] See Aloisi/Potocka-Sionek/Ratti CML Rev. 2025, 1407 (1417) ('The Directive, therefore, does not standardize the employment classification in the platform work cases across EU Member States.'); Gräf ZFA 2023, 209 (214); Kocher NZA-RR 2024, 449 (452); Krause NZA 2022, 521 (527); Chandna-Hoppe ZEuP 2025, 9 (31 et seq.); Fischels/Sokoll NZA 2024, 721 (726).

[75] See Schubert in Giesen/Junker/Rieble, 2023, p. 69 (77, 85); Rosin Ind. L. J. 2022, 478 (491 et seq.); Kullmann ELLJ 2022, 66 (68).

[76] Skandalis DEE 2025, 450 (454 et seq.).

[77] Compare Kullmann's ELLJ 2022, 66 (77) view that 'Ultimately, however, a rebuttable legal presumption will not entail a material change to the EU definition of "worker" or the national definitions of the employment contract or relationship, but will involve an amendment of an evidentiary nature.'; Aloisi/Rainone/Countouris, p. 8, 12, 17.

[78] Aloisi/Potocka-Sionek/Ratti CML Rev. 2025, 1407 (1417).

[79] Kazakos in Ladas/Papadimitriou, p. 85 (138); Skandalis DEE 2025, 450 (454 et seq.).

[80] Skandalis DEE 2025, 450 (457).

[81] Compare Countouris/De Stefano ELLJ 2025, 432 (444).

feature of an employment contract and a criterion thereof. For this reason, its use as an element of the presumption should be framed in such a way that the presumption retains its specific procedural function. The conditions to be satisfied for the presumption of an employment relationship between the service provider and the platform should therefore not be understood as requiring a point for point replication of the criteria of the employee concept in the context of platform work.[82] Otherwise, a person performing platform work could, in substance, have to prove almost the same criteria in order to trigger the presumption as would be required to establish the employment contract directly.[83] In this case, the Directive's requirement that the presumption must operate as a 'procedural facilitation for the benefit of persons performing platform work'[84] could lose some of its practical effect[85] (see also → Art. 5 mn. 5 et seq.).

III. Need for transposition

26 The Greek legal presumption against the existence of a contract of employment (Art. 69(2) L. 4808/2021) is incompatible with the Directive.[86] The presumption is misguided because it does not favour the existence of a contract of employment and, at best, leaves the service provider in the same position[87] and is based on the wrong subject matter: contractual clauses rather than the factual performance of work. The other existing general legal presumption in favour of an employment relationship (the nine-month rule) can be retained as a matter of national law.[88] The Directive-specific platform-work presumption would then operate as a lex specialis, resolving platform-work disputes. Although Art. 5(3) excludes the Directive's presumption from tax, criminal and social-security proceedings unless national law extends it (→ Art. 5 mn. 24), a separate question remains whether Art. 4 nonetheless requires appropriate and effective procedures based on the primacy of facts also in those areas (→ Art. 4 mn. 9–15).

27 The Greek legislator has a range of options when designing preconditions of the presumption.[89] Under the current rule on platform work, the legislator simply adopted the

[82] Wank EuZW 2023, 747 (751); De Stefano ILLe-J 2022, 1 (3 et seq.); Aloisi/Rainone/Countouris, p. 14 et seq.; Krause NZA 2022, 521 (528).

[83] Compare Greiner/Baumann ZESAR 2023, 409 (415) (The burden of proof for the criteria that trigger the presumption remains in any case with the service providers).

[84] See Art. 5(2), first sentence Platform Work Directive ('effective rebuttable legal presumption of an employment relationship that constitutes a procedural facilitation for the benefit of persons performing platform work.'); cf. recital 31 Platform Work Directive.

[85] Compare European Commission, Report Expert Group – Transposition of the Directive (EU) 2024/2831 on improving working conditions in platform work (12.1.2026), 31.

[86] So too the prevailing opinion in Greece: Skandalis DEE 2025, 450 (455 et seq.); Kazakos in Ladas/Papadimitriou, p. 85 (138); Travlos-Tzanetatos EllDni 2021, 1608 (1621); Theodosis in Stylianidis, p. 452 (457); Zografidis, 'Implementing the Presumption of Employment of the Platform Work Directive' (Global Workplace Law & Policy 23.04.2025) <https://global-workplace-law-and-policy.kluwerlawonline.com/implementing-the-presumption-of-employment-of-the-platform-work-directive> (last accessed: 15.08.2025).

[87] The Platform Work Directive requires 'effective procedural facilitation': See Art. 5(2); cf. recitals (14), (25), (30) ('effective procedural facilitation').

[88] Art. 1(1) L. 2639/1998 as substituted by Art. 1 L. 3846/2010 ('An agreement between an employer and a person engaged for the provision of services or the execution of result-based works, for a fixed or an indefinite term—in particular in cases of piece-rate remuneration, telework, or home-based work—shall be presumed to amount, in substance, to a contract of employment where the work is performed personally, exclusively or predominantly for the same employer for nine (9) consecutive months.').

[89] Compare European Commission, Report Expert Group – Transposition of the Directive (EU) 2024/2831 on improving working conditions in platform work (12.1.2026), 30–31.

case-specific criteria used in *Yodel*[90] (→ Art. 5 mn. 20) and, in effect, created a 'definition' of a self-employed 'platform worker', which was enacted as a legal presumption. Accordingly, when implementing Art. 5 of the Platform Work Directive, one plausible and Directive-conforming transposition option would be to link the presumption closely to the Directive-specific notion of 'digital labour platform' itself (Art. 2(1)(a)) and its organisational features.[91] A relationship can be rebuttably presumed to be an employment relationship if a service is provided via a digital labour platform, at least in part at a distance by electronic means and at the request of a recipient. This must involve the organisation of work performed by individuals in return for payment, as well as the use of automated monitoring or automated decision-making systems. Such an organisation of work, which is primarily assessed by reference to actual performance, including automated monitoring and decision-making systems, is to be treated as indicating 'direction and control' within the meaning of Art. 5(1). Genuine, purely intermediary portals are not covered[92] due to the lack of the organisational element required, because they merely provide the means by which service providers can reach the end-users (→ Art. 2 mn. 18 et seqq.). Another reason to support such an implementation is that platforms have proven to be 'institutional chameleons',[93] capable of adapting their direction and control mechanisms in response to changes in the regulatory frameworks.

Grounding the presumption in the organisational element renders the legal characterisation plausible without exhausting the concept of an employee. It strikes a fair balance: The operator can effectively rebut the presumption by proving that the characterisation is incorrect and identifying an alternative legal relationship. The service provider should not be required to establish evidential requirements so burdensome that the presumption loses its function as a procedural facilitation (→ Art. 5 mn. 5 et seq.). 28

D. Algorithmic management

The national provisions that introduced the first statutory framework on digital labour platforms to the Greek legal order contain no specific regulation of algorithmic management (→ Preliminary remarks to Art. 7–12 mn. 29–37).[94] In contrast, a subsequent statute on emerging information and communication technologies[95] imposes pre- 29

[90] ECJ 22.4.2020 – case C-692/19, ECLI:EU:C:2020:288 – B v Yodel. See Patsourakis DEN 2020, 809 (813 et seq.); Patsourakis in Ladas, p. 639 (684).

[91] Compare Kocher's NZA-RR 2024, 449 (452) similar proposal for Germany. This approach may equate to an unconditional presumption of employment in platform work: compare Kocher, 'A Timid Proposal: Employment Status in the Proposal for an EU Directive on Improving Working Conditions in Platform Work' (Verfassungsblog 18.7.2023) <https://verfassungsblog.de/a-timid-proposal/> (last accessed: 15.8.2025) ('But why condition the presumption at all?'); Zografidis, 'Implementing the Presumption of Employment of the Platform Work Directive' (Global Workplace Law & Policy 23.4.2025) <https://global-workplace-law-and-policy.kluwerlawonline.com/implementing-the-presumption-of-employment-of-the-platform-work-directive> (last accessed: 15.08.2025).

[92] Kocher, 'A Timid Proposal: Employment Status in the Proposal for an EU Directive on Improving Working Conditions in Platform Work' (Verfassungsblog 18.07.2023) <https://verfassungsblog.de/a-timid-proposal/> (last accessed: 15.08.2025); Krause NZA 2022, 521 (524).

[93] About this adaptability: Aloisi/Potocka-Sionek/Ratti CML Rev. 2025, 1407 (1421); Hießl ILLe-J 2022, 13 (25); Krause NZA 2022, 521 (529).

[94] Art. 68–72 L. 4808/2021; see also Zerdelis, Labour Law, p. 49; Zerdelis in Papadimitriou, p. 139 (164).

[95] Art. 9(1)–(2) L. 4961/2022 – 'Obligation to inform about the use of artificial intelligence in the field of employment

1. Every private-sector undertaking which uses an artificial-intelligence system that affects any decision-making process concerning workers or job applicants and has an impact on working conditions, selection, recruitment or evaluation shall, in any event prior to its first use, provide each worker or job applicant with adequate and clear information, which shall include at a minimum the parameters on

use transparency where an AI system affects decision-making about employees or job applicants and extends that duty to digital platforms,[96] covering both employees and independent contractors.

30 This provision, though, only partially meets the requirements of the Directive.[97] Under Greek law, the 'parameters' of an AI system must be disclosed only once prior to its first use.[98] Consequently, it does not establish a duty to give case-specific reasons when a concrete decision affects a worker. The EU legislature, however, mandates per-decision rights (→ Art. 11 mn. 2–6). Nor does Greek law provide a right of access to a designated human contact person to discuss and clarify the facts, circumstances, and reasons for the decision. One point of alignment is the personal scope: Greek law extends the transparency duty to platforms in respect of employees and independent contractors.[99] This extension is therefore compatible, but the per-decision rights remain missing.

31 These provisions are useful as horizontal transparency clauses, but they are far from sufficient to transpose Chapter III of the Directive. Greece will require new, platform-specific provisions[100] that (i) extend coverage to all automated systems used by digital labour platforms and to all persons performing platform work irrespective of contractual label; (ii) add the Directive's content, timing and recipient requirements for transparency; and (iii) create rights to per-decision explanation and written reasons, access to a designated human reviewer, binding deadlines, rectification or compensation, and adverse decisions taken by human. The transposition rules on algorithmic management must be drafted in technologically neutral terms, referring to 'automated monitoring systems' and 'automated decision-making systems' and should not be tied to the technology-sector notion of 'artificial intelligence' (→ Preliminary remarks to Art. 7–12 mn. 14).

32 For completeness, note that national law[101] provides an institutional basis for information and consultation on 'new technologies' and 'methods of control',[102] but it does not guarantee the explicit timing and scope of information required by the Directive,[103] and does not expressly extend to representatives of non-employee persons performing platform work.[104] Likewise, national law[105] lays down horizontal conditions for exclusively automated individual decisions and prohibits discriminatory profiling. However, being rooted in the law-enforcement data-protection regime,[106] it cannot substitute for

which the decision-making is based. This is without prejudice to cases requiring prior information and consultation, and the undertaking shall ensure compliance with the principle of equal treatment and the prohibition of discrimination in employment and work on grounds of sex, race, colour, national or ethnic origin, descent, religious or other beliefs, disability or chronic illness, age, family or social status, sexual orientation, gender identity or sex characteristics.

2. The obligation in paragraph 1 also applies to digital platforms within the meaning of Art. 68 of Law 4808/2021 [...], in respect of natural persons connected with them by contracts of employment or by contracts for independent services or for work.'

[96] Art. 9(2) L. 4961/2022 cross-referring to Art. 68 L. 4808/2021.

[97] Especially of Art. 11 Platform Work Directive.

[98] See Theodosis in Stylianidis, p. 452 (458).

[99] Similarly, Art. 11 Platform Work Directive applies to 'persons performing platform work' (employee or not).

[100] Similarly, Skandalis DEE 2025, 450 (462).

[101] Art. 12 L. 1767/1988.

[102] See Theodosis in Stylianidis, p. 452 (458).

[103] Art. 13–14 Platform Work Directive.

[104] Art. 15 Platform Work Directive.

[105] Art. 52 L. 4624/2019.

[106] Theodosis in Stylianidis, p. 452 (458).

the Directive's sector-specific labour obligations (→ Preliminary remarks to Art. 7–12 mn. 45–53, 70–77).[107]

Under Greek law, digital labour platforms are subject to the same duties of care, health and safety in respect of providers as if those providers were employees, irrespective of the contractual nature of the relationship.[108] Self-employed persons providing platform-based delivery or transport work are entitled, given the special features of that relationship, monetary substitution for a protective helmet and payment of a 15% uplift on the statutory minimum wage where own equipment is used.[109] For transposition, these provisions should be specified to address risks from automated monitoring and automated decision-making systems (including psychosocial/ergonomic risks) and to require regular, participatory risk assessments and preventive measures (→ Art. 12 mn. 1–4).[110] 33

Before services commence, platforms must, under the same domestic legal framework,[111] give service providers, irrespective of the nature of their contractual relationship, a copy of the contract, which must state inter alia the characteristics of the services, collective-organisation rights, the platform's health-and-safety obligations, and the data-protection measures the platform adopts for providers' personal data. This is a general, information duty; it does not secure per-decision explanations, access to a designated human contact, binding timelines, or rectification and compensation after adverse automated decisions. Targeted transposition is needed to add the content, timing and recipient requirements of the Directive.[112] 34

E. Collective rights

Under national law, service providers engaged by digital platforms through independent service contracts enjoy comparable trade union rights to employees. They can establish organisations to call and conduct strikes[113] and conclude collective agreements.[114] The domestic legislature has extended these rights to persons performing platform work, even if they are not party to an employment contract. Despite the absence of an employment contract, the Greek legislature considers this category of providers to be working in conditions requiring protection similar to that afforded to employees.[115] These provisions therefore could be seen as recognising the existence of an **intermediate** 35

[107] Art. 7–12 Platform Work Directive.

[108] Art. 71 L. 4808/2021. See also Skandalis DEE 2025, 450 (466); Zerdelis in Papadimitriou, p. 139 (163).

[109] Art. 71(2) L. 4808/2021 extends the rights laid down in Art. 56 L. 4611/2019 to platform service providers.

[110] Art. 12 Platform Work Directive.

[111] Art. 72 L. 4808/2021.

[112] Art. 9–11 Platform Work Directive.

[113] As regards the right to strike, the familiar procedural framework of Art. 19–22 L. 1264/1982 (prior notice, safety/minimum-service requirements, prohibition of lock-outs and strike-breakers, and expedited judicial proceedings) applies mutatis mutandis.

[114] Art. 70 L. 4808/2021.

[115] Art. 70(3) L. 4808/2021 cross-refers to Art. 1(2) L. 1876/1990, which permits collective agreements covering those natural persons, who are considered as a third category between employees and the self-employed.

category[116] between employees and self-employed persons, the economically dependent self-employed platform workers.[117]

36 Much of this framework remains theoretical.[118] For example, the Greek legislature introduced the possibility for economically dependent service providers without an employment contract to conclude collective agreements in 1990, but this has not yet been utilised.[119] This is not only a problem in Greece, but in many Member States.[120] Although the law permits platform service providers to unionise, strike and bargain collectively,[121] such permission alone may not necessarily fulfil the requirements of Art. 25 of the Directive to promote the role of social partners and encourage collective bargaining in platform work. These provisions should be coupled with a clear and detailed institutional framework for the representation of persons engaged via platforms.[122] Without such a framework, these rights risk remaining merely formal, which may not fulfil the obligation to 'promote' and 'encourage' collective bargaining in platform work. Moreover, according to the prevailing opinion in Greek scholarship, any statutory extension of collective bargaining rights to platform workers should be confined to solo self-employed persons or those who are economically dependent, in order to minimise concerns regarding Art. 101 TFEU.[123]

F. Results

37 In Greek labour law scholarship, the criteria of 'personal dependence' or 'subordination' are being adapted through interpretation and development in line with labour law's goals, particularly in view of the new social reality of platform work. The focus is shifting from managerial prerogative, binding instructions and directions, to the broader **concept of the heterodetermination of work**, which is understood as combining elements of the criteria of integration into the organisational structure of the platform, as well as the missing assumption of entrepreneurial risks and opportunities on the part of the platform worker. Greek case law has not yet clarified its position

[116] See Vergis EErgD 2021, 1025 on third categories from the point of view of English law; Skandalis DEE 2025, 450 (452). See also Zerdelis in Ladas/Papadimitriou, p. 47 (58); Zerdelis in Papadimitriou, p. 139 (157); Koukiadis, Individual and collective labour law, p. 105; Lampropoulos DEE 2022, 1038 (1045 et seq.); compare Travlos-Tzanetatos, EllDni 2021, 1608 (1616); Vergis EErgD 2023, 717 (724 et seq.); Giannakourou EErgD 2021, 983 (993); Palli EErgD 2021, 1015 (1016).

[117] Compare Koukiadis, Labour Law, p. 232; Zerdelis, Labour Law, p. 48 et seqq.; Zerdelis EErgD 2023, 667 (674); Kaisari EErgD 2021, 1079 (1119); Skandalis in Ladas/Papadimitriou, p. 225 (229 et seq.).

[118] Due to various constraints imposed by legal and practical obstacles, compare Aloisi/Potocka-Sionek/Ratti CML Rev. 2025, 1407 (1430 et seq.).

[119] Art. 1(2) L. 1876/1990. See Lixouriotis EfDD 2021, 216 (222); Koukiadis, Labour Law, p. 423; Zerdelis in Papadimitriou, p. 139 (156 et seq.).

[120] Eurofound (2022), Regulating minimum wages and other forms of pay for the self-employed, Publications Office of the European Union, Luxembourg, p. 53 et seqq.

[121] Art. 70 L. 4808/2021.

[122] Similarly Skandalis DEE 2025, 450 (465), correctly noting that the rights provided for by Greek law are consistent with Article 25 of the Directive; to similar effect, see Patsourakis in Ladas, p. 639 (688 et seqq.), who sets out domestically relevant legal mechanisms for the practical implementation of the rights provided for.

[123] European Commission, 'Guidelines on the application of Union competition law to collective agreements regarding the working conditions of solo self-employed persons', 30.9.2022; Cf. recital 29 Platform Work Directive; Ladas DEE 2021, 749 (757); Skandalis DEE 2025, 450 (465); Skandalis in Ladas/Papadimitriou, p. 225 (239); Zerdelis, Labour Law, p. 46 et seq.; Zerdelis in Papadimitriou, p. 139 (163); Travlos-Tzanetatos, EllDni 2021, 1608 (1616 et seqq.); to similar effect Patsourakis in Ladas, p. 639 (690 et seq.); in general for the limits that competition law imposes on collective bargaining see Rainone/Countouris, passim; Aloisi/Potocka-Sionek/Ratti CML Rev. 2025, 1407 (1429).

on platform work from a labour law perspective. Overall, the EU legislator points in the same direction as the prevailing opinion in Greek scholarship regarding the legal characterisation of platform work.[124] Although the concept of personal dependence is not legally defined, the legislator has adopted a presumption against the existence of an employment contract that might amount to a negatively framed definition of employee status in platform work. Amending domestic law is therefore necessary. Nevertheless, the view that existing employment relationship rules or concepts like dependence are not fit for purpose at all when it comes to platform work is too far-reaching.[125] Even in the digital world of work, **the issues at stake are traditional ones**, as the fundamental conflict between capital and labour persists.[126] With appropriate interpretation and development, existing concepts can address most of the issues associated with platform work while still respecting the intentions of the – democratically legitimised – national legislator. Additionally, the Directive addresses legal loopholes and corrects market failures in this area.

In Greece as in other Member States, it is only through an employment contract that all protections of labour law come into full effect. However, platform work legislation has emphasised once again that labour law provisions may sometimes not depend on the employment contract.[127] Recent national legislation on collective rights and health and safety in platform work is moving the legal framework away from labour law structured around the employment contract. New sub-fields structured around work via digital platforms cover also self-employed persons whom the legislature deems to be in need of selective protection under some labour laws with different levels of benefits **beyond the binary divide** in the employment context.[128] This reflects the fact that the practical scope of the employment contract has shifted in recent years alongside the growth of the platform economy, and that existing legislation is not fully responsive. This development elevates civil-law contracts, creating a third category of individuals positioned between employees and the self-employed who are granted only a subset of the rights enjoyed by employees. Similarly, EU legislation cuts across the traditional national **taxonomy of contract types**[129] and aims to protect persons performing platform work to some extent, regardless of their contractual classification. The concept of employment is becoming more pragmatic, addressing protection gaps regardless of national contract form systematics. 38

124 Cf. recital 3 Platform Work Directive ('prohibiting the abuse of atypical contracts'); recital 4 ('power imbalances'); recital 7 ('platforms exercise de facto direction and control over those persons, often integrating them into their main business activities'); recital 25 ('to combat false self-employment'); recital 30 ('Direction and control can take different forms […] platform economy model is constantly evolving. […] not only by direct means but also by applying punitive measures or other forms of adverse treatment or pressure.').

125 To similar effect Aloisi/Potocka-Sionek/Ratti CML Rev. 2025, 1407 (1435, 1443): 'resilience of the (broadly understood) concept of subordination in the context of digital and highly atypical work arrangements'; Schubert in Giesen/Junker/Rieble, p. 69 (89) (Existing concepts can cover platform work).

126 Preis RdA 2019, 75 (86).

127 Compare Aloisi/Potocka-Sionek/Ratti CML Rev. 2025, 1407 (1443) ('beyond the scope of traditional labour legislation'). Several scholars have already argued for decoupling the scope of labour law from the contract of employment, see for example Fudge Osgoode Hall Law Journal 2006, 609 (634); from the perspective of CJEU case law Menegatti ELLJ 2020, 26 (40 et seqq.). See also Kocher's NZA-RR 2024, 449 (451 et seqq.) criticism of the traditional legal systematics of contract forms.

128 On a selective protection of certain groups under some labour laws with different levels of benefits beyond the binary divide in the employment context, compare Davidov OJLS 2014, 543 (553 et seq., 556).

129 Compare Simitis 1994, p. 1097 (1099) (The national approach could be curbed as part of the Europeanisation of labour law).

Italy*

Literature: Ales, 'Article 27 CFREU. Workers' right to information and consultation within the undertaking' in Ales/Bell/Deinert/Robin-Olivier (eds), International and European Labour Law. Article by Article Commentary, Baden-Baden 2018, p. 214; Ales, 'Protecting Work in the Digital Transformation: Rethinking the Typological Approach in the Intrinsically Triangular Relationship Perspective, in Ales/Curzi/Fabbri/Rymkevich/Senatori/Solinas, Working in Digital and Smart Organizations. Legal, Economic and Organizational Perspectives on the Digitalization of Labour Relations, Cham 2018, p. 11; Ales, 'In favore dell'etero-organizzazione come "concetto" autonomo: timeo danos et remedia ferentes', Massimario di giurisprudenza del lavoro (MGL) special issue 2020, 19; Aimo, 'Trasparenza algoritmica nel lavoro su piattaforma: quali spazi per i diritti collettivi nella proposta di direttiva in discussione?', Lavoro Diritti Europa (LDE) 2024, 2; Aimo, 'Dalle schedature dei lavoratori alla profilazione tramite algoritmi: serve ancora l'art. 8 dello Statuto dei lavoratori?', Lavoro e Diritto (LD) 2018, 585; Bellavista, 'Il nuovo art. 4 dello Statuto dei Lavoratori' in Zilio Grandi/Biasi (eds), Commentario breve alla riforma "Jobs Act", Padova 2016, p. 717; Biasi, 'La salute e la sicurezza dei riders al tempo del Covid-19', Diritto delle Relazioni Industriali (DRI) 2020, 841; Brino, 'Il lavoro attraverso piattaforma digitale: profili regolativi emergenti e questioni aperte', in Amoroso/Di Cerbo/ Maresca (eds), Diritto del lavoro, Milano 2025, p. 1146; Carinci/Giudici/Perri, 'Obblighi di informazione e sistemi decisionali e di monitoraggio automatizzati (art. 1-bis "Decreto Trasparenza"): quali forme di controllo per i poteri datoriali algoritmici?', Labor (L) 2023, 7; Corti, La partecipazione dei lavoratori. La cornice europea e l'esperienza comparata, Vita e pensiero, Milan 2012; Dagnino, 'Il diritto interno: i sistemi decisionali e di monitoraggio (integralmente) automatizzati tra trasparenza e coinvolgimento' in Biasi (ed), Diritto del lavoro e intelligenza artificiale, Milan 2024, 147; Delfino, 'Lavoro mediante piattaforme digitali, dialogo sociale europeo e partecipazione sindacale', Federalismi.it (F) 2023, 174; Donini, 'Profilazione reputazionale e tutela del lavoratore: la parola al Garante della Privacy', Labour & Law Issues (LLI) 2017, 35; Faioli, 'Trasparenza e monitoraggio digitale. Perché abbiamo smesso di capire la norma sociale europea', Federalismi.it (F) 2022, 104; Falsone, 'What Impact Will the Proposed EU Directive on Platform Work Have on the Italian System?', Italian Labour Law e Journal (ILLeJ) 2022, 99; Ferraro, 'Collaborazione coordinata e obbligo di sicurezza del committente', AmbienteDiritto (AD) 2023,1; Ingrao, Il controllo a distanza sui lavoratori e la nuova disciplina privacy: una lettura integrata, Bari 2018; Lazzari, 'Gig economy e tutela della salute e sicurezza sul lavoro: Prime considerazioni a partire dal «caso Foodora', Rivista del Diritto della Sicurezza Sociale (RDSS) 2018, 455; Lunardon (ed), Informazione, consultazione e partecipazione dei lavoratori, Milano 2008; Menegatti, 'The Evolving Concept of "worker" in EU law', Italian Labour Law e Journal (IlLLeJ) 2019, 71; Nogler, 'La subordinazione nel d.lgs. n. 81 del 2015: alla ricerca dell'"autorità del punto di vista giuridico", Argomenti di diritto del lavoro (ADL) 2016, 47; Otto, 'A step towards digital self- & co-determination in the context of algorithmic management systems', Italian Labour Law e Journal (ILLeJ) 2022, 51; Pascucci, 'Note sul futuro del lavoro salubre e sicuro... e sulle norme sulla sicurezza di rider & co', DSL 2019, 37; Perulli, 'The legal and jurisprudential evolution of the notion of employee', ELLJ 2020, 117; Perulli, Oltre la subordinazione. La nuova tendenza espansiva del diritto del lavoro, Turin 2021; Purificato/Senatori, 'The Position of Collective Rights in the "Platform Work" Directive Proposal: Commission v Parliament', Hungarian Labour Law e-Journal (HLLeJ) 2023, 1; Recchia, 'Condizioni di lavoro trasparenti, prevedibili e giustiziabili: quando il diritto di informazione sui sistemi automatizzati diventa uno strumento di tutela collettiva', LLI 2023, C.34; Rota, 'La tutela prevenzionistica dei riders nella legge n. 128/20190', Labour & Law Issues (LLI) 2020, 62; Sartori, Il controllo tecnologico sui lavoratori. La nuova disciplina italiana tra vincoli sovranazionali e modelli comparati, Turin 2020; Senatori, Rappresentanza collettiva dei lavoratori e ordinamento europeo. La prospettiva dei diritti fondamentali, Turin 2018; Spinelli, 'Industrial Relations Practices in the Digital Transition: What Role for the Social Partners?', Diritti Lavori Mercati International (DLM.int) 2024, 461; Trojsi, 'The confirmed, indeed reinforced, Centrality of the GDPR for the Protection of Workers' Personal Rights in the light of subsequent EU Legislative Acts', Italian Labour Law e-Journal (ILLeJ) 2024, 355; Zoli, 'I diritti di informazione e di c.d. consultazione: il d.lgs. 6 febbraio 2007, n. 25', Rivista italiana di diritto del lavoro (RIDL) 2008, 161.

* The report is the result of a shared reflection by the authors, however, the paragraph lett. A) can be attributed to Edoardo Ales, paragraph lett. B) to Iacopo Senatori, paragraph lett. C), no. I,II,III to Federica Palmirotta, and paragraph lett. C), no. IV to Ilaria Purificato.

A. Introduction

1 Decree-law 3 September 2019, n. 101, as converted into law by Act 2 November 2019, n. 128, amended Legislative decree 15 June 2015, n. 81 by introducing a Chapter V-bis (Art. 1(1)(c)). In that Chapter, for the first time, the Italian legal order was confronted with the issues of platform work protection, although with specific, if not exclusive reference, to delivery services, provided by self-employed. Art. 1(1)(a)(2) Decree-law n. 101/2019 also provided the extension of the personal scope of application of the regulation concerning hetero-organised autonomous collaboration to platform work, consequently enjoying the same protection of subordinate workers.

2 Art. 11 Act 13 June 2025, n. 91 (2025 European Delegation Act), delegates the Government to implement the Platform Work Directive[1] by laying down principles that refers to: the adjustment of Chapter V-bis, there included the definition of digital labour platforms; the provision of effective procedure to guarantee the proper qualification of the legal and contractual status of platform workers, to be intended in a broad sense, also including self-employed workers, for the purpose of this paragraph; the introduction of an adequate data protection system in case platforms resort to algorithmic management; the provision of information to platform workers, their representatives and public authorities, if needed, on algorithmic management; the adoption of algorithmic management decision-making mechanisms monitoring and control systems; the adjustment of the occupational safety and health regulation to platform workers; the provisions of transparent information on working conditions to platform workers.

3 Those are the topics that will be addressed in the following paragraphs.

B. Employment status

4 The purpose of improving the working conditions in platform work, as stated by the Platform Work Directive (→ Art. 1 mn. 25–27), has been pursued in Italy through a **combination of judicial action** on provisions of general application and **sectoral legislative** interventions specifically targeting the phenomenon[2].

5 The key reference, in this regard, is Art. 2 Legislative Decree n. 81/2015, which provides for the application of subordinate work provisions to any individual providing services under a coordinated self-employment contract performed personally and on a continuous basis, whose performance is organised by the client, without any codetermination of work patterns, including place and time of execution (so called '**hetero-organisation**'). As already mentioned, that provision has been subsequently amended by Decree-

[1] With regard to the interpretation of the Directive, it should be noted that the Expert Group on the transposition of the Platform Work Directive has recently published a report, see European Commission, Report Expert Group – Transposition of the Directive (EU) 2024/2831 on improving working conditions in platform work (12.1.2026).

[2] Brino, in Amoroso/Di Cerbo/Maresca, p. 1146.

law n. 101/2019, which extends its scope to platform work by clarifying that it also applies when the contractor organises the performance through digital platforms[3].

Judges have frequently relied on this provision to bypass the stalemates and loopholes of the classification procedure, whose established criteria are poorly suited to the specificities and nuances of work performed through the mediation of a digital platform. **6**

Initially, case-law that addressed the employment status of platform workers (namely food delivery riders) classified them as independent contractors, based on their **freedom to refuse the tasks** assigned by the platform, which was considered incompatible with the employee's subordination to the managerial prerogative as defined by Art. 2094 of the Civil Code.[4] **7**

The potential of the notion of hetero-organisation, as devised in Art. 2 Legislative Decree n. 81/15, became clear in later judgments. While maintaining that platform workers are self-employed, the courts held that the specific modalities of how their work was organised (like the unilateral assignment by the client of the deliveries and the corresponding scheduling) qualified them as hetero-organised, hence granting those workers all the protections afforded to subordinate employees.[5] In this way, the workers' freedom to refuse an assignment, which is a key argument in favour of the classification of such workers as self-employed, becomes irrelevant. As the Court of Cassation held in in a landmark ruling, the autonomy exists only in the formative phase of the agreement but not in the functional phase, concerning the execution of the performance, and this is enough to meet the criteria set out in Art. 2.[6] **8**

However, other courts, especially in more recent cases, have opted plainly for the classification of platform workers as employees. Notably, this line of jurisprudence advocates a **'modernisation' of the concept of subordinate worker** under Art. 2094 of the Civil Code, to adapt it to the forms of the work performance enabled by the new technologies, which often involve a more subtle and opaque exercise of the managerial prerogatives.[7] In particular, the courts, also drawing from the (more extensive)[8] notion of worker elaborated by the **Court of Justice of the EU**,[9] noted that the combination of remote surveillance and algorithmic management enables platforms to exercise the typical forms of direction, control and even disciplinary power that characterise subordinate employment, despite the merely formal and fictitious autonomy granted to the workers. **9**

Against such background, while it can be argued that the Italian legislator has established a solid way to grant adequate protections to platform workers, regardless of their classification as employees,[10] the lack of consistency of judicial approaches to the classification of platform workers as employees or independent (albeit hetero-organised) contractors testifies that the legal system still lacks the 'measures to facilitate the determination of the correct employment status of persons performing platform work' required by the Directive (→ Art. 1(1)(a) mn. 28–32). **10**

---

[3] With regard to the relationships that may arise among the various parties involved, Ales in Ales et al., p. 11, refers to a trilateral work relationship, not comparable to agency work, to capture the growing empowerment of clients, which may extend to their active participation in the design and production of the goods or services provided by the business.

[4] Trib. Turin 7.5.2018, n. 778.

[5] Court of Appeal Turin 4.2.2019; Trib. Milan, 19.10.2023.

[6] Court of Cassation 24.1.2020, n. 1663.

[7] Trib. Turin 18.11.2021.

[8] Menegatti ILLeJ 2019, 71.

[9] Trib. Milan 28.09.2023.

[10] It is worth mentioning in this regard the set of special protections afforded to platform workers that do not fall under the category of hetero-organisation by Art. 47-*bis* et seq. Legislative decree n. 81/15.

11 To be more specific, the Italian system appears to comply with only some of the requirements set out in the Directive in respect of the correct determination of the employment status of platform workers. The requirement that judicial scrutiny on the existence of an employment relationship should be guided by the '**primacy of facts**', as stipulated by the Platform Work Directive (→ Art. 4 mn. 27–29) is a well-established principle of Italian labour law, constantly upheld by the courts including in the aforementioned cases concerning platform work. In this sense, the procedures currently in place in Italy to determine a workers' correct employment status could be considered as 'appropriate and effective' (→ Art. 4 mn. 22–26), especially insofar as the recent rulings, as it was mentioned above, have shown the inclination of the judges to take into consideration the case-law of the Court of Justice of the EU and to assess the factual circumstances also in the light of the use by the platform of automated monitoring and decision-making systems.

12 The same cannot be said with regard to the **legal presumption** that the Directive requires to put into place (→ Art. 5 mn. 4 et seqq.).[11]

13 The view that the mechanism set out in Art. 2 Legislative Decree n. 81/15 constitutes a presumption of employment status has been authoritatively supported in the scholarship,[12] but it has not been endorsed by the Court of Cassation in the first decision in which it ruled on the employment status of platform workers.[13] The Court characterises Art. 2 as a '**remedial provision**', whose purpose is to circumvent the limitations of the procedures for the determination of the employment status. This approach has been strongly criticised by some legal scholars, particularly for its failure to identify the elements that distinguish the concept of hetero-direction, that characterises subordinate employment, from that of hetero-organisation.[14] However, viewed from the Court's perspective, Art. 2 represents a regulatory approach that diverges from the one adopted by the Directive: the latter still based on the traditional dichotomy between subordination and autonomy, the former pursuing the expansion of labour law through the 'annexation'[15] of certain areas of self-employment.

14 However, even if one accepts the argument that Art. 2 sets out a presumption mechanism, this presumption does not allow for a **rebuttal by the presumed employer**.[16] As a result, it cannot be considered consistent with the requirements of the Directive.

15 Furthermore, Art. 2 provides for a series of **exemptions** from the application of labour law protections to hetero-organised workers, which appear inherently incompatible with the Directive, which does not authorise such exemptions. They concern activities carried out in specific sectors and, more significantly, cases in which collective agreements provide for specific employment conditions in light of the particular productive and organisational needs of the sector. To the extent that this provision authorises collective agreements to derogate from the (alleged) legal presumption, it constitutes a clear violation of the requirement that collective agreements aimed at improving the employment conditions of genuine self-employed persons performing platform work shall not undermine the correct classification of persons performing platform work with regard to their employment status (recital 29).

---

[11] A different view is expressed by Falsone ILLeJ 2022, 99 (104).

[12] Nogler ADL 2016, 47 (60). For a different view, more aligned with the prevalent judicial interpretation; Perulli ELLJ 2020, 71 (127).

[13] Court of Cassation 24.1.2020, n. 1663. The Court reaffirmed its position in the subsequent ruling of 31.10.2025, n. 28772.

[14] Ales MGL 2020, 19 (20).

[15] Perulli ELLJ 2020, 117 (126).

[16] Nogler ADL 2016, 47 (60).

An alternative approach to complying with the required legal presumption could be found in the method traditionally employed by courts to determine the existence of an employment relationship in cases where the exercise of managerial prerogatives of direction and control can not be clearly demonstrated. In such instances, the courts rely on **subsidiary factual elements** that can presumptively indicate the existence of an employment relationship: a technique often referred to as the '**typological method**'.[17] However, aside from the circumstance that the application of this method is not mandatory for the judges, the main impediment to its use is that the factual elements typically considered by the courts, such as the stable integration into the organisational structure of the company, regular working hours, and exclusivity of the work relationship, do not adequately capture the distinctive features of work performed through digital platforms. Nevertheless, this should not preclude the courts from re-elaborating their interpretative parameters to the emerging forms of employment, particularly given that, according to the Commission, the Directive does not require national legislators to explicitly predetermine the applicable presumptive criteria.[18] 16

In light of these considerations, Art. 11 Act n. 91/2025 provides very broad delegation principles to the government on the matter. 17

Under Art. 11(1)(c), the Act commits the government to 'identify appropriate and effective procedures to verify and ensure the correct classification of the employment status of individuals performing work through digital platforms'. However, it does not clarify whether these procedures should include a codified legal presumption: the element which, as stated above, represents the main gap in the current Italian legal framework with respect to the requirements set out in the Directive. 18

Art. 11(1)(a) authorises the government to introduce all the necessary amendments, additions and repeals to ensure the full and correct implementation of the Directive and expressly identifies Chapter V-*bis* Legislative Decree n. 81/15 as the primary focus of the legislative intervention. 19

That piece of legislation was introduced by the already mentioned Decree-law n. 101/2019 with the aim of providing minimum protections to riders who do not fall within the category of 'hetero-organised' workers, as they provided services only on a casual basis.[19] The wording of Art. 11(1)(a), suggests that the intention of the legislator is to make Chapter V-*bis* the central framework for the specific regulation of platform work in Italy. 20

Indeed, this approach would seem more reasonable than amending Art. 2 Legislative Decree n. 81/15, given that this latter provision covers a range of employment situations broader than platform work only. However, this gives rise to a possible paradox. In fact, persons performing platform work who do not meet the employment status criteria under the new rules implementing the Platform Work Directive may still be classified as 'hetero-organised' and granted access to the labour law protections through Art. 2. 21

A related question is whether the transposition of the Directive will necessarily entail the repeal of the current provisions of Chapter V-*bis* Legislative Decree n. 81/15, granting minimum protections to a group of genuinely self-employed platform workers. The answer is negative, insofar as the scope of the Directive does not extend to the rights of self-employed platform workers other than those related to data protection. Hence, although the non-regression clause set out in the Directive cannot be invoked to solve the question, as it only refers to the preservation of more favourable provisions for 'platform workers' (Art. 26), it may be argued that any legislative intervention exceeding the scope 22

[17] Court of Cassation 30.4.2021, n. 11424.

[18] *See* European Commission's Report Expert Group (n 1), 31.

[19] For a detailed analysis see the next section of this chapter.

of the Directive would represent a breach of the delegation criteria established in the European Delegation Act.

23 A specific requirement stipulated by Art. 11(1)(b) is the alignment of the **definition of 'digital labour platform'** in the current legislation with the one set out in the Directive.

24 The existing Italian definition, enshrined in Art. 47-*bis*(2) Legislative Decree n. 81/15, construes a digital platform as 'software and IT procedures used by the contracting party which, regardless of the place of establishment, are instrumental to the delivery of goods, determining the remuneration and setting the conditions for how the service is to be performed'.

25 This definition shares with the European one the central role of the platform in organising the work performance, but besides that the two concepts differ significantly. For the Italian legislation, the platform is conceived as the **technological infrastructure** used to provide a service. In contrast, for the Platform Work Directive the platform is the legal entity providing the service and acting as the counterpart of the worker. Furthermore, the European definition adopts a broad and comprehensive notion of **work organisation**, potentially encompassing any form of managerial prerogative, on the condition that it is carried out through automated decision-making and monitoring systems. On the other hand, the Italian definition is focused more narrowly only on the functions of remuneration-setting (which the European Commission does not consider necessarily inherent to the definition of platform work)[20] and determination of the conditions under which the activity is performed.

26 To conclude this section, the European Delegation Act also provides for the adaptation of the social security framework, by calibrating protections according to the status of platform workers as employees or self-employed.

C. Algorithmic management, data protection, ex-ante and ex-post transparency

27 The protection granted by the Platform Work Directive to persons engaged in platform work irrespective of their employment status are centralised in the III Chapter of the Platform Work Directive entitled '**Algorithmic Management**'. Aimed at mitigating and regulating the capability of digital labour platforms to implement algorithmic management, this chapter is focused mainly on the enhancement of core safeguards in the following areas: data protection, **ex-ante and ex-post transparency**, **health and safety**, as well as **involvement of workers' representatives.**

28 To fully grasp the impact of its provisions and protections, it is firstly essential to understand the concept of 'Algorithmic Management' as defined in the Directive. Despite its seemingly redundant nature, this premise is pivotal in light of the considerations outlined in the previous paragraph since, as it will be shown, this interpretation inevitably spills into the protective statute afforded by the Italian system to platform workers and, as a consequence, it influences the degree of protection in the four core safeguards highlighted above.

29 Algorithmic management commonly refers to the use of Algorithmic Management Systems, which are automated or semi-automated computer processes, to manage re-

[20] As stated in the European Commission's Report Expert Group (n 1), the Commission services confirmed that Art. 2(1)(a) does not contain a limitation to services whereby the platform processes the payment in return for the work, European Commission, Report Expert Group – Transposition of the Directive (EU) 2024/2831 on improving working conditions in platform work (12.1.2026), 16.

lationships with personnel and support organisational decisions dealing with all the operations related to the working relationship. Within the Directive, these management operations are subsumed in: (i) monitoring, supervision and evaluation of the work performance by the use or with the support of automated systems; (ii) decision-making operations taken with the use or with the support of automated systems related to any aspect that significantly affect persons performing platform work, including the working conditions of platform workers (such as, decision on recruitment, the organisation of work assignments, their safety and health, etc.).

These functions inevitably reflect the power to organise work which is not merely a unilateral prerogative of the digital labour platform but rather a 'necessary and essential component' (→ Art. 2 mn. 12–20) for platforms to fall within the scope of the Directive. Furthermore, the organisational power does not necessarily entail the exercise of direction and control but may also take the form of unilateral organisational conditioning by the platform of the extrinsic modes of execution of the service, which does not annul the worker's freedom to organise the means employed in the performance of their work.[21] **30**

Consequently, the requirement of the 'organisational power' for digital labour platforms, as stipulated in the Platform Work Directive, implies that any platform worker and, most importantly, almost any person performing platform work is subject to hetero-organisation, according to the Italian legislation, thus, enjoying the application of the protective status of employees, although formally qualified as self-employed. **31**

Given this background, it is now possible to shift to the specific content of the core safeguards, taking into account the differences stemming from the employment status and highlighting how the provisions of the Directive fit into the current Italian regulatory framework as well as what changes the European Delegation Act recalls. **32**

I. Data Protection

The **protection of personal data** for all persons performing platform work is one of the main objectives of the Platform Work Directive, alongside the improvement of working conditions for platform workers. The former is, indeed, recognised as a gateway for protection of workers, irrespective of the contractual relationship. **33**

In this context, the first strategy of protection is the limitation of processing of certain category of data (→ Art. 7 mn. 2–8). To this end, the European Delegation Act, at Art. 11(1)(d), mandates the Government the definition of procedures for restricting the processing of personal data by automated monitoring systems or automated decision-making systems. This limitation duty, however, seems to fit into the prohibition already established in the Italian legislative framework, pursuant to Art. 8 Act 20 May 1970, n. 300 that forbids the investigation from making enquiries, including through third parties, into the employee's political, religious or trade union opinions, or into facts irrelevant in the assessment of the employees' professional capability[22]. **34**

Such prohibition, whose infringement is also a criminal offence,[23] should apply not only to platform workers (i.e. employees) but also to persons performing platform work, either hetero-organised (Art. 2 Legislative decree n. 81/2015) or in a coordinate continuative collaboration (Art. 409, n. 3, civil procedure code) as well as to self-employed individuals performing delivery services through digital platforms (art. 47-*ter*, Chapter V-*bis* **35**

[21] This is the notion of 'hetero-organisation' according to Perulli ELLJ 2020,117 (372).
[22] Aimo LD 2018, 585; Donini LLI 2017, 35.
[23] Art. 171, Legislative decree 30.6.2003, n. 196.

Legislative Decree n. 81/2015).[24] Nonetheless, the scope of Art. 7 Platform Work Directive, in terms of subject matter whose processing is prohibited, is wider. It includes also emotional and psychological state of workers, as well as biometric data.

36 Apart from this 'substantive' limitation, the Italian legislative framework also recognises a teleological and procedural constraints at Art. 4 Act n. 300/1970, governing the employers' power of control, which inherently involves the processing of personal data.[25] More precisely, the use of audio-visual systems and other tools that enable remote monitoring of workers' activities – and thus, also any automated monitoring system – is permitted only following an agreement with trade unions or, alternatively, authorisation from the competent administrative authority, and solely for purpose related to organisational and production needs, workplace safety and the protection of company assets. Such procedural safeguard set out in Art. 4 currently represents the only instance in national legislation where trade unions are granted a formal right to co-determination.[26]

37 Additionally, the Platform Work Directive also provides more specific rules for consulting platform workers and their representatives during data protection impact assessments[27] (→ Art. 8 mn. 1 et seq.), an aspect that likewise calls for implementation at the national level.

38 Lastly, it must be noted that *ex-ante* and *ex-post* transparency safeguards are corollary of the strengthening of data protection, but, on account of their breadth, they warrant individual consideration in the following sub-paragraph.

II. Ex-ante and ex-post transparency

39 The opacity and information asymmetry faced in the context of algorithmic management, in general, and especially by persons performing platform work, is a critical aspect tackled by the Platform Work Directive through the establishment of safeguards strengthening **transparency** – individually or collectively – both *ex ante* and *ex post*.

40 With regards to **ex ante transparency**, it must be noted that with the Legislative Decree 27 June 2022, n. 104, adopted to implement the Transparent and Predictable Working Conditions Directive, the Italian legislator has departed from the specific aims and has further expanded protections by recognising a specific obligation to provide information on the fully-automated decision-making and monitoring systems used by the company, which impact the execution of work tasks, pursuant to art. 1-*bis* Legislative Decree n. 152/1997.[28]

41 This information duty largely matches the information rights set out at Art. 9 Platform Work Directive with regards to the recipients and subject matter of information. Furthermore, it has the same subjective scope of Art. 8 Act n. 300/1970, described above, covering also hetero-organised platform collaborators and self-employed riders.

42 As noted, however, this discipline does not fully align with the requirements of the Platform Work Directive. The aspects that remain uncovered and, therefore, need to be

[24] Art. 47-*quinquies*, Chapter V-*bis*, Legislative decree n. 81/2015 provides that rules protecting the freedom and dignity of workers provided for employees – and thus also art. 8 included in Title I of the L. n. 300/1970 – apply also for workers falling within the scope of Chapter V-*bis*. Perulli ELLJ 2020, 117 (204); Sartori, p. 313.

[25] Ingrao, p. 32 et seqq.; Sartori, p. 220 et seqq.

[26] Bellavista in Zilio Grandi/Biasi, p. 717; Sartori, p. 220.

[27] Spinelli DLM.int 2024, 461 (470 et seq.); Trojsi ILLeJ 2024, 355 (366).

[28] Recchia LLI 2023, C.34; Carinci/Giudici/Perri L 2023, 7; Dagnino, p. 147. Some scholars have argued that the legislator did not respect the Directive's 'effet utile': in this regard *see* Faioli F 2022,104 (107 et seqq.).

implemented as required by the European Delegation Act at Art. 11(1)(f) are essentially twofold: 1) the inclusion of non-fully-automated monitoring and decision-making system; 2) the written form requirement.

Despite the need of adjustment, this national regulation has – and has proved to have – a wide potential. On one hand, it broadens the scope of application to any worker subjected to algorithmic management beyond the dimension of digital platforms, compared to the Platform Work Directive. On the other hand, by 'duplicating' information channels, it places a substantial amount of information in the hands of the union organisation. Indeed, it has also been already enforced by Trade Unions to contest the anti-union nature of the refusal of a food delivery platform in the relationship with its riders.[29] Furthermore, it is relevant to add that, thanks to the information received under Art. 1-*bis*, as mandated by the judge in the ruling of the 20th June 2023, the unions Nidil CGIL Palermo, Filcams CGIL Palermo and Filt CGIL Palermo were able to build a further case of collective discrimination.[30] 43

Additionally, as regards monitoring devices adopted to exercise – either directly or indirectly – the power of control over the workers' performance, Art. 4(3) Act n. 300/1970 already obliges employers to provide the worker with adequate information concerning the modalities of use of the tools and the procedures by which monitoring activities are carried out. This provision applies not only to platform employees but also to hetero-organised platform worker as well as to self-employed performing delivery services through digital platforms.[31] 44

Conversely, the greater impact of the Platform Work Directive is expected to affect the legal instruments to foster **ex-post transparency** provided by Art. 10 'Human oversight of automated monitoring systems and automated decision-making systems' and Art. 11 'Human review' of the Platform Work Directive (→ Art. 10 mn. 1–4; Art. 11 mn. 1–6). Indeed, the national legislative framework currently lacks any right of explanation or the right to request a review of the decision – with the exception of the contestation of charges concerning disciplinary sanctions, according to Art. 7 Act n. 300/1970, which, however, has the same subjective scope of Art, 4. Similarly, there is no procedural framework on the impact assessment of decisions taken or supported by automated monitoring systems and automated decision-making systems on persons performing platform work. 45

Hence, in the exercise of the delegated authority conferred by the European Delegation Act at Art. 11(1)(a) and (g), the most significant amendments will concern precisely these aspects, including the requirement that all decisions to restrict, suspend or terminate the contractual relationship, as well as any other decision of equivalent detriment must necessarily involve human intervention, as provided by Platform Work Directive. Up until now, the minimum protection provided by Chapter V-*bis* Legislative Decree 81/2015 for self-employed individuals performing delivery services through digital plat- 46

[29] The reference is to: Trib. Palermo, 31.3.2023, between Nidil CGIL Palermo, Filcams CGIL Palermo and Filt CGIL Palermo, as recurring parts, and *Uber Eats*, as defendant; Trib. Palermo, 20.6.2023, between Nidil CGIL Palermo, Filcams CGIL Palermo and Filt CGIL Palermo, as recurring parts, and *Foodinho*, as defendant, Trib. Turin, 5 August 2023, between Filcams CGIL Torino, Filt CGIL Turin, and Nidil CGIL Turin, as recurring parts, and *Foodinho* S.r.L., as defendant.

[30] Tribunal Palermo, 17.11.2023, between Nidil CGIL Palermo, Filcams CGIL Palermo and Filt CGIL Palermo, as recurring parts, and *Foodinho*, as defendant.

[31] As noted above, Art. 47-*quiquies* provides that rules protecting the freedom and dignity of workers provided for employees – and thus also art. 8 included in Title I of the L. n. 300/1970 – apply also to workers falling within the scope of Chapter V-*bis*: Perulli ELLJ 2020, 117 (204); Sartori, p. 313.

forms has only prohibited exclusion from the platform and reductions in work opportunities due to non-acceptance of the service.[32]

III. Health and safety

47 The significant risks for **health and safety** faced in platform work are addressed in the Platform Work Directive at Art. 12, despite exclusively in consideration of platform workers, who are employees, and therefore already fall in the scope of Council Directive 89/391/EEC (→ Art. 12 mn. 1–4). In this regard, the Platform Work Directive calls for a specific evaluation of the risk entailed by automated monitoring and decision-making systems, also ensuring the involvement of representatives' of platform workers and platform workers themselves – a necessary clarification given the low unionisation as well as the absence of representation at the workplace – especially in concern of work-related accidents, psychosocial and ergonomic risks, as well as violence or harassment in order to identify the appropriate preventive and protective measures. With the European Delegation Act, the Italian Parliament had delegated the Government to adopt the necessary changes and additions to Legislative Decree 9 April 2008, n. 81 (Consolidated Text on health and safety in the workplace) to ensure the health and safety protection of platform workers.

48 Nonetheless, it must be acknowledged that in Italy, thanks to the extension of the protective status of employees-platform workers, hetero-organised persons performing platform work, and coordinated and continuative workers already enjoy the OSH obligations applied to employees. For the latter, however, the protection arises only where the work takes place in the premises of the client.[33] Furthermore, some residual yet mandatory protections in the Italian legislative framework are also applied to other self-employed collaborators in delivery platforms, who are outside the scope of Art. 2 Legislative decree n. 81/2015, as they perform occasional work, pursuant to Art. 47-*septies*[34].

49 The vagueness of the provision raises questions about the scope of its reference to the Consolidated Text on health and safety in the workplace – specifically, whether it encompasses the entire regulatory framework or merely entails its limited application. In the latter case, the obligation imposed on principals would be confined to organising and financially supporting training and health surveillance for self-employed riders who choose to avail themselves of such measures, without extending to the supply of personal protective equipment.[35] Alternatively, the provision might be interpreted as shifting the entire burden of safety-related costs onto the principals, including those associated with personal protective equipment.[36]

[32] Art. 47-*quinquies*(2) Chapter V-*bis*, Legislative decree n. 81/2015.

[33] Art. 3, par. 7, d. lgs. n. 81/2008. *See* Ferraro AD 2023, 1 et seqq.

[34] Rota LLI, 2020, p. 62 seqq.; Lazzari RDSS 2018, 455 seqq.

[35] Pascucci DSL 2019, 37 (48).

[36] This is the interpretation shared by Perulli, p. 218 and Biasi, p. 841 (847). This interpretation has also been endorsed in case law: Trib. Florence, 1st April 2020; Trib. Bologna, 14 April 2020, both recognising a right for riders to receive personal protective equipment to prevent Covid-19 and more recently, Trib. Milan, 8 July 2025, recognising the obligation to consult the local workers' safety representative also for self-employed riders.

D. Role and Involvement of workers' representative

The Platform Work Directive regulates forms of **involvement of workers' representatives** (or workers), whether they are platform workers or persons performing platform work, in several Articles. Reference was made to the Data Protection Impact Assessment (DPIA) and to the involvement of representatives in matter of health and safety protections, as well as to additional forms of participation that are recognised domestically but not foreseen by the Directive itself. This paragraph will focus on analysing two institutions in particular: information and consultation, and human oversight. 50

Information and consultation rights are one of the forms of workers' representation regulated by the Platform Work Directive in order to protect employee[37]. In Italy, information and consultation (I&C) on matters of a general nature are regulated by Legislative decree 6 February 2007, n. 25[38], which transposes the provisions of Directive 2002/14/EC (I&C Directive). As indicated in its title, the legislative decree is intended to establish a general regulatory framework for I&C. In practical terms, this means identifying the matters covered by I&C, defining procedural rules[39], and outlining the circumstances in which the employer may claim confidentiality or be exempted from the obligation to inform and consult[40]. At the same time, the mentioned decree entrusts collective agreements[41] with the task of defining spaces, times, modalities and contents of these rights. 51

In Art. 13(1) (→ Arts. 13, 14, 15 mn. 13 et seqq.), the Platform Work Directive clarify that 'without prejudice to Directive 89/391/EEC as regards information and consultation and to Directives 2002/14/EC or 2009/38/EC of the European Parliament and of the Council', then it identifies the elements of the I&C Directive to which it refers (in particular, the definition of I&C and practical arrangements) and those new elements (the matters covered and the optional assistance of an expert). These issues, in turn, have implications for the transposition of the Platform Work Directive into national law. 52

More specifically, one may question whether those aspects not expressly referred to by the Platform Work Directive but regulated under existing domestic legislation should continue to apply, bearing in mind both the initial premise set out by the Directive itself and its standstill clause. 53

Indeed, the provisions of Art. 13 Platform Work Directive may affect the scope of application of the current rules. On the one hand, the directive confirms that its beneficiaries are limited to employees and their representatives[42]; on the other hand, it does not refer to the minimum number of employees for companies, which is set at 50 employees by Legislative decree n. 25/2007. 54

Pursuant to the text of the Platform Work Directive, the procedures regulating I&C coincide with those laid down by current national legislation, which (pursuant to Art. 4) refers the detailed regulation of these procedures to collective agreements, while establishing the general principle that I&C must take place in an appropriate manner in terms 55

---

[37] Purificato/Senatori HLLeJ 2023, 1; Otto ILLeJ 2022, 51; Aimo LDE 2024, 2 (5–11).

[38] Lunardon; Zoli RIDL 2008, 161; Corti.

[39] Art. 4 Legislative decree n. 25/2007.

[40] Art. 5 Legislative decree n. 25/2007.

[41] The definition of collective agreement provided in Art. 2 Legislative Decree n. 25/2007 is 'the collective agreement concluded between the employers' and trade union organisations which are comparatively most representative at the national level.'

[42] In particular, we refer to both Art. 13 (information and consultation), which refers specifically to platform workers' representatives and not to representatives of persons performing platform work, and Art. 15, which does not include Art. 13 among the provisions – and therefore among the instruments – that may also be extended to representatives of persons performing platform work.

of timing and content, as also enshrined in Art. 27 of the Charter of Fundamental Rights of the European Union[43].

56 A specific issue addressed by the Platform Work Directive concerns the matters falling within the scope of information and consultation. The directive expressly provides that these shall also include 'decisions likely to lead to the introduction of or to substantial changes in the use of automated monitoring systems or automated decision-making systems.'

57 However, drawing on the provisions of Directive 2002/14/EC, Legislative decree n. 25/2007 already refers, in Art. 4(3)(c), to 'decisions likely to result in significant changes in work organisation or in contractual relations', thus the measures envisaged by Art. 13 of the Platform Work Directive could arguably be regarded as falling within this scope. This would mean that the Italian regulatory framework on I&C would not, in principle, require substantial amendments regarding to this element – at most, for textual clarifications, as has occurred in other instances[44] – while continuing to reserve the role of defining the modalities of I&C to collective agreements, in this case taking into account the 'technical complexity of algorithmic management systems'[45].

58 The new feature stated in the Directive under analysis with respect to the domestic law currently in force is the possibility to be assisted by an expert to examine the issue and prepare an opinion during the consultation phase, recognised to workers' representatives[46]. This solution should strengthen not only the substantive protection of workers but also the technical capacity of trade union representatives to understand highly technological choices, thus promoting more 'qualified' bargaining.

59 Critical issues in the implementation of the Platform Work Directive may arise with regard to the identification of the actors entitled to these rights, namely workers' representatives. According to the definition provided under national law, these are understood to mean 'workers' representatives as defined by applicable legislation, as well as by the intersectoral agreements of 20 December 1993 and 27 July 1994, and subsequent amendments, or by the applicable national collective agreements in cases where those intersectoral agreements do not apply.' In practice, this typically refers to company-level trade union representatives (rappresentanze sindacali aziendali, RSA) and unitary workplace trade union representatives (rappresentanze sindacali unitarie, RSU). However, the organisational and structural characteristics of platform work hinder the establishment of RSA and RSU, thereby weakening the effectiveness of the legislative provisions, as they would lack a collective interlocutor through which dialogue could take place.

60 Secondly, a critical issue could arise from the difficulty in this sector in concluding collective agreements, which play a central role in defining information and consultation procedures[47].

61 As mentioned in paragraph II) of this Chapter, the Italian legal system currently lacks a human supervision system. This institution, to be carried out – according to the Platform Work Directive – with the involvement of workers' representatives, aims to ensure an *ex post* transparency, with potentially significant effects, as it could lead to a change in the automated monitoring system or automated decision-making system, or to the ces-

[43] Spinelli DLM.int 2024, 461 (470 et seq.); Ales in Ales et al., p. 214; Senatori, p. 69.

[44] For instance, Art. 2 Legislative decree n. 81/2015. In this case, paragraph 1 was supplemented by the provision stating that 'The provisions of this paragraph also apply when the methods of performing the service are organised through platforms, including digital platforms' through Act 24 February 2023, n. 14.

[45] Recital 52 of the Platform Work Directive.

[46] Art. 13 provides that the cost of the expert must be covered by the undertaking, when it employs more than 250 employees.

[47] Delfino F 2023, 174.

sation of its use when it may lead to a risk of discrimination or if it has violated the rights of people who work through digital platforms. Therefore, in implementing the European Delegation Act, a participatory procedure will need to be introduced, which will take place at least every two years and involve platform workers' representatives and human resources from digital platforms, as well as the digital platform itself. In particular, the former should receive the information collected by these human resources, while the modalities of worker participation will have to be specified, as this aspect has not been clarified by the Platform Work Directive. However, this should not be limited to simply receiving information, but should also allow for the expression of opinions. The involvement of workers' representatives beyond mere information seems to be confirmed by the Platform Work Directive itself, which in Art. 15 includes among the provisions applicable to persons performing work on platforms not the entire Art. 10, but only the part that establishes that the information collected for the assessment should be shared with their representatives.

E. Postscript: Recent legislative developments

Subsequent to the completion of this chapter, a new Law Decree has been enacted that may, to some extent, affect certain aspects of the legal and regulatory framework examined herein. Indeed, on April 30, 2026, the Law Decree no. 62/2026 was published in Official Journal, which establishes, at Chapter III, urgent provisions against illicit intermediation and labour exploitation in the digital economy, also known as 'caporalato digitale', by introducing four Articles explicitly dedicated to such matter. The act, however, anticipates also some safeguards endorsed by the Platform Work Directive, which is expressly cited in its recitals. **62**

A brief overview of the most relevant provisions is deemed necessary in order to contextualise the analysis in light of the evolving legal framework. However, it must be noted that, as this chapter is being finalised pending the parliamentary conversion of the Law Decree, the observations set out below are necessarily preliminary and limited to the text currently in force. **63**

With the aim of preventing unlawful labour intermediation and exploitation, the Decree amends several provisions of Legislative Decree No. 81/2015, including by introducing requirements to verify riders' identities (Art. 15). According to this provision, the access to digital platforms is permitted only via secure identification systems, such as the Electronic Identity Card (CIE) and the sharing or transfer of access credentials is expressly prohibited. Moreover, the platform operator must ensure compliance with these measures and may face administrative sanctions or suspension of activities in the event of non-compliance. **64**

In line with the Platform Work Directive and implementing the delegation contained in the aforementioned Act, the Decree also regulates the classification of the employment relationship for workers intermediated by digital platforms (Art. 12). The provision reaffirms the well-established jurisprudential trend regarding the primacy of factual circumstances over the formal classification adopted by the parties. More original is the introduction of a legal definition of specific presumptive criteria, which are nonetheless consistent with the indicators already employed by case law for the classification of an employment relationship. These criteria include the exercise of powers of organisation, direction, supervision, evaluation, restriction of access to work, and the unilateral determination of remuneration. While the European Commission had excluded the necessity of such an explicit list,[48] this choice may prove useful and effective in providing a procedural facilitation for workers seeking a correct classification of their employment status. Finally, Art. 12 explicitly establishes the existence of a legal presumption of an employment relationship where elements of control or hetero-direction are found.

65 Furthermore, the Decree establishes a formal right to algorithmic transparency, both *ex ante* and *ex post*, although uniquely in its individual dimension. In particular, Art. 14 imposes dual obligations on digital platforms. First, platforms must provide workers with clear, accessible, and comprehensible information concerning the automated or algorithmic systems used for the allocation of tasks, the determination or modification of remuneration, the evaluation of performance, and the suspension, restriction, or termination of access to the platform. Secondly, upon request, workers are entitled both to receive a clear explanation of automated decisions affecting their working conditions or remuneration and to obtain human review of such decisions.

66 In its current formulation, however, the transparency regime appears to present several shortcomings concerning both the form and the subject matter of the information obligations. As regards the former, the provision does not fully replicate the safeguards established under the Platform Work Directive. Notably, it does not require information to be provided in written form, nor does it establish binding rules concerning the timing of disclosure obligations. As regards the latter, the provision appears to conflate the subject matter of the information duty with the operational functions of the automated systems themselves, thereby risking a dilution of the substantive scope of transparency obligations.

67 Should this formulation be confirmed during the parliamentary conversion process, one positive aspect may nevertheless be identified in the breadth of the provision's scope of application, considered that it would include also non-fully-automated monitoring and decision-making systems, in line with the Platform Work Directive.

---

[48] European Commission, Report Expert Group – Transposition of the Directive (EU) 2024/2831 on improving working conditions in platform work (12.1.2026), 30.

Spain*

Literature: Aloisi, 'Boss ex machina: employer powers in workplaces governed by algorithms and artificial intelligence', in Lo Faro (ed), New technology and labour law, Italy 2023, p. 15, p. 4; Baylos Grau, 'Cambio digital y poder en la empresa: fortalecer los derechos colectivos', RDS 2024, 17; Baz Rodríguez, 'Responsabilidad algorítmica y gobernanza de la inteligencia artificial en el ámbito sociolaboral. Entre la perspectiva y la prospectiva', T&D 2022, 1; Beltrán de Heredia Ruiz, 'Nadie da duros a cuatro pesetas (transparencia algorítmica y representantes de los trabajadores: el nuevo art. 64.4.d ET)' in Ministerio de Trabajo y Economía Social (ed), Digitalización, recuperación y reformas laborales. Comunicaciones del XXXII Congreso Anual de la Asociación Española de Derecho del Trabajo y de la Seguridad Social, Spain 2022, p. 985; Bini, 'L'informazione algoritmica nel diritto del lavoro spagnolo: orizzonti espansivi di democratizzazione' in Ludovico/Nahas (eds), Diritti fondamentali, lavoro e nuove tecnologie, Italy 2025, p. 207; Blasco Jover, 'El derecho de información algorítmica de los representantes de los trabajadores', T&D 2023, 1; Blázquez Agudo, La protección jurídico-laboral de los 'riders'. El trabajo en plataformas en la encrucijada de la laboralidad', RDS&E 2021, 38; Extremera Méndez, 'Al fin la Directiva 2024/2831 sobre condiciones de trabajo en plataformas: retos y oportunidades de su trasposición al Derecho español', LS 2025, 1; Gallego Moya, 'Encaje de la reciente normativa española sobre riders en la propuesta de directiva comunitaria sobre plataformas digitales' in Bellomo/Mezzacapo/Ferraro/Calderara (eds), Improving working conditions in platform work in the light of the recent proposal for a directive, Italy 2023, p. 35; Gil Otero, 'La protección de datos en el trabajo en plataformas digitales y las decisiones individuales automatizadas' in Pérez de los Cobos Orihuel/García Piñeiro (dirs), El estatuto jurídico del trabajador en la era digital, Spain 2024, p. 221; Gil Otero, La economía de plataformas ante las categorías clásicas del Derecho del Trabajo, Spain 2024; Gómez Gordillo, 'Algoritmos y derecho de información de la representación de las personas trabajadoras', TL 2021, 161; Gorelli Hernández, 'Algoritmos y transparencia: ¿pueden mentir los números? Los derechos de información', T&D 2022, 1; Mateescu/Nguyen, 'Algorithmic management in the workplace', D&S 2019, 1; Jarrahi/Sutherland, 'Algorithmic management and algorithmic competencies: understanding and appropriating algorithms in gig work' in Taylor/Christian-Lamb/Martin/Nardi (eds) Information in contemporary society, USA 2019, p. 578; Mercader Uguina, 'Plataformas digitales y trabajo' in Pérez de los Cobos Orihuel/García Piñeiro (dirs), El estatuto jurídico del trabajador en la era digital, Spain 2024, p. 197; Miranda Boto/Brameshuber, 'El impacto de la digitalización en la representación de las personas trabajadoras: posibilidades y desafíos para los derechos de información y consulta y la negociación colectiva', RT&SS CEF, 2024, 21; Pastor Martínez, 'Los derechos colectivos de información, consulta y negociación del uso de algoritmos y sistemas de inteligencia artificial' in Ginés I Fabrellas (dir), Algoritmos, inteligencia artificial y relación laboral, Spain 2023, p. 335; Pérez del Prado, 'AI, right to information and new forms of participation: the Spanish experience', FLPT 2025, 261; Rodríguez Fernández, 'La participación de las personas trabajadoras en la gobernanza de la transición digital: las experiencias de la Unión Europea y de España', RDS 2023, 107; Rodríguez-Piñero Royo, 'La Ley Rider dos años después. Enseñanzas de una experiencia particular', REJL&SS 2023, 13; Sánchez-Urán Azaña, 'Digitalización de la economía y trabajo. Fronteras de laboralidad' in Pérez de los Cobos Orihuel/García Piñeiro (dirs), El estatuto jurídico del trabajador en la era digital, Spain 2024, p. 245; Sánchez-Urán Azaña/De Torres Bóveda, 'El trabajo en plataformas digitales' in Gil Plana (dir) La construcción internacional y europea del derecho social, Spain 2025, p. 169; Serrano García, Los derechos en el trabajo desarrollado en plataformas digitales. aplicación práctica de la Directiva, Spain 2024; Todolí Signes, 'La regulación de la inteligencia artificial en la Directiva de trabajo en plataformas digitales', LRDT&PS 2024, 26; Valle Muñoz, 'El derecho de los representantes legales de los trabajadores a ser informados por la empresa sobre el uso de algoritmos o sistemas de inteligencia artificial', REDT 2023, 1.

* This paper has been conducted in the framework of the Research Project I+D+i 'Internacionalización y europeización del Derecho del Trabajo: desafíos en un contexto globalizado de los instrumentos de flexibilidad' (ref. UCM-PR12/24–31563).

A. Introduction

1 The rapid development of digital technologies has created new ways of managing work, enabling companies to control, manage and discipline their workers[1] remotely and in real time through the use of algorithms[2]. One of the first sectors to implement algorithmic systems for this purpose is the digital labour platform sector.[3]

2 In recent years, Spain has proved to be one of the European Union countries where more digital labour platforms existed,[4] and where more people depended on the work they performed on them -as it meant their main source of income.[5] It is because of this sector's importance, among other things, that in 2021 the Spanish legislator showed its efforts to regulate work on digital platforms, through a series of reforms. However, these legal reforms have proven to be insufficient in practical terms and, of course, in terms of complying with the provisions of the European Platform Work Directive. At present, Spain does not have a draft transposition and, discussions have not yet started.

3 The aim of this paper is to examine different ways of transposing some of the fundamental provisions of the European Directive into Spanish law[6]. To this end, we will first analyse the existing regulatory framework in this area. This will serve as a basis for studying the provisions of the Directive, allowing us to assess the best way to transpose them into Spanish law.

B. The existing regulatory framework on platform work in Spain

4 The digital platform sector in Spain was regulated for the **first time in 2021** with the enactment of Royal Decree 9/2021[7] and then Law 12/2021, to guarantee the labour rights of persons dedicated to providing services for digital delivery platforms (popularly

[1] In this Article, the term 'worker' refers to persons providing services under a labour contract. When referring to independent contractors the term 'self-employed' person is used. The term 'service providers' is also utilised as an umbrella concept to refer to any contractual relationship with the platform, regardless of their subordinate or autonomous nature.

[2] Which results, among other things, in the intensification of the employer's powers and, at the same time, the reduction of workers' self-determination. See Aloisi in Lo Faro, p. 15 (27 et seq.).

[3] Mateescu/Nguyen D&S 2019, 1 (1); Jarrahi/Sutherland in Taylor/Christian-Lamb/Martin/Nardi, p. 578 (579).

[4] The third, according to available data (year 2021). European Comission, 'Digital labour platforms in the EU: Mapping and business models', May 2021, 31.

[5] It was the fourth country with the highest number of providers generating their main source of income from the services they provided on digital labour platforms. Data from 2022. Piasna/Zwysen/Drahokoupil, 'The platform economy in Europe: Results from the second ETUI Internet and Platform Work Survey', ETUI, 2022, p. 46 et seq.

[6] It should be noted that only some of the most important provisions of the European legal instrument have been selected, as the extension of this work does not allow for a full analysis of the Directive and its transposition into Spanish national law.

[7] Real Decreto-ley 9/2021, de 11 de mayo, by which the revised text of the Workers' Statute Law, approved by Real Decreto legislativo 2/2015 de 23 de octubre de 2015, is amended to guarantee the labour rights of persons dedicated to delivery in the field of digital platforms. It was challenged as

known as '*Ley Rider*' or 'Riders' law'). This law was the result of social dialogue between the most relevant social partners at national level[8] and the Government. Social dialogue provided the law with a greater degree of legitimacy and balance between the different social and business interests; although, probably as a result of this compromise, we can note some of its shortcomings.[9]

Law 12/2021 aimed to reform Spain's fundamental labour law, the Workers' Statute[10] (WS), by incorporating: (1) an express presumption of employment in the digital delivery platform sector and (2) the creation of a new right to information regarding algorithmic systems used to manage work. 5

Through this legislation, **Spain became one of the first European countries** to regulate important aspects of work on digital platforms and, in general, algorithmic work management. In this sense, some authors have referred to Spain as a 'pioneer'[11] and even a 'European referent'[12] in the legislation of this sector of work. Below we address the content of this law. 6

I. Legal status of persons performing platform work

The debate around the legal nature of the relationship between service providers and digital labour platforms has been and continues to be controversial[13] given the variety of elements that operate in these relationships, often indicative of both autonomy and dependence at the same time.[14] 7

Spanish labour courts have dealt with the legal classification of these individuals since the entry of the platforms into the national market,[15] resulting in disparate rulings on the issue. In September 2020, the controversy reached the Supreme Court,[16] which concluded that the relationship between a rider and the platform (Glovo, in this case) was an employment relationship. According to the Supreme Court: 8

> The company has established instructions that allow it to control the production process. Glovo has established means of control that operate on the activity and not only on the result by means of algorithmic management of the service, ratings of the delivery drivers and constant geolocation. The driver does not organise the production activity on his own, nor does he negotiate prices or conditions with the owners of the establishments he serves, nor does he receive his remuneration from the end customers. The individual had no real capacity to organise his work performance, lacking the autonomy to do so. He was subject to the organisational guidelines set by the company.

---

unconstitutional, not because of its content but because of the type of law chosen to regulate it. See, Spanish Constitutional Court judjement 147/2023, of 6 of November 2023 (n. 4469/2021).

[8] The most representative trade unions (*CCOO* and *UGT*) and employers' organisations (CEOE and CEPYME) in Spain.

[9] Pastor Martínez in Ginés I Fabrellas, p. 335 (337).

[10] Real Decreto Legislativo 2/2015, de 23 de octubre, por el que se aprueba el texto refundido de la Ley del Estatuto de los Trabajadores.

[11] Mercader Uguina in Pérez de los Cobos Orihuel/García Piñeiro, p. 197 (203); Pérez del Prado FLPT 2025, 261 (263); Todolí Signes LRDT&PS 2024, 26 (37).

[12] Gallego Moya in Bellomo/ Mezzacapo/ Ferraro/Calderara, p. 35 (49).

[13] And in general, as Sánchez-Urán Azaña rightly points out, 'the issue of the labour frontiers is a timeless and universal question'. Sánchez-Urán Azaña in Pérez de los Cobos Orihuel/García Piñeiro, p. 245 (246).

[14] Not surprisingly, it has been argued that the legal classification of these persons is one of the most problematic issues in the work on digital platforms. Mercader Uguina in Pérez de los Cobos Orihuel/ García Piñeiro, p. 197 (201).

[15] In particular, the first two rulings that addressed the legal classification of these service providers were the social court (*Juzgado de lo social*) judgments: SJS n. 6 de Valencia, de 1 de junio de 2018 (núm. 244/2018), and SJS n. 39 de Madrid, de 3 de septiembre de 2018 (núm. 284/2018).

[16] STS 805/2020, de 25 de septiembre de 2020 (núm. rec. 4746/2019).

> This reveals an exercise of corporate power in relation to the way in which the service was provided and a real-time control of its execution that evidences the existence of the subordination requirement inherent to the employment relationship.

9 While the Court's judgment is of great significance, it did not put an end to the controversy over the legal status of these persons. It is a judicial interpretation applied to a particular case. In any way, this judgement influenced the decision to regulate on the matter, leading to the enactment of Royal Decree Law 9/2021, of 11 May[17], which eventually led to the aforementioned Law 12/2021. The latter added to the Workers' Statute a new provision, the twenty-third additional provision (hereinafter, 23AP WS). According to which:

> By application of what is established in Art. 8.1, it is presumed to be included within the scope of this law the activity of persons who provide paid services consisting of the delivery or distribution of any consumer product or goods, by employers who exercise the business powers of organisation, management and control directly, indirectly or implicitly, by means of the algorithmic management of the service or working conditions, through a digital platform. This presumption does not affect the provisions of Art. 1.3 of this regulation.

10 This presumption transfers the judicial interpretation to the legal text,[18] highlighting the need to provide greater flexibility to the backbone elements of the employment relationship: provision of services for the benefit of a third person (what we call '*ajenidad*' in Spain) and subordination,[19] adapting them to the new employment realities. However, it should be noted that it does **not automatically** recognise the relationship between a service provider and a digital delivery platform as an employment relationship.[20] The worker must provide sufficient indicia to trigger the presumption, after which the platform may present evidence to prove otherwise.

11 The presumption has been criticised by a sector of the Spanish labour law doctrine.[21] Firstly, because of its restricted and excessively specific scope of application -it only covers one type of platform providers (delivery drivers or 'riders').[22] Moreover, it does not alleviate the burden of proof of the employment relationship,[23] as the individual still has to provide enough indicia[24] to activate this procedural mechanism.

12 Hence, it would seem that we are back to where we started,[25] since in reality the presumption does not really bring anything new with respect to what already existed[26] (we already had the general presumption of employment which did the same as the specific one, set in 23AP),[27] and all that is done is to expressly recognise algorithmic work management as another employment indication.

13 Consequently, the resolution of these disputes is, once again, in the hands of the courts.

---

[17] Mercader Uguina in Pérez de los Cobos Orihuel/García Piñeiro, p. 197 (203).

[18] Gallego Moya in Bellomo/ Mezzacapo/ Ferraro/Calderara, p. 35 (45).

[19] STS 805/2020, de 25 de septiembre de 2020 (núm. rec. 4746/2019). Moreover, in this way Poquet Catalá, p. 16; Gorelli Hernández T&D 2022, 1 (6); García Rubio, p. 131.

[20] Gil Otero, p. 31.

[21] Sánchez-Urán Azaña in Pérez de los Cobos Orihuel/García Piñeiro, p. 245 (275); Baz Rodríguez T&D 2022, 1 (16); Gil Otero, p. 31.

[22] Blázquez Agudo RDS&E 2021, 38 (44).

[23] Gil Otero, p. 32.

[24] Gorelli Hernández T&D 2022, 1 (9 et seq.).

[25] Sánchez-Urán Azaña in Pérez de los Cobos Orihuel/García Piñeiro, p. 245 (279); Blázquez Agudo RDS&E 2021, 38 (46).

[26] Gallego Moya in Bellomo/ Mezzacapo/ Ferraro/Calderara, p. 35 (46).

[27] Blázquez Agudo RDS&E 2021, 38 (44).

The entry into force of this regulation gave rise to reactive positions by some platforms, in particular *Deliveroo*, which decided to end its activity in Spain in 2021 (being their last day operating in Spain the 29th of November).[28] Notwithstanding this drastic reaction, the presumption has proven to be of limited practical effectiveness as some digital platforms have not opted to hire their service providers as workers, but rather to modify their algorithms to give workers more freedom, in an attempt to escape from the employment status.[29] 14

II. The right to information on algorithms

Secondly, Law 12/2021 introduced a letter (d) to Art. 64(4) WS by virtue of which a right to information on the algorithms used by the company in the workplace is recognised. In this regard, and as a preliminary, it is necessary to make **three clarifications**. Firstly, that we are dealing with **a purely labour-related right to information**, given that it is introduced in the Workers' Statute. Consequently, persons providing services on these platforms on a self-employed basis are excluded from this right. Secondly, it should be emphasised that this is a provision whose subjective scope is **not limited to the digital platform sector**, but extends to all sectors of employment, since it is recognised in an article that applies to all workers regardless of their occupation or specific sector. Thirdly and lastly, it is essential to consider that the right to information recognised here is of a **collective nature**, i.e. it is for workers' representatives to exercise, and not for individual workers. 15

Art. 64(4)(d) WS provides that the works council shall have the right 'to be informed by the company of the parameters, rules and instructions on which algorithms or artificial intelligence systems are based that affect decision-making that may have an impact on working conditions, access to and maintenance of employment, including profiling'. 16

1. Personal scope

The Spanish worker representation system consists of a dual channel, made up of both elected representatives (personnel delegates and works councils[30]) and trade union representatives (trade union sections and trade union delegates[31]). Both representative formulas coexist and relate to each other, to such an extent that in some cases they may even coincide.[32] 17

The collective right to receive information (including algorithmic information) is recognised **for all elected representation**, both the works council (Art. 64 WS) and the personnel delegates, who 'shall have the same competencies as those established for works councils' (Art. 62(2) WS). Furthermore, trade union delegates -not trade union 18

---

[28] Deliveroo, 'Deliveroo announces agreement to end operations in Spain' (Deliveroo, 18.11.2021) <https://corporate.deliveroo.co.uk/investors/news/deliveroo-announces-agreement-end-operations-spain/> (last accessed: 21.06.2025).

[29] Rodríguez-Piñero Royo REJL&SS 2023, 13 (28 et seq.); Gil Otero, p. 33.

[30] They are elected by all workers. The determination of the existence of delegate/s or council depends on the size of the workforce.

[31] They are elected from among the members of a trade union and act within the company. Trade union sections are established by trade union members in the company; union delegates are appointed only by those trade union sections that meet the requirements of Art. 10 of the Organic Law on Trade Union Freedom and act as spokespersons for the section vis-à-vis the employer.

[32] Since works councils are often composed not only of workers, but also of trade union members. The latter being also elected by direct ballot among the workers of the workplace, in accordance with the electoral process laid down in Section II of Title II WS (Arts. 69 to 76).

sections- shall have the right to be informed on the same matters as the elected representatives in accordance with Art. 10(3)(1) of the Organic Law on Trade Union Freedom.[33] Therefore, one can observe that, in the case of the trade union channel, not all representatives will benefit from such rights, i.e. trade union sections. The recognition of information rights is not full in this case.

2. Material scope

19 Workers' representatives have the right to know 'the parameters, rules and instructions on which algorithms or artificial intelligence systems are based that affect decision-making'. It can be observed from the provision that the information obligation is not only activated with respect to decisional systems, but regarding all those that 'affect' decision-making. This includes, for example, information on monitoring systems whose outputs are used to make the decision.

20 The parameters, rules and instructions refer to the configuration of the system used by the employer, and the purpose of providing this information to the representatives is so that they are aware of the logic of the system's functioning.[34] This means that there is no right to information with regard to the training and test data used to prepare the system, nor with regard to the input data. Furthermore, there is no right to information on the results produced by the system. All of these are decisive aspects that may compromise the proper detection of irregularities in its use, such as, for example, the existence of biased data or discriminatory results.

21 Access to information on the configuration of the algorithm is foreseen with respect to systems that may affect decisions on access to and maintenance of employment, and working conditions. Therefore, the material scope of the rule is broad, covering not only the duration of the employment relationship, but also the previous stages (personnel selection and recruitment), as well as those decisions that may result in the termination of the relationship.

22 We cannot define this right as a collective version of the right to information in the field of data protection (Art. 13 in connection with Art. 22 GDPR). Although they share similarities in part of their content (both seek to know the logic of the system), **there are substantial differences** that do not allow for such an analogy. The first and most obvious is its labour nature, which limits its application to persons providing their services on an employment basis, whereas the GDPR's right of information is recognised for all citizens regardless of their employment or contractual relationships. Moreover, as already noted, the Art. 64(4)(d) WS right of information is recognised in respect of all systems that affect decision-making, so that, unlike the GDPR, there is no requirement that the system that is the subject of the information makes the decision *de facto* itself. Nor does the right to information in the workplace require a certain level of impact on the individual to be triggered, but it is sufficient that workers are merely affected. Finally, it is a right to which one is entitled, irrespective of whether or not there is a processing of personal data,[35] which enables the inclusion of decisions and systems using anonymised data or non-personal data, such as those linked to productivity.

---

[33] Ley Orgánica 11/1985, de 2 de agosto, de Libertad Sindical.

[34] Academic doctrine agrees in this regard. See, Blasco Jover T&D 2023, 1 (7); Gorelli Hernández T&D 2022, 1 (18); Gómez Gordillo TL 2021, 161 (176); Gallego Moya in Bellomo/ Mezzacapo/ Ferraro/Calderara, p. 35 (48); Rodríguez Fernández RDS 2023, 107 (133); Bini in Ludovico/Nahas, p. 207 (209).

[35] As Gil Otero rightly points out in the framework of data protection, there is no right to information with respect to input data that is not of a personal nature. Gil Otero in Pérez de los Cobos Orihuel/García Piñeiro, p. 221 (225).

3. Temporal and formal requirements

According to Art. 64(4) WS algorithmic information has to be provided 'at appropriate intervals'. So the temporal requirement is clearly indeterminate, potentially leaving it up to the employer to arbitrarily set the times of delivery. In this respect, majority of scholars have considered that in order to make this right effective, the information should be provided by the employer at least at the following times: prior to the implementation of the system and each time the system undergoes some kind of change or modification.[36] In this regard, it is necessary to point out that according to the wording of the provision (which refers to systems that 'affect'), one could argue, in fact, that the information corresponds to an ex post stage, i.e. after the company configured the system[37], meaning that worker's representatives would not have the right to be informerd in the design phase, but only after it is completed and conducted unilaterally by the employer. 23

As far as formal requirements are concerned, the Spanish legislation merely repeats what is already laid down in Art. 4(3) of Directive 2002/14/EC, on the framework for information and consultation rights of workers, through Art. 64(6) WS.[38] Thus, instead of creating rigid criteria for each of the matters subject to information, the Spanish legislator chooses to assess compliance based on the very purpose of the right, i.e., to enable the examination of the information and, in some cases, consultation. 24

Although this right has some shortcomings – which we will not address in this paper, as they go beyond the scope of our analysis – it has been welcomed by the doctrine as a step forward in the regulation of algorithmic work management. 25

C. Avenues and recommendations for the transposition of the European Platfotm Work Directive

Despite the legislative advances that Spain has adopted in this context, the entry into force of the European Directive requires **unquestionable changes**. In order to carry out these changes and adaptations, it is necessary, as a preliminary step, to determine the most appropriate transposition strategy. In this regard, there are two fundamental options: (1) to develop a new law that regulates all the aspects required by the Directive and (2) to examine the existing regulations and make the relevant alterations and additions to comply with the provisions of the Platform Work Directive. 26

The second option is the most appropriate since, on the one hand, we are dealing with two different legal regimes (employment – self-employment) and, on the other hand, because the matters to be transposed are extremely varied (data protection, health and safety, participation, etc.), each of which is regulated by its own specific legislation, determined, among other things, by its own specific legal nature. A nature that determines, in itself, the type of rule that should be used to regulate it. For example, the right 27

[36] Beltrán de Heredia Ruiz in Ministerio de Trabajo y Economía Social, p. 985 (998); Gómez Gordillo TL 2021, 161 (178 et seq.); Miranda Boto/Brameshuber RT&SS CEF 2024, 21 (52); Valle Muñoz REDT 2023, 1 (14); Pérez de los Cobos Orihuel, 'Sobre la "guía" práctica de información algorítmica laboral' (Oleart Abogados, 1.7.2022), <https://www.oleartabogados.com/sobre-la-guia-practica-de-informacion-algoritmica-laboral> (last accessed: 3.7.2025).

[37] Baylos Grau RDS 2024, 17 (34).

[38] According to which the information shall be provided by the employer to the works council, without prejudice to any specific provisions in each case, at such time, in such manner and with such content as are appropriate to enable the employees' representatives to examine it properly and, where necessary, to prepare the consultation and the report (Art. 64(6) WS).

to personal data protection is a fundamental right (Art. 18 of the Spanish Constitution) and, as such, must be regulated through a specific type of law: organic law.[39]

28 The above makes it clear that regulating all the contents of the Platform Work Directive in a single piece of legislation is inoperable, as not all matters can be regulated by the same legal instrument. The Spanish legislator will have to make the necessary amendments to the existing legal texts.

I. European presumption and its transposition to the Spanish legal system

29 Some have argued that the presumption set in Art. 5 Platform Work Directive was **inspired** by the Spanish legal presumption,[40] mn. → 3 et seq. so it would seem that, at least in principle, it would not be necessary to make major changes to domestic legislation.

30 The Spanish presumption, like the European, is a quasi-generic presumption, since it does not require the fulfilment of specific criteria to determine legal status[41] (Art. 5 Platform Work Directive), is based on the facts (principle of primacy of facts) and not on the denomination (*nomen iuris*) that the parties give to the relationship (Art. 4(2) Platform Work Directive) and has a *iuris tantum* (rebuttable) character, requiring activation (Art. 5(1) Platform Work Directive). Thus, some authors have argued that 'the transposition of the future Directive could be done as simply as removing, from Law 12/2021, the restriction to the delivery or distribution sector'.[42]

31 In addition to extending the scope of application to all digital labour platforms (understood in the terms of Art. 2(1)(a) Platform Work Directive), it would be advisable for the national legislator to expressly include the possibility that 'the presumption of employment also applies where the service provider does not have a contractual relationship with the digital platform that manages and controls his/her work, but with an intermediary to whom the latter has outsourced the services'.[43]

32 The rebuttable presumption of Art. 5 Platform Work Directive is a minimum mandate, hence Spain will have to decide whether just maintaining the presumption of the 23AP WS -with the aforementioned extension of its subjective scope- or, on the contrary, to develop it, requiring the fulfilment of specific criteria applicable to this context. According to some voices, the latter option is more ambitious[44] as it would make it possible to define more clearly the contours of this particular contractual relationship. This greater degree of certainty as to 'what it takes to be reclassified', would presumably make it easier for the individual to provide the necessary evidence to trigger the presumption. However, other authors have considered the opposite, arguing that narrowing the presumption of employment would compromise its effectiveness.[45]

33 We will have to wait to see which of the options will end up being chosen by the Spanish legislator by the end of 2026.

---

[39] According to Art. 81 of the Spanish Constitution.

[40] Mercader Uguina in Pérez de los Cobos Orihuel/García Piñeiro, p. 197 (213); Gallego Moya in Bellomo/ Mezzacapo/ Ferraro/Calderara, p. 35 (54).

[41] Sánchez-Urán Azaña/De Torres Bóveda in Gil Plana, p. 169 (193).

[42] Gallego Moya in Bellomo/ Mezzacapo/ Ferraro/Calderara, p. 35 (55).

[43] Gil Otero, p. 37. In a similar way, Extremera Méndez LS 2025, 1 (36).

[44] Gil Otero, p. 37.

[45] Aloisi/Rainone/Countouris, 'An unfinished task? Matching the Platform Work Directive with the EU and international "social acquis"', 2023 International Labour Organization, 17; Rainone/Aloisi, 'The EU Platform Work Directive What's new, what's missing, what's next?', 2024 European Trade Union Institute, 9.

II. Common rights

34 The common regime of rights and safeguards of the Directive (Arts. 7 to 11 Platform Work Directive) have as their legal basis Art. 16(2) TFEU, i.e. data protection. This basis allows the extension of the provisions to all platform service providers irrespective of their contractual relationship.[46] When considering the transposition of this first part of the contents of Chapter III Platform Work Directive, we must take into account this rationale, as it allows for a unified transposition in a single national legal text. Moreover, the regulation of data protection cannot be articulated through just any law, so that the dispersed transposition of the common regime – i.e. in the WS (labour law) and in the Statute of Self-Employment (law regulating self-employed persons) – would not comply with the aforementioned constitutional mandate.

35 The fundamental Spanish law in this matter, the Organic Law on Personal Data Protection,[47] lacks provisions such as those in the Platform Work Directive (Arts. 7 to 11) and, even less, aimed at such a specific group as the one addressed here. However, the national law has a final title, Title X, dedicated to the 'Guarantee of digital rights', which we believe would be the most appropiate title to incorporate the rights and protections that the Directive recognises for all service providers.[48] This Title recognises a series of general rights for individuals in the digital age, as well as specific rights in the field of employment. The Spanish legislator could include these provisions as separate articles or create a specific chapter within the Title, which would bring them all together. In our view, the second option would be the most advisable, so that the content of Title X would be organised into three possible chapters: (1) on citizens' rights in the digital age, (2) on the digital rights of workers in the company and (3) on the rights of persons providing services on digital platforms. The latter could start with an article defining the scope of application of its provisions and continue with a second provision incorporating the definitions of Art. 2 Platform Work Directive. This could be followed by the limits on the processing of personal data (Art. 7 Platform Work Directive), the participation of representatives of persons performing platform work in the impact assessment (Art. 8 Platform Work Directive), the individual and collective information rights on the systems, and the right to portability of personal data (Art. 9 Platform Work Directive), the rights of supervision and human review (Arts. 10 and 11 Platform Work Directive, respectively) and, finally, the right to have communication channels between providers and with their representatives (Art. 20 Platform Work Directive).

III. Employee-reserved rights

36 These rights constitute the second part of Chapter III of the European Directive and, as a consequence of their strictly labour-related nature, will have to be transposed exclusively into national labour law. It would be advisable for the WS to establish an article alluding to the article of the Organic Law on Personal Data Protection that contains the definitions, so that they do not have to be repeated.

---

[46] Sánchez-Urán Azaña/De Torres Bóveda in Gil Plana, p. 169 (178).

[47] Ley Orgánica 3/2018, de 5 de diciembre, de Protección de Datos Personales y garantía de los derechos digitales.

[48] Something that has also been considered by Extremera Méndez LS 2025, 1 (24).

1. Information and consultation

37 To the aforementioned right in Art. 64(4)(d) WS must be added the contents of Arts. 13 and 14 Platform Work Directive, albeit the Spanish legislator should not make any major changes, with the exception of the right to individual information provided for in Art. 14 Platform Work Directive.

38 Firstly, in relation to Art. 13 Platform Work Directive, **Spain already has a provision**, Art. 64(5) WS, which recognises the collective rights of information and consultation regarding 'all decisions of the company that could lead to relevant changes in work organisation and employment contracts in the company'[49]. To these rights is added the workers' representatives right to issue a written report, prior to consultation, when these relevant changes arise from 'the implementation and review of work organisation and control systems, time studies, establishment of bonus and incentive systems and job evaluation' (Art. 64(5)(f) WS). These provisions cover the implementation and review of algorithmic systems[50] to which Art. 13(2) Platform Work Directive refers to.

39 On the other hand, in relation to Art. 13(3) Platform Work Directive, although the Workers' Statute does not expressly recognise the right of workers' representatives to be assisted by experts, this recognition exists implicitly through Art. 65(2) WS when the experts, together with the workers' representatives, are required to observe a duty of confidentiality with regard to sensitive company information. Yet still, with the transposition of Art. 13(3) Platform Work Directive, the Spanish legislator will have to expressly recognise this right in Art. 64 WS (dedicated to information and consultation rights), and also provide that the platform will be responsible for covering the costs derived from it -which must be proportionate- when it has more than 250 workers in the country. A more favourable transposition for the social side could consider extending the coverage of expenses to two experts or, instead, reducing the number of workers required for the platform to be responsible for financing this assistance to the representatives. Moreover, in order to guarantee the expert's neutrality[51] in advising the representatives, it would be useful for the legislator to expressly state that this professional must be chosen by the representatives themselves, regardless of whether the platform is responsible for paying for his or her services[52]. In any case, collective agreements may establish more beneficial conditions in favour of workers.

40 In our opinion, the greatest transposition challenge in this area is to be found in Art. 14 Platform Work Directive, which recognises an individual labour right to information in those cases where there are no workers' representatives on the platforms. This is a very positive development, although it breaks with the Spanish paradigm, which configures information (and consultation) rights as strictly collective rights. This has traditionally meant that, in the absence of workers' representatives to exercise them, these rights are inoperable. A situation that occurs with some frequency due to the Spanish productive structure -mainly made up of micro-companies that do not reach the number of workers necessary to constitute a representative body- and to the fact that

---

[49] According to the recently published European Commission, Report Expert Group – Transposition of the Directive (EU) 2024/2831 on improving working conditions in platform work (12.1.2026), 64, the application of this obligation to platform workers should be made explicit in national legislation.

[50] See, Gorelli Hernández T&D 2022, 1 (17); Blasco Jover T&D 2023, 1 (9); Valle Muñoz REDT 2023, 1 (8); Pastor Martínez in Ginés I Fabrellas, p. 335 (352).

[51] Something that has concerned some authors. See, Serrano García, p. 92.

[52] The European Commission, Report Expert Group – Transposition of the Directive (EU) 2024/2831 on improving working conditions in platform work (12.1.2026), 64, acknowledges that this should be the case, i.e. is for worker's representatives to choose who is the expert assisting them.

the reference unit for the determination of the representantives is the workplace (establishment) -which normally does not exist in the context of digital labour platforms.

41 The transposition of Art. 14 Platform Work Directive into Spanish law could end up being a mere addition of a specific provision for the context of digital labour platforms or, in the best-case scenario, it could be the necessary push for a change of direction with regard to the exercise of information rights.

2. Health and safety

42 The transposition of the health and safety mandates (Art. 12 Platform Work Directive) is to be carried out by means of the Spanish Law on the Prevention of Occupational Risks[53] -specific labour law in charge of regulating this matter. The requirements to carry out an assessment of the risks posed by automated systems, as well as the establishment of the necessary measures by the platform to prevent their occurrence (Art. 12(1) Platform Work Directive) would be included in Art. 16(2) Law on the Prevention of Occupational Risks, which establishes the obligations of the employer to carry out the risk assessment and the risk prevention plan. On the other hand, the rights of workers to information, consultation and participation with regard to the assessments and preventive measures required by Art. 12(2) Platform Work Directive are already recognised in Art. 18 of the national law, although this recognition is made in a general way with regard to occupational health and safety matters.

43 The protection of workers from excessive pressures and other risks to their health due to their interaction with or affectation by automated systems (Art. 12(3) and (4) Platform Work Directive) can be embedded in Art. 15(1)(d) Law on the Prevention of Occupational Risks, on one of the principles of preventive action, that is, 'adapting work to the individual, in particular as regards the design of workstations and the choice of equipment and working and production methods, with a view, in particular, to reducing monotonous and repetitive work and its effects on health'. With regard to the protection of workers against violence and harassment and the establishment of channels of complaint (Art. 12(5) Platform Work Directive), we also have general provisions, but equally applicable to this sector and type of labour management: (1) Art. 4(2)(e) WS recognises the right of workers 'to due regard for their dignity, including protection against harassment' in all its dimensions, (2) the establishment that harassment of a worker constitutes grounds for disciplinary dismissal (Art. 54(2)(g) WS), (3) all health and safety regulations, which are fully applicable to this type of misconduct, and the Law for the protection of persons reporting regulatory infringements[54] which protects the disclosure of these wrongdoings.

44 In general, it can be observed that the general health and safety rules remain in force and can be applied to the specific risks that arise as a consequence of the use of these technologies to manage workers. Platforms will have to include in their risk assessments and prevention plans the use of these systems as an additional content -something they were already obliged to do before the Directive, although it was not expressly established. The same applies to the protection of workers from undue pressure and from violence and harassment. Therefore, it would not seem necessary to create new articles to transpose Art. 12 Platform Work Directive, although an express mention could be made of the framing of these specific risks in the Law on the Prevention of Occupational Risks.

[53] Ley 31/1995, de 8 de noviembre, de Prevención de Riesgos Laborales.

[54] Ley 2/2023, de 20 de febrero, reguladora de la protección de las personas que informen sobre infracciones normativas y de lucha contra la corrupción.

3. Protection from dismissal and equivalent measures

45 Art. 23 Platform Work Directive requires member States to establish measures to prevent employers from using dismissal or similar actions to punish and discourage workers from exercising their rights under the Directive. These measures specifically require workers to be able to request from the platform a written document stating the causes or reasons justifying the dismissal or equivalent measure. This requirement is **already fulfilled** by the Spanish legal system, which requires employers to provide a 'dismissal letter' containing the reasons justifying the termination measure, whether objective (Art. 53(1)(a) WS) or disciplinary (Art. 55(1) WS). Moreover, under the current legislation, if the dismissal is appealed, the platforms would already be obliged to prove the grounds for termination alleged in the dismissal letter. If the platform succeeds in proving the grounds, the dismissal would be 'fair' (in accordance with the law); otherwise, it would be classified as 'unfair' (the causes are not proven or the legal formalities are not complied with – for example, if the dismissal letter is not delivered), in which case the employer would have to choose between readmitting the worker or compensating the worker, or 'null' (if the court finds a violation of fundamental rights), which would mean the immediate readmission of the worker to the company, and a potential compensation for the damages caused.

46 It is noteworthy that the Platform Work Directive extends these protections beyond employees, covering service providers who have a contractual relationship as independent contractors with the digital labour platform. The protection of these individuals against contractual terminations with the above guarantees (written notice) does not currently exist. The self-employed individuals with the greatest protection against termination of contract are what we call 'economically dependent self-employed workers (trabajadores autónomos económicamente dependientes or TRADE)[55] through Art. 15 Statute of Self-employment[56], although even in these cases the provisions of the Directive are not complied with. It is for this reason that Art. 15 should be reformed for TRADE and a new provision should be added for the classic self-employed that incorporates the provisions of Art. 23 Platform Work Directive.

D. Concluding remarks

47 The analysis carried out shows that the existing legal framework does not allow Spain to comply with many of the provisions set out in the Directive. The majority of the articles that will entail the greatest reforms at national level have proved to be those relating to the 'common' rights of service providers, which, for the most part, are completely new to our legislation. However, as regards the specific rights of service providers under the employment regime, it is clear that the adaptations required are often minimal, requiring solely express references in the existing articles to show that their scope of application extends to this sector.

48 Another of the areas that will hardly require any changes is the rebuttable presumption, which Spain already had prior to the Directive proposal itself.

49 All in all, it can be concluded that although the transposition of the Directive will require national adaptation efforts, Spain already has a legal framework that, in our opinion, will facilitate this work. In this sense, it would be very positive, as has already

[55] Those who receive at least 75% of their income from the same client (Art. 11 Statute of Self-employment).

[56] Ley 20/2007, de 11 de julio, del Estatuto del trabajo autónomo.

been advocated by other voices,[57] to urge the Spanish legislator to extend the rights and guarantees recognised by the Directive with respect to algorithmic management to all workers regardless of their sector of activity; thus avoiding the creation of unjustified inequality between the levels of protection provided for each sector.

57 Gil Otero in Pérez de los Cobos Orihuel/García Piñeiro, p. 221 (240 et seq.); Todolí Signes LRDT&PS 2024, 26 (46); Extremera Méndez LS 2025, 1 (37).

Index

Bold numbers refer to articles, normal ones to margin numbers.

Index

Index

Index